WELLER'S WAR

BY GEORGE WELLER

NOVELS
Not to Eat, Not for Love
Clutch and Differential
The Crack in the Column

HISTORY
Singapore Is Silent
Bases Overseas
First into Nagasaki
Weller's War

FOR YOUNGER READERS
The Story of the Paratroops
The Story of Submarines

TRANSLATION
(AS MICHAEL WHARF)
Fontamara, by Ignazio Silone

BY ANTHONY WELLER

NOVELS

The Garden of the Peacocks
The Polish Lover
The Siege of Salt Cove

TRAVEL

*Days and Nights on the Grand Trunk Road:
Calcutta to Khyber*

HISTORY (EDITOR)

First into Nagasaki
Weller's War

GREECE UNDER HITLER!

Six Graphic Eyewitness Articles

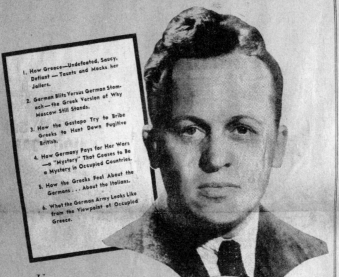

1. How Greece—Undefeated, Saucy, Defiant — Taunts and Mocks her Jailers.

2. German Blitz Versus German Stomach—the Greek Version of Why Moscow Still Stands.

3. How the Gestapo Try to Bribe Greeks to Hunt Down Fugitive British.

4. How Germany Pays for Her Wars —a "Mystery" That Ceases to Be a Mystery in Occupied Countries.

5. How the Greeks Feel About the Germans . . . About the Italians.

6. What the German Army Looks Like from the Viewpoint of Occupied Greece.

by
GEORGE WELLER

George Weller, embattled Balkan correspondent of The Chicago Daily News, who stood his ground in Greece when the Germans came, has at last found an opening in the armorplate of Nazi censorship. Now—from somewhere in Europe—he's ready to tell the things he saw . . . in Greece under Hitler!

* * *

Weller's personal experiences have been grim. He was "quarantined" in Athens by the Germans for more than two months—"held incommunicado by the Vienna Gestapo for 21 hours"—taken by special guard to Berlin—and finally "excluded by Germany from no fewer than eight countries."

But it is of Greece in irons that Weller writes—an incredible Greece under Hitler. Be sure to read George Weller's searching, searing, eyewitness story of what happens to a land when German occupation begins.

Starting TOMORROW *in*
THE CHICAGO DAILY NEWS

WELLER'S WAR

A Legendary Foreign Correspondent's Saga
of World War II
on Five Continents

GEORGE WELLER

EDITED BY ANTHONY WELLER

THREE RIVERS PRESS
NEW YORK

for

Gladys Lasky Weller

(1922–1988)

in loving memory

Originally published in hardcover in the United States by Crown Publishers,
an imprint of the Crown Publishing Group, a division of Random House, Inc., in 2009.

Library of Congress Cataloging-in-Publication Data

Weller, George, 1907–2002.

Weller's war / George Weller.—1st ed.

1. Weller, George, 1907–2002.   2. World War, 1939–1945—Personal
narratives, American.   3. World War, 1939–1945—Campaigns—Europe.

4. World War, 1939–1945—Campaigns—Asia.

5. War correspondents—United States.   I. Title.

D811.5. W4425 2009

940.53—dc22   2008039988

ISBN 978-0-307-34203-4

Printed in the United States of America

DESIGN BY LEONARD HENDERSON
MAPS BY MAPPING SPECIALISTS, LTD.

10 9 8 7 6 5 4 3 2 1

First Paperback Edition

Contents

THE WAR IN EUROPE
AND THE MIDDLE EAST

Germany and her allies
Height of Nazi expansion

FINLAND

SWEDEN

NORWAY

Oslo

Stockholm

ESTONIA

LATVIA

DENMARK   Copenhagen

Baltic Sea

LITHUANIA

EAST
PRUSSIA

Danzig

North
Sea

Bres

IRELAND

GREAT
BRITAIN

HOLLAND

The Hague   Amsterdam

London

Dunkirk   Brussels

Berlin

Warsaw

Lublin

GERMANY

POLAND

ATLANTIC
OCEAN

BELGIUM

Paris

LUXEMBOURG

Prague

SLOVAKIA

FRANCE

Vienna

AUSTRIA

HUNGARY

Budapest

R

Bern

SWITZERLAND

Vichy

Turin

Trieste

Danube R.

Belgrade

Bay of
Biscay

Genoa   Bologna

YUGOSLAVIA

PORTUGAL

Madrid

Lisbon

SPAIN

Marseille

Figueras

Barcelona

Corsica

Livorno   Paestum

Skopje

Va

ITALY

Rome   Monte Cassino

Anzio

ALBANIA

GRE

Monte Fortino

Capri

Sardinia

Tangier

Bizerte

Sicily

Malta

Mediterrane

Casablanca

MOROCCO

ALGERIA

TUNISIA

N
W   E
S

0   250   500 kilometers

0   250   500 miles

LIBYA

GREECE

Skopje · · BULGARIA
YUGOSLAVIA · Pithion
THRACE TURKEY
ALBANIA *MACEDONIA*
· Salonika · Mt. Athos
Corfu · Metzovo *THESSALY*
Neokhori *EPIRUS* · Larissa *Aegean Sea* *Lesbos*
GREECE · Domokos
· Kapenisi · Lamia *Euboea* *Chios*
Agrinion · · Thermopylae
· Idoriki · Amphissa · Parnassus
Ithaca · Delphi · Distomo *Chios*
· Patras · Thebes · Marathon
Corinth · Piraeus · Athens
· Olympia · · Kaisariani
Nauplion
PELOPONNESE
· Sparta
Ionian Sea
· Kranai · Gythion
Cape Matapan N
Kythera Island
W 0 100 200 kilometers
· Canea
0 100 200 miles E. · Suda · Herakleion
S · Malemi *Crete*

Leningrad

A

VIA · Moscow

U   S   S   R

· Minsk
st-Litovsk · Stalingrad
D · Kiev
Lvov
· Rostov
Caspian Sea
RUMANIA
Sinaia ·
Black Sea
· Bucharest
BULGARIA
Sofia · · Shipka Pass · Tehran
STRUMA *BALKAN*
VALLEY *MTS.* · Istanbul
ECE · Mosul **IRAN**
· Smyrna **TURKEY**
(Izmir) · Khorramshahr
· Athens Andimeshk · · Dizful
SYRIA · Baghdad Ahwaz · · Bandar Shapur
· Basra
Crete **IRAQ**
LEBANON · Rutbah *Persian Gulf*
CYPRUS Beirut · · Damascus
an Sea Haifa · · Tiberius
· Mafrak
Tel Aviv ·
Jerusalem · · Amman
PALESTINE **TRANS-**
JORDANIA
· Cairo **ARABIA**
EGYPT

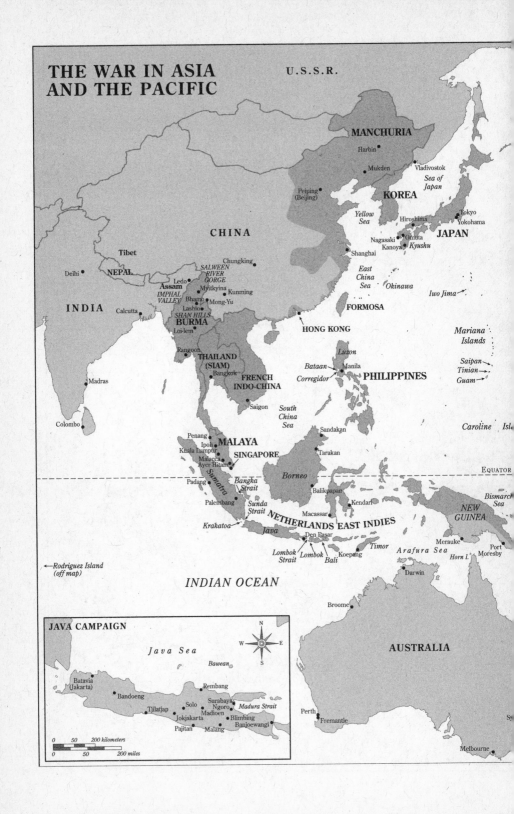

THE WAR IN ASIA AND THE PACIFIC

U.S.S.R.

MANCHURIA

Harbin

Mukden

Vladivostok

Sea of Japan

Peiping (Beijing)

KOREA

CHINA

Yellow Sea

Hiroshima

Tokyo
Yokohama

Tibet

Chungking

SALWEEN RIVER GORGE

Nagasaki
Kanoya

Omuta
Kyushu

JAPAN

Delhi

NEPAL

Assam

Ledo

IMPHAL VALLEY

Myitkyina

Kunming

Bhamo

Mong-Yu

Lashio

SHAN HILLS

BURMA

Loi-lem

Shanghai

East China Sea

Okinawa

Iwo Jima

FORMOSA

Mariana Islands

INDIA

Calcutta

Rangoon

THAILAND (SIAM)

Bangkok

FRENCH INDO-CHINA

HONG KONG

Luzon

Bataan

Manila

Saipan
Tinian
Guam

Madras

Saigon

South China Sea

Corregidor

PHILIPPINES

Colombo

Caroline Isl

Penang

Ipoh

MALAYA

Sandakan

Kuala Lumpur

Malacca
Ayer Hitam

SINGAPORE

Tarakan

EQUATOR

Sumatra

Padang

Bangka Strait

Borneo

Bismarc Sea

Palembang

Balikpapan

Sunda Strait

Kendari

NEW GUINEA

Krakatoa

Java

NETHERLANDS EAST INDIES

Macassar

Den Pasar

Merauke

Port Moresby

←Rodriguez Island (off map)

Lombok Strait

Lombok
Bali

Koepang

Timor

Arafura Sea

Horn I.

Darwin

INDIAN OCEAN

Broome

AUSTRALIA

JAVA CAMPAIGN

Java Sea

N
W   E
S

Bawean

Batavia (Jakarta)

Rembang

Bandoeng

Surabaya

Tjilatjap

Solo
Madioen

Ngoro

Madura Strait

Perth

Jokjakarta
Pajitan

Blimbing
Malang

Banjoewangi

Fremantle

| 0 | 50 | 200 kilometers |
| 0 | 50 | 200 miles |

Melbourne

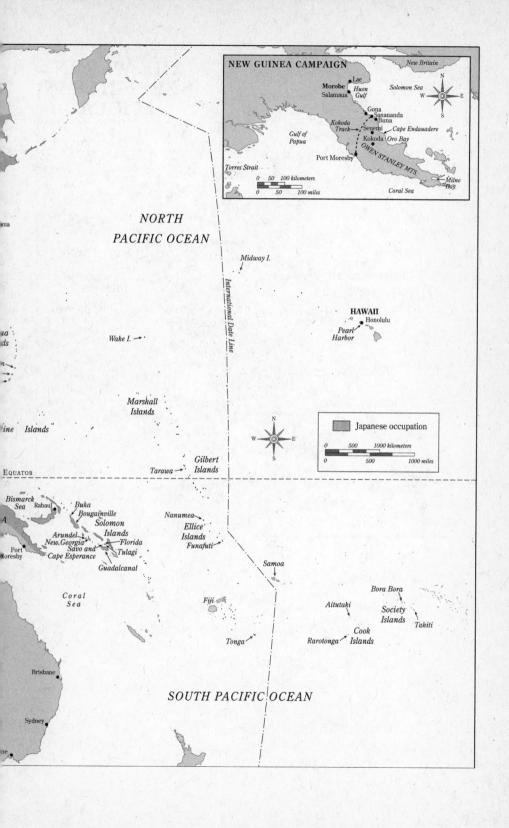

NEW GUINEA CAMPAIGN

New Britain

Lae
Morobe
Salamaua
Huon
Gulf
Solomon Sea

N
W   E
S

Gona
Sananada
Buna
Kokoda
Track
Senemi
Cape Endauadere
Gulf of
Papua
Kokoda
Oro Bay
Port Moresby
OWEN STANLEY MTS.

Torres Strait
Milne
Bay

0   50   100 kilometers
0   50   100 miles

Coral Sea

NORTH
PACIFIC OCEAN

Midway I.

HAWAII
Honolulu
Pearl
Harbor

Wake I. →

International Date Line

Marshall
Islands

ine   Islands

N
W   E
S

Japanese occupation

0   500   1000 kilometers
0   500   1000 miles

Gilbert
Islands
Tarawa →

EQUATOR

Bismarck
Sea
Rabaul
Buka
Bougainville
Solomon
Islands
Arundel
New Georgia
Florida
Savo and
Tulagi
Cape Esperance
Guadalcanal

Port
Moresby

Nanumea →
Ellice
Islands
Funafuti

Samoa

Bora Bora

Coral
Sea

Fiji

Aitutaki
Society
Islands
Tahiti

Cook
Islands

Tonga
Rarotonga

Brisbane

SOUTH PACIFIC OCEAN

Sydney

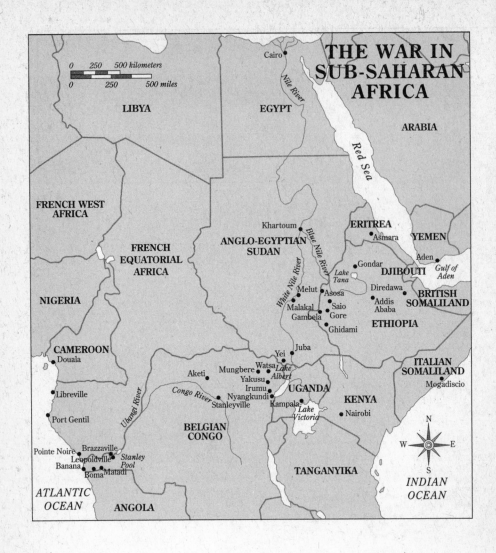

THE WAR IN SUB-SAHARAN AFRICA

Scale: 0 — 250 — 500 kilometers / 0 — 250 — 500 miles

LIBYA

EGYPT

• Cairo

Nile River

ARABIA

Red Sea

FRENCH WEST AFRICA

FRENCH EQUATORIAL AFRICA

ANGLO-EGYPTIAN SUDAN

Khartoum

Blue Nile River

White Nile River

ERITREA

Asmara •

YEMEN

Aden •

Gulf of Aden

DJIBOUTI

Gondar •

Lake Tana

BRITISH SOMALILAND

Diredawa •

Addis Ababa •

Melut •

Asosa •

Saio •

Gore •

Ghidami •

ETHIOPIA

Malakal •

Gambela •

NIGERIA

CAMEROON

Douala •

Libreville •

Port Gentil •

Ubangi River

Congo River

Aketi •

Mungbere •

Yakusu •

Irumu •

Nyangkundi •

Stanleyville •

Yei •

Juba •

Watsa •

Lake Albert

UGANDA

Kampala •

Lake Victoria

KENYA

Nairobi •

ITALIAN SOMALILAND

Mogadiscio •

BELGIAN CONGO

Pointe Noire •

Brazzaville •

Leopoldville •

Banana •

Boma • Matadi •

Stanley Pool

ATLANTIC OCEAN

ANGOLA

TANGANYIKA

N
W — E
S

INDIAN OCEAN

Foreword

Warfare profoundly changes not just its combatants but also its eyewitnesses. A war correspondent—the professional eyewitness whose task is to get as close as possible and report as much as possible while surviving as long as possible—is in a peculiar position. Neither victim nor killer, he still risks injury and death. Meanwhile, he must stand aside as portions of the truth he attempts to convey to a readership back home are siphoned off by censorship. It is, ultimately, a frustrating profession that one way or another can destroy many of its bravest and most honest practitioners.

George Anthony Weller (1907–2002) was among the eminent American correspondents of his era, recipient of a 1943 Pulitzer Prize and a 1954 George Polk Award, both for foreign reporting. He first made his name as a courageous reporter during World War II, one of the few to cover every principal theater of war on all the continents. To revisit his diverse work now, sixty-five years later, is to be reminded of how very much the foreign correspondent—a vanishing profession—can and should provide, and how much has been lost along with the reading public: not just the skill, in wartime, to evoke unforgettably a battle large or small, but also the rigorous ability to analyze the politics that lies behind it, and give voice to the rich personal stories and complex levels within any human struggle.

One self-flattering aspect of a purely contemporary viewpoint is to imagine that correspondents today are more daring or endangered than in the past. This detailed look at a single reporter's World War II odyssey should put such notions to rest. It is also a chance to follow the effect of five years of continuous war on an exceptional man. Here he is in 1943, after seven months of steadily worsening malaria in the jungles of Papua New Guinea, writing to his editor from a portable hospital near the front about when he might be coming home for a much-needed break: "You may wonder why it takes me any time at all to cut loose from this war, when others are able to flit from one theater to another like swallows. It is because I have been deep in it. It takes time to free oneself and get ready to come back."

When George Weller left New York by ship in December 1940 to report from Europe for the *Chicago Daily News,* he was professionally successful and well prepared for the task at hand. At thirty-three, he had managed to survive the Depression as a writer. He was a mature, highly praised novelist and sometime translator, fluent (albeit with a Boston accent) in German, French, modern Greek, and Italian, conversant in Spanish and Portuguese. He had placed more than a hundred articles and short stories in the leading magazines, including a dozen pieces for the *New Yorker.* He had spent much of his twenties in Europe, writing two novels and working as a Balkans stringer (1932–1936, a dollar per day) for the *New York Times.*

Widely published yet still barely solvent, once he left America behind for good and became a full-fledged foreign correspondent, he was immersed in nonstop war. In the opening year alone he endured at close hand a series of upheavals as the Axis took over the world. From Portugal and Spain he moved to more-familiar terrain and watched the Nazis seize Rumania, Bulgaria, Yugoslavia. His baptism of fire came as his beloved Greece fell to German assault. As the last reporter out of a burning Salonika (by fishing boat), he was "quarantined" by the Nazis in Athens and taken to Berlin. Freed after nine weeks, he headed south. He tramped to the heart of Central Africa to find tribesmen who had fought the explorer Stanley in the prior century. In Brazzaville he managed a controversial interview with General de Gaulle, head of Free France, who soon tried to deny the overtures he had just made behind Churchill's back.

From there Weller followed Belgium's Congolese army on an obscure campaign against the Italians in the highlands of western Ethiopia. He met Haile Selassie on his recovered throne and, after the attack on Pearl Harbor, was sent east by his editor to Singapore. For six weeks he covered the doomed British colony, strategic key to Asia's sea lanes, as the Malay Peninsula fell to the Japanese. He got away on one of the final ships through Bomb Alley and spent the next month covering the collapse of Java, fleeing under heavy strafing and shelling on the last boat to escape. (*Time* magazine called him the "much machine-gunned George Weller.") Reaching Australia, he sent out the first account of the epic Battle of the Java Sea, an Allied disaster. All these classic stories are in this book, seen through his skeptical, sympathetic, and fiercely intelligent words.

That was his opening fifteen months; the rest of his war was equally eventful. Amid bouts of malaria he covered the struggle for the Pacific, principally from New Guinea, the Solomons, and Australia. He trained as a paratrooper, the first reporter to do so, and received his Pulitzer for the account of an appendectomy performed by a pharmacist's mate aboard a submarine in enemy waters. After home leave he returned to the Pacific via Italy; a violated Greece in the early throes of civil war; across the Middle East through Palestine, Iran, Iraq; a spell with guerrillas behind enemy lines in Burma; by tumultuous road to China, thence the Philippines, finally Japan. The relentless struggle pared and galvanized his writing, and shaped his vision of the world. In sending back not only the guts of war but the thinking behind it, too, the dispatches transformed him irrevocably.

A gusty man with extraordinarily alive blue eyes and a head suggesting steel-reinforced bone structure, Weller always seemed larger than a mere six feet. As someone who felt at home everywhere and went deep into what he called the secret history of each place, his reportorial gift was a mask of complete innocence that was misleading and often trapped his subjects in unwitting revelations.

Having begun as a novelist, he had more literary style than most reporters. ("You could hear the bomb singing as it came down, singing like a bomb that loved its work.") He joined the *Chicago Daily News* in late 1940. All but forgotten now, this afternoon newspaper's foreign staff was syndicated in over eighty papers—far more than even that of the *New York Times*. Thus Weller's coverage, with a readership of ten million, appeared regularly in the *Boston Globe,* the *San Francisco Chronicle,* the *St. Louis Post-Dispatch,* and the *New York Post.* Besides him, the *CDN* could boast such correspondents as Leland Stowe, Paul Ghali, Robert J. Casey, Richard Mowrer, Edgar Ansel Mowrer, Webb Miller, Helen Kirkpatrick, John B. Terry (killed in the war), William H. Stoneman (wounded), Archibald Steele, John Whitaker, Walter Robb, David M. Nichol, Allen Haden, Hal O'Flaherty, and William McGaffin—four Pulitzers, one Medal of Freedom, and one French Legion of Honor among them. *Time* called their reporting of World War II "the best in the U.S." They were under the direction of foreign editor Carroll Binder, whom Weller compared to a manager on a baseball team. "As events come to bat, he moves about his infield and outfield." That might mean, for Weller, being shifted as rapidly as possible from an old war in Africa to a new in Asia: "When one war ends, another is quick to begin."

Weller was a man of the world, in an old-fashioned definition: an American type who existed midcentury, charming, stubbornly confident, at ease in any situation. At the same time, he never forgot growing up poor—his Harvard tuition was generously paid by a man he caddied for as a teenager—and he remained frugal all his life. A career under fire or stuck in difficult places stopped him from worrying about eating well or dressing stylishly.

His second job after college, during a year of study at the University of Vienna, was as an actor with Max Reinhardt's theater company, partnering the young Hedy Lamarr. Freelancing from Vienna, Capri, and Athens, through the 1930s he managed to publish reportage and fiction regularly in *Story,* the *Nation, Esquire, Collier's, Harper's, Vanity Fair,* the *New Republic,* the *Atlantic,* and the *New Yorker* while getting a political education for the *New York Times.*

He also published two novels that secured his early reputation but made him little money. *Not to Eat, Not for Love* (1933) was a modernist work about Harvard whose diverse language held tinges of Joyce's influence and whose technique owed much to Dos Passos. Praised by luminaries such as Conrad Aiken, it went through five printings and is still remembered. *Clutch and Differential* (1936) fared differently. A panoramic attempt to portray American life through linked stories—connected by interludes using the automobile as allegory—the book received strong, if puzzled, reviews and sold fewer than seven hundred copies "in the heart of the Depression," as Weller put it, "when people on bread lines couldn't wait to read an experimental novel."

His last novel, *The Crack in the Column* (1949), set in Greece during the Nazi occupation and subsequent civil war, was written during his stint as a Nieman Fellow. It was dedicated to George Polk, the CBS newsman whom Weller had met as a naval officer in the Solomon Islands and whose murdered body was found in Salonika Bay in May 1948. (Seven months earlier, in Greece, Weller had been Polk's best man and loaned him his wedding suit.) The dedication does not explain any of this, but reads simply: TO GEORGE POLK / WHO KNEW THE GREEKS / AND DID NOT FEAR THEIR GIFT.

From the 1950s, Weller covered principally the Mediterranean and the Middle East, but also the Soviet Union, Eastern Europe, South America, Africa, and the Pacific. He added to his résumé by being a prisoner of the Communist Chinese in Manchuria and the Germans in East Berlin. Once he traveled for a year and a half with never more than a week in one place, and often only a night or two; he roamed so constantly that one editor, looking over his expense sheets with dismay, said: "You can always count on Weller—he proceeds from A to B by way of Z." He also wrote several plays that enjoyed the distinction of actually being produced. In 1972, six years before the *CDN*'s untimely demise, he "retired" but continued to write and was awarded Italy's Premio Internazionale di Giornalismo. Most of his life was spent overseas—he died at ninety-five in his seaside villa, south of Rome—and across seven decades he reported from nearly every country.

Weller's War can be read not only for his accounts of dramatic events but, beneath this, as a wartime journey of the soul. It appears at a moment when World War II is about to leave the domain of the recent past, recalled in detail by some of our elders as an individual conflict in which they participated, and become a mythology.

"I should have felt remiss in the correspondent's duty toward history if I failed to record this before liberation had sicklied over the sharp memories," he wrote in a letter to his editor near the end of the war, and often in these pages you can sense, behind his toil, a determination that what he has seen not be forgotten.

The toll on Weller's colleagues quickly becomes evident. Many reporters wound up dead. At the same time, the more outlandish episodes were typical; people feared lost in one country turn up alive, years later, on the other side of the world. The scale may seem immeasurably vast, but these dispatches show that it was a personal war, with its coincidental meetings, its quick friendships, its quirks of fate.

Chronologically, the five years contained in *Weller's War* lead up to the three weeks already covered in *First into Nagasaki: The Censored Eyewitness Dispatches on Post-Atomic Japan and Its Prisoners of War* (2006). As the first outside observer to reach Nagasaki (September 6, 1945), four weeks after the bomb, he defied MacArthur's blackout forbidding reporters from entering either nuclear site. After daring to make his way into the scorched city before any American soldiers or doctors, and brazenly telling the Japanese military he was not a newspaperman but a U.S. colonel, he wrote dispatch after dispatch of the greatest scoop of his career—indeed, one of the greatest of the century—only to see it all snuffed by MacArthur's censors. The stories were blocked from reaching his editors back at the *Chicago Daily News*.

After a week among the ruins and makeshift hospitals, speaking both with doomed Japanese and with their doctors cataloging the effects of radiation, Weller left Nagasaki to visit several nearby Allied POW camps—most of whose prisoners still didn't know the war was over. He took down each tortured man's saga of years at slave labor in treacherous coal mines. Those dispatches were suppressed, too.

As a result of the interviews, he wrote "The Death Cruise," a long narrative about the worst Japanese hellship, whose cargo hold carried sixteen hundred prisoners from the Philippines to the prison camps. After seven weeks of dehydration, starvation, murder, bombing by our own planes, and even cannibalism, only three hundred survived.

Thwarted by the censors, Weller finally gave up on Nagasaki and moved on. His carbon copy of the dispatches soon went astray. It was one of the frustrations of his later years that these stories, among the most important of his career, were lost to posterity, erased by his own government. Six months after he died, amid the chaotic archive in his villa by the Mediterranean, I discovered the missing typescripts in a mildewed wooden crate—crumbling, moldy, still afire with all they had to say. They had been waiting, one room over from where he sat, ever-more faintly remembering; and my triumph was tempered by a sadness that he had died believing them vanished.

That book has made possible *Weller's War*. When I began assembling it, I was unaware of how very much my father had written during five years of war, or all he had survived to see the atomic conclusion. Because I grew up hearing story after story, I thought I had a notion of what his World War II had been like—the first war of his professional life. When I read all the dispatches, I realized I could not have been more wrong.

It was not just that in many parts of the world he reported from, the airplanes and trucks looked antiquated and rickety, or that what he called modern armaments seemed to belong to an age long before the atomic bomb. I'd imagined the war as a twentieth-century struggle, but so much of his experience—landscapes, empires, and people—instead seemed to leap fully grown from the nineteenth century. He had given me a sense of the heroism, the humor, and the bloodshed, but what he'd seen was more poignant, more funny, and far more horrible than what he later recounted. Best of all, I could watch it happening right before his eyes, before all his senses.

Inevitably, the present book is as much about being a war correspondent as it is about what one man witnessed. The ease of modern communications can make us overlook the fact that, until recently, a reporter's challenge lay in surmounting the problems not only of "getting in," but of swiftly being able to get a story out. During World War II there were no instantaneous satellite links, only cable offices within reach if one were lucky, where— along with normal, excruciating delays—the tendrils of political and military censorship could be too muscular to remove.

The articles in this book were sent back in four ways. After being censored locally, most early dispatches were relayed to Chicago by telephone or radio. Those Greek dispatches following Weller's release by the Nazis seem to have been mailed from neutral locations, probably Bern and Lisbon, before Weller left for Africa.

The bulk of the book's dispatches were cabled via New York to Chicago, where *CDN* stenographers expanded them from a ready-for-telegram language that foreign correspondents wrote in directly. Due to the cost of sending stories across the globe (often forty cents a word), this compressed "cablese" removed everything obvious. Numbers, acronyms, and punctuations were spelled out. Each text was dated with the day and hour when a reporter was typing, since a dispatch might sit in a telegraph office for many days awaiting transmission. In 1942, for example, the South Pacific had only two cable routes, and one was the slow way around Africa; a reporter covering the war on New Guinea while nominally based in Australia might queue up behind a logjam of four hundred coded government messages.

To illustrate cablese—this lost language in which most of Weller's articles were composed in the field—here is the beginning of a dispatch from Nagasaki, typed at 1 a.m. on the morning of September 9, 1945:

```
press collect via rca chicagonews newyork
nagasaki 90100 article to follow nagasakis hospitals stop
atomic bombs peculiar quote disease unquote comma
uncured because untreated and untreated because
undiagnosed comma is still snatching away lives here stop
men women children with no outward marks injury are dying
daily in hospitals some after having walked around three or
four weeks minimum thinking theyve escaped stop doctors
here have every modern medicament but candidly
confessed in talking to writer dash first allied observer
reach nagasaki since surrender undash that answer to
malady is beyond them stop their patients though skins
whole are simply passing away under their eyes
```

This, when expanded, becomes:

The atomic bomb's peculiar "disease," uncured because it
is untreated and untreated because it is undiagnosed, is
still snatching away lives here. Men, women and children
with no outward marks of injury are dying daily in hospitals,
some after having walked around for three or four weeks
thinking they have escaped. The doctors here have every
modern medicament, but candidly confessed in talking to
the writer—the first Allied observer to reach Nagasaki since
the surrender—that the answer to the malady is beyond
them. Their patients, though their skins are whole, are
simply passing away under their eyes.

In our era of instant electronic transmission it may be difficult to con-
ceive of any blockage interrupting the smooth passage of news from reporter to editor. Yet the correspondents' version of World War II was only
what the censors failed to stop. For any reporter who tried to defy censorship, there was always the threat of dire punishment: the withdrawal, in a
war zone, of accreditation, without which a reporter could not function,
leaving his newspaper, magazine, or radio network without a berth in an
important dateline. Throughout the war, then, there was another war
going on, all along, and it did not end with any treaty of surrender.

In my father's archive I found a list, penned in 1945, of censored stories. It includes: "The B-26 squadron commander in northern Australia who in deadly seriousness ordered the officers of the entire squadron to grow moustaches and carry swagger sticks. I have a copy of that order, but I'm going to try it on our censors in the next war . . . In Tahiti, our lend-lease bicycles and trucks were on public sale—the admiral there, the largest physically in the U.S. navy, suppressed the story and would not see me . . . In Brazzaville, Governor-General Eboué—could not interview him because he was black—or I could interview him but not say he was black. . . ."

The astute reader will enjoy watching Weller do his best to slip forbidden political analysis under the rug and out the other side. Unfortunately I have not been able to lay hands on the lost dispatch he wrote criticizing the Yalta Conference of February 1945, which MacArthur's determined censors blocked because he called it a defeat of the United States by Stalin. Late in life he wrote: "Wherever the censor's pencil falls on your copy, he is hurting you terribly. But he is also teaching you. Learn from the censor. Freud said it well—'Wherever there is a repression, there is a neurosis.' Follow that twinge. Find the unwelcome fact and give it a home. A censor knows exactly what he doesn't want you to write. Let him guide you."

Since American World War II reporters were often in generic military fatigues, they wore brass shoulder tabs that said *War Correspondent* and carried the assimilated rank of lieutenant—"a painful disparity," Weller wrote, "with Italy's fascist forces, where they were splendid colonels with orderlies. Still, I could hardly expect MacArthur and his colonels to promote me. After all, I refused to promote them."

In the days before credit cards, each foreign correspondent carried a letter of credit for, say, $5,000, which was presented, on arrival in a new country, to a bank. The total would diminish as operating funds in the local currency were withdrawn. Gradually the letter of credit would have to be replaced, which presented other obstacles; a message from the accounting office of Weller's newspaper, written to him in Australia in May, stated that a letter of credit sent him in November had just been returned to them after "considerable traveling." Due to bank regulations it could not be easily canceled, so off it went again to try to find him.

For this work Weller earned an annual salary of $6,000, or $500 a month. His personal mail took two years to catch up to him.

This volume represents about 10 percent of what Weller wrote from January 1941, when he arrived in Europe, until October 1945, just after he left Nagasaki. His output was prodigious despite challenging conditions; I have sifted every issue of the *Chicago Daily News* for his best published dispatches. And I have included a few "missing" ones, either killed by censors and never transmitted, or simply never published, which I found in his papers. Among these are what would have been the first graphic ground-level description of the results from the firebombing of Tokyo.

Through 1943, the *CDN* provided the date on which each dispatch was filed (unless that was so far back it made the material look questionable). In 1944 the paper ceased this useful practice, so from then on in the book the date for a dispatch becomes the day it appeared. Multiple dates mean I have combined dispatches.

The volume also contains a half-dozen longer pieces, written for magazine publication. Weller had an understanding with his editors that fuller articles could be handled by his literary agent, Harold Ober, if they did not fall within the *CDN*'s confines. Written with details and gestures of style inappropriate for a daily paper, they add another dimension to the dispatches.

The novelist in Weller is always present in his ability to put a scene before us through dialogue, describe a battle concisely, or summon up an elusive atmosphere, and throughout the war he wrote short stories. I have selected three. I have also included a few of his letters and even a soldiers' verse—Weller was a great collector of ragtag bits and pieces. As in the prior volume, there is a section of photos chosen from thousands in his archives (though he found the task annoying, the *CDN* insisted he carry a Leica, and use it). And pertinent documents are reproduced before each chapter—such as his Nazi travel papers, and an apology from a brutal Japanese POW camp commander.

The volume offers abridged versions of his three wartime books: *Singapore Is Silent, "Luck to the Fighters!"* and *Bases Overseas*. It is impossible to compress 350 pages into 65, but I have tried. In another sense, there are two other "books" implicit here. In 1941 he saw Greece fall, and in 1945 watched its liberation turn into civil war; he also spanned a year and a half in New Guinea, the only reporter to cover all its major campaigns.

I have written brief introductions for each section. Some provide the story behind the chapter's adventures, some the basic political background presumably familiar to an average reader of the day. Obvious as it may sound, it is useful to recall that for much of the war Weller and his readers had no idea how it was going to end, nor how long that end would take.

No doubt there are characterizations and expressions that will bother some readers, but they speak to the racial nature of this war. It is always problematic to try to inhabit the past, to enter its differences; to re-create its assumptions, all it took for granted—for we must first try to understand it on its own terms before we judge it on ours. It is no use reading a reporter's words from the past and trying to frog-march them into the present. The goal, while remembering what you know that he did not, is to ask yourself if he knew anything that you do not.

I have chosen to maintain the spellings of place-names as used in the dispatches, rather than update them.

I have abridged every dispatch while preserving the writing. Most frequently cut have been lists of soldiers' names, mentioned in a dispatch as a way of not just giving credit but letting their loved ones know where they were and that they were alive. Weller was a boots-in-the-mud reporter, able to talk to men of any rank, but considerations apply to a book that do not apply to a day's newspaper article. If I have offended anyone by removing those names, I apologize.

No writer can second-guess posterity, which has its own hunger. Weller, like all serious correspondents, was well aware of the responsibilities of a reporter—to accurately and unsentimentally convey the truth to his readership, for they deserved no less—and of his duty toward history. The American instinct to simplify all politics, to look for an unpolitical, emotional right or wrong no matter what and to avoid thinking, stymied him. He believed it was the reporter's duty not to simplify, and like many correspondents, he thought the political naïveté of his countrymen total. In *Singapore Is Silent,* written the year after the United States entered the war, he was blunt: "Asia is the kindergarten of American geopolitics, and the American people are the reluctant pupils who dislike the lessons they must learn, and have not yet understood that the old, simple life of play in the garden at home is gone forever."

As with many foreign correspondents, a globe-girdling life ultimately made it impossible for Weller ever to belong in America. Home became somewhere else. A dissatisfaction with the sleepiness of his country, and the habit of being overseas professionally, kept him away even while sharpening his skills of observation. In a letter to a friend sent from the Pacific in September 1942, he wrote:

> I never felt that it was more necessary than at present to have at least one ornery correspondent with a disputative Yankee mind on the scene. Everywhere I go in the world I marvel at the narrow margin by which the truth gets into print, when it does. My job, and doing it well, never seemed so important to me as now. Sometimes I get the old egotistical feeling that the pulse of things here beats for me and me alone. At least I can say one thing positively, and that is that I know more people on more widely separated parts of this front than any other newspaperman. I try not to stay anywhere very long. I have already made up my mind how I can serve my country best . . . The war correspondent job is the one where I fit—no medals, no promotions, but plenty of personal satisfaction.

Over the years he witnessed as much death and destruction as the world has to offer, yet he never lost his unflagging humor, his sense of beauty or of the grandeur of human achievement.

As Walter Cronkite wrote: "George Weller was not only one of our best war correspondents but he had that quality that imbued his copy with lasting importance. He wrote in the present tense but always with the recognition that he was writing the history of his time." Our need to understand the past is not nearly as strong as the present's natural determination to erase it. My hope is that this book may delay that erasure and, in its precise evocation of war, even achieve a kind of timelessness.

—*Anthony Weller*

It is no one's fault. . . . Everybody struggles
as hard as he can to make war like war.

—A<small>NTOINE DE</small> S<small>AINT</small>-E<small>XUPÉRY</small>,
Flight to Arras

December 11, 1940
(Date)

PERMIT OF LOCAL BOARD FOR REGISTRANT TO DEPART FROM THE
UNITED STATES

This is to certify that __GEORGE__ __ANTHONY__ __WELLER__
(First name)   (Middle name)   (Last name)

Order No. __8__ , Serial No. __2914__ , Class __3__ , Division __a__
(Number)   (Letter)

a registrant of this Local Board has applied for a permit to depart from the United States, and this Local Board, being convinced that said registrant is not likely to be called for military service during the proposed absence and that the granting of such permit will not result in the evasion of or interference with the execution of the Selective Service Law, hereby authorizes the said registrant to depart from the United States and to remain absent therefrom for __three years__
(Designate period of absence)

In his application the registrant gave this information:

1. Countries to be visited __Eastern Europe__

2. Individuals or organizations represented __Chicago Daily News__

3. Nature of business __FOREIGN CORRESPONDENT__

Description of registrant:

RACE		HEIGHT (Approx.)		WEIGHT (Approx.)		COMPLEXION	
White	✓	5' 11"		195		Sallow	
		EYES		HAIR		Light	
Negro		Blue	✓	Blonde	✓	Ruddy	✓
		Gray		Red	*	Dark	
Oriental		Hazel		Brown		Freckled	
		Brown		Black		Light brown	
Indian		Black		Gray		Dark brown	
				Bald		Black	
Filipino							

Other obvious physical characteristics that will aid in identification _____

Date of birth __July 15, 1907__

C. C Clark, Secy
Member of Local Board.

I

Early European Dispatches

Portugal, Spain, Rumania, Bulgaria, Yugoslavia

When Weller stepped off the SS *Excambion* at Lisbon in January 1941—having left New York mid-December and written two dispatches on board, about the ship's barber and about fellow passenger Laurence Olivier, who took training as a Morse code operator—he hit the ground running. From neutral Portugal and the refugee situation coagulating Europe's borders, he moved on to Spain, which was suffering enforced food deprivations under Franco, then briefly on to Rome.

Though the United States was still a year away from entering the conflict, Europe was already a year and a half into the war. Hitler had successfully invaded Poland in September 1939, with the Soviet Union's aid; then Denmark and Norway in April 1940; followed by Luxembourg, the Netherlands, and Belgium; then France, which surrendered in June. (When Churchill refused to surrender, Hitler began air attacks on Britain's bases and cities, with an eventual invasion in mind.) Such victories helped impel Fascist Italy, under Mussolini, to join forces with Nazi Germany. They, with Japan, would constitute the principal forces of the Axis.

The value of Weller's earliest dispatches lies in their portrait of the fall of the Balkans—far more complex and personal than any

summary can suggest, from the collaboration with Germany of
Bulgaria and Rumania (whose oil fields were so crucial to Hitler)
to early atrocities against Jews. Here, too, are hints of the coming
invasion of Russia (June 1941), and the diplomatic dithering of
the British prior to their wholehearted defense of Greece.

—

Red Tape Bars Refugee Road to U.S. Havens

Creative Exiles in Lisbon Wait for Papers That Come Too Late

Lisbon, Portugal—January 11, 1941

Traffic on the "underground railroad" from France through Spain and Portugal to the United States—operated seamlessly through the autumn by
American rescue committees trying to save European intellectuals—is virtually at a standstill. This is due partly to increasingly stringent war conditions and partly to the indiscretions of some of its most distinguished
"passengers."

Americans here and in France, working day and night to save men and
women whose artistic and creative achievements entitle them to sanctuary
in the United States, find the jungle of red tape separating refugee-choked
Marseille from Lisbon's wharves growing gradually more impenetrable. The
last group of seven persons to leave France was imprisoned at Figueras, forty
miles from the border. Two are now charged with espionage and none of the
others, though released several days ago, have yet reached here.

These refugees do not resemble the fur-coated fugitives, both foreign
and American, who sit upon piles of smart luggage in the anteroom of
the United States consulate here, calmly waiting for the overworked vice-
consuls to arrange passports and steamer or clipper accommodations.
These are mostly drab little people with thin overcoats and papier-mâché
suitcases—not important enough to be known in America but just sufficiently interesting to rate inclusion upon secret police lists of the author-
itarian states. Few in numbers, they are minor rather than major artists.

The more famous refugees who entrained on the "underground" earlier have soaped the rails by talking freely of their experiences upon their arrival in New York.

The authorities of all countries concerned agree that, to function successfully, the railroad must not be underground but above board: an American-administered organization unattached to any political party or faith, openly aiding non-revolutionary persons across boundaries to countries already willing to accept them.

While the control of entrance into the United States has been governed by the strictest consular standards, in intermediate countries the wartime conditions—varying from regular to chaotic—have impelled refugees occasionally to use irregular methods in crossing frontiers. Such means, regarded now as normal wartime procedure, had been employed only to get the fugitives through unfriendly countries to where their legitimate papers would be valid.

Several prominent creative artists safely settled in America, including a well-known German novelist, were so elated over their escapes that they dramatized mildly adventurous details for the benefit of Manhattan ship reporters in a manner now reacting painfully upon colleagues still marooned in France.

While conditions of rescue work change almost hourly, the chief difficulties are two: (1) the unexplained reluctance of the French authorities to grant exit visas to guests whom they regard with the most open disfavor, and (2) the fact that Spain is becoming an ever-deepening gulf where the committees are unable to gain adequate representation. A Portuguese transit visa, good for one month, and a Spanish, valid for a fortnight, must be secured before France will even examine the United States document which replaces a passport for denationalized wanderers.

Usually the exit visa from France must be passed by a German or Italian armistice commissioner, or both. Frequently visas expire before exit is approved and the melancholy fugue of bureaucracy must be started over again from the beginning. Almost no one of military age is allowed to move, and that term is subject to the widest wartime definition.

The "railroad's" traffic also is hampered by communication difficulties, since only diplomats and others specially authorized can telephone to France. Telegraphic exchange through French censorship usually takes four days, while five weeks often elapse before letters containing indispensable documents sift through the Spanish and French censorships.

It is estimated that about a hundred intellectuals, with their American documents approved, are trying vainly to get exit visas from French, German and Italian authorities in Marseille.

—

MILLIONS OF SPANIARDS GROW THINNER AS BRITISH BLOCKADE GETS TIGHTER; FAMINE NEAR

Barcelona, Spain—January 15, 1941

When Federico Vega, a common Spanish dockworker, arose from bed one morning this week, stepped into his single pair of work pants and tightened his belt, his pants sagged down disconsolately from his muscular hips. With a whispered oath Federico unbuckled the belt, drew out his clasp knife and stabbed a fresh hole in the heavy leather. The new punch is about three quarters of an inch beyond the last hole, forced a fortnight before Christmas.

Federico is getting thinner as the British blockade is getting tighter. It is a blockade directly around his belly; since July his belt has gained so many new holes that it looks as though it possessed several different owners. Four times since July he has amended his belt to fit his shrinking silhouette. Federico's government is sympathetic to the Axis, but his gastric juices are in rebellion.

Like millions of other Spaniards, Federico's face and figure have changed in the last six months. His cheeks, which were rosy and full, have become sunken and pale. His black eyes have lost their sparkle and his small paunch, which aided rather than impeded his heavy work, has now disappeared. He is leaner, quieter and more easily fatigued. Federico is suffering from Europe's commonest ailment this winter—undernourishment.

In good times Señora Vega was able to give her husband at least one big loaf of bread daily. Today, by standing in line every morning from darkness at 7 until 9:30 or later, in the bitterest weather Spain has known in years, she can provide them each a single piece of bread weighing two and one half ounces, or about the size of a Parker House roll.

At his work of moving crates Federico has never fainted yet, but he must pause often for rest. He refuses to weigh himself to find out how much he has lost. His belt holes tell him all he needs to know.

Like many women and children, Federico's wife shows the effect of the blockade in her legs, which are blotched with a case of rickets. Although she waits many hours in consumer lines, she often finds that the day's supply is exhausted. Outside the ration system eggs cost 12 cents apiece, sugar is 65 cents a pound and butter $2.25. All are virtually unobtainable except in restaurants, which are better supplied than families.

A restaurant dinner, priced at 60 cents in the United States, costs $3.70. Official prices are deceptively low, rationed sugar, for example, being ticketed at 12 cents a pound. Actually, it is obtainable in needed quantities only by stealth. The small Spanish cigarettes are limited to forty weekly at a cost of 36 cents, and must be purchased between 3:30 and 5:30 Monday afternoons in Federico's city.

Only a handful of the wealthy who are able to afford a car can get poultry or potatoes because it is necessary to go to the country and persuade the farmers to sell behind the barn. The extra gasoline necessary costs $1.40 a gallon and is obtainable in quantity only by undercover payment of American dollars.

In the shops, finicky buyers get scant satisfaction. If questions are asked, goods are returned to the shelves because the storekeepers would rather keep their supplies than sell, fearing a time when they may have nothing marketable to offer.

Thousands of families from smashed villages have emigrated to the towns and big cities. Since their homes are unrepaired, they prefer to eke out an existence on urban food lines rather than return to their shattered dwellings.

—

400 CRAFT LAND; TROOPS STREAM TOWARD DANUBE

Total of 1500 German Planes Are Poised for Balkan Action

Bucharest, Rumania—February 15, 1941

The German Army celebrated the British departure from Rumanian territory by bringing almost an entire air division into Bucharest. Four hundred bombers, arriving in flights of 24 each, landed yesterday at the Chitila airdrome. (Attack planes for their protection had already been on hand about a fortnight.) They did not fly over the city, and the population remains uninformed of the strength of the Nazi forces, whose totals are estimated at three air divisions of 500 planes each.

Today the expeditionary forces are streaming south toward the Danube. Roads are carefully studded with German signs, hospitals being openly marked, military quarters in code. Rumanian censorship expressly forbids mention of the movements of the officially designated "forces of instruction," on their way to new "classrooms." The Giurgiu bridgehead has been protected with German anti-aircraft guns for more than two weeks. War materiel has been flowing steadily across.

Wearing the wings of the motorized columns that make even the plainest infantryman look like an aviator to Rumanians, the blue-clad, ruddy Germans came into Bucharest by truck from the north. Their officers, in ankle-length grey or green leather coats, led them in fast campaign cars, some of American make.

Everything is moving fast, and they stop in the capital barely long enough to eat one warm meal, go to the threat-and-scare picture on movie row, buy themselves one of the German cameras which cost much less here than in the Fatherland itself, take pictures of each other and the Rumanian soldiers and embrace the girls in a cheap bar. Then they are off again, clambering into the covered wagon truck, sitting in motionless and expressionless rows in the dark, without even rifles because the arms and ammunition are going south by train disguised as freight.

Bucharest looks fantastic to the young Germans. They don't understand the broad Slavic squares, the mixture of streamlined and gingerbread architecture, the deserted palace modeled after Versailles but bigger. And they don't know the police wearing tall astrakhans, or their new "comrades"—the brown-clad farm boys of the Rumanian army, in their ill-fitting greatcoats, who patrol the streets by threes, searching and questioning pedestrians.

As these cogs rolling down the assembly line of war reached the capital, they were photographed by German official photographers in intimate poses with their Rumanian colleagues, about 1,200,000 of whom will be mobilized by March 1. The officers are rarely used for propaganda purposes, however, possibly because many have an uncannily British look cultivated during Carol's regime.*

Probably no two armies ever had less idea what they were supposed to mean to each other or where they are going. Who is the enemy? The Germans thought it might be the Bulgars, and now it is either the Greeks or the Turks, or both, and the British too, and possibly even the Yugoslavs.

The Rumanians admit it may be any or all of these, but the idea they nurse hopefully is that it may be the Russians. If not now, then eventually.

The German officers, several of whom resemble American college boys, some lively professors, and a scarred, monocled minority who resemble Broadway Prussians, are quartered in the best hotels. The general staff, which will take over when the war operations commence, is housed at resort hotels, a few hundred yards from the palace where King Michael† is living.

Along the chief country highway, field telephone corps are at work. German engineers already have unrolled the cables of a new system for the capital. In front of staff headquarters at the urbane Hotel Ambassador stands a sentry box striped with the German colors, the object of covert comment by anti-Axis Rumanians. Before other hotels stand mud-spattered cars, all sizes and shapes, with numerals omitted to baffle the supposedly numerous agents of the British intelligence service.

The columns of machine-gun motorcycles and hooded trucks that fill the capital's squares by night, replaced every few days, are kept under sentry guard, but there is an almost carelessly open style about all the troop movements. The probable German force here is about 510,000, and the speed of arrival about 6000 daily.

In January the German officers had orderlies check on the identity of their neighbors at tables in the large hotels, but now—as Rumania is whipped into the shape already made for Hungary—there is an easy air of behind-the-front.

In the countryside, where only German correspondents are supposed to go, the scene is more businesslike. The environs of Bucharest, one vast

---

*Carol II, the "playboy king" who ruled from 1930 to 1940, enjoyed diverse wives and mistresses across Europe. His son Michael, for whom he abdicated, spurned him thereafter.
†Carol II's son (b. 1921), powerless for most of the war under pro-German prime minister Ion Antonescu, against whom he led a 1944 coup—resulting in occupation by the Soviets. Decorated by both Truman and Stalin, he had to abdicate in 1947.

air field, are lined with hundreds of dark-grey attack planes and bombers. Barracks for 4000 flying troops are being finished, and they look exactly like cantonments seen by the writer in America in December. Rumanian soldiers still guard the railroad bridges, but never far from German observation.

Every room in every tavern along main highways is taken. At first, some conscientious attempts at concealing the size of the columns by moving them out of sight of the roads were made, but this has been dropped.

Hours of negotiations with the badly disrupted police secret service are necessary for even one villager to travel to the next village to sell his produce, and while in Bucharest life is imprisoned within the capital—so that none may visit the surrounding countryside—rural life is virtually frozen where it stands. Except for the Ploesti oilfields, and the endless lines of Reichsbahn freight cars bringing war shipments south, the only movement is the flying German columns, lines of hard-bitten motorcycle riders between them. When they come down the highway, every rude wooden telegraph pole of the Rumanian constabulary jumps instantly into the air. But where Hitler's men are bound, after Bulgaria, no one is sure.

It is still an army exerting more political than military pressure, because it has not yet found an antagonist.

—

BLAST OF HATRED FORCES PRO-NAZI EDITOR TO RESIGN

Sofia, Bulgaria—February 19, 1941 (Delayed)

The name of Ilya Radelescu has disappeared from the masthead of the leading pro-Axis newspaper, in Bucharest, and although the circumstances still remain unknown to the Rumanian public, no one acquainted with them can deny that there exists a way to express public opinion in a totalitarian state.

Radelescu, a lawyer by training, an editor by profession, and a strong Axis adherent by faith, is the publisher of the newspaper *Parunca Vreme*, the only out and out pro-Legionary (pro-Guardist) sheet which has survived the Antonescu purge. The paper was originally called merely *Vreme*, meaning "Times." When Radelescu's five-year-old daughter, Parunca, whose name meant "order," died tragically from the effects of an accidental pencil thrust in the eye, Radelescu was grief-stricken. He published her picture on his front page and incorporated her name into that of the newspaper: "Order of the Times."

Premier Antonescu, the Army officers composing the military cabinet, the heads of the banned political parties, and the editors of all the Bucharest newspapers received this week copies of a letter addressed to the Iron Guard editor. It read:

Dear Mr. Radelescu:

When your daughter died, you published her picture to show your grief. I inform you, herewith, that I lost my eighteen-year-old son in the recent street fighting, on which day I do not know.

After I waited three days for my son to come home, I went to the slaughter house. What I saw there I shall not forget the rest of my life. I saw human beings hung up like animals; I saw a little girl, five years old, suspended by her feet from the hooks where the calves are hung. Her entire body was smeared with blood.

I ran away at the sight. Then I went hunting for my son in the morgue. I saw hellish sights there, hundreds and hundreds of dead, who no longer resembled human beings. I saw men whose tongues had been torn out. I saw women's bodies torn to pieces. I saw children whose corpses were smashed beyond recognition.

I fell down in a faint. They took me to the Strada Roma (location of the Legionary headquarters) and there, finally, I found my son dead, with his head pierced with bullets.

Such was the end of an upright, eighteen-year-old young man, who, thanks to your activities, became a fanatical nationalist.

Dr. Ilya Radelescu, I say to you that not the bullets of the soldiers that killed my son are responsible, but you yourself are the murderer of my son; you, who for years on end have tirelessly fanned the flames of hatred, and through the shallow phrases of anti-Semitism led my son along the road of evil. For ten years you have been a tireless fighter against the Jews. I tell you that you are a liar. You published in your newspaper a fable about Jews and in it you insisted, among other things, that in the County of Muscel there are about 6,915 Jews.

Now I come from Muscel myself and I know that county very well. I know that in that county there are only two Jews, one a clockmaker

and the other a tinsmith. Both are poor and work from early morning till late at night. I want to know where you got the other 7,000, or
so, Jews. Out of your imagination, naturally. You lied so remarkably
in this instance, I believe all your other stories are probably lies. But
with this campaign of lies you have led the ignorant and inexperienced
upon the high road which ended in the reign of fire of the Strada
Roma.

It does not interest me in whose service you have done this. The one
thing that interests me is that my child is dead. And in return for this
I give you my curse for the balance of your natural life.

(Signed)
Ekaterina Paraskivescu.
CALLEIA AGRIVITSA 55.

The mother's letter was barred from publication by the censorship, but
the wave of official disapproval in ministerial and journalistic circles was
too much for Radelescu. On Wednesday he withdrew the use of his name
from his own newspaper.

—

NAZI PILOTS FLY BRITONS IN BALKANS

Sofia, Bulgaria—February 25, 1941

With all rail communication in the Balkans placed by war conditions in the
hands of the German Lufthansa, British journalists are faced with the
dilemma of riding swastika-bedecked planes, with Nazi reserve officers as
pilots, or missing the story. Usually they fly on the enemy's wings and are
treated with total courtesy.

The Lufthansa crews seem to enjoy having an English passenger because it gives the male steward a chance to practice a particularly discon-
certing form of the war of nerves. The other passengers are usually all
German. The flying steward waits until the Englishman has dozed off to
the drone of the motors, and then, approaching close behind him, says, in
something as near to Cockney as he can manage: "Tickets, please, sir."

A more serious hazard is weather, which may deliver the correspondent into the yawning mouth of a concentration camp instead of at his office. The perilous jump is from Belgrade to Budapest, which few Englishmen now dare. The plane, which has left Bucharest and Sofia early the same morning, continues to Vienna. Occasionally, however, the bad weather shuts down the Budapest field and it is up to the Nazi pilot, in midflight, to decide whether to turn back to Belgrade or to fly onward. If he turns back, the Englishman is safe; if he selects Vienna, the Briton goes to a concentration camp.

The Nazis bagged two Britons of subordinate diplomatic standing in this way several weeks ago, but after keeping them as guests for a few days, turned them back without even asking an exchange of prisoners.

While boundary regulations get more stringent, the Germans' conception of passenger rules is much less severe than that of American flying lines. Seat belts are almost never fastened at take-offs or landings, and the view from the windows of the cabins remains unobstructed even when, as in Rumania, flying over fields lined with camouflaged bombers and fighters and surrounded by aviation barracks.

—

GERMANS IN BULGARIA AWAIT THE SIGNAL TO DON UNIFORMS

Just Like Cinderella They Look Forward to the Witching Hour

Sofia, Bulgaria—February 27, 1941

The hour of the midnight ball has almost struck, the 8000 or so hobnailed Cinderellas who have crossed the Bulgarian borders from Rumania by airplane, train, ferry and pontoon bridge in tanks, armored cars, automobiles and motorcycles are all in their chimney corners, and it remains only for Hitler to pronounce the word and the magic transformation will begin.

The two jolly-looking young men who seem like tennis players except for their scarred cheeks, and beside whom one sat in the coffee house this afternoon, will appear in the same grey-green uniforms that fill the streets of Bucharest. The sober, erect gentleman of fifty with the top-laced boots, who tried to be polite when the BBC came in booming, will appear in the striped red trousers of the Reichswehr general staff.

Was that a naval officer for whom the Bulgarian admiral put on his dress uniform with all his medals this evening? Whoever he was, he forgot himself and gave the Nazi salute. When midnight strikes, as suddenly as the cheering section of an American college game shifts its cards upon signal, all the German traveling men are to become soldiers.

It is probably the most perfectly trained army in mufti that one has ever seen. In Bucharest, where they come from, their routine of greeting is complicated: first, Hitler salute, then handshake, the army salute, then Hitler salute again. Here, it is only a slight lift of the eyelash.

This business of being part of one large machine, and yet pretending to be isolated all day long, is a wearisome test for army nerves. About one o'clock in the morning, when a handful of other guests had taken their keys and gone up to bed, and even the American newspapermen, having given up looking in alleys and behind garages for the one uniform that would operate as a catalyst of the whole situation, have fallen asleep on their typewriters, the visiting firemen have retired to an old-fashioned German get-together down in the back room of the lobby.

What do these Germans talk about? What did the Greeks lying inside the Trojan horse talk about? Probably the moment when they would get out.

The tanks are in Bulgaria, the artillery is here, a few airplanes are at a new air field at Dolna-Orekovitza—at least they were last week—the munitions and food stores are ready, the motorized columns are waiting in the country roads, on the rolling uplands of the Danube to the snowy Balkan Mountains. The air is full of German radio messages. A huge army truck, dirty with miles of travel, its grey curtains flying wildly and the empty screws where its license ought to be, went hurtling through the streets at dusk, and the Sofia policeman abruptly found something wrong with the button of his glove.

A staff campaign car without side doors, bearing Reichswehr plates, got itself tangled in the narrow downtown streets, and acted as embarrassed as a fireman who falls through a skylight. At four o'clock this morning two German agency correspondents telegraphed Berlin that the invasion had occurred. This afternoon the German legation had a press conference for its own newspapermen and told them that nothing of the kind had happened, at least not yet.

The news of the death of Bulgaria's independence was greatly exaggerated. It was not midnight, but half-past eleven. All the uniforms went back into the suitcases again. The shoes put out in the hall tonight to be shined were the simple, sturdy kind, affected by army people in their civilian interludes. What will tomorrow night's boots look like?

About the only rights the Germans and Bulgarians are still ready to concede the British remaining here, is a question of etiquette. After all, decorum was always the Britons' forte.

How then, Mr. British Minister? Is this still a visit or is it an invasion? How many German officers, busily ignoring each other, are enough to make a diplomatic protest? If they get together stealthily late at night for beer, and if they all produced papers, would you say that they were nothing but arms salesmen?

The best witticism was coined at the German legation, when they called up the press department of the Foreign Office to ask the name of the so-called German officer who slugged U.S. Minister George Earle with a bottle. It must have been a mistake, the legation suggested. First, the assailant was not in German uniform. Second, there was no German officer with a bottle-scar on his nose, not, at least, attached to the staff at the legation.

And the buxom, jolly German lady of sixty, dressed in black, with spotless white linen, who arrived on the plane from Rumania just after Marshal General Siegmund Wilhelm von List (commander in chief of Nazi troops headquartered at Sinaia, Rumania)—who is she? Has she a uniform of some kind? What does it look like? Or is she just somebody's mother who came to see the show?

The British simply must do something about this soon. The suspense is not only terrible; it is getting a little ridiculous.

—

Nazis March While Britons Dally in Sofia

Belgrade, Yugoslavia—March 7, 1941

The presence in Bulgaria of forty Britons—plus about fifty Dutch, Belgian and Polish diplomats who have lost their status—became today a military advantage greater than five divisions in the Nazi attack on Greece racing south for the border.

Until the diplomats of the three governments and the English are evacuated on Sunday and Monday the British bombers waiting in the Greek air fields cannot check the heavy German columns now passing down the Struma Valley road. Nor can they, for fear of having their nationals held as hostages, blast the pontoon bridges over the Danube, across which the Nazi troops are following their Luftwaffe predecessors.

Thus while the Britons (many of whom insisted until the last that the Bulgarians would not let in the Germans) are getting health certificates for dogs, automobile cachets and German military permissions to drive to the Turkish border, the Germans are formally taking over the anti-aircraft posts, listening stations and air fields upon which they have been working for the last several months with the collaboration of the Bulgarian general staff and the government.

For the British and their allies Bulgaria has been a second home that they are saying farewell to in the measured English fashion. Meantime the Germans speedily are converting it into a fortress and base to strike the English in Greece.

How many of the approximately 25 divisions and 1500 airplanes in Rumania have crossed the Danube into Bulgaria is uncertain because the sudden step has caused exaggerated figures. Judging from the strength of the general staff in Sofia, under Field Marshal General von List, the number probably does not exceed six divisions, and possibly a single division of the Luftwaffe.

Since correspondents are not allowed to leave Sofia, besides having their communications severed for the past three days, it is impossible to say how many soldiers have been routed around the city and how many sent through the Shipka Pass. The German technique has been to strive for air mastery south of the Balkan Mountains first. Nearly all the trucks in campaign cars passing from Sofia bear the license *W. L.,* meaning Wehrmacht Luftwaffe.

In a column of about 120 armored cars, trucks and officers' cars passing the palace of King Boris* Wednesday noon, the writer counted 22 of the

---

*Boris III (b. 1894), who ruled from 1918 until his death in 1943 amid a succession of Balkan upheavals. An uneasy and powerless ally of the Nazis, he is alternately reviled for the assistance he gave to Hitler and admired for all he refused to give.

type of German anti-tank guns which is also used for anti-aircraft defense. Evidently the Germans recognize that, in the mountainous terrain along the Struma, the single narrow road with its small bridges and small-gauge railroad are easy marks for British bombers unless they first gain air mastery here.

The writer saw a single sign of humor in the entire phlegmatic invasion: a big army truck, caked with mud, bearing the words, scrawled by a soldier's finger, *Grand Balkan Express*.

On the boulevards the Bulgarians stand around the formidable German field cars as Americans on Michigan Avenue when a new model runabout appears. Many trucks bear nets and green cloth screens on top for camouflage against bombing. Kitchen trucks and mobile mechanical shops accompany each column.

Thanks to the British still being here, the Germans are able to break every rule for military communications, long columns of trucks being seen without any defense whatever. Since no fuel trucks are in evidence, it is believed that the Bulgarians have opened their roadside military depots for these very heavy vehicles.

Special posts have been built on several Sofia routes for soldier lookouts to watch for British or Greek planes. The Germans are quoted as having pledged to destroy Athens if a single bomb is dropped upon Sofia. Not having been there, the writer is unable to say whether Athens is technically an open city under the military definition. Sofia has at least three anti-aircraft cannon believed of British make, mounted on the roof of the national bank in the heart of the city.

For 72 hours, up to last night, telephone communications have been interfered with or severed by the authorities, apparently under German influence. When the writer left the city on Thursday, the director of the foreign press was reported in conference with three German officers, presumably arranging the details of the formal censorship to replace the present irregular one.

CABLE AND WIRELESS LIMITED.

ΤΗΛΕΓΡΑΦΕΙΟΝ ΑΘΗΝΩΝ

ΤΗΛΕΓΡΑΦΗΜΑ

26 APR. 1941

| Date
Ἡμερομηνία | 26 4 41 | 0955 | Time handed
Govt Office | 1000 |

(Ἡ κάτωθι πρώτη γραμμή δὲν ἀφορᾶ τὸν ἀποδέκτην. Ἡ δευτέρα γραμμὴ περιλαμβάνει κατὰ σειρὰν : τὸν αὔξοντα ἀριθμὸν τοῦ τηλεγραφήματος, τὸ Γραφεῖον προελεύσεως, ἀριθμὸν λέξεων, ἡμερομηνίαν, ὥραν καταθέσεως καὶ παρατηρήσεις).

GOA T11 CHRIST

NYZ122/ CHICAGOILL 25 25 1044

LC WELLER AMERICAN LEGATION ATHINAI

YOUR COURAGEOUS BRILLIANT COVERAGE DEEPLY APPRECIATED BUT

IMPORTANTEST YOU UNSUBMIT HEINIE SUPERVISION PREFERABLEST

TURKEYWARD OTHERWISE CRETEWARD OR WHATEVER FEASIBLEST

BINDER +

"Via Radio-Athinai"

Auswärtiges Amt

Berlin W 8, 26. Juni 1941
Wilhelmstr. 74-76

Nr. P XIII Auslandspresse

Der amerikanische Journalist Georg Weller, der
ursprünglich direkt von Wien über Buchs nach der
Schweiz ausreisen wollte, fährt auf Veranlassung
der Presseabteilung des Auswärtigen Amtes über
Berlin nach der Schweiz. Aus diesem Grunde ist
die Grenzausgangsstelle nicht Buchs, sondern
Basel. Es wird gebeten, Herrn Weller ungehindert
passieren lassen zu wollen.

Im Auftrag

II

The Fall of Greece

George Weller radios that what makes his experiences at the Greek front "almost unbearably terrible and at the same time sublime . . . is the patient belief of good, ordinary human beings that freedom, like a big, benevolent stork sitting upon his nest above each village square, will return to his vacant home."

—*Chicago Daily News*

Greece mentored Weller as a history-minded reporter. Saturated in the classical world, he had known the country well since the early 1930s. He'd lived in Athens for years as a Balkans correspondent for the *New York Times,* and written a book about Greek politics. Thus, at age thirty-three, when he returned from April to July 1941 to witness its fall to the Germans, he had a special perspective on its struggles—a deep grasp of both languages, both peoples, and a strong dose of political realism. (A good friend, the brilliant young reporter Spyros Vlachos, had committed suicide two years earlier after being tormented by the Metaxas dictatorship, which Weller termed "a four-year police state of extremist Fascist nature.")

The four months Weller witnessed are among the most momentous of Greece's century. Late in life, he had no more ardent wish than to visit, one last time, the islands he had known seventy years earlier.

In October 1940, Mussolini—without telling Hitler—gave an

ultimatum of invasion to Prime Minister Metaxas, who defied him. The Greek army, deployed throughout their familiar mountains, defeated the Italian forces and pushed them back into Albania, where they had to wait out the winter for reinforcements. This delay is now considered the first Allied land victory of World War II.

For the Axis, Greece held enormous strategic importance. Without it, they could not hope to seize the British-held Middle East, nor protect their easy gains in the Balkans, nor control the eastern Mediterranean.

Hitler, eager to break his nonaggression pact with Stalin and attack Russia yet unable to leave his southeastern flank unconquered and vulnerable, took over the Greek invasion from the Italians with a Nazi blitzkrieg in April 1941. (Metaxas had died in January.) Winston Churchill sent British troops from Libya and Egypt to try to prolong the defense, but by May, Greece was occupied by Axis forces. Some historians believe that the delay of the Nazi assault on Russia—enough to put that army at the mercy of the Moscow winter—can be credited to the doomed Greek resistance.

Once Athens was overrun at the end of April, Weller was forced to stay and fell silent for a month. "Quarantined" by the Gestapo for nine weeks, he was unable to communicate with his editors. His early dispatches about the invasion, sent by official German mail to his *Chicago Daily News* colleague in Berlin, David Nichol, got through. With the help of third parties he was able to smuggle out only a single later dispatch, also published here. None can have pleased his captors, who gave him a protracted, convoluted departure.

The tragedy, human and military, of Greece matured Weller rapidly as a reporter. From his narrow escape in Salonika (present-day Thessaloniki), to enduring his first air raids in the countryside, to his portraits of a besieged but uncowed Athens, to his weeks under the Nazi bureaucratic thumb, the author of these dispatches is a changed man and a stylistically leaner writer from the rather elaborate Balkans observer of a few months earlier. He is now a war correspondent.

—

A Tale of Two Cities—Rome Shorn of Glory, Athens a City of Honor

Athens, Greece—April 3, 1941

Today's picture of Rome and Athens:

Two worldly-wise cities lie blacked out under the brilliant Mediterranean starlight tonight, contemplating the same destiny that has reversed their ancient cousinship. Imperial Rome is in the descendance, the Germans have come again into the Forum, but this time Greece, once conquered by the Roman legions, holds the advantage.

How are the two peoples, fundamentally different by lineage but related through Mediterranean culture, adapting themselves to the fortunes of war? How are ordinary Italians and Greeks affected by the incredible reversal that has filled even the enemies of Italy, including the Greeks, with pity for those who, following Mussolini's dictum, have believed, obeyed, fought—and died?

Because the writer is the only American newspaperman who has visited both Rome and Athens in this fateful new year, he undertakes to hazard a description of the changes war has wrought in the psychology of the peoples of the two countries.

A visit to Rome was made in January, when the Italian situation was more hopeful. Mussolini had not yet tried for a personal victory in Albania and failed. The battle of Cape Matapan—"No battle at all," a captive sailor in a Greek naval prison told the writer this morning, "because we never fired a shot"—was unfought. Yugoslavia was quivering with uncertainty, instead of bristling with confidence.

All these brutal blows to fascism were still to come and there was hope of a spring Albanian campaign and stopping the British at Bardia and holding Eritrea and Ethiopia. Yet it was hard to imagine a more dangerously subdued city than Rome in midwinter. The air was electric with suffering and unspoken resentment.

Meanwhile, on the opposite side of the Adriatic, even while Hitler's Trojan Horse was leading the German divisions along their zigzag way from Vienna to the Black Sea and across Bulgaria toward the Greek border, a resignation to die if necessary was giving the Greeks fortitude.

There was resignation in Rome, too, but it was acceptance of death itself. Something that had been real and even idealistic was dying; it was unmistakable and could almost be smelled in the tense Roman air. A whole political philosophy was lying upon its bier, breathing as steadily as it could, trying to conceal from the worried faces at the bedside that it would never rise again, as death is unmentioned when the malady is hopeless and the slow illness final.

Then one has walked through both the Roman Forum and the Athenian Temple of Zeus by moonlight. One has touched Italian as well as Greek sandbags and heard overhead Greek as well as Italian planes. One has groped through Italian as well as Greek blackouts along the slippery walls of streets where not only Metaxas and Mussolini but also Aristotle and Cicero have walked. And one can say without the wish to favor either people's pride, but merely to report the truth, that Greece has had an advantage of spirit more than of arms.

Greece has suffered deeply in the war, she has lost many sons in saving her honor, but honor is still left. In Italy there is an inexpressible feeling that it is honor rather than victory that is slipping away, as the arms that seized Albania and attacked Greece never invented any moral justification except a superficial one and disclaimed needing even that. The Fascist blow has been force, and with its failure there is a sense of emptiness in the Roman streets.

The battle of Cape Matapan has brought evidence directly to Greece's shores. Italian sailors who spent twenty-three hours swimming in the water amid mangled comrades, who knew only that they had been roused from sleep to find their ship pinned in the glare of British searchlights and were blown instantly into the sea, were very clear and emphatic when they were asked today why they were fighting.

"When we left Taranto and were told we were going to meet the British we were happy," they said. "We wanted to prove that we were brave. We had no Germans with us, either. We wanted to revenge ourselves on the offense of the Treaty of Versailles."

One of the handful of officers who survived was asked by the writer whether he still believed in an Axis victory. "As long as the Germans continue every day to sink 100,000 tons of ships carrying American food," he said.

When told that such figures were fantastic, the officer stared steadily at the twinkling Bay of Salamis, where the Greeks once repelled the Persian galleys.

"I don't know," he replied, standing there pathetically in prisoner's dungarees. "A hundred thousand tons a day was what we were told in Rome."

—

LOVE OF COUNTRY DRAWS WEALTHY TO BATTLE LINE

An Italian Prince and a Greek Millionaire Both Do Their Share

Athens, Greece—April 4, 1941

In Greece and Italy the attitude of the wealthy toward the war is sharply different from the public psychology.

Rome, in midwinter, when the writer passed through, was overshadowed by the death of the 23-year-old son of one of the two oldest Italian families, Prince Camillo Caetani. He was the last of his line and a 700-year-old family died out with him. He met Greek fire in Albania's mountains, and because it took too long to get him to a dressing station, because of half-prepared Italian support, he bled to death.

Prince Caetani left one witticism that may be remembered after the war is over. In the first days, before German anti-aircraft gunners arrived, the Italians placed all their guns around the edge of the Sacred City. When the first practice alarm was sounded, and the guns began firing, something went wrong. The barrage formed an umbrella and shells began dropping in the boulevards. The Forum was peppered, the Coliseum chipped, and shrapnel fell even in the Piazza Venezia.

"What is this, anyway?" asked Prince Caetani, "the Italo-Italian war?"

What has war meant to Greeks of the same class as Prince Caetani?

In an aristocratic club of Athens, a sleepy retreat with red-leather lounges full of brooding gentlemen, the writer met yesterday a Greek merchant of Paris. He was a member of a clique of men between fifty and sixty who regularly discuss politics.

A millionaire, fat and as fond of life's good things as Prince Caetani, but twice his age, the Greek displayed himself to his friends. He was dressed in the khaki of a private of the lowest grade, wearing the rolled leggings and forage cap.

"How do I look?" he asked his friends, extending his huge hobnailed marching boots above the waxed floor. "Isn't this a handsome jacket they gave me? The designs I'm wearing show everybody that I'm in the signal corps." He turned around slowly so they could admire him rear and front. "My captain says I'm very fit for a man of my age, and if we go to the front I'll handle myself very well. I may not be good enough to get a medal but I ought to be able to grab a few Italians."

A retired Greek general, looking like an old fox, watched the rookie over the heads of his fellow members with a tinge of envy. The millionaire private, to whom everyone listened respectfully because of his uniform, began giving a lecture.

"I don't believe in giving the poor everything they want," he said categorically. "Our poor people seem to think they can have this war all to themselves, but they can't. I have just as much right to get in it as my chauffeur. I got a little soft sitting around this club with you so long, but I guess my figure is as good as Mussolini's. Want me to show you again the way I salute my captain?"

—

Greek Salonika Retreat Told by Eyewitness: Saga of Heroic Greeks

Correspondent of Daily News Reveals Feat

Athens, Greece—April 14–15, 1941

The only truthful and complete eyewitness account of the fall of Salonika could be written by Greek officers who were forced to abandon the second city of the nation, and by the population, which has now become merely a pawn in Adolf Hitler's plans for empire. But since these voices cannot speak and their stories can only be pieced together by historians, your correspondent offers herewith the single, authentic, first-hand story of the passing of Salonika.

As fortune would have it, the *Chicago Daily News* was the only foreign newspaper or agency with its own correspondent in Salonika during the two days preceding the German capture. The present story—composed after a three-day passage aboard a tiny fishing boat, upon which this writer had to sleep on deck and exist upon a diet of black bread and army oranges—may stand temporarily, despite its unavoidable incompleteness due to the fact that the writer had to flee from the Macedonian capital with the last boat full of refugees.

The Greek retreat by sea from Macedonia and Thrace, one of the least known but most extraordinary strategic feats of the war, is coming to a successful close.

Most of the Greek army holding the northern frontier against the Germans was able to withdraw from around Salonika Bay, blowing up bridges as they went and preparing a line of steel that now awaits the Germans—the rules of the game prevent saying where—between the sea and Albania.

But in order to save the heavy equipment, artillery, materiel and the invaluable technical heads of the general staff of the eastern campaign—and .to accomplish thoroughly the work of sabotage—relatively small Greek forces had to hold the breach during the withdrawal. When surrender was imminent, these men, having loyally done their job as a stopgap, were given the choice of yielding or making their way to the sea, where vessels of all sizes and shapes awaited them.

They could either become prisoners or back slowly toward the tiny ports of the Macedonian shore, hoping to board dingy little fishing craft. Some made the characteristic choice of the independent Greek spirit. They went on fighting.

Although no fresh reports have come from that region, evacuees assert that fighting is continuing, the Germans having the greatest difficulty ferreting out the harassing Greek bands.

This gallant rearguard action—strictly voluntary—has slowed and thinned the German progress westward, because a substantial number of *Schnelltruppen* ["fast troops"—i.e., motorized infantry] and airplanes were forced to keep their attention in the area bordering Turkey.

Salonika was abandoned according to an orderly plan whereby the city was recognized as a liability in a long campaign. Though this may seem a loser's excuse for a setback, it is the truth. Such a policy of recognizing that a superior line of defense existed south of Salonika, and that the city itself was a military liability, could only be taken in secrecy, despite the heartaches involved. This fact cannot rub from the writer's mind the haunted eyes of Salonikans walking the streets last Tuesday afternoon, searching the face of each well-dressed person or braided officer for the answer to the unspoken question: When are they coming, and from where?

The military decision for withdrawal was taken around dawn Tuesday morning, when the general staff's telegram was filed at Salonika. The man in the street knew only at 4:10 that afternoon that something terrible was happening when a huge black pillar cloud rolled directly over the city from the broad, beautiful bay.

Only a few minutes before, all had been heartened by the sight of four German prisoners marching quickly under guard toward the railroad station, bound for Athens. They were treated, as this correspondent knows because he interviewed them in a railroad shelter during an air raid and later in a coach, with the greatest courtesy and understanding. They were stared at, but the only man who ventured to jeer aloud from the crowd was speedily silenced by policemen.

Their businesslike march through the downtown temporarily restored hope that rumors of Teutons nearing the city, having broken the Serbian lines, were false. But when it was evident that the enormous black cloud was because a camouflaged oil tank banked up on the western end of the waterfront had been fired, the portent was unmistakable. Perhaps due to stoical Greek courage, no panic occurred.

At six the last train departed from a tiny boxlike station in Salonika, carrying what it could in huge packages of army stores piled upon the platform. Since few believed that bridges still existed, there were only a few persons at the station.

In the meantime, the heaviest Greek motorized equipment—which will not be detailed here for obvious reasons—went pouring through the main boulevards. The army was saving everything that could be saved. Departing soldiers tried to cheer the crowds by shaking their fists toward the north, but the pedestrians merely stood and watched, a few sadly raising their hands.

Giant oil reservoirs plumed up. The demolition squads, determined that the Germans should not find even the little advantage of fuel tanks, moved to a second yard, and soon another terrific column of smoke and flame mounted skyward.

By six o'clock it would have been natural to expect some such mass rush upon the few vessels at the waterfront as occurred at Smyrna and upon the occasion after World War I of the burning of Salonika, but none occurred. There were pathetic scenes at the docks, where civil administration employees were bidding goodbye to their relatives, and at a tiny dock behind a villa east of the city, where British citizens were being carried by tender down the bay to a waiting vessel.

So great was the rush among Cypriots, Smyrniots and Jews carrying the authentic blue passport that the small camouflaged yacht was unable even to accommodate two Americans desiring passage. In the end, the tender simply failed to return after taking off British diplomatic pouches that had come from Athens with the writer the day before, leaving a small knot of pathetic people upon the quay for care by the imaginary financial resources of the American consulate. Meanwhile the two columns of oily smoke had joined at a great height over the city.

While soldiers, federal constabulary and civil employees, including those of the telephone, telegraph and railroad services, crowded aboard two freighters in the bay, the overflow was obliged to take caïques, coastwise sailing vessels, averaging about forty feet long, with diesel power. After the six o'clock train left, the oil tanks continue to blow up briskly in a manner probably extremely satisfying to the demolition squads. A new and deeper note came about seven o'clock, from the western marshes: bridges going heavenward.

Most of the small army of aged taxis probably got through—at least those that left before three o'clock. The first Nazi motorized equipment was coming down the road from Doiran, Ghevgheli and Torex, straight for the ruptured end of the communications. Refugees dropped their papier-mâché suitcases tied with string, their clothing wrapped in bed linen. (A no man's land between today's lines is apparently cluttered with household goods.)

Most soldiers carried merely a rifle, a blanket, and a large round loaf of bread under their arms, and as soon as they had the safety of the deck underfoot, lit the omnipresent Greek cigarette and turned their eyes north to the low, bare foothills of the Rhodopes, where their comrades were still struggling to stem the Germans in the Strymona pass. Few wounded were aboard the boats, most apparently having been taken aboard the southward train.

By sunset, all the big freighters and war vessels (undefinable here) had weighed anchor and slipped down the gulf, leaving the bay, which in the afternoon had been dotted with ships of every size, unnaturally bare. Around eight o'clock, warehouses in the harbor's free zone caught fire. The personnel of the Yugoslav area, mostly Serbians, left on whichever sailboats would carry them, heedless of destination. The last train from their homeland had passed the Ghevgheli-Idomeni frontier the night before, having been attacked by nine Stuka dive bombers at Skoplje and abandoned by the passengers seven times while their papers were being examined.

After darkness fell, with the city still blindingly alight from waterfront fires, two deep booms were heard—the powder magazines of the chief fortresses guarding Salonika had been blown. Soon afterward fire leaped up from a flour factory which would have furnished nutriment to the oncoming German divisions, which reports number at five. Previously, according to a statement of the Greek authorities, army foodstuffs were distributed to the population so it would not fall into enemy hands.

It is rare today to see a fire burning almost unchecked. Salonika firemen, alone among the civil employees, were required to stay at their posts and see that fires, while consuming thoroughly, should not spread to the remainder of the city.

From eight o'clock communication with Athens, except the last military radios, had ceased. Since bridges had been blown up, the remainder of the troops directed themselves eastward, beginning the seaward evacuation.

Through being the only foreign correspondent in northern Greece, the *Chicago Daily News* representative was able to choose between: *a)* going south by motorcar or railroad with the general staff's equipment and the majority of troops—arriving at Athens within two days and, *b)* taking a chance on embarking with the ragamuffin flotilla, which began leaving Macedonian and Thracian seaports 48 hours after the last bridge over the Cestos had been blown up and mobile retreat westward voluntarily cut off.

Luckily, the writer chose the latter, slower course. Although this account must mention, by name, merely those places positively in German hands, it is the only testimony available by a journalist, either Greek or foreign, taking part in the withdrawal by sea—a withdrawal equivalent to Dunkirk, and testimony that seafaring Greeks have lost none of the cunning of Homer's time.

The writer was accompanied throughout the 3½-day journey by Mrs. Ray Brock, wife of the *New York Times* correspondent, who had arrived from Belgrade aboard the last train before the Nazi invasion overran the Vardar Valley.

Five different caïques—as the Greeks call their small fishing boats—all with soldiers aboard, conveyed us from the burning Salonikan waterfront to the foothills above Piraeus, reached by taxi while the fiercest night raid by the Germans was directed against the port.

The caïques were similar: high rounded prow, poop low amidships, canvas-lined rails. In each, the captain was absolute master until a ranking Army officer stepped aboard.

After saying goodbye to the American consul and vice-consul, the writer went aboard a small sailboat, supposedly destined south for Chios. The engine stalled in the harbor, and it was nearly one and the moonlit bay was deserted when the motor finally caught. Occasional shots were audible. As the city fell completely silent, illuminated by brilliant flames, the distant reverberation of artillery began, volley after volley. (Already German motorcyclists were near, encountering no resistance.) It was the beginning of the great Aegean embarkation.

The entire bay, in fact the entire northern Aegean, was the scene of a sea retreat organized upon the waves, with characteristic Greek willingness to make up the answers to emergencies when they were encountered. Majors and colonels upon the poops of dozens of crafts, most less than forty feet long, talked over the situation with old island salts who guided their craft by standing erect at a ten-foot-long helm, hewn out of a single piece of wood and held between the ankles.

The sailing courses were discussed within hearing of all as in the days when Agamemnon's fleet was returning from Troy, and the waters were approximately the same, the vessels no bigger, nor was the map consulted even once. The menu, consisting of soft, black bread and oranges, with hardtack as dessert, was served by passengers tossing it from hand to hand. Although many of the passengers had known what it was to try to hold a Bulgarian border fort while it was being dive-bombed by countless German planes, not one complaint was heard.

Officers and soldiers, who could escape the war forever by crossing the Turkish border, were calmly making new plans to meet the Axis forces upon the northwestern fronts. Some expressed the wish to return to Athens briefly, or see their families before taking up again the strain of war. Doubt of final victory never once was expressed.

The grizzled skipper, who had served on freight ships on both American coasts, pointed up. A huge bomber, flying at about 5000 feet high and probably laden with a deadly cargo for the German columns, was passing to the north. No one paid any attention to it, except ourselves; and several soldiers, busily cleaning rifles and submachine guns, scarcely glanced overhead, while half a dozen hung seasick upon the rails had not even heard the motors.

The caïque left Salonika Bay three hours before the Germans arrived, with firing audible in the suburbs and an unearthly glare from oil tanks fired by British demolition experts reddening the sea. The fire lay ahead, off the port bow. It was soon discernible as the mighty headland of Karaboun, where the Greeks had a fortress and a small naval air station listening-post guarding Salonika Bay.

Two large buildings topping the peninsular cliff were walls of flames as the caïque passed. A Greek patrol boat waited in the choppy waters below the headland for the last of the demolition squad, in this case Greeks, to descend to safety.

As the sun came up, the horizon ahead bulked with the outline of Cassandra, first of the three peninsulas extending southeast. As we ran along the coast, the odd passenger list, including Polish refugees, Salonikan merchants and several employees from as far east as Alexandropolis, stood upon the heaving deck in overcoats, watching the headland with the same sleep-befuddled eyes as the soldiers'. Were the Germans coming this way yet?

When we slipped into the narrow quarter-mile canal at the village of Potiri two big army trucks and three cars were waiting at the end of the road. Could they be Germans? The boxlike ferry being pulled across the tide rip was full of soldiers wearing welcome brown. They were members of the fast transport that connected the field base and Salonika headquarters, headed by a husky young sergeant.

The Germans were close behind. Although there were no signs of panic, the sergeant insisted that the boat leave immediately without pausing for provisions. Mrs. Brock and the writer bade adieu here to the first caïque, whose captain, anxious to obey the sergeant, quickly sailed for a remote island in the mid-Aegean, taking the luggage of both Americans, as well as their overcoats and food.

About an hour after the caïque left another was found at the canal's eastern end. The bewhiskered captain lingered, despite reports of oncoming Germans, until two rowboats had been loaded with cases of oranges and bread as well as more soldiers at one time than the vessel probably had passengers in her entire history. Finally the sail was hoisted, the engine panted and the vessel began clipping the waves southward. Barely half an hour later German squads reached Potiri, making themselves masters of the peninsula.

With the giant conelike peak of Mount Athos—the clerical republic where monks of the Greek Church dwell in perpetual celibacy—looming, the overladen craft began to be overtaken by other craft coming from tiny white villages perched upon the green surrounding hills.

One small, blue-rimmed dirty-white craft passed, apparently superpowered, bearing demolition officers. When another lumbering caïque overtook us, the colonel ordered the ships, in constant peril of entangling their bowsprits' rigging, to be brought together. Many soldiers, constabulary, and troopers in blue-green were ordered overside. Learning that a new caïque had been found on an island a few hours from our baggage, we also clambered from one bucking vessel to the other.

The officers and soldiers were eager to get to the mainland as soon as possible, but although the weather was clear blue, a terrific wind was blowing. Eventually the craft began to slip out and the two Americans found a fourth vessel, bound for a nearby island where their luggage and clothing and the records of the *Chicago Daily News* Foreign Service had ended their wanderings.

On the second night the sea grew rougher, the wind was contrary and the cold too great for sleep upon the rainswept, crowded decks. Soldiers, gendarmes, women and children dragged canvas through the craft's single hatch, spread it upon the naked ribs of the keel, and used a handful of cold bags for covering. The skipper, seated in an ordinary kitchen chair, hugged the huge helm under one arm as the rain blotted out the islands. The soldiers, now having acquired sea legs, calmly shared half their cigarettes.

Before dawn, the craft had picked her way into the harbor of a landlocked island, far to the south—another white-walled town, cast like a deck of cards upon a moonlit hillside. The harbor was crowded by dozens of caïques and the worried portmaster, who had an American high school education, was pacing the stone quay, endeavoring to persuade the skippers to leave promptly to eliminate the danger of air raids. Here we rejoined the original transport squad and, surrounded by soldiers, spent the night upon the relative comfort of a wooden bench.

In the starlit morning we were set, with soldiers, in a tiny motorboat piloted by a giant Greek, once a resident of Indiana Harbor. We reached the small island of Euboea about noon. After a two-mile hike to the nearest village, we procured a car which brought the entire company to one of the principal towns in central Greece.

From the matter-of-factness with which the villagers received the cavalcade, it was evident that many defenders of Thrace and Macedonia had already passed the same way. In an unnameable harbor, we saw a Greek hospital ship.

After the mayor himself turned out a force of constabulary to find a taxi, your correspondent set forth on the long drive to Athens. En route he saw many familiar faces and a considerable number of soldiers, indicating the general staff's plan had been carried out as well as could be expected, considering the sudden Serbian retreat.

Repeated air alarms which were scrupulously enforced in the countryside, even at night, obliged the passengers, more for form's sake than for safety, to take refuge under bridges and in fields while pom-poms made punching noises in the darkness and the night over Piraeus was ablaze with flaming onions.

Athens itself was wild with joy because a German bomber had been seen falling in spectacular flames a few minutes before. The cool, well-managed retreat by scores of invaluable officers and hundreds of valiant men determined to fight the Germans again, wherever found, was little known, but for an American witness it was proof of Greek resourcefulness, cooperation and capacity to think fast when hard-pressed—as well as the first victory for a midget fishing fleet.

—

GERMANS POUR DOWN HAIL OF LEAD FROM GREEK SKIES

With the British Forces in Central Greece—April 22, 1941 (Delayed)

Here in the shadow of cloud-enshrouded Parnassus, where blue valley mists make the long snowy summit seem to float in clear air, the hum of a

German bomber scatters men across the landscape as if the droning were itself a bomb.

When you hear a Messerschmitt's vibration or the pulselike whoomwhoom of a big Junkers or Dornier you select the pilot's probable object— tents, trucks, supply dump, railroad cars—and run as far as possible in the opposite direction. While running you attach your helmet, canting it instinctively toward the plane.

With your breath coming short and fast and the nape of your neck feeling exposed, you pick possible places ahead—trees, big or small ditches, stone walls, old foundations or simply deep grass. Soon you learn to line up shelter spots away from the target by planning successive future dashes from bush to ditch.

You run with your shoulders huddled low, ready to throw yourself to the ground as soon as the machine guns begin uttering their short epithetical bursts of hatred. If the plane is high you can run several seconds longer but you must be motionless and hidden before coming within the pilot's eyerange. Your face must lie flat against the earth though your back feels pierced with hundreds of bullets even before the ratcheting sound begins overhead. The lightest movement may mean the hose of death which, like a gardener's watering can, is carefully pouring bullets upon every tree and shelter within reachable distance of the road.

Olive trees make ideal cover for the convoy that breaks into a wide circle, resembling pioneer covered wagon trains defending themselves against Indians.

During a recent fourteen-hour bombing and machine-gunning in a dozen places behind the front, your correspondent experienced what has been the daily dose of exposed British and Greek troops. Camped in a stone barn below Parnassus, he had just emerged from a sleeping bag and was picking haystraws from his ears when a cry arose: "Here he comes!" *He* always means Jerry, who is an early riser.

I ran across the meadow, half slipped and fell against a stone wall. The Heinkel came down leisurely from the morning sun and sprayed the barn tiles with bullets from about 2000 feet. No bomb fell; the two small trucks seemed probably unworthy game. The spurts of fire, which sounded like members of a motorcycle club starting their engines, abruptly ceased.

One could almost feel the searching eyes of the pilot. He fired three sustained bursts. Then, humming contentedly to itself, the plane disappeared over the shoulder of the Parnassus foothill. Absolute silence ensued.

I noticed for the first time that the meadows were filled with red poppies. From behind the hill a machine gun thrice chewed into the silence. Not far away was the village where I had bought big round loaves of bread, lettuce and olives the night before. Suddenly the earth rocked and the pumping noise filled the air. A bomb had fallen in the village. Machine guns spoke again faintly, like a far-off typewriter, with a motor's soft sounds dying away. Silence again.

After a few minutes, heads appeared above the ditches and walls. It was too soon for shouts, because those lying in ditches always converse in whispers, like people in city shelters. A few figures emerged from the grass, brushing off dirt.

Another motor was heard, this time from the direction of Athens. We hoped it was a British Hurricane but its pulsating engines showed that it was a big Junkers. The psychological effect of being approached from the rear was calculated to give us the impression of being surrounded. While the Junkers bombed the village, I left my stone wall and ran across the meadow to the river and jumped into the shelter of the overhanging bank. A thin, transparent cloud hung at about 3000 feet and the Nazi pilot, though unmolested by any ack-ack, entered the veil, churning his way through and leaving a wake like a ferryboat.

He passed over without even firing but before he was out of sight another Messerschmitt appeared from a third direction, coming fast and low. At the same time over the mountain pass toward Lamia appeared three Nazi bombers. Along the railroad the earth gushed upward in six places while the ground rocked. Overhead the Messerschmitt began machine-gunning.

When a faint, screaming wail began behind the riverbank I knew a bomb was coming. *How near, how far?* A giant bomb went through the earth behind me and the river's water leapt in a dozen places. Two more planes appeared from the direction of Salonika and began bombing the railroad line. A machine gun atop a freight car replied to the bombs which missed the track by several yards.

For a quarter-hour the valley was filled with buzzing motors and bursting bombs, machine-gun fire dusting all the treetops near the highway. The attack was the antithesis of bombardment by armadas flying in echelons; it was like a circus with too much going on for comprehension, single planes attacking whatever they wished and unmistakably enjoying the sport of diving from all angles, showering machine-gun bullets at will. The effect of seeing such an attack upon encamped troops, with the only reply cautious, intermittent machine-gun fire from the ground, was bewildering and unsettling. The effect of lying absolutely still, while death went squeaking through the grass and bombs rocked the earth beneath you, was a feeling of rage then, as the punishment continued, of degradation and defilement. It was like being asked to remain immobile while being beaten from head to foot.

The bombing and machine-gunning went on at least a dozen times more during the day. I found a rock crevice on the mountainside giving protection against the thinly singing machine-gun bullets. From here I saw a Nazi bomber, disdaining even to dive upon its target, drop two bombs from at least 4000 feet, hitting a road less than twenty feet wide. Bombs could be seen falling slantwise, like quotation marks sliding down the face of the blue sky. But when these hit, nothing happened.

"Duds," muttered another American correspondent. Then, with a roar, the road flew into the air. The dive-bombs had been timed for delay to allow the plane to make an upward sweep. A New Zealand truck driver, a few feet away, who had emerged from cover, was blown from his feet and shaken up, the only ascertainable casualty of the day except three or four trucks whose spotters were already lying in the grass. But many useful hours had been lost.

—

BRITISH STRIVING TO HOLD OFF NAZIS AT THERMOPYLAE

Handful of Troops Fighting Stout Delaying Action in 'Forlorn Cause'

Athens, Greece—April 24, 1941

Fighting a stout delaying action in what is admittedly a forlorn cause—the defense of Greece's sacred city against the Germans—a handful of British

Imperial troops are trying to hold the mountain defenses above Thermopy-lae, and the pass itself, against German attacks from Lamia, the ravaged city on the opposite side of the marshy plain. There, between mountain foothills and the sea, three hundred Spartans died under a shower of Per-sian javelins, and today calm, stubborn men whom your correspondent saw digging in two days ago are meeting the combined attacks of German dive bombers, tanks and infantry.

The sea now is shrunken, widening the passable area along the Euro-pean Gulf to about 300 yards. Toward this slender line scores of trucks filled with men moved past for hours Monday morning while the stars paled. Few men spoke. Their mission was to hold the line as long as possible—with lit-tle or no aviation to help.

Last week, when there was still hope that the line north of Larissa would hold, the writer slept in a deserted farmhouse beside the warm sul-fur springs which emerge from the mountain. At that time it was thought the Germans would be stopped at the mountain stronghold of Domokos, but aviation protection was unavailable.

Your correspondent's car, passing down the mountain on Sunday, was almost the last to traverse its hairpin zigzags because British demolition experts blew up the culverts the same afternoon. The serpentine road is garnished with vehicles that lost their footing during the retreat and now offer shelter for battle snipers. But even should the British fight their way forward into the Lamian plain, they could not hold it long because the line of communications from the highway downward is cut off.

Thus the troops are literal successors of their Spartan heritage, fighting along the seaside corridor in order to protect their comrades far behind them at Thebes, Athens and in southern Greece. Their action is twice as important because it also permits King George* to establish his govern-ment safely on Crete while German planes dominate every highway in northern Greece, except the actual boulevards of downtown Athens, which remain unbombed.

During this terrific travail of Greek-British friendship, even neutral ob-

---

*George II (1890–1947), who "ruled" Greece from 1922 to 1923, and again from 1935 to 1947. In between came thirteen coups and twenty-three changes of government. He spent those years in Britain, as he spent World War II after the events in this chapter.

servers are deeply moved at the trust and esteem with which this sad stage of collaboration is closing. Contrary to German claims, the attachment of the two countries remains unshaken, and the British are defending Greece as though it were England.

German planes caused the same alerts today as yesterday, but Piraeus was left untouched, the attackers concentrating on air fields where British planes were based.

Only two members of the British-American newspaper colony now remain in Athens, this writer and the Associated Press correspondent, Wesley Gallagher.

—

BRAVE ATHENIANS DEFEND SKIES

Athens, Greece—April 24, 1941

This capital continues to defend itself against aerial attack with a valor worthy of the warrior goddess whose name it bears. Dorniers, Messerschmitts and Junkers must fly high over Athens, for the spears of its anti-aircraft guns still are pointing upward in an encircling ring.

In their repeated attacks upon Athens' port of Piraeus, only a subway ride distance from the Acropolis, and their morning, noon and evening bombardments on the airdromes surrounding the capital, the Germans still avoid the puffs of black and white smoke the "ack-ack" (anti-air defense) sends up around each marauder.

Respecting Athenian gunners as much as the city's status as a shrine of antiquity, they attack by coming in from the sea or stealing over the backbone of Mount Parnes or Hymettos for a quick blow and a quicker getaway. A single siren begins the warning moan, then others take up the sound from a dozen roofs. The Parthenon's tawny marble columns stand serene above the scurrying streets, unmoved, untouched and eternal. The guns crack and white puffs appear in the sky.

People, fully aware that only a narrow line of British troops at Thermopylae is protecting the city they love, linger at the entrances to *kataphygion* (raid shelters), unwilling to miss vicarious participation in this testimony of the unbroken Greek spirit. Only a single German bomb has fallen in a suburb since the war began.

Every trail of white vapor means for them that a German has been shot down, though oftener it is simply a stiff dive through atmosphere. The authorities, once extremely strict about shooing people into shelters, have relaxed. Photographs taken in daylight by German reconnoitering planes after their moonlight raids probably show hundreds of upturned Greek faces and upward-pointing fingers.

Although the stars over Athens hang low and bright they are not enough for raiding these days. Should the British hold the mechanized German attack along the Euboean Gulf a week longer, the unforgettable spectacle of night raids will begin anew. No one who has ever seen one can forget it. The sky is like one vast black photographer's plate, illuminated by the moon's immeasurable luminescence.

Before the first German motor is audible in the sounding board of the surrounding hills, the siren sends the cautious to the cellars and the curious to the roofs. One searchlight goes on, then another. From the seacoast, from the hills, others take the hint and point their fingers in the same direction. "There he is!"

With difficulty one makes out a tiny flying creature, so intensely bathed in searchlight that it resembles one of those gnats with transparent wings and organs. Rarely does he dodge or twist, though he sometimes goes into a dive to escape.

Upon the night's huge moon-saturated face everything appears to happen so slowly and leisurely it seems incredible that it is the performance of the fastest instruments known to man. The ack-ack, like a chain of solemn glowworms, mounts the searchlight's beam. When the German is somewhere outside the beam, four glowworms usually seem enough to handle him, but as soon as he is pinned in the light a whole host of lightning bugs come from all directions. At the same time, powerful aerial bombs burst around him with an eardrum-cracking concussion, despite the great height.

The interplay of searchlights is fascinating. Sometimes they seem to make a bag of lights around where he is heard, slowly tightening until the German's attempt to break through reveals his position.

Planes seem only rarely to fall in flames. The spectator on the crowded roof is usually cheated of the ultimate spectacle because the pilot is killed, rather than the gas tank ignited, and the plane plunges in the darkness, too fast for the searchlights to follow, and lands where the wreckage cannot be illuminated. But since raids are usually made by individual planes, cessation of the engine tells its own story.

Perhaps the most fascinating sight is when a cornered pilot, perhaps half-blinded by the searchlight's rays, orders his gunner to return fire, not against the guns, but against the searchlights. Then, single file, the Nazi glowworms, usually yellow, begin crawling down the beam as though walking upon it. It would seem impossible to miss the target which continuously offers a trajectory, but actually, as far as is ascertainable, not a single searchlight has yet been darkened.

When the flier flees across the clouds like an insect crossing the frosted glass of a skylight, sometimes a searchlight winks out after the plane sends fire down against it. Invariably it merely passes its prey to another on the opposite side of the city. As soon as the next Nazi comes over, all the polyplike fingers of Athens again go feeling for him and the searchlight just fired upon is as busy as ever.

—

ROLE OF ATHENS: A STOPOVER ON NAZI DRANG NACH OSTEN

(Editor's note: This is the first dispatch to be received from the Daily News *correspondent in Greece in more than a month.)*

Athens, Greece—May 24, 1941 (By Mail to Berlin)

Still dazed by its month-old defeat, Athens is waking slowly to the fact that, although a city under German control, it is not yet a German city.

Big military road signs in German remind Athenians that their city is now only the metropolitan capital of Hitler's drive to the Middle East. Athena, spear-bearing goddess of the Greeks, who has been pushed aside by flying Valkyrie with tommy guns, still hardly grasps what has happened.

On the burning, dusty sidewalks wander hundreds of returned soldiers, bearded, hatless in the sun, their shoes broken from three weeks of hiking from Albania, with castoff jackets over their army breeches to give them a civilian status. Sometimes they buy garlic, lemons and peanuts, virtually the only grown foods easily obtainable from truck gardeners, and peddle them. Oftener they supplement the Tsolakoglou* cabinet's bread allowance by begging.

Both the German and Greek governments are attempting to evolve a labor plan but with capital still timid, flown, or uncertain of its own worth and southern Greece still a war zone, reconstruction will be slow. Thrice weekly the *Deutsche Nachtrichten* [the German News Agency's troop newspaper] suggests an analogy between food conditions and what Germany suffered after the last war. Exhorting the public to "work for unity," the paper affirms that this recipe saved Germany and Greeks must sacrifice their individualism. "The Germans are not to blame," avers the editorial.

An official of the American relief organization, which has helped Greece for 25 years, said that food needs still outstrip supplies. In the industrial quarter of Piraeus 5000 persons appeared for family handouts of 320 portions, consisting of bread the size of grapefruit and a cupful of olives. In another suburb, where there are 160 portions, 3000 persons appeared. Like postwar Vienna, Athens is undergoing the hunger pangs of an overgrown metropolitanism and a shrunken hinterland.

German army and air force members are quartered in requisitioned private homes and public buildings at fixed rates of about 35 cents daily for an officer's single room to one cent for an infantryman, payable by the municipality. For them, many filled with the traditional *Sehnsucht nach Sueden,* or "southern longing," the emotional partner in the German soul of the sterner *Drang nach Osten* ["drive to the east"], Athens has not much more to offer than antiquities and sunlight.

Even while the sky over Hymettos booms with troop-carrying planes bound for Crete, other Germans are marching up the sacred steps of the Acropolis, unarmed except for cameras. Scores have been purchased with the ubiquitous *Reichskreditkassenscheine* (credit scrips used by Germans in conquered territories).

The Germans eat more and drink less than the British and, like their

---

*General Georgios Tsolakoglou, who surrendered Greece to the Germans on April 20 and was their collaborationist prime minister until December 1942. After Greece was liberated (see Chapter XVII), he was sentenced to death, but died in prison in 1948.

predecessors, are forbidden to dance in the cabarets or to have more than desultory acquaintance with Greek girls.

As for the Greek himself, he is conforming with German plans for him within the bounds of his temperament which is fundamentally critical. He is reading frequent new ordinances in the press, picking his way through streets buzzing with an enormous variety of German military vehicles, and growing accustomed to seeing German traffic officers in trench helmets at key streets or guarding hotels.

Two Greeks have been executed on order of the German court martial for looting but the shock of defeat has dulled the impulse to plunder. A German order expressly threatens anyone cutting telephone wires, but sabotage, if any, has occurred on a scale so small as to be unnoticed.

The Greeks are intensely curious about the wonders of Nazi mechanized warfare. Whenever a motorcycle column stops the Greeks stand by gazing in wonder at scores of implements, useful or deadly, that the Germans are able to produce from its sidecar.

It is unforgettable to see one of the approximately 30,000 Cretan veterans of the Italian war, while the island is being infested by parachutists, standing in the gutter humbly counting the letters on a road sign reading *Wehrmachtzahnarztselle*. There is no one to tell him, although an astounding number of German officers speak perfect modern Greek, that the formidable word means simply "army dental clinic." He reads amid the humming of hundreds of propellers and to him it is one more incomprehensible manifestation of this bewildering war.

—

WELLER RELATES HIS EXPULSION BY GESTAPO AGENTS

'Escorted' from Athens to Berlin, Then Put Out of German Territory

Somewhere in non-German Europe—July 9, 1941

After a nine-week quarantine in Greece, two American newspapermen and a woman radio announcer have been sent out of the country under military surveillance, by order of the German Foreign Office authorities, and banned from further reporting or traveling in any Balkan country whether neutral or involved in conflict. After being flown by the Lufthansa to Belgrade then by military plane to Vienna, the Americans were held incommunicado by the Gestapo for 21 hours at a police hotel in the Danube along with interned Russians, and later taken to Berlin under Gestapo guard. No charges of any kind were expressed or implied by these actions.

Wes Gallagher of the AP, Betty Wason of the Columbia Broadcasting System and this reporter were those expelled from Greece. Nila Cram Cook, an occasional writer for *Liberty* magazine who was ushered out of India by the British several years ago—after an episode involving Mohandas Gandhi—and her son became members of the ejection party, but outwitted the Germans. Despite a warning to ready herself for the special plane northward, from which the Americans were specifically forbidden to alight in Sofia, Belgrade or Budapest, Miss Cook disappeared, to the discomfiture of the German legation and the distress of the Americans.

A three-day search by American authorities failed to discover any trace of her or her son.* Her last statement was that she "was going to visit her father's grave." George Cram Cook, a poet and novelist of Davenport, Iowa, who staged Eugene O'Neill's early plays, is buried at Delphi. It is presumed, therefore, that Miss Cook has taken refuge in the wild fastnesses of Parnassus, above Delphi, where she spent several years of her girlhood. At least a regiment of Austrian Alpine troops would be needed to find her among the hundreds of caves of the enormous mountain block.

In Berlin the press bureau spokesman, Dr. Emil Rasche, handed the few newspapermen a verbal expression of regret that the Foreign Office order, intended to be carried out by the military and boundary authorities, had nevertheless put the correspondents, without charges being preferred, under confinement by the secret state police, who specialize in dangerous political and military crimes.

The German ban against these American correspondents on traveling through and residing, visiting, or working in any Balkan country must nev-

---

*Cook left an irregular trail. Weller ran into her again in April 1945 in Tehran, Iran, where—having escaped Greece via Turkey and Afghanistan, and converted to Islam—she was the director of the Persian state theaters and censor of all performing arts, including movies. She also ran a ballet studio in her villa for the daughters of good families. Her eighteen-year-old son became a lieutenant in the Greek army.

ertheless remain in effect, said the spokesman. Although the ban did not specifically affect American newspapermen, it was stated in Berlin that the ban would make it impossible for Balkan correspondents to enter Hungary, Rumania, Croatia, Bulgaria, Montenegro, Albania, Greece or Turkey. The ban was also said to have been in effect since before the German-Russian conflict. The fact that Gallagher and the writer had just been issued valid Bulgarian visas and been promised Rumanian visas would not reopen access to the independent countries closed by the German authorities.

A renewed request to be allowed to go to neutral Turkey, which had been named as the exit destination on an original note by the American minister to the German legation in Athens, was once again denied by the foreign office. The single facility available to American newspapermen working in the Balkans, the spokesman stated, was to leave Germany, Germanophile and German-conquered countries as promptly as possible and proceed homeward.

This interview with Dr. Rasche in the Berlin Foreign Office, courteous throughout, was the conclusion to nine weeks of uninterrupted efforts on the writer's part to leave Greece in a correct and authorized manner. In the course of repeated visits to German military and diplomatic officials, he was given assurances every time that he could leave as soon as the military situation was clarified.

On June 23, Major Kliemann of the boundary administration assured him flatly and without qualification that when the Cretan mopup was over, he could go anywhere the *Chicago Daily News* might designate, in the Balkans, or Near East; to Turkey, or Syria, "Even to Egypt, if you wish."

Satisfied on the honor of a German officer at this promise, the writer chose to remain in Greece instead of taking several means of clandestine departure. The refusal of permission to go to neutral Turkey, and the subsequent expulsion via Berlin through Switzerland, became even more groundless, for reasons of military secrecy, when both American military attachés in Athens were given permission by the Germans to go to Turkey only ten days prior to the invasion of Russia [June 22].

Since transportation to Turkey was available, it seems impossible to interpret the German order other than as a blanket shutout of American correspondents from even nominally free Balkan countries. The only correspondent now there is Leigh White, CBS and *New York Post* writer, who is convalescing from a German bullet wound received in Athens and could not be expelled for medical reasons.

We three expelled American correspondents passed from military hands to the Gestapo in Belgrade, where the Lufthansa plane was grounded due to Russian operations. In a small, single-motored Junkers reconnaissance plane we were flown to Vienna and landed at a military field, where a Gestapo car took us to Gestapo headquarters at the old Hotel Metropole beside the Danube Canal. Being completely bewildered as to why we were in Gestapo hands, we were questioned by the Gestapo chief commissioner, a burly man with pince-nez spectacles.

The writer, who studied a year in Vienna as a good-will fellowship holder of the Institute of International Education, and who never expected to come back as a police prisoner, acted as interpreter.

"What were you three carrying on in Greece?" the commissioner inquired.

When we replied that we had simply received a German order to quit Greece immediately by way of Switzerland, and asked to be allowed to take the next train for the Swiss border, the commissioner asked what guarantee we could offer that we would not alight from the train and evade the expulsion order.

When we suggested that—having already taken tickets from Vienna to Switzerland at German orders—the Gestapo might take us to the frontier, the commissioner said he must hold us in Vienna overnight. Before leaving Gestapo headquarters we asked the commissioner, who refused to reveal his name: "Do you accept the responsibility for not allowing us to telephone the American consul? And do you accept the responsibility for not allowing us to go to Switzerland according to Foreign Office orders?"

"I assume both of those responsibilities," the commissioner replied gravely.

We were led to the Hotel Dianabad, where a number of Russians were held in rooms adjacent to us, and given strict instructions by our guard— those men in plus fours—not to attempt to leave the building, to write any letters or to telephone.

The next morning we were taken to the city police headquarters and ordered to fill out applications for residence. After registering, we were handed formal orders of expulsion on the so-called *Aufenthaltsverbot* form, effective immediately.

We were then asked to sign the expulsion orders in acknowledgment but, inasmuch as they provided for penalties and cited by number unfamiliar articles of the Nazi legal code, the writer suggested our signatures should be withheld until our plea to get in touch with the American authorities was granted. This decision was communicated to the police, with unsettling effect. We were returned again to the police hotel, to be taken again that afternoon to the Gestapo.

The Vienna police in the meantime made our refusal to sign our own expulsion orders the subject of a letter to the Gestapo. The Gestapo commissioner disclosed that he had received orders from the Berlin Foreign Office that we were to be sent that night to Berlin rather than expelled through Switzerland.

No other accommodation being available, we spent the night with one of our Gestapo guards on the wooden benches of a 3rd class railway coach, sleeping upright. Before leaving Vienna we were permitted to summon the American consul and make a report to him—21 hours 25 minutes after our arrival—of our situation, which he then conveyed to the American embassy in Berlin by telephone.

The next morning in Berlin the Foreign Office dismissed the Gestapo guard after explaining that the Viennese commissioner had mistaken their use of the word *Schutz,* which in German means either protection or guard. Though not technically arrested, we had been held under military or Gestapo surveillance constantly since leaving Athens two days before.

In Belgrade, the militant adjutant of the air force had instructed us that we were expected to remain in full view at all times, and particularly not to attempt to visit the bombed city, which, he said, was closed even to German citizens.

These expulsions took place June 23. The details have been withheld until now by agreement with American correspondents in Berlin. It was feared that, were the facts announced earlier, the high feeling in America against Nazi methods would be reflected in retaliations on German correspondents in America. Such steps would be swiftly followed by aggravated steps against American correspondents in Berlin, whose position is already difficult but who have received verbal assurances that they will be allowed to leave in the event of a break in relations.

The single exception to this promise is Richard Hottelet, imprisoned United Press correspondent, who was at first accused of communicating with invisible ink to his fiancée, employed in the British Foreign Office, but who is lately said to be charged with Russian espionage.

The three expelled correspondents do not desire to start a cycle of retaliation with personal tragedies to innocent correspondents in both Berlin and Washington.

The writer's expulsion, though groundless, simply carries out a German intention expressed in January, one week after his arrival in Europe, by the *Sudost Echo,* German weekly of Balkan economics. In a front-page editorial two columns long entitled "Weller in Belgrade," the *Sudost Echo* suggested that a *Chicago Daily News* article about the food situation in Spain was "cannibalistic" and displayed "a bestial joy" in human suffering, and demanded that the Yugoslav government "give the creature his walking papers" before he could similarly abuse Yugoslav hospitality.

Prospering military circumstances in the Balkans have made it possible for the German government to carry out, themselves, the suggestion made six months ago to the Yugoslavs. In this example of German foresight and planning, the Lufthansa, Army, Luftwaffe and Gestapo have united to carry out the original inspiration of the propaganda ministry.

Few of his fellow newspapermen, the writer may say without false modesty, have been kicked out of the Reich itself in such a magnificent and complicated fashion as he has been expelled from the *Lebensraum* ["living space"]. Until now the correspondent had been able to keep his professional record completely free of expulsions. Now he finds himself overnight excluded by Germany from no fewer than eight countries. This must be the jackpot of being undesirable.

—

Greek People, Unconquerable, Jeer Invaders

Heroic Little Nation Proves More Glorious in Defeat than in Victory

Athens, Greece—July 25, 1941

Under the slow-motion, repeat performance of mechanized war that laid the entire country waste, Greece lies defenseless today, submitting to the immediate mutilation and continuous exploitation that Hitler and Mussolini have decided shall be the lot of tiny powers daring to defend themselves.

But Greece is unconquerable. In this lean summer when the German Army has picked the country so clean of food that even Italians have been moved to send milk to Greek babies, the Greek is as undefeated, as saucy, as defiant as six months ago when, with fingers freezing upon the trigger, he fought in mountain cold until his ragbound feet and legs had to be amputated from a half-starved frame. Hungry, unemployed soldiers, wandering the streets in grotesque costumes, often burst into uncontrollable tears when they speak of their comrades lying in unmarked ravines in what are now greater Bulgaria and greater Albania. But the next minute a crust of bread and a handful of olives will set them singing openly anti-Mussolini marching songs under the noses of Italian gendarmes patrolling the streets.

Since the Germans entered Athens twelve weeks ago, the Greeks have been fighting the same lonely battle as prisoner nations all over Europe. The Axis has locked Greece into solitary confinement, where only the thin voice of forbidden broadcasts and hopeful rumors, mostly exaggerated, support the war-shocked spirits. The Greeks have been left alone with what the world calls their defeat, with nothing but memories of Tepeleni, Argyrocastro, Pogradetz, and the bloody defense of Ruppel Pass against the Germans to sustain them. Heroes of war are obliged to remain unhonored and heroes of occupation unknown. Greece is held beneath the black tent of Berlin-controlled Europe where nothing comes up but the harmonious tidings of newborn states, plus the occasional interruption of firing squads.

Cretans were executed by the scores when, after being disarmed by the government of the late General John Metaxas for liberal sympathies, they used hammers, sickles and kitchen knives, the only weapons they had, to meet German bombing planes and parachutists armed with tommy guns.

To write the following account of the occupation, your correspondent made over two months' observation of history clamoring for expression but only part of which can be described even now because of the danger of retaliatory measures.

The Greeks have been far more glorious in defeat even than they were in victory. It was miracle enough that they fought their first war united, without party schism; it is incredible that they have been able to endure defeat without any break in ranks or recrimination. Perhaps because the government that fled to Crete, headed by King George, was largely composed of remnants of the Metaxas dictatorship—which attained popular tolerance only through defending the country against its Axis friends—the people show no signs that leadership's absence worries them.

Because the war against Italy and later Germany was the people's war from the beginning it is still continuing in the form of pinpricks of civilian resistance to the military administration. The Metaxas dictatorship left Greece as well prepared for occupation as for war. German and Italian field staffs have invented no trick for shackling the population that could surpass those tested during the four years when Greek brains were turned against Greek, and parliamentary liberties nonexistent.

Against German Stukas dive-bombing Greek hospital ships—all five were sunk—the Greeks had no protection. Nor have they been able to prevent systematic carpetbagging by the German military machine, which is specifically organized for that purpose. But when the Germans began, a day after arriving in Athens, to issue *Verordnungen*—ordinances, regulations and laws—on arm-length handbills repetitiously pasted upon the walls, the Greeks knew exactly what to do. They read them, snickered and, when the blackout came, quietly tore them down.

And they talked. They are still talking, not so much about the Italians because everybody, even in Greece, has begun to be sorry for the Italians, but about the Germans. The Gestapo chief, according to the Greeks, was the biggest victim of a whispering campaign that turned the *Stadtkommandantur* into a bundle of nerves. As the story runs, he resigned, saying: "There are two countries where I cannot work—Japan, where nobody dares talk, and Greece, where everybody talks."

Although neither democratic power did much to deserve the blind loyalty of the Greek man-in-the-street—the British campaign having been a retreat from the beginning and the Americans failing to deliver a single promised airplane, cannon or equipment—the Greek continues to hang on to the belief that rescue will come.

A minority echoes the view that if Great Britain could send no better than 60,000 men and 250 airplanes, mostly of outmoded design, to face an army known to number 500,000 men with about 2000 aircraft, she would have done better to send nothing whatever and let Greece make peace on her own terms. But a 90 per cent majority rejects this thesis. They say that when Greece decided to fight Italy she embarked on a road without any return. With Metaxas dead, there was no leader in Greece capable of inducing the army that had defeated the Italian generalissimos, including Mussolini himself, to sell out its victory before Hitler's threats.

Only the knowledge that Greece defeated Italy makes it possible for the Greeks to endure the humiliation of German occupation. The Nazi rationale that Greece was invaded only to attack the British is laughed at. The Greeks know that it would have been necessary for Hitler to come through Turkey or Greece in order to attack the Middle East. And Italy's flounderings in Albania had to be aided by Hitler or else fascism's falling wingtip would have pulled the plane into a tailspin.

What comforts Greece is that her slender strength caused sufficient delay so that the Nazi drive to the Suez met blistering summer heat and had to turn northeast against Russia. But the Greeks are proudest of all that they were the first to teach the British the weakness of Italian arms— that their rout of the Italians along the Albanian frontier was the green light for the Ethiopian and Libyan campaigns.

Their attitude toward the democracies may be summarized thus: "We have fought for your rights; now what are you going to do to recover ours?"

—

GREEKS HUNGRY AS NAZI ARMY GRABS THE FOOD

Athens, Greece—July 26, 1941

Much has been said of German concentrated foods, powders and juices that turn sawdust into nectar and make every Nazi soldier self-sufficient for eight days upon the hoof. But when the Greeks—who know plenty about food—discuss how the blitzkrieg can be stopped they answer, "Close up the restaurants." For when German meets German here the first thing he does is to enter a restaurant and eat.

From the experience of the Balkan campaign, the Greeks believe that the Nazi advance toward Moscow has been slowed down because there is not a lunch cart, tea room or nut sundae spot in Russia.

The secret of the lightning Nazi advances, according to the Greeks, is that every moment spared from strafing is used in diligent, continuous eating. It took some time for the Greeks to understand that the first thing the German Army does after bombing a city is to eat everything in it. When they grasped this epicurean feature of the blitzkrieg it was already too late to close the restaurants. Instead they raised the prices. As a result the proprietors of Athens' most aristocratic and expensive eating places, Kostis and Maxims, both have been in jail. They are now forced to keep their doors open, accepting Axis funny money for wines and foodstuffs that cost thousands of gold-backed drachmas when bought.

To some people the most disillusioning feature about the Greek campaign was that British officers, suffering continuous unprotected bombing and machine-gunning by Nazi planes on exposed roads, stubbornly continued to travel country-club style in American-built station wagons that have no overhead visibility and whose doors invariably jam at the moment when only a quick dive into a ditch is protection against death. But the German occupation revealed an even more prosaic fact, that the deadliest weapons in the Nazi arsenal are not bombs, flame throwers and machine guns but knives, forks and spoons.

While the British conscientiously imported almost all their foods from Egypt, the Germans brought almost nothing but enough ersatz to tide them over between towns. The Agoranomia, or food control section, was captured everywhere. In Athens the Germans asked where the food administration was even before they demanded the surrender of hidden arms.

All Hellenic eating records collapsed from the time when the first German *Feldwebel* [sergeant-major] planted his feet under a table at Zonars and pounded for attention. The record of sixteen chocolate cakes consumed at a single sitting—at a time when ragged Greek officers, having marched for three weeks from Albania eating grass, were begging for food at back doors—was seized by the infantry from the Luftwaffe gourmands, who specialized in rich, American-style sundaes.

In any occupied town it is a common occurrence to see a German blitz straight down a menu consuming double orders throughout and tripling anything really toothsome. Such decathlon eating records would be merely a pleasantly human counterweight to Nazi asceticism if the factory girls in Athens were not fainting repeatedly at work for lack of sufficient nourishment.

Every restaurant from Alexandropolis to Calamata has its own incredible German eating records. Flocas, a famous meeting place in Salonika—the city whose only flour mill was burned down the night before the Nazis entered—is still talking about five Germans who demanded five orders of bacon and eggs with three eggs each. At the time only smuggled eggs were obtainable, at 12 cents each, about five times the normal price. When the Germans finished the first order they commanded another. After that they commanded a third, still with three eggs on each plate. Before invariable successions of rounds of sundaes they insisted on having two large orders of ham apiece.

This was at a time when the marketplaces were bare to the boards and the writer was unable, regardless of cost, to get anything but string beans, cherries and bread. It has been common in Athens for civilians to be denied eggs with the proprietor's answer, "Must save all my eggs for the Germans or I will be arrested."

For several weeks it was impossible for restaurateurs even under threat of imprisonment to supply all the food the Germans wished. In order to be sure the Reichswehr's strength did not fade, the *Stadtkommandantur* farmed out wholesale orders to the Greek middlemen. The writer has studied several such orders. They say nothing about price. Price is never an object to the Reichswehr, because they print their own money wherever they go and their bayonets do the legalizing.

The large supply of tinned beef and other food left behind by the retreating British for the American Red Cross was taken away by the clique of Germanophile Greek generals who preceded the Tsolakoglou government. When the American relief man tried to recover the food for distribution in refugee quarters in Piraeus and Athens, where rickets and malnutrition are rampant, he was turned down with the bluntest discourtesy. Later two truckloads of the same food were distributed by the Germans in the same suburbs while Nazi cameramen ground busily.

At the present rate of approximately five ounces daily per person—one-sixth the normal diet of the Greek laborer—wheat stocks mixed with corn meal will hold until the new crop late in July. But the ration cannot be extended and the workman must simply tighten his belt over the hollow place caused by lack of essential food.

When German officers, suspicious that they are not to get everything on hand, insist on visiting kitchens and ice chests, Greek cooks receive them with scant courtesy. But simply by ignoring politics and fighting with the Greeks strictly about food, many members of the Reichswehr have picked up a surprising command of the Greek language. Three sitting in a tavern below the Acropolis the other night ordered in German, as the cap to an enormous meal, "Three coffees, bitter."

"Three poisons," yelled the waiter in Greek, with a malevolent look.

One Nazi raised his head: "Make that two poisons and one coffee," he said in perfect Greek. "I happen to be Austrian."

—

GESTAPO FAILS—BRITONS STILL HIDING IN GREECE
Athens, Greece—July 27, 1941

Although the purpose of the Greek campaign announced by Adolf Hitler was to drive the British from Greece, the British are still here. The Gestapo, ordered to round up the surviving members of the expeditionary force, has been at the job for twelve weeks and is about ready to give up. For when the Greeks hide anything, it stays hidden, and since mid-April they have been hiding Australians, New Zealanders and English technicians who failed to catch the last boats.

The Germans do not know exactly how many British the Greeks, at the risk of their lives, are hiding, but they have become sufficiently bothered by the phenomenon to start a separate Greek department of the Gestapo to catch them. These manhunters are chiefly Greeks who have lived in the United States or British colonies and speak English freely. It is short-term work, but pays well—twenty-five hundred drachmas (about $20, in normal times) for 10 days' work, plus expenses.

The job of the Greek sleuth is to go into the vast ranges of mountains, where the Aussies and Kiwis have fled, and represent himself as an agent of a secret rescue committee, preparing a motorboat for the escape of soldiers. Such committees exist, and because many Greeks aided British to escape in this way before Crete fell, the excuse is plausible. The Greek gets instructions from the Germans not to enter into direct contact with the Britons, but merely to obtain the names of people hiding them, and the place. The Germans do the rest.

It is a good plan, but with Italians in Greece it has outlived its usefulness. The Gestapo no longer has sufficient staff men to carry out the captures, and as for going up in the frowning Greek mountains alone, the Italians suffer from squeamish memories of the inhospitable Albanian highland. The Italian is more courageous than either the Germans or Greeks give him credit for, but he doesn't want to have the Germans send him up in them thar hills again.

These German attempts began after the fall of Corinth when, as a propaganda move intended to carry a pointed slur, the Germans offered 150 drachmas "head money" for every Aussie or Kiwi captured, and 100 for every Englishman. There were no takers. After the parachute attack on Corinth a store clerk hid twenty-three Australians in a public bomb shelter while paratroops searched all the city's homes. Afterward he led them by night through the German lines to the chief embarkation port at Nauplia, where they got away safely.

Other Britons were lost in Athens and could not find their outfits in time to pick up with any coastal evacuation parties. Some bought grey Greek suits and cheap shoes and set out for the hills. Many were hidden in private houses.

The Greek police, whose officers were discharged by the Germans for non-cooperation when the German battle flag was purloined from the Acropolis, gave the fugitive Britishers every help. In one instance, a Greek living on Lycabettos, the conelike hill in the center of Athens, learned that a uniformed Englishman was hiding in the ravine behind his house. To be sure that his record was clear with both the Germans and the police, he sent a small boy to guide the police to the hideaway. A patrolman went to the spot, dismissed the boy with thanks, changed clothes with the Englishman, gave him money, and sent him away.

While Britons who have been able to pass the closely guarded roads and get up into the mountains are secure once they get in the hands of shepherds, those taken into family homes and apartments in Athens suffer not only from confinement but fear of exposing their hosts to risk. Arguments, mostly in sign language, occur almost daily, the Briton maintaining he must give himself up, the Greek family that he must remain where he is. When children in the family would be confused by a stranger speaking an alien tongue and might make an accidental betrayal, the fugitive is lodged in an adjacent vacant building. Incredibly enough, many Britons go out regularly at night, attend cinemas and mingle with crowds. Cockneys of short stature with dark hair are particularly free in their movements. A considerable number have dyed their hair; German efforts to trace them have been unavailing.

This freedom sometimes leads to excessive confidence and mishap. In a resort near Athens a saloonkeeper hid seven Australians in an outbuilding. Taking compassion on their confinement, he kept them primed with generous quantities of retsina, the strong Greek wine. One evening he joined in, and becoming somewhat awash, suggested a procession with himself as leader. A victory march through the village to the tune of *Tipperary* ensued. The celebration ended when the parade marched straight through an astonished German motorcycle column, which was almost too dumfounded to do its duty, but not quite.

—

PORTABLE PLANT PRINTS CASH AS NAZIS ROLL ON

Italians Imitating Nazis—Go on Spending Spree in Greece
with 'Phony Money'

Athens, Greece—July 29, 1941

The mystery of how Germany is able to pay for her wars is no mystery at all for citizens of occupied countries. The German people have paid for the actual tools of killing and its training, but as soon as the Reichswehr crosses a new frontier by force, the invaded people begin meeting the Nazi bills.

The mechanics are simple. They consist of two hooded German army trucks, backed up together so the combined printing plant operates in a line. The supply of money, that is, army purchasing power, is limited only by the supply of paper and ink. The Germans fix the rate of the new currency—*Reichskreditkassenscheine,* national treasury notes of credit—at any exchange rate that seems convenient. Because the supply is unlimited, the rate does not matter. In Greece the exchange happens to be 50 drachmas per occupational mark, as the notes are usually called.

Besides his salary, every soldier on leave in Athens was given 100 such marks, or about 5000 drachmas, the equivalent of a month's salary for a Greek civil employee of the middle class. (A parachutist earns 250 marks monthly.) Large illustrated posters appeared in all banks and shop windows by German order, showing the marks and their Greek equivalents.

The soldiers quickly spend their allotment—worth $40 if the currency were not being simultaneously inflated—for clothing, soap, pajamas, silk stockings for German womenfolk, the many things in which Germany is deficient. Multiplied by an army numbering at least 350,000 men, the purchases swept Greek shops clean of the few things left over from the war. Tailor shops, particularly, were left bare. The purchases would have been serious in peacetime, but in war, with Greece totally cut off from importing either finished or raw materials, they were disastrous.

Some Greeks attempted to close their stores to conserve their stocks, but were ordered by the Reichswehr to remain open. The Greeks observed that there was no signature of a responsible official on the *Reichskreditkassen-scheine,* but the alternative of nonacceptance was imprisonment. Nazi officials paid all purchases in big bills; one was seen on Stadium Street, crossing from shop to shop, breaking one 5000-mark note after another.

This form of refined looting—whose effect was to leave the Germans in possession of all vendable articles and the Greeks with fistfuls of paper— has since been kept under control so that it has never broken dangerously out into the open. All that the uneducated Greeks understand is that the Germans have the money and they do not. Prices have climbed steadily except where forcibly pegged by the government, and in such cases merchants are literally giving away their articles. Food prices, except for bread and milk, have tripled.

The practice of offering military money on a bayonet in beaten countries after hostilities are over goes back at least as far as the leather-punched thongs distributed by Kubla Khan's army in Asia, and continues up through the armies of Louis XIV to the rubles printed by the German forces in Russia during the last war.

The suffering among salary- and cash-dependent Greeks has been great. Topping the German Army's inflation is the 5000-mark note, worth 250,000 drachmas—the price of an automobile. Now a new Italian inflation has come along, just as after the conquest of Albania. Although the Greek cupboard is bare, the Italians have demonstrated their hopes by printing money as high as 100,000-drachma notes. Issued by the Cassa Mediterraneano di Credito per la Grecia, a hitherto unheard-of organization, and in drachmas, not lire, it proves that Italy assumes the state privilege of printing Greek currency. From this it is reasoned that the Duce may be planning to draw Greece permanently within the empire.

Greece's newest funny money is pale green, with a head of Mercury on one side and a head of wheat on the other. Printed both in Greek and Italian, it gains little popularity from two Greek inscriptions which both contain mistakes.

The issuing bank itself translates its own name wrongly as the "Mesogeion Tameion" instead of the Mesageiakon Tameion. The only other Greek sentence—"The present note must be accepted for its nominal value"—is translated into Greek in thirteen words which contain four grammatical errors and a misspelling.

—

Greeks Pay Fines—for Future Too!
Athens, Greece—July 31, 1941

In taking possession of the Ionian islands when occupying Greece, the Italians pasted up on all the principal buildings of Cephalonia—birthplace of the late dictator Metaxas—large posters of Mussolini in belligerent attitude, his jaw outthrust. This proved to be too much for the Cephalonians. When morning came all the posters had been torn down.

The Italians fined the entire population ten drachmas (about eight cents at the official rate of exchange) per head. The Cephalonians came obediently before the courts and paid, but some of them when summoned placed twenty drachmas upon the magistrate's desk.

"What's this for?" asked the judge. "The fine is only ten drachmas, not twenty."

"That's for tomorrow," was the reply.

COMPANHIA PORTUGUESA RADIO MARCONI

TELEGRAMA

Transmitido pela linha _____   *Taxa simples:* ____ $____

à estação de _____ *às* _____   *Taxas acessorias:*

por _____   _____ $____

Número local	Indicações de serviço	Destino	Origem	Número	Palavras	Data	Horas	
	nlt							_____ $____
							Minutos	TOTAL _____ $____

Indicações eventuais: Código:

Via "EASTERN" ou Via "RADIO DIRECTA"

Nome e residência do destinatário:

SIr John Stavridi

Ionian Bank   London

Correspondência e assinatura

~~Yxrxhex~~   Her ten days nursing as only woman in thickest

fighting at western end Crete makes your daughter Joan   in

my judgment Greeces greatest heroine war STOP Shes now safe

healthy free in Athens where eye left her late June STOP shall
try send you further particulars George Weller   correspondent
Chicago Daily News Hotel Palacio Estoril

Nome, morada e telefone do expedidor dêste telegrama:

George Weller Hotel Palacio Estoril

Hora da apresentação dêste telegrama

____ horas _____ minutos

do relógio da estação.

RECIBO

Foi paga a quantia de ____ $ ____ taxa do telegrama _____ , n.° _____

para _____ depositado às ____ h. / ____ m.

PAP. L___ ___RA. Li___ó:

III

Canopies over Crete

Fruitlessly awaiting permission from the Gestapo to leave Athens, Weller woke early one May morning to droning German planes embarking on the first paratroop invasion in history. Beyond what Weller uniquely saw, these dispatches (merged into one) contain valuable eyewitness material, the result of interviews with veterans of Crete's defense nearly a year later, who told him their story.

It was necessary for the Nazis to take the island of Crete to complete and solidify their hold on Greece. (Though the mainland was occupied by Bulgaria and Italy as well, the most important areas were occupied by Germany.) About twenty-five thousand British troops joined the fourteen-thousand-man British garrison already defending Crete. Greek forces numbered about nine thousand. The Greek government of George II, which had retreated to Crete, retreated onward to Egypt. In the last days of May, only sixteen thousand British troops were evacuated by ship; all Crete had surrendered by June 1.

Whatever dispatches about the island that Weller wrote from Athens in May or June never reached Berlin via his underground mail railroad; no copies survive. Those given here were sent from Portugal just before he left for Africa.

Despite heavy German losses, the military potential of paratroopers stayed with Weller. Chapter XII contains his evocative writing about how it feels to parachute, and his archive contains notes for a never-completed book on the history of ballooning. Indeed, his penultimate book, for younger readers in the popular Landmark Books series, was *The Story of the Paratroops* (1958).

Canopies over Crete

Somewhere in Australia—May 20, 1942

Today is the first anniversary of the airborne invasion of Crete. Exactly a year ago, German parachutists came floating down upon Malemi Airdrome and opened a wedge for the capture of the strategic island. In a tactical sense this invasion ended one chapter of military history and opened another—one that is still incomplete.

Crete was taken, held and mastered entirely by air-conveyed troops. Seaborne reinforcements were sunk but airborne forces continued to arrive. Crete was purely an aerial triumph, although not so planned. The first steamer bearing Germans arrived only after the Nazis, by mastering the air and land, had mastered the sea.

This correspondent has obtained previously unpublished details of the epochal attack by talking with Australians who defended Crete. Up to now the German winged invasion has been described coherently only from the Axis point of view, because no Allied correspondents were upon Cretan soil at the time and because survivors' narratives were curbed by military exigencies.

Three reporters—Wes Gallagher of the Associated Press, Leigh White of the *New York Post* and this correspondent—remained in Greece on invasion day and were overtaken by the German wave. Through circumstance— White and Gallagher being elsewhere in Athens at the time—this correspondent was the only actual witness of the Luftwaffe's launching of the air armada.

I watched the paratroop invasion from Mount Lycabettos, a cone-shaped hill 700 feet above the Athenian plain and overlooking the Acropolis, the Saronic Gulf and Peloponnesus peninsula. Across the eastern side of this seaward-sloping rectangle I was destined to see the beginning of the world's first airborne invasion.

For weeks the Germans had been assembling gliders at Tanagra, a small airdrome north of Athens. It was Germany's big chance for a rehearsal of the air invasion of England and Der Fuehrer was not inclined to let the opportunity pass untested. Yet the secret was well kept.

Small Greek steamers and schooners at Piraeus were held to be the an-swer to how Crete would be invaded. Nobody had any intimation the Luft-waffe would attempt more than isolated chutist attacks upon exposed points. The Germans, through plasterings of Crete's airdromes, had re-duced the British bombing threat to a point where, upon German-held air-dromes around Athens, blinking beacons revolved all night. Thus the German glider bases were rid of the bombing threat in the rear.

The first intimation that events of unprecedented proportions were stirring was a drumming sound, faint and far away, but very powerful, which this correspondent heard in his sleep shortly after dawn on May 20. It was at first impossible to discern the cause of the steady purring drum-ming, like hundreds of bees imprisoned under the eaves of the roof. Except for old women, who went each morning at four to the deserted stalls of the public market in old Athens in hopes the German quartermasters had al-lowed a few vegetables to get through to the starving city, no one was stir-ring. The Greeks are early risers, but in occupied countries people cling to sleep as their narcotic against hunger.

Hearing the many motors, Athens collectively turned its face to the wall and this, too, was my first impulse. But the noise persisted, different from the motors of Messerschmitt-109s and 110s, which regularly crossed the center of Athens for propaganda effect upon their bombing missions. It sounded steadier, more extensive.

Then from the terrace I looked eastward, and saw what it was. Length-wise, over the hump of Hymettos, a long line of black-winged creatures was flying south. Rubbing the sleep from my eyes, I was at first doubtful that it was not birds. For planes, they were flying in the most peculiar and contra-dictory formation—a long cavalcade, like camels crossing the desert. They were so far away—the Germans were taking this precaution against any Athenian with a secret radio informing the British what was afoot—that they could be seen only from high upon Lycabettos and were invisible to the hungry, sleeping thousands below.

What puzzled me was that their formation seemed composed of big and little planes in equal numbers. Every big plane had a little plane directly behind it. The whole procession was moving very slowly. This indicated that the big planes must be transports, probably the slow "Auntie Jus," the Junkers-52s. What then could be the little planes following so closely behind, with the unsubstantial bodies of fighters? Perhaps the Germans were trying a new protective idea for fighters to follow tightly upon a transport's tail. But why experiment on such an enormous scale?

Furthermore, the Junkers were creeping along at hardly 110 miles an hour. What kind of fighters were these which were able to throttle down to that pace and follow their lumbering Aunties at a fixed distance?

The Germans had taken Corinth airdrome and bridge by parachutists and earlier used skymen in piercing Rupel Pass on the Yugoslav border, but nothing had indicated that they contemplated an experiment upon so vast a scale.

Actually, the general prediction that big events were in the making had been formulated by Major Nicolas Crawe, American air attaché at Athens, a veteran of many RAF raids and co-designer of the first Flying Fortress. Crawe had formulated his views in a report to the War Department, but it was not transmitted because the Nazis cut off all communications even between the United States legation and Berlin and Rome, to say nothing of Washington.

Once the magnitude of the operation began to be understood, other things began to fall into place. One understood why scores of trucks bearing license plates *WL* for the Wehrmacht-Luftwaffe (German army air force) had gone purring through the boulevards from the city barracks late the night before, laden with thin-faced youths wearing the mountaineer's edelweiss upon their shoulders. Around eleven that morning the Junkers began streaming back, diminished by about one in five. Their "fighter planes" no longer were tailing them. Still the Greeks knew nothing of what was happening.

Not until a BBC broadcast the next day did the word seep through. But at two o'clock another long procession of Junkers moved southward, but gliderless. From a rooftop above the office of a friendly dentist, I counted 53 planes, but some were Messerschmitts and Dorniers. Our hopes increased because this seemed to mean that the gliders were exhausted and Crete's resistance was stiffening enough to require new bombardments by "Flying Pencils" and "Schmitters."

There are times when one can unmistakably see the future written upon the visage of the present. This correspondent had such a view as he saw the long line of big and little aircraft filing slowly away, laden with hundreds of men, disappearing into the southern blue. The historical moment transcended any fact of whether the planes were German, British or American. The door upon the future opened slightly and one caught a quick but unmistakable glimpse of what the war was becoming and would be by the time the United States became a participant.

"Only one thing was constant in the battle between German parachutists and ourselves for possession of Malemi Airdrome," said an Australian officer who took a leading part in the defense of Crete. "That was the sound of bells."

The officer was attached to the anti-aircraft unit defending Malemi, which consisted of four 40-mm Bofors guns manned by English troops, and six of the same caliber served by Australians. A brigade of three shrunken battalions of New Zealanders and Maoris was the force defending Malemi against land attack.

"Only a few hundred yards west of the red patch of dust we called Malemi was a monastery named Mongonia. It was built solidly, like a fortress. From the field, the monks could often be seen moving about outside with their tall stovepipe hats, stroking their beards as they walked and murmuring their meditations.

"As the Messerschmitts and Stukas began to rain bombs upon us, parachutists floated down. While the still-unsunk British cruisers in Suda Bay threw shells at them, the monks disappeared behind the ramparts of the cloister. But the chimes remained constant. Each time we heard them we asked ourselves whether we would live to hear them the next time.

"The bells went on pealing every quarter hour, day and night, through three days of fighting during which we not only battled parachutists but watched the German invasion convoy wiped out by our destroyers. Even before the screams of the sinking Germans, the bark of guns and the blast of bombs, the bells of Mongonia Monastery went on chiming. I suppose they are still chiming today."

In dispatches describing an isolated Anglo-Greek nurse, the heroine of the 7th General Hospital on the shore between Suda Bay and Malemi, this correspondent told ten months ago how Nazi planes carefully reconnoitered and photographed every inch of ground beforehand.

The Australian officer confirmed the carefulness of the German preparation. "Almost every chutist had a small mapcase showing in a three-dimensional drawing, relief and profile, what he would see upon landing. He was able to orient himself immediately for attack.

"During the ten-day period when they tried to bomb us into submission, I saw one of the most gallant deeds I ever hope to witness. Eighty Messerschmitt 109s, which are fighters as well as bombers, came over. The whole remaining Royal Air Force, consisting of three Hurricanes and two Gladiator biplanes, went up to challenge them. There could be but one result, but it was gallant beyond description."

The little force of Anzac [Australian and New Zealand Army Corps] defenders had almost no intimation that the invasion was coming except the general warning that "something is expected." The customary morning bombing by Messerschmitts, which probably came from Melos or Rhodes, as well as Corinth, Argos and the three Athenian airdromes, seemed heavier than usual.

"But my first real idea that the parachutists were upon us was when I looked up and saw a pair of wheels belonging to a mortar sailing down as though it possessed wings."

The Australian guns began to speak immediately. The Junkers came over in three lines of three planes, each towing a glider. Each group of chutists, stepping out of the nine-plane, nine-glider formation, also dropped a mortar and several machine guns. Stories about three or four gliders being towed together were false; one was the maximum.

"Our fire began to take effect. One glider was loosed and began to sidle downward. We shot off the nose. You could see men falling to their deaths from the open nose, like peas falling from a pod."

On the airdrome, the 5th Regiment of New Zealanders and Maoris grappled immediately with the first batch of 300 chutists and wiped them out, securing badly needed tommy guns and pistols from their bodies. But the parachutists kept coming. The Germans dropped officers with walkie-talkies in the less accessible hills to the south, above the airdrome. They communicated directly with the pilots of the planes which came over in waves. They helped the parachutists by bombing our anti-aircraft guns, which were able to sweep the airdrome as well as overhead.

"We could hear these parachute observers in our radios, taking over the direction of the air bombardment from the bombardiers and giving unciphered directions to the planes. They worked exactly like front-range artillery observers, speaking corrections for each new run and giving landmarks to the pilots as guidance to camouflaged positions. It was naturally difficult to ferret them out, with our positions bombed and dive-bombed simultaneously."

While the parachute convoys were coming from Athens and possibly also Rhodes, the Stukas which intensively dive-bombed Australian positions were based on the airdrome on Kythera Island within full view of Malemi.

"It was a simple matter for the Stukas to get a load of bombs, gain height and descend upon us. The whole operation required hardly half an hour for the round trip. Lacking reconnaissance aircraft for nearly a week, we had no way of knowing that the Nazis had established a Stuka airdrome, toolshed and bomb dump within full view of Crete."

Junkers with gliders kept coming between ground-directed bombings, shellings and machine-gunnings of British positions.

"I looked toward Peloponnesus and as far as I could see there were two continuous black lines of aircraft moving in opposite directions like two flights of locusts. One was coming toward Malemi with parachutists and bombs, the other was going north empty to get more."

These transport planes were taking heavy losses, too. Forty-three planes and gliders were downed by smoking guns that the Stukas and Schmitters tried to destroy.

"I never shall forget the bravery of one English sergeant who had his arm shot away at the shoulder by a shell. He propped himself against the Bofors and kept on directing the fire until he fainted and fell. And every now and then would come the uncanny, slow pealing of the bells from Mongonia Monastery."

Englishmen, Australians, New Zealanders and Maoris, fighting desperately to hold Malemi Airdrome against Nazi parachutists, knew that they were guinea pigs in a rehearsal of the hoped-for Nazi air invasion of England. But they had little time for reflection as they fought for their lives under the merciless sun of Crete.

Directing their Stuka attack by walkie-talkie radios, in the hands of observers dropped by parachute, the Nazis slowly, and at a terrific cost in men, began to make gains in their effort to silence the Bofors guns buried in pits around the red rectangle of Malemi. Their losses in men and aircraft were heavy. The Cretan airdromes became so glutted with smashed Junkers, Messerschmitts and gliders that it was impossible for the troop-carrying Junkers to land.

Then the Germans were commanded to land anywhere, regardless of cost. The only place left was a narrow strip of rocky beach between Malemi and Suda. They landed there, aided somewhat by the Junkers' low-landing speed, but often crashed. Every hundred yards there was a crushed, emptied troop carrier.

What really decided the battle for Malemi Airdrome was a tactical maneuver by German parachutists upon the ground (never mentioned in previous accounts) that became the turning point due to their daily reconnaissance and photographic knowledge of the terrain. Malemi is a long, clay-dust air field running parallel with the rocky southern Cretan shore. Northward, bordering the airdrome, lie ranges of stony hills and mountains, out of which comes the Tavaritos river that winds past the western end of the air field, where its stony course enters the sea.

The builders of the airdrome, to keep the sudden heavy rains that rush down the hills from washing away the air field, had devised a big masonry drainage ditch twelve feet deep. The month being May, when rains are unknown, the channel had only a few inches of water in the bottom. Learning their lesson from the annihilation of the first parachutists, the Germans dropped succeeding batches at the eastern (open) end and the western (river) end of the long, deep drain. Instead of attacking the New Zealanders or English and Australian anti-aircraft immediately up the rocky hills or across the fire-swept runway, the Nazis dropped into the bottom of the culvert and remained there while British positions were dive-bombed.

Even after the severest pounding the anti-aircraft guns were still unsilenced. At times they played dead, withholding fire. The Nazis were uncertain whether the crews were killed or not.

"At this point Jerry did something I never expected to see again," said an Australian officer. "He sent down a two-motored Messerschmitt 110 to test whether we were really silenced. First he 'dragged' the field at ever-descending heights. We held our fire. Then he flew directly over without firing a shot, at a 15-to-20-foot height, practically begging us to give away our situation. Still we held fire.

"Finally, he came down and landed amid wrecked gliders and Junkers on the field. Like a mother partridge he taxied back and forth, up and down, over and over again. Ten times. Then he cut loose. He gunned his motors and his wheels were just lifting from the runway when we hit him. He crashed into the sea."

Attacks by Stukas and 109s based on the islet at Kythera became ferocious. Of the eighty-two men who had manned the original positions, only sixteen escaped. Mortars and artillerymen dropped by parachute combined their fire with Stuka bombs and rendered the guns useless. There began a game of hide-and-seek in the stony hills. The Anzacs had by no means given up hope of recovering the airdrome. Although cut off, they were encouraged by seeing the Navy chop to pieces a German convoy of Greek fishing boats and small steamers when they tried to land.

But the Nazis not only dropped elite parachute troops upon Malemi. Giving great depth to their operations, they continued dropping many Bavarian mountain troops in the hills. Besides, loads of ordinary Reichswehr landed in crashed Junkers along the beachfront. The entire operation was thus conceived: shock troops—seventeen- and eighteen-year-old parachutists—followed by mountaineer regulars using parachutes as conveyance, and finally airborne regular troops for reserve.

Three days later the New Zealanders were still maneuvering to recapture the field and had a good position for attack. The Nazi commander, knowing this, sent a message by a prisoner to the New Zealand commander, Colonel Allen, saying: "Surrender or we shall send more Stukas to dive-bomb you out of existence."

The message had an ironical side because the Stukas were already dive-bombing intensively. Colonel Allen, who was later killed in the western desert, wrote carefully in pencil at the bottom of the Nazi warning: *You can go to hell.*

The German master-plan, in taking Crete wholly by airborne troops and parachutists, is of particular importance because the Nazis, having failed to invade England by sea, may drive a preceding wedge of air troops into some remote corner of the British Isles (such as southern Ireland or northern Scotland) in an attempt to divert British aircraft there while invading elsewhere.

In reckoning the possibilities, it must be kept in mind that in taking Crete, Germany had only one small warship—a single Italian destroyer which was blasted when trying to bring in an armada of German-laden Greek schooners.

Everything else, from the opening bomb to the last Red Cross packet, was carried by air. Even the daylight aspect of the seaborne convoy had Messerschmitt protection. After the British fleet got among the mosquito fleet of Greek coastal boats, the latter simply did not exist. When the few survivors returned to Piraeus, this correspondent there ascertained that the terrified crews had deserted, leaving the Nazis without sea conveyance. Yet the invasion went on anyway, by air.

The Germans were discreet about the number of troops carried by air to Crete because of its bearing on a possible mass invasion of England. But at least 20,000 men were carried in a week of constant shuttling by Junkers. On the first day alone in the neighborhood of Herakleion, General Freyburg estimated, Junkers averaged sixty landings hourly for ten uninterrupted hours.

Have Americans grasped the idea that once air domination is obtained over an area of 500 miles, any number of troops up to and including a full division can be transported there with full equipment?

Malemi yielded much more slowly than the Nazis expected. The original plan called for 500 parachutists, 5000 paratroops and 15,000 seaborne troops. The parachutists were supposed to get Malemi in two hours. Actually, it required more than 1000 chutists to obtain mastery in three days. And three days later the Nazis were still being pounded at a range of about 4000 yards from the village of Galata to the east by New Zealand gunners. Even on the second day the Maoris, shouting war dance songs, were able to make a two-mile charge with fixed bayonets directly into the teeth of the rapid-firing guns of the Nazis in the culvert north of Malemi. Furthermore, at Herakleion not a single parachutist was left alive from the scores dropped within the city.

"We kept everything within the city's perimeter absolutely clean," said one anti-aircraft officer, who after his gun was destroyed escaped the Nazi dive-bombing in a small rowboat from the end of Herakleion's jetty. Picked up by the cruiser *Hobart,* he witnessed the destruction of nineteen German schooners in three days.

The layman may ask, where were the British aircraft while English, Australian, New Zealand, Maori, Black Watch, Argylls and Royal Marines were suffering punishment from the air? Another officer, who was at the

RAF field in Libya when Hurricanes left for Crete, spoke with admiration of the pilots. Few returned.

Why, it may be asked, did Britain not send transport planes laden with her own parachute troops, from Africa to Crete? The answer is that Britain was simply not prepared, either by training or in quantity of planes. Germany was transporting troops from Athens, a distance equal to that from Cairo to Crete, but Germany was wealthy in Junkers and had obtained fighter domination over Crete through bombing attacks from Kythera and Rhodes.

The military principle for use in the coming parachutists' war in the Far and Middle East is that, if the invader's reconnaissance planes are driven off or his vertical photographs made meaningless by camouflage, he cannot estimate the defenders' forces. But the defending force must be able to deploy itself with scouting patrols in the broad periphery around an airdrome because the chutists, while they prefer to land upon an open surface, can land in open countryside. In the Rethymnon engagement the tide was eventually turned by 500 parachutists who landed the first day 3½ miles west of the airdrome.

Crete's lessons are therefore applicable in the event of a German attack upon England. Perhaps American troops would go by air from Ireland to the attacked area. Only when thousands of soldiers and eventually an entire army is ready to buckle on parachute and leap into action from plane doorways as readily as from the aprons of motor trucks can the foot soldier's full mobility be considered achieved.

Anything that can be carried can be dropped. Only lack of that priceless quality, imagination in warfare, limits its future application. Mercury was the first winged god who flew over the Aegean; parachutists dropping upon Crete opened the future.

—

HEROINE BORN IN HOLOCAUST OF CRETE WAR

Athens, Greece—August 1, 1941 (Delayed)

Hospital No. 7 has given Greece its greatest heroine of the war, an Englishwoman of Greek lineage who went through, on the island of Crete, ten days of the fanciest kind of hell the blitzkrieg can provide. She is Joan Stavridi, daughter of the London banker, Sir John Stavridi. She is a tall, attractive woman in her early thirties who looks like a champion tennis player. Taken prisoner at first by the Germans, who were astonished that a woman could go through what she has experienced alive and unruffled, she was immediately released and is now living here, unmolested.

Although the Axis-controlled cabinet of General George Tsolakoglou dare not recognize her heroism, the Germans tended by her admit that her spirit is the kind that has left Greece, though defeated and starving, still uncrushed and defiant.

Hospital No. 7 was located, for the inscrutable reasons that governed many things in the British campaign in Greece, in the perilous no man's land between the island's two chief strategical objects. Grouped around a two-story central building with a 40-foot red cross painted on its roof were forty tents, fifteen of which were wards for wounded and the rest shelters for personnel. The tents were unmarked by red crosses. So thoroughly and repeatedly was Hospital No. 7 bombed after the blitz began that Joan decided it had to be moved. She was not only the only nurse, and chief superintendent of the hospital; she was the only nurse left in western Crete, the New Zealand nurses having been evacuated two days before "it" began.

Attired in a brown-trousered battle costume and wearing above it only her white nurse's insignia, she ordered the transfer. The only place to go was a chain of caves under the shelflike Aegean seashore. Hospital No. 7 had lost all its own regular doctors a few seconds after the blitz struck. They had been having a swim off the beach, and were machine-gunned to death in the water by a passing plane. They were replaced, but there was never anyone to replace or relieve Joan Stavridi.

When the first 800 German parachutists came down upon Malemi they were wiped out by Australian sharpshooters. "I've just spent an hour of the best duck-shooting I ever had," said one Australian. This was before the bombing of Hospital No. 7 began. Wounded Germans were placed in tents beside the wounded Imperials.

Many chutists had broken thighs from being dropped too close to the ground. None seemed more than twenty. They had nervous, glassy eyes; their glances were wild and unseeing. They could not talk clearly. They remained in that condition for two hours, then had simultaneous seizures like patients emerging from a drug. The Australians claimed to have found chocolates with a peculiar taste in their equipment.

Then came the heavy bombing of Hospital No. 7. "They may have thought we were an army camp with a hospital in the middle," said Joan, "but they had photographed us so many times I don't see how they could have failed to know that we were undefended and had wounded." When the bombing broke loose, she was in the second story of the hospital building. "I could look out the window and see the planes strafing after they had bombed, and they seemed lower than the second story."

For 2½ hours of the intensest raid she lay in a slit trench beside an Irish Catholic priest, her tin helmet over her eyes. It was impossible to move the patients until night, when they began carrying them, bombed Britons and bombed Germans, down to their cave hospitals.

The next day the Stukas and Dorniers started work on the warships in Suda Bay. It required almost two days of dive-bombing to reduce the cruiser *York* to helplessness, but on the first day fifty sailors were wounded by a single hit. Hospital No. 7 now had bluejackets as well as Australians, New Zealanders and Germans.

Then the Germans came hard at Malemi again, having lost the intervening sea battle when about fifty small Greek schooners were sunk. The Luftwaffe pilots pancaked down the big, slow Junkers-52s wherever they found an opening. This time, having bombed the anti-aircraft thoroughly beforehand, they got a force on the ground who moved fast along the shore and captured Hospital No. 7. They sent back to Malemi all the British and Germans able to walk. That lasted a couple of hours.

Then the Australians attacked along the road and won back Hospital No. 7. The Germans fell back toward Malemi. Joan Stavridi had more wounded, of both sides, for the few cots left by those the Germans had forced to walk.

"By this time we had pretty well broken all the rules of war for both sides," says Joan. "I don't think either the British or the German manuals approve of a nurse trying to operate a hospital permanently in advance of the front line. Do they?"

Once the Maoris made a surprise attack on Malemi with fixed bayonets, and when it was over there were dark-skinned islanders as well as Nazis on the beds.

Hospital No. 7, for the last nine days of the siege, consisted of five caves on a fire-swept shingle of beach. It was a ten-minute walk of death from the westernmost cave to the easternmost, always under either German or British fire. The hospital was badly in need of food and there was no way to get it. Then a bright New Zealander took a captured Nazi flag and spread it on the ground for the Luftwaffe to see. Food began to parachute down in abundance.

After the Nazis took Malemi things got really difficult for Hospital No. 7. Supplies had been destroyed in the first bombing. Although by some miracle there were no deaths, there was only a single vial of morphine for hundreds of cases of screaming pain. When the parachutists began calling for anesthesia, Joan Stavridi held up her two hands and said: "This is all I have left now to quiet your pain."

The British, though dive-bombed by clouds of Stukas, refused to take the fleet out of Suda Bay as long as Malemi could be bombarded and there was a battleship gun to do it. All day and most of the night a continuous yowling archway of shells passed over the hospital, 14-inchers that landed among the encamped parachutists. Once again they started for Canea and took back Hospital No. 7.

But that did not end activities in the no man's land around the hospital. The Australians had, meantime, occupied a height behind Joan Stavridi's hospital, a place called Galata. From there they commanded the road, both ways, to Malemi and Canea, and were able to enfilade the German advance.

Nobody in the cave dared raise his head above the shelf of rocks. But Joan Stavridi had to find a way to get operations done, because wounded were still being brought in by scurrying stretcher bearers. She spread the last sheets on a slab of rock outside the cave mouth and kept on saving and sometimes losing the lives of patients. When bombs began to fall again on the beach and in the sea, Joan decided the cave hospital had to be better marked than the tent hospital had been. A daring messenger stole up by night to the abandoned hospital building, sawed the red copper screenings out of the windows and brought them back to the cave. That night the international patients sat up together by the light of hurricane lamps, forgetting their pain and helping Joan sew red crosses onto the sheeting.

The wounded continually asked for more water, but the nearest spring was ten minutes away. Joan asked the Germans whether they would allow her to send for water. "Yes, if you can find two orderlies willing to go." Two Britons volunteered, and shortly one came panting back. "John's hit," he said.

He was, and in a few seconds died with a bullet from Galata through his spine.

The agony ended only when the Germans took Canea, and the Aussies holding Galata had to fall back into the hills. When the German staff found that there was a woman at Hospital No. 7, who had been caring for all who fell for the past ten days, they could not believe it. "A woman here?" they said. They put her on a plane taking wounded back to Athens, and there she is today.

There are many Greek women who served the British and Greeks well without having opportunity for such heroism—fifty-two nurses were killed in the three weeks of fighting and all five of Greece's hospital ships were sunk—but the place of Joan Stavridi is the highest among those whose courage is known.

—

NAZIS WIPE OUT MEN IN VILLAGE TO AVENGE ATTACK ON CHUTISTS

Athens, Greece—August 2, 1941

The harvest is good this year in Christomathos, one of the Cretan villages that fell under the German parachute attack, but it will rot in the fields. There are not enough hands to pick it.

When the parachutists came down with their tommy guns blazing, the Cretans went out to meet them. Because the Metaxas government (of the late dictator) had disarmed them for their anti-royalist sympathies, they had few rifles, but they had knives and sickles. Before they were overcome, they gave as good an account of themselves as the Middle Ages could in fighting against the blitzkrieg.

The parachutists passed on, leaving five dead. On the fourth day after the island was in German hands, a detachment of soldiers headed by an officer, with a captured Greek Army doctor, a surgeon, as interpreter, came up from Canea to Christomathos. The Germans called the village population to assemble in the little square. Almost all were women and children.

"Where are your men?" asked the German officer.

"There are not many left."

"I need twenty-five men. I want men that are strong and healthy, none younger than 18 and none older than 42."

Only sixteen men could be found within these age limits. They sidled curiously into the square, and were counted.

"Not enough," said the German officer. "I must have the full count of twenty-five. I will extend the age limit from 16 to 55."

Twenty-three were found. By including one boy of 15 and one old man the quota was eventually rounded up in about an hour. In their farmers' working jackets and sag-seated Cretan trousers, the peasants were guided into the square. The German soldiers drew up on each side, facing inward upon them in two lines of a broad V formation. At a sudden signal from the officer, the machine guns began to speak. The entire manhood of the village was wiped out.

The Greek doctor almost fainted. "What is the reason for this?" he asked.

"We are following orders," said the German officer. "I am ashamed that I must do a thing like this, but I must, because it is the personal order of the Fuehrer."

"What are his orders?"

"Where snipers instead of regular soldiers kill our men, we are ordered to execute an equal number of civilians in that place. But where our men's bodies bear traces of mutilation—not bullet wounds but knife thrusts or slashes—the Fuehrer has ordered that we must exact five lives for the life of every German soldier."

The Greek doctor, turning pale, turned to go away.

"Wait, doctor," said the officer. "We have orders to visit several other villages, and you must go with us."

"You can kill me if you like," said the doctor, "but I cannot take any more part in this."

The Germans allowed him to go. But other peasants, who came to help bury the bodies of the villagers of Christomathos after the Germans had left, tapped the doctor on the shoulder.

"We have some cases up in the mountains that need care," they said guilelessly. "Come with us."

But the doctor read their intentions in their eyes: they took him for a traitor. He fled the island and is now hiding in Athens.

Telegrama

Modelo n.º 72

Recepção n.º

Nos telegramas recebidos pelos ... mpressores
o primeiro n ... ção expe-
didora é o nú ... ctf 88 mots ... ica as pa-
lavras e os res ... hora do depósito.
Este impresso deve acompanhar qualquer reclamação
que o expedidor ou o destinatário fizer sôbre erros de
transmissão ou demora na entrega.

Registou

Expedido às

Por

Número local | Indicações | Destino | Origem | número | Palavras | Data | Horas
20036 est chicago ill   88169 89 10 =
minutos

Via   Código

= two previous messages addressed legation pending   receipt
extower detailed instructions how reach next assignment
which brazzeville book passage freetownward availablest plane or
ship stock large quantity quinine hydrochlorate begin immunization
taking one tablet dily if uninnoculated yellowfever paratyphoidba
take precations stop carry washable clothing sweaters colonial
helmet paragraph if getaway quick youll monopolize
this promising colourful assignment for which excellent facilities
prearranged passpor extension already requested washington
paragraph keep me advised developents paragraph anticipating greek
series which should completed prior your departure cordially
= carroll

BELGISCH - CONGO

CONGO BELGE

INSCHRIJVINGSBEWIJS

N

ATTESTATION
D'IMMATRICULATION

N

INSCHRIJVING
OP HET BEVOLKINGSREGISTER

AU REGIS

Te vertoonen op elk verzoek
der overheid.

A exhib

IV

The de Gaulle Debacle in Brazzaville

Following Weller's liberation from the Nazis in Bern, his editor, Carroll Binder, sent him a telegram in Portugal on July 20 instructing that his next destination was to be Africa—once he finished sending in his series on Greece. *"If getaway quick, you'll monopolize this promising colorful assignment."*

From Estoril he went by ship to the Congo seaport of Banana, by car to Boma and Matadi, and by boat up the Congo River to Léopoldville (now Kinshasa).

Besides Weller's memorable portraits of Léopoldville and Brazzaville—and a ride in an experimental airplane—his encounter with General Charles de Gaulle had significant repercussions for both men (as biographers, and A. J. Liebling in *The Road Back to Paris* [1944], have pointed out). I have used not the original dispatches but a more reflective piece that Weller wrote later in the war. Beyond the loss of a reportorial naïveté which he perhaps exaggerates, the encounter shows Weller was already focused on the strategic importance of bases. This thinking bore fruit in his 1944 book, *Bases Overseas* (Chapter XIV), whose thesis of worldwide strategy annoyed nearly everyone.

A phrase that occurs often in this collection bears explaining. From March 1941, through the program known as "lend-lease," the United States supplied Britain, the Soviet Union, China, Free France, and other allies with $50 billion worth of arms, aircraft, motorized transport, and matériel—over $700 billion in today's money. Three-fifths of this aid went to Britain, largely in return for the use of bases; it was a way for America to take sides six months before it declared war.

—

Wild Congo Jungle, Not War, Takes Life of a Belgian Planter

Boma, lower Belgian Congo—August 20, 1941

Trop parler peut tuer ("Too much talk can kill"), says a wall poster with a black Bangala warrior—like those now trickling back from the Ethiopian victory—lying crumpled upon it.

The poster is nailed upon the veranda wall of the administration building in this town of 250 whites and countless thousands of blacks, the second stopping place on the two-night upriver trip to Matadi, seaport of the Congo.

Below the poster, scattered upon the veranda floor in pathetic array, lie the disordered household effects of a white man who died, not from talk but from double pneumonia—an incidental victim of the Congo's economic effort to put its shoulder to Great Britain's wheel.

The only one among the civilian casualties in this civilians' war, which reaches into the jungles of the Congo watershed as well as into metropolitan air-raid shelters, Georges Paquay was swept to his death a few hours after this correspondent's launch, fighting up the tricky channels through crocodile and boa constrictor country, reached Boma's quay.

At midday he was considered only slightly ill, but before the jungle moon arose he was dead. Now, in the morning sun, his friends, as the quickest way of settling his affairs, were auctioning off his possessions among themselves. A handful of colonial officials, river pilots, banana company executives in white puttees and sun helmets, accompanied by wives of several of their number, made bids casually from positions along the veranda rail.

Below, against the background of the tawny river, Cabinda blacks with store trousers and tattooed cheekbones occasionally made bids.

"What am I offered for this handsome set of living room chairs?" asked a roly-poly little colonial administrator who traditionally officiates at these auctions. "Examine that beautiful upholstery," he cried, snapping his suspenders with a professional air.

The upholstery consisted of American flour bags turned inside out to show less of the lettering. They were stuffed with straw. Chipped enamel plates, battered knives and forks, a Flemish-French dictionary and an insecticide gun all bore the unkempt look of a womanless household.

"They're not worth much," said a woman nearby. "His wife and two children in Brussels may discover only after several months that he's gone, and even then we won't have much money to send them."

The small pistol, which once made the jungle nights seem less dangerous, went for less than $5 to a newly arrived member of a British propaganda mission.

How had this planter died?

"Well," was the explanation, "we ordinarily buy in the United States our trucks for hauling to port the palm oil which is essential for British fats. But shipping is slow and uncertain, and now most American trucks are going to the Middle East. We're forced to take our chances and make old equipment last.

"Two nights ago a native boy drove Paquay's remaining American truck into the river mud. A murderous chill comes from the Congo now at the end of the tropical winter. Paquay worked all night in hip-deep mud, sweating and chilling himself alternately, because he knew he was unable to get another truck from the United States. By morning he had double pneumonia."

"What bids do I hear for this beautiful American-made home lighting plant?" cried the auctioneer.

He threw a switch and the motor began to hum. The auctioneer pointed to the manufacturer's plate.

"Made in Weesconsin, Ooo Esss Aah [U.S.A.]," he said.

The Cabindas and Senegalese crowded closer. The sun made the whitewashed walls of the Portuguese fort in Angola, across the river, gleam whiter. Beyond tin-roofed sheds and river dredges the sleek, brown Congo moved patiently and disdainfully toward the sea.

FREE BELGIANS AND FREE FRENCH BURY RIVALRY

Jointly Mark First Birthday of Liberty Tomorrow on Banks of Congo

Brazzaville, French Equatorial Africa—August 26, 1941

A rivalry native to the chilly lowlands of Flanders and northern France is being buried by the banks of the mighty Congo near the equator tomorrow, when liberated France and the unmolested Belgian Congo celebrate together the first birthday of Free French Africa.

Across the two-mile eddying expanse of Stanley Pool, above where the Congo is forced into a bottleneck of rapids so terrible they are still unconquered, the dusty little cities of Léopoldville and Brazzaville, whose white inhabitants number hardly 6000 against a total of nearly 100,000 blacks, face each other. They are the headquarters for most of what remains free of France and Belgium.

Here on the watershed of the wild crystal mountains the relations of old Europe are reversed. Each little capital is named in honor of its founding father, the Belgian for Leopold I, grandfather of today's prisoner king, and the French for Count de Brazza, Stanley's intrepid rival. Although Léopoldville—Brussels on the Congo—represents a smaller European country, it is bigger, more ornate and more pretentious than Brazzaville— Paris on the Congo. Neither is large enough to shut out the green wilderness around the brutal river flowing between them.

Each city extends about four miles along the riverbank. Each is fringed by native encampments, airports, hospitals and wireless stations. But the Congo is broader than either narrow strip of civilization. The current races between them faster than an automobile can traverse either city.

Only about 28,000 Belgians—less than the number of immigrants the United States absorbed from Europe during a single month at the height of the refugee exodus—rule some 12,000,000 blacks. They have taken over the shipment of vital supplies to the Allies as their responsibility and are content not to need a de Gaulle as an emblem of unremitting battle.

Among the colonial men and women in sun helmets on the streets of both Léopoldville and Brazzaville, the charge by France's former Premier Paul Reynaud that Leopold III laid down his arms without being beaten has now been buried and forgotten. Both parties are prepared to admit King Leopold's innocence. Such forgiveness has not been easy because for years the French and Belgians, in their frankest moments, used kinship of language to criticize each other with the same candor, sometimes acerbity, as Americans and Canadians.

Free France's birthday finds both in the same position of following Great Britain's marching tune because Britain is intact and has veto control over all American arms assignments, without which neither can fight. Finding himself obliged to carry on the war strictly upon British lines, both the Frenchman and the Belgian has found tolerance in seeing a cousin in the same position.

Even celebrating de Gaulle Day, Brazzaville seems more of an African city and Léopoldville more European. Even more, Léopoldville resembles Mississippi River towns of the Deep South. Its single large hotel reaches four stories. Although a government seat and headquarters of would-be tourist traffic, it is actually a business center operating a handful of large corporations that own the Congo commercially, with a fleet of American taxis to conquer its enormous distances.

Brazzaville, smaller, is more picturesque and more military in tone, content with its "push-push" monocycle rickshaws using two native runners.

Both cities have responsibilities far beyond their dimensions and even when they are putting on their brightest show, the Congo seems mightier than either. At six in the evening, when the bluish autumnal dusk ends the twelve-hour equatorial day and the sun drops like a burning orange behind the hills, the 25-foot launches to take Europeans and natives alike across the spinning whirlpools cease running, fearful that in the darkness they may be swept into the rapids. After ten even telephone conversation between tropical France and Belgium is severed and the Congo splits this miniature African Axis until morning.

With Brazzaville celebrating and Léopoldville helping, the trans-river traffic now has mounted to two launches hourly, which is the equivalent of a traffic rush. Each side's Ellis Island consists merely of an official in shorts, studying a book resembling a hotel register, under the veranda of a small cottage with a pair of native soldiers to help him. All persons crossing the river sign this book.

In the waterside customs houses both apply regulations with a severity and thoroughness as though this were Central Europe. The war has heightened the Congo's closed door policy and it is far easier for harassed Europeans to enter the U.S.A. than the relatively unpopulated and unexplored Belgian and French Congos.

Both sides are especially watchful against Vichy spies. Long ago all provincial maps of the Congo and French Equatorial Africa were collected from the bookstores by military authorities. Today it is impossible to buy even a large-scale map of Africa in either Congo capital.

—

THE GENERAL CHANGED HIS MIND

1944

It is doubtful if a newspaperman remembers any event more sharply than his original loss of innocence. For a reporter, particularly in politics, his own descent from the mount of belief and entrance into the valley of distrust (whence few travelers return, because the going is easier) retains a bitter sweetness he likes to savor again. As paratroopers recall their first jump, as schoolgirls remember their first kiss, as lawyers argue again their first case, the newspaperman remembers the day he found out that men can be liars. The pain is gone now, and understanding has decanted some of the indignation. But still he feels a wry tug, remembering when the world caved in—the day a man told him a story to publish, then repudiated it.

How can a man say a thing today and tomorrow deny that he has said it? This is a mystery, at least it is to a newspaperman until it happens to him. If the denial is equivocal, with many an "I said" and "You made me say," and the writer is young and conscientious, he will argue out the affair with himself abed, till weariness puts his shredded mind finally to sleep. But if the denial is bold, flat and unequivocal—if the statesman or the cinema star or the military man baldly repudiates in public what both the journalist and himself know he issued for publication—then the shock is great. Now he lies sleepless until morning, and dawn finds him a different man.

"Confidence," the French say, "is a plant which does not sprout a second time." Yet it is a callow scribe who allows his bitterness to be permanent. The intelligent one understands that this is the upturn in his career. Until today he was only a journalist; he believed in ethics. Now he has become a newspaperman. He believes in people . . . people whose ethics he knows.

This writer's tumble into maturity occurred in French Equatorial Africa.

Mobile governments often have "old" and "new" capitals. Brazzaville, the old capital of France's Fourth Republic, is the first capital of the regime of General Charles de Gaulle—a torpid town of yellowish plaster houses beside the muddy Congo, just above the toothy white rapids discovered by Stanley. The Congo is here the boundary between France and Belgium, the colonies properly called *Afrique Equatoriale Française* and *Congo Belge*. The opposite Belgian capital, with speeding muddy river between, is Léopoldville.

On both sides, tugged with tight hawsers against the riverbank, lie gaunt paddlewheel steamers, Mississippi-built and Congo-assembled. These steamers go on month-long journeys up the Congo and Ubangi. A smell of smoke drifts pleasantly through the air, and the black women of Brazzaville and Léopoldville, draped in gaudy cottons, bend over washing stones on each side of the racing brown flood and pound and slap and scrub with trading soap and pound again.

Two gasoline launches bear passengers between the two capitals of empire from six o'clock in the morning, which is dawn on the equator, to six in the evening, which is sunset. Then the capitals are cut off from each other. The honorific choice of Brazzaville by de Gaulle as his capital did not make the slightest difference.

One dark night de Gaulle's predecessor, the Vichy governor of French Equatorial Africa, straitjacketed in blankets, was bundled across the river after a *coup de main* jointly prepared by British and de Gaullist agents on the Belgian side. This snatch called for a special motorboat to cross the Congo after the cocktail hour. Otherwise the routine dominated by the great brown river was undisturbed by the coming of de Gaulle to Central Africa.

Above French soil rose the webby tall towers of the voice of France. Through this radio station alone, of all those in the world, the tall general could speak his mind. In London and Cairo he had to submit to the censorship of the British, who were paying the costs of his political administration and keeping a correspondingly close watch. This dependence on Britain approximated that of Haile Selassie, similarly inhibited in Addis Ababa, but with the important difference that in Brazzaville de Gaulle was free.

De Gaulle lived in a suitcase. His life was a constant *V-for-Victory* three-way shuttle 8000 miles long: Cairo-Brazzaville-London, then back again London-Brazzaville-Cairo. Unpopular with Britons, frequently irked by them, the general must often have felt, seeing the tempting antennae of free speech soaring above his own French capital, an impulse to tell the world his intensely patriotic hopes and troubles. He knew the consequences. If he spoke his thoughts today in Brazzaville he would have to answer for whatever he said in London or Cairo within the week.

The Congo town was a symbolic rather than a real capital. De Gaulle spent little time there. While other overrun empires like the Dutch and Belgian were content to have their administrative headquarters in London, since the uninvaded portions of their empires were too remote, being on French soil was important to the general. Brazzaville was little, hot and dirty; it was clique-ridden, poor, uncertain. But it was France and it was his own.

At this time the United States had neither entered the war nor recognized the de Gaulle regime. American recognition of [Marshal Philippe] Pétain was sustained by a game of bluff and counter-bluff. Vichy was a kind of buffer state between the Germans and the Americans. Their mutual recognition of Vichy kept them both, though actually already at war, frozen in a neutral pose, like boxers divided by a referee in an old-fashioned sporting print. Germany wanted time to beat Russia, America wanted time to tool up for war. The silver cup was Northwest Africa; each power was ready to make war as soon as the other reached for it. Neither America nor Germany foresaw that Japan would push them into war before either was ready.

In supporting Britain the United States was supporting de Gaulle. Churchill supplied him headquarters in London and Cairo, and money for the salaries of his officers and men, thus controlling him politically. British credits in the U.S. were exhausted, but there was enough on hand to keep going the tall leader of the fallen ally, and uphold the old *entente cordiale*.

Of the American lend-lease arms supplied to the British, a small trickle went to de Gaulle. It was nothing like the heavy stream that would eventually flow, but it whetted the general's dry throat. After the Americans entered the war the British retained financial control of the Free French army, while the Americans completely outfitted one French division after another by lend-lease.

While Brazzaville was capital of Free France, the vastness of Northwest Africa was in Vichy hands, with German plainclothes men and Gestapo watching the same "neutrality" which American consuls were also overseeing. The southern Sahara and the humid little French mandates of the Gulf of Guinea were the line between Vichy and de Gaulle. At the same time all de Gaulle was divided into three parts: Central Africa, the Middle East and London.

The general chafed under unilateral British control. His American aid was coming through British brokerage, closely safeguarded. He wanted more American support and he wanted it directly.

In the relation between America, Britain and the Soviet Union, de Gaulle has always tried to work a little more closely with the rising member. Because the other two powers must come to terms with the ascendant power, they must come to terms with de Gaulle. The United States was the rising force, for Russia was reeling back before Hitler's armor and the British were barely holding out in the desert while awaiting more American tanks and aircraft.

De Gaulle decided to do exactly what Britain had in the period before lend-lease: to make the United States an offer of strategic advantage for her coming participation in the war. Churchill had offered Roosevelt a ninety-nine-year lease on certain Atlantic bases in return for fifty four-stack destroyers of the old Atlantic Fleet. De Gaulle decided to make Roosevelt a similar offer, but go one step farther. He would offer the United States bases beyond the Atlantic—bases in Africa.

In some respects the offer was more attractive than Churchill's. American participation in the war was certain. Already American freighters were unloading lease-lend aircraft at British ports in the armpit of western Africa. These aircraft were flying across the Chad—first of the African colonies to go de Gaullist—to the Sudan and Middle East. To fly the same route, would the Americans not welcome ports of entry under their own supervision? As well as naval bases in the Gulf of Guinea to meet the submarine menace and prepare to strike Dakar? As soon as Hitler got himself unencumbered in Russia, he would edge across to French Northwest Africa, and then where would an American expeditionary force land?

So de Gaulle began formulating his offer. It was of the greatest importance that this step, taken as leader of Free France and without Churchill's knowledge, should succeed. If it failed, if Roosevelt ignored or neglected the offer, de Gaulle would be exposed without support between the mighty Anglo-American opposites.

If Roosevelt accepted the offer London would probably go along in the interest of unity. Acceptance of African bases would be an American step toward war, hence in the British interest. If Roosevelt refused, de Gaulle would be out on a cracking limb. Without having gained new support, he would have shown his wish to gain more independence of the old. Churchill would not put him overboard, but he was sure to be displeased. "Whose bread I eat, his song I sing," goes the proverb.

Any French statesman (except possibly Pétain) would have considered the risk fair and the offer sound and reasonable. Storm flags rode over Africa as submarine sinkings increased. Washington was wondering whether the Atlantic Fleet would have to storm the new, reinforced Dakar and take it by surprise. In the United States the unchangingly large body of Francophiles were pressing hard for Secretary of State Cordell Hull to drop Vichy and recognize de Gaulle. The general had not yet taken Washington, but New York was his.

At this time the British were as reluctant as Roosevelt later became to grant Free France easy recognition. Churchill had not even broken with Vichy, and his confidence in de Gaulle was less than whole. But if the Americans recognized de Gaulle he would have powerful backing, making him even more difficult to handle in the Middle East. Was this desirable? Free France, weak but enterprising, would be able to establish that genteel rivalry between great supporters which has more than once benefited the small and dependent.

De Gaulle was discreet. He did not fly to Washington. Instead, he made his offer to a State Department officer in the Middle East five months before Pearl Harbor. His offer was ignored. Perhaps de Gaulle's equivocal status caused the snub. Perhaps Washington did not wish to offend Britain by accepting. Perhaps Roosevelt and Hull concluded it was more valuable to dangle Pétain, thus keeping the French fleet immobilized and the Nazis from seizing Northwest Africa.

De Gaulle waited a few days in the Middle East for a definite answer.

Then, impatient, he resolved on a bold expedient. As he had gone over the head of the British government to offer the bases to the United States, so he would go over the head of the American government (which kept the offer secret) and reveal his bid to the American people. With the future American armies already being mobilized for battle in Europe, but the Atlantic war unwon, the advantage of possessing secure African bases would be unmistakable. And he hoped that his offer would add power to his plea for a break with Vichy and formal recognition of Free France.

For de Gaulle to reach the American public was not easy. Cairo and London outlets were cut off by British political censorship. His offer would have to come from Brazzaville, the only capital where he was supreme. A special broadcast was impossible; lacking the American tubes that had still not arrived, the Congo phone transmitter could be heard only with freakish rarity in North America. . . . Nor could the announcement be too bold. Nothing like an "open message" would do. The offer had to come out casually, to offend the British as little as possible.

The foreign newspapermen who had visited Brazzaville during the war could be counted on the fingers of one hand. A few had sped through en route to or from the Middle East on the flying boats of the Lagos-Congo-Lake Victoria-Nile run. But neither the American news agencies nor the newspapers maintaining foreign services considered it worthwhile to place a correspondent in either French or Belgian Congos. De Gaulle did not dare make an official announcement through the Free French news agency; its British sources of revenue would dry up instantly. The ideal circumstance for the general's launching of his first trial balloon would have been to find in Brazzaville an itinerant American newspaperman representing a journal of good repute, and to send him aloft.

Such a test aeronaut was precisely what de Gaulle found waiting when, late in August of 1941, he arrived from Cairo to celebrate Brazzaville's first birthday as capital of the legitimate empire. The *Chicago Daily News,* one of the oldest foreign syndicates in the United States, published in more newspapers than any other non-agency service in the world, had sent a correspondent to Brazzaville to write about the Free French and if possible to interview de Gaulle.

In celebration of the same *fête* the Flying Wing, a highly experimental plane without fuselage, in which a dozen passengers could sit parallel in the thickened wing, arrived in Brazzaville piloted by Jimmy Mollison to become the flagship of the Free French Air Force. A British firm stopped production after two Flying Wings. Even unpious pilots blessed themselves before they put their hands on the controls. Since few officials in the Congo were interested in previewing the aerial future, the Chicago newspaperman, while awaiting de Gaulle's arrival, had been able to go on the plane's baptismal essay over the Congo. He found a quarter hour's experience exhilarating but unsettling. He had no apprehension whatever that he would shortly accompany de Gaulle himself on a transatlantic ballooning mission of an even more tentative and experimental nature.

One afternoon two days before Brazzaville's birthday Karl Quigley, a hefty, straightforward American in his late twenties who had served as ambulance driver under fire in France's great retreat and escaped from a Nazi prison camp, arranged an interview. Quigley was a former Los Angeles newspaperman and writer, honest and intensely loyal to de Gaulle. As head of the American side of the Free French propaganda establishment in Brazzaville he lived in a mosquito-netted little room on the ground floor of the lemon-colored, arcaded building, set in the country, where the clicking machines of persuasion operated all day. Because Quigley, as well as his French superiors, would bear the responsibility of seeing that the eventual story corresponded with the interview and of censoring it politically, the reporter asked that he be present. The hour was six in the evening. The only other person in the room, after his aide left, was de Gaulle.

It was not easy to put questions to a man in his position. The difficulties in Syria between the French and the British had reached Africa by the jungle telegraph, but one could not allude to them. The matter of American and British recognition was equally delicate. De Gaulle wanted both deeply; his followers repeatedly said so; but anything he added would seem an undignified supplication.

Friendly ground being thus crevassed, the easiest and most courteous thing seemed to be talk about Vichy, the common enemy. De Gaulle was contemptuous of the Vichyists in an unhurried way. He spoke cautiously, as though he wanted to be extremely careful what he said to the world. Asked whether he thought the United States should sever with Vichy he said, "I do. Without delay. Immediately."

Was there no evidence to hope that Vichy might resist Hitler, if British fortunes in the Mediterranean improved?

"Not only is there no evidence, but the men of Vichy could not turn back if they wanted to," said de Gaulle. "They have taken three direct steps, one after another, and they cannot retrace them even if they should develop a desire to do so. The first step was when they lost the military campaign. The second was that they concluded an armistice with Hitler. The third was that they undertook to collaborate with Hitler's plans. Those steps were taken separately. Each closed a new door to retreat. They cannot go back. They can only go farther in the same direction."

But why should not the British sever with Vichy before the United States?

Without a second's hesitation, de Gaulle replied: "England is afraid. (*L'Angleterre a peur.*) What, in effect, England is carrying on is a wartime deal with Hitler, in which Vichy serves as go-between. Vichy serves Hitler by keeping the French people in subjection and selling the French empire piecemeal to Germany. But do not forget that Vichy also serves England by keeping the French fleet from German hands. Britain is exploiting Vichy in the same way as Germany does; the only difference is in the purpose. What is going on is an exchange of advantages which keeps the Vichy government alive as long as both Britain and Germany agree that it should exist. If Vichy should lend or lose its fleet to the Nazis, Britain would quickly bring the suspense about recognition to an end. And if Vichy should cease serving Hitler, Germany would dismantle Vichy herself."

However, with Vichy and London thus intertwined with Berlin, how important was it that Washington cut off Vichy?

"In my opinion," said de Gaulle gravely, "the effect of an American severance with Vichy would be very great."

Less sure of this than the general, the interviewer asked—with a suggestion of irony which de Gaulle did not fail to catch—whether an American political attitude ever meant much to the average Frenchman.

"I am not suggesting that the French public is looking to America for its political opinions," said de Gaulle. "But at least the situation would then be clearly defined. It would be seen that America at last had taken an unmistakable line against all those helping Hitler. We know already what the average Frenchman's feelings are toward Vichy. The severance of relations would indicate to him that the American government felt the same way. Moreover, it would demonstrate that American policy toward Vichy was consistent with its policy toward Berlin."

Vichy thus pigeon-holed, we talked of progress in the colonies, Brazzaville's birthday, the spirit among the troops. These topics were tame, but the interviewer had been warned to expect little, and was prepared to get nothing. In the small, closed room with its scant African hangings the interviewer, seeking a ground agreeable to de Gaulle, evaded the truly searching questions. Out of courtesy for the general, from whom answers came like taffy from a pull, and out of knowledge that anything critical the general might say would never pass his own censorship, the reporter kept to questions within the public domain. He was also on guard against that kind of off-the-record confidence which statesmen employ to stifle an embarrassing truth which the newspaperman is likely to know from another source.

It was the general himself who tired first of this talking about nothing-at-all. With military decisiveness he suddenly took command of the interview. He ceased being the questioned and became the questioner. With an abruptness which took both the interviewer and his own publicity man off-guard, he leveled an inquiry like a gun at his visitor.

"You mention the achievements of the Free French and you say that America is following them closely," said de Gaulle. "Why, then, does the United States not take cognizance of our accomplishments?"

He did not use the word *recognize,* a term of such fetish importance in his mind that he rarely allowed himself to utter it. He left that to the interviewer.

"You mean, recognize your movement, *mon général?*"

His disproportionately small head nodded a bare fraction. Yes, *recognition* was what he meant.

During a little silence, the interviewer felt for words that would not wound this proud and extremely sensitive soldier. "I am a newspaperman. I do not know what is in the mind of Monsieur Roosevelt."

The general seemed to warm a little at finding an American as nonplussed as himself. "Well, tell me what you *think* is the reason." He sat back expectantly.

"I do not think America is refusing to recognize you out of any love of Pétain."

De Gaulle was not satisfied. "What is it, then? Not love for Vichy. *Et alors?*" *Pétain* was a word like *recognition* which meant too much for him to use it. The Brazzaville radio, too, shied away from the name, since the underground had reported that attacks on the old man's character—instead of his perspicacity—boomeranged as propaganda. "Well?"

"I think that you realize, general, that America never has what you could call an inventive government politically. We citizens often notice that our diplomats wait for the British to make up their minds, then imitate them two days later, looking the other way to pretend they never noticed." (De Gaulle did not smile; something earnest was on his mind.) "And so, since the British are your formal ally but have not yet recognized you formally, we have no example to follow." (De Gaulle tossed his head impatiently.) "I think two things will have to happen before America recognizes you: we shall have to be formally at war and hence your ally, and Britain will have to break with Vichy and recognize you first. You must always remember that the Americans are politically a timid and unaggressive people."

During these words de Gaulle's immobile face seemed to grow tense and impatient. His tone, however, more than his curiously passive countenance showed dissatisfaction with what he perhaps regarded as more American evasiveness. With pent-up unrest he shot out the words, "But with me offering them bases in Africa!" (*"Mais puisque j'ai mis des bases en Afrique à leur disposition!"*)

Neither of his hearers was sure they had heard aright. They looked at him, and at each other. The room was perfectly silent. At first his two listeners were too astonished to say anything. Then the reporter ventured: "Bases, general? Where?"

"On the coast of French Africa."

"On the Atlantic coast?" It was a wasted question, indicative of the agitation in both hearers. The general was hardly able to dispose of Bizerta or Casablanca, and Vichyist Djibouti was blockaded under siege by a British handful of King's African Rifles . . . Quigley was saying nothing, simply staring at the general. As news, this was a Koh-i-Noor.

"And have you announced your offer yet elsewhere?"

"No, not before this."

"Where was your offer to the Americans made?"

"I cannot reveal that just yet." Pleased, the general sat back easily. He rarely smiles, but he seemed to be smiling faintly at his flabbergasted hearers, as though gauging the public effect of his offer by its effect on the two Americans in his room.

"How many bases?"

De Gaulle hesitated, as though he had not expected a question so precise. He took thought. Then he said, "Four."

"All on the coast of that part of Africa held by your forces?"

De Gaulle bowed an affirmative.

There was a short pause, while Quigley and the questioner drew breath. De Gaulle stirred slightly, as though that was all he wished to say. He was ready for his hearers to go.

"And what did you ask for in return? Destroyers? Arms?"

"Nothing," said the general.

"Did you offer the bases for ninety-nine years, like the British?"

"For the duration of the war," said the general. He explained the dangers of the Nazis occupying the Dakar-Casablanca corner if they were successful either in Russia or Cairo. "It is an act of prevention," he said, as though the step were already accomplished.

A horrid fear touched the reporter. De Gaulle was then known as a firebrand, a visionary. Was he perhaps, in the way of such luminaries, saying what he intended to do, rather than what he had done? "Pardon me, general, but I am not sure whether we understood you correctly. Did we understand you to say that you planned to offer these bases later, or that you have already offered them?"

"I have offered them already," said the general.

"When?"

"A few days ago."

"And have you an answer yet?"

The general gave his two hearers an eloquent look, as though of a hard-tried patience. "Not yet," he said. Again one had the feeling that he wished to conclude the interview here. But many questions crowded to be satisfied.

"If Roosevelt accepts the West African bases as he did Britain's Atlantic bases, what do you think Vichy's reaction will be?"

"Possibly nothing very much will happen," said the general calmly. "At least, not until Germany is able to ease up in its struggle against Russia.

Both the United States and Vichy will simply coast along, more or less as at present. Of course if you are asking about strategic rather than political considerations, that is different."

"Please explain, general."

"Examine any map showing the route and frequency of British convoys and you will find that the most traveled path is around the bulge of Africa. For the protection of these shipping lanes, the Nazis cannot be allowed to use Vichy's African soil in combined airplane and submarine attacks, or Britain's Middle Eastern lifeline would be severed. Britain has Bathurst and Freetown, but they are so small that Dakar easily dominates them. They are too near and weak to serve as bases."

De Gaulle's mention of this key to the Mediterranean and South Atlantic opened the way to a strategic question. "Do you think the U.S. fleet can take Dakar?"

"Not without a battle of considerable dimensions," said de Gaulle. "The support is the question as much as the battle. Nearby British ports are exposed by nature and furthermore they have inadequate facilities for their present needs. The same thing applies to Accra and Takoradi on the Gold Coast, and Lagos in Nigeria."

"Then you do not believe that the United States should attempt to take Dakar by force at any time, but rather that the American fleet and air arm should establish bases within the Gulf of Guinea as a check on the German advance into Africa."

De Gaulle's heavy-lidded eyes seemed to lift a little. "You have grasped," he said gently, "the reason for my offer to the United States."

The United States would soon need French bases in the Pacific, too, if Japan entered the war, the general pointed out. . . .

"Would these bases be equally available to the American fleet?"

"Without any fuss whatever," said the general. He moved to rise, putting his hand on his papers.

"Have you any objection to saying which bases you have offered in Africa, general?"

"Duala," he said. "And Port Gentil." He waved his hand, as though this were an annoyingly small detail. "And Pointe Noire." He moved toward his risen guests, edging them toward the door. He never named the fourth port, though Quigley later hazarded it was Libreville.

"You are confident America will make good use of these bases, general?" said the interviewer, moving backwards, sun helmet in hand.

The general made a little parting speech, with that here-is-one-more-thing-for-you air common to interviewees. "I have always had faith in the United States keeping her word and I know that America does not covet territorial aggrandizement in Africa. I am sure that France's African possessions would be in safe hands if strategic points were occupied by the American navy. I observe that one of the cardinal points of the Atlantic Charter is respect for the integrity of all nations. And finally, I believe in the American concept of international honor."

"And general, what will be your answer if Monsieur Roosevelt accepts your offer and you are accused by Vichy of bartering French African ports for American aid?"

"My answer," said de Gaulle, "is that there is no more reason to believe that the United States would break its word of honor and keep the French bases beyond the term of the lease of the period needed as defense against Hitler, than there was in the last war to safeguard Brest and Bordeaux against the United States before accepting your help against the same enemy."

With this small speech, delivered in a simple and altogether comradely manner, the general saw his guests out, receiving and returning their salutes.

Written promptly in Quigley's room at the propaganda office, with one remark of the general's about the Syrian campaign omitted because Quigley believed it would offend the British, the interview was stamped and passed. One copy was handed to the English-speaking French officer who headed the press office. He read it, approved it, and authorized its transmission.

The Brazzaville radio charged more per word for news transmission to the United States than the Belgian station in Léopoldville. The interview therefore was sent from the Belgian side. There was a reciprocal agreement between the Belgian and Free French authorities, to prevent evasion of censorship, under which neither would allow transmission from its station of anything about the other colony unless it was stamped by both. Flashed to Chicago, New York, London and South Africa, the interview was published in the newspapers of August 28 [1941].

An hour after the interview was filed with the Belgians, a Free French officer phoned under the Congo to the writer at the A.B.C. hotel in Léopoldville. Though the interview had been stamped, read, censored and passed by all the competent authorities, there were other persons who had asked to see it . . . No, not the general . . . other persons . . . impossible to be more precise . . . oh, well, if the Belgians were already transmitting it, never mind. . . .

The next day a follow-up story on the African bases, duly censored and stamped by both Free French and Belgians, was flashed to the United States. Two days later, on a Saturday, de Gaulle flew in a British flying boat to Nigeria. Things immediately began to happen.

While the United States had only that gifted Gael from Yale, Patrick Mallon, with a malaria-stricken aide, to carry the diplomatic burden on both sides of the Congo, the British kept consular staffs in both Brazzaville and Léopoldville. In the late afternoon of the morning when de Gaulle landed on British soil, the British consul in Brazzaville informed the Free French that some hours after his arrival in Nigeria General de Gaulle had issued a public denial of the interview.

Eventually de Gaulle sent a peculiarly worded message to his press chief in Brazzaville. It said: "Inform the American correspondent Weller that I am not in agreement with his making me say that I have offered French bases to the United States." He succeeded in satisfying the British by repudiating the interview without absolutely denying it. In other words, he simply hauled down his trial balloon.

To complete the disavowal, the turning of the Koh-i-Noor to paste, Cordell Hull denied knowledge of any such offer to the State Department. He had a legal right to do this, since he could not well admit to having received offers from de Gaulle for the disposal of territory over which he still recognized Vichy's authority. It was easy for the unlucky aeronaut, however, to ascertain that de Gaulle had repeated his offer to another diplomatic official, that the original offer had been made in Cairo, and that de Gaulle had already announced it in Stanleyville to a meeting of Free French.

Quigley was a stricken figure in whom sorrow struggled with indignation. His first act was that of an idealist undone; he asked to be taken off press duties and sent to fighting service in the field, by preference with the oasis-raiding parties . . . In any governmental propagandist, an attachment to truth is a liability.

In London, as A. J. Liebling remarks in *The Road Back to Paris* (p. 156), this interview made de Gaulle "a very naughty boy" in official circles, and obliged him to make "public expiation" by disowning it. Liebling remarks: "This sort of thing contributed to what one of my best-informed and most British friends called de Gaulle's 'justified Anglophobia,' but it did nothing to encourage him in further gestures toward America."

What Africa eventually heard via the verbal telegraph was that on arriving in British Nigeria, de Gaulle was faced with a demand from Churchill to repudiate the offer. Why? The guess was that Churchill was not desirous of having de Gaulle undersell him in the strategic market, trading bases to Roosevelt for recognition or less where Britain had traded bases for destroyers. . . . No official explanation ever came from London. This much was certain; de Gaulle opened a door into Africa for America, and Britain shut it.

As for the interviewer, while making full allowance for de Gaulle's difficult position, he vows that he will never again ascend, even unwittingly, in a trial balloon. Never again, he hopes, will he find himself drifting alone over Africa under a leaking envelope of propaganda in a basket from which the chief pilot has bailed out. Let the general mount to the skies. The lesser aeronaut has grounded himself for the duration.

Chicago Daily News expense account

George Weller
September 7---October 4, 1941

Credit outstanding favor CDN as of Sept.6 $1452.11

EXPENSES
Communications

Domestic telegrams $16.62
Local phones and postage   ~~XXXXX~~
                                         8.54
                                       $25.16

General and Travel

Transportation: Irumu--Watsa--Sudan--
            Western Ehtiopia --Sudan--Watsa $264.30
  Local transportation   72.61
  baggage fees   36.90
  camp equipment   32.12
  porters   26.20
  hotels and lodgning   133.65
  food   127.44
  newspapers and source material   19.66
  tips and gratutities   15.62
  entertainment in line of service   11.45
  messengers   8.19
  exchange fees (Sudan and Ethiopia)   8.54
  medical treatment (amoebic dysentery)   18.65
  visa   4.90
                                               $805.39

SUMMARY

Favorable balance CDN Sept. 7, $1452.11
less Sept.7-Aug.4 expenses   805.39
      balance carried over $ 646.72

(signed)

George Weller
George Weller
Batavia, February 9,1942.

V

The Belgian Campaign
in Ethiopia

This remains the unique eyewitness account by a reporter of a forgotten, yet important, military campaign between colonial empires in Africa. Much was at stake—more than just Haile Selassie's rule in his country, an ousting of Italy, and a sense of vindication by a defeated Belgium in striking a victorious blow against the occupying Axis power. Also up for grabs was who would control crucial access in Africa to Sudan, to the Red Sea, and to the Arabian Peninsula.

The Emperor Haile Selassie (1892–1975) had ruled Ethiopia— often called Abyssinia by Europeans—since 1930. Once Mussolini's forces invaded in 1935, and took the capital Addis Ababa in 1936, Selassie went into exile in England after giving an impassioned speech before the League of Nations that described how freely the Italians used chemical weapons on unarmed civilians. (They would also execute both his sons-in-law; a daughter died in captivity in Italy.) Mussolini now held an important chunk of African territory, alongside Somaliland, in the Italian Empire. Selassie, with the help of British, Belgian, and Free French troops, was unable to leave exile and recover his capital until May 1941.

Following the de Gaulle interview and its aftermath, Weller proceeded up the Congo River by boat. He stopped in Stanleyville (present-day Kisangani) and nearby Yakusu and caught several stories there. Then, thanks to the pilot Dewez and his aging Fokker—flying over the Sudan—Weller joined Belgian Congo forces in Saio at the end of a twenty-five-hundred-mile odyssey across the continent's waist. There he witnessed what resembled a conflict from the prior world war: African against African on behalf of European powers. Weller's photos show open-cockpit biplanes, rattletrap trucks, bygone rifles. His expense reports tell their own story: $26.20 for a month of porters, $32.12 for camp equipment, $127.44 for food. (He came down with amoebic dysentery.)

The seven stories, which ran in early October, were finished in Juba in Anglo-Egyptian Sudan and sent from Léopoldville the third week of September, upon Weller's return. A Belgian information office in New York soon proudly published the dispatches in a booklet. Mistakes which appeared both in the newspaper and the booklet have been corrected here against the cablese.

As a thank-you for helping him in the field, Weller cabled the *CDN* to purchase subscriptions to *Time, Harper's,* and the *Atlantic* for Major General Auguste Gilliaert, Belgian Congo.

—

CONGO'S ADVICE: BRIBE HITLER OR BUMP HIM OFF

Yakusu Station, River Stanleyville, Belgian Congo— September 17, 1941

"When is the war going to end? How can two tribes continue fighting so long? Why does your tribe not give a big present to this chieftain, Hitler, to persuade him to surrender?"

Such are the questions two tribes of Congo fishermen, the Lokeles and the Yawembes, and three tribes of forest hunters, the Esoos, the Bambolis and the Torumbus, are continually asking the courageous band of missionaries who have undertaken their material and spiritual improvement.

Less than a dozen quiet, hard-working men and women have made themselves responsible here for keeping 150,000 black people physically healthy as well as at peace with each other and themselves.

Congo boatmen, who nightly face the jaws of crocodiles and hippopotamuses to spread their fishing nets across the violent river, arrange their tribal difficulties to end in early armistices. They think whites ought to do the same. Their proposal for handling Hitler is simple: offer him a bribe in the form of a valuable woman of the allied tribe. This method has brought an end to hundreds of jungle wars and the tribesmen believe it would be similarly successful in Europe.

For a week World War II was not known in the jungle. The long, hollow drums, whose muffled tattoo sends the news of every marriage and death from village to village, were silent. Then paddlers in dugout canoes, who had gone upstream as far as Stanleyville, began asking the mission staff searching questions. The Belgian government gave orders that all native queries should be answered with absolute honesty and straightforwardness. No attempt was to be made to whip the villagers into war frenzy or to complicate their lives with political dogma.

These river and forest people are genuinely mystified over why the war is continuing so long. If offering Hitler a woman fails, they have a second solution ready.

"It would be easy to defeat your enemy," they tell British missionaries in this American-financed station, "if your tribe would all go on a fast. Starve yourselves for two days. Being hungry will make you strong. When you feel at your strongest take your spears and knives, get in your canoes and cross to your enemy's side of the river and kill them all."

—

Aged Crate Shows Need for Airplanes in Africa

Stanleyville, Belgian Congo—October 11, 1941

When you have been piloting the same military transport for one full year over Central Africa's sea of trees, you start watching the new American designs and wondering when they will be available for service here.

When you have landed the same ship at postage-stamp jungle airports for two years, you begin peering over your mechanic's shoulder for flaws. When she has had three years of tropical sun and rain, you are ready for new wings. When she has had four, you pack two parachutes. After five years in trans-African service, you are on your own and the passengers on their insurance.

Lieutenant Jean Joseph Dewez, the Belgian Congo's ace military pilot, has passed the limit and has been on his own for several years now. At the controls of his flying crate, which is the flagship of little Belgium's Congolese air arm and was the mainstay of the recent heroic campaign in Ethiopia, Dewez has winged more hours than younger jungle pilots have miles. The bush people call him "Ndeke Lipumbu," meaning beautiful bird.

Dewez is a small, shy, Thurberesque man in his middle thirties. His pockets are always filled with orders, memoranda, maps, Ethiopian thalers, Sudanese pounds, Egyptian piastres and countless letters. What pocket space remains is occupied by small green lemons with which he bulges all over.

Dewez is the kind of man who is always trying to do favors and never asks any. Nevertheless, he has been getting restless lately. He walks around the hangar in the brown shorts of the Congolese *Force Publique,* with his sun helmet pulled down over his eyes, concealing the misgiving upon his face.

Hardly anyone could blame Dewez for getting worried. He is flying the oldest transport plane in Africa. It was assembled in 1929. It is a Fokker ten-passenger monoplane, of the type the Dutch airlines to the Far East discarded five years ago for American Douglases, which themselves are outmoded today.

The Fokker is the grandpa of today's trans-African Lockheed. But Dewez still goes groaning impartially across the broad brown Congo, the great equatorial forests, the Mountains of the Moon, the glassy Sudanese marshes, the rolling Kenya uplands and far up Ethiopia's forbidding highland. Whenever protests of senile rage come from the three 240-horsepower Gnome-Rhone engines—which may be above the uninhabitable Nilotic swamps, or over Ituri Forest, where pygmies hunt in the shadows of 200-foot trees—Dewez wheedles, humors and nurses the motors along until the next patchpocket airdrome comes in sight.

To bring Dewez' three-horse buggy into the field is a task suitable only for a man with five arms. Besides manipulating the stick, the enormous wheelbrake and three separate motor controls, Dewez must somehow manage to wind, organ-grinder fashion, the hand lever leveling off the tail elevator. The lever is cunningly tucked away behind him, two feet above his head. Try using full wrist action back up there yourself and imagine how pleasant must be an ice cream freezer in motion, operated overhead and backwards, when the cabin temperature is 100° and the tropical trees are rushing up toward your face. Dewez literally cranks his ship into the field.

Your correspondent got acquainted with Dewez' hack through riding it from the Belgian field headquarters in Northeastern Congo to Ethiopia and return. Dewez is pleased with his ability to keep his relic pushing 115 miles an hour, and small wonder. He has neither a copilot nor a parachute. At the other set of controls, carefully avoiding touching them, sits Lulengo, the totally black son of cannibals from Matadi in the lower reaches of the Congo. He is Dewez' mechanic.

If the thin crack in the cowling above Dewez' windshield, now admitting light, should open under air pressure—as surely it would if Dewez put the Fokker into a steep dive—and something loose should hit Dewez between the eyes, Lulengo would simply fold his hands and await the inevitable.

Dewez usually addresses Lulengo in Lingala, which is the lingua franca among Congo tribes, and Lulengo calls Dewez "master." Dewez retains Lulengo because, unlike white mechanics, he always confesses frankly when he doesn't know what is wrong. Lulengo's chief duties are refueling and winding the propellers before the takeoff. This he accomplishes with an old-fashioned pole looped with leather. Lulengo's only two words of English were learned when Dewez recently was doing flying ambulance work with the South African forces in southern Ethiopia. They are: "No good."

When engaged in errands of mercy, Dewez indicates that he is no longer a military pilot by painting a large white circle upon the Fokker's crackerbox fuselage with a bright red cross inside it. When the ambulance work ends, he whitewashes the cross. Dewez is conscientious about this change. Aboard the plane he keeps a Bible in his map case, with cotton batting for his passengers' ears and molasses kisses that Lulengo offers to all seatholders.

While piloting it is necessary for Dewez to keep the side windshields open to hear the first protest in the three engines. Sitting six to eight hours daily with 720 horsepower hammering less than six feet away has made him partially deaf.

During the height of the Ethiopian campaign, Dewez often flew more than ten hours daily carrying British wounded along the Diredawa-Mogadiscio-Nairobi route. Two hundred hours monthly is still his average. The wheel must be gripped and the plane steered every second because the Fokker was already old when automatic pilots began to be installed. Furthermore, a permanent combination of indigestion and dysentery is an ailment common to tropical flyers who sleep on alternate nights atop mountains and in the desert. Dewez is no exception.

Few pilots' eyes can hold out against the burning Sudanese plain which, when flooded, is one of the most blinding terrains in the world. But Dewez, sitting at the Fokker's cracked wheel, simply glances for guidance within the cowling, which he has made to look like a downtown telephone booth, with numbers indicating compass directions and crude pencilings outlining the principal mountain passes. Time was when Dewez dared to slant the Fokker's nose downward and watch a giraffe nibbling a tree or a herd of elephants blundering through the grass.

But he will not be able to indulge in such whims again until United States factories are able to deliver the planes already ordered for the Congo.

While spending the night at Juba, in the Anglo-Egyptian Sudan, somebody lifted the ninety hard-earned dollars from his trousers pocket which Dewez planned to send to his wife in Nairobi. Yet he refused to delay our takeoff. He earnestly felt his pockets to see whether he had enough lemons, much needed among the Belgian forces encamped in the Ethiopian highlands. They stave off beriberi; also, the soldiers have discovered that if you offer an Ethiopian girl a lemon and she accepts, that means she wants your friendship to ripen rapidly.

Keeping pasted above him as a talisman a 1931 Congolese airmail stamp, which bears the pioneer picture of his Fokker showing the same license and lettering as today, Dewez cocked his sun helmet forward and stared ahead through the Ethiopian mountains. Through his sunglasses he studied his British engine gauge, his German altimeter and Italian horizon lever. The latter often rotates during level flight in a manner the Fokker itself could not possibly do under any circumstances. He can read his Scotch compass, even in blazing sunshine, only with the aid of his flashlight. Dewez is prouder of the altimeter than of any other instrument in the plane. It was made in 1914.

THE BELGIAN CAMPAIGN IN ETHIOPIA

A Trek of 2500 Miles Through Jungle Swamps and Desert Wastes

Saio–Gambela–Bortai Brook–Saio, Western Ethiopia– October 3–9, 1941

Blitzed at close quarters in Europe, Belgium has crossed the entire African continent to take revenge on the Axis. In a tropical campaign whose like for hardship has not been witnessed in this war, Belgium has bested Italy in Ethiopia.

Belgium has hewn her black police force of the Congo into a modern army. To strike at Germany's partner, that army—the *Force Publique,* with another army of patient porters to bear food and munitions up dizzying mountain trails—has traveled from the damp groves of the Congo jungles, homeland of gorillas and pygmies, across the watershed lying between the Congo and the Nile, down the other side into the Anglo-Egyptian Sudan along the White Nile and, finally, across the salty wastes of western Sudan to the mighty rampart of mountains guarding inner Ethiopia.

To carry provisions, the Belgian expedition transported a Congo fleet of twelve 10-ton barges with a 33-foot baby tugboat across the African continent. The journey began above Stanley Pool near Léopoldville and ended at the foothills of the Abyssinian highland. From Léopoldville to Aketi the midget navy traveled 1000 miles up the Congo River. From Aketi they rode narrow-gauge flatcars 450 miles through Paulis to the railhead at Mungbere, then motored 400 miles to Juba where they re-launched into the White Nile, then by water across the Sudan to Ethiopia. Bridges limited to eight-ton loads were required to carry thirty-ton trailers and one collapsed in the Sudan. Another proved a tight squeeze, being barely an inch and a half wider than the baby tugboat's beam. In navigating the turbulent White Nile, the Belgians found that the tug drew five inches more than the deepest channels. The difficulty was met by running the tug at top speed into a mud bar, then seesawing it across by shifting the crew and the cargo forward.

To reach the Italian stronghold the Belgians also had to surmount heavy tolls of dysenteric and pulmonary diseases. In the face of an army superior in numbers, firepower, strategic positions and not inferior in personal bravery, the Belgians have seized for the British—with whose campaign their own was coordinated—the natural mountain fortress.

The British, now besieging the last Italian forces near Gondar, aim to recover control of the Blue Nile's Ethiopian headwaters in Lake Tana. Thanks to tiny Belgium's daring expedition, England no longer needs to worry about the White Nile's headwaters—the other source of lower Egypt's indispensable fertile topsoil and life-giving water. Congolese troops have delivered this to Britain, with a corresponding effect on London's bargaining power with the Egyptian government.

The Italian army under General Pietro Gazzera, Mussolini's one-time war minister, had its headquarters in this mountain town. At 5621 feet, Saio commands a matchless view of the mountains toward Addis Ababa as well as of the broiling Sudanese swampland, which the Belgians conquered before assaulting the chain of Italian garrisons.

In the bitter engagements culminating in the siege of Saio, the Belgians were outnumbered three or four to one. For as long as two months, due to impassable roads and ebb conditions on the White Nile's tributaries, the Congolese troops were cut off from supplies. Their condition was continuously more precarious than their antagonists'.

The Italian-built network of smooth *autostrade* ends more than 300 miles away. (A cavalcade of Belgian trucks bearing prisoners to Addis Ababa, trapped in the mountains, will not be able to return until the dry season turns mud into dust.) Although Haile Selassie has succeeded in sending sixty loyal guardsmen to nearby Gore, capital of the province, where they are under British command, a leader of one such mission in the area outside Belgian operations has been decapitated. Control of the province of Galla Sidamo is closely disputed between "patriots" and guerrillas, armed with rifles and ammunition stolen from Italian magazines.

Suggestions a year ago that Italy should be attacked were considered premature; the Congolese army, organized chiefly as a colonial constabulary, had defense obligations of greater importance. Risks of taking the force upon a trans-African expedition several times as long as any similar caravan ever had attempted, through virtually uninhabited country, were closely studied by the Congo's war staff and the Belgian refugee cabinet in London.

Mussolini's forces had deeply indented the British in Kenya and there was the possibility they might seize Sudanese air bases along the White Nile, severing Africa horizontally and preventing American arms from reaching the Middle East.

Although some Belgian officers here have been too far from London and too close to Italian machine guns to know or care whether Belgium and Italy are formally at war—several Saio staff frankly confessed uncertainty today as to how things stood legally—the pattern was already complete before the black sons of the Congo embraced their wives and children the last time and faced eastward.

The counter-invasion of Ethiopia developed rapidly after the Sudan frontier was crossed on February 2. Belgium's heroic campaign has been curtained in secrecy not only for military reasons but because Congolese troops were inaccessible. Foreign correspondents following the army's progress around Asmara (Eritrea), or north from Mogadiscio (Italian Somaliland), were separated from the Belgians by the Italian lines. Coming from the Sudan, heavy rains had erased the trans-swamp road to the foothills of the Ethiopian mountains. As far as Belgium is concerned, hostilities are suspended and the army's only task is to ensure order while the British complete the cleanup. Your correspondent is the first to don a Belgian uniform and join the trans-African force in the field.

While preparing a definitive story of a hitherto unknown campaign, the writer is using as his quarters the former bedroom of General Gazzera. The only battle he has engaged in is against hundreds of tiny aggressors, too small for the Belgians to capture, who are still defending Gazzera's mattress against all comers.

Before reaching the Ethiopian rampart held by Italian troops, Belgian colonials from the Congo had to hold together an armed column of trucks carrying soldiers, porters and munitions 1400 miles across almost uninhabitable country. The first aim of the attack was Asosa, in the region drained by the Blue Nile, about 300 miles north of the Italian headquarters at Saio.

Starting from Watsa, in northeastern Congo, the first battalion to depart climbed slowly out of the Congo watershed, whose crest is marked by the Sudanese frontier, and descended by way of Yei. En route the troops pitched camp where the aging Theodore Roosevelt came before the great war for his last shooting expedition; where the scarce white rhinoceros still hides, and giraffes and elephants abound.

At Juba, with the burning bowl of the Sudanese plain before them, the column turned north along the White Nile. River boats brought them in five days to Malakal where dwell the strange, long-legged Shilluk people, a cattle-keeping tribe of extremely thin physique who wear tan, knee-length tunics. When the clothespole Shilluks first saw the sons of Congo cannibals, with their sharpened teeth and tattoo-corrugated faces, it was difficult to say which were the more surprised.

At Melut the column turned east, pushing their American trucks through two days of blistering, waterless desert. Major Isidore Herbiet, known to his battalion as *Tata*—meaning father—prepared for attack. The King's African Rifles, consisting of natives from East Africa, commanded by Colonel William Johnson, were already moving into line and awaited Belgian help.

Asosa is surrounded by hills and possesses barracks, a radio station, a hospital and an airdrome. It required three days for the battalion, with sweating porters carrying machine guns on their heads, to mount from Kurmuk, a Sudanese border town, to hill positions outside Asosa, at over 5000 feet.

The combined attack of Congolese troops and the King's African Rifles began March 11, just six weeks after the Belgians left the Congo. The Italians were taken by surprise and abandoned Asosa, pushing south to join their next garrison along the Ethiopian massif at Ghidami, 120 miles distant.

Belgian losses were chiefly through bacillic dysentery, whose mortality is 30 per cent, and amoebic dysentery, whose death rate is 5 per cent. Sudden changes of climate worked devastatingly upon the Congolese porters, who also suffered from pulmonary diseases caused by exposure aboard the double-decker Nile barges. Accustomed to the warm, damp nights of the humid Congo basin, they caught bronchitis and pneumonia in the parched and grassy Sudanese lowland, where days were hot and windless and nights chilly and breezy.

At Asosa the Belgians discovered porters who receive wages of 1 franc (2½ cents), the same amount second-class infantrymen would have spent on sandals from the Congo. The terrific heat of the Ethiopian paths had burned their bare, calloused feet nearly to the bone.

Asosa finished with virtually no losses except by disease. The battalion was given the far harder task of doubling back across the Sudanese desert to the Nile port of Melut (225 miles), ascending the river to Malakal, then doubling back east again to the Ethiopian foothills (275 miles) to close the bag. The Italians had already killed the single Englishman guarding the Sudanese highway frontier post in this utterly lonely land of yellowed grass and mosquito-infested swamp.

There was a growing danger, when the Italians were still strong and well organized, that their withdrawal into western Ethiopia might abruptly turn into a dangerous attack upon British positions in the Sudan. At almost all points the Italians were better armed and provisioned than Allied troops. Everything depended upon a single Belgian battalion moving fast and intact around three sides of a Sudanese desert square, then advancing east along the torrid road to Gambela in time to prevent General Gazzera from striking first along the same road.

The Belgian battalion, composed of 700 men and about 400 porters, made the 800-mile journey through country where the temperature ranged constantly above 100 degrees. This meant eleven days of the severest hardship for men alternately buffeted brutally in trucks, then forced to descend to heave them from the sand.

Belgian commanders knew their battalion could not enter the first habitable place, Gambela, at the foot of the mountain rampart below Saio, without fighting. Lacking air protection, they were completely exposed to reconnoitering Italian planes.

The King's African Rifles, trying to force the Italians south along 120 miles of ravines of Italian highland, were in the meantime halted by Gazzera. The Italians were planning, if not to strike at the Sudan immediately, to summon their energies for a bitter defense of Saio's natural fortress and agriculturally rich plateau. Besides having ample munitions, an excellent system of trenches and artillery emplacements and a first-hand knowledge of the country, the Italians had selected one of the few areas capable of supporting a colonial army living upon the land. Although harsh Sudanese swamp lies below Ethiopia's back doorstep, the mountains are comparable to Switzerland for green fertility. Here is the same rich, reddish soil which, passing into the White Nile, helps furnish lower Egypt every floodtime with virginal topsoil.

The province of Galla Sidamo is the storehouse of western Ethiopia. Gallas, despised by Ethiopia's ruling Amharites as second-rate warriors, are excellent farmers and cattlemen. From the writer's window standing corn rivaling Iowa's can be seen in dozens of upland pastures.

Gambela is the first village in Italy's Ethiopian empire captured and held by Belgium's expedition from the Congo. It lies where the Sobat River emerges from the Ethiopian mountains into the Sudanese plain, about forty miles from the Italian headquarters at Saio. Today its dusty little square beside the 200-foot-wide river is lined with fast little Fiat campaign cars and seven-ton Lancia trucks. On the Lancias are painted designations like *Gruppo Motorizzata di Harar* ("Motorized Unit of Harar"), showing the distance the Italians retreated across Ethiopia when striving for a final punch against the Anglo-Egyptian Sudan for possession of a chain of air-dromes along the White Nile, and to cut off the West African sources of American supplies. The single battalion of Belgians forestalled the blow.

Belgian subalterns, some with experience in the French Foreign Legion, sleep on cots in these Italian trucks. By day they watch 80 Italian drivers temporarily saved from a British prison camp because they alone know the secret of the Lancia's eight changes of gearshift. The Italian chauffeurs are thankful, since Ethiopian guerrillas' notion of squaring accounts is mutilation. They are being paid wages plus living expenses, in accordance with international law, and appear happy their war is over.

The Italians defended Gambela bitterly. They knew that if they lost the village they would be forced to retreat up into the mountain stronghold of Saio where General Gazzera had established his headquarters. Gambela was the only point whence either a motorized or river expedition could start. As long as Gazzera held it, he might take the offensive. If the Belgians won it, the Italian position would become defensive only. The Fascists would be walled inside Ethiopia.

Gambela is barely large enough to support its country store, full of tin pans and cheap candy beads, operated by an Ethiopian Greek. However, several one-story barracks and a radio station show that England has understood Gambela's political importance. Here, many miles inside the Ethiopian frontier, the British flag floats overhead. The Sudanese policemen—recruited from the tall, cranelike Shilluk people—defend this tiny British possession.

The British had obtained from Haile Selassie a territorial concession here the size of an American city block. This outpost of empire—"Little England"—serves as an excellent listening post for politics along the Ethiopian watershed and is legally as British as Hyde Park. Curiously, the Italians had allowed Major John Morris, who has been here sixteen years, to remain with his garrison of Sudanese.

Morris is a tall, blonde Briton in his later fifties. He spent several rough and tumble years in the western United States before America became too tame for his taste. His old friendship with the Duke of Aosta was rewarded when Aosta, then Italy's viceroy, sent a private warning that a declaration of war by Mussolini was impending. This enabled Morris to escape to the Sudan. Aosta also gave orders that the Gambela territory should be respected regardless of the war situation.

Three months after the Belgians gained Gambela, Aosta was imprisoned by the British in the same Sudanese resthouse where Morris took refuge after receiving Aosta's message. When Morris returned to Gambela he found everything intact.

To storm Gambela—key port of the Ethiopian White Nile and gateway to the Sudan—the Belgians, fatigued by their 800-mile, eleven-day journey from Asosa, had to make a frontal attack. The Italians placed machine guns under sycamore trees along the river, making an attack by water impossible. A second line of eight machine guns covered the road from the Sudanese desert as far as the Sugarloaf, a 300-foot, conical hill. The flanks of the peak were ringed by Italian machine guns.

The Belgians sent Congo infantrymen creeping through the brush, led by a white officer. They silenced the machine guns on the river and prepared to handle Sugarloaf.

The Italians called the Belgians' tribesmen *Niam-Niams*. A "Meat-Meat" is a black so meat-hungry that he is a cannibal. Gazzera termed the Belgians' use of Niam-Niams barbarous. The Congolese, aware of Italian worries about their appetites, asked to charge the sides of Sugarloaf with bayonets. They wiped out the machine-gun nests.

The Belgians lost three infantrymen killed, plus three white officers and fifteen Congolese wounded. Belgian losses increased the next day. The Italians refused to tell their casualties, but numerous bodies were found in the streets here.

After the Belgian battalion took Gambela, the Italians retreated by mountain road 4000 feet to Saio in orderly retirement. Belgian officers here pay tribute to the fighting of the younger Italian officers, particularly the Askari subalterns from Eritrea.

Exhausted and suffering almost to a man from dysentery, the Belgian battalion settled down to hold Gambela against the Italians behind and above them. The Belgians were alone between the hostile Ethiopian rampart and the Sudanese plain, without either artillery or aircraft. However, the African radio brought the news that another battalion was en route across the Sudanese plain and a third was assembling in northeastern Congo, preparing to dare the same journey across Africa.

This chain of mountains, source of the White Nile's waters and lower Egypt's life-renewing soil, is crisscrossed by ravines. Although Belgium's battle against Italy is over, death still lurks. Everywhere along the steep road up to the Italian headquarters at Saio, signs protrude in the eight-foot elephant grass: WARNING! LAND MINE!

The Italians, though ill-starred upon the battlefield, are probably the world's experts at making pursuit dangerous. They not only mine the roads but set sensitive traps in the tall grass, some so close that if two cars meet along a one-way mountain road whichever turns outward has an excellent chance of being blown up.

Yet the Belgians, after taking Gambela, started up toward Saio. The columns of reddish rock rising from the grass offered an ideal situation for guerrilla warfare. Gazzera waited to make his resistance atop the plateau. There a violent torrent called the Bortai, crossing the road at a right angle, was the first natural division between the Italians on the heights and the Belgians in the bullet-swept ravines.

The Belgians, strengthened by a company of Stokes 80-mm mortars and a battalion, moved to attack, led by Lt. Colonel Vandermeersch, who, because of his exceptional height is called *Kasongo Mulefu*, "awfully tall." Their forces, totaling about 1500 men and 600 porters, were insufficient to seize the heights. The Italians were reinforced until they had 7000 men, and became so bold that the Belgians had to take the offensive to conceal the small number of their forces.

In the first battle of the Bortai, on April 15, the Belgians lost two valuable officers. Lieutenant Simonet, scouting alone between the lines, stumbled into an Italian ambush and was killed. Sergeant Dorgeo, a former Foreign Legionnaire, who had arrived in the Congo after escaping from Narvik, was unfamiliar with his surroundings. He was surprised by three Italian officers who emerged from the brush holding up their hands and shouting: "We're English." Not sure the King's African Rifles, supposedly fifty miles to the north, might not have sent a liaison party to the Bortai, the Belgian officer lowered his revolver. He was mowed down by Italian snipers in the bush. In the ensuing fight the Belgians lost a native corporal and four soldiers. But 3 Italians and 40 Eritreans were killed, and 70 wounded.

During the first struggles at the Bortai, the Belgians learned to respect the Italian spotting system. The Italians posted an observer in a tree with a sniper; a squad of infantrymen hid around the tree. But the artillery barrages following such observations were often wastefully long. Usually the Italians continued pounding with 77s an hour after the Belgian patrols had stolen back to their own lines.

Nine days later the Italians took full advantage of their superior positions and armament. After a two-hour barrage they attacked. It was the first time the men from the Congo had heard the terrible concert of modern gunfire in full chorus.

Using machine guns, automatic rifles, baby machine guns and hand grenades, squads of Eritreans, with Galla snipers, filtered through the Belgian left and right.

One hero of the unequal struggle was a porter who rushed unarmed into the gunfire to aid two radio operators. He rescued their apparatus intact. (Belgian officers often were saved by their men.) The Belgians were forced to withdraw beyond a pair of hills that screened them from view.

Following the two battles, the Belgian situation in the rear became critical because of weather and a break in the slender trans-Sudanese communications.

May 1 until June 15 is the end of the dry and the beginning of the rainy season. During these weeks the single road across the Sudanese plain turns to mud. The water levels of the rivers Sobat and Baro, flowing into the White Nile, are insufficient for Nile barges. While the Italian troops ate plentifully on their highland gardens, the Belgians between Bortai Brook and Gambela were on half rations. The heat mounted to 110 in the shade, 128 in the sun. Clouds of mosquitoes rose from the plain.

The Gambela airdrome, whose single hangar still bears the ironical words *Roma Doma*—"Rome is Master"—was too short for planes carrying food. Some could be dropped from the skies, but it was impossible to feed 2500 men this way. Lt. Colonel Martens, a small man known for his ability to absorb tropical heat, was hard-tested to hold the situation together.

Several porters obliged to carry food to the front lines, forty miles away on a cold rainy plateau, died from undernourishment and fatigue. The officers, living on canned beef and rice, were also affected.

Beriberi broke out and even today the writer finds cases still being treated at Gambela. The food supply fell so low that the officers took the camouflage nets covering the trucks and seined the river for fish.

The month of May, when no fighting took place, was the most difficult and tragic for the Belgian *Force Publique*. But victory was nearer than any knew.

Trapped by rains, the Belgian expedition was in a precarious situation until early June when the rivers Sobat and Baro rose, enabling reinforcements coming from the Congo via the White Nile to reach them.

The Belgians' first plan was to cut off Gazzera's army—strongly encamped up in Saio—from Mogi, another town on the uneven, 5500-foot plateau. Mogi is the garden center of the thickly ravined highland, and Italian porters were bringing the principal fresh foodstuffs for the Saio garrison, numbering about 8000 men against the Belgians' 2000.

To hold Bortai Brook, the Belgians atop the plateau facing Mogi could spare only about 250 men from their two battalions. These Belgians had to descend from the plateau and launch their attack from Gambela, the fever-infested port where the Congolese themselves had been isolated for the past six weeks.

From Gambela it was a two-day climb on all fours by mountain goat path to the Mogi positions, and another day for each porter to descend. The maximum burden the most courageous black bearers from the jungle could carry upon their heads was 35 pounds each. Nine of this was food they ate en route. The bearers' legs were cut by the razor-sharp elephant grass, their bodies weakened by dysentery and malnutrition. Porters with names like Katanabo, Bungamuizi, Kabome and Sawila are still being cited for bravery and endurance in the officers' reports.

The Mogi siege was even more expensive in soldiers than porters. The hope to cut off Mogi was that the King's African Rifles and the British East African Regiment, blocked farther north in an attempt to take Ghidami, might be able to press south and join the Belgians.

Under Captain-Commandant Pierre Bounameau, they attacked Mogi on June 9, shortly after taking Gambela. Their rear was covered by the arrival by river of another Congo battalion under Major Antoine Duperoux.

The Italian garrison, of about 300, held their well-fortified position stoutly. Realizing Mogi could be taken only at heavy cost, the Belgians dug in around the town and sent patrols to ambush the road to Saio on which Italian food was carried.

Lt. Colonel Martens ordered his Belgians to increase patrols upon the Saio Plateau to make the Italians believe they were facing superior forces. Elephant grass, which the Italians had burned in April in order to have a sweeping line of fire, had grown high again, so the Belgians used a ruse familiar to American pioneers in fighting the Indians; they moved their cannon and machine guns frequently to suggest multiple points of fire. Meantime the alarmed Gazzera tripled the Mogi garrison, bringing it to 900 men.

As the Belgians grew bolder the Italians grew more discreet. The South African Air Force began to send daily patrols of three Fairey-Hartebeest biplanes, which bombed Saio and machine-gunned the roads.

Then solidly built, six-foot Major General Auguste Gilliaert arrived from the Congo. Known to his men as *Kopi* ("leopard"), he is a quiet and catlike man. It was decided that the plan for taking Mogi should be dropped and the meager forces entirely concentrated upon Gazzera's headquarters at Saio.

While preparing for a broad-scale attack across Bortai Brook, Gilliaert, with Martens, was several times under fire in the front lines. An Italian machine-gun officer, when told his fire had almost wiped out the Belgian general staff, expressed astonishment that the Congolese commanders should be in the front line trenches. "With us nobody above the grade of captain comes that far up," he said.

The 3500 white Italian troops occupying Saio Heights outnumbered the total Belgian force. The Fascists also had the 45th, 181st, 187th and 188th battalions of Eritreans whose battle pennons were covered with honors conferred by Mussolini. Italian officers and men retreating from Addis Ababa and Jimma, under British pressure, were coming daily into Saio.

While readying a master plan to storm Saio, Gilliaert kept in touch with British headquarters in Khartoum. "I based our chances of success upon continuous aggressive activity along Bortai Brook against Mogi," Gilliaert told me, "applying Kitchener's maxim that you can try anything against an enemy who refuses to budge."

On July 1 the British radioed the Belgians that they had cut the 450-mile-long Shio-Addis Ababa road about 200 miles from Haile Selassie's capital. Gilliaert prepared to close the mouth of the Belgian bag into which the Italians were streaming.

Believing British pursuit closer than it was, Gazzera blew the bridge over the Indina River, forty miles east of Saio, thus buttoning the eastern mouth of his own bag himself. But the Congolese offensive was still a dangerous gamble because the Italians were better armed and fed, held superior positions with more firepower, and outnumbered the three Belgian battalions between three and four to one.

When the first battles of Bortai Brook were launched they were preceded by three days of rain and cold which took bitter effect on men and officers. This time a morning sun warmed the Congolese and put them in battle mood. At dawn on July 3 the Belgian advanced posts opened fire and half an hour later all the batteries of artillery entered into action. The Italians replied with the full intensity of their superior cannonading power.

Duperoux's battalion went forward to take the two dumpling hills flanking each side of the road, which the Italians had gained in April. Duperoux's men crept through the brush and high grass toward the hills, infested with machine guns.

The battalion in reserve, commanded by Major Boniface Robyn, crawled behind Duperoux's left. Simultaneously Gilliaert sent the third battalion under Vandermeersch upon the assignment that was the key to the entire operation: a long, swinging movement around the right, through grass higher than a man and along a goat path carefully plotted by scouting parties over a fortnight.

The entire surprise operation was successful. The Italians, falling back from the two dumplings, found themselves flanked upon their left by Vandermeersch's forces and unable to hold the ravine of the Bortai between the dumpling and the Italian secondary line of fortifications strung across Saio Mountain. They melted away downhill toward the Sudanese plain on their right. They dared not use the road for direct retreat, for it was under continuous Belgian artillery fire.

At 1:40 p.m., the encircling battalion was preparing an assault upon the Italian heights. Two Mitalia motorcars were seen descending the serpentine road toward the newly-won Belgian positions, bearing white flags.

Gilliaert met the enemy a short distance from the Belgian side of Bortai Brook. The *Force Publique* of the Congo had crossed Africa to gain Belgium's first victory against the Axis. Sweet revenge for the invasion of the faraway homeland!

Gazzera's surrender to Gilliaert—following the Duke of Aosta's surrender to Wavell of the British Middle East command—leaves the Allied arms in Ethiopia today with mastery as far as Mussolini is concerned. Final liquidation of the Fascist empire will come when the Italians holding out around Gondar give themselves up to the British troops that have been surrounding and starving them since July.

Vastly outnumbered by the Italians, even after surrender, the Belgians have been hard put to handle 15,000 prisoners in all of Galla Sidamo. At Saio alone nine generals, 370 lesser officers, 2575 Italians and 3500 native soldiers surrendered to the Congolese force which, with 2000 porters, made hardly 5000 men.

The first Congolese officers who entered Saio to complete the negotiations told your correspondent today: "We literally waded in Italians. We were embarrassed to find how many enemies had fallen into our hands. The Italians were chagrined to find that we numbered only three battalions instead of three divisions with South African reinforcements, as their intelligence service had led them to believe."

The proudest achievement of the Belgian general staff is that the public market in Saio has been functioning normally since three days after the fall and that no looting has occurred. At nearby Mogi, when 900 Eritreans found that all but 50 of the 250 Belgians originally besieging them had been withdrawn, they wished to start fighting but were dissuaded by their Italian officers.

Belgian deaths were 462 men, both white and black, four-fifths of whom died of disease. The Italians probably lost about three times as many, although casualty figures are not available.

The younger, more belligerent Italian officers taken prisoner by the Belgians blame their defeat on the inertia and fear of older generals. Although sympathetic with Il Duce's imperialist ambitions, they have an intense dislike for the Fascist party coterie around Mussolini, whom they consider parvenus. Officers of all ranks seem to reserve their chief loyalty for the members of the Italian royal house.

Being outnumbered three to one, the Belgians were hard put to handle large numbers of prisoners like the battalion of captured Blackshirts. They have solved this by taking the Italian *carabinieri*—Mussolini's constabulary—returning their rifles loaded, and setting them to watch the herds of prisoners. The *carabinieri* show no objection to guarding masses of other Italians.

Captured Italian officers were allowed to keep their sidearms as a sign of honorable defeat. One officer offered for sale to the Belgians a dazzling revolver entirely plated with gold from muzzle to butt.

In surrendering, Gazzera asked safe conduct for the Eritreans to British prison camps. This request, granted by Gilliaert, was a needed precaution because the Ethiopian "patriots" who fought at Bure and Gore under British officers considered the disarmed Italians fair game. The 650 Italians who surrendered at Bure came into the Belgian lines almost naked, their garments having been purloined by Ethiopians.

The Italian governor at Gore asked the Belgians to provide at least two of the feared Niam-Niams for each truckful of prisoners to prevent molestation. An Italian priest who insisted on going into the countryside, against Belgian advice, is missing.

Your correspondent has been unsuccessfully attempting to undertake the ten-day journey to Addis Ababa. Belgians here state that at least fifty men would be necessary as escort on the journey to the capital. The settlement of old differences between the Gallas and Amharites, who served in Mussolini's army and who have lately revealed their faithfulness to Haile Selassie, is still proceeding actively, with all participants amply armed.

The Italian decision to surrender doubtless was accelerated by the desertion of an entire battalion of mixed Gallas and Amharites under Eritrean officers, who are now roaming the western highlands fending for themselves. The Negus—Selassie—has sent sixty members of his personal constabulary as the nucleus of a force intended to bring order. But until the region becomes more pacified such measures may not prove effective. Dajazmach Wayessa Bakako, political boss of Saio, upon whom your correspondent paid a courtesy visit yesterday, stated he had about 100,000 Gallas under his jurisdiction. However, a rotogravure newspaper picture of Haile Selassie, with his family, hung prominently upon the mud wall of Bakako's residence and the chieftain expressed his warm loyalty to the Negus. Bakako also presented the visiting press a gift of ten eggs and two live chickens.

An attack upon the Belgian Congo, no matter from what quarter, can be made only at great cost to the invader, now that the Belgian forces have the experience of their successful campaign against Italian strongholds in Ethiopia.

Soldiers of the Congolese *Force Publique*—in peacetime a sort of police constabulary—fought under the most difficult conditions in their first foreign war. They have learned the secret of resting through days of terrific heat, scouting strange territory under protection of the cool night and attacking at dawn. They have learned the laborious routine of camouflaging positions with bundles of elephant grass changed daily because it yellows in the tropical sun, revealing critical points.

Through Gilliaert's and Martens' tactic of continuous aggression, the Belgians have learned how a small but mettlesome force, even in a strange land, may keep a large and irresolute army upon its own territory permanently in a state of uncertainty and self-defense.

Major Duperoux, leader of the battalion now administering Saio, told your correspondent today: "Colonial warfare is the only form of encounter in battle remaining where the forces are sufficiently small that the meaning of conflict is comprehensible to the participant. In such a campaign you feel the clashing wills of the opposite leaders directly instead of remotely. Colonial warfare retains here what has been lost in the mass conflict of Europe."

Much curiosity has been felt as to why Gazzera failed to descend from the Ethiopian highland and invade the Anglo-Egyptian Sudan before the arrival of the Belgians. When Gilliaert asked the Italian general's chief of staff, Damico replied: "Gazzera did want to attack the Sudan but received contrary orders from the Duke of Aosta, who preferred that the expedition be withheld for political reasons."

The Italians then possessed ample provisions. When they hoisted the white flag they had hardly two months' supplies left.

Being without political aspirations and responsibilities in Ethiopia, the Belgians are withdrawing fast, leaving the police problem between the British and Selassie.

Gradually the rows of round grass huts, constructed in Congo fashion from elephant grass by Belgium's soldiers, will cease to be alien features of the Ethiopian highland. Eight 77s will soon be added to ten cannon which already have made the trans-African journey back to the Congo. Seventy machine guns, 122 automatic rifles, 6900 rifles, 15,000 hand grenades, twenty tons of radio equipment, and substantial medical supplies, most in excellent condition, make up the total booty.

Belgian road crews are preparing the dizzy Gambela-Saio highway which still bites mouthfuls from the tires of their American trucks. A dozen Italians are at large here and their claims for recovery of property seized by Mussolini are being heard.

The British have sent two officers with subordinates to take charge of western Ethiopia, in cooperation with Major Morris, administrator of the British territorial concession at Gambela, where the Union Jack now floats.

At Bure, which was taken jointly by Belgian cyclists and the King's African Rifles, a chieftain named Licht Lakau holds authority, reportedly for the Negus. At Gore the famous Ethiopian patriot, General Mosfin, a refugee in the mountains throughout the Italian occupation, has emerged from hiding, and, with numerous followers already gathered, will probably take a leading role. The western Ethiopian situation will continue to count much in British policy towards Egypt.

In summary of this hitherto unwritten fragment of the history of World War II, it may be said that while the King of the Belgians is prisoner among his own people, honored pictures of Leopold III and his tragically deceased Queen Astrid are hanging today above the officers' mess table here in the remotest part of Ethiopia—symbols that Belgium in Africa remembers Belgium in Europe, and has begun to exact the prices of invasion from the Axis.

—

Sweet Music in the Jungle

(*Never Published*)

Gambela Province, Galla Sidamo, western Abyssinia— probably mid-September 1941

A son of the Congo jungle who crossed the entirety of Africa as a member of the Belgian expeditionary force was stimulated by Major General Auguste Gilliaert's ban upon looting to a degree that managed, through legitimate manipulation of exchange, to build four packages of cigarettes into a modern phonograph with sixty records.

Stuffing his pockets with four packages containing twenty cigarettes each, the Congolese hiked to the former Italian headquarters of Saio, forty miles away and 5500 feet up a mountain. Italians in the prison camp were cigarette-famished, many of the lower grade officers not having smoked for over a year.

The untutored jungleman sold the cigarettes at a piaster each—that's about five cents. Meanwhile, the bottom had fallen out of the market for Italian lire, replaced by Selassie's thalers. With eighty piasters of capital, the Congolese bought in the Saio marketplace a bale of lire thick enough to stuff a cannon's mouth. He then returned to the Italian prison camp without even bothering to count the lire.

He swapped the bundle of Il Duce's useless currency for an Italian officer's phonograph plus the records. The phonograph originating in Rome is now playing merrily in a grass hut somewhere in the Congo jungle.

Chicago Daily News expense account

George Weller
October 5 to November 1, 1941

Credit outstanding favor CDN as of Oct. 4 $646.72

EXPENSES
Communications

Domestic telegrams	$17.89
Local telephones and postage	6.57
News cables from Nairobi paid in advance, itemized below, receipts being enclosed	72.96
Advanced US consul in Nairobi for despatches to be filed from Ethiopia via Nairobi, to Joseph Palmer, to be accounted for, as of Nov.1.	$202.00
	$299.42

General and Travel

Transportation: Watsa--Irumu--Goma--- Usumbura--Astrida--Kampala, by car	$205.70
Kampala to Nairobi, plane and car	38.90
Nairobi to Mombasa, sleeper and car	23.12
local transportation--taxis, ferries, cars	68.15
baggage	26.05
British uniform,1 dress, 1 camp (required)	51.60
porters	15.19
Hotels and lodging	136.44
Food	122.07
Entertainment in line of service	7.94
newspapers and source material	17.75
tips and gratutities	23.25
messengers	8.62
exchange fees (Uganda and Nairobi)	6.21
	$1050.41

Favorable balance CDN Oct.4	$646.72
less expenses as above	1050.41
unfavorable balance CDN, dredit GW	$403.69

NOTE: news cables   Oct.27   53sh.60   (signed)
itemized   "   "   74sh72
                    "   29 10sh40   George Weller
                    "   "   81sh68
                    "   "   38sh80   Batavia,Feb.10,1942.
                    Nov.3   102sh
                             361sh 20   George Weller
361 shillings 20 equals $72.96 debited above
      all receipts enclosed

VI

"In Darkest Africa"

After the Belgian campaign in Ethiopia, Weller returned to Léopoldville to send his dispatches. From Stanleyville, he proceeded east for about two hundred miles, part of the way on foot with porters, to the village of Irumu. There he looked into the veracity of Henry Morton Stanley (1841–1904), the Welsh-born, American-bred explorer and journalist most famous for having tracked down the missing Dr. Livingstone.

Weller's interest was, specifically, an expedition described in Stanley's 1890 bestseller, *In Darkest Africa*. Remarkably, Weller was able to locate several older tribesmen who had fought against Stanley and had their own version of the historic events—to which the reporter clearly gave credence. Late in life he wrote: "Only Pearl Harbor could have brought me out of this African wonderland."

—

TALKING DRUMS OF CONGO SAVED BY MISSIONARY

Keeps Telegraph of Jungle Alive as Interest Begins to Wane

Congo River Station, Yakusu, Stanleyville, Belgian Congo—October 10, 1941

In the nick of time to save the vanishing art of talking drums, John Carrington, a young missionary at this jungle outpost, has prevented the younger generation of Congo peoples from losing forever a unique method of communication.

Aided by a tall, deeply tattooed old drum master named Lifindiki Tuay-tolo, which in English means "Quarrelsome Smith," Carrington has been able within the last year to instill the river tribes centering around this Baptist station with sufficient interest in the jungle telegraph so that it will probably survive a few years more.

Nearby a swimming hippopotamus' nose, barely appearing above the Congo's brown flood, made a ripple upstream. Carrington, who is a tall, blond Briton twenty-nine years old, stood beside a six-foot village drum beating out messages for the correspondent.

"As soon as the tribesmen leave the villages and get acquainted with the white man's telephone and telegraph, they begin to disdain the drum," he said. "They even forget their drum names, given to them by their fathers at birth."

At the correspondent's request Carrington, in drum language, asked the fisher people of the village, for whom meat is a rare delicacy, why they had failed to enter their canoes and spear the swimming hippo.

Carrington translated the reply: "We cannot overpower majesty of his jaws."

The drum language is more elaborate than human speech, Carrington has found. When Germany invaded Belgium the jungle drums called it not simply a war, but a "war of spears and knives."

In drum language every word becomes a full phrase. The reason is that each drum, like the spoken language of the Lokele fisherfolk, uses only two tones, obtained by hollowing wood to different depths on opposite sides of the drum's soundhole. Contrary to human tones, the high note is called the man's voice because it carries farther, and the low note is called the woman's voice. One drumstick strikes the woman's side of the drum, the other the man's. Each blow corresponds to a syllable, but since many spoken words when drummed would sound identical, names are expanded into long synonyms to bring out variations. Thus the jungle telegraph has become a kind of poetry.

Big bluish-black clouds were piling over the opposite side of the river. The villagers began fearfully closing the doors of their wicker huts when Carrington pounded the rain call, which goes: "Badman, son of disease, is coming down upon clods of earth." Quarrelsome Smith took over the two rubber-ended drumsticks and began hammering out the call to frighten away the rain: "Don't come, rain; the men of our village don't want you."

The drum-making village of Yafolo, forty miles upriver, carves drums from the bolondo, a species of pterocarpus wood. Drums require a fortnight's work, cost $20 and up and last a decade. Eight-foot drums carry about fifteen miles, but, contrary to explorers' stories of the Congo, drum messages cannot be sent long distances. They cannot be sent to tribes with different languages.

The polite drum word for a white is "white man spirit from the forest," but until recently the synonym, "death on the river," was common. Grief is "tears from eyes and crying from the mouth." To express death the Lokele drums were saying long before missionaries like Carrington arrived: "Spirit has left body and body has returned to ground."

—

"In Darkest Africa"

Stanley's Trip into Africa as Seen by Natives

Nyangkundi, Territory of Irumu, Province of Stanleyville, Belgian Congo—October 23–27, 1941

The history of white exploration of inner Africa has been exclusively written by the white man himself. The black African, in such accounts, plays the role of a patient porter or foot soldier when upon the explorer's side, and of a clever thief or hostile warrior when on the opposite side.

With conquest, friendly and hostile savages merge into law-abiding natives. In Africa as little is known today of what the black man thought about the white man's coming as is known in the United States about how the American pioneers seemed to the Indians.

Diaries, journals and memoirs of white explorers remain in printed texts. But Africa's version, compounded of word-of-mouth testimony of its natives, a version which in some cases differs deeply from those of the white man, remains alive only as long as do the old men who witnessed the happenings in question.

When Africa's patriarchs, whose memory is sharp and clear because it is independent of book learning, pass away their histories become tales for evening campfires that grow distorted as each narrator adds his dime's worth of embroidery.

In an attempt to rescue at least a single important chapter of the African story from oblivion before it is too late, your correspondent traveled to the little-visited country between the Congo and the Nile. Here Henry M. Stanley, explorer of the last century, met and overcame the warriors of King Mazamboni, the fierce tribe of Undussumas, in the most critical struggle of his career.

The rolling green farmland where the battle was fought lies almost at the absolute center of Africa, on a 4200-foot plateau abounding in elephant and antelope. The plateau, the continent's heart, is the home of the "duckbill women" who uglified themselves against the danger of being sold as slaves to the Arabs by placing enormous plates in their upper lips. They are frequently seen even today.

On the western side of the plateau, which Stanley approached from the darkness of the great equatorial forest, tiny rivulets begin their 2000-mile journey to empty into the Atlantic Ocean below the equator. On the plateau's eastern edge, hundreds of small waterfalls facing British Uganda tumble to the almost uninhabited, swampy, hot shores of Lake Albert.

Although the plateau gives the Undussumas crops of bananas, tapioca and corn as abundant as in Stanley's time, only a single white farmer dwells here now.

On December 6, 1887, near what is today the frontier village of Irumu, Stanley joyfully emerged from the misty shadows of the equatorial jungle where he had known famine, theft and petty harassment by the natives. He had been forced to abandon many of his followers at a "starvation camp" by the junction of the Ituri and Epulu, upper tributaries of the Congo.

The last tongues of forest emerge directly upon the Undussumas' plateau, and the British-born, American-naturalized explorer believed that he had hardly a forty-mile journey ahead. This was about five days' march for his heavily burdened column—numbering 171, plus four white men— to the plateau's brow 2000 feet above Lake Albert's marshy and humid shores.

Hundreds of the same Undussumas this writer has been interviewing blocked Stanley's way. Shouting imprecations, they sent flights of spears and arrows from the lower heights of the mountain chain paralleling the trail across the plateau. They brought Stanley's column to a standstill and compelled it to give battle.

The region, almost uninhabited except for the natives' battlefield along the Talolo stream—known to Stanley only as the "Tributary Ituri"—naturally is unmarked. When further opened the region will become as familiar as a California trail. Stanley, after his armed victory, showed that the plateau was the safest trans-African route between the Congo and Nile basins.

In 1938 two Belgian officials, Lieutenant Fernand Depotre, former administrator at Irumu, and Raoul Dufour, the late provincial governor of Stanleyville, found two Undussumas who said they had seen Stanley's battle. But until the present trip by your correspondent, there had been no attempt either to map the battleground or to record the testimony of the scant surviving warriors.

In interviewing tribesmen who witnessed the Stanley battle he had the help of William Deans of Alameda, California, the young missionary representing the station of the Plymouth Brethren that lies directly on Stanley's route. Deans, despite his boyish appearance, has lived twelve years in inner Africa.

In discovering the surviving Undussuma veterans, Deans and the writer gained the support of Prince Lifungula, leader of the four clans making up the Babira race, of which the Undussumas are a single branch. Prince Lifungula, himself an Undussuma whose name means "door-lock," has for eight years held the office that Stanley's enemy, King Mazamboni, did when his scouts brought the first word that the jungle, always thought to be exclusively inhabited by pygmies, was disgorging white men and Arabs.

Prince Lifungula, son of Mazamboni's successor, is due to receive the same title of king from the Belgian government as soon as he attains a greater age. Already he enjoys full regal powers.

Before the journey to the battlefield, Prince Lifungula received Deans and the writer in the round, triple-doored building, with earthen floor and thatched roof, supported by timbers, which is the Babiras' tribal council house.

After the missionary explained our errand it developed that Prince

Lifungula, a Roman Catholic convert, could speak a few words in French. The audience was informal. The prince wore only a single loose white tunic. His place was inside a small, half-circular, knee-high enclosure resembling a dais, upon the same level as the dirt floor. The Americans sat across the room, against the opposite wall.

Reposing in a low-slung canvas chair, showing his sharply-filed front teeth in frequent smiles, Prince Lifungula readily consented to the expedition through his territory. He promised to round up tribesmen known to have fought Stanley.

Prince Lifungula's aides displayed to the guests one of the heavy wicker shields woven in black and brown that the Undussumas who rushed Stanley carried. Eventually Prince Lifungula showed the Americans a spirally-carved horn of a waterbuck that sounded the charge into battle, terrifying Stanley's Arabs.

As our intention of rendering the native story of the battle became understood, the prince grew captivated with the idea and eventually offered to accompany the expedition. His offer was gladly accepted.

To compare H. M. Stanley's own account with the African version of what occurred when warriors blocked his way between the great equatorial forest and Lake Albert, your correspondent has traced roughly the explorer's route. From jungle near the present village of Irumu, Stanley advanced twenty miles across open elephant-grass country, dotted with conical grass huts, to the battleground.

Comparing native accounts with what appears in Stanley's book, *In Darkest Africa,* it seems today that his expedition was threatened with extermination if the Undussumas had carried out their intentions. But these tribesmen were never able to muster sufficient rifle fire seriously to jeopardize Stanley's safety.

Stanley indirectly admits this by stating that only one Arab was injured during the four-day engagement. Both Stanley's account and illustrations in the original edition of his book suggest fighting at close quarters across Talolo stream. But such fighting never occurred, according to stories obtained by the writer from Undussuma warriors who actually participated in that battle.

Moreover, there exists another discrepancy. Your correspondent possesses carefully checked, first-hand African versions of this battle, certainly the most critical of Stanley's career. If these are believable, the heavy slaughter among the Undussuma suggested—but not statistically estimated—in Stanley's account ranks as the work of adventurous rather than accurate reporting.

Without detracting in any way from Stanley's genius and courage, one must match the African measure of his military prowess against his own.

"As soon as we discovered that the white man had sticks that could kill at a much greater distance than our spears we ran away as fast as possible," several woolly-haired, elderly Undussumas unabashedly told your correspondent through his translator, the American missionary Deans. The Undussumas' sovereign, Prince Lifungula, was present to ensure the accuracy of the narrative.

The Undussumas unanimously agree with Stanley's story that they were able to halt the explorer's column, place it under siege and prevent its breaking camp. Without any prompting or suggestions the aged braves corroborated that on the third day of the siege they attacked Stanley anew and fought all day, being stopped only by Stanley's troops setting fire to their villages.

Like his earlier errand of rescuing Dr. Livingstone, Stanley's purpose in crossing the Undussumas' plateau was one of relief. Eventually his expedition laid the political lines for the conflicting African imperialisms which lie beneath today's Anglo-German struggle.

A committee of private Britons shared expenses with the Egyptian government in sending Stanley to save the German pioneer called Emin Pasha. The Khedive of Egypt had dispatched Emin Pasha into the central African province of Equatoria with the title of governor, in order to protect the upper waters of the Nile from falling into non-Egyptian hands.

The German pasha had been marooned for five years upon the borders of Lake Albert, adjacent to the Undussuma country, with a few hundred Egyptian officers and soldiers and some 5000 camp followers. The German was serving under the Khedive on the same basis as the more famous British General Gordon. But Gordon's massacre at Khartoum in January, 1885, by the fanatical Sudanese followers of the Mahdist leader, Mahomet Ali, cut off the German governor's only way of escape through the Nile Valley to Egypt.

The year before Stanley set forth, the cornered German pasha sent the British a secret note offering to leave the Khedive's service and surrender the African basin of the Nile to the British flag. The British published the note before sending Stanley to the German's rescue, with the result that, discredited, Emin feared more to emerge from the heart of Africa than to remain.

Stanley's defeat of the Undussumas, like Kitchener's taking of Khartoum, paved the avenue toward today's British hegemony over the sources of the Nile, and it resulted in control of the Egyptian cornerstone of Middle East strategy.

Had Stanley been unable to vanquish the Undussumas, reach Emin and persuade him to leave the upper waters of the Nile by way of Zanzibar, the Germans instead of the British might have gained control of the Nile.

As our party traveled single file along a muddy footpath through a green tunnel of tall elephant grass our guide, Prince Lifungula, sent out runners to bring in from outlying villages the old men who had participated in or witnessed the four-day encounter between Stanley's forces and the Undussumas.

For a while we followed Stanley's own trail through the valley that Stanley's account said was the scene of his hottest engagement. The valley was dotted with villages of round and conical thatched huts precisely as in Stanley's day, and the blue smoke of numerous brushfires lay cloudy in the ravines.

Circling around behind Mount Nyangkundi ("Mountain of Love"), which slopes about 1500 feet above the 4200-foot plateau, we finally veered upward along an old tribal path on the mountainside.

It was when 300 dancing and yelling Undussumas, "shaking their flashing weapons, gesturing with spear and shield," came running along this path that Stanley recognized that he would have to fight to reach Lake Albert. Eventually, the explorer found himself surrounded. The Undussumas at the right, toward the mountain, and others on the left, toward the Talolo stream, harassed his march. He was finally forced to encamp on a spur of the 120-foot hill of Nzerakum.

As our party reached the foot of Nzerakum, Prince Lifungula halted the column. He then commandeered the furniture of a grass hut—consisting of two folding camp chairs. Porters carried these up the summit of Nzerakum after us. It was considered necessary that Missionary Deans and the writer, while hearing native history, should have formal seats. Stanley wrote of the position: "Fifty rifles could hold a camp here against 1,000."

As the old warriors arrived, toiling up the steep slope with perspiration showing through their kinky, whitening hair, Deans acted as interpreter to put the writer's questions to Prince Lifungula. Stanley never was referred to by name but as Bula Matari, meaning "Breaker of Stones," the title the explorer gained when he used dynamite to blast his way through the lower Congo portages.

The warriors, although averaging seventy years of age, showed no trace of senility. Most were attired in cast-off European trousers and shirts befitting an important occasion. One was clad simply in a tunic of blue cloth. Despite a broiling sun, several had donned patched and dilapidated top-coats—their ultra-formal attire. They had slender, erect figures and replied to questions calmly and positively.

The first to tell the battle story was Gayomba, the grizzled ancient in the blue tunic, whose name means "They Are Talking." Gayomba held up his hand, palm outward, at eye level. When asked his age at the time, he indicated that he was about seventeen. Stanley mentions first noticing the natives in Talolo Valley between one and three in the afternoon, but Gayomba said: "Our frontier guards first saw the Breaker of Stones shortly after dawn, and we kept his party under observation throughout the morning. The border watchmen saw him as soon as he crossed the river and emerged from the forest where the Bambutis (pygmies) live. The guards sent runners to warn King Mazamboni in the royal village over there."

Gayomba pointed to a site about half a mile from the hilltops beyond the curving Talolo.

Asked whether he knew which was Stanley, Gayomba said: "Not then, but later I learned to recognize him because he wore a curved visor under his helmet shaped like a half moon."

Asked whether he fought, Gayomba said: "No, because I was considered immature. But I did not run away with the old men, women and children either. I stayed with the warriors on Mount Nyangkundi and watched."

Shown pictures in Stanley's book for the first time, the Undussumas remarked sharply: "The battle tunic looks like cloth but our warriors wear only leather. Furthermore, our tunics come only below the hips, never to the knees."

Stanley treats with skepticism, in his account of the battle, the excuse that King Mazamboni gave after his defeat, that he personally had never wanted nor participated in the battle.

According, however, to what was volunteered to your correspondent by Dadumbi (translated "We Have Departed for Good"), Mazamboni's nephew by his royal brother Singoma, the King unceremoniously gathered his regal robes about him and scurried high into the mountains at the first tidings of the "Stone Breaker's" arrival. Dadumbi, whose appearance today belies his sixty-odd years, accompanied his royal uncle. Dadumbi was then a boy about twelve.

Dadumbi said: "The reason Mazamboni fled was that the Breaker of Stones sent messages ahead demanding that the King of the country come to see him because he wanted to palaver. Mazamboni feared that Bula Matari really meant to capture him as a hostage or to murder him. So the King left the situation in the hands of sub-chiefs and climbed to the forest Bubongo on the mountain, where he hid with the old men, women and children."

Dadumbi related this hitherto unrecorded evasion by King Mazamboni, who is one of the most prominent figures in Stanley's memoirs, without a blush for his uncle's cowardice. "All Mazamboni said was: 'This white man shall never look upon my face.' "

An agreement achieved by Stanley with his foe under the shadow of Mount Nyangkundi, in almost the exact geographical center of Africa, remains respected in this day of broken pacts. It was a compact etched in a blood ritual.

Stanley was represented by an Arab subaltern; King Mazamboni by the father of Bungamuzi, one of a coterie of veterans whose testimony to your correspondent tends to amend the explorer's chronicle of his battle here in early December, 1887.

The two deputy treaty makers each took a knife and made three cuts on the other's body—between eyebrows, between breastbones and on one wrist. Then each took a fresh baked potato, rubbed it in his own blood and gave it to the other to eat.

That sealed the peace.

Only a handful of Undussuma tribesmen remain of those who witnessed or participated in Stanley's last and hardest battle in his trans-African trek. From these the writer heard it was almost a bloodless skirmish. He heard also of the dissent in their ranks when the first white man they had ever seen appeared from the depths of the equatorial forest, leading white-clad Arabs armed with American rifles.

Their testimony was intoned upon the site of that battle in tribal language.

"When King Mazamboni fled into the mountains and evaded his royal responsibilities, his younger chieftains decided to make war," these elderly warriors told your correspondent. Asked who were their chiefs—not mentioned in Stanley's account—the aged braves said they were led by Kembarani (whose name means "Fighter"), Mapero ("Little Man"), and Mbulangba ("Left Behind").

Were any relatives of those three chieftains present?

A man, apparently in his fifties, stepped forward and announced himself as Ledjiabo, "Scout with Far Vision."

"I am Mbulangba's son but I did not notice much fighting because I was too busy drinking the milk at my mother's breast," said Ledjiabo, provoking a roar of laughter from the surrounding Undussumas.

Then a very old man stepped forward. His name was Bungamuzi, "Lost His Home." He was asked why the Undussumas refused to allow Stanley passage as the other tribes had done. "The runners sent back by the frontier guards all agreed that the enemy's numbers were few," explained Bungamuzi. "When we saw the column coming across the valley in exposed country, we knew that we had many more warriors than they had. We did not even bother with the war dance. We said to ourselves, 'This task will be easy. We shall annihilate them.' "

In general outline, the native version of the four-day encounter agreed with Stanley's. But the warriors' stories contradicted the explorer's account that the "riflemen did execution among the mountaineers." They all insisted that their casualties were but one killed and two wounded.

Stanley never committed himself on the exact number of Undussuma casualties. But his book states that King Mazamboni, in beseeching peace, declared that he had been prevented from negotiating sooner "by the clamor of young men who insisted upon fighting. But now, as many of them have been killed, he was ready to pay tribute."

Perceiving your correspondent's doubt that so few Undussumas could have been hit by Stanley's Askaris, armed with the most modern American carbines, the gathering of veterans finally produced an elder named Kinsala, "Multitude." In a firm voice and fixing his interrogators with his eye, Kinsala declared: "I am the brother of the only man killed by the followers of the Stone Breaker."

Asked whether Stanley participated in the shooting, the Undussumas replied: "No. The Stone Breaker wore a revolver but used it only to kill cows for beef."

Had Stanley lost any men?

Ngonjaibo, "He Likes Them," another veteran, contributed a further incident not mentioned by Stanley but which all present confirmed.

"The Breaker of Stones lost no men in the battle with the Undussumas but afterward, when he returned through our country from Lake Albert, he lost one traitor soldier by hanging."

As for the peace terms—omitted by Stanley—the Undussumas said: "We pledged to give them passage and not to molest them. We promised not to run away and hide in the bush but to remain in our villages and behave in a friendly manner."

The aged Bungamuzi interjected: "And we gave them guides to take them to the lake."

How many?

He replied instantly, "Seven," and with octogenarian triumph ticked off their names upon his skinny black fingers.

As the red African sun sank low on the wooded western horizon Bungamuzi described the blood rite whereby the peace terms were sealed.

Stanley's peace pact, in the blood of his Arab subaltern and an Undussuma warrior, opened the way for Bula Matari's many subsequent journeys through the Undussuma country which dominates the Nile's headwaters.

Breaker of Stones is gone as well as most of the Undussumas of his day, but his pact remains as an example to a cynical world.

ለ ኢ ት ዮ ጵ ያ · ሹ ማ ም ን ት ና · ሕ ዝ ብ ።

ይህንን · ማናተም · የያዘ · ሰው · የእንግሊዝ · መንግሥት · የጦር · ሹም · ነው ። ኢትዮጵያን ·
ለመርዳት · የመጣ · ነውና · በደኅና · ተቀበላችሁ ፤ ጉዳት · እንዳያገኘው · ጠብቃችሁ ፤ ምግብና
መጠጥ · እየሰጣችሁ · በሚቻላችሁ · ሁሉ · ረድታችሁ ፤ ወደሚቀርበው፡ የእንግሊዝ · ወታደር
ሰፈር · እንድታደርሱት · አደራ · እንላችኋለን ።

አዲስ · አበባ ፤ ጥቅም ት

CHIEFS · AND PEOPLE OF ETHIOPIA!

The bearer of this document is an officer of the British Government. As he
has come to help Ethiopia, receive him and protect him in order that he may not
suffer. Give him food and drink and help him in all possible ways and take him to
the nearest British military camp. This is our recommendation.

Addis Ababa, October, 1941.

VII

With Haile Selassie in Addis Ababa

There was nothing simple about African travel in wartime 1941, even on an expense account. Having cabled his dispatches from Léopoldville, to return to Ethiopia to cover the British siege against the Italians in Gondar, Weller had to make a circuitous route to avoid Axis forces: first by car to Goma via Irumu, south to Kampala (Uganda), plane down to Nairobi (Kenya), and train to the port of Mombasa; by ship and sailing dhow to Mogadiscio; across the Indian Ocean to Aden (described herein); back across the strait and overland to Addis Ababa, then Gondar. This journey took more than two weeks and cost the *CDN* a thousand dollars—almost $15,000 in today's money. Also, his Leica was stolen in Gondar.

The articles in this section are in the order written rather than the order published. Presumably the dispatches appeared as they were received, and the newspaper left out Weller's dates of writing to avoid confusion. Other dispatches in the archive, omitted here, were killed by British military or political censors.

Missing from the interview with Selassie was a far more spirited statement of support for the American people. Just after Weller's first dispatch was sent, a second dispatch, "a personal message to the American people in the hour of their national defense," was soon killed by British political censorship in Cairo, "who seemed to have forgotten that there was in Africa such a person as Haile Selassie. Of course he had to be censored, whoever he was." Here is how Weller recalled the incident:

Two days later the Emperor wrote out, by request, a message to the people of the United States of America. He wrote it out in his own hand, and studied it for a full day before sending it to [my] basement room in the Hotel Imperial. The Emperor, accustomed to being pinned somewhere between Great Powers, lets them wait. Neither London nor Rome can hurry him. He does nothing hastily.

"America, which has always respected the rights, liberty, and integrity of all nations however small and has never recognized any conquest of aggression; America, one of the most peace-loving nations of the world, is now attacked without provocation by a brutal aggressor. The whole world will recollect America's effort through her illustrious President to prevent the outbreak of the war which now rages throughout the world. Japan has made war against America and has thrust aside all offers of peace in the Pacific.

"People of America! Great is your struggle, but liberty and justice are on your side, and you will crush the warmongers. Great will be your victory and through it peace will be given to the world. You have the full sympathy of the people of Ethiopia and of myself.

"Rest assured that God is with the Army which fights under the standard of Liberty and Justice."

—

INDIAN OCEAN TURNS HEAT ON SOLDIERS

Somewhere in the Gulf of Aden—December 6, 1941
(written mid-November)

If the pores of troopships were not of iron, one would say that they perspired too.

It was hot in the Indian Ocean and it is hotter now in the Gulf of Aden. They say that when we get into the Red Sea, where Africa and Asia lie to the left and right of us, that oven will really turn on the heat.

This is the route plied by the giants of Great Britain's maritime fleet, their tween-decks choked with troops, their forward and stern bulkheads cluttered with squatting Africans and Asians. It is a hot way to go to war, no matter where you come from.

From Nairobi, Kenya Colony, to Addis Ababa, capital of Ethiopia, it takes four hours by plane for anyone from a colonel to a major-general. If your rank is between an African tent-carrier and a Sandhurst lieutenant colonel—this is where a foreign correspondent belongs—you have fourteen days of travel before you.

Ten are spent aboard ship, mostly in convoy. Although the nearest transport with its grey-brown uncamouflaged sides and lackadaisical smoke wreath is about three hundred yards away, you soon get the impression that it is crowding you. In this heat it is too close for comfort. You don't want anything or anyone near you, even if it's a ship. What you would like is a cold Atlantic breeze. Between equatorial Africa and Arabia there isn't any such thing.

Even the stateroom fans get tired whirling all day. They pause inexplicably, as though to rest. After a few hours they resume work again. Nobody knows why they stop, and nobody knows why they start again.

There was an electric flat iron aboard. After pressing sweat-saturated uniforms all day long, it finally rebelled and refused to heat up anymore. Someone suggested dropping it overboard but nobody felt strong enough to carry it as far as the rail. Besides, we might run into a breeze. Perhaps it will start working then. Until that, you simply keep your wet shirts hanging in rows before the electric fan.

Under the drab awnings to cover the top deck, peculiar eddies of heat are waiting to entrap the fool who thinks there may be a breeze up there. It is hotter under the canvas than July at the circus. Look upward and you see black smoke pouring from a funnel—straight up. It is not true that there is no breeze. There is, but it is traveling in precisely the direction we are steering, at precisely our speed. The long canvas windtraps, meant to catch the air and carry it down the ventilators into the broiling engine room where the temperature is 114, are motionless.

The gunners in the anti-aircraft towers, built above decks, sit directly in the sun. You would not be surprised to see the pith helmets catch fire on their heads. They have cooked for hours, long past the point where perspiration is possible. Their faces have the look of a Thanksgiving roast that needs basting. An acute ear could probably hear the sound of their brains simmering.

At breakfast and luncheon officers and non-coms eat in two separate

relays. Dinner they take together. Dressing for dinner consists of tucking in
your damp shirttail. The food is what people in more humane latitudes describe heartily as a "good, nourishing hot meal"—usually of soup, thick
and hot enough to get the pores nicely opened. Then broiled fish. The chief
dishes are roast beef, veal, or chicken served piping hot, with baked or
boiled potatoes so hot they have to be handled with a spoon, and warm vegetables like carrots or parsnips. Every dessert is the same—pudding with
hot sauce. The beverage is hot coffee.

Old King's African Riflemen and gold coasters tie extra napkins round
their necks like hotel chefs and go patiently through the entire menu. It is
perfectly good usage to wipe your streaming face, neck and arms with your
napkin. But don't try to wring out the napkin surreptitiously between your
legs. It is not done. Simply allow it to drop with a wet plop to the floor and
ask for a new, dry one.

The armed merchantman, who is our watchdog, cruises about a mile
ahead. Apparently it spends most of its time at night watching to see that
nobody aboard us allows a gleam of light to emerge when stealing a breath
of air upon the deck. Our deck entrances, as a blackout precaution, are
hung with triple curtains of canvas. Going out is like feeling your way
through a labyrinth. Reaching forward, you touch something that feels
slippery as a snail and realize it is a human arm.

But if the curtains are moved aside and a beam of light momentarily escapes, the night watch aboard the merchantman—whom the captain calls
in convoy terms our "commodore"—never fails to notice. Immediately his
blinker blue light begins scrolling across the mile of water and someone
comes from our bridge to remind us in dour, Scotch waterfront accents:
"Thairs a warr on." He usually stays under the blue light outside the bar
and has a quick one before mounting bridgeward again.

For nondrinkers of alcohol the little barman offers lime juice. He first
brewed the drinks individually but soon found himself knee-deep in limes
and verging on a nervous breakdown. Rummaging in the storehouse, he
turned up a baby bathtub from the days when the ship was on a Far Eastern passenger run. Now the drinks are dipped directly from the bathtub
where Indian amahs once bathed the sons of Poona colonels.

Most of the passengers prefer canned beer to bathtub juleps. Gliding
over the waves from hot latitudes to hotter we leave bobbing upon the surface behind us a serpentine trail of tinkling beer cans. By day, they catch

the glint of the sunlight. By night, they excite tiny phosphorescent animals who gather around them as they depart down our wake. The deepest, steadiest drinkers and perspirers claim they are rendering a public service by sowing the cans astern. If an Italian submarine or German raider slipped up behind the armed merchantman plowing ahead it might not hear. But we ourselves, standing by the rail, would certainly catch the sound, for the rattling beer cans against the invader's steel sides would give ample warning.

This Falstaffian school of anti-submarine defense thinks the battle of the Indian Ocean could be won if the breweries of Chicago, St. Louis and Cincinnati would introduce gallon-size kegs of tinned beer under the lease-lend act. They are themselves perfectly willing to defend the Atlantic convoys under the same plan.

Among the approximately 1500 military and naval proletarians aboard are only two women—girls rather—clad in the neat khaki of the auxiliary forces. One is married; the other married an officer after knowing him four days.

Yes, there is a war on. But the song they endlessly play on their portable gramophone comes from the United States and dates from the days of black-faced Bert Williams, even before World War No. 1—*When That Midnight Choo-Choo Leave for Alabam*. Played upon a troopship in the suffocating Gulf of Aden, outside the cabin window of the only American aboard, it unquestionably deserves to be called a hot number.

—

WRITER WATCHES ITALY'S SUN SET IN EAST AFRICA

Gondar Is Taken by British After 7-Month Siege

British Advance Battle Headquarters, Northwest Ethiopia—November 26–27, 1941 (Delayed)

Italy's last foothold in Ethiopia was blasted from under her today when a blazing six-sided attack upon her mountain stronghold, under the direction of Major General Cyril Fowkes, brought the commanding Italian general, Guglielmo Nasi, to plead for terms.

Your correspondent writes Italy's epitaph in a trench a thousand feet above Gondar and five miles away as the crow flies, and the air rings with the detonations of Italian stores by General Nasi's demolition squads, continuing from Lake Tana to the northern escarpment of Ethiopia's network of canyons. Every hill and mesa is spouting smoke—either signal fires started by the King's African Rifles and the Ethiopian patriots as they took one summit after another, or the last traces of Italian positions, blown skyward by African and Indian artillery.

From half an hour before dawn until now, at 5:30 in the afternoon, your correspondent has been watching the tremendous panorama of the battle—infantry creeping uphill directly into the fire, airplanes dive-bombing and machine-gunning the ground troops, and Italian artillery firing until annihilated in positions deeply dug into the mountain. Although the British field radios picked up General Nasi's message to his outlying batteries, saying that surrender was imminent, further machine-gun fire can still be heard from Gondar.

Probably never has the awful chorus of modern warfare—the clatter of machine guns from aircraft and ground, the deep terrible boom of bombs and the stabbing note of field guns—been echoed against a setting so magnificent as from this sandbagged hillside brink, with a sheer 2500-foot drop to the pastures below.

The dozen officers composing General Fowkes' general staff stood by with binoculars pressed to their eyes, sending quick orders by telephone and radio to dozens of different positions. Though an airplane could cross the whole, vast battlefield in ten minutes it will be days before all the forces converging through these valleys can unite in Gondar.

Your correspondent slept last night under a hill shaken by Italian shells, which were seeking to wipe out eight field guns hidden nearby. At five o'clock this morning, with the stars still shining, he arose to watch the first barrage shoot its yellow tongues up over the hill toward Gondar.

Why has it taken the British forces in the wild country north of Lake Tana nearly as many months to isolate and suppress Italy's last remaining troops as it has taken them to sweep over all the rest of eastern Africa?

That is the unspoken question buzzing like a bothersome bushfly over the glories of the Ethiopian victory.

It was first predicted that Gondar would fall in days, but the time length-

ened into weeks and months. It was stated that starvation would compel besieged forces under General Nasi—the bespectacled sixty-two-year-old Italian commander—to yield before General Fowkes, brisk, vigorous British
commander in chief, who, as a brigadier in the King's African Rifles, already
has bright successes at Addis Ababa and Jimma behind him. The popular
image has the Italians high upon a castellated hill, defending against vastly
superior forces and unable to take retaliatory action. Seen against the
panorama of rapid Italian collapse elsewhere, Gondar's continued failure to
fall seems to reflect upon the enterprise of its besiegers.

Even foreign correspondents, British, American and South African,
have left the forces in this canyon-ridden, awesomely savage country to
their thankless task. Your correspondent is the only newspaperman with
them, the others apparently driven away not only by the studied lack of
emphasis upon Gondar in the Allied communiqués, but by the slow, rudi-
mentary method of press communication of military news that has characterized the entire Ethiopian campaign.

The Italians themselves have eschewed the subject, little desiring to salt
the wounds of a shrinking empire. Thus Gondar has been forgotten and
one of the interesting conflicts of the war ignored.

Actually, the struggle is different from the rest of the Ethiopian campaign. The first difference from Italian withdrawal elsewhere is that here
the Fascists are fighting. With all lost except honor, they seem determined
to rescue that. General Nasi is the general chiefly responsible for the Italians taking British Somaliland in August, 1940, and never has received
credit for it. As Governor of Ethiopia, he was ordered to use harsh policy,
but refused, and successfully introduced appeasement. Thus his native
troops are more loyal to him than to the average Italian general. He has instilled the Italians with something resembling willingness to die for this
cause, admittedly forlorn from the start.

Only two days ago, upon the towering, pointed Venticinque Hill, your
correspondent saw where a lone Italian machine gunner cut off from his
comrades continued holding his post until he was wiped out by artillery fire.

Hand-to-hand fighting has occurred over almost every foot of the green
mountain pastures, cornfields, wheatfields, yellow and grey, as the lines
slowly closed in on the white spatter of buildings in Gondar. The slow bump
of artillery fire shook the hills and puffs of smoke jumped in the air as ring
after ring of hillside forts were penetrated. Yet, when bayonet charges were

attempted uphill in the face of machine gun fire, the Italians failed to flee, as elsewhere, but stood their ground to meet the Uganda, Tanganyika, Nyasaland and Kenya riflemen.

Against the Ethiopian patriots led by British officers and against detachments of Haile Selassie's own army, the Italians frequently fought as if victory were possible. As a result death tolls are high and if General Nasi were to continue to resist, the vultures that tirelessly circle above the hills would have more work than the prison camps already waiting.

Your correspondent spent most of today in an artillery command position with the air overhead constantly swishing and crackling with a concussion of great shells. Time after time the infantry in the valley below advanced under covering fire against Fascist artillery shells which punished their advance. One after another the Italian field guns were wiped out and the East African armored cars first took Azozo Airdrome then entered Gondar from the south. Italy never put her single remaining Fiat into the air.

The sun is almost down upon Italy's last day in Ethiopia. Now street-fighting has started in Gondar. Snipers' shots and the crack of pistols can be heard, but a last Hartbees-Wellesley (an American-built Mohawk) is settling safely upon the lone airdrome. Smoke from cannon mouths lies in the valleys below us in blue wreaths.

The sun has finally descended in red glory behind the mountains of Lake Tana and tomorrow all Ethiopia will belong once more to Haile Selassie.

From the point of view of altitude, fighting for Gondar has been tougher on the troops engaged than any other campaign of the war. Here soldiers have battled at 10,000 feet. At night they have camped in drafty tents pitched in chilly hollows at anywhere from 9500 feet upward.

The rarefied air has been the defenders' best friend and the attackers' enemy. Without effort one grows sleepy; with even slight exertion the lungs begin to cry out for air.

In the bowl of green hills covered with acacia trees and marked with rocky declivities where the Italians have entrenched themselves, complicated trench systems could be taken only by uphill bayonet charges. There was little cover for troops to lie down and gather strength.

The Italians never forsook a position without planting it thoroughly with mines. Sappers from West, East, and South Africa had to cover the small glades of forest and the nearby fields watching carefully for hidden mines before the infantry could move up.

Gondar is seven days by motor convoy from Addis Ababa (Ethiopia's capital) and three days from Asmara. Virtually all supplies except fresh meat had to be brought the entire distance into the field.

The final attack on Gondar would have begun earlier but the northern roads were inaccessible as the rains lasted extraordinarily late this year.

Through regular air reconnaissance and the interruption of clandestine mail service through the mountains from Gondar to Asmara—where live the families of many of the besieged—the British had a fairly complete picture of life within Gondar, even before its surrender. Children were evacuated long ago and only five women remained within the city, all reputedly ladies of frail frame.

Rome radio complained that the British bombed Gondar's hospital. South African airmen at first thought they knew exactly which it was. Originally there were only half a dozen red crosses upon Gondar's roofs, but with the Mohawks, dozens of red crosses appeared upon Gondar's roofs.

Some points which ordinarily would be sought out by bombers have been untouched in an effort to avoid unnecessary destruction. It would have been easy for the British, commanding a powerful air force, to wipe out Gondar in a two-hour air raid as the Germans did Coventry, but the city itself has been spared.

Bringing peace to Ethiopia is costing Britain about $15 million a year in public maintenance but the magnificent Italian roads are already showing signs that they will not last forever.

As your correspondent finished this dispatch, a chieftain muffled in a white scarf and with a black sun helmet like Haile Selassie's rode by upon a dappled horse. Behind him followed his gunbearer, a bearded man in draped clothes trotting to keep up with his master. Thus the Ethiopians are content to go from one pathetic little bone-littered village to the next.

—

WRITER FINDS GONDAR A CITY OF CONFUSION

Gondar, Ethiopia—December 3 & 5, 1941

Wrecked by the continuous bomb and shellfire of the fierce days of the battle, Gondar, the city of castles, today is a confused scene of rejoicing by the incoming British troops and even of a cocky acceptance of defeat by the gold-braided Italian officers who held out so long within the embattled citadel.

Airplanes buzzed back and forth from the 9000-foot tableland above Gondar as your correspondent, covered thickly with dust, came into the town after an all-day drive in a tiny campaign car that negotiated the un-believable curves of the 30-degree slopes of the mountainside road that was the secret of the Italian undoing.

Gondar stood figuratively athwart the only highway controlling the route through western Ethiopia connecting Asmara in the north with Addis Ababa in the south. But precisely where the ramparts are dizziest and even the talented Italian road engineers never attempted to go, British engineers with East African labor built a secret highway over the heights. Three to four hundred trucks of the infantry brigade, often pulled by trac-tors in danger of toppling into the abyss, descended from the tableland to-ward Lake Tana and, aided by Ethiopian patriots, took the Italians from the rear.

Far from being an obscure mountain town, Gondar is—or was—a full-grown city with three-story office buildings and many villas and large, deep air-raid shelters now scarred by the siege and virtually without food, cloth-ing, or supplies.

The British authorities have confined many prisoners in the Portuguese castle dungeons, but since these total approximately 12,000 Italians and 11,000 Africans, the problem is difficult. Many officers have been allowed to return to their modest homes. Their healthy appearance belies reports of starvation; their demeanor is self-assured and chatty and in some cases verges upon the bumptious.

Unlike the defeated General Nasi, who is a Sicilian, most of the officers seem to originate from northern Italy and many are physically large and well set-up fighting men. They were outnumbered by the rainbow mixture of the British forces more than two to one but fought bravely against supe-rior aircraft and are fully aware that whatever military honors remain to Italy in the Ethiopian campaign are theirs.

The colonel of aviation in charge of Gondar ordered the single remain-ing Italian plane burned before the British armored cars entered Azozo Airdrome, a mile south of Gondar. When your correspondent photographed it today in the bomb-pierced hangar, the pails of the last remaining gasoline which had been used to destroy it still hung on the landing gear and the nosecap.

All through the night, rifle and machine-gun fire was heard from the surrounding hills and fires blazed up as irregulars discovered stores of cordiate. The city itself, with doors ajar and unremoved bodies lying in many buildings, was absolutely dark except for flickering candles behind closed shutters. The dynamo that supplies the city's power is halted for lack of gasoline, pending the opening of a direct road from the northern tableland where the removal of mines may take several days. One party of peace negotiators was blown up by a mine and a British major had both legs broken.

General Nasi surrendered unconditionally to officers of a Kenya armored car unit Wednesday, November 26, at 4 p.m., after a final eleven-hour battle brought the attacking forces into the very streets of the city. The same officers to whom General Nasi surrendered had been in Gondar earlier in the afternoon, but they had been forced to withdraw.

I was with infantry detachments all that morning and watched magnificent assaults on hill after hill in very tough going. When these infantrymen marched into Gondar that night they were very tired after fighting all day but not too tired to sing and cheer. The Ethiopians spent the night celebrating, blowing horns and building huge victory bonfires on the hills around the city.

—

HANDY ANDY BUILDS TANKS; FOOLS ITALIANS

Gondar, Ethiopia—December 4, 1941

One of the mysteries of the long battle for Gondar and Lake Tana—the unexplained appearance of an unidentified plane over the no man's land between the British and Italian lines—was solved today when a young engineering officer from Cape Town confessed that he was the pilot of the phantom plane.

In an interview on the summit of a 10,000-foot escarpment where he was helping to build a new highway, Alfred Stadler, a young lieutenant who is a member of the engineers corps, told this correspondent the story.

"We engineers were working upon a swamp section of the road a few weeks ago when we found an abandoned Gloster Gladiator fighter," said the young, flaxen-haired engineer, who spent time in Aurora, Illinois, and Cedar City, Iowa, studying tractors. "The pilot had been hit by ack-ack and forced to land. Since the $20,000 plane was under shellfire from Italian artillery and located in an inaccessible spot, no attempt at salvage was made after the pilot walked safely into our lines. But we engineers, who never get much chance at anything but hard labor and little glory, became curious. One day I had a look at the plane. I found she had a bullet hole through the oil-cooling system and instrument board but nothing else wrong.

"We got a little of this and a little of that and I fixed her up. Finally, the boys said to me, 'Why don't you fly her?' We waited until the enemy artillery was busy on other objectives and then went out again. The elephant grass was six feet high around her. We used the propeller as a lawnmower and taxied her up and down, clearing a path for a take-off. Italian artillery kept landing shells on the hill behind the plane but we kept on working.

"I took off with the rest of the engineers all waving at me. I flew over brigade headquarters and several other places, astonishing everybody. Wishing I were an aviator instead of an engineer, I flew until all the petrol that had been left was used up and then I landed near our camp."

It is unlikely, however, that the engineers will part with the demon pilot without a struggle because Stadler's talents are fully in accord with his "Handy Andy" appearance. During the last two battles involving the fortifications outside of Gondar, he constructed the only 60-ton tank ever seen in Ethiopia. It was made from three-ply and beaver board, superimposed on a bulldozer used in road construction. It had sewage pipes of six-inch caliber for armament.

When the phony tank ran across the meadows it crushed the elephant grass so completely that the Italians were convinced it was genuine. Eventually, Stadler's tank drew so much artillery fire—which disclosed the location of the enemy gun positions—that the inventor was obliged to abandon it and flee across the meadows back to his own lines.

When the war is over Stadler plans to continue selling American-made tractors to South African farmers. If a tractor can be made to fly and fight battles, he would like to make it.

BRITISH CENSORSHIP

(*Killed by British censors*)

British headquarters at the front, Gondar, Ethiopia—probably December 6, 1941

Why Britain lost upon the publicity front one of the most glorious campaigns she has ever won in the field—the war against Italy in Abyssinia, East Africa—is illuminatingly revealed here. Not knowing why both British and American war correspondents deserted the field with an alacrity comparable only to that shown by the Italian army, at a time when the difficult campaign around Lake Tana remained unsettled, this writer crossed Africa to write at least one definitive account of this heroic and fragmentarily understood victory.

From his brief experience here it is clear why the glories of this campaign have become known only in a mutilated and inconsecutive form. Abyssinia is a place where a *No Priority for Journalists* sign was hung out at the earliest moment and remains prominently displayed as the difficult Tana campaign nears its close.

Some hard things have been said about British military censorship, not all of them deserved. Censorship is not the trouble here. What is faulty, and ensures that the African campaign will come close to being muffled in the same obscurity as the past year, is the misused and inadequate technical means for transmitting news, and the inability of any authority high or low to recognize and correct this condition.

For months, British and South African journalists (and a sole American) who followed earlier phases of the campaigns were restricted to 400 words daily—not 400 each, but a *total* of 400 words. When Haile Selassie entered Addis Ababa, one of the greatest days of moral vindication in the history of the British Empire, the correspondents through hours of persuasion got their total raised to 800 words. In this way, the Germans—with triumphant details of sweeping the Balkans, which occurred at the same time—were able to blanket completely the British victory in Abyssinia, obtained against far greater odds. This blunder ranks with some of the biggest of the old London Ministry of Information in the days before the Blitz.

Learning that the chief battle for Gondar was imminent, this writer set out for the scene by the quickest means possible. This involved sixteen days' journey by train, motorcar, steamer, airplane and Arab dhow, the elapsed distance between headquarters at Nairobi and here being a circuitous route of about 4000 miles.

By a last-minute airplane journey across the Gulf of Aden, and from Addis Ababa to this front, the correspondent was able to arrive two days before the conflict which separated Italy from Lake Tana and made Gondar's capture inevitable. He witnessed the entire progress of the battle and was given every facility but communication. By returning to the air field and interviewing observer pilots, the correspondent was able by a peculiar fluke to get details of the Italian surrender before either military press officials or indeed the general staff itself.

Such good fortune was unavailing against the ironclad *No Priority* rule which still holds. The correspondent's story was delivered into the hands of press officers at about five o'clock, approximately one hour after the Italian surrender. It was brief, covered a single typewritten page, and contained nothing which required censorship. However, it was marked by a competent officer with the *No Priority* instructions provided by military regulations. When the official communiqué was transmitted at eleven that evening—six hours after the *Chicago Daily News* story was prepared—the latter still reposed on the desk in the signal tent. Night gave way to morning and while the communiqué was already in London, this correspondent's story still awaited transmission from the front. No mistake was involved; the entire stoppage was completely in accord with practices which have dominated this entire campaign. Eventually the dispatch departed at nine in the morning, having been held for ten hours after the official communiqué.

A novice might think that once transmitted from the Gondar front, a dispatch of such importance would go directly to the western hemisphere by not more than a single re-routing. But the transmission method is almost unique in its inadequacy. This message had to go to Addis Ababa, to there await again its *No Priority* turn, and be transmitted to Nairobi. There it had to be re-censored and thence transmitted to London. From London, it was sent to Canada and the United States.

Under such circumstances it is small wonder that British and American newspaper owners considered it wisest to withdraw their correspondents from a campaign which, however interesting in itself, was hopelessly bogged down in mishandling from a publicity standpoint. It would cost Britain millions of dollars to buy the space thus thrown away—and it is not for sale. If Britain's African victories fail to match her continental defeats in their impression upon the American public, it is because her soldiers' courage cannot become known under present conditions.

—

WRITER IN BOMBER'S PLACE IN AFRICAN RAID ON FASCISTS

With the Advance Wing of the South African Air Force, Northern Ethiopia—December 22, 1941 (Delayed)

One of the strictest rules of this unit forbids taking war correspondents upon bombing raids. The danger of complications is far too great.

In the recent siege of Gondar, South African pilots did most of their attacks upon the entrenched Italian positions not at night, the least dangerous time for bombing, but by daylight. Their Hartbees biplanes, whose maximum speed was once 180 mph but which the rigors of a long campaign had cut down to 150, were not precisely vehicles in which headquarters would prefer correspondents to fly. Furthermore, the Hartbees are opencockpit two-seaters. Since the fuselages were cramped and bomb loads relatively heavy, taking a correspondent along would mean displacing the rear gunner. Obviously, no correspondent could be allowed the responsibility for protecting the plane's tail against diving attacks from the rear.

But, recognizing this rule as inflexible, it is interesting to imagine what his experience would be if he were permitted to take part in a raid, or should do so by a subterfuge. Within this field the impossible becomes the possible.

Our mythical correspondent sat long upon his canvas cot in a patched tent upon this chilly Ethiopian plateau discussing with the pilot what should not be done.

"Whatever you do, don't shoot off the tail of your own plane," said Luke, chunky elder gunner and intelligence officer of the squadron.

The oily-black, gas-operated Vickers, which the gunners dismount each night and keep as tenderly as babies in their tents beside them, was then brought in.

"You can shoot anywhere, even straight down if you need to. But you must stand up in the cockpit in order to take aim. I have found most success in leaning as far out as possible and firing under the tail. The angle of deflection is much less noticeable that way and you can easily sweep around crosswise."

Asked what ensured against being ejected from the cockpit when standing up, Luke said: "You have a strong cord—we call it the monkey's tail—attached to the rear of your parachute harness, enabling you to stand without being thrown out."

Lying in bed in the morning, our correspondent heard the first sortie leave. He then arose before his pilot—a small, modest, quiet young South African named Al—and tested his parachute harness. At 7:30 the Hartbees' 750-H.P. Rolls-Royce motor was already whirring. At 8:38 the two planes taxied to the head of the bumpy mountain runway, and departed at 8:40.

The pilot and gunner of the second plane waved to our correspondent in the cockpit of the lead plane as they came in sight of Gondar. Two murderous-looking fighter monoplanes were approaching from the brown canyon to the east. The writer swiveled the gun around and prepared for action but they proved to be American-built Mohawks. At twice the speed of our correspondent's machine they passed 1000 feet below and whirled over the green hills like sharks over the seabottom.

After finding the ground signals from the King's African Rifles, the plane slanted toward the Italian lines. From the air almost nothing could be seen of a living human being. Puffs of smoke from shells landing upon the hillside betrayed where the Italians were hidden. As the plane's phone system was broken, our correspondent was unable to communicate with the pilot. But before leaving he had asked Al to indicate when the bombing dive was approaching.

Over one hillside position the plane began dipping, turning and sideslipping. Anti-aircraft fire had begun. The plane twisted and turned, and the Vickers gun trembled in its clip at the top of the fuselage.

Suddenly, Al swung about and tugged at our correspondent's sleeve.

Half a second later the sky was all around and an invisible hand jammed the correspondent firmly into his seat. The Vickers gun came loose and its butt dealt him a starmaking blow upon the cranium. With a fighting effort our correspondent recovered control of the treacherous gun. The invisible hand jammed him deeper and a tremendous roar filled the air. With a jolt, the hand was lifted from his shoulder and there was a sensation of relief.

Then there was a bumping sound as though a giant drum had been kicked. Then again. The green hilltop, which had been circling seconds before, suddenly appeared at the right hand side, much larger and clearer than it had been before. Two puffs of smoke were floating away from its top, taller and thicker than those caused by artillery. Hardly visible over the right-hand side, the fortified hilltop was snatched away. A moment later it appeared again on the left-hand side with higher puffs of smoke. A second later it was back on the right again and disappearing.

Ground-marking troops appeared below. The continual banking and turning, professionally known as "evasive tactics," were beginning to confuse the vision of the correspondent. Climbing turns over our lines, Al took the plane up again to 3000 feet above the ravines and 2000 feet above the Italian fortifications. Uncertainty as to whether ack-ack, invisible in the daytime unless one is directly in the line of fire, was continuing, made bank dips continually necessary.

In a moment our correspondent saw a secret signal from the troops' observation post indicating that they were suffering artillery fire from a specified direction. Al saw the signal too and set off thither.

Smoke shells from the East African gun batteries below eventually pointed like a finger to the hill where Fascist artillery was located. This time Al didn't bother to give warning. Again it seemed the plane's floor could not hold the push of our correspondent's weight. Again came the soft kick of release from below.

This time there were three strokes from the giant drum. Our correspondent's stomach began to swing with the plane, but slightly slower. Before the next dive he was what the British euphemistically call "ill." After that he knew little except endless circling, and tops of hills peeping into the cockpit from both sides.

Climbing out of the cockpit at the field, he noticed that the entire front of the engine was smeared in black oil, and oil covered the wings.

"Thought we'd better come home after they hit us," said Al. A single Italian bullet had penetrated the oil pump below the engine.

Note: Any resemblance to living persons or places in the above narrative is purely "evasive tactics."

—

VICTORY SURE, HAILE SELASSIE DECLARES IN MESSAGE TO U.S.

Addis Ababa, Ethiopia—December 15, 1941 (Delayed)

In ringing words of encouragement from the first and weakest victim of the aggressor powers to the latest and strongest, Haile Selassie today delivered a message to the American people that they be of good hope in their struggle against Japan.

"The battle will be long but victory is certain," said the Negus Negusti in a message given to your correspondent in an exclusive audience at the royal palace today. It was the first interview of any kind for Ethiopia's Emperor since Gondar's fall to British troops on November 27 sealed Italy's fate in East Africa and at last restored the Negus to his entire kingdom.

The Emperor announced for the first time that Ethiopia was formally at war with Japan. "I have sent President Roosevelt word that all America's efforts at stamping out aggression have our prayers and our warmest moral support. While Ethiopia cannot yet offer more than this to the common cause, we give this heartily," said the Negus.

The Emperor and his interviewer were seated in the great walnut-trimmed study of the palace. The Negus, a slight figure, was attired in the tunic of a general of the Ethiopian army, with crossed cannons upon his shoulders and triple campaign ribbons upon his left breast. His brow was patterned by many wrinkles, for peace has not brought answers to all of Ethiopia's difficult domestic problems. But his halo of dark hair and his curly beard seemed to add to the intensity and spiritual quality of his face, whose deep religious feeling has impelled many observers to compare it to the face of Christ as imagined by artists.

"In my farewell message to the League of Nations five years ago, I predicted that what happened to Ethiopia would happen to many other powers, both small and large," said the Negus in a low, warm voice. "Tell me something. Why did not England and America check these aggressor powers long ago?"

Your correspondent replied that many peoples have been asking their governments the same question without getting any answer.

"Wars will end only when the Kingdom of God prevails over all," said Selassie. "Until then it is inevitable that they will continue with all their suffering."

At the same time the Emperor demonstrated that his preoccupation with spiritual matters had not allayed his interest in Ethiopia's political welfare. He revealed that Ethiopia had already laid claim to Eritrea and Italian Somaliland as the parts of Mussolini's empire she seeks to have deeded to her after this war.

"Ethiopia earnestly desires her own outlet to the sea, independent of French Djibouti [capital of French Somaliland]. She must have a port in order to be able to sell our products, import others and thus raise her standard of living. Now that we have roads to Massaua and Assab [Red Sea towns of Eritrea], Mogadiscio [in Italian Somaliland] and others, we need the right to use those ports. The purpose of my first visit to Europe in 1924 was to try to obtain outlets to the sea, which Ethiopia needs more than ever today."

Your correspondent inquired whether the evacuation of Italians from Ethiopia, now being carried on by the British, should, in the Emperor's view, be extended to Eritrea and Italian Somaliland.

"I think it would be necessary in order to ensure stability along Ethiopia's borders," replied Selassie readily. "The Italians left many cotton, flour, woolen and other mills and factories, some under state auspices, some with private capital. I am recommending that a certain number of Italian technicians remain temporarily until the Ethiopians can take over their work, or until British, American and other foreign experts can assume their jobs. I suggest you make known as widely as possible that Ethiopia needs and wants as many trained, high-caliber men as the United States can spare," volunteered the Emperor.

Asked what would be the mechanics of application for work in Ethiopia, Selassie said: "The best course would probably be for the applicants to write the American consul in Aden, and make known their qualifications."

SINGAPORE
IS SILENT

by

George Weller

VIII

Singapore Is Silent

What boots it at one gate to make defence
And at another to let in the foe?
                    —JOHN MILTON, *Samson Agonistes*

On the day after Christmas 1941, Weller arrived in the most important British base in Asia and the Pacific: invulnerable Singapore, the prosperous island at the end of the Malay Peninsula. His assignment was to cover the colony's defense. It soon became clear to him that it could not hold. He was there nearly six weeks before managing to escape, on a freighter under attack, to Java.

The fall of Singapore, for the British Empire, has in psychological terms been compared to the attack on Pearl Harbor—except that it was far worse. The U.S. Navy could be and was rebuilt. The notion of Singapore, as impregnable as Troy, the empire's firmest foothold in Southeast Asia, being smashed and forced to surrender was unthinkable; 130,000 British troops were taken prisoner, their largest defeat. Strategically it was like the fall of several countries, for a glance at the map shows its dominant location. From it the Japanese could control air and sea lanes in all directions. In Cecil Brown's words, "To watch the city crumbling under the crash of Japanese bombs was pure, naked tragedy . . . a great bastion of heroic Britishers wiped out by Whitehall indifference and Singapore stupidity."

Although the *Chicago Daily News* carried constant dispatches from Weller in Singapore, these were subject to the strictest censorships, both military and political, that he suffered until Nagasaki. Little of what he or other reporters experienced and wrote filtered through in any authentic form to their newspapers, magazines, or radio broadcasts. After escaping to Java in February and from Java in March, over the next few months Weller worked in Australia on what is possibly his finest book, which appeared in March 1943 to unanimous praise. As Singapore colleague Brown wrote in the *New York Times Book Review*, "His indifference to danger is equal to his skill in writing and reporting."

Because only in *Singapore Is Silent* was Weller finally outside the censors' control, rather than use the original bowdlerized dispatches, I have abridged excerpts from the book. Here he was able to write in long, thoughtful chapters rather than in brief, monitored articles, and he could give voice to his frustration at how much was being endured, and how little understood, from thousands of miles away.

In an early chapter that I have omitted, Weller discusses how he came to be transferred there from Addis Ababa:

In a message relayed to Chicago through Intelligence C at Nairobi, the newspaperman offered to go to the Pacific front. Gondar had fallen, the last Italian in Ethiopia was a prisoner, and Chicagonews, as the cable companies called both the paper and its representative, had received the only first-hand account . . . Now all that was over. When one war ends, another is quick to begin. The new war in Asia must be quickly met and witnessed before history drowned its new participants in the same sea of violence where Haile Selassie and his millions of tribesmen were struggling to keep afloat.

The catcher of the *Chicago Daily News* team is Carroll Binder, a playing manager . . . He accepted the suggestion from the outfield. He lifted his mitt to send a signal to the player, moving him from the African right field to deep center: Asia.

GRATEFULLEST SINGAPOREWARD AIRWISE IF POSSIBLE

Weller would solve the problem of what to call himself in the book—since he was often acting not as an individual but as representative of an institution—by referring to himself not as "I" but as "Chicagonews." There is also a glimpse of how complicated the chess game of correspondents could be. "It is not often that one *Chicago Daily News* war correspondent on trek meets another, for they are few in number and their paths fly wide apart." After a long week of air travel from Cairo—stopping in Basra, Karachi, and Calcutta—Weller reached Rangoon and found a *CDN* colleague, Leland Stowe, who became a lifelong friend:

It was not easy to work out a modus operandi with Stowe, because there was no truly uninhibited outlet for news in the Far East. There was the further possibility that Arch Steele, the regular correspondent in Singapore who had been summoned into Russia, would be called back again. Nor would it be easy, once we parted, either to speak to each other across the barriers or to explain our problems to Carroll Binder and Paul Scott Mowrer far away in Chicago. The best plan seemed to be for Stowe to write the Burma campaign from Rangoon while the new partner went on to Singapore. If Singapore should hold and Rangoon become static, then Stowe could bypass Singapore southward to Batavia. If Chungking woke up, Chicagonews would go there, leaving Stowe in Rangoon.

Two philhellenes had met. Stowe learned from the newcomer, his successor in the Balkans, that Greece, in the hour when it fell under Germany, had already prepared thousands of copies of a booklet containing Stowe's early dispatches on the struggles in Albania. His work was felt to be the best that had come out of the Albanian phase of the Greek war. His booklet was intended to be placed in the hands of the Greeks before they met the Germans. Stowe could not have received a better Christmas present; his face lighted up happily.

Weller was about to witness the Allies' greatest, most inexcusable defeat. And for the next two years he would cover the war in the Pacific.

His account of Singapore's fall begins in late December 1941,
when he arrived, and takes it to the end, a month and a half later.

—

Singapore

Over by the harbor of the Chinese fishermen one saw the low-slung greenish, pink, and yellow four-story buildings, and the closely tethered junks in
Singapore River, ranked like slippers in a closet. On the far side, opposite
Victoria Memorial Hall, was a pillbox guarding the foot-and-rickshaw way
across the river. Singapore was at heart metropolitan, not colonial, a seg-
ment of finance capital and government dropped on an Oriental island. The
first bombs had hit in Raffles Square.

The name, associated for Americans only with genteel burglary, slowly
took on its special Singapore meaning. Sir Thomas Stamford Raffles, a be-
ginner with the East India Company at fourteen, had landed at Penang in
1805. He took Java from the Dutch in 1811, but on getting his fever-shaken
body finally home, died young. In Raffles Square, flanked by department
stores, banks, and office buildings, the traffic policeman's kiosk was already nicked with bomb splinters.

The names of the streets full of bustle and purchase were difficult to
sort out. There were the honest Imperial names of the East India period:
Raffles, Waterloo, Queen Victoria, and Sofia, and there were also Penang,
Malacca, and Pekin streets. There were names like De Souza, too, re-
minders that it was the Portuguese who took Malaya from its own King
Mahmud in 1511. There were also one or two Malay names, such as Brag-
Basah Road. Along Orchard Road was the California Sandwiche Shoppe,
intended to attract the citizens of a certain World Power better known for
their wandering habits than for any resultant political education.

The Singapore Club with its tall French windows facing out upon the
harbor—with its perfectly ordered tables bearing a *Sphere,* a *London
Graphic,* the morning copy of the *Straits Times,* and the last copy, now ten
days old, of poor Penang's newspaper—was an ideal place to sit and discuss
with the army press officers what was known as "the situation." In the
crowded roadsteads of the gleaming bay—holding everything from Chinese

junks to the ferry puffing down from Penang that had once connected Prince of Wales Island with the mainland—there was clear indication of what was happening. Singapore's ships were not being bombed. Did the Japanese hope to capture these too? The Japs did not bomb the harbor until Singapore's last days. Why they spared it and allowed ships to escape, even to return and take off more refugees, no one ever knew.

"We expect the natives to panic like rabbits," was what they said in the Singapore Club. They didn't.

On Christmas Day the Japanese began their series of pamphlet propaganda. The first shower suggested that Malays, Chinese, and Indians mark the coming birthday of Jesus Christ by "burning all foreign devils in a holy flame." The Japs hoped that Singapore's Asiatics were inflammable. Actually the "natives" were learning how to rescue people from the cracking walls of a house with a spitting incendiary bomb in its middle. They were saving foreign devils, not burning them.

The best commentary on the division of populations in Singapore came when the blood banks at the hospitals began to grow low, when from 60 to 90 planes were coming over every day, when even the official figures admitted 75 to 450 dead. This was the time when people, as strange a mixture as could be seen walking along the arcades by noon or shuffling in the bazaars by twilight—Chinese women in black smocks and wide oyster-shell trousers, Sikh taxicab drivers with carefully curled beards, Malay boys from the Jesuit School, and Portuguese Indian clerks from the social rooms of the Goa Society—all lined up at the clinics to give their blood for the emptied veins of the mutilated and moaning people taken out of smashed buildings. If blood was short, the volunteer nurses, the much-criticized "idle wives of Malaya," gave theirs, and so did the fresh-faced Australian nurses. For the first time in Singapore's history, the blood banks did as big a job as the money banks. Here was the true mingling of the races; white gave red blood to yellow and the lazy brown Malay bared his arm and let his heart pump for the hated chiseling little yellow merchant from Canton or Hainan. The blood brotherhood of Japanese power is well known, but the blood brotherhood of the donors in Singapore, selfish capital of the selfish East, had to be seen to be believed. There was no Malayan armed force except the comic-opera guardsmen of the so-called Independent States, but when blood was asked for there was a line of will-givers ascending the hospital steps. They had no weapons, but they were ready to give their blood for Singapore.

Perhaps part of the energy of Singapore's civil population was due to the fact that although the island is only 73 miles above the equator, its temperature is never oppressive and frequently is cool. Singapore's climate is never so insufferable, for example, as that of New York City on a muggy day in June. There was more energy on the island than elsewhere in Malaya, and at times the city almost attained the wasteful bustle of a Western metropolis. The banks were so choked with people, almost all refugees, that it was nearly impossible to push through the doors.

Besides private banking negotiations, there were other matters of banking magnitude afoot. All the bulky bonds of the war loans, in the name of the Federated Malay States and Straits Settlements, had to be destroyed lest they be captured, as they were negotiable on sight. The Chartered Bank kept three women busy cutting off the bond numbers and sending them to the Treasury building vaults.

The means of transfer would have shocked an American surety company. Every morning the sheared bonds were loaded into a dhobi's wash basket, placed on the seat of a rickshaw. The wife of the director mounted beside it. A guard from the bank walked beside the coolie. The bond shipment moved off at a barefoot trot for the Treasury, £5,000,000 of war effort in a rubber-tired rickshaw.

The British bank-managers often worked attired in the fire warden's khaki in which they had watched the night before, a peculiar brassy helmet riding their desks amid the flotsam of checks, flimsies, and government permissions. As a rule their tempers held under the deluge, but sometimes burst into a thunderbolt of rage. There were few adding machines and no bookkeeping apparatus. Everything was done by pen and pencil and longhand computation. People never gathered in lines but always in clusters around the cages, exchanging horror tales—particularly about Penang's nine hours of bombing raids—and naming ships' names with a freedom that would have made every hair of the Admiralty stand on end.

Penang was the first city to demonstrate the depths of Chinese courage and Malay stoicism. The Asiatics refused to take cover, and were machine-gunned in the streets. The hospitals filled; they were still bringing in terribly wounded people two days afterward. Here sat a wrinkled old man, his body curled like a seashell around his grandchild, the only living member of his son's family of eight. They found an old woman, wounded, with both her legs broken. When they brought her to the hospital grounds and laid her on the bare floor—there were not nearly enough cots—she piped up: "I'm not going to die yet. I'm going to live to see the Japs beaten."

Most truths can stand tempering. All refugees and escapees are alike, including correspondents. They all came out on the last train, saw invaders enter the town, knew themselves inefficiently protected from the first but were never able to do anything, slept on hard train floors, had only canned milk for the baby on the way down, left the silverware in the sideboard and the radio blaring. War upsets family routine. Invasion followed by flight leaves everybody distraught and dispossessed.

Pressure was being put upon Sir Shenton Thomas, the tall, sharp-nosed Governor, to evacuate women and children from Singapore, but he found this order difficult. He had already pledged that all races should receive equal rights at the gangplank. To carry this out would mean evacuating 400,000 women and children, Chinese, Indians, Malays. Where were they to go, and who was to support them?

Many native families returned to Madras and Calcutta. White women and children who possessed the means arrived in the Indies and Ceylon, sleeping in the holds of freighters, and proceeded to Australia and Africa. Until the end, from a governmental point of view these escapees were merely making use in wartime of the privilege of going wherever they pleased. They were not officially evacuees. Some 3000 white women and children, along with thousands of Chinese, Indians, and Malay mothers and children who wanted to get away, were left behind.

What about the Singapore of Joseph Conrad, Somerset Maugham, and the early Bruce Lockhart? What about the island Raffles had bought, Manhattan-style, for only £13,500 from the Princes of Johore? Had it ceased to exist? Had Singapore Sal* reached her blowzy end at the foot of some greenish pier where feeble equatorial tides sucked and sighed? Or was Singapore just another of those seaport cities that have lost their character through the leveling influence of marine industrialism?

---

*Voluptuous and masked piratical villainess, armed with both cutlass and automatic rifle, who opposes steely Steve Conrad in several 1940 issues of *Adventure Comics*.

At first it was hard to say, for ten brothels do not make a Singapore, nor twenty. There were rickshaws, yes, drawn by toothpick men with gaunt runners' faces and sunken, leather-colored cheeks. But these coolies looked not starved and filthy but clean and somehow healthier than nearly anyone else. They obeyed winking traffic lights, as modern as in Atlanta. For short runs, the canny Chinese rickshawman charged as much as the fat, bearded Hindus did for their groaning taxis.

This was a different Singapore, home port of broad fishing junks that creaked beside the watery staircases of the river, but also port of call for the "Australian fishing fleet," that December sea caravan of eligible and enthusiastic Australian girls who cast their lines in the clubs from Penang to Singapore, who fished in the Malayan grounds where lurked the timid bachelor hornpout, and for whom a single catch, landed and basketed, would satisfy each fisherwoman for a lifetime.

Another un-Singaporean thing about Singapore was that it did not smell of opium or tar, of smoke or whisky, of lamp oil or sawdust, of perfume or sweat. Singapore, in fact, did not smell at all. It was scrubbed and clean, and even where it was poor it was not dirty. The very rickshaw runner, sweating through his thin cotton shirt as his scuffing sandals rose and fell, seemed to perspire odorlessly.

The only sign of food restrictions was that at the Singapore Club one had to be satisfied with two principal dishes instead of three, and a single pat of butter. There was plenty of rice, even though Indo-China was cut off. Transport going up to the front had hurt but not halted the trucking of fruit and vegetables into Singapore Island. Mangoes, passion fruit, and pineapples were abundant.

There had been three "cabarets"—large Oriental dance halls—the New World, the Great World, and the Happy World. The first Japanese bombers, with impeccable symbolism, not only hit downtown in Raffles Square, but placed a direct hit on the Happy World. Sadly smashed, the aviators having probably mistaken its rambling broad roofs for the hangar buildings of the adjacent Kalang airdrome, it remained closed. That left the Japanese with two Worlds still to conquer.

All the Worlds were more or less alike, with a curved and fretted Oriental archway over the entrance. Inside was a long pavilion, flanked by booths under whose blinding white lights had been sold sea-chest keepsakes, conch shells with maps of Singapore Island, pocket combs decorated with nude Chinese Junos. The church was once the mother of the theater; in Singapore each dance establishment looked like a rather noisy and blatant temple. The central shrine was the large dance hall, with the nearly continuous music of the big Eurasian dance band pumping through the dragoned doors. The architecture was a pastiche of Buddhist temple, Teutonic modernism, and World's Fair 1939. Inside were the Chinese hostesses, sitting together in slit-legged flowered silk dresses. "I come Canton. I splik English, yess." Not one in a hundred did speak English.

When war came, the big temple remained and the dance music went on. The room was vast, and domed high. Thick heavy curtains were hung about the doors and windows. The hostesses stayed, in their tubular flowered dresses covering their flat tiny breasts and narrow hips. None needed a brassiere. They wore high heels to gain a little on the soldiers and sailors with whom they danced. The girls sat in fours and fives by the dance floor, their big red and white handbags lying on the tables.

Soon the Great World was closed; more raids were coming. But the New World went on, through the bombings and the deaths all around, straight through to the fall of Singapore. It was the hugest and hottest of the Worlds. There was a ceaseless come and go, because there was no admission fee. One was expected to drink, and the charges were not more than at a soda fountain. From the waiters one purchased tickets to dance with the girls, for about 4¢ each. The dance ticket said: *Night dance—good for one dance only. N.B. Coupons not bearing the Chop of the Managing Director, Mr. Ong Peng Hock, are not Valid.* The atmosphere was so shadowy that it was necessary to take a girl out under the central lights to see her face.

Some girls seemed no older than thirteen or fourteen, and most were far from being Singapore Sals. When asked to dance, they never showed either vivacity or enthusiasm. For many the New World was undoubtedly not a way of either being wicked or earning a living, but simply a way of seeing what the world was like and meeting men. The Chinese are businesslike people, but these girls never would ask to collect the dance ticket from the man, as would a Broadway hostess. She would receive it with uncommercial negligence, flipping it carelessly into her handbag. Singapore's judgment of these girls ran: "The Chinese girl who has been kept by a white man and then put aside is on a higher social stepladder than the girl

who is still a virgin. But she can never give you love, because she is not capable of it."

It was probably true. The girls seemed to make no effort to attract men
or to hold them, other than the scrupulous and identical cultivation of their
own beauty. Their eyes were expressionless. When men failed to show interest, they danced with each other, using a fast lindy hop and shag step.
No one can say what conversations went on, after the band played *Good
Night, Ladies* and *God Save the King,* and Chinese girls and Occidental
men went out and stepped up into one-and-one-half-seat rickshaws, usually
with the soft rain of the Malayan night pattering on the canvas canopy
overhead. But many of the girls, even pretty ones, went home alone.

To send in anything American larger than a destroyer, it was recognized, would be useless in the face of Japanese aircraft superiority. The
Japs had started by getting air superiority through aircraft-carriers in the
South China Sea, and now they were rapidly taking bases in northern
Malaya and getting land-based and sea-based superiority. The distinction is
important because if the British had been able to control the land bases,
even though their fighters were inferior and few, they might have held off
the larger naval force. Now the Japanese had both, and their carrier-based
fighters were superior to the best British land-based plane (the American
Brewster). After the Japanese got air fields and put extra gas tanks on their
fighters, the margin of their Army 97 and the Zero over the Brewster was
even greater.

Singapore was a naval base, but almost as empty of activity as the great
dock was of warships. On the south side of the island was the cruiser *Exeter,*
a hospital ship, and dozens of other interisland ships and international
freighters. There was little dispersal; the only place where Japanese
bombers could have found more compact targets was Rangoon, where the
freighters had lain in the Irrawaddy River like sucking pigs alongside a sow.
After a little experience one looks on ships and harbors and military stores
and field quarters with the same questions: How well are these objectives
dispersed, how many would be lost in an intense air raid without fighter
protection, and where will the human beings take cover nearby? With more
experience these queries are supplemented by another: Where shall *I* take
cover? Only two phases of the invasion of Malaya and the attack upon Singapore could be treated reportorially with any frankness: (1) the creeping

jungle-seashore-and-road fight southward, and (2) the simultaneous air attack upon Singapore itself.

Major Fisher and Captain Hooper were ready and eager to arrange a trip to the front. An advanced correspondents' base had been established in Kuala Lumpur, the Federated Malay States' capital, which one early learned to refer to as "K.L." A train with sleepers left for it every night; and, although jammed to the luggage racks with human beings on the way south, it was usually empty going north.

On the matter of equipment the situation was characteristically Singaporean. There were plenty of water bottles, web harnesses, belt boxes for emergency rations without the emergency rations, and combined ponchos and ground sheets of greenish-grey rubber. There were gas masks, hundreds of gas masks. The Japanese had not used gas, although a smoky shell had been mistaken as such. Everyone was supposed to carry a gas mask over his shoulder, through all the six weeks. Fisher and Hooper never failed to have theirs, as regulations specified, hung upon their thin shoulders. They grew a little lopsided, like caddies, in their gas-mask direction, but mercifully did not insist that correspondents be so scrupulous as themselves.

But what about tin hats? With the Japanese concentrating upon air attacks, strafing buildings, dive-bombing, high- and low-level bombing, how about a tin hat to go to the front with?

"I'm dreadfully, terribly sorry, and we're trying to do everything we can about it," said Fisher, "but we've just received word that no helmets can be issued to correspondents."

—

FRONTWARD

"Going to the front" in a battle area where the enemy controls the air is a metaphysical term. Nobody can go to the front. Everyone is at the front already. The front is too much with one, not only late and soon, but all day and all night. The only time when the front is not there overhead is when it rains. Sometimes there is position bombing even in the rain, when the target is as familiar by landmark as were Singapore Island's four chief air fields. But one still speaks of the front as a place where men are fighting, tommy gun against tommy gun or even hand to hand. The front, like Doctor Faustus's Hell, was everywhere, nor were we out of it.

It was the first trip to the Malayan front for General Pownall also. From the train, which was about an hour late reaching Kuala Lumpur, he stepped down from his compartment, gave a friendly wave and a "Hello, Weller," and went into the shadows of the station. Captain Emerson, an Englishman who had been leader-writer for a Calcutta newspaper and was now press officer for Indian troops, met Chicagonews. There was breakfast in the deserted little waiting-room, then off to the press headquarters. These consisted of two long rooms in a warehouse. They had wooden bunks, without mattresses, for correspondents with bed rolls but unable to get rooms at either of the two comfortable hotels. The place was clean and busy.

In a few minutes, with the Malayan morning still hesitating, trying as usual to give showers upon the mountains and ricefields, with blue skies over the roads and villages, the mustard-colored car was pulling north along the rock-ballasted highway.

It was a green country, green and wet. Flooded paddy fields alternated with rubber plantations right and left. The rubber trees, their trunks slitted herringbone fashion, sped past in one long artificial forest, their glades clean and neat.

It was a country soft and wet, like a brown girl standing in a foggy shower. The shoulders of the low Malayan mountains could be seen on the right-hand (east) side of the road. Wet grey clouds moved over the shining leaves of the jungle trees, making them glitter. As the sun tidied up the day, evaporating fragments of morning dew, by nine it was all blue overhead. Morning was the time, in this early phase of the campaign, for bombing and machine-gunning by the Japanese. Unless there were raging storms, morning visibility was perfect. Around one, the atmospherics usually changed, and a heavy solid block of cirrus clouds moved across the sky at about 6000 feet. The Japanese could not see if they flew above this blanket, and knew themselves silhouetted targets for anti-aircraft fire if they flew below it.

The Japanese suffer from the defect of the scheming mind; they always behave as though a trap has been set for them. They are brave in combat, since to be taken prisoner is worse in the Nipponese culture than to die, spelling loss of citizenship, loss of property, and loss of the right to marry and have children. But they are cautious in planning action, and their plotters' mentality sometimes slows them down. They were under the illusion that British anti-aircraft guns existed in Malaya, whereas except for Singapore, the only thing north of Johore causeway bigger than .50-caliber machine guns was a battery of Bofors 40-millimeters, which first appeared at Ayer Hitam.

The Anglo-Indian officer drove at about 50 miles an hour, although the road where it passed through the shadow of rubber plantations was still wet and slippery. He drove fast because there had been occasional sniping from the side, perhaps by single infiltrated Japanese or Malayan fifth-columnists. The rest of the press party came suddenly into view, under the leadership of Captain Henry Steel, a slim man of about thirty, one of the few undisillusioned press officers anywhere in the world.

Most newspapermen who begin to work for the services start glowingly, kindled by an enthusiastic resolution to see that word of the war, hitherto garbled and watered by professional military men, reaches the public in a form that while maintaining all the needs of security is still lively and real. Within a short time they find that they are limited in power by their rank. Those who emasculated the word before them are now in power above them. The only difference between their status outside the forces and inside them is that they are now obliged to say "sir" to the same comptrollers. There follows a painful period when the former newspaperman makes up his mind whether to become a company man in the great corporation of the service. Sometimes he decides to ask for a transfer to a fighting post, and to postpone his dream until that ideal war which can be described as it is being fought.

Somehow Steel seemed to have managed to go around this alternative. He had his moments when he wished to renounce it all, but then he would bounce back again. Nothing takes the place of energy, and Steel had the gift of energy. Where he could not smuggle the correspondents actually into the confidence of the general, he smuggled himself in, standing negligently by during telephone conversations and putting in questions where he could. He was absolutely honest about the military situation, and treated American correspondents with the same confidence he treated the British. He had capacity to plan, and ingenuity about getting stories back from the front: two rare, invaluable characteristics in a press officer. Sometimes he anticipated dangers that did not arise, but this was refreshing in an atmosphere where so many in authority tended to pooh-bah sensible premonitions. But when a correspondent wanted to go up to a post under fire, Steel never refused to take him.

The party got as far as Ipoh. Japanese bombers were over the town. For a hundred miles back toward Kuala Lumpur every shop had been shuttered and closed. At Ipoh the streets were full of youths. Where most women and children had gone nobody seemed to know; back "into the rubber." People with wheelbarrows and tiny carts pulled behind bicycles crowded the streets, their faces taut with fear. One man was going into the rubber with nothing on his bicycle but a big sack of rice. It was too heavy for him to pedal, so he pushed it. Women went by with babies twisted like dolls into their sarongs and clinging like limpets to their hips.

Chinese merchants in Ipoh were frightened, for they knew how long the Japanese had been trying to incite the Malays against them. In the Japanese political pattern for Malaya, the Chinese had the role that Jews had in Poland, France, and the Balkans. They were the shopkeeper class who exploited the Malays and led them away from their old ideals as warriors. They were urban parasites, and the Malays were the rural producing peoples. They were the money-chasers, and the Malays were the fighters. . . . The Chinese, like the Jews, developed their own clannishness; in Singapore there was even the Tiger Swimming Pool especially for Chinese.

When the Japanese took a town in Malaya, they troubled less to humiliate and degrade the white administrators by the methods used in the Netherlands East Indies than to draw the Malays close by degrading the Chinese. The Chinese were forced to clean out cesspools. A Malayan woman was safe, but no Chinese woman could be protected against the whim of the Japanese soldier. There was a simple rule in all the towns that the Japanese had taken—no door was to be locked.

The Japanese do not disdain marriage with Malays. Their blood dominates such matings. Their plan is that the 120,000,000 Malays assume a junior partnership in Japanese hegemony as a labor race, kept integrated by flattering references to their racial unity while being kept divided by political decentralization.

The attitude of Malays toward the British is of cooperation without affection, obedience with indifference. In the Netherlands East Indies the Malays were never as antagonistic to their Dutch masters as to their potential Japanese conquerors. Intermarriage is, as always, the answer. The Dutch believe that if a Malayan woman is good enough for a white man to sleep with, there is no reason to exclude her from becoming a wife. There were thousands of mixed marriages in the Netherlands East Indies and aside from country-club intrigue, nearly all seemed happy and successful. In Malaya there was a British master class far more tolerant, hardworking, and well-meaning than it was given credit for being. But a land, like a woman, needs to be loved to be possessed, and for Malaya the sweetness of first love was over.

The Dutch are close-fisted and stubborn and can do any American and most Englishmen out of their eyeteeth in a business bargain, but they happen to be the only nationality of the white race except the Russians who have put into practice the Christian principle of the spiritual equality of races. They do it imperfectly, and race pride exists in Indonesia, but the legal premise of equality is there.

The Chinese of Malaya were sharply different, according to what part of China they came from. The bottom of the laboring class worked in the mines but considered themselves a cut above the Tamils from southern India, who worked for a plodding wage. Other Chinese, however—shopkeepers, servants, houseboys—had different ideas. The cream of the Chinese were the babas, educated and particularly prominent in Malacca. They were good lawyers and excellent physicians; many an Englishman went by preference to a Chinese doctor for natural remedies.

These Chinese, knowing that Malay was an easy language, took the trouble to learn it. (Malay sometimes has a peculiar quaintness when spoken by a foreigner. A houseboy unable to get along with the cook complained to his master: "He has a sweet mouth, but his heart is bitter.") British merchants learned a few words, but the military was singularly unenergetic, given that they expected to fight in the jungles.

Pushing centralization, the British drew four states into a group known as the Federated Malay States, with their capital at Kuala Lumpur. In 1927 legislation was taken from the native sultans into British hands.

The Straits Settlements comprised the vital seaport areas: Singapore; Penang; and the old Portuguese port of Malacca. By 1927 not only their sultans but also the British Residents consulting with them were deprived of their powers.

Besides the four Federated Malay States and the four small but vital Straits Settlements, whose strings came tightly together at the top in Sir Shenton Thomas, there were five independent, "unfederated" states. Johore, whose skyscraper capital was visible across the causeway from Singapore, was the best known. Then came Kedah, lost early to the Japanese, outflanked by Thailand to its east; Kelantan, in the wild center; Trengganu, the big state on the China Sea; and lonely little Perlis which the Japs, when they jumped the Thai border, inhaled before they began to gobble.

This scattered galaxy was also firmly in the hands of Sir Shenton Thomas, their affairs being referred to his desk in Singapore by the English officers at each native court. It was a system based chiefly upon the English capacity to know in a complicated and violent world what the Malays, Chinese, Singalese, and Tamils needed, more coherently than they knew themselves, and to give it to them. Outside the tragic error of misjudging Japan, it was an honest, stodgy administrative system.

Our party dropped in at the Ipoh airdrome, a few miles off the road. The two hangars were still burning, their roofs smashed in. A demolition party had finished the job of the Japanese bombers. The sun was going down, and the jungle's profile was turning dark upon the western horizon. It was a scene of industrial desolation amid Malaya's never-dying luxuriance. Showers and sun had made the grass more green, and there were a few well-meant, amateurish craters caused by demolition engineers. The Japs had dropped nothing on the runway itself, so the engineers had attempted to blow it up. It was like trying to blow up twenty football fields at once.

In the ruins of the little aviation clubhouse, papers were scattered all over the floor; the furniture had been hacked to pieces and windows smashed so the rain beat in. On a wall was a picture of the first Imperial Airways plane from London, a four-motor cabin job, which had landed on the inaugural flight over a decade before. Since then the runway had been broadened and lengthened. One learned that it was impossible for Japanese bombers to use the Ipoh airdrome. They did, nevertheless.

As a precaution against being surrounded in burning Ipoh, the party fell back for the night to Kampar, a crossroads marked by a club with little more than a lounge to hold dances, two billiard tables, a bar. Dues notices were thumbtacked on a board, and the draw for a forgotten tennis tournament. It might have been a small country club anywhere, with committees for this and that. Here was the usual gathering of Home Defence Corps men in their fifties, who had sent their families down to Singapore weeks before and put themselves at the call of any general who wanted their services. "Hello, boys, come in!" they cried. "How about a drink?"

Whatever one might say of others, the hearts of these men were in their fighting. Most were small-scale rubber planters and tin-miners. A few had been in the last war. Their companies were composed of one European platoon and three Asiatic. Braver than Penang's civil servants, they wanted to fight the Japanese. Indeed, they had stopped a dangerous movement through back roads by the enemy.

The next morning the bombers were at work early. The sky was blue and clear. The air, except when a convoy truck came hammering down the highway, was quiet with the soft country stillness. On such a day there are only a few hesitant breezes across the rice paddies and the treetops; the leaves are silent. The voice of Malaya is a trickling of water purling down from one rice-paddy outlet into the next, the voice of the brown water that feeds the rice and, feeding it, feeds men.

It happened that Chicagonews heard the bombers first, a murmurous buzzing. As it grew louder, it was evident the flight was large. Finally one could see them, purposeful and remorseless in their ordered flight. People were running off the road. Drivers of trucks, seeing terror in the faces, slewed onto the soft green shoulders, jumped down, and headed running into the rubber. Everything stopped. It was like Greece again. Again the long convoy-filled road of the retreat, again the imperious airplane overhead. The airplane creates a cone of immobility beneath it in every direction. The human beings lie flat, submitting. Whom will the plane kill? That is the question to be decided. The trucks and cars try to hide in the trees. The men go far back from the telltale strip of the road. Everybody stares up, death wrinkles in the brow, fear in the shifting eyes, forgetting the cares of the earth. Everything stops until the airplanes attack. Everything stops. "Don't fire a rifle, anybody," said Steel.

These bombers did not attack. Through the binoculars one could count 26 pairs of silver wings. They were very busy and certain of formation; their goal was somewhere south. It was probably not Singapore; the Japanese were not attempting that yet, because there were one or two Brewsters still at Kuala Lumpur, which was their objective. In hours Ipoh would be in their hands.

The planes were about 12,000 feet high and not escorted by fighters. They kept west of the parallel lines of railway and highway. In this way they ensured that if there were any Bofors anti-aircraft guns, the planes could not be taken by surprise, since the guns could be only moved by two methods. The Japs were still suspecting greater force than was there. The planes passed, glinting like symmetrical silver confetti, the rhythm of their motors playing strange tricks among the headlands of the forest, loud when they were approaching, almost dying as they came overhead, then growing loud again as they moved down the road. No one had given an air-raid signal, but after they passed, a whistle shrilled out. All-clear or tardy warning?

What should the party do? Once more the correspondents had discovered, as they were to discover over and over in the succeeding days, that you cannot go to the front in a jungle war unless you are winning. The next best thing was to find out what places had been struck by the bombers. "What do you think, boys?" said Steel. "George here suggests we go back to the first place that was hit. What do you say?"

"Here they come again!" yelled a voice from the road. There was a clatter of hobnailed boots running fast, then shouts in Malay. The trucks, burring for the getaway, stopped again. Everyone ran across the road toward the Frenchman's villa and the river gulch behind it. This time the noise was different, low and nearby and increasing fast. Far away the bombers had seemed almost too high to discern. This noise, one could tell before it arrived, was too low for them to be seen.

Then it came, looping around the bend in the road, a single-motored two-seat plane, dull grey. It was hunting for something, and it looked as though it knew what it wanted. Was it that little railroad station? It went over to the station, slid down upon it and *pump, pump, pump, pump, pump.* But no bombs. Did it have any bombs?

Another motor's drone began murmuring in the north: another hunter coming to help the first. He came into sight, watching us out of his left slant eye. He went a little farther down the railroad, disappeared for a while from sight while he *pump-pump-pumped* something, then *pump-pumped* it again.

Meantime the other plane had tired of the little station and was coming straight for the Frenchman's villa on the edge of the river gulch, a cleft about 300 yards wide and 40 feet deep. The Jap was cautiously high again, 1500 feet, but something about the villa made him think this the brigade headquarters he was looking for. He had received a tip from below, probably, perhaps some flour in arrowhead shape on the road, a favorite device of his agents.

The party was not together; they were scattered like pheasant's chicks under every leaf and tree or hugged close to the walls of the coolies' outhouses. He looked them over and decided that they were worth the trouble.

The Jap's dive was not a dive at all; it was a long toboggan slide, leisurely slanted. The whistle of the wings for once outdid the motor. The most ominous thing of all was that there was no sound of a machine gun. He was taking aim.

Faces went down against the mud. There were only two or three helmets in the party. Chicagonews put his doubled fists over his head. You could hear the bomb singing as it came down, singing like a bomb that loved its work. In the last moment one pressed altogether hard against the earth. Then it hit.

There always seem to be two voices to a bomb's landing in earth: the bomb's voice and the answer of the earth. The bomb's voice is a sharp call, but the answer of the earth is as different as the earth itself. The note is almost one, and yet the second stroke is audible. And it is the second voice, the voice of earth, that man feels as well as hears. In Greece the whole desiccated length of the Valley of Parnassus had shuddered as from a blow delivered upon the body of a hard-muscled athlete, resistant and rejective. In the Malayan earth the blow was received as though it had been struck against a woman, soft, muffled, and yielding.

The clods fell, pattering here and there through the leaves.

The bomb had landed on the other side of the house; the Jap had overshot. The rear gunner flayed away nastily again with his machine guns as the plane climbed for height.

Several other things were happening. The second plane had come back. And there was a third somewhere, its nasal voice ruminating about what it intended to do.

The Jap in the second plane had seen the first miss, and he intended to better the marksmanship. He came over the red New England barn of a rubber godown and turned his head down upon his work. At the top of his dive he pumped briefly from his machine guns as though announcing it was his intention to kill. Then his guns chopped off, and there was no sound but the all-pervading whistle of his dive.

It was very silent, there among the green leaves. One could almost hear the beating of hearts all around.

Chicagonews slipped to the wet edge of the gulch, a brown wall of mud as high as a three-story building. There was no foothold on its slippery wet side, but there were a few weak bushes loosely attached on its upper rim. The American clung to these, his body hanging down over the gulch, his fingers interlaced with the stems of the bushes.

The squeal of the wings had stopped; the plane must have turned upward. That meant the bomb was falling. Now you could hear it—that intense little song. The correspondent let loose one hand and with his other tried to cover the top of his head. Why does a man who in other days would have covered other parts of his body want first today to cover his brain?

When bombs are falling, water is as handy to have nearby as a mirror is for a suicide. The face of the water, if it is smooth, will tell you what is happening, even though the pliant earth and the deep grass try to conceal the story. Only a curling thread of smoke out of the grasses will inform you that the plane is using tracer bullets. But the water, if it is smooth, tells all. There may be a great splash, silence, and then a watery pillar thrown straight upward. Or if the bomb lands on the earth instead of in the water, there may be spurts and shoots and cones of water all over the surface jumping up violently and irregularly as the shrapnel violates the water. Or there may be nothing but merry little skips and scars and ripples, as though boys were scaling stones across the surface. This time there were several little fountains that jumped a foot or 18 inches high, and also a number of little thuds in the bank.

The machine gun was pumping away, and there began to be ticking sounds in the leaves. This gunner was better.

Chicagonews prepared to scramble up, but the third plane was coming. There was a stinging sensation in his right arm. The arm was covered with red ants. The ants had been living in the bush and were angry. They crawled up the arm, bare in bush jacket to the elbow, and ran inside the sleeve biting furiously. There was nothing to do; to be bitten or to fall 30 feet into the ravine, that was the choice.

The other plane was attacking, and one could not scramble up the bank. *Pump-pump-pump.* As the plane dived, Chicagonews changed hands, putting the ant-covered hand on his head and grasping a bush with the other. The bush hand was covered with red ants too, and they began stinging scalp and hand simultaneously as the bomb began dropping, monotonously calling— in Japanese—the undecipherable name of its enemy.

Not the bomb, the bombs.

There were two, and they fell in two double beats beyond the battalion's villa, too far away even for jumps in the river.

The Japs saw that they had missed; probably there was a curse exchanged in the cockpit. The rear gunner pumped his gun steadily as long as he was in range. The other two planes, ahead, were already coming down the railroad line, turning this way and that to see what they could find, coming to peer at the rubber godowns and send shells into the freight cars. They ignored the bridge over the ravine. The Japanese never bombed railroad bridges; they envisaged them as being of greater importance all the way to the causeway at Singapore, the most important of all.

Nobody was hurt. The bombs were wasted and the cannonfire was wasted and the machine-gun fire was wasted. But in hurting through delay, the raid was successful. Such patrols held up convoys. This the Japanese could have done almost as well by being close overhead without shooting, breathing down everyone's necks. Later they spared their ammunition.

This raid, extended infinitely in time and space and intensified in both, might be taken as a symbol of what was happening to thousands of men all over the Malayan front. Wherever the British made a fixed position, they were photographed from the air and quickly thereafter machine-gunned and bombed. There were no aircraft available. Many men fought for six weeks without seeing a single Allied plane, just as they fought for days without seeing a Japanese afoot.

Calculating by speed and time of flight, it seemed as though the 26 bombers would be over Kuala Lumpur in about an hour's flying time. Thus they could be expected back in about two hours. The party started south to overtake the trouble.

The first badly smashed place was Tanjong Malim. Seeing a supply train in the station, the Japanese broke their rule about leaving railroads un- harmed. Smashed by a direct hit, the train had buckled back like a mur- dered snake dead in mid-coil. The locomotive and end cars were on the rails; those in between had twisted away.

The bombs had been heavy. There were holes through all the station's windows. The sign hung from the iron girders of the pedestrians' overpass from one side of the station to the other was sagging on one hook. It read: *Persons are warned to look both ways at the approach of a train.* There were three or four dead and some wounded. "Come on, let's get cracking," said Steel. The party climbed back into its vehicles, placed its spotters with binoculars on the roofs, and started off again.

It grew cloudy, and there were a few showers. The roads were not crowded as at Ipoh. The Malays seemed to be intelligent enough to push into the rubber rather than flee south to the catchpot of Singapore. Rural populations are more self-reliant than urban ones, who flee from town to city to metropolis, hoping to hide where the swarm is greatest. The coun- try's empty ceiling is broader and safer.

The Malays and the Chinese loaded what they could on bicycles or wag- ons and disappeared humbly rubberward. Only the Eurasians and the na- tive clerk class of pen-pushers went toward Singapore, sometimes by train, sometimes in wheezing automobiles. A slightly intoxicated middle-aged English planter was driving a low-slung black roadster around in circles in a deserted village crossroads, muttering to himself. "Which way to the front, boys?" he cried. "That way or *that* way?"

"That way," the retreating party answered, pointing toward Singapore.

"I doubt it," he said under his breath. Seeming to remember something, he got out and bent his flushed face over his gasoline gauge and peered at his tires. "Wife and kids left long ago," he said out of the corner of his mouth to nobody in particular.

Malaya was prepared for only one kind of attack: a full-scale offensive by an old-fashioned armada of destroyers, cruisers, and dreadnoughts entering Singapore's mine fields. It seemed impossible that the enemy would refuse to do the act which every preparation had made perilous for him, and would seek another way.

A delaying action like the British withdrawal through the Malay Peninsula deserves to be called deliberate only if the delay is fully exploited. The Greek campaign may be considered a delaying action for the defense of Crete, just as the withdrawal across France may be considered a delaying action for the defense of England. But England could have been taken then had the Nazis dared, and Crete was taken. Is the history of Allied defeats one of withdrawal where the defenders have failed to exploit the interval they have gained?

Americans have hitherto understood politics as a science of relationship between peoples. Strategy, inseparably connected with formations of land and water, has always remained vague and abstract in their minds. At the Imperial conference in June, 1918, at which the British Empire decided the apportionment of colonies when the Germans were to be defeated, there was no American representation. Thereafter at the peace conferences Woodrow Wilson, while giving away to Japan without protest the Mariana, Caroline, and Marshall archipelagoes—thus creating between America and the Philippines the screen of Japanese defenses that were to make MacArthur's pleas for help unanswerable—spent his time quarreling over Papua with the adroit William Hughes, Premier of Australia. "You don't understand Papuans, Mr. President," said Uncle Billy. "They don't want plebiscites. Up in Papua, people eat each other." Wilson, whom Uncle Billy once described to Chicagonews as "a man of mulish obstinacy," knew as little of his country's political stake in Asia as most of his countrymen did a generation later.

—

PROBLEMS OF CENSORSHIP

Having been to the jungle front, one saw the inevitableness of the British retreat. Nowhere was the withdrawal disorderly or panicky. But the movement was too fast to offer any truly delaying resistance to the Jap.

Now Chicagonews experienced a sensation strange to a war correspondent—he did not wish to meet the leaders of his own forces. In a way, they were speaking to him, as to the public, through the communiqués.

Understatement depends for its force upon there being somewhere a catalytic agency speaking the whole gravity of the situation. At Singapore this should have been the correspondents. But it was too late for plain speaking; it could no longer be allowed with safety to the forces.

The British generals were not actually as much like ostriches as they seemed from afar. But when the Japs hit, it was too late for the truth to keep Singapore free.

The reluctant recognition that Malaya could not be reinforced and Singapore would probably not hold must have been made in the first fortnight of January, when General Pownall was transferred back to Java, there to submerge quietly and perhaps not wholly reluctantly beneath new Allied staff announcements and the reshuffle of the Southwest Pacific Command. There was a feeling for a newspaperman that those who were intelligent knew that Singapore would be lost and could not say so, those less intelligent thought it might be held and would affirm it with a confidence far out of proportion to their actual beliefs, and the Governor would simply predict it would be held. Under these circumstances it became embarrassing to visit Singapore's leaders—embarrassing because their views could not be expressed in print without adding to the spirit of error which characterized much journalism in wartime, and betraying the journalist's obligation to the people he informs. It is not much better to be silent than to lie. But when all tongues are bound by crisis, and there is no hope of revealing the truth even if one hears it, perhaps it is a little better. The "Singapore will be held" of the military changed, as it always does, to "Singapore must be held." Generals and admirals, quite properly, sometimes say retreat but never say surrender.

What was the use of visiting public men with the appetite of journalism when they too were imprisoned in a situation where they could not speak the truth without being accused of pessimism or defeatism? Let them alone with their consciences, their deciphered signals, their dossiers, and their in-baskets and out-baskets. Men at work, do not disturb. Wavell himself never gave a press conference or even received formally any newspapermen. One or two who knew him, like the sensitive and courageous Ian Morrison of the *London Times,* stole a word with him when he came up from Java briefly to visit the front. He was noncommittal. It was against the code even to say he was in Malaya until after he left, and unlawful to quote him. Wavell was serving as the boy at the dike while waiting for the United States to take over the Pacific, and he knew it. As the retreat went on, the amount anybody could truthfully say shrank in proportion with the distance between the "line" and the Strait of Johore.

There was a discussion by correspondents with the military after the causeway was blown, when the red-balled bombers began to appear daily and nightly. General Percival* said: "Today we stand beleaguered in our island fortress"—he did not speak of siege. The censors hated the word, saw that inevitably it would be used, and were determined to hold it off, as though it were Japanese, to the last minute.

Nearly every ship that left southward was bombed. The air was completely in Japanese hands. Yet the censors still blue-penciled "siege."

At this time the Japanese used to threaten to drop parachutists on Singapore Island; they never did so, but only because they were moving southward too rapidly by other means. Today any area, whether surrounded by water or land, is fortified only when it has both fighter and interceptor aircraft. The land or sea approaches had become the equivalent, after Crete, of the portcullises of the castle. It is always possible to scale the walls downward with parachutes as one once scaled them upward with ladders. But there were words that Singapore dreaded, and one was *siege*. To the censors this still meant a surrounding. The earthbound military refused to realize that when you have lost control of the air on all sides you are surrounded.

After the causeway was blown, the troops having retreated across it, there was a conference which would have made Noah Webster smile in the pressroom at the tall Cathay building—the thirteen-story Cathay riding the sea of Oriental three-deckers. "Can we refer now to the 'siege of Singapore' as having begun?" the correspondents wanted to know. The army's strategist-lexicographer hesitated. The enemy were mounting artillery in Japanese estates on the shores of Johore; it was a matter of hours, perhaps minutes, before the very room in which the correspondents were sitting, fully exposed to observation posts, would be under Japanese shellfire. But had Singapore's siege begun? The military censor did not like to think so.

---

*Lieutenant General Arthur E. Percival, operational commander of the British army.

"I still don't like that word," he said. "I still don't think it's justified."

There was a burst of expostulation.

"But surely you can't deny that we are besieged," said someone.

"Besieged, yes," said the military censor, "but I object to the noun 'siege.' "

"We cannot say that 'the siege of Singapore has begun.' Can we say that 'Singapore is now besieged'?"

The censor nodded. "Yes, I will pass 'besieged.' *But I still don't like the word 'siege.' "*

At least one newspaperman who missed the conference, and could not seem to get the hang of this rule even after his colleagues patiently explained it to him, led his dispatch off with "The siege of Singapore has begun." The next morning, when shells were dropping on the island, he received his censored carbon back, and it read "The besiegement of Singapore has begun." Naturally "besiegement" was changed in London and New York back to "siege," the cable editors reasonably considering that this was a time for plain language.

Perhaps more frankness of mind would have helped, and perhaps not. The British still seemed to believe that they were bluffing the Japs. As the conservative *Straits Times* rudely put it, they were not successfully bluffing even themselves. There was also a latent and baseless fear of Malays and Chinese running loose in race riots if the truth were told them. Actually, during Singapore's disintegration nothing unlawful occurred beyond petty pillage that would be normal in any country under the same circumstances, and an ordinarily well-disciplined Malay policeman whistled at a white woman. Singapore's Asiatics were ready to face the truth.

Considering into the bargain the Eurasian air-raid wardens and bank clerks, the Chinese and Hindu debris-cleaners, the blood-givers of every race and age, and considering the great swarm of the bereaved through the heavy bombing raids when Singapore was provided no fighter defense whatever and the official figures for a single raid were 453 dead and 1100 injured—considering all this, the balance of behavior is so far on the side of the Asiatics that nothing more can be said.

It is difficult to mention the military, naval, and RAF censors temperately. They held the correspondents' noses fast to the grindstone of the communiqués, even when the communiqués were two to three days behind the facts. The idea was that if a place was admitted lost, the enemy would move through it faster and with less caution. It was not an imaginative concept.

It was never clear whether the military censors were superior to the Governor's two civil appointees, Duckworth and Fearon, who topped the staff of robot censors beneath. Some were ferocious; a particular practice was to cut the leading paragraph off a narrative then send it 10,000 miles away to enter the newspaper office headless, its statement of topic, place, and circumstances amputated, a victim of amnesia.

The newspaperman's malady is to accept the inhibitions of a bad censorship and to discourage himself by precensoring his work. A good correspondent has a lively sense of responsibility, but guards himself against any feeling that he is an apologist, whether for groups, officials, or attitudes. The Singapore censorship made semiapologists out of a great many through fear of being disaccredited by the London War Office, an ever-present weapon on British territory.

The first of many disagreeable events was the imprisonment of Thomas Fairhall, a thirty-year-old correspondent for the *Sydney Daily Telegraph,* who on Christmas Eve was thrown into jail for some observations about the military situation he had received on a visit to Australian troops. The message had been censored both militarily and politically, and passed. But after an inquiry from Canberra, the military used several Intelligence officers to induce him to name his source. Fairhall refused, and was released on Christmas afternoon.

Next, the War Office ordered Major Fisher to disaccredit E. R. Noderer of the *Chicago Tribune,* who describes himself as "a little guy with glasses." An energetic reporter, after covering Dunkirk from the German side he left Berlin for Cairo. In Malaya, Noderer managed to get bombed and machine-gunned more than almost any other correspondent. It was embarrassing for Major Fisher to have to tell him the War Office had deprived him of the privileges of the war zone. Everyone, even the censors, did his best to try to persuade the War Office to forgive the isolationist *Chicago Tribune,* but the War Office did not forgive. The reasons given for Noderer's dismissal were that he had never reported to the Cairo authorities (not true), that his Iran dispatches were unfavorable to British interests, and that press accommodations were overcrowded. The reasoning was like Singapore itself: inept, but hopeless to correct. No pleas had any effect. The London order stayed, as London's orders do.

There were at the time twenty-nine radio and newspaper correspondents in Singapore, of whom seven were feeding American outlets. Thus the United States, vital as its interests were in Singapore, received its non-British information through seven fallible human beings: Noderer, Harold Guard of the United Press, Yates McDaniel of the Associated Press, Tillman Durdin of the *New York Times,* Cecil Brown of the Columbia Broadcasting System, Martin Agronsky of the National Broadcasting Company, and George Weller of the *Chicago Daily News.*

Then came the third step: Cecil Brown, who served *Life* magazine and was correspondent for *Newsweek* as well as for the C.B.S., a regularly British-accredited correspondent who had suffered expulsion from Italy for his struggles against the censorship there, also found his accreditation canceled.

All three cases were thrusts at American information, because Fairhall's newspaper had entered into an agreement with *Time.* This move left four American newspapermen and one broadcaster providing news from Singapore. There was still the question of whether America should send naval help in spite of Britain's loss of air control over Malaya. Following Pearl Harbor, America was no longer neutral, but a full-time belligerent; the obligation of informing the American public honestly was getting greater as the quantity of news shrank and the quality deteriorated.

Brown, a tall and likable drink of water, pressed a little too hard on the weak spots to be popular with the authorities. He had gone on a gratuitous lecture tour of British jungle camps before the war and made a characteristic journalist's mistake of trying to mend matters by working upon the military rather than the public. So much depends in military life upon morale that criticism is liable to wound some frail characters. After the line began falling back, some officers who returned from the front thought his predictions too exact to be innocent. For a time Brown teamed with Odie Gallagher of the *Daily Express* in trying to break through with tidings of what was happening. Gallagher finally gave up and went to Burma; Brown remained. Living with him and Martin Agronsky at the home of two men of the Texaco Oil Company, Chicagonews followed their querulous battle and listened for the snap as each nerve string parted. Brown and Agronsky got along well enough with Duckworth and Fearon, but with the subordinate censor they were similar to caged animals trained by torture. In this censor's office there was a kind of hurricane fence erected from ceiling to wall. The censors, who included several women, were locked in. Their desks were at the end of a great dark room artificially illuminated even by day. Through the fence one saw only women, pencils upraised to pounce.

When Brown and Agronsky tried to write tame pieces they would have to wait for the underling censors to communicate with superiors. This exasperated them. Often in the afternoon they could be seen clinging to the hurricane fence—their wailing wall—pleading for someone to listen to their troubles. Agronsky, a heavily built athlete, looked like a distraught orangutan; Brown resembled, stretched against the wire, a Russian wolfhound. "Can't someone come to the screen and talk this over in a friendly way?" Agronsky would cry in forceful Brooklynese. Not a head would turn. Brown would drop his long arms from the bars of the cage and moan: "It's no use, Martin, it's no use. Forty million listeners don't matter. They just don't matter."

It was never possible to ascertain exactly why Brown was disaccredited. Nobody claimed he had tried to evade censorship. His messages went under the eyes of the authorities; they had been responsible for what he was allowed to say. A strong hint was dropped that he was being punished for matter whose submission indicated he was not disposed as he should have been. Not all the correspondents, not even all the Americans, rallied to his defense; there was no aggressive defense even from his home organization. Brown's expulsion coincided with a severe article in *Life,* passed by censorship, in which he described the Malayan campaign. It was evident Singapore would fall, and the authorities might more adroitly have held their move against him. But they did not, and said that curbing him had been under consideration for weeks.

A publisher had already signed Brown for a book on his Far Eastern experiences, and Chicagonews saw him off in a Qantas flying boat. In Batavia the Dutch authorities, exercised about his effect on morale, would not consent to his broadcasting. From Soerabaya Brown flew to Darwin, then back to the United States. The free press in the Empire were more eager than any American organization to hear his story; both the *Express* and the

Sydney Telegraph offered him a chance to tell his side, and even to pay him. Not wishing to have a *succès de scandale,* he refused.

A year before, under the misapprehension that American diplomats were qualified to regulate the country's press, Duckworth—a man of integrity—had come to an understanding with the U.S. consul general by which American correspondents, in return for having their dispatches discussed rather than censored without right of appeal, were to hold secret all matters concerning the Singapore censorship. None of the correspondents in Singapore had ever heard of this agreement.

Military censorship always ends by being political. Since in a military sense Singapore had very little to conceal except the location of its big gun emplacements, its ammunition stores, and its gasoline dumps, and was, in the plain words of the *Straits Times,* "a bluff," the censorship had to be turned around and begin by being political in the guise of being military. In other words, it had to sustain the illusion that Singapore was adequately fortified. This meant no one could say that Singapore was not adequately fortified. Perhaps one might do a little guarded carping, but an out-and-out flat denial that worthwhile defenses existed was out of the question.

Censorship was necessary before the war ever opened, not to conceal what was there, but to simulate what was lacking. A censorship is supposed to keep political criticism under control. Is there any point at which a correspondent would be hauled before the authorities for being too optimistic? It never occurred to any correspondents in Singapore to attempt this unusual experiment by filing a dispatch that outbuttered the most complacent greasers of public opinion, that brought together all the paper armies, typewriter machine guns, and handout airplanes used to pooh-bah the enemy and insomnify the public. Perhaps they should have done so.

Getting back a dispatch from which everything had been slashed except the little reservations that showed the situation was not entirely hopeless, one American correspondent contemplated building a great dispatch of all these inanities, molding them into a big paper ball, and rolling it down the Strait of Johore the evening after the causeway was blown. "Singapore can and will be held," the message would begin, then it would roll on and on.

Can a critic, a war correspondent for example, be more fatheaded than the authorities? No one ever heard of a public statement so gooeyly optimistic that before being fed to the public it stuck in the censor's throat.

Words, words, words. But these were words to remember. Those tiresome discussions in the Cathay involved the principles for which people were offering all they had, blood and sweat, tears and toil. The American and British peoples were fighting to be informed. They did not want to be fooled. They wanted to hear the truth. They could take it.

It is through knowing the truth that the people discover their hidden will.

—

THE RAIDS

After the first heavy raid, when the sign *They can't stop our clock* was hung up opposite the Victoria Theatre, the broken fuselage of a navy Zero was left on the lawn of the Cricket Club. Most of the club's windows had been smashed. It seemed impossible, touching this doll plane, that this small fuselage possessed the margin between holding and losing Singapore. The tail was so tiny it seemed rather to belong to a child's wagon made to imitate an airplane than to the real thing.

The Zero was made to be fought and used up quickly; whether the Jap pilots were meant to live or die, their planes were designed to fight hard, never to be repaired, but only replaced, and to perish soon. Chicagonews talked with two pilots who had fought Zeros, and they said: "The Japs are afraid to dive them, because their wings come off, but they can outmaneuver us. What really counts is being able to turn inside the Jap. We can't do that yet." The Zero was a butterfly, and looked like one, but in this case the butterfly had a vicious sting. A plane which can "turn inside" another plane, by a single simple loop, can turn itself from prey into pursuer, dealing death where it was taking it two seconds before.

Airdrome control is like checkers; every move is felt in its consequences all the way back along the line. After Singapore became untenable, the Japanese raiders exploited every scrap of advantage they knew they had. Their schedule was simple. They merely calculated the fighting time of the Hurricanes over Singapore plus the length of fuel time needed to return to

Palembang. Then they would lead meager defensive fighters on a chase all over the island—high-speed climbing is a devourer of fuel—and when the Hurricanes were forced to turn home, the bombing of Kalang and Thailand would start. The Hurricanes could either land under the bombing and be destroyed, or make for Palembang and be ineffective. The British could not meet this attack by dividing their forces, because they were too few.

A raid by day was as different from a raid by night as man from woman. Singapore was the first gratuity of the war to suffer regular bombing by day and by night, something more than London ever endured. Furthermore, it was ceaselessly under the threat of invasion. That threat was two-dimensional: it could come across the water or it could drop through the great sea of air above.

Raids by day are costly, because they usually involve the loss of many bombers. But they pay off heavily. When directed against a great city they either tie up all its affairs completely or they slow them down so greatly that it amounts to paralysis. The human being awakens in the morning alive, rested, full of vitality, and open to new impressions. If the first flush of the day's activity is dampened by a scurried flight to an air-raid shelter, if the whistle and stamp of bombs and the great shudder of the earth beneath them are the opening chord of his day, subsequent work will be carried on slowly, vaguely, and with a kind of absence of mind.

It is possible to take a raid calmly, and to rationalize the required concessions to the fear of the mind. But the fear remains in the body. The body is still fearful when the mind is either courageous or resigned. The body in this hour is more timid than the mind, for though the mind says "Your chances of escape are ten thousand to one," the body responds, "Yes, but that ten-thousandth chance is annihilation. I am near Death, and I know it. And it is a Death which is not coming from within the body, but a brutal stranger falling out of the sky upon my head. This Death does not meet me walking down the street or in a quiet room; he falls on me suddenly, carelessly, indifferent whether now or later, whether it is myself or someone else. The great indiscrimination of this tumbling Death, this purposeless designation as to whether he kills me or someone else—this is what makes air warfare terrible."

At first the revolt of the body, directed against the induced calm of the

mind, is hard to take. The body rebelling against the unnaturalness of this
kind of war has no shame. Pulses beat in the throat that never were felt before. The eyebrows contract with premonition. The voice falls to a whisper,
as though the enemy could hear. (Some Chinese believed the Jap pilots
could not only hear but see them.)

The final indignity is this: The fearful bowels, where the Greeks rightly
situated the terrible emotions, turn and give up holding power, and finally
abjectly yield. It cannot be denied: the body is unreasonable, but it is afraid.
For the first underground shelters in London to have been without toilet
facilities was a neglect the importance of which only those who have seen a
large number of frightened people can understand. Water was always lacking in Singapore after the siren sounded; the demand was too great for the
big pipeline from Johore.

The Singapore sirens placed all over the city, from the police station on
Bukit Timah Road to the top of the Cathay, were the usual rising and
falling wailers. It is astonishing that the Allies criticize the fear-making
whistles attached to German and Japanese bombs while committing a deed
of terrorism against their own populations with the unholy banshee cry of
warning. The siren's moan has in it something that does not merely inform, but terrifies, preying on the public nerves. What is needed is a siren
equivalent to someone stepping up and saying quietly: "Let's look around
for a bit of cover, shall we?" rather than "Here they come—run!"

Over Singapore, after feinted raids started around eight o'clock, the
real thing would begin about ten, usually from 25 to 27 planes flying
tightly in an open V. (An American flier who underwent raids at Nichols
Field told Chicagonews it was "the most nearly perfect formation flying I
have ever seen, including our own.") There was a high degree of organization in the Japanese squadron, all aircraft depending strictly upon signal
by hand or radio from the leading bomber. The Japanese strive to lay the
same V-shaped scheme upon their target as they maintain in the air. This
is pattern bombing. If the sights taken by the leading bombardier are accurate, the target will be obliterated by the other aircraft. In bombing,
each takes the signal from the one ahead, and the Japanese are experts at
this coordination.

It is hard to express a raid in words. A raid is at once more terrifying
than a description, and less so. Singapore had piled sandbags before its

downtown arcades. Behind the mighty granite of its bank buildings anyone could be protected against splintered hits. But by daylight women and children are not downtown. And it was in the homes of the poor down the waterfront near Kalang, and in the hundreds of flats and tenements along the North Bridge Road, that most deaths occurred. It was terrible to see humanity, confused, lost, shelterless, hacked down by the bombs.

And not only humanity was outraged; every living thing felt the ordeal. Particularly pitiful were bomb-shocked animals, unwounded—dogs and cats, pet monkeys, and parrots with their eyes staring from their heads, glittery with terror, clinging to the earth with frightened claws, sometimes unable to recognize owners who had been the whole world of their affection a few minutes before.

North Bridge Road lay parallel with the Singapore waterfront, three blocks back from the harbor. Here lived all the girl jitterbugs who helped support families with what they brought home from the cabarets. Some with country relatives moved to the villages in the western part of the island, putting notices in the personal columns: "Miss Dolly How Cheng informs her friends and clients of the New World cafe that she is absenting herself for a short sojourn in the country." The reason frequently was that Dolly's home was now a cascade of bricks and mortar, with the face of the little shop across the street punched in like that of a battered witness.

The Air Raid Protection was the most efficient organization in Singapore; its Chinese, Indian, and Malay youths worked with authority, speed and courage, and there was common sense hidden under their plain grey steel helmets. "If I want the most efficient in Singapore," said an Australian officer, "I go first to the Scotsmen, then the Chinese." Japanese bombers would fly the length of the waterfront pumping long sticks of bombs onto North Bridge Road, where there were no shelters, not even the six-foot-deep stone culverts that lined parts of the Bund and Orchard Road.

The only really efficient shelter in Singapore was the ramp of the Cathay, and it was always thick with squatting grandmothers in black, little boy babies, and Chinese mothers with faces white with rice powder. Malays rarely sheltered there.

For one who went through most of the raids in Room 32 at the Raffles, the moment of greatest tension came when the rooftop watcher, the irascible engineer of the hotel, blew four whistles from the cupola above. This meant the droning silver planes were practically overhead, and their leader was making the decision that meant life or death. The lookout had some peculiar ideas; one was that the church behind the Raffles had been placed to make a line with its spire directing bombers to the Cathay. This would have been like a cricket pointing his antenna at an elephant.

The slow crunch of bombs as they marched up the street was unforgettable. It sounded like a giant walking. Once two big ones landed in the rear of the Raffles, plastering against the wall the Indian porter who frequently carried the dispatches of Chicagonews to the telegraph office. There was little of him to be found, but what there was the other porters gathered up in a cloth, the engineer standing nearby, his dusty sleeves rolled to his elbow, as the elderly bellboys carried away their comrade. A black cat that prowled around the washhouse was shriveled, its skin stretched taut. There had been no fire; only complete disemboweling of the buildings in the rear.

If one can see the planes in the blue sky, and observe the direction of their flight, one can say either "They can't get me on this run" or "It may be mine this time." Either way, the tension is short. But a daytime raid was a continuous ordeal from the first rising sigh of the warning siren to the last all-clear. From the rational strategist in the operations room of the fighter base to the terrified mother, lying perhaps in the maternity room of the hospital with her baby beside her, all feel alike a sense of being made ignoble by helplessness to retaliate. There is a degradation in being bombed, and that selfish "Thank God they're hitting someplace else" rising from within ignores that the whole body of humanity is vulnerable.

Indeed, no one who has heard a bomb land nearby even in countryside can doubt that the earth itself revolts against the unfair and unnatural blow; there is a protest, a muffled shudder of revulsion, in the tremor even when a bomb lacerates only wet and open earth. Half the raids upon Singapore were made when the whole island was covered with the thick mist of the monsoon. Even had bombers dared to descend to 500 feet, they could have seen nothing of their target. Perhaps they came over hoping to find rifts that would enable them to aim, but when no rifts appeared, they dumped their bombs through the rain, sometimes accurately, sometimes indiscriminately. Especially in a rainstorm there is something about being bombed that debases the whole human race. It seems pure unaimed hatred; the striker has not the faintest notion where his victim is, and seems to care not who he is.

One day from the terrace in front of Room 32, Chicagonews watched a heavy raid in the middle of a slashing rain. The engineer on the roof, soaked to the skin, shouting wild orders down into the courtyard, had no idea where the bombers were and was blowing his whistle like a distraught policeman. The bombs were falling; you could hear them biting into the waterfront, kicking into the houses with a noise like a big boot kicking a bass drum. The rain spattered on the black pavement and went hissing and whispering through the deep gutters where the coolies, their rickshaws carelessly upended against the buildings, stood knee-deep in the cold running water, huddled down against the sideways flash of the bomb. A great smoking hole was open in the sidewalk; nearby an automobile that had puffed into flame slowly burned up blackly through the raindrops.

And in the middle of the rain-washed street, quite alone and neatly placed together, was a pair of coolie's sandals. Why had this unknown coolie, having run all his life in those sandals, thought in the last moment that he could now flee faster in his bare feet? Abandoned in the shining black street with the water running all around them, they seemed like the empty sandals of all humanity. They remained there side by side while the bombs fell and while, in the languid tropical way that slowed down everything but the bombs, the rain continued falling and falling.

The most terrible death tolls, like the 453 killed and 1100 known wounded already noted, were mostly the work of sunlit raids. Sometimes when there were fewer dead it seemed more tragic; it is easier to realize what 9 deaths mean than 90. A single raid on the Bund wounded 135, mostly workmen, and killed 56. Three days later, January 21, the bloody totals were 304 dead, 725 wounded.

Beside the naked day raids, the night raids were almost sporting affairs. The Japanese tried to murder the city's sleep and in a measure they succeeded. But the defense had its effect. Unless blinded by clouds or by the radiance of the moon that makes the sky a milky pearlish opacity, the searchlights quickly found the Japanese. There were one or two night fighters based on Kalang, but the heavy day raids soon chopped them up. After that it was anti-aircraft guns versus high-level bombers.

At night the Japanese bombed only in good weather and were able to ori-

ent their attacks upon the four airdromes and the naval base by the twinkling waters of Johore Strait and the harbor. Bombs falling by night claimed
fewer lives, because many workers had gone by bus to their homes in outlying kampongs and kangkars (Chinese villages), which unless they were near
the naval base rarely received hits. At night these little villages became isolated when the great sirens in downtown Singapore were heard moaning
across the dark roads and valleys of the island. But by night transport went
on, trucks groping across the island taking supplies toward the causeway up
to the front, and there were no crowds downtown to be terrified. Night was
the dark coverlet that seemed both to excuse the indiscrimination of the invaders' bombing and to soften the victims' apprehension of it.

The game in the sky, up among the sharp stars, was enthralling. But the
Japanese never tried spectacular stunts like the Luftwaffe over Greece,
where one had seen a harried pilot, cornered in a persistent searchlight,
dive straight down the blinding beam, firing tracer bullets until it sputtered out. There were no man-to-man duels over Singapore. The Japanese
kept at fingertip length from the searchlights. There are few things so
beautiful to see as a perfect maypole of them, with streamers coming in
from every circumference to meet in a crowning halo, within which moves
the steadfast attacker, while starry death twinkles in the sky, and the earth
lifts and shakes with the upward-leaping shells, and finally with the total
thunder of the fallen bombs. Sometimes the air plays strange tricks, and
one feels a pushing thrust in the face from far off before the grunting impact is heard.

Even after the bombs dropped it was not quite over, for the lights held
the planes, banking slowly away, which did not break formation. Still in
their tight V, still held loosely by the beams from below, they faded into the
iridescent moonlight, evaporating away till the searchlights winked off. One
woman found the perfect image for the appearance of a Japanese formation
in a searchlight. "It was like a silver brooch hung in the sky," she said.

When a plane was hit by night, there was no flaming torch; rather there
was a momentary gap in the V as one member fell back and was lost in the
darkness. The next moved up into position, so one had to keep counting the
bombers over and over again to be sure how many the antiaircraft guns
had brought down.

Moonless nights were ordinarily without heavy raids, but the Japanese tried to deprive the city of sleep by sending over planes in pairs every two hours, creating a continuous alert. In this way they sought to map the anti-aircraft defenses at low expense and find out where the immovable search-lights were. This effort failed, because after the siege began the salient searchlights of Singapore were dragged to the northern shores of the island to illuminate the crossing of the Japanese troops. And there the search-lights, those great moon-faced creatures that had served so well, met their end, smashed by Japanese artillery and mortars firing at a range of a mile.

Counting up aircraft lost in battles over Singapore gave little indication of the true losses, because 5 or 10 planes were lost on the ground for every one in the air.

For several days the people of Singapore were dying faster than the people of London in the Blitz. Open graves were dug each day in the cemetery, awaiting those who would be killed by explosives that were even then being loaded upon Japanese bomb racks in Kuala Lumpur and Sungei Patani. Whoever thinks that Singapore's people were anything less than noble may keep in mind that more people died in the four heaviest raids than in two years of bombing of Malta, and twice as many were wounded in a single raid as the 583 "seriously injured" in Malta's first two years.

In the hundreds of mourning Malay homes, the words of Mohammed for the dead were read. On little altars in the Chinese homes Pu-tai, the laughing Buddha with the fat creased belly and almost audible merriment, was a god to whom the wounded could no longer turn. The Chinese not only hate the Japanese; they despise them, and laugh at them. But it was not a time for laughter. It was a time, every other recourse having failed, to turn to Kuan Yin, the goddess of Mercy, "She who looks down and hears the cries of the world." The Chinese, the tin-miners and the houseboys, the baby-loving amahs and the swing-loving taxi dancers, in their temples and in their homes were calling on Kuan Yin to hear the cries of Singapore.

Earlier the Japs had announced that large numbers of Indian troops had surrendered and were fighting the British. This was a somewhat awk-ward build-up for an ambush the next day, when the enemy dressed as In-dians and approached the British lines crying "Do not shoot, we are friends!" The radio-planned disguise was a new one. In spite of help from the Penang radio station (which, left undemolished, was sending Japanese propaganda a day after Penang fell), the attack was a failure.

Sometimes, however, the Japanese, in order to lend efficacy to their constant radio threat of dropping parachutists on Singapore, would promise simpler things elsewhere and carry them out, a kind of institutional advertising to instill the idea that Nippon, like Gimbel's, always told the truth.

For example, Penang announced that in seventy hours from the broadcast, the hospital at Malacca would be bombed, and that if the British allowed their wounded to remain they would do so at their own risk. The hospital was bombed in seventy hours. They announced similarly that they were going to bomb the Johore hospital just north of the causeway, where many of the worst wounded cases from the front were concentrated and where many brave doctors and nurses remained behind. Right on time, they did so. No military purpose was served in either case, but by the announcement they thought they took the sting out of the atrocity while they built up institutional credit for doing what they promised, with the hope of winning more credence for their threats to drop parachutists on Singapore, which were lies.

The leaflet campaign was not open to description by correspondents for some reason vaguely related to morale. The leaflets were not precisely snowed down over the city, and probably most got lost. They were on cheap paper, colored to attract attention as they fluttered down, designed to ingratiate, to terrify, or to encourage "honorable surrender in a hopeless struggle." One had a picture of Japanese soldiers distributing gifts, cigarettes, food, and sweets to the Malay and Chinese populations. In the background, peeping timidly from behind a rubber tree, was a British soldier. One leaflet even asked the Chinese—who hated the Japs more intensely than did any other group—to illuminate their homes "to protect them from being bombed."

The Indian pamphlets showed Indians being wiped out in the front lines by Japanese bombing and mortar fire while behind the lines in far-off Calcutta, and at Singapore, British officers frolicked in safety and lust. Such propaganda might have had some effect on the Indian troops—though certainly never on the Gurkhas—were it not that most of them had seen their British officers die in the brow of battle.

The Japanese also went to work on that minority of Anglophobes present in any group of Australians. They dropped one pamphlet reading: *English not only name the Australian sheep farmer, but treat you as the*

*countryman and make you stand in the first line on the battlefield while be-
having as rearguards watching you fight and die.* It is doubtful whether
many were able to unscramble the ideas.

After the siege began, the responsive Yamashita* changed from threats
to baby and mammy themes. One photograph of a small chee-ild was cap-
tioned *Come home, Daddy, before it's too late.*

The troops on Singapore Island were tired and embittered by the lack
of aircraft support, but they were not yet ready to bite at such ham propaganda as this. They expressed what they felt, occasionally what they
thought, by scribbling something upon a wall. Walls not only have ears; to
political minds they sometimes have voices too. The *Daily Mail* said of
Malaya: "It is heart-breaking to reflect that so much might have been
saved by so little," and an Australian plodding back from Johore scrawled
upon the wall his weary rejoinder: "England for the English, Australia for
the Australians, but Malaya for any son-of-a-bitch who wants it."

—

CLEARING FOR BATTLE

One who believed that Malaya was all pampered wives and drunken
planters and complacent officials needed only to see the morning train of
evacuees from Kuala Lumpur coming into the station, disgorging worn-out
women with babies, followed by frightened amahs and bewildered children.
They had said goodbye to their husbands, who were fighting somewhere in
the Volunteers. They did not know where they were going next, and frequently received little help from the mining and rubber companies that had
employed their husbands. The government officials did well; exiled in Australia and India, they still drew heavy salaries before going on to new jobs
in the East and West African colonies. But for the planters little was done.

The Dutch in Singapore were self-possessed and cool and left no one behind, even bringing out two final planeloads in the last week of January.
Only a handful of Chinese ever got away; there was nowhere for them to go.

---

*Lieutenant General Tomoyuki Yamashita.

To give the Chinese a chance, Australia was induced to let down its barriers. Immigration for Malay's two million Chinese was restricted to fifty families annually; granted permission for a single year's stay, they had to offer as security enough funds for two years.

For months the Singapore widow was a familiar character in the planless unrolling of war in the Pacific. You found them everywhere, these wives who had stammered goodbye to their husbands amid hasty cautions about what to do with the silver, which houseboy should have the big radio, and where to address letters. They did not know when they would see their husbands again. They went off, sleeping in freighter holds with hundreds of other worried women and frightened children.

When they arrived in Java, the overcrowded Dutch put them up in convents and schools and did their best as invasion darkened over the islands. Then once again the wives had to go from one steamship office to another, the companies themselves unable to say when rescue ships would arrive because Japanese bombers and submarines were pounding them through Bangka Strait into the Java Sea. Things were rapidly approaching a pass where women and children would have to be dropped behind to carry the essential executive personnel of the war to be.

Few Singapore widows received letters from their husbands before the island fell. They were in doubt even whether their husbands had remained in Singapore. As the Japanese bombers intensified their attacks, they feared rather that their husbands had got away and gone down with one of the burning or exploding ships. Everything was anxiety and the uncertainty that makes for more anxiety. Most women had little money or none; though the unsung heroes of institutions like the Hong Kong and Shanghai Banking Corporation steadfastly telegraphed money southward, some was lost and some necessarily misdirected. Women and children who had left fathers in Ipoh saying they would go to India found themselves at the Singapore docks obliged to go to Java or not at all. Sometimes it was the other way round. But Colombo wanted as little of these refugees as did Java; they had to be sent from one back door of the war to another, sitting on stoops as long as they could before being pushed on, feeling the tether to a lost husband and father growing weaker and weaker, and eventually spreading themselves from Bombay to Capetown, London, and New York, and around the world from Perth to Auckland or Spokane to San Diego.

Far different, these pathetic fugitives, from those "refugees" of Central Europe whom one had seen playing for $100 greenbacks outside Lisbon, and who struggled and fought to have priority over American evacuees returning by plane—American Export line was not good enough—to the United States. The Singapore wives had no plans, and the last airborne clipper for California had left long ago. Perhaps those who were childless were the most pathetic; they drifted from clerical jobs with the U.N. headquarters outside Batavia to other jobs with the American Army and Navy in Australia. Few had training for office work, almost the only kind open. Although participation in the war effort can be exhilarating, the atmosphere of general headquarters—making war seem a problem of in-baskets and out-baskets—was not happy for such wives, their minds uneasy with their missing husbands.

Some sent their children to sheep stations or country schools in Australia; some tried to settle down in South Africa. They haunted the offices of the Malayan Far Eastern Information bureaus, much different from the institutions of propaganda they resembled by name. There you could learn by hearsay, when official sources were mum or uncooperative, which ships had been sunk and which had come through, whose husband or sweetheart had sent a last letter mentioning a precious name or two of the friends still with him, and alive. Then the Singapore widow could go to the boarding-house of the one who had received this news and hunt for the name of her husband, son, or lover in the letter of another Singapore widow.

Usually the information was far out of date. Noel Martin, say, whom one had once met at a party, thought he had seen your husband—or it might have been your husband's brother—in a Bren-gun carrier coming up toward Malacca about the third week in January. Noel had waved and shouted, but your husband—or brother-in-law—could not hear above the clatter. There had been many retreats; some had been cut off on the mainland, and some had fought on the island. Had the Japanese captured all those left in Sumatra? Perhaps they did and perhaps they did not. Where was he?

Men as well as women civilians went through the experiences of Singapore widows. There was the Chinese clerk at the transfer window of the Chartered Bank, which kept a Punjabi to knock down any European or Asiatic who tried to fight his way into the vaults when the air-raid siren sounded. This Chinese was in his fifties, bald, with the subdued face of a slave of documents. The Friday morning before the causeway was blown, the people—Australian, British, Malay, Dutch—were clotted close around his window, Chicagonews among them. The routine was maddeningly slow, as in all Far Eastern banks, but the crowd was patient. The Chinese wrote, took out tissuey carbons, rewrote them, signed, checked them, counterchecked them, wrote something extra special sideways in their margins and suddenly pushed them all violently away from him. Throwing up his hands in a completely un-Chinese way, he lifted his face to the people at the bars of his cage and cried passionately: "What am I doing here, will you tell me that? My house was bombed and destroyed last night. My young wife and I were in the shelter, and she had a miscarriage. I took her to the hospital this morning. I should not be here"—he pointed to the papers—"I cannot concentrate. I know this work is very important to do, I know you want to go away, but I cannot concentrate. What am I doing here, will you tell me that?"

No one moved, no one had anything to say, no one had an answer. Finally the Chinese took up his pen. There was moisture at the back of his eyes. He reached out and took a paper, any paper, from the pile. He looked at it seriously for a moment, but it was strange to him. Then, for the third time that morning, the siren went.

Slowly the Chinese clerk of Singapore put down his pen, and slipped like a rag from his stool. He followed the evacuees to the shelter under the vault.

Three months after Singapore fell, the Naval Intelligence officer at Fremantle received a visitor. He was a small man, probably unfit for military service, about fifty years old. He looked like the little men who are aged messenger boys, dishwashers, busboys, and pushers of rolling stretchers in hospitals, those who try to work up to be assistant bartenders and streetcar conductors.

"I want to get some information," he said, "about a ship. It's a ship that left Singapore for Ceylon in the first week of February. Look, I've got the name." He unfolded the piece of paper with the name of a ship penciled in another hand.

The Naval Intelligence officer read the name of the ship, but did not change expression. It was against the rules for him to give any answer. But sometimes you have to bend the rules. "Can you take it?" he said.

The little man looked him in the eye and nodded.

"She went down."

The little man did not move. Finally he picked up his hat.

"I think I'll go out," he said. "I think I need a beer."

He came back again in a few minutes. His step was not altogether steady.

"There's something I didn't tell you," he said. "My family was on that boat."

"What kind of family did you have?"

"I had the five kids and my wife." (He said them in reverse order, as the husband who has long been a father is liable to do.)

The Naval Intelligence officer did not know just how to put it. "We do not have any list of survivors from that one," he said.

"And it's almost three months now," said the man. "Is that right?"

The officer's eyes were mild. "Yes," he said.

"And still no survivor list?"

"Except for a lascar seaman on a raft."

The little man took his hat. "I guess there isn't much left for me to do," he said. "Not until I get out of these clothes." He put his hat at a wrong angle on his head. "Where do you go when you want to ask them to take you?"

He never came back. The Naval Intelligence officer does not know whether they took him. He could hardly have made a good sort of soldier. Perhaps they made him a storekeeper or a military watchman. A security job, the army would think, would be the right place for a small man, a man no longer young, whose dearest reasons for living slept forever, slept in each other's watery arms at the bottom of the dark well of the sea.

—

THE LAST STAND

When complete histories are written, the valiant fighting of the Indians will not be a lost chapter. The 9th and 11th Indian divisions, together with two battalions from the 6th Punjabis and one from the Southern Punjabis, fought intermittently all through the campaign, some with Indian officers, some with white, some with both. The Indians were everywhere, from when they backed the Argylls [Scots] in the early campaign to when they camped in the road below Caldecott Hill radio station, sleeping in trucks and using the same shelter from bombings as Chicagonews.

White officers of Indian regiments are in many cases the most liberal-minded of English forces, for they know that the Indian is a hard-bitten soldier. A member of a Gwalior regiment lost his rifle, a true crime. "Can I make amends in my own way?" he asked. Permission was granted. He crawled out in the night, bearing only his long knife. He came back with three rifles and seven Japanese ears.

The Indians suffered greatly through Japanese tanks and anti-tank fire. In armored cars they were withdrawn from roadhead to crossing to coast-line village, regrouped and resupplied, then attached and moved some-where else. The fact that it was impossible for a war correspondent to be with these troops and stand better than an even chance of getting back made the narratives of their courage so incomplete.

Better, but still only fragmentary, justice can be done to two battalions which held the frontal road blocks through the hardest days: the Gurkhas, and the Argylls and Sutherland Highlanders. Mile after mile the little men from Nepal in the highest mountains in the world, and the freckled Scots-men who had waited for battle for twenty-six months of draining tropical heat, held the "line" while the withdrawal proceeded. Not many of either battalion came through.

When the Australian force on the main road pushed fresh troops before the Japanese offensive, the hard-hit Gurkhas were beckoned to coastal po-sitions on the western shores of Johore, and the worn-out Argylls took up rear positions behind the line. This was the first breather for either. Five weeks of fighting, day and night, was behind them; the island's defense lay ahead. Such uninterrupted dive-bombing and machine-gunning has seldom been suffered for so long.

The Gurkhas were almost unmentioned throughout the war. Only by finding their one remaining major was Chicagonews able to uncover part of their story.

Since Kipling's day there has always been comradeship with the "John-nies" [Gurkhas]. Even though they do not speak the same language, the British soldier and the Johnny sit down, smoke, and gamble together. The mutual respect of fighting men has broken down racial barriers. Like the Maoris, the Gurkhas have never been beaten in the field. Proud to be Nepalese, they serve under the condition that they must always have British and never Indian officers; these officers in turn have an obligation to expose themselves to fire in the front lines with their troops, and do so. The Johnnies went into action in northern Malaya with not much more than Gurkha tradition to hold them up. "Please remember our men are little more than seventeen or eighteen," the major said. "They're in a strange climate, almost more oppressive to them than to a white man. Six months ago most had never seen a machine gun or a lorry, to say nothing of a tank. Furthermore, our own officers are new, and many have just been learning to speak Gurkhali and to tell a kukri from a bread knife."

The Gurkhas took the Japanese onslaught from Thailand in a series of bloody crossroads the length of Malaya. The Japanese had stored their tanks just across the border, where the single road comes in, and thanks to Thai complicity, were able to strike the Gurkhas with three light tanks led by a heavy tank. The Gurkhas still had their equipment and were able to knock out the first tank and thus delay the column. However, the Japs pressed onward, using more heavy tanks equipped with cannon and also mortars. The Gurkhas were obliged to fall back. Until the last moment they tried to hold bridges, but totally lacked aircraft support. "I give you my word that for five weeks we positively did not see a British aircraft of any kind," the major said.

At Simpong, where the Japanese were already slipping coastwise up the Kedah River, the Gurkhas established their headquarters in a duplex house with two large wings. Japanese fighters dropped a stick directly across the house. In one wing ten men were killed. In the center passage twenty-five were wounded. In the other wing four officers, the operations staff, were sitting in a room working over maps. The bomb came through the roof and landed in a far corner. Two walls were blown away, and the officers were left sitting in the open air, completely unmarked.

One beardless boy had both his legs blown off and was bleeding to death. The major leaned down and said: "You're a Gurkha, aren't you? What about a smile?" The boy just got a Gurkha smile going, but died before it was fully upon his face.

After falling back, the Gurkhas fought the rest of the campaign without gear. Their lorries, munitions and stores were gone. They had only machine guns and rifles. They depended on the Chinese for food, "and the Chinese never let us down."

One thing that astonished them was the minuteness with which the Japanese fighters pursued them. A single Army 97 would come down from as high as 5000 feet to kill a single man on an open stretch of road. Twice they fought for three days without getting any food of any kind, and the airplanes never left. The major said: "It wouldn't be so bad if they just machine-gunned and bombed us while we're eating and sleeping and trying to prepare positions. What I object to is their coming down to look at my maps and study my orders over my shoulder." The Japanese maintained a continuous flagellation over one Gurkha encampment for thirty hours.

There were never any boats to cross rivers on, and the bridges had long since been blown up on the withdrawal of the main body of troops. "It seemed as though we swam our way southward almost as much as we walked." Through 150 miles of Kedah and another 200 of Perak, from Ipoh halfway to Kuala Lumpur, the Gurkhas fought their little-known, never celebrated rear-guard defense. Their most terrible ordeal awaited them in the middle of Malaya. They pitched their camp south of the Slim River, in a hairpin curve where a rubber estate was three-quarters encircled by a loop in the main highway. Japanese planes hugging the tops of the trees kept them under observation. The machine-gun fire from overhead had been slackening, and the colonel in charge took this as a sign that no attack was imminent. Other troops still held with Bren-gun carriers the road on the north side of the river. By now the Gurkhas were so accustomed to being machine-gunned by planes all day that any pause seemed a vacation. Men and officers sprawled out for a delicious hour of rest.

Then someone heard the rattling of tanks on the highway.

"Sounds like Bren-gun carriers coming up," said one officer.

But he was wrong. It was eight Japanese tanks coming *down*. They had pierced the road block north of the river, run across the unblown bridge, and with the aircraft to guide them were now sent to annihilate the Gurkha headquarters.

They took their time. They ran tanks halfway around the loop, then shifted the turrets round to aiming positions. Not bothering to be evasive, they called out an occasional "Banzai!" They even delayed long enough to hang a Rising Sun flag on the lead tank. These formalities having been carried out in the best taste of *bushido,* they fired shells through the unprotected rubber. English officers and Gurkhas were caught. All they could do was lie behind trees barely ten inches in diameter. As the men crawled, it was like shooting rabbits at 100 yards. Occasionally the Japanese amused themselves by machine-gun fire. Finally they decided the job was finished, and started out of their tanks. Suddenly a grenade whizzed, and exploded against a tank. The Japs hastily jumped in, and resumed fire. More trees were smashed to bits. The wounded and dying lay on all sides. Nine more Jap tanks arrived and joined in.

After a while some tanks went on southward. There was nothing to stop their going on to Singapore except the selfless bravery of an ordinary sergeant-major of an artillery battery in the rear. On his own initiative he had a single 18-pounder dragged out to the middle of the road, in full fire of the Japanese force, and stood by his breech. He stopped the tanks, and paid for doing so by his life. The captain of the artillery battery, who had his left arm entirely shot off and three fingers of his right hand shot away as well as a bullet through his right leg, somehow got out a revolver, crept forward, and killed two Japs who attempted to emerge from their tanks. Finally the advance tank force turned back, returning to the grove of death where the Gurkhas lay, for more sport. For ninety minutes all seventeen tanks turned their full fire upon the grove where the Gurkhas crawled amid their dead and dying. Both colonels were killed. But the Japanese never did compel a surrender, and never dared emerge from their steel caissons to face the Gurkhas' grenades. Their tank force, Rising Sun flag and all, withdrew again north of the river.

"We've been through something that makes Norway, Dunkirk, and Greece look like a weekend show," said the surviving brigade major of the Gurkhas.

The Scots, though continuously scourged by aircraft, managed to get loose occasionally. During a battle at Kuala Dipang, one of the eleven battles they fought, seventeen Japanese coolly walked into the railway station to the west. They soon were attacked by an armored car and barricaded themselves in the station. Meanwhile an Argyll captain, his company sergeant-major and orderly crept around the side. The captain had a tommy gun. He used it to beat open the door. By the time he got inside he was out of ammunition. He used it to club the Japanese over the head. There were still three Japanese hiding, somewhat ridiculously, in the ticket office. The sergeant-major, who was made of more than parade-ground stuff, burst open the ticket office and killed the three Japs who were left with his fists and his tin hat.

—

THE FALL OF SINGAPORE

For the last three weeks of its life Singapore's sky was almost never clear of smoke, sometimes thin, grey, and wan, sometimes black and overpowering. The Japanese were in the dilemma of knowing they had Singapore within their hands and being unable to decide what to preserve and what to destroy. Except for human life and the will to resist, there was not much they could destroy. The bombers left untouched the large oil reservoirs on the island of Bukum, where 40,000,000 gallons of fuel were stored, to be set aflame at night in the last hours of the fall of the city. The man with the pistol in his hand was nearly parched to death as he rowed away.

About two weeks after the first Hurricanes were landed at the navy yard and unboxed, about thirty more Hurricanes were flown in from an aircraft-carrier on the western side of Sumatra. By this time Singapore's air fields were smashed, the Japanese were so close that the warning system no longer functioned, and the possibility of regaining control of the air had slipped beyond reach.

A whole shipload of other RAF fighters, full of courage for the task, arrived in the last days of the siege, but were never used. Because they had no regular commanding officer and no word had been sent of their arrival, they sustained considerable casualties through being bombed at the piers.

The withdrawal of troops across the causeway took the Japanese by surprise; apparently they expected to be fought more stiffly. The quick retirement had to be made suddenly to gain a little rest for the weary men and time to prepare. The British command counted on an interval when the Japanese would not know what ambushes were awaiting them. Washington sent word that if Singapore could hold out thirty days, help would come. Singapore did hold—for exactly thirty days.

Single reasons are usually the offspring of simple minds, but certainly one important thing was that the coastal defense guns were not movable, could not be turned around to fire along the network of roads in the jaw of Johore. This jaw held Singapore like a bone in the mouth of a dog. Chicagonews, in the last conference before leaving the night that the causeway was to be blown, made the atmosphere in a tranquil press conference—characterized by the usual superficial questions and evasive answers—momentarily discordant by asking how many coastal guns pointed out to sea and how many pointed at the Japanese. The answer given by the army spokesman was discreet: some pointed one way, he said, and some the other.

Were there many?

Candidly, the spokesman could not say that there were very many.

The able G. W. Seabridge, editor of the *Straits Times,* remained the one voice no one could suffocate. A month to the day before the first Japanese barges crossed the straits the paper had said: "Time after time we were told of the arrival of large convoys of troop ships, quantities of aircraft, tanks and all the other paraphernalia. Where is that immense strength? . . . Everybody in this country appears to have been lulled into a sense of security by confident statements regarding our armored might. The only people who have not been bluffed are the Japanese."

Singapore was so big that it had a man-power problem. In spite of all the troops pulled back down the peninsula—even the Japs claimed only 5000 dead and 7800 prisoners for the 600 miles of fighting—there were not enough men on the island to fight for it. The fortress was, of all things, too big for its garrison.

When General Percival and Lieutenant General Gordon Bennett went to inspect the lines they found companies separated by distances of one or even two miles. For a wall of men, half a million troops would have been necessary—instead there were clusters marooned on three sides by tidal waters. Among these little forces the Japanese sampans and barges could easily penetrate.

But Yamashita was as cautious as ever; the only thing the Japanese fears is surprise. The Japs pushed their little mortars into position in the rubber groves and behind the buildings of Johore. They began throwing shells, their fire directed by aircraft and balloons. They could take fixes on the fall of their shells; and always the Japs had the abundant advantage of the thousand-eyed planes.

The night when a 75-yard opening was blown in the causeway—whose $12 million cost had gone into making it too solid to destroy—Sir Shenton Thomas made an address on the MBC. He said: "Today we began the battle of Singapore. Before I say more, let me set your minds at rest on a most important matter. The general officer in command told you that our forces will stay here and carry out the high task of defending the island and fight on till victory is won. This is a total war in which the whole population is involved. Let not, therefore, the Asiatic population of this island imagine for one day that they will find themselves abandoned."

Thomas kept his promise. The Asiatic population was not abandoned. Singapore was never evacuated.

By the time the causeway was blown, the question of evacuating the troops from Singapore was simply theoretical; the losses in bringing them to Java would have been terrible, even had the ships been available. Every vessel that went through "bomb alley" (Bangka Strait)—and every vessel had to—was severely bombed.

The enemy landing was expected hourly. Wavell cabled MacArthur in the Philippines, offering to fly there. About this time three loaded freighters under army commission were allowed to start the perilous journey toward Corregidor, and there was some hope MacArthur could be reinforced. MacArthur's reply to Wavell was: *Thanks but consider the life of the supreme commander of the Southwest Pacific is too precious to be jeopardized.* He was right. Only one of the freighters got through.

Although there were no ships to take away the troops, troops continued to arrive. The liner *Empire Star* brought in nearly 9000 tons of cargo, including tanks and many crates of Hurricanes. The captain remained nine days, unable to obtain orders either to unload or to leave. Finally he unloaded anyway, and left. The tanks and Hurricanes fell into Japanese hands, to be used in the battle of Java.

But Singapore's hope did not die, and its routine went on. The littlest waiter at the Raffles, who had declined to leave even when two heavy bombs fell upon the laundry in the rear, still stood at the door in the mirrored hall after the evening tea dance, offering outgoing officers the same unpurchased yellow Teddy bears he had been offering for weeks past.

Months before, perhaps, he must have sold them all and become temporarily very rich; he always seemed to believe that another day for them would come back again, inexplicably, as the first had come. When all the Chinese roomboys and the Malay waiters fled he was still there, offering them for sale. Seeing him, one wondered whether when Yamashita first came through the blackout curtains, the little porter would try to sell him a fuzzy yellow Teddy bear.

On Friday, February 6, with Wavell already gone, Percival gave his message to the troops: "We will hold Singapore! There is no question about it. Just because we do not see so many of our aircraft overhead and large naval vessels about, it does not mean the air force and navy have abandoned Singapore."

There were four full raids that day between dawn and nine in the morning. By this time it was clear that the rising and falling note of the siren and the long note of the all-clear might be ignored. Singapore was under continuous air raid.

The first shells fell upon the downtown suburbs on Saturday. The Japs had been saving this bombardment for their first attempt to cross the strait.

In "European" villas people had begun to destroy what they had of value. The broadcasting company suddenly announced that Singapore would be held and demolition must cease. It was the same contradiction that had dominated the entire campaign; nobody knew whether the island could be held or not. If it could not be held, the task of demolition was so enormous that it had to begin immediately. But if it could be held, the task of uncrating and putting into action the materials that had arrived had to begin immediately. There was no safety in either the godowns, being bombed daily, or the air fields, over which the Japanese scouted ceaselessly.

Yet hope was very far from dead, and spirits were high. Malta had held, and Corregidor and Bataan were holding; why should not Singapore hold too? The sight of one or two Hurricanes coming over hastily from Palembang and skipping back again raised hearts. The will to hold Singapore was there; everyone felt it.

With the island jammed with refugees, civilian and military, and its roads clogged with vulnerable trucks and cars, shortage of food would have made the work of the Japanese much easier. But no one was going to starve Singapore out, whatever direction he came from. Food was divided into truckloads, each containing enough for a family for six months: bacon, crackers, tea, sugar, butter, corned beef, and canned milk. From these stores many who escaped in small boats laid away their provisions. At Singapore, unlike Corregidor, there was food for years of siege.

Every villa was crowded. Most roomer-boarders were strangers to each other and only vaguely known to their hosts. One Singapore hostess who found herself with eleven house guests put up a sign which met this emergency in etiquette well. "Do not imagine it is necessary to appear," it read, "except at meals." This left her unsatisfied. She attached a postscript: "And do not be excessively polite."

Hopes as grotesque as gargoyles roamed the streets. The cruelest rumor was that Wavell had landed at Penang heading a fleet of American warships. A British and American column had jumped on the beach from the accompanying convoy, the tale went, severed Japanese communications in mid-Malaya, and was racing south to relieve Singapore. The tragic thing about such hopes was that they were not feather-bed escapism, but indicated an honest, optimistic frame of mind. There was a spirit here which could have been used—had weapons been available, had the people's army been mustered.

There was no more withdrawal possible; everyone in the island knew that. In the past weeks those voices at the Singapore Club which spoke with premonition of what "the Asiatic population" would do were now ready to give tribute to its self-decision and dedicated spirit. Something like comradeship came to Singapore.

Asiatics had no illusions about the inadequacy of the protection given them. Where they were unorganized, they were fearful and ran for shelter in the deep culverts. But where they were organized, whether to withdraw the wounded from the rubble of a fallen building or to fight fires, they did their work to the end with full gallantry. And the Cricket Club and the Singapore Club boasted about their boys that all were "magnificent."

But it was too late even to be magnificent.

After the first spasm of indignation passed in the London press, Churchill asked for and received the vote of confidence necessary to carry his government over the coming fall of Singapore. Even in Singapore itself there was evidence of that effort to understand faraway difficulties which is one of the most admirable things in the British character. There was none of the bitterness that might have been expected. Singapore had been strong, and perhaps it still was. Perhaps Singapore could hold. The *Straits Times* still did not demand the resignation of Churchill or his Cabinet. Far from bellowing at the head of the pack, Singapore hung in the rear, waiting and hoping for London to do something, realizing that London and Washington, once so near and so big, were now small and far away.

As Singapore began its death watch, the lull that follows recrimination and regret spread over the watching world. Nothing more could be accomplished by criticism. Did London and Washington realize what was happening?

Chicagonews remained until all other American special correspondents of both newspapers and radio had left. Two American agency men, Yates McDaniel of the AP and Harold Guard of the UP, stayed behind and sent the best accounts of the battle. One or two British and Australian correspondents remained, departing at ragged intervals past the point where intensive shelling began. The military bureau of press relations departed the day before Chicagonews, leaving the trusty Steel in charge of final withdrawals. Among the unrecorded losses was a huge bookkeeper's typewriter which Chicagonews had personally looted from an empty barracks south of Ipoh and brought back for the use of Major Fisher and Captain Hooper.

The office in the Cathay building was deserted, where Chicagonews had flattened out on the floor and crawled to the inner rooms when the bombs came down upon Fort Canning and Orchard Road. Here he had crept to the window and peeped mously over the sill to see the big brown rolling clouds of bomb dust rising from the buildings, and the tiny red brushwork of the newborn flames reaching up. Secure behind the masonry and knowing that the planes had passed, he had looked out the window and seen a Chinese fire warden standing on a roof while the smoke and yellow dust rose round him, beckoning and shouting in three languages to the fire engines ranged around the building. Singapore had had its heroes.

At the same time, even in its hour of agony, Singapore had its traitors and fifth-columnists, Chinese, Malay, Indian, and Eurasian. Even when the island was surrounded, the spying continued. The Straits Settlements police, excellent men with steadfast officers, were kept busy following the tricks of the agents of Japan.

One clever device was the bamboo lamp to signal bombers during a blackout. A thick hollow length of bamboo rested leaning against a house, inconspicuous in the darkness, its top perhaps twenty feet above ground. No glow or reflection was visible; no smoke could be smelled. Yet inside, well below the top, there was a lamp burning. Two houses away was another pole propped carelessly against a house, and along the kampong street was another. They made a dotted line of light, invisible from the ground, but bright as a flashlight to aircraft over the blacked-out island.

Most irritating and dangerous was the concealed radio transmitting station, traced as far as a marshy wild area, but not ascertainable beyond that because the radio direction-finder was not acute enough.

Exactly a week after the blowing of the causeway, the Japanese started to use their sampans and barges on the eastern side of Singapore, first eliminating Pulau Ubin, where the granite for the causeway had been mined. By taking this small island the Japanese could not only prevent the British sending river gunboats through the strait; they also ensured themselves granite for filling in the open 75 yards of the causeway.

The tall Cathay skyscraper, sticking above Singapore's hills and houses like the Empire State Building above Manhattan, furnished a handy point of range for the Japanese gunners and spotter aircraft and a good place for British counter-observation. The Cathay was the jewel in the treasure chest of Singapore, and the Japanese, while shelling indiscriminately, left the skyscraper almost unmarked.

In the heavy raids while the Japs were massing their invasion barges, the black-pyjamaed Chinese women still gathered on the marble ramp of the Cathay's cinema. One day a baby was born on the ramp; *The Philadelphia Story* was playing inside. After three or four days, while the Japanese advanced across the island, the Chinese families began to desert their towering air-raid shelter. On the roof the two lookouts with their direct telephone to headquarters began to hear singing sounds. *Whee, whee* said the tiny voices in the air, and the observers knew for the first time that they were under rifle fire. The lookouts could see everything, every dogfight over the city, every flight of low-hurrying bombers, and occasionally even the betraying flash of a Japanese gun before the shells burst. They watched the new artillery placed on Pulau Ubin methodically demolish Seletar airdrome. Then the Japanese guns swung around and began dropping shells on Government House.

From then on no place on the island was safe. The finger of the guns had reached the heart of Singapore. Shells began to fall in Change Alley, through whose hardware and gimcrack bazaars one had been able, as through a tunnel, to see from Raffles Place to the lively waters of the bay.

Time was when the observing officers on the Cathay had had difficulty in keeping away intruders who wanted to see the struggle; as soon as bullets began twanging overhead, visitors appeared no more. For a while a policeman who possessed a seized collection of the indecent photographs that seem a stable part of Japanese colonial families' household effects had kept the observers' minds upon terrestrial matters. Then he too disappeared. At length, feeling lonely, the observers dropped a phone line down fourteen storys to the small private villa of R. E. Marriott, who lived with his American wife in a small villa by the Cathay's parking. It was a strain being fired at continuously day after day, and the observers liked to know occasionally what was going on in the nether world of the streets.

Among the paradoxes of Singapore, perhaps the most extraordinary was the voice of the radio. Between news bulletins from the front and abroad, most of them discouraging in character, seething swing numbers came jumping, jittering, jiving out over the kampongs and villas, the shell-racked hotels and flats. Nothing much stranger could be imagined, while shells crisscrossed overhead, than the shrill clarinet rollicking merrily away, the deep bass thumping out its offbeat rhythms, and the muted trumpet inviting all the world to dance. Most of these records had been made far away, the work of big American dance bands playing in security in some Manhattan studio. But America was in the war too. Why so gay?

As one heard this whipping hot music, one's feet could hardly keep quiet; a fast and jittery pendulum swung inside the body. Then the siren on the police station at the crossroads would begin to wind up its warning. Across the trampled green padang of the house at the foot of Caldecott Hill, with the broadcast radio towers poking their invitation to the Japanese bombers up in the sky, there would come two or three Indian gunners, asking for shelter from the morning's raid. "And so it's goodbye to Horace Heidt and his Musical Knights until tomorrow morning. . . ."

Japanese artillery fire kept growing thicker and heavier, breaking up the roads with craters. Bombing was intermittent, but shelling was persistent and endless. Almost the entire sky was black. The big brick-lined oil tanks by the causeway's head went up in towering pillars of smoke. Every boom signalled the destruction of new millions of gallons of hard-won fuel.

The Japanese fighters never ceased patrolling the roads, machine-gunning everything and searching beneath trees and beside deserted villas for motor trucks, particularly of the Indian divisions. The Japanese specifically avoided bombing the Alexandra Hospital. An improvised hospital, unmarked, was hit by incendiary bombs and burned in a high wind before the wounded could be removed.

The Japanese never ceased trying to obtain a surrender. Repeatedly they called across the lines, sometimes in Hindustani, sometimes in English: "Why not give up this useless fight?" Leaflets signed by Yamashita told the cramped forces to give up because "the Japanese forces desire to refrain from seeing the city reduced to ashes."

Shells were falling all over Monday and Tuesday, the more dangerous because the fire was unpredictable. There were shell holes everywhere, and no longer anyone who cared about filling them. The Japanese were now playing at newsboy. *EXTRA* in large letters topped the leaflets, saying that President Roosevelt was negotiating a separate peace with the Japanese and had asked for a declaration making Singapore a "neutral zone." This last attempt, with the smoke so thick it shut out the sun and the shells falling ceaselessly through it, was beyond ridicule.

The Japanese had penetrated almost into the suburbs of Singapore. By 2:30 on Wednesday afternoon they actually were in possession of the chief police station on Bukit Timah Road, less than six minutes from the Raffles and the waterfront. Then, with more Australians blocking them, the Japanese became cautious.

Thousands of vehicles, the sediment of the entire Malayan campaign, stood crammed on the overhanging lip of the island, among the granite colonnades of the deserted banks and shipping companies. Shells came over in some places every fifty seconds; the 5.9s hit Government House and the waterworks. The Argylls, fighting beside the marines, were overrun. Colonel Stewart told Chicagonews: "As we lay in the ditches the noise of Japanese tanks passing was incessant through the night."

Until Singapore fell, its entire southeastern coast, almost 15 miles, was still in British hands. On Wednesday the RAF blew up its own headquarters at Sime Road. The Japanese had never bombed the RAF headquarters, though they claimed to know where it was, because—so the Penang radio said—"We consider the RAF our best friends." Perhaps they did not know exactly where its headquarters were.

All males, including civilians, regardless of age were refused permission to leave Singapore. It was too late to leave, anyway. The harbor front was under almost constant bombing and bombardment. On Wednesday the Sultan of Johore and Yates McDaniel lunched together, and far from being pleased that the British were losing, as his enemies represented him, he was according to McDaniel "a broken man." In his demeanor of defeat he stood far above the playboy reputation with which he had been saddled by Singapore's gossips. He started back alone, to find a place where he could give himself up and ask the Japs to return him to Johore Bahru. He left it to his wife, a Rumanian Jewess, to decide whether she would join him or escape and go abroad. All that afternoon she was unable to make up her mind, but by evening she started back, following her husband. About twenty British and Australian nurses stayed too, to care for the 4000 wounded forced back into the island.

On Thursday the guns finally found the range of Singapore's general arsenal. It blew up with a mighty roar. One or two barge-loads of bombs from the RAF base, which were to have been destroyed by engineers, fell intact into Japanese hands. The engineers had always more jobs of demolition than they could possibly handle.

Although they must have been bewildered, Percival and Thomas rolled up their sleeves and helped to fight the fires catching everywhere. A new spirit came to Singapore. The *Free Press,* still carrying on amid the falling shells (never failing to tell of the narrow escapes of its Chinese reporter), informed all who were still able to obtain the paper that they might now open the gates of any villa and take shelter underneath the trees of any padang. There was no more private property. Under a sky full of death Socialism had flown in and roosted, of all places, in Singapore.

With dawn Thursday morning headquarters announced that a demand for surrender had been dropped by Japanese airplanes, and no reply had been made. Admiral Spooner sent his aide to the chart office to collect the last maps for the long and dangerous run to Colombo. Steel and McDaniel drove a car to the waterfront and pushed it off, photographing it toppling into the harbor. They made their way down the coast and turned up in Batavia. Most of the military censors appeared in Java, but the civil censors, Duckworth and Fearon, went to Colombo. Duckworth's wife, a refugee in Australia, later joined him in Durban.

The eminences on Pulau Ubin in the eastern strait had been figured out by Yamashita as the best places for artillery, so fire would fall on the city. In this way the Japanese troops could cross from north to south without passing under their own artillery barrage from the east. A general can use lateral artillery fire on a retreating enemy like a housemaid sweeping a room with sidewise swipes of a broom.

It had become apparent that resistance was hopeless. A British officer carrying a white flag approached the Japanese lines.

The interview between Yamashita and Percival on February 15, 1942, in the Ford Motor assembly plant, was hard and peremptory on Yamashita's part, without any trace of that respectful address which the Japanese customarily use on formal occasions. Although such Allied humiliations, when offered to the Japanese people, are frequently exaggerated to set an example of ruthlessness—it is hard to say, for example, whether the captive crew of the *U.S.S. Houston* was beaten with whips, as the Japanese people were told—the Japanese version of the conversation is worth giving, if only to indicate what they believe such a submission should sound like:

Yamashita: I am not asking whether you wish to surrender or not, and, if you wish to do so, I insist it be unconditionally. What is your answer, yes or no?
Percival: Will you give me until tomorrow?
Yamashita: Tomorrow? I cannot wait. It is understood, then, that Japanese forces will have to attack tonight.
Percival: How about waiting until 11:30 P.M. Tokyo time?
Yamashita: If that is to be the case, Japanese forces will have to resume the attack until then. Will you say yes or no?

Percival was silent.

Yamashita: I want to hear a decisive answer, and I insist upon unconditional surrender. What do you say?
Percival: Yes.

Yamashita said he would "consider a triumphal entry into London" but had "no plans to hold one for the fall of Singapore." He had little time to dawdle; the glorious conqueror was needed on Bataan to handle the stubborn Americans.

Lieutenant General Bennett escaped two hours after the surrender. His aide, Captain Gordon Walker, swam from the waterfront to a sampan and with several other officers started down the strait. They got aboard a junk crowded with British officers, slipped past the silent guns of Blakang Mati, and so south for five days. Walker has said: "All of us were in a bad state of nerves and everyone wanted to run the boat. After twenty-four hours we began to eat, and took a cup of water a day, a handful of rice and some carefully divided cubes of pineapple and bully beef." From the junk the Bennett party transferred to a launch and went through Sumatra to Java.

The Japanese spent a week, beginning February 15, sweeping up mines. Then their vessels came down the South China Sea and entered the harbor. They claimed to have taken 26 transports and warships, including a "boat evacuating British women and children." Singapore to the end was never taken by sea.

Two map rooms were the centers of Singapore's operations. One was in the green-camouflaged building in the hollow cut by the Japanese golf course. Here Chicagonews had seen General Percival produce his identity card before entering. (Had the Japs substituted another Percival in his place, they would have been foiled.)

Five hundred miles to the south, by the great Java volcano of Bandoeng, were the master charts of the vast South Pacific, Wavell's overwhelming responsibility. Here, among others, was a map of Singapore Island. When the maps were not in use a white curtain was drawn, to be raised each morning when staff conferences began.

Then came the day when the Japanese crossed the island, their tank column finally bisecting Singapore.

The next morning, when the maps of Sumatra, the Philippines, Borneo,

Java, Celebes, New Guinea, and Australia stood revealed in vast array, their isinglass covered with crayoned lines and scribbled numbers of units—American, British, Dutch—over one chart the white shroud had been drawn down, covering the line in orange pencil from the causeway of Johore to Pasir Panyang. And the blank face of the map, white and empty, looked out upon the last staff conference, asking an unspoken question.

When would the deliverers of Singapore come?

Chicago Daily News Expense Account
George Weller.

February 22, 1942 to March 21, 1942.

--

Unfavorable balance CDN - Feb 21 - $4,374.61

EXPENSES
Communications

Local phones - Java	...	24.20
Long distance within Java	...	33.07
Messengers - Java	...	16.08
Local phones - Australia	...	5.62
Long distance - Australia	...	12.44

Transportation

Tjilatjap, Java to Fremantle -
(eleven days at sea)   FREE
Batavia-Soerabaya-Banjoewangi-Malang-
Madioen-Djocja-Bandoeng-Tjilatjap - by rail
to Soerabaya - car thereafter   217.56
Porters and baggage fees   ...   18.61
                                    $327.59

General

Hotels (Java)	...	98.60
(eleven days aboard boat not included)		
Hotels (Australia)	...	76.94
Food	...	142.06
Tips and gratuities	...	33.17
Radio hire (Java & Australia)		18.06
Newspapers & source material		9.16
Postage	...	4.56
Exchange fees	...	7.80
Stationery (Australia)	...	8.32
Entertainment in line service		9.45
Total expenses		735.60

Unfavorable CDN balance   ...   4,374.61
plus expenses, Feb 22 to Mar 21   735.60
            Balance due GW Feb.21 $5,110.21

---oOo---

IX

The Collapse of Java

George Weller Lands in Java from Singapore

Batavia, Java—February 4, 1942

Seventy-seven American refugees have arrived here from Singapore aboard a freighter, the bridge of which was scarred with shrapnel from Japanese bombers.

The radio officer was slightly wounded in the attack. Men, women and several children remained below deck when Japanese bombers straddled the ship.

The Daily News *correspondent stepped over the body of a badly wounded coolie when he boarded the ship and slept in his clothes out of doors on the ship's bulkhead during the four nights required for the journey.*

—Chicago Daily News

Having escaped Singapore barely a step ahead of the Japanese, Weller's twenty dispatches from nearly a month on the huge island of Java show he was under no illusions that the heart of the Dutch Indies empire could hold. By early March the Japanese would take prisoner thirty-two thousand Allied troops.

Years later, Weller remembered: "Laurens van der Post, caught with me on Java when it fell, asked me to join his private underground to hold out against the Japanese till a British submarine should come. . . . Having been stood up by a British consul on the shores of burning Salonika, I declined. . . . He spent three and a half years in a Japanese prison camp."

After the loss of Java and the rest of the Dutch East Indies to the Japanese, Australia and New Guinea could only be next.

This section contains the first of the three short stories included in this book: "Farewell in Java." A dispatch covering the same material was published by the newspaper, but the short story contains better detail.

The heroic actions of Navy doctor C. M. Wassell (1884–1958) were first described in Weller's dispatch about his own escape by island steamer from Java and in the later dispatch solely devoted to Wassell. After the doctor was awarded the Navy Cross by President Roosevelt in the spring of 1942, the story caught the attention of the public and of the movies. Cecil B. DeMille asked the government if it might be amenable to him making a film about the doctor; it immediately transferred Wassell to U.S. Navy Public Relations and moved him to Hollywood to serve as technical adviser. DeMille hired novelist James Hilton to produce a "nonfiction" book about the *Janssens'* voyage which was only partly accurate. Still, *The Story of Dr. Wassell* (1943) was a modest bestseller and set up the Gary Cooper film of the following year, which was the whole idea.

Amid all this Weller, on home leave for the first part of 1944 to get over severe bouts of malaria, did a few joint interviews with Wassell, who after the furor died down returned to active service and finished as a rear admiral. The doctor's share of the book and film money all went to charity.

This is the first of several chapters—along with the Australia, New Guinea, and Islands sections—which roam far forward chronologically. Though Java was in Japanese hands until the close of the war, Weller continued to write about it as information came his way. I have included some of these later dispatches.

BOMB VICTIMS 'DIED BUT THEY DIDN'T CRY OUT'

Batavia, Java—February 5, 1942

An American oilman who had just arrived from Singapore aboard a freighter passed his hand across his eyes. He doesn't wish to remember what he saw. He was the only American among sixty-five refugees crammed aboard the vessel.

When three Japanese bombers discovered the freighter somewhere along the sea route to Java, he found himself saving victims of the Jap air attack. Three times in two hours, big two-motored bombers attacked the ship from an altitude of 1000 feet. Sixteen bombs were dropped but the only one that struck home penetrated the engine room. Let's have the Yank tell his own story:

"A few minutes before the attack," said the oilman, "a blonde Danish engineer—a youthful, cheery fellow—had borrowed my stock of American magazines. Then a Chinese scholar, a graduate of Cambridge University, offered to change my submarine watch from eleven o'clock onward for his later trick on deck.

"I surrendered the magazines but kept my own watch. The next thing I was doing was cutting the shoes off the feet of the engineer and leading the young Chinese scholar, critically wounded, to a lifeboat.

"The Chinaman kept crying in his Cambridge English: 'I cannot see. I cannot see.' Finally he crossed his arms before his face. The flesh had left his finger bones. The blast had blackened as well as blinded him.

"God knows how the big Dane was able to walk from the engine room after the bomb hit. He was bleeding all over his body. I didn't know what to say. I said: 'Want a drink, Peterson?'

"He just shook his head. His yellow hair and fresh-looking face were burned black. After the fire was extinguished and he had been carried to the lifeboat, he tried once to use his lips. I couldn't make out at first what he was saying but I finally understood. It was: 'Where have the women been put?'

"He died in a warship's hospital. Eleven died altogether. Some weren't hurt badly but cried for help. Some didn't cry out at all. Two little apprentice seamen never opened their mouths. One was ten years old, the other fourteen. They were, in the Chinese phrase, 'little learner pigeons.'

"The skins of some Chinese were peeled by flame from yellow to ghastly white. But these kids were blackened. One little apprentice died quickly but the other tried to crawl upon his charred knees to the edge of the lifeboat. There he tried to pull himself over the gunwale into the water—the only cool thing he could see. Yes, we used picric acid. But both boys died.

"How many wounded I put into the lifeboats, I don't know. I remember there were four lifeboats full of bodies, spread lengthwise under the thwarts. We had lowered the lifeboats to the water's edge when a squadron of our warships was sighted over the horizon."

—

FAREWELL IN JAVA

A Short Story

At twilight the correspondent stood on the hill above the pier at Banjoewangi, the easternmost tip of Java, and looked across the strait to the green, smoking volcano of Bali. To the Dutch commandant of the last two unsunk PT boats he said, "I'd like to put foot once on Bali before we lose it entirely. The Japs have the air field at Den Pasar, but you'll still be evacuating native troops tonight from the northern coast. Take me over with you tonight, will you?"

The green-clad commandant conferred with three other officers. They shook their heads. Nothing doing. So the war correspondent saluted them and turned and walked bitterly back toward town. Bali: another good story that would never be told.

In Banjoewangi every house was dark and still. Many had fled after a Zero machine-gunned a schoolhouse. The American went to the little hotel. In the bar the talk was of the battle of Straat Bali. Two sailors from the *Piet Hein*—the Dutch destroyer sunk when the mixed force of American and Dutch warships had pressed through from the Java Sea to the Indian Ocean to attack the landing Japs—were being toasted at the bar. One had kept afloat in the sucking tides of the Straat for three days with a life preserver, the other for thirty-six hours without one.

"We cannot sleep you here," said the innkeeper. "We have no room. You will have to drive back to Soerabaya. But use no headlights, or you will be shot by the anti-paratrooper patrols."

Soerabaya was too far. Besides, the war correspondent had to get back to Malang air field to wave off the Nineteenth Group's battered Fortresses, falling back to Australia. Sleep in the army car? In the damp Javanese night an intestinal cold creeps into one's vitals.

"Could you put up with a bed on a coffee plantation?" said a voice. It was a short, dark-haired Dutchman, in his early fifties. He was the antithesis of copybook Dutchmen, sallow, slim and brown-eyed. There was no mistaking his kindness.

The correspondent accepted. With army car and soldier chauffeur following, the planter led the way in his old American car, and crept out of town through the mists and up into the coffee highlands.

"I drive slowly for two reasons," explained the Dutchman carefully. "First, because headlights are forbidden. And second, because I have explosive in the back of this car. You see, I am a planter, not a soldier. I do not know much about things that explode."

His home, about the size of any American suburban middle-class house, lay upon the saddle between and below two volcanoes. It overlooked the sea across which the Japs were expected.

His wife, a blue-eyed Dutch blonde off a Delft plate and perhaps a decade younger than he, was waiting for them with coffee and spicecake. Their two sons, fourteen years old and seven, were studying their lessons. Was it possible, the correspondent asked himself, that this home would soon be in the hands of Japan?

"While you were gone, I was out on the *padang* talking to the women," said the planter's wife. "The phone rang and I thought it might be the signal. But it was only the chief of police making a general call to all the planters. The Americans bombed the Japanese at Bali and disorganized them. He does not think they will be ready to cross the Straat to Banjoewangi until the day after tomorrow."

The two boys looked up. The eldest, thin like his father, but taller, said, "Has the guest seen our American diesel? Did you show him the electric pump we bought from Chicago? And the new American bean sorters?"

"I do not want to take our friend into those wired buildings now," said the planter. "Remember, we are only amateurs with explosives. We are obliged to blow up all our valuable machinery after the enemy lands. But not ourselves beforehand." The younger boy, all golden and blue like his mother, looked up at this and smiled faintly, then returned to his book.

Taking the correspondent out to the porch, the Dutchman explained their preparations for the destruction of the small rubber plant, the coffee sheds, the barns. "This will burn, that will blow up," he said, pointing to everything that meant the life of the homestead. He spoke without sadness and with extreme simplicity. "It is too bad to destroy all that machinery from America. It took us many years to save enough to buy it. But we shall. Nothing must remain which the Japs can use."

Even the American car was doomed to go, though this effectively marooned the family in the country.

That night there were fires visible on the beach across the Straat on Bali. Japanese campfires? Nobody went to bed because the army captain in his office down by the quay telephoned that the Jap convoy, escorted by warships, was visible over the moonlit sea. But the "stand-by" signal for destruction never came.

The morning broke and everybody, sleepy-eyed, sat dozing over coffee. The sun climbed behind Lombok. The convoy was gone, the sea empty. Again the phone sounded an air-raid alarm. The father went forth and did what he had repeatedly since February 3—he beat upon the gong hanging upon his porch, warning all the plantation workers and coolies that planes were expected. He drew out a small notebook, noted the hour and date in the methodical fashion of the Dutch.

"That was our thirteenth alarm," he said.

The Eurasian assistant manager already had left the porch, checking once more the demolition plans.

"Do you think the Japs will want to take my boy?" asked the mother.

The eldest was already a six-footer, despite being only fourteen, but with pretended competence the correspondent replied, "No."

"Yesterday a Jap Navy Zero from Bali, on reconnaissance, flew round and round only a few feet above us," said the planter speculatively. "But somehow the pilot did not use his machine gun."

Candles were set out for when the electric lighting plant was blown. Where the assistant manager of the encharged demolition would hide afterward was a family secret. Nothing but the house structure and the bil-lowing wet, green hills of rubber and coffee would remain when the Japs came up from the harbor.

The phone rang again. "The lookouts say the Japanese have begun un-loading invasion barges," announced the planter after he hung up. "You had better not go back to Banjoewangi. You might be caught. We want you to get away. Somebody must tell Java's story."

"What are you going to do with your family?"

"We are going to wait here. We have laid enough fuses. Everything will be blown up except this dwelling."

"Why not destroy everything now, and escape? We can all go in the army car. I can get you aboard a freighter at Tjilatjap. In a week we can be in Australia."

The father looked at his wife and two sons. "This plantation is ours," he said mildly. "It does not matter how many Japanese come here, with how many airplanes or tanks. We have our workmen to take care of. We have our plantation. Java is still Dutch."

Suddenly a bell began to toll dolefully in the workmen's quarters. "Air raid," said the planter. "Here they come again." The camouflaged army car was already at the gate, the soldier chauffeur scanning the sky toward Den Pasar. The war correspondent shook hands with the Dutch family and jumped in.

"Goodbye," said the planter. "I'm sorry for your not being able to get your story about Bali."

"That's all right," said the correspondent. "I got another."

—

OFFICERS AT FRONT IN PERILED JAVA TELL FEARS

Bandoeng, Java—March 3, 1942

Besieged Java looks now to Australia, Great Britain and chiefly the United States for the aid it has been promised to arrive unstintingly after the Japanese invasion, a canvass of military opinion behind the lines revealed today.

For the Dutch generals it is a life-and-death question. The attitude this correspondent encounters is: "We are perfectly willing to sacrifice if we are certain that greater offensive aims are served elsewhere. But the London and Washington leaders, because of their unfamiliarity with the South Pacific, still do not fully comprehend what Java's peril means in terms of Japan's future striking power."

Pictures of America's fighting lanes adorn local magazines, and placards beseeching Indonesian Dutchmen to contribute to Spitfire funds for the defense of Britain strike a paradoxical note as the first top-flight American fighter or Spitfire has yet to be seen in Javanese skies. What Dutchmen cannot make out is whether the Americans and British want a fluid war in the Pacific, with Japan kept busy everywhere, or a frozen war, with Japan merely checked by temporary stopgaps. The Dutch want a fluid war. They want the Javanese front to keep the Japs as busy as MacArthur's Philippine front, until an American naval offensive relieves both. Here is how Dutch, and many American officers, too, see the fateful alternatives:

1. Holding Java means forcing Japan to pump men and resources constantly along extremely extended and exposed lines of communication, because an invasion force is far more dependent on its basis of origin than an occupying force.
2. Losing Java means backing up to northern Australia, which, because of lack of harbors, exposure to aircraft and insufficient means of feeding forces, means a clogged, static position. An American front there will be awkward and expensive.
3. Holding Java means subtracting some pressure from MacArthur, and increases Jap uncertainty as to whether he will receive reinforcements.
4. Losing Java means giving the Japs control of the naval base of Soerabaya, better than any other nearby base except Jap-held Singapore, and far superior to Darwin down in Australia, America's next best.
5. Holding Java means diverting Jap land forces that might otherwise be used in Burma; Burma cannot tie up the Japs as Java can, because only air and land forces are needed there, the navy's role being minor.
6. Losing Java means depriving the Allies of an opportunity for the safe recovery of the Sumatra and Borneo oilfields.

7. Holding Java means giving Russia a chance to resist Germany's spring campaign and possibly launch a trans-Balkan offensive.

8. Losing Java means empowering Japan to attack Russia as she desires.

9. Holding Java means the Allies' second chance to defend Holland, thereby upholding the last spiritual capital for the prostrate but rebellious peoples of Europe.

10. Losing Java means the removal from the 26-nation front of the last small country able to throw an effective rather than a token force into the field.

11. Holding Java means a springboard for the desire growing in every American's heart to avenge Pearl Harbor and create a permanent pattern for security and economic opportunity in Asia. Without Java the offense cannot get underway.

12. Losing Java means opening the door to the Japs' movement of welding 70 million British and Dutch Malaysians into a bottomless reserve of manpower for the already foreseen war in which Japan intends to lead Asia's millions against the European and American hemispheres.

13. Holding Java means fighting Japan from a base where the native population is friendly to Allied purposes.

14. Losing Java means transferring the chief theater of resistance to Burma and India, where the natives vary from apathetic to rebellious.

15. Holding Java means fortifying China by reducing the pressure against the Burma Road and making the Jap Navy's interference with war supplies entering the Bay of Bengal less effective.

16. Losing Java means releasing Jap warships from convoy work in the Java and China seas, not only for blockades of Rangoon and Vladivostok but interference with American convoys to Australia and agitational sinkings off the Pacific Coast.

17. Holding Java means honoring the Americans here risking their lives in submarines, destroyers, fighters and bombers against odds varying from four- to ten-to-one and sending them the help everyone would like to be able to send MacArthur.

18. Losing Java means giving hard-working U.S. forces here a choice between evacuation, which is unfair to the Dutch, and being lost with the island.

—

STIRRING STORY OF FLIGHT FROM JAVA AND JAPS

George Weller Tells How Ship Dodged Attacks to Reach Australia

(Missing since March 2, when he filed his last dispatches from Java, George Weller, the Daily News *correspondent in the Far East, has finally reached safety "somewhere in Australia." In his story herewith, he relates the story of his miraculous escape.)*

Somewhere in Australia—March 14, 1942 (Delayed)

For correspondents lucky enough to obtain transportation on B-17 Flying Fortresses, Java was hardly six hours from Australia and safety. But for any who stayed after the last American Navy unit sailed on Sunday, March 1, and the last bombers departed at dusk the same day from Jokjakarta, Australia was much farther.

After being bombed in Batavia, bombed in Soerabaya and bombed in Bandoeng, this correspondent on Monday, March 2, with William Dunn of the Columbia Broadcasting System and Frank J. Cuhel of the Mutual Broadcasting System, the last remaining radio reporters, started for the southern Java port of Tjilatjap. DeWitt Hancock of the Associated Press and William McDougall of the United Press were the only Americans remaining and they planned to leave immediately in another car.*

Our start was made amid a raid in which Jap Navy Zeros were attempting to destroy the eleven fighters and four bombers which alone remained as defenders of Java's western plateau, where the Netherlands East Indies Commander-in-Chief, Lieutenant General Hein Ter Poorten, once planned a Bataan-style stand. There were unashamed tears at our final handshakes with the men and women of the Dutch press bureau, headed by L. H. Rittman, the jovial and lovable director of that singularly honest and fearless governmental propaganda department.

---

*Their eventual ship was bombed and sunk March 7; Hancock drowned. McDougall made it to the coast of Sumatra, where he was imprisoned for three and a half years. Cuhel died in a 1943 plane crash in Lisbon, en route to North Africa on assignment.

In Tjilatjap's small cemetery lay, under walnut-colored wooden crosses, the bodies of American sailors who died defending Java. Others were there alive, the wounded with reddish scarifying marks from bomb blasts. Like ourselves they were placed aboard a small Dutch island steamer.

All day we waited in the tiny harbor expecting raids, but Jap fighters, based on Bali, were harassing the defenses around Rembang and only one alarm sounded and no bombs were dropped.

Naval physician Lieutenant Commander C. M. Wassell of Little Rock, Arkansas, laid his bandaged, wounded charges out upon the steamer's bulkheads. One topic of conversation was our chances of piercing the Japanese submarine blockade. At darkness we slipped out through the mine-dotted harbor, clouds obscuring the moon.

There were about six hundred aboard, with cabins for less than forty. Many were officers fresh from the destruction of the Soerabaya naval base. About ninety per cent of the passengers were Dutch navy people. Two were sailors I had interviewed at Java's easternmost end, Banjoewangi, after they spent two days and nights in the water seven miles off Bali following the sinking of their destroyer.

Past mine fields, a friendly thunderstorm took us in charge, convoying us under cloak of darkness and rain through whatever submarines were waiting. We expected, even with the steamer's labored eight knots an hour, to be a hundred miles at sea by daybreak. But dawn found us far closer to Jap bombers.

The Dutch Admiralty having other last ships to send from the harbor the same night, one bearing enemy alien internees, spread them variously over the sea. Our ordered course lay straight along Java's shore directly toward the enemy base at Bali and about two miles from shore.

Out of the rising sun came the Japanese bombers, the same distance offshore as ourselves to evade listening posts. First came nine, then seven, then nine again. They were directly overhead, their motors humming incessantly. The day was blue and bright, but they had bigger prey than our ship in mind. Their missions were to bomb Tjilatjap.

We still pursued our creeping course along the shore. The captain knew the inadequacy of six lifeboats to carry a hundred times as many people and did not dare to turn to sea. The passengers, fat with life belts, clogged the passageways, uncertain whether they would be bombed from below or above.

A burning sun beamed upon the greased lifeboat davits. I gave an unknown woman the journal of my fourteen months of wartime evacuations with the request that if her lifeboat reached shore she send it to the *Daily News*.

Nine returning bombers passed, parallel to the ship. Then, before the siren could even blurt the first peep of the quadruple signal meaning air attack, machine-gun bullets and the cannon shells came directly into the main saloon below the bridge. Sixty persons were instantly upon the floor, trying to crawl under benches. Somehow I crawled into a B-deck passageway. Then came more hammering of steel and splintering of wood.

Whether we were being shelled by a submarine or attacked by an airplane was impossible to tell. I saw a curl of blue smoke arising beside one bulkhead door from an incendiary bullet.

"Stop pushing me," said the little Eurasian woman ahead of me on the jammed stairs. When she discovered that I was attempting to lace her huge, mattresslike life jacket she grew quieter.

For an interval we arose. Then came again the terrible hammering and tearing of wood, running like a xylophone the full length of the ship. No motors could be heard, nothing but explosions. Each time the corridors were jammed with bodies. As we struggled downward attacks began upon the sides of the ship, increasing our belief that we were being shelled from shore by the Japs, who had already crossed the island. Then we were machine-gunned and shelled also from the seaward side.

Between attacks, we lay sweating and prone, some Malays and some whites, too, covering their eyes like the evil-fearing monkey curling into an embryonic ball.

I found the whole right shoulder of my bushjacket uniform drenched with blood, which had soaked even my glasses case. But I was not wounded. Three wounded lay in the corridors, but none whom I could recognize as having been beside me. Four times the death tattoo was played upon us. The rear gunner got a bullet through his hat, another across his uniform.

For more than an hour after the last attack, all of us lay on the iron decks and in the darkness of closed compartments. Then slowly arose bodies dented with their own lifejackets, the cork of which was in some cases torn away.

There had been two Navy Zeros. One lifeboat was shot open. Hardly a ventilator, or stretch of canvas, but had been riddled. The Japs simply had shot all their ammunition at us.

But nothing could make us go faster than our eight knots. The sun was still high, it was hardly noon. We crept toward shore and entered the tiny harbor of Patjitan. There were no natives visible. The captain lowered the boats and asked all who wished to row ashore to leave. He said that we had only a "slight to perhaps fifty-fifty chance" of escaping. About three hundred went ashore and were last seen trailing up a narrow path into country where the Japs spearhead was hardly twenty miles away.

Under cover of darkness, we again crept out to sea. Eleven days of sleeping upon open decks with life belts always entwined on one arm brought us, with our American wounded, to safety.

—

TELLS HOW JAVA LEVELED BASE BEFORE INVASION
Somewhere in Australia—March 17, 1942

How successfully Singapore's naval base was destroyed by British demolition squads remains uncertain, but Soerabaya's annihilation by the alert, well-prepared Dutch navy men was accomplished with complete thoroughness. Nothing that flames could consume, explosives rend or sea water engulf was left when the first Jap patrols entered the smoking naval base.

Although the Dutch had failed before the war to sell the Allies on the fact that Soerabaya was the superior base, events proved the claim. Singapore's huge, empty buildings, underground oil stores and great drydock were liabilities after Jap bombers gained the upper hand and their artillery began shelling the island.

But even after enemy bombers from Bali were pounding Soerabaya, Allied warships, limping back from the sad battle in the Java Sea, still found succor and help. British submarines long depended upon Soerabaya's big, excellent workshops for the outfitting that Singapore's yard was never able to supply. American destroyers and submarines found little lacking there.

This correspondent paid his second visit to Soerabaya three days before demolition began and accompanied a party of Dutch naval demolitionists aboard the last ship that ran Japan's cruiser and submarine blockade south to Australia. Without panic, following a prearranged plan, they had carried out their total destruction on three separate sites—the naval airbase at Morokrembangan, the naval base at Oedjoeng, and the commercial harbor at Perak, all parts of the Soerabaya waterfront.

With Dutch method they had divided the demolition into two phases, manual destruction and heavy destruction. Manual destruction began on Sunday, March 1, after Vice-Admiral Helfirch, formerly commander of the United Nations' naval forces in the Southwest Pacific, had left by plane carrying the Netherlands East Indies' most secret documents. Manual destruction was done by navy executives themselves. All documents were burned. With fire axes—ordinarily used to fight air-raid fires—file cases, desks and chairs were smashed into small kindling. Telephones and switchboards were smashed into bits with heavy hammers.

The radio workshops alone employed 250 mechanics. Hammer in hand, the superintendent walked down the line of scores of big American-made radio tubes, each worth more than $500, shattering them like wine glasses. The office staffs ended their work by sprinkling kerosene over the interiors of old buildings.

The heavy destruction occurred on Monday, March 2. Fifty specially deputized members of the naval police carried out the task in 6½ hours.

On the Sunday, Jap fighters and bombers had been sent in nine raids over the base, each time attacking from a different direction, like spokes running in toward the hub of a wheel, with characteristically careful synchronization. The flames from Monday's demolition told the Japs that destruction was afoot on a far greater scale than they could accomplish and they took their bombs elsewhere.

With cotton in their ears, Dutch naval police first destroyed the coastal guns, exploding dynamite within the barrels. The drydocks were a harder problem. First the pumps in all were destroyed. The fifty-ton little dock for the use of seaplanes was quickly demolished. Next two floating drydocks of 2000 and 3000 tons were disabled—they are so heavy nothing on earth can float them—and sunk.

A 1500-ton floating drydock proved a harder nut because, not being so heavy, it was unsinkable after the pumps were ruined. A disabled Dutch destroyer was placed inside. Eventually the sides were blown open with bombardment shells from the submarine drydock. Then it sank.

Next came the 4000-ton drydock at Perak. A disabled Allied destroyer was placed within. Water was allowed to enter, causing the destroyer to turn slowly upon its side and sink within the drydock. Then the drydock itself was submerged, both sinking together to eternal rest on the sea bottom inside their harbor home.

At exactly 10 o'clock, the magazines on the island of Madura were exploded in 62 huge concussions. An air-raid warning sounded so that all precautions would be taken to protect children against the blasts which, it was thought, might get out of control. Five great hangars, long the mother-sheds for the American Navy's PBY flying boats, were blasted. The engine workshop, after the lathes and motors were all smashed, blew heavenward. Once 2000 of the base's 16,000 men worked there.

Torpedo magazines holding from five to six hundred torpedo shells each were exploded individually, while N.E.I. submarine commanders—forced only the night before to the sea bottom by cavalcades of Jap destroyers preceding their convoys—watched with set faces. One sub commander told this correspondent that he had lain upon the sea floor, in 150 feet of water, from six Saturday evening till noon Sunday, while depth charges made his little submersible, which looks like a toothpick beside American subs, shake until its gauges were all smashed. Overhead passed the churning propellers of 34 Japanese transports, accompanied by 11 warships. The destroyers lingered above him, depth-charging for eighteen hours.

Once charges of picrine were laid, the flames began their work. The smoke grew into monstrous billows, carried westward across Java by a high wind till the long funeral train spread the entire length of the shore. Black clouds shut out the sun. Those who had seen the destroyed oilfields of Tarakan and Balikpapan (both in Borneo) and Palembang (capital of Sumatra) said they had never witnessed anything comparable.

Thus the Dutch carried out punctiliously, systematically and completely the final destruction of their greatest eastern fortress. Few naval officers had time even to see their families. A train was waiting to take them to Tjilatjap. Their wives and children are in Jap hands—and some are known to be dead—but their war goes on.

A 'TRAVELER' OF ARKANSAS IS JAVA HERO

Perth, Southwest Australia—March 20, 1942

A grey-haired Yankee doctor whose fourteen years of fighting malaria in the Orient has not deprived him of his Ozark Mountain twang was awarded the United States Navy Cross in record time here.

Lt. Commander C. McAlmont Wassell, the 58-year-old physician, brought out the last American Navy wounded from Java on the same little inter-island steamer on which this correspondent escaped.

The doctor was standing by the wounded in the hospital at Jokjakarta, to which they had been transferred to provide safety from the incessant bombing raids on Soerabaya. There, under Dr. A. C. Zwaan, famous surgeon of the Netherlands East Indies, wounded sailors, three of them unable to walk, were given "as careful, efficient and thoroughly modern care as the best hospital in the United States could've offered," Dr. Wassell said.

But the American Flying Fortress base, where all machines had been concentrated after the destructive surprise raids by Jap fighters on Malang, was also at Jokjakarta, and Jap reconnaissance soon discovered this. The Army Fortress command, when it departed from Java on Sunday, March 1, at six o'clock, had the cabins of its ships crammed with ground personnel and the original hope to fly the wounded to Australia was of necessity abandoned.

The morning after the last Fortress left, Dr. Wassell's wounded lying in their beds heard a big Jap bomber fleet pound the deserted field to bits. The Japs were approaching overland to cut Java in the middle.

After repeated attempts to telephone the American embarkation party at Tjilatjap, Dr. Wassell decided to take the initiative. Amid the beds of the wounded he explained that if they remained they would become prisoners and asked how many could endure the hundred-mile journey over mountain roads to Tjilatjap.

Every hand was raised except that of a single yeoman, obviously unable to move. Most of the wounded were survivors of bombings on their cruisers. Several of their shipmates had already been buried in Tjilatjap.

With the unfailing, cool cooperation of the Dutch authorities, Wassell managed to obtain automobiles and gasoline and the agonizing journey began.

This correspondent first saw Dr. Wassell on the morning of March 3, shortly after I arose from my billiard-table bed. "If you can get my wounded aboard your bow you'll be doing me a great favor," the doctor said to me in an unmistakable Arkansas drawl.

The Dutch authorities at first demurred at the risk because the ship was already chartered for a demolition party from Soerabaya and sinking was considered probable. But, through Dr. Wassell's efforts, consent was finally obtained. It was fortunate because the ship, although fiercely shelled and machine-gunned by the Jap Navy Zeros, was the last to run successfully the cordon of Jap submarines and cruisers in the Indian Ocean exits from Java.

Dr. Wassell stayed loyally with the wounded during the raid, helping the Dutch Red Cross men bind up new casualties among the approximately six hundred passengers. "What I think was most interesting was that I gave out more than five hundred glasses of water after the planes left," said the doctor. "That shows how fear makes human bodies exude perspiration."

Again, when the Dutch captain sneaked his vessel into the little Javanese inlet of Patjitan and half the passengers accepted his offer to place them ashore, Dr. Wassell put the question to the American Navy men, recumbent upon the bulkheads, whether they wished to take the risk of being sunk by the Japs. Unanimously they decided to risk the open sea, even though the Dutch gun crew, machine-gunned in the action, decided for the shore.

When the Dutch doctor was obliged to stay behind with the non-American wounded, Dr. Wassell became the ship's physician and served as such throughout the eleven-day trip to Australia.

Dr. Wassell's investigations in preventive medicine, particularly malaria, have brought him three Rockefeller fellowships, one being held at Peiping [Beijing]. Despite his hillbilly accent, this Arkansas traveler speaks flawless Chinese and his war career, like MacArthur's, is just coming to public notice.

Dying Java's Last Message Picked Up by Fleeing Ship—Malayan Youth Stays at Post

Perth, Western Australia—March 24, 1942

Java's last faint message still lingers in the minds of those who were able, by luck or providence, to slip through the Japanese cordon of cruisers, submarines, destroyers and aircraft carriers that before and after the Java Sea battle sank several Allied warships including the U.S. gunboat *Asheville*, south of the Indonesian island barrier in the Indian Ocean.

The message was heard aboard the little inter-island Dutch freighter carrying a naval demolition party and this correspondent. The naval party had aided in the destruction of Soerabaya. The freighter, the radio of which caught the weak valedictory, was itself attacked by Japanese fighters and now proves to have been the last vessel escaping from Java, subsequent vessels being many days overdue.

The radiogram was sent by one of these Malayan youths, westernized in dress and speech, whom the Dutch, as the English in Malaya, used to carry the burden of fighting fires after air raids, succoring the wounded, sounding alarms, enforcing blackout restrictions, delivering messages and doing everything else that required quick, intelligent action and a self-sacrificing spirit. They were impressionable teenage youths, eager to serve long hours and trustful that the British and Dutch leaders would protect them, as they had filled their minds with western culture.

In Malaya, many such Eurasian "Andy Hardys" had passed what corresponds to American college entrance examinations and, although barred by preferential standards and financial handicaps from further advancement, were intellectually at the same level as English public school boys entering Oxford and Cambridge, having passed identical London-made examinations.

In Java and Sumatra, a more liberal Dutch policy sent many such young men to Holland for advanced study and, provided they had even a touch of Dutch blood, gave them full citizenship.

Java, Sumatra, Celebes and Borneo were covered by a network of air-raid listening posts, mostly upon the beaches of outlying islands and promontories, manned by these young men.

Binoculars in hand, they would stand on lookouts, watching Jap planes from Kendari, Balikpapan, Macassar, Bandjermasin, Palembang and Bali concentrate upon their home island. In scores of lonely outposts like Madura, Billiton and Bangka Islands, with only a little knapsack of food beside them, in camouflaged huts, they waited by an automatic radio. When Jap bombers and fighters appeared, they transmitted the height, distance and direction of the flight, enabling the handful of American fighters to meet the attack.

The dialogue that our freighter's radio feebly picked up was between one of the three chief Dutch air-raid warning headquarters—in western, central and eastern Java—and a youth who was sitting in a beach hut directly at the point where the Japs were making one of their supplementary landings after the first triple invasion. Here's how the interchange went:

"I see enemy transports with troops getting into barges offshore. What shall I do?"

"Remain at your post. Continue sending details."

"Many barges are now approaching shore. I have no revolver. What shall I do?"

"Remain at your post. Continue sending."

"The Japs have begun firing at my hut. I cannot escape."

The dialogue ended there. Whether the young man, who remained at his post like Herculaneum's famous sentry, until the end came, was killed or captured was not revealed.

Unless the United States can promptly begin political as well as belligerent activity in the South Pacific, what will happen to 5 million such youths, among 70 million Malays, after the Japanese take over the responsibilities the English and Dutch have been forced to surrender?

—

JAPS TOOK 900 TEXANS IN JAVA, REFUGEE REVEALS

Guerrilla Band in Java Awaits Allied Invasion

Somewhere in Australia—October 13–14, 1942

Somewhere between 800 and 900 American soldiers, chiefly members of the Texas National Guard, were taken prisoner in Java, together with some few of the Army Air Corps. Furthermore, a certain number of Navy men, survivors of the cruiser sinking in Sunda Straits, are known to have been held in Java.

A handsome Dutchman in his late twenties provided this correspondent with the first authentic account of what has happened to prisoners in the East Indies since the triple Japanese landings, under an umbrella of bombers and fighters backed by a heavy cruiser and destroyer force, overwhelmed Java.

This boyish-faced infantry leader, who cannot be named for reasons of security, is one of the most remarkable officers who has yet emerged from the war scene. His modest, gentle manner and his dark, sensitive, lean and rather un-Dutch face belie his astonishing adventures.

His escape from Java was his second successful flight from an Axis prison camp. He was captured by the Germans in the invasion of Holland and was first incarcerated in a Silesian prison camp in eastern Germany. From there he escaped last spring and traveled on foot completely around the bayonet-guarded borders of the Bohemian protectorate, through Saxony and Bavaria into Switzerland, thence across France, Spain and Portugal to England, joining the Free Dutch forces there.

Despite having a wife and three children who were hostages in the Hague, he departed immediately for the East Indies to join the colonial army. As an officer of native infantry in the area west of Solo, in central Java, he met and fought the Japs who landed near Renbang. He is probably the only officer thus far among the Allies who has fought both the Germans and Japanese, surrendered to both, been captured by both and escaped from both.

After several weeks in Japanese hands, by means which he has not divulged the young captain escaped from camp and reached the shores of northwestern Java from the central Java prison camp. Being slight, darkskinned and black-haired, instead of brown and rosy blond like most Dutchmen—even though not an "India boy" or half caste—the fugitive was able to pass as a Javanese. He joined forces with two other white Dutch army officers, one of whom, who had amateur yachting experience, managed to procure a 25-foot motorless open-cockpit catboat. The Japs had apparently discounted the possibility of any escapes after commandeering small boats, feeling secure because the prevailing monsoon wind blows away from the nearest point of Australian coast, seven hundred miles distant.

The Dutch soldiers outwitted the Nipponese by heading their tiny craft to Africa, across the waters of the Indian Ocean between Madagascar and Java, whose mastery still is disputed between the Jap, American and British navies.

Sneaking past the great volcano of Krakatoa, where the American cruiser *Houston* went down off Prinsen Island, and passing through Sunda Straits, using a small steamship chart torn from a tourist booklet, the trio sailed more than 2700 miles as the steamer plows and nearly 4000 miles, actually, to make their first landfall. This was Rodriguez Island, a speck about two hundred miles east of Mauritius and about six hundred miles from Madagascar.

"We had never expected to make it," said the Dutchman, candidly. "The wind drove us along at a terrific speed. Because the Japs' patrols were out, on both the Javanese and Sumatran shores of Sunda, we could not make shore and hide. We had to sail straight through under their eyes in broad daylight."

The voyagers were fully aware of starting off on a trip rivaling Captain Bligh's, which in sailing distance approximately equals that from New York to Italy.

"We took along forty-five days' provisions—all we could carry. A few miles south of Sunda a heavy wind suddenly snapped a mast in two and carried away our sail. Up to then we had plenty of water caught in the tarpaulin from rains. Then we had to rig our tarpaulin with blankets to make new sails. Our greatest treasure was our chronometer and two sextants, which made up for the crudity of our map."

The voyagers lived chiefly on rice, boiled in rainwater over a small power stove. Their only other food was potatoes and corned beef. When the dim outline of Rodriguez showed over the bow of the gunwale the trio shook hands.

So that first-hand knowledge of conditions in Java be known in the three chief centers of the refugee government, one voyager started to America, another to England, the third to Australia.

Escapes from the Japs in Indonesia have been extremely rare and this is the first balanced account of what happened to the many stranded British,

Dutch, Australians and Americans during the first six months of the Jap occupation.

Guerrilla forces, remnants of Allied troops who held on in Java to the last, are now battling on in the island's mountains, awaiting an Allied offensive to take over. "I believe our guerrillas would give active support to any landing attempt by the Allies but these forces can, at present, have only nuisance value and little means for offensive operations against Japan," the Dutch officer said frankly.

Java, with its forty million people crowded upon a small island, is too highly civilized to offer more than a few mountain hideouts. The Japs hold garrisons in Batavia, Soerabaya, Rembang and cities in central Java like Jokjakarta and Solo, but prefer to avoid losing prestige in a campaign against guerrillas. The mountainous refuges above the gardenland of Java's terraced ricefields are relatively isolated and restrict the guerrillas' offensive activities. Moreover, the Japs are eager to avoid any fighting which would disturb their "peace and prosperity" campaign.

The treatment of Dutch civilians and colonial administrators was liberal and decent during the first few months, when the Japs made an intensive effort to persuade the Dutch to make a separate peace. In June, however, all white males from sixteen to sixty were snatched from their shops and plantations and herded into concentration camps. Women and children were ordered to leave their villas, and occupy houses in restricted sections closely watched by Jap-controlled police.

Japan's political plans in conquered regions where relatively large white populations exist—as in Java and Sumatra—are now clear. During the period of "rehabilitation and stabilization," the Japs imprison the highest functionaries and military officers, along with troops, both white and native.

Complete disruption of economic life, after the conquest, means that the civilians must work for the Japs or starve. The Japs are holding out pledges of merciful treatment to enlist white civilians or retain those already engaged, especially technicians, granting them in return considerable freedom of movement, but paying them in Jap-fabricated inflationary "guilders."

The duty of such temporary employees is to get the war-crippled public utilities, like railroads, power plants and waterworks, functioning again. If they refuse, or accede halfheartedly, they go to concentration camps and their families are forced to live from hand to mouth. If they agree, they can stay at large so long as they are useful and the Japs have no Japanese or native executives to replace them. When this period passes, all are indiscriminately packed into concentration camps and their enterprises taken over by Jap companies.

The troops are disciplined; no cases of Dutch women being molested have occurred in Java. Looting is not by force but by pumping out Jap "guilders" via a printing press. The object is to leave native or Dutch owners with their hands full of paper and the Japs with their hands full of manufactured goods. A rise in prices makes no difference because the presses simply run faster and print more money.

Like the Germans, the Japs had difficulty keeping shops open because the natives prefer to shut the doors, take what articles remain and flee to the hills, making caches there rather than to be continually cheated by this non-violent looting. The Japs have decreed that all shops must remain open and no articles be concealed. The shopkeepers, getting poorer with every Jap purchase, tried to cut down hours of business. Jap Army commanders retaliated with an order obliging all to remain open until ten at night—four hours beyond the usual closing time.

The Dutch captain described how yawning proprietors, barely able to stay awake behind their counters, are obliged to keep themselves available for Jap purchasers during all but their actual hours in bed. Once in Javanese hands the false guilders are legal tender and the Javanese are in a position to plunder each other just as the Balkan people vainly are trying to absorb huge quantities of occupational marks. Such is the first monetary phase of the Japs' imperial policy. The best that can be said of it is that looting shops prevents looting homes.

The second stage of plundering by manipulation is now opening, in which merchants are offered a chance to exchange their valueless "guilders" for yen which they need in order to make purchases of Jap goods to replenish their shelves. By comparison with the Jap guilder the Jap yen is solid gold. With the second stage of the exploitation under way, a host of carpetbagger Japs are beginning to arrive, offering to fill the empty shelves with their gimcrack products. Since there is no competition, the merchant has the choice of buying Jap or closing up his business and starving. The

Jap administration, when it gets back its own "guilders," simply pays them out again in salaries and the whole paper chase recommences.

—

JAP CULTURE: MALAYS FORCED TO HANG THEMSELVES PUBLICLY

Somewhere in Australia—November 18, 1942

The Japanese invaders of the Dutch East Indies have invented a method of death through self-inflicted torture to check Malay looters, according to a Dutch officer. This officer, an eyewitness, escaped recently from the island.

Malay looters are hanged, but instead of having their spinal cords mercifully snapped, according to the Western method, they slowly hang themselves. And they die standing up, untouched by the hands of the executioner and without their feet ever leaving the ground. The ritual is as follows:

A Malay condemned by a Jap military court is led to a public place, the favorite being the garden of Batavia's Survey Building, which has a picket fence and offers an unimpeded view to passersby. A cord is knotted firmly but not chokingly around the victim's throat, and the loose end attached to an overhanging balcony or tree. Heavy weights are strapped on the doomed man's shoulders and his wrists are loosely tied behind his back. The man can stand easily and breathe normally. But he cannot slouch or relax because his windpipe immediately is constricted.

After hours of suspension the weights begin to drag him down. As his weakness grows, his knees cease to support him and sag more and more. The man thus gradually throttles to death in full public view.

"Dutchmen executed by the Japs were rather few. I cannot say whether the method of self-strangulation was used with them," said my army officer informant. "But I saw three men forced to strangle themselves this way in Batavia. Many Malays watched them die through the fenceposts. Two were nearly dead, or rather showed only occasional signs of life after two days of this. The knees of the third were just giving and he was beginning to choke. Many, many natives are thus executed all over Java. A few tried to steal from the Dutch, as expected, but most tried to break into small Chinese 'Toko' shops to purloin trinkets."

Americans, wary of atrocity stories since the other war, may well reflect upon this fully authenticated story which was not issued by any governmental propaganda machine. It is a lesson as to the character of the Japanese.

—

[probably somewhere in Australia]
July 9th, 1943

Mrs Bertha Bauers,
FLORENCE, <u>KENTUCKY</u>

Dear Mrs Bauers,

My reply to your letter of March 2nd has been delayed by my work in New Guinea. It happens that I have been writing a history of the squadron of which your son was a member. Publication has not been arranged yet, but Dr. Wassell is correct in saying that I know something about the group.

You received word on May 17th that your son had been reported missing. According to my information, your son was lost on February 28th, not February 25th [1942]. He took part in the last gallant attempt by the American fighters to stop the Japanese invasion fleet which had already landed about 70 miles west of Soerabaya.

The Japs were on the beach in the early morning and he was one of the force that went out to attack them. Nothing could give me more happiness than to be able to say to you that there existed a strong hope that he is still alive.* You are familiar with the War Department practice in carrying men as missing until they are considered certainly to be dead.

---

*In fact, 2nd Lt. Cornelius Reagan survived his crash (on March 1). He was taken prisoner and spent three and a half years in a Japanese POW camp. See *"Luck to the Fighters!"*

Not until we recover Java, and perhaps not then, will we know exactly what happened to your son.

All the fellow pilots of his squadron have left the Pacific months ago. But I have unearthed a ground-crew man of the squadron who tells me that he talked to one of the pilots. This pilot said that he saw your son's plane afire and tried to signal him to bail out, but without success.

This is the second report I have had that your son's plane was seen afire in the air, but it may be a case of duplication. I give it to you for what it is worth.

You have my sympathy in your loss.

Sincerely,

George Weller

Correspondent: Chicago Daily News.

Printed in England. Sept. 1940. (8,000 pads.)

THE EASTERN EXTENSION AUSTRALASIA AND CHINA TELEGRAPH COMPANY, Limited.
(ASSOCIATED WITH CABLE AND WIRELESS LIMITED)
(INCORPORATED IN ENGLAND)

CABLE ROUTES ————
WIRELESS ROUTES ————

OFFICE OF ISSUE
PERTH
19 MAR 42

Circuit FS193	Clerk's Name.	Time Received.	
SYP90V	GN		

CHICAGOILL 33 16TH   COLLECT2/7

RETRANSMITTED FROM SYDNEY

LC GEORGE WELLER CARE IMPERIAL CABLES ADELPHI HOTEL   PERTH

TREMENDOUSLY RELIEVED HAPPY SAFE ARRIVAL HEARTIEST CONGRATULATIONS

BEST WISHES FROM ALL STOP SUGGEST ROUNDUP DISPATCH ENTIRE JAVA

CAMPAIGN

          PAUL MOWRER

MARK YOUR REPLY "Via Imperial"

NO ENQUIRY RESPECTING THIS TELEGRAM CAN BE ATTENDED TO WITHOUT PRODUCTION OF THIS COPY.

Printed in England. Sept. 1940. (8,000 pads.)

THE EASTERN EXTENSION AUSTRALASIA AND CHINA TELEGRAPH COMPANY, Limited.
(ASSOCIATED WITH CABLE AND WIRELESS LIMITED)
(INCORPORATED IN ENGLAND)

CABLE ROUTES ————
WIRELESS ROUTES ————

OFFICE OF ISSUE
PER
20 MAR

Circuit.	Clerk's Name.	Time Received.	

SYP109V   CHICAGOILL   24   19TH   10 33AM

          RETRANSMITTED FROM SYDNEY COLLECT 1/11

     LC GEORGE WEBLER ADELPHI HOTEL PERTH

CONGRATULATIONS FINE JAVA NAVAL STORY CAN YOU DO SAME FOR

JAVA LAND BATTLES

          PAUL MOWRER

M 1055
MARK YOUR REPLY "Via Imperial"

NO ENQUIRY RESPECTING THIS TELEGRAM CAN BE ATTENDED TO WITHOUT PRODUCTION OF THIS COPY.

X

"Luck to the Fighters!"

The Story of the American
Fighter Planes in Java

To those in Java,
living and dead,
who await the return of America's wings

"Luck to the Fighters!"—abridged here in details but not in scope—took Weller a year to write after he escaped from Java in March 1942. During this fury of work, he was covering the war from Australia and from New Guinea, and also writing *Singapore Is Silent*.

Originally, the fighters saga was to be one-third of a long book about the Pacific; the other parts were to cover the fall of the Dutch Indies and the war in New Guinea (Chapter XII). A dispute with his publishers led him to set aside the larger Pacific scheme before the Singapore book even appeared. (Weller and his agent thought that Harcourt Brace held up its release so as not to compete with a book by Theodore White, then later refused to put out the Java fighters as a short book of its own for the same reason.) This kind of crisscrossing author-publisher-agent argument, due to wartime mail delays, dragged on for months. The demands of the *CDN,* coupled with serial malaria, doomed any longer book.

By that time Weller's manuscript of the young American pilots who had saved Java for a crucial month was a year and a half old, then two years old . . . and soon it seemed a very remote story in a dense war producing ever more sagas, more defeats, and more courage than the purchasing public could conveniently absorb. It remains today a virtually unknown corner of the war, and of American heroes. (The "American war correspondent" rearranging beds at Batavia's Hôtel des Indes is, of course, Weller.)

In the end this chronicle appeared not as a book, but carved up as three long installments in a military history quarterly during 1944 and 1945. Weller's literary agent, Harold Ober, subsequently did his best to find a hardcover home for it, without success. By then the futile defense of Java must have seemed a long way off to any editor assessing the reading public.

It remains an eyewitness account of a dramatic chapter of the war that only Weller took the trouble to see. Among his Java dispatches are several that cover episodes from this material, but as he was scrupulous about not writing anything that could be useful to the enemy, until Java fell to the Japanese the story of the Seventeenth Pursuit was neither finished nor could be told. (He was eventually able to interview surviving pilots in Australia and New Guinea.) His frustration at not seeing it all in book form sprang from his sense of responsibility to history. "They fought unknown . . . Someone must speak for them."

That might serve as a partial statement of the correspondent's duty, in any war.

—

FOREWORD

Official reports, personal memoirs and the dispatches of war correspondents are said to be the stuff of which history is made. If this be true, an adequate account of the American fighter pilots in Java may never be written.

For four weeks a squadron of American fliers and ground crew, cut off from all sources of supply and maintenance, held the air over Java against an enemy that was their superior in every respect but fighting ability and courage. For much of this time these Americans were virtually the only force of modern pursuit planes defending the Dutch East Indies.

Official reports of the American fighters in Java are extremely meager, fragmentary and sometimes inaccurate; the originals, such as they were, had to be destroyed in the evacuation of the island.

Finally, the eye of the war correspondent, searching for valor unrecognized and wishing also to honor those who serve humbly but serve well, passed by the Seventeenth Pursuit Squadron, Provisional. These men fought too far outside the tentacles of communication to win equal respect with those whom proximity helped on the way to recognition.

Neither general nor war correspondent ever visited the hidden runways of the Seventeenth Pursuit. They flew unrecorded. They fought unknown.

One of the inequalities of war is that those who serve nearest the outlets of information become most familiar to the world. The work of the Eagle Squadron, the Flying Tigers, and the gallant twelve fighters of Bataan all became known. The efforts of the Americans who flew for their flag in Java were written across her coppery sunsets, but they vanished with the final fading of invasion.

While the Indies yielded little by little to their enemy's savage enterprise, the American army's Fortresses and dive bombers, the navy's big and vulnerable PBY Catalina flying boats, and this hidden hive of hard-pressed fighters all strove together to sustain the doomed and disintegrating chain of islands that stretched across from north of Australia. All fought in the vicinity of Soerabaya, 400 miles from the headquarters of General Wavell, General Brett and Admiral Hart, 400 miles from the Bandoeng radio station and the censorships military and political.

Something was told of the Fortresses and dive bombers. A little was tardily revealed of the gallantry of PatWing Ten, the émigrés of Cavite. But what the creaking "Forties" (P-40s) of the American fighters at Blimbing did to win time for General MacArthur's eventual defense of Australia has never been disclosed.

Having served as war correspondent in Java after leaving Singapore, the writer of this account felt sharply the neglect of the American fighters, in which he was himself a balked and unhappy accomplice. Although he traveled four times the length of Java, visited nearly every field where Americans touched landing gear, recorded all he could within the bounds of military and political security, and remained in Java two days after the last fliers themselves had gone, the writer felt sharply the incompleteness with which he and others in identical predicament recorded this important instant in American history.

Itself written in the field, this account of what happened in Java should be considered an elementary nugget, unfinished and awaiting the treatment of other hands. Three of the four commanders of the Seventeenth Pursuit are missing or dead. Someone must speak for them. This account is offered out of debt to those who fought and are still fighting, as well as those who lie forever in the Graafplaats Kembang Koening at Soerabaya, in the blue recesses of the Java Sea, in Bali's soft jungle, or in some forgotten rice paddy high on Java's curved terraces.

Too little to honor fully those whom it celebrates, perhaps this word will not arrive too late.

George Weller
Somewhere in New Guinea
1 March, 1943

"LUCK TO THE FIGHTERS!"

Twenty-seven big Mitsubishi bombers, fifteen Zeros hovering above them like gnats, arose from Kendari in the eastern Celebes, swung into their great geese-like triple V, and marched methodically over the blue waters of Madura Strait. It was a big raid on Java, and Soerabaya was going to get it.

Soerabaya, the chief Dutch naval base in the Indies, had no radar listening apparatus to give warning before the bombers came up over the horizon. Nowhere upon its hilly shores did one see the black-armed monster that saved England and could tell the approach of aircraft nearly a hundred miles away.

The Dutch system of warning was voice radio sets, manned by courageous Javanese youths and Eurasians in shacks on lonely beaches, who relayed word if the Japanese flew over within hearing distance or eyeshot.

But the Japs flew high, often above 20,000 feet. If they were seen, it was lucky. If they were not, it was too bad.

The Japanese were already beginning to exploit the indirect approach. Their base was so close that their Mitsubishis had plenty of time-over-the-target and could hit Soerabaya from any direction except directly south. And on successive raids, comparing the time of the warning on the Dutch radio with the position in the flight leader's log, the Japs could determine which approach gave Soerabaya's thousands the narrowest margin of warning, or no warning at all.

This time the makeshift warning system, like a network of fire wardens protecting a national forest, happened to work effectively.

Among those Japanese fighter pilots flying above the bombers was a dead man. He did not know yet that he would soon be dead. With his rubber-sneakered feet on the sensitive needle-like controls of his butterfly plane, he kept his eyes on his squadron leader, his oxygen mask tightly closed. He was flying at nearly 30,000 feet, where no American Kittyhawk could reach him. The Dutch pilots' Brewster Buffaloes, already wallowing at 16,000 feet, could do no more than look up.

Yet he was a dead man. For at that moment the P-40E that was to accomplish his ending was searing down its runway and taking off, with an American, a plain-and-simple, uncomplicated human being in heavy drill trousers, furred boots and a leather flying jacket.

The flying garment of the Japanese pilot was not a zippered army leather jacket like the American's. He wore a funeral shroud, suitable for a corpse. He meant it to be such. The shroud was long and black. He must have known that when the Zero is hit it usually burns up or blows up. He did not know that he would die, but if he did, he was dressed for it.

American and Jap met at 22,000 feet over the Java Sea, met and fought. The American's guns won. The Jap, still alive, began to fall. But this Jap did not burn. His engine was hit, not his fuel tank. This is rare, because in the Zero the tank is directly behind the engine, and when one goes, usually the other puffs into flame too. The Jap's propeller, from being invisible before him, slowed and became an almost visible wall. Then as the plane began to fall the prop whirled faster, the earth grew larger, the prop grew invisible again then with an awful simulacrum of safe flight the wings screamed loud, the rooftops came closer and closer—

They found him over a garden wall, still in his burial shroud. His wish had been to die for the emperor. Neatly he dressed for death and neatly he got it. The American, nonchalant and slovenly, dressed for life in a leather zipper jacket, remained alive.

Enemies form each other's natures. This pilot's antagonist was an American. Not any particular American; it's aimless in this war to attribute acts to individuals. He was one of perhaps the bravest, least known group of fighter pilots in the war in the Far East. He fought at a time when we were losing the war, and losing it fast. Australia had to be saved many times, and he gained time to save it.

This nameless American pilot was the American boy whose two slim hands—he was hardly twenty—were thrust into the Dutch dike at Java and held long enough for the American and British High Commands to get away, held long enough for Soerabaya to be destroyed by the Dutch with fire, axe and explosive and thus denied to the Japanese navy, held long enough for Australia to get sufficient additional American aircraft to stop the Jap on the Java-Solomons line.

The boys at the Java dike were part of the Seventeenth Pursuit Squadron. We can name it, because it is gone forever, scattered and dispersed. Everyone knows the work of the Flying Tigers in Burma and China, or of PatWing Ten in the Philippines, Java and Australia. Everyone knows how the Fortress bombardment groups fought there. But few have heard of the Seventeenth Pursuit. Their work remained almost unknown even in Java. Like angels, nobody knew where they came from. Only their works were famous. Why?

First, because they were secretly based at Blimbing—a village between Soerabaya and the Fortress base at Malang. Only a handful of correspondents ever went from western Java, where the ABDA [American-British-Dutch-Australian] Command was located first in Batavia and then in Bandoeng, to eastern Java. And no correspondent was allowed to visit their field.

Some of these pilots died in Java striving to stem the Japanese. The honor they deserve is long overdue. To realize what they accomplished necessitates knowing how the Seventeenth Pursuit came into being, how it fought until every plane it had was destroyed, and how its members, now scattered forever, are fighting still to avenge those who will fight no more.

The Seventeenth Pursuit Squadron was born not in Java or the Philippines, but Brisbane. The man who brought it into being was stocky, peppery little Major-General Lewis Brereton, who was the spark plug of the fighter forces in Java after Brett moved into position as Deputy Commander of the patchwork Allied force.

If pilots were as superstitious as sometimes represented, the Seventeenth Pursuit might well have taken its number for a talisman. On the field at Brisbane in early January, there were seventeen P-40Es ready to fight—if they could get to Java. The tiny expedition consisted of seventeen pilots, seventeen crew chiefs, seventeen armorers, one line chief, one first sergeant and three radio men—the barest bones of a skeleton force rushing into an emergency. It was a kind of defensive commando. Only thirteen pilots in the Seventeenth Pursuit had experience flying under Brereton in the Philippines. Four pilots newly arrived from California made up the rest.

The squadron commander selected by Brereton was Captain Charles "Bud" Sprague, a slim young redheaded Irishman from Bridgeport, Connecticut, who was soon to acquire a status with his men that amounted to worship. Commissioned only after arriving in Java, his majorship, like almost everything about the Seventeenth, was just dealt off the arm.

Time, time, time was what Australia needed. "You—well, you—er—just go up there and fight," Brereton said.

Send us American fighters was the signal being tapped out in different codes from a dozen places, from Tulagi in the Solomons and Rabaul in New Guinea to Rangoon and Colombo.

New Guinea's Port Moresby, undergoing daily punishment by low-flying Zeros and high-level bombers, wanted fighters. So did Singapore, 2800 miles away across the great half arc of the southwestern Pacific. The only forces opposing the Japanese at this time were half a dozen badly shaken P-40s still remaining on Bataan, the handful of Wirraways still striving to endure Japanese attacks upon Moresby, the slow Dutch Brewsters and curious CW-21s that were rejected by our army because it took a genius to land them—both to be massacred in the first heavy raid on Soerabaya—and the doomed RAF Hurricane fighters debarked in late January on Singapore.

Across the enormous panorama there were air fields galore, but no planes. Had all one hundred and twenty American pilots been able to take off instantly from Australia in fighters for Java, it would hardly have been enough.

Scrappy little Brereton—who through his spectacles can give a look which pins you to the wall—peeled the gilt from the golden apple of the Indies before he tossed it into the lap of the Seventeenth. While the flies of Darwin practically kidnapped him, he gave the boys a straight talk, delivered in the challenging let's-see-anybody-say-different Brereton manner. Nobody was there to write down his sulfurous views, but the boys felt they would never forget what he said. They cannot give you the exact words, but as they remember, it went like this:

He said that we would be heavily outnumbered from the beginning.

He said that we could expect some support from the Hurricanes if any got out of Singapore, but probably not very much because things were looking tough. He said he would be coming up himself as soon as he got things straightened out . . .

And what did they think about it?

We understood two things. We understood that he was a pilot's air general. And we understood that if Java fell we probably would not be coming back.

Taking the fourteen planes to Java by air could be planned in only one way. There was no choice of air fields as there had been across Australia; there was just a single causeway of islands, good as long as the Japs left it alone. Due to Portuguese neutrality, the Americans had to fly from Darwin to Koepang. Beyond that the only airdromes were on the island of Soemba, or Bali. The next landing had to be Java.

In the October conferences in Java before war broke out, it was arranged for Dutch fighters to take part in the defense of Singapore and British fighters to take part in Java. No one could foresee that American fighters would be the principal defending force for Java. Nor had the Australians and Dutch come to any agreement nor made any preparations for the transport of planes from Australia to Java.

The whole idea was that the British fighters, if the Philippines fell, would drop back from northern Malaya, and if Singapore fell, would pull back to Sumatra and Java. A good plan, but Singapore and Manila both lost all their fighters.

The day came—it was January 23 [1942]—when the pilots strapped on their goggles, walked across the red clay RAAF field at Darwin, and climbed in. Then they were off over the big abandoned meat factory. They saw Melville Island on their right, and soon they were gone.

A leathery-faced American pilot, who flies an aged bi-motored Beech-craft and has remained anonymous while accomplishing some of the most incredible scouting flights of the Pacific war, led the fighters safely to Koepang, like some Daniel Boone of the Indonesian archipelago. Though separated by twenty-five years and 17,000 hours flying time, they were his gang, the Philippine bunch he'd flown out in this rickety plane, announcing his arrival from Australia with a telegram, *One Beechcraft, one nitwit en-route*. But for him [Paul "Pappy" Gunn], they would be with the other young pilots on Bataan. He brought them because he wanted them to fight with six machine guns on wings instead of a Garand that most couldn't handle.

Another pilot, Lieutenant Ben Irvin, caught dengue fever at the Penfoei airdrome and was forced to remain when the final flight took off for Wain-gapoe. Two days later a whip of Japanese fighters swept in and destroyed his Kittyhawk; his sergeant, Angelo Prioreschi, was working in the hangar when six Zeros strafed methodically for twenty-five minutes. "I ran around that hangar like a chicken, trying to dodge those bullets," said Prioreschi, a stocky blackhaired crew chief from a Pennsylvania coal-mining town. He went on to Java and became one of the squadron's three decorated enlisted men. Irvin (later to win almost every flying honor America could give) flew back to Darwin to plead himself another P-40.

No, there was nothing secret to the Japs about the stepping-stones from Darwin to Soerabaya.

Curiously enough, many of the ground crewmen had never in their lives flown before they took wings for Java. As Perry says: "We left Australia over the Timor Sea on our way to 'the front.' We flew until almost six p.m. and finally were over Timor itself. We landed at Koepang, taxied up to the concealed hangar, got out and there wasn't a soul in sight. A few minutes later the Australians manning the 'drome began drifting out of the jungle. They were amazed to see us. We had come in from the wrong way, and thinking it was two Jap bombers, they took to their slit trenches in the jungle. The Japs had been raiding at nine in the morning and five in the afternoon for the last two weeks. They had just left, they said. We went up and had our supper, along with a cold bottle of Dutch beer.

"We stayed in a grass hut and took turns through the night standing guard with the brilliant moon overhead, silhouetting the swaying palm trees and ferns. The lizards croaking in nearby bushes, and the night birds uttering their hoarse shrieks, made it unforgettable. At last dawn came and we took off as soon as the runway was visible. All this time we'd been looking for our Forties to arrive to accompany us. We were getting worried about them, and also for our own safety, since Japanese planes were in the area and we had no guns at all on the transports. We had not seen the other transport for a long time and we were all alone in the sky.

"Suddenly a plane dived out of the clouds above us, went below and came up under our belly. Instantly: Jap! From each side we expected flashes from his guns. Twin flashes came blinking at us. It was the other transport! The sigh of relief was audible. 'Don't ever do that again,' said one of the men, talking to the other plane."

Less than three weeks later, Japanese parachutists were to descend on Koepang, breaking the golden thread to the Indies.

Koepang to Waingapoe, for the gnatlike P-40Es, was only about 240 miles over the Savu Sea. The next hop would have been only 300 miles if the P-40s could have landed at Den Pasar. But at this time on Bali there was only the air field, no fighter fuel. They had to push through to Soerabaya, a jump of over 450 miles.

The fighters got only a glimpse of Bali, that unspoiled paradise of the creative craftsman. They did not know, then, that over Bali and little Penida, the island in Lombok Strait, Major Sprague was to fight his last battle as their commander.

Thirteen planes arrived in Soerabaya on January 24 and 25.

Two days later the big American transport planes came winging in from Darwin. The boys in tan duck caps who knew about machine guns and carburetors jumped to the ground with: "How did the engines stand up?" on their lips.

It's a cramping, deafening and fatiguing experience to fly fighter planes over long stretches of water. Fighter pilots are not navigators by nature. Sprague had brought his whole force through intact, but they were tired.

The marathon was over; they prepared their maneuvering muscles and sea-weary eyes for the sprints.

The British troops fell back upon Singapore, and the Japs took Ambon, the northern keyhole to the Banda Sea. Would Singapore hold? The Japs were making preliminary photographs of the Soerabaya navy yard—the last usable Allied naval base above the south coast of Australia—for the raids to come. Small wonder the Jap bombers would be able to place a bomb directly amid the thatched camouflage the Dutch had so painstakingly built over the drydock for our refugee Asiatic Fleet.

For five days at Soerabaya the pilots learned to distinguish the Dutch and American aircraft already on hand, which in the Dutch case consisted of Dorniers, Ryans and barrel-bodied Brewsters, together with a handful of old Curtiss CW-21Bs plus a small force of PBY Catalinas. The Americans also began practicing with the interceptor control operated by the Dutch air officer at Soerabaya, to whom they were subordinated. "Those Dutchmen certainly were gutty," said one American armorer who saw them fight. There was something challenging about receiving the duty from men who died as the Dutch did in the first raids.

The CW-21, their best plane, was a radial engine job like the Zero, with four .303 Browning machine guns. But the Zero had about fifty miles an hour margin over the old Curtiss interceptor, and could practically turn cartwheels inside it.

The first time the Japs hit Soerabaya, thirteen of these anachronisms went up; only seven came back. At night the Dutchmen sang and laughed and drank beer just the same, and the American enlisted men felt a wonder that men could die like that.

Those five days in Soerabaya, the Allies got to know each other. Dutch pilots and American enlisted men lived only a few doors apart. Before dying, the Dutch knew who was taking over.

When the seven went up, to meet the next overwhelming raid, only two came back. The hard-boiled Dutchmen, with the strong suicidal streak that came of desperation, merrily told the Americans: "If the Japs come tomorrow, we'll both go home, too. It's time we knocked off work, like those other boys."

About the Dutch, the Americans say: "They might be a little quick reaching for the old guilder, but they sure knew how to fight as a people, and you couldn't move them with anything. They certainly tried to show their appreciation for us."

On January 27 Sprague took out a flight of ships to protect a Dutch sub crippled in the shallow water attacks off Borneo. After the weather worsened under the prevailing monsoon, and the sub was no longer in danger of air attack, all the P-40s were pulled back to Soerabaya. Lieutenant Frank Neri, landing in bad weather after a mission to Bali, spun in and crashed. His face and head were terribly cut and his ear sliced off cleanly, as by a razor. He went to Bandoeng for more treatment. After Neri had gone, a couple of his friends went out to the scene of the crash and saw something white in the grass. It was the ear. They put it in a small blue box and carried it around awhile, intending to return it formally to its owner. But the ear became impossible to live with and finally, like a lot of things, got lost.

The Dutch, realizing that heavy bombings were imminent, hastened to get the Americans moved back to Blimbing, behind Soerabaya. There was one thing the Dutch were rich in, and that was air fields.

Blimbing (not to be confused with the Blimbing near Malang, the American Fortress base) was a little kampong on an inconspicuous road six miles south from Djombang, a station on the railroad through central Java. From a fighter's view aloft, Blimbing looked like a button set deep in an upholstered divan. It was ranked on every side by climbing *sawis,* the terraced ricefields by which Java's 40,000,000, a population denser than almost any in Europe, were able to feed themselves.

The field was typical of Dutch ingenuity. They had taken several ricefields, drained them, and planted grass. From the air it still looked more like a ricefield than anything else. It was six miles by the squadron's two "peeps" [small jeeps] to Blimbing the village, where the men lived in the deserted homes of executives of a sugar mill. Then it was another six miles out to the main road, and about twelve to Djombang, where one could take a crowded local train to Soerabaya, full of women in sarongs and babies in tiny sarongs, sweets, chickens and lively Javanese chatter.

For twenty-seven days the Japanese could not find the Blimbing air field. Our pilots often had difficulty finding it themselves. (The Dutch called it "Ngoro" after a nearby town.) The ex-ricefield that was the bulwark against Japanese invasion of eastern Java was shaped like a cross on

the ground, with the long arm pointing east and the three short arms running north, west and south. The Seventeenth arranged its planes so at least
sixteen—if they were in repair—could get off the cramped runways in
three minutes, spiral up and gain enough height for a diving attack at oncoming Zeros and Mitsubishis. Considering that the best pilots had to take
off on the short-armed north-south runway, over choppy dangerous air
drafts exhaled up from flooded ricefields, the speed of take-off could hardly
have been beaten by a crack outfit from those all-outdoors fields where
fighters trained back in the States.

The idea was that the American fighters could protect either Soerabaya from a head-on attack over Madura Strait, or Malang against an attack coming from Bali. Meantime bombers from the Seventh Group as
well as the more famous Nineteenth were to strike Japanese ships wherever they were, to destroy their air fields from Jolo to Kendari, from Balikpapan to Kuala Lumpur in faraway Malaya, from Singapore to
Palembang. These were the days when the B-17 was only a high-level
bomber, when moonlight skip-bombing was unheard of, and anything
below 5000 feet by daylight was considered wild and wasteful for the
bombsight-obsessed monsters.

The Seventeenth moved to its new field after Lieutenant Geurtz, their
hard-working Dutch liaison officer, and Captain Willard Reed of the Marine
Corps had perfected arrangements and finished preparations. Because the
field at Blimbing was well-hidden, accommodations were plain. You
couldn't have everything. One customarily cheerful pilot wrote: "The food
was terrible, prepared by native cooks, and had no similarity to anything
appetizing. So all we would eat was peanuts, bananas and beer. We would
only plan from hour to hour, not knowing if we would be alive the next
hour. Everybody was in good spirits despite our predicament."

The day of the ground crew was long and hard. The early shift had a
breakfast of bread with powdered chocolate, took the peeps out to the field
and had tools in their hands by 2:45 a.m. The regular shift could loaf in
bedded ease, provided only they were on the field by 4 a.m.

There was no engineering department and no supply department. They
simply borrowed things back and forth. "Could I trouble you, McBride, for
a cupful of presto?" "If you can give us the use of two hundred rounds of
clean .50s for the day, Goltry." They swapped like housewives.

At 9 the grease gang had another light breakfast consisting of cottile roots plucked fresh from the nearby field and prepared by the Dutchman, his wife and two daughters who fed them. The cottile is a white rooted plant that looks in leafage like a fig and has a straight root. Stripped and boiled, they were good.

Sometimes in this late breakfast they had fresh coconut. There were a hundred fifty coolies working at the strip, rolling gasoline drums and building shelter revetments out of bamboo, matting and tar. It was enough to point to a tree and one of the little Javanese would hitch back his sarong, plant his knife more firmly in his belt, and go up the best-inclined coconut palm.

Blimbing had no anti-aircraft; the Dutch idea was apparently that when this field was discovered by the Zeros, there were plenty in Java to take its place. The Americans started some protection against strafing. They dug four or five round holes about five feet deep, and took .50-caliber guns from damaged or foundling P-40s to arm them. In the plane the guns had been electrically fired, but there was no electrical system on the ground. They rigged up selenoid magnets from the planes as triggers. How all this would have worked out in a raid nobody knew. After a couple of weeks the Dutch sent out some native gunners, who lived in the shacks between the eastern and southern arms of the runway and manned the guns by day.

Sprague tried to keep everyone alive to the fact that they might be attacked any time, by land as well as by air. As early as February 2, four full weeks before the day of invasion, he told the men: "The Japs are due any moment."

The Japanese hunted patiently for the field. They found and struck not only Batavia and Soerabaya, but Malang, Madioen and Jokjakarta, the three Fortress bases, and the headquarters of Wavell at Bandoeng. But until the very day their landing barges grounded on the sands of Java, they could not find Blimbing.

One morning they almost found it. Four Zeros came over the little field and hung over the rice paddies like the ever-circling hawks of Java. As Perry said: "If they had been able to spot the field, the Seventeenth Pursuit Squadron would have had its career ended. They would have bombed it out completely. As it was we were able to operate a while longer and the Jap radio still reported 'swarms of fighters rising from hidden fields all around Soerabaya, armed with six cannon.' . . . In reality it was our twenty- or thirty-odd P-40Es armed with six .50-caliber guns, rising from *one* hidden field. But the Japs couldn't do anything, and Tojo kept losing planes."

In the broiling Javanese noon—sometimes broken by petulant thunderstorms—the squadron's truck would circle the field with lunch: usually fried rice with some fruit like mango or pineapple. The truck stopped at the east end revetments, the north end revetments, and "Operations," a twenty-foot-square grass hut pushed in the corner between the southern and eastern arms of the runway. The grass huts for armament and engineering were a little farther down the eastern arm.

Before the thunderstorm that often follows sunset in Java, the tired men crammed aboard the two peeps and the truck to go back to Blimbing. Supper, the best meal of the day, was waiting: a big tureen of soup, water buffalo meat with cabbage and rice, and finally *manggas,* the Malay for "mangos," which they learned to call by the native name.

Busy though the men were getting the P-40s ready to fight, there was still enough zest in them to want their planes to look terrifying, so they painted on the leering shark mouths that go so well with the underslung jaw of the P-40. Some thought a dragon was the thing, and soon there were a few dragons. Usually officers did this fancy brushwork themselves, spurred by suggestions from mechanics lying on the ground beneath the awkwardly placed underwing feed system of the P-40.

It is customary, when officers and enlisted men have faced death together, to find in retrospect that they were so close the barrier of rank actually vanishes. Blimbing was this kind of situation. The best testimony of such comradeship is that enlisted men are its chief witnesses. "We knew we were all in it together. The officers behaved this way to us, and we behaved the same toward them."

Discipline was strict, but it came from below rather than above. Sprague was no prude. When they asked him about leave in Soerabaya, he said: "After you get the planes ready and can give them no more work, your time is your own. You can go anywhere and do anything. There will be no leave passes; you issue your own. But you have to be in the revetment long enough before dawn so that when your pilot comes out, his ship is ready to fly and fight." To the officers, speaking apart, he said: "There will be no saluting and stuff around here for awhile. We can't waste time in non-essentials. Our job is to hold the Japs out of Java as long as we can."

Then, just to make sure the grease gang understood obligations were mutual, he called them in again. He said: "We're operating under bad conditions. We have one armorer, one crew chief and one pilot for each plane. If anything big goes wrong, we can't fix it. It's up to you to see that your ship is ready to fight. Besides the guns in his plane, every pilot has a .45 in his shoulder holster. If something mechanical goes wrong with his ship or his guns in the air, and the pilot gets back, he has the privilege of landing, pulling his .45, and shooting you on the spot." No groundlings were shot.

"Jess" Willard Reed was one of that group of American naval and Marine Corps pilots who had been hired by the Dutch Government to give instruction in piloting Catalinas. Small, round-faced, dark and vivacious, one of the most beloved Americans who ever visited Java, Reed was to be a kind of unofficial foster father to the Seventeenth Pursuit. He was not only ready to guide them, as he had the Dutch, he was ready to fight with them.

Two days after the Squadron settled in at Blimbing, Sprague flew to ABDA headquarters in Bandoeng to explain the lack of repair equipment in Soerabaya. The Dutch had no radar; the Americans had no spare parts, tires or anything else.

Almost upon the hour of the redheaded commander's departure the Japanese sent their first great wave of bombers against Soerabaya.

The lookout system gave the Americans between twenty and twenty-five minutes' warning—when it worked. The Japanese bombers usually came in at 21,000 feet and were able to get over Soerabaya and open their bomb hatches before the Americans could reach them.

On February 3 the Americans were 4000 feet below when they saw the first formation. There were seventeen enemy, in two lines. The Americans chased the bombers, twin-motored Mitsubishi Type 1 Bettys, far out to sea. But the Japs had to pay for their blow at Soerabaya. Bill Hennon of Mound, Minnesota, gained the squadron its first bomber by sneaking in alone from the rear and picking one off.

Hennon, who earned his Silver Star in one of these raids, had been arguing with a Dutch pilot on a Soerabaya airdrome when the Japs came over. "A Brewster can't turn inside a Zero," he said. The Dutchman said it could. He went up to prove his ideas, and in ten minutes he was back sitting in the same slit trench. "You vere right, Bill," he said. "Brewster cannot turn inside Zero."

On this same day the Seventh and Nineteenth heavy bombardment groups of Fortresses received their heaviest blow at Singosari field, a few miles from Malang. Five Fortresses were destroyed on the ground—four that day, the fifth puffing into flame the next. This last Fortress fathered a saying not found in books of Javanese lore. Its number was 27; the saying, whenever an unexplained bolo knife or binoculars was found in the hands of a new owner, was that "I got it out of 27." The limits of 27 became as extendable as passenger accommodations on the *Mayflower.*

The next day Sprague flew in from Bandoeng. The ABDA command had not been able to offer much in supplies or equipment. There were no other Kittyhawks in Java; only a few Brewsters and some Hurricanes from Singapore that already had their hands full trying to protect the east coast of Sumatra, where every escaping ship was being terribly punished as it passed southward through Bangka Strait.

The Seventeenth began to sense how remote it was in the extemporaneous, under-equipped scheme of Java's Allied defense. Batavia, at the other end of Java, was a commercial port, of little importance except as a refuge for ships fleeing from Singapore. But on the defense of Soerabaya— a naval base in some respects better equipped than Singapore and far more active—the Allies had bet their hope of stopping the Japs north of the barrier islands. If Soerabaya was to remain a mother port for warships, particularly for American subs meant to halt the Jap convoys, the eleven Kittyhawks of the Soerabaya fighter force would have to be kept in the air.

The lack of radar equipment to defend Soerabaya, giving the Seventeenth time to meet the invaders at sea, was keenly felt in the grass huts at Blimbing. There were also difficulties coordinating the telephone-radio warning system, with long-range Jap fighters approaching Java from the south and east as well as the north.

An adequate warning system might have saved Java. As it was, the boys listened for the warning gongs of the villages, which traveled faster than the tattoo of African drums.

In this first raid on Soerabaya, of February 3, the Japs sent over seventy bombers in all, killing 33 people and injuring 141. The red-circled bombers claimed to have got eighty-five Dutch planes besides five Brewsters shot down.

The next day Blimbing saw its first tragedy: the lovable and popular "Jess" Reed, the Marine captain who had been a kind of guardian angel to the Seventeenth. He had no right to be bringing in an army P-40; his job was on the PBY Catalina training side. But he wanted to help. He was a flying commander, and knew he could not give Bud Sprague full cooperation with the Dutch unless he understood the take-off problems at Blimbing's compact *sawi*-surrounded field.

Jess took off smoothly, but coming in, perhaps due to the twinkling illusion of the flooded ricefields, he made a mistake, and his motor cut out. What Reed probably did was to reach for the throttle and pull back on the mixture control, which is next to the throttle in a P-40, not bent away from it as in a PBY.

Almost everyone in the squadron was standing on the field watching him. His plane disappeared behind a hilly ricefield. Then they heard the sloppy noise of the crash. He must have got the engine going again, because they heard it catch once before striking. Then Bill Hennon and Cy Blanton reached him. Only his arm was broken; it seemed to everyone as though he had been drowned in the *sawi* rather than killed. He had tried to stretch his glide, possibly after shutting off his mixture control and being unable to get it going again. Besides having turned over, the plane had come completely around and was facing away from the field.

The Dutch mourned Reed, eldest of their American instructors, and wanted to bury him, but the Seventeenth decided to take care of this marine who was their own. One staff sergeant had operated a funeral parlor, and Reed was borne away by the hands of the men who admired him. They buried him not far from the *sawi*, and there he rests awaiting the day when his own marines go back to Java.

New reinforcements were on the way from Darwin. After the raids on Koepang and Bali, every flier knew there was no safety in the Darwin-Soerabaya island stepping-stones.

A lag is necessary in describing to the public the deterioration of any military situation. At this time, when encouraging statements were coming

out about the prospect of Singapore holding, the Japanese were busy saw-
ing off the arterial system of supplying fighters upon which the whole
Dutch East Indies depended.

Down in Australia the U.S. Army was working to do the impossible and
keep the planes flowing. Not only P-40 Kittyhawks but also navy-built A-24
Dauntless dive bombers were urgently needed to stop the invasion convoys
the Japanese were assembling for Java. Neither the British nor the Dutch
possessed any dive bombers.

Meantime American mechanics in Brisbane were diligently trying to
put together a navy dive bomber with army weapons. A dealer in old iron
was patching up new gun mountings for the rear cockpit, to fit army
machine guns on the navy supports. Hammering things out by hand
blacksmith-fashion, he was also attempting to make over navy bomb
catches to hold army bombs. The army was paying, in those feverish
makeshift hours in Australia, for its reluctance to accept the ten-year-old
navy experience in dive-bombing, just as the navy was to be tardy in discovering the value of the great land-based reconnaissance bombers used
by the army.

When the dive bombers, which were to be operated out of Java under
top cover furnished by the Seventeenth, finally started flying there, they
faced the same difficulties of having no intermediate bases—like champions of the springboard forced to swim the English Channel as a warm-up
for their diving.

One A-24 en route across northern Australia lost its way and came
down in the desert with a belly landing, scraping off its lower pan and
bending its propeller. The pilot began sending telegrams back to the miniature American headquarters. He imagined he was still in the middle of the
American system of supply and behaved accordingly. His first telegram
went about like this:

FORCE LANDED PLEASE SEND GROUND CREW.

This message being unanswered, he sent another:

WASHED OUT BELLY PAN AND PROP PLEASE SEND SPARES.

There were none to send, so there was no reply. The flier in the bush waited another couple of days, then had the Australian homesteader who was boarding him send another:

STILL GROUNDED HERE WHAT SHALL EYE DO?

This time the reply was:

WHY DONT YOU MARRY AND SETTLE DOWN.

The lieutenant thereupon took part of the corrugated iron roof from the farmer's shed and made himself a new bellypan. He removed the propeller, drove to town and stood by while the local blacksmith hammered it roughly into shape. Then he flew the plane back. He was learning how wars are fought.

No substantial group of fighting planes has ever traveled to battle so far under their power as did the Seventeenth to save Java. If they had never brought down in flames a single Jap, or failed entirely to delay the enemy's onslaught, a forefinger following on a map the crooked, death-strewn line of their travel would necessarily pause in awe at their achievement.

In another part of Australia a big transport plane was about to leave for Java with two dozen "odds and sods" of servicemen. The colonel in charge accidentally learned that the fighters en route there in P-40s—newcomers to the Seventeenth—were going to leave without parachutes, because none had yet arrived.

"I don't order or even suggest you give up your chutes," he said to his fellow passengers. "I merely put the situation before you, and ask you to do as you see fit."

Every man entered the transport, took his chute, carried it out and threw it on the fighter sector truck nearby. The fighters took off for the long seat-pounding race for Java, and there was a reassuring chute under every pilot.

Though Soerabaya was only a tree-top jump from Blimbing, the newcomers had to be guided in personally, because Blimbing was almost unfindable in the cushioned Javanese hills. Somebody always had to go over to Soerabaya to bring in the new boys.

The former newcomers were now the old-timers. They gave hints about what to do and what not to do. The food in the hotel at Djombang was terrible, but you weren't supposed to complain. Every third day or so you could go into Soerabaya and fill up on the delicious twenty-course *rijstaffel*. The unit of Dutch money was a guilder but it was always called a "glider." And it glided away, just like that.

Nine new pilots brought the fighting strength of the squadron to twenty-two. Besides Egenes, Reynolds, McWherter and Jackson, they were blond and blue-eyed Wallace Hoskyn of Seattle; Lester Johnsen of South Bend, Washington (a sprite of Norwegian descent who had been a champion relay runner at Stanford); stocky Bernard Oliver of Prescott, Arizona; short, thin-haired James Ryan of Oklahoma; and talkative little Roger Williams of Sterling City, Texas, of whom hangar fliers said: "That guy jumps around like spit on a hot stove."

The fighters were up and active by six on the morning of February 9. Just before eleven o'clock the expected warning came. Even when the air defense control was not working well, the Dutch were heartening to work with.

"Do you see them, fighters?" The call, in a strong Dutch accent, would come over the little phones in the cockpits. "Look a little north and east of where you are. Do you see them now?"

And whoever was leading the flights—Sprague, Coss, Dale, Lane, McCallum or Kiser—would answer: "Sure, we see them! Here we go."

Then the never-failing Dutch answer would come back, clear for everyone to hear: *"Luck to the fighters!"* (The Dutch said later, "We liked to hear them answer. They often said: 'Okey-doke! We see them.' And then we would say again: 'Luck to the Yanks! Luck to the fighters!'.")

All four flights set off to meet the Japs. This time it was eighteen Mitsubishis. Williams was the first to sight them, but his "enemy bombers ahead" was not clearly heard by all the pilots, partly because the P-40s were scattered out to cover the square of danger as broadly as possible.

Five fighters got into the bombers, which split upon being attacked into two flights of nine each. The attack was made at 24,000 feet and Coss, Williams, Jackson and Hague all got in at least one pass, while McWherter, using tactics invented by himself, got in four. The left engine of one Mitsubishi began to smoke under McWherter's bullets, but cleared up again. Then the Dutch lookouts reported that they saw a bomber go down into the sea northwest of the naval yard. It was given to McWherter in view of his having made more passes than anyone else.

By this time the Seventeenth had its own bulletin board and Sprague had scribbled the total:

> *One Seversky*
> *One Messerschmitt 110*
> *Two Mitsubishi 96 heavy bombers*
> *Three Zeros*

On February 10 the fighters began to clear decks for action. Wasted hours of operation against non-existent bombers had to be eliminated; of twenty-three P-40Es, only sixteen were in operation. More were added when Hennon and Egenes went over to Djember and brought back two ships that had been forced down. But they were not ready for combat. Fighter planes are delicate creatures, even when as heavily armed and underhung as the P-40s. The redheaded major and Cy Blanton spent a half hour each of early daylight trying to screw up the loose places.

Even more P-40s were on their way, this time including several veterans of the Philippines (led by the slim handsome Grant Mahony of Vallejo, California) who had fought against shoals of Zeros and bombers.

The squadron was feeling its strength and eager for battle. There were now 47 officers, including two transport pilots and two Dutch liaison officers. There were three Dutch radiomen but only 81 American ground crewmen— less than two to a plane. Two pilots were still marooned in Bali and two were in Soerabaya hospital.

It was sixty miles to Soerabaya, and the enlisted men went to town whenever they could borrow a jeep, or a truck. Once in Soerabaya, as Perry said: "When you wanted to go somewhere, you gave a native boy a Dutch five-cent piece to hail a taxi, then you hung onto your hat and prayed, while the driver drove through streets crowded with hundreds of bicycles, ox-carts, and pedestrians at a pace twice as fast as the traffic would permit. A driver that honked his horn first had the right of way. The horn was continually blaring and beeping and many times two taxis could not come to an agreement on who hit the horn first.

"We had learned by this time to pay the driver, then turn and walk off. We used to ask them: 'How much?' and paid them according to the number of fingers they held up. It was usually four times too much, and the Dutch people told us the average rate was a guilder an hour. So after that we would pay them what we thought it was worth and walk off. They never got underpaid.

"We learned other things about associating with natives. Another thing was: Never give a native beggar money. Many times syphilitic beggars would approach us for money, and finally a young Dutch soldier told us to tell them in no uncertain terms to be on their way. 'The government takes care of them,' he said. He told us to say *pikki!* when they came around. Pronounced *peegy*, it meant 'Get the hell outta here.' They knew very well what it meant; they were used to it.

"One night a couple of us went to a native stage show. Against a background of fantastically weird, unforgettable music, on a stage elaborately decorated with beautiful curtains and brilliant colors, native actors, dressed in the most luxurious of costumes, acted with grotesque and exaggerated motions, telling the old story of the eternal triangle. Man's wife has another man; man kills other man in a terrific sword fight. It was the most amazing thing I had ever seen, and I knew I would never forget it. A Dutch friend translated the words as best he could, so we were able to follow the story. It was fascinating and that alone paid for all the discomforts we had had. I will never be able to forget the beauty and luxury of the spectacle."

Lincoln's Birthday was a big day for the Seventeenth Pursuit; important visitors were coming. Billed in advance only as more P-40Es, they turned out to be A-24s. They dove fast, all right, but you had to start pulling them out of the dive so far from the ground that your bombing was liable to be inaccurate. (Eight days later, the A-24s were destined to take part in the first dive-bombing raid in the history of the United States Army. The writer was on the field at Malang to watch this flight.)

The wet fields, due to the monsoon rains—which lasted intermittently all afternoon and much of the evening—were causing as much trouble as the lack of facilities for repairing the temperamental Kittys. The squadron had only twenty-four flyable planes for its 47 pilots, and seven more under repair. The ground men puttered and adjusted and soon there were two more Kittys ready.

The Japs, however, having tested Soerabaya's fighting strength, decided to postpone their bombing activities in the eastern part of Java to concentrate upon the situation at the west created by the fall of Singapore. At this time the Japs were already nearly a week on Singapore Island, and the overcrowded garrison, with its backs to the sea and the wharves, knew that it also was doomed.

Timing two blows at once, the Japs prepared their parachutists on Borneo for the airborne attack against Palembang, Sumatran home of the Dutch and American oil refineries. Already the Japanese invasion fleet, ignoring burning Singapore, was feeling its way south to Palembang. The mixed force of American, Dutch, and British destroyers and cruisers was hunting this fleet in the waters between Sumatra and Borneo, but had to steal its way by day against Japanese bombers.

Of all this the men of the Seventeenth Pursuit knew nothing. The afternoon of February 14, the canopies of enemy parachutes first mushroomed in the blue sky over Palembang. That night Bud Sprague was summoned to Bandoeng. When he took off from Blimbing on Sunday morning, two ugly things were happening.

1. An officer with a white flag from the camp of Lieutenant General A. E. Percival had asked for terms for the surrender of Singapore from General Tomoyuki Yamashita, and
2. The Japanese invasion fleet had reached the mouth of Sumatra's Moesi River, and started up toward Palembang.

The airdromes at Palembang, called P1 and P2, were already deserted. Although the Dutch had wiped out every one of the Jap parachutists, the godowns of Palembang's Chinatown were burning in a great fire of which the refineries of Standard and Shell were the tinder. On the Sunday before, the Japanese had caught on the ground most of three squadrons of Hurricanes, and destroyed them, too.

If fighter planes were to defend the skies over Java, it would have to be the Seventeenth. Of the handful that had reached Batavia for the RAF, about six had been assembled. The RAF had lost most of its records and nearly all its procedure books for the Hurricane in Singapore and Palembang. In the backyards of cottages around the Batavia airdrome, raided sometimes at high noon by the Jap low-level strafers, they were assembling Hurricanes at a rate of one every twenty-four hours.

Sumatra was falling, and it was up to the Americans to do something about it. But Palembang, for a P-40E, was miles away around the elbow angle of Java, Sunda Strait and Sumatra.

At Blimbing the first team of the Seventeenth Pursuit took off for Batavia.

The manager of the Hôtel des Indes at Batavia could accept no more guests. The dining room was closed at nine. There was no more food. Well, perhaps he could get some food. But there was no room; there was positively no room. All the hotels in Batavia were overcrowded. There were so many refugees, from Singapore and Sumatra; there were British refugees, Dutch refugees, American refugees from the big ship that had tried to leave Padang and was bombed before it got its anchors up. The manager would be glad to help if he could, but he could not eject guests from their rooms. The crew of the American Fortress would have to go elsewhere.

The Seventeenth Pursuit was not too pleased at being called bomber pilots. The point of view of a fighter pilot to a bomber is sometimes—though not always—that of a despatch rider toward a brigadier's chauffeur. The Indies, delighted by the long-range raids of the Fortresses in Malaya, had gone a little Fortress-crazy. In Soerabaya the Dutch women knitted sweaters for "Yankee fighters"; in Batavia they thought the Seventeenth was just some little adjunct of the B-17s.

(The Fortresses served their uses. When Stauter got his flying jacket riddled and his messkit shot up—at Blimbing everyone lined up together, tin pans and cup in hand—and there were no replacements, an enlisted man thought of an errand at the Singosari bombers' field. He came back with a new jacket and shiny mess gear.)

The boys who had come in to the Hôtel des Indes were too tired to argue. They were grimy with the long flight from Soerabaya. They had no ground men of their own to service their planes. Batavia was a strange and dark city, and everything was closed.

On the way over, the eight pilots—Sprague was to meet them in Batavia—had stopped at Madioen to transform themselves into bomber pilots at this sub-field of the Fortresses. Bending and manipulating with the makeshift bomb catches, they somehow managed to attach to the wings of each plane four 20-kilo bombs, then made Batavia. Most of all they wanted to get out of their clothes and get into bed.

An American war correspondent, one of those who maintained simultaneous quarters in Soerabaya, Bandoeng and Batavia, heard that a "Fortress crew" were in the dining room of the des Indes. It seemed a lot of men even for a Fortress. He went in and sat down with them. They looked tired and he asked them where they were going to sleep. They replied, "It looks as though we'll have to go back to the field and sleep under the plane." The American correspondent went to the manager, who said he could do nothing. Then the correspondent began to move things around.

First he wandered through the darkened rear arcades of the des Indes to the door of Big Bill Dunn of the Columbia Broadcasting Company, who looks so much like Hermann Goering that few can believe him the son of a midwestern minister. Bill was sharing a room with Syd Albright of NBC. While the fighter pilots were finishing up their rice and chicken the three correspondents prowled the dark arcades of the hotel. In some rooms there were two beds and only one person sleeping. In some rooms there was no one, the army or navy officer incumbent having gone up to the mountains to Bandoeng to confer with the ABDA command.

Where there was a single vacant bed, it was quietly commandeered. Where there were double beds, and only one occupied, the man who hired the room for his exclusive use woke up to find himself rooming with a war correspondent. And the fighter pilots moved into the rooms of the war correspondents themselves.

You could hardly tell the leader of the raid from his officers, except by his red hair. None wore any insignia of rank. They looked like a tug-of-war team at the end of a fraternity picnic. They were not too dirty or tired, however, not to be curious where they were going. When the correspondents told them of the 'chutists over Palembang one said: "Oh-oh, so that's it."

It was.

Mahony, being Irish, stayed up a little longer than the others, and so did the slit-eyed and quiet Coss. Mahony told how Walt Coss had escaped the Zeros over the northern shore of Luzon. It was just after one of his pals, dying, signed a statement that he had been machine-gunned after bailing out.

When the Zeros caught Coss their first bullets chopped into his tail, then bit into his cooling system. Coss climbed out but kept his clenched finger on the rip cord without pulling. When the waves began to look toothy and white, he had to open up. The canopy snapped out just in time. The Zero chased him down to the water and the canopy lit flapping on the waves beside him. Coss struggled out of his yellow swimming jacket as the Jap's bullets ate into the canopy. His lungs were suffering. But he dove under, hearing the rap of bullets on the water.

When he came up there were holes in both parachute and yellow vest. Every time the Jap dived, Coss dived. Finally he reached the beach at Aparri and walked all the way around to Baguio, where he reported for duty again.

Mahony could not be induced to talk about his Philippine days, but finally one episode was pulled out little by little.

It seems that as soon as the Japs got their hands on Legaspi field in southern Luzon, using formerly American equipment, they began trying to jam the radio communications of the American fighters there. Mahony knew the station well, and was even acquainted with the Filipino who had lived in the shack with his family. Mahony decided to eliminate the jamming nuisance by a one-man raid. Dodging around bays and valleys he reached the field safely, and dove upon the radio shack.

"What happened was like one of those old two-reelers of Mack Sennett's that we used to go see as kids on Saturday afternoons." He grinned a little. "Remember how the first shot would be just a telegraph pole standing on a street corner? Then the head of a cop would stick out from behind the pole. Then he would put out his whole torso and look around. Then he would step out himself. Then he would go back behind the telegraph pole and ride out on a motor cycle. Finally a whole patrol wagon full of cops would ride out in a big open truck, all waving their nightsticks and yelling—all of them coming from that one skinny telegraph pole.

"It was like that when I dived on the Legaspi radio shack. The Japs came pouring out of that little building first by ones and twos, then by half-dozens, then by what looked like scores. Maybe I'm exaggerating, but it certainly looked like at least a hundred came out the windows and through the doors and went tearing down the hill to take cover in foxholes.

"As soon as I began my dive their AA gunners began winking little lights at me from over in the corner of the field. I turned away, and they kept on winking. I dove down to swing over the trees and what should I see tucked away very cutely in a corner of the 'drome but twelve big bombers of the kind that were hitting Cavite, about 28 Zeros, and a Lockheed transport of the kind the Japs bought to use as a model for construction. I thought: *This is mine.* I was just putting my stick over to go for them when I took a quick look up just to be sure everything was all right.

"Everything was not all right. There were four Zeros standing straight up and down, falling on my tail as perpendicularly as raindrops. I swung over toward the parked bombers and fighters, leading them out of their dive. We reached a place over the aircraft about the same time, and everybody was shooting, the Japs at me, and I at the Mitsubishis and fighters. I don't know whose bullets did more damage to the aircraft. But they hardly touched me.

"I went over Mount Mayon, and they were still chasing me. They could do everything better and faster than I could and I thought I was a goner. I decided to try playing ring-around-a-rosy. The mountain is about a mile high, with a perfect cone-shaped peak. I went around it twice, while they hunted in both directions. But they got so confused guessing which was themselves and which was me that I was able to slip down to tree-top level and make a getaway through the valleys."

Next morning the weather was misty with monsoon clouds and rain, a providential consideration for the Japanese unloading their barges at Palembang. Monday was ugly weather too. Over the low land between Batavia and its port of Tanjong Priok, whose canals gave it a strange resemblance to Holland, a low soft mist lay upon the ricefields and the godowns. For the P-40s it was no use taking off to find a place one had never seen, under weather where it could not be observed.

The delay meant that the Japs would have established their fighter protection on P1, Palembang's fighter airdrome where most of the British Hurricanes had been destroyed a week before the parachutists fell upon Palembang.

The morning of February 17, eight Jap fighters met the Seventeenth as the Americans came in over Sumatra from the Java Sea and got the lie of the Moesi River. This time the Japs had no bombers to protect. The Americans, intact, had themselves to protect: in Madioen they had become dive bombers.

The Jap fighters were not Zeros, but 97s—a low-winged monoplane used principally for ground strafing, scouting, and light bombing jobs, such as troops on a tropical highway. Six of these 97s came in on the heavily laden Kittyhawks. Sprague shook off the weight of his bombs, and Coss, McCallum, and Kruzel got rid of their own to fight as the 97s came in. Egenes coolly made a good bombing run first.

Sprague got one 97 immediately. McCallum and Kruzel, now feeling light as angels, went into the 97s with their fingers on the button. Two more 97s went down.

The 97s did not blow up like a Zero in a puffball of flame; they fell away smoking, like matches fallen to the ground.

Mahony had already led the way down onto the Japanese ships in the river. His bombs fell away among the landing barges on the Moesi bank, lightening his wings of machine gun bullets, and emptying his cannon. Egenes got another fighter.

Kentucky "Kay" Kiser wanted to be in on both strikes, fighting and bombing too. He held greedily to his bombs. Even though he knew what would happen if a Jap bullet should hit one, he went in among the three 97s that were left. He got the cone of his fire leading one of the 97s the right number of inches and sawed him apart. Then he peeled off and went down among the river craft with his bombs.

The Seventeenth were happy when they got back to Batavia and came in one by one. None was lost.

The dive-bombing of Palembang had been a peculiar mission for fighters. But it was typical of the shoestring methods necessary to stop the leaky Dutch dike, at which the waters released by the fall of the dam of Singapore were now rushing.

While Sprague had been leading his pilots over the smoking refineries of Palembang, things had been happening at the two home fields of Soerabaya. The Dutch handed over operation of the interceptor control to Bill Fisher, a major who'd been with the American bomber command. This transfer was made with the best of good will on both sides. Now Soerabaya had no more Dutch Brewster fighters to send up against the Zeros. Cavite had fallen. Singapore had fallen. The defense of the only naval base remaining in Allied hands was up to the Americans.

The change was timely, though it did not remedy the basic need of a

radar. The Japs, possessing Palembang, were ready to work the eastern
half of the pincers round Java. In spite of daily flights over Soerabaya to
check American submarines and other craft in the harbor, they did not intend to strike yet with full force.

At this time a Japanese aircraft carrier had crept down into the Arafura
Sea. The Dutch bases on Timor, meant to defend the Indies as far east as
New Guinea, were already swept clear of fighters.

The Japs were preparing a raid against Darwin that was to be one of the
most terrible and tragic of the war. Their plan was to begin at the outside
and work across the stepping-stone islands from Darwin through Timor,
Soembawa, and Bali to Soerabaya. The intention was slowly to cut off Java
from the east or Australian side, stop the flow of fighters at their source,
and cut off in Java the whole withdrawal of forces from Singapore. In this
scheme the Japs were in general successful.

The Allies had anticipated this plan in part. The American aircraft tender *Langley* had already left Darwin for Fremantle, due to sail on for
Burma with thirty-two more Kittyhawks and pilots. If necessary the *Langley* could turn toward Java and drop her fighters there. This was what she
eventually attempted.

The Japs usually sent their bombers from the southeastern Celebes
(possibly also from eastern Borneo) and allowed the Zero fighters, with
belly tanks beneath, to overtake the bombers over the target. Japanese
timing is excellent; one noon this same week, within minutes the writer
saw four Zeros run off a beautiful crisscross on the airdrome at Batavia,
piercing the warning system and raking the Hurricanes and Brewsters on
the field with two 90° sweeps. But this day for once Japanese timing did not
function perfectly, and the new Dutch-American warning system did.

Because Bud Sprague was in Bandoeng, Cy Blanton—who comes from
Earlsboro, Oklahoma, and is very proud of it—got his chance to lead the
squadron into battle. Cy is a boy with thin blond hair and a tremendously
friendly manner. He was a little older than the others, and that was why he
got the call.

The Japanese bombers were caught in the unhappy position of having
their arrival forewarned adequately for the first time, without their fighters having yet reached the rendezvous. The first Americans left Blimbing
at 10:45, zipping down the field with tails high, leaping over the terraced
ricefields.

When the Japanese bombers saw them, and knew their own nakedness without fighters, they must have known they were facing death. What happened in that melée of spitting machine guns was this: The Japs knew that they could not turn away. Blanton led the four flights in, and got his own bomber immediately. His was the lead bomber, and it fell in smoke. The enemy formation began to break up.

The Japs were in the position of flying toward the sun and toward Soerabaya, with more P-40s concealed in each than they could see or guess at. Almost every Kittyhawk got in one, two or three passes at the bombers. The Japanese turret and belly gunners fought back, but there were simply too many P-40s around them.

The Japanese bomber rarely bursts into flames. Instead the motors begin to smoke. The head of the bomber droops as though weary. The glassed-in nose sinks. Rarely does the fire spread. But the smoke from the engines gets thicker. The nose gets heavier and nods lower. The bomber slopes away, sags, droops until it passes the oblique angle and becomes perpendicular. Then it goes down, straight down.

Four were flaming as they fell.

This was the first time that the American pilots, free of the buzzing Zeros, were able to meet enemy bombers on fighterless terms. As far as this correspondent has been able to keep record, it was the only time in the Pacific war that Japs failed to provide top or bottom cover for their bombers by daylight. Even over Singapore, when the Japanese were positive that they had grounded all but a scattered residue of Hurricanes, they never failed to send a protective sheet of fighters across the island under the blanket of bombers. When the Japanese commander knows the bottom sheet of fighters is already on the bed, he always separates his blanket of bombers with another sheet of fighters. Sometimes he puts another sheet on top of the blanket, just to be sure that nothing gets close to those precious bombers.

When you lose Zero pilots, as the Japs figure, you lose nothing. You simply throw butterflies into a furnace. But when you lose bomber crews you lose a *team* of men. There is far more team play called upon within the big complicated mechanism of the bomber than among wasplike fighters. An attack by fighters starts orderly and ends disorderly; there are only about two seconds when interplay counts (though some commanders believe formations should be drawn up again). A bomber crew is functioning as a team from the moment it leaves the airdrome, and the battle is only an accentuated form of that team play. The bomber cannot dodge; each crew within each fuselage is a part of the greater phalanx of the bomber formation itself.

The gunners of American bombers have to take handling Zeros as a matter of course, and have learned to rely upon their own firepower. Japanese bomber crews have not yet been pushed to this point, because their air generals have followed—necessarily—the principle of not sending their bombers unaccompanied by Zeros.

Seen over time, this appears a good way to conserve bomber reserves and keep crews intact. Sometimes called the Seversky system, it is ideal for a frugal nation like Japan. The fighters get no bigger; they merely carry more fuel. The big economy comes in the size of the bombers, and their equipment. The bombers cut down on armament and defensive armor, while increasing the bombload. Although the Jap bombers do have machine gun blisters and tail gunners, their firepower is weak compared with the B-17 and B-24. They can be built much smaller, effecting great economies of metal, and still carry an efficient bombload. For night raiding they can do about as good a job—providing no night fighters arise to meet them—as the big American bombers. The Seversky system is ideal for the hard-hitting nation short of raw materials, which hopes to get them by the stab-in-the-back method. If she can catch her enemy bending, as the army likes to put it, and can get her raw materials, she may be able to change over to the big bomber plan of production.

But the Seversky system is harder to work out than it sounds. A fighter must be built to fly fast; a bomber, fast in the pinches, cannot cruise long distances at fighter speeds. The two planes cannot start together; they must rendezvous. And anyone who has tried to rendezvous in the sky, even by good weather and broadest daylight and at determined altitudes, knows how difficult it can be.

Another difficulty with the Japanese system when it faces a fully alert and equally armed enemy is the number of imponderables that go into computing fuel for the fighters. Britain lost most of her Hurricanes in the battle of Crete through their being based in Africa and falling into the sea, because fighting had used up their homing fuel. When the Japs tried to raid Darwin after American fighters and warning planes had been put into operation, the same thing happened; the Zeros, chased by P-40s, fell like the dry and weary flies of autumn into the Timor Sea.

The Seversky system, with which the Japs *opened* their war, places almost the whole burden on the Zero pilot. When good planes and fast-working warning systems put him to the test, the disadvantages of interdependence begin to show.

Our Fortresses and Liberators take occasional lickings, but have initiated a period of self-protected heavy bombers which, operating like submarines of the air, can go by daylight anywhere along the enemy's coasts—anywhere except within his anti-aircraft-fringed harbors—and persecute any unescorted freighter or transport ship. This commerce-raiding, also effective in knocking out isolated enemy dumps and garrisons with inadequate anti-aircraft, is something the Japs cannot do yet.

Bomber crews want fighters overhead whenever they can get them; it is difficult to be in a bombing run over the smoking volcano at Rabaul, be attacked, and keep on target while fighting off a hornet swarm of Zeros. But whereas at the beginning of the war the bombers were asking—sometimes a little querulously—for fighter escort both ways to any targets fighters could reach, now all they ask is protection when actually making their bombing runs. Give them peace for these three minutes, and the .50 calibers will take care of the Zeros the rest of the time.

So much for the contrasted views of American and Jap bombers. We like fighter protection; they must have it.

The Japs, preparing their plans of conquest, used the Seversky idea of a long-range fighter protecting the long-range bomber. When fighters drop belly tanks to defend bombers, their fuel margin narrows even though the first intake is from the belly tank. This cascade—"It's raining Jap belly tanks," the Seventeenth's pilots used to say—occurs just when the fighter is avidly pulling gas for fighting speed.

What happens inside a Japanese bomber when attacked? What happens to the hard morale, the desire for self-sacrifice for the Emperor? Ordinarily it would be hard to say. The processes of the Japanese mind are alien to ours. But one principal diversion of fighter pilots is listening to each other's radios, and it so happens that a Japanese-speaking American aviator who listened in on one such conversation during the battles over the Pacific is able to furnish us with a pretty good idea.

This American fighter pilot dived upon a bomber and set it aflame and had the unusual experience of overhearing—and understanding—what the Japanese commander said to the tail gunner. It went like this:

Pilot: "We have been hit. We are burning. For the eternal honor of the Emperor and the glory of Japan I am about to cause this plane to dive upon that American warship down there."

Tail Gunner: "I don't care what you are going to do for the honor of Japan and the glory of the Emperor, but this plane is burning and I am going to leave it by parachute immediately."

If any such conversations went on in the burning bombers outside Soerabaya that day, the Seventeenth did not know. The Dutch saw nine come down, with at least 45 Japanese crewmen. Fuchs and Williams got their first officially credited bombers.

Another nine enemy bombers appeared, making eighteen in all. But by this time the twelve Zeros that were to furnish "cover underneath" appeared, and rolled the Americans into a wildcat fight.

The Japs were flying a stepdown formation of nine bombers, each tail gunner in the staircase protecting the belly of the bomber above. To attack meant to face the concentrated fire of all the tail gunners. Jock Caldwell, flying in close as usual, had several tail trifles *(empennage)* entirely shot away. This student of the Orient, whose perfect physique had earned him the name of "Little Tarzan," decided to attack.

He made his way straight down the staircase. He set the top bomber afire, and the bottom one. The staircase lost its upper and lowermost treads; they fell away in flame and smoke into the sea. The staircase flew on. Jock stretched his dive over the rice paddies, and bailed out. Somebody saw him; someone else picked him up.

That day Jock, who was just twenty-five, earned the Silver Star that General Brett was to give him. Little Tarzan's armorer, square-built Sergeant Lewis McNeil of Lubbock, Texas, was not the only member of the squadron for whom Caldwell was like a god. There is a tendency, after death strikes a group of fliers, to elevate those who have offered their lives, and by reminiscence to give them an influence in the squadron that they had not possessed. Although Jock Caldwell never became squadron leader, he might very likely have carried that responsibility.

Caldwell got a severely wrenched back out of his two bombers, but used nevertheless to help his armorer plugging in cartridges. He did not smoke or drink himself, and when he heard that the merry McNeil was slightly awash, whether at the Trocadero in Brisbane, or the Shanghai, the Café Royal or (till the Japs hit it with a bomb) the Tip Top Café in Soerabaya, he would find a rickshaw or taxi, whatever the hour of day or night, and bring the errant home.

Caldwell was the one to whom the squadron looked for its slight political education. He had been brought up in China, and taught and studied in Japan. "I've seen Japs at war for five years and I know what to expect from them as enemies," he used to say. Of his parachute jump after being shot at by the nine Jap bombers he said merely: "I found I was in the cockpit, falling to pieces, but still indicating 450 an hour. I tried to get out, and the slipstream pushed me back. I decided it was all over and that I might as well let it happen. Then I thought: 'What the hell, let's have another try.' That time I managed to get out."

Although a teetotaler, Caldwell was no absolute puritan. He had McNeil paint the names of girls on the guns: *Lois, Beatrice, Helen* and on the smoky other wing *Elizabeth, Ruth* and *Lavelle*. "Beatrice jammed up on me today," he would say after landing, pulling back his canopy. "Beatrice always was a bitch," McNeil would answer. . . . The Japanese thinks of the Anglo-Saxon, particularly the American, as weakly uxorious. But there are reasons that are not purely affectionate why a pilot may name his guns after women.

The afternoon after this big interception under Blanton's leadership, the Palembang force came back. There were handshakes; the little force had fought at two places in the dike six hundred miles apart. The score in favor of the Seventeenth, confirmed and ascertained—which meant watching them all the way to the water—was four Zeros, four 97s, one Messerschmitt 110, and fifteen heavy bombers.

It was impossible for the Seventeenth to intercept the raids that occurred over the middle of Java, which was simply too enormous for them to hold everybody off. They were stopping everything thrown at Soerabaya, when they had time to climb high enough. With more planes they might have protected Batavia and Bandoeng, at the other end of the six-hundred-mile island.

But the Japs had to have Soerabaya. The moment was coming for the great attempt to break the lifeline of the barrier islands. Soerabaya was the last unburned hangar of Allied air strength. Soerabaya had to be silenced.

At times they sought Soerabaya to forget Blimbing. There were planes with 400 hours on them that should've been taken down 200 hours earlier. You shouted at the coolies as they rolled the big drums across the field, and watched that the gas did not dribble onto the field as they pumped, their brown backs running with sweat. The planes had brakes that were worn out; the tachometers were gone or broken. "Wild Man" Morehead, wild no longer, was the thrifty armament officer who kept reminding the armorers as he walked in the sun from revetment to revetment: "Save every loose round. We might not get any more. The ammo isn't coming through from Australia. Keep looking around the grass and grab any rounds you see. Never let a round get corroded. We need every round. We might never get any more."

We might never get any more . . . we won't get any more . . . there's no more coming . . . when this is gone, we won't get any more. . . .

The ships had to be kept on alert, and when they rusted, the armorers were hard put to keep them firing. There were too few ships; there was no relief. When an engine had to be taken out they rigged a pulley under a tree and hoisted it that way. Often the pilots had to attack the Japs from the right or left wing, instead of aiming dead-on, because only half the guns were working. When "enemy aircraft sighted" came to the thatched Operations shack, the pilots had to be reminded before they ran for their ships to clear their guns at every 5000 feet, otherwise they would freeze up.

And we probably won't get any more . . . no more. . . .

No wonder they had to go to Soerabaya, sometimes.

Bud Sprague used to get them together, when mess was over—"and I've seen the major standing twenty-fifth in line." His talks came about two or three times a week. They met in the abandoned sugar factory where the Dutch had installed a ping-pong table and a pool table. The windows were blacked out, and it had a tile floor. "I just called you in to say that you needn't be worried if the Japs come here," he would say. "This isn't the best America can do; you know that. It just happens to be the best right now. But don't think you're going to be just sacrificed to this thing. We'll fight as long as we can. But if things get hot, we'll leave with three days' start. This war is just beginning and we're going to be in it for a long time."

They could not know, then, that they would get away, but he would be the one left behind.

Anyhow, they went to Soerabaya. Some of them looked at the brown girls. Most, however, did things like Sergeant Perry: "We visited the famous Soerabaya zoo, the aquarium and the city in general. We were each ceremoniously presented with an Air Raid Warden's badge. A Dutch friend gravely pinned it on our shirts and explained that we were the first ever made 'Honorary Air Raid Wardens'."

Air raid wardens indeed, guardians of Soerabaya.

"After we got our badges, our Dutch friend took us home and introduced us to his daughter Doreen and his wife. Doreen was a little taller than me, with long blond hair, more on the beautiful side than cute or pretty. I stayed there till late that night talking to Doreen, she telling me Dutch words and I telling her the English counterparts. We really had a good time and I promised myself to see her again."

On the 19th of February, a black day, the Japs went for both Soerabaya and Darwin simultaneously. The Australians had no radar to give Darwin any warning and paid dearly for the omission. This, the only successful Japanese attack against Australia, was to be revenged within a matter of minutes.

The day at Blimbing began with a false alarm, the squadron taking the air at 9 and getting back at 10:30 without any bombers coming over. At noon they were up again and two flights of ours met eight Zeros: exactly even terms numerically.

Half the Zeros were shot down. Mahony and Lane each got one. So did Hague, whose plane was called *Colleen,* and Kruzel, whose armorer (Lyman Goltry of Glenwood, Iowa) loved a girl in a San Rafael chainstore. Kruzel thus carried into battle against the mystified Japs a sharkface with the inscription *J.C. Penny-Lou.*

The other two flights moved in on the bombers, which fled without opening their hatches. But when it came to nose-counting time on the field at Blimbing, there were three pilots missing: Gilmore, Blanton and Fields. Gilmore was shot down and was burned, but the Dutch doctors took care of him and saved his life. Blanton was thought lost, but it turned out that he had only brought down his ship on a beach along the Straits of Madura. But Fields never came back.

Fields—a full-blooded Cherokee tribesman from Grove, Oklahoma, with the curious first name of Quanah—was the first American Indian flier lost in the war. He got out of his plane alive, but when they found him he had bullet holes through the canopy of his parachute. One bullet had gone through his head. He was buried, like the others, in the Graafplaats Kembang Koening in Soerabaya, and went to his rest in the wet dark soil of Java. Like the Maori pilots from New Zealand who in aged Brewsters met the Zeros over Singapore, flying wingtip to wingtip with the white kiwis, the American Indian died a warrior.

The invasion of Bali was the knot in the noose with which the Jap garroted Java. On February 20, with Soerabaya saved by the "Forties" but Darwin's harbor filled with sinking ships and her streets with bodies, the great simultaneous invasion of the island chain got under way by night. A Japanese fleet with two cruisers, four or five destroyers and four transports slipped down the east coast of Bali, swung around and prepared to attack from the south. The Japs landed on this side because they knew most of the Dutch, British and American warships were operating in the Java Sea. Having already made Den Pasar's field useless, they could protect the landing operations by getting through Lombok Strait—thus closing both it, and the Bali Strait, with patrolling destroyers.

At the same time, the parachutists came down upon Koepang. The Japanese had broken the lifeline in two places. Just to be sure of having the first stepping-stone, the Japs also landed on this day in Portuguese Timor, forcing the Australians there back into the mountains.

The chain of islands was severed. Now no more fighter reinforcements could be flown to Java. And the little band of P-40s already there could not be flown out. They would fight until their end.

The fleet moving upon Bali had been under observation since two days before. On the night of the 19th, Bandoeng sent down orders for a bombing mission against the force on the bay by Den Pasar, and its destroyers and cruisers.

For the mission to Bali the P-40s took off early on the 20th, led by Sprague, to rendezvous over Malang with the A-24 dive bombers and three LB-30s flown over from Jokjakarta. These A-24s, seven of fifty-two landed at Brisbane before Christmas and assembled by Fortress ground crews, had made the same hazardous pilgrimage to Java as the Seventeenth. Their pilots were experienced, their gunners were nothing but pickups from B-17s who had never dive-bombed in their lives.

The writer had gone up to Malang to see this first take-off. It was a bright blue morning. The A-24s came in and circled the green hangar. The dive bombers were navy planes, converted for army use, and the mechanics had some difficulty fitting the big bombs to the attachments. As "raid time" approached, one by one the pilots and observers pulled down their goggles, climbed in and took off on the first army dive-bombing raid in history. This little group of dive bombers, with an occasional loss here and there, was to go on fighting the war all the way to Papua.

The P-40s had the hazardous job of staying over the enemy in Bali and protecting the dive bombers and the LB-30s as they came over from Malang. Time after time the Zeros attacked from above. All four flights fought to protect the bombers. But when the sweaty and drawn pilots got back to Blimbing four faces were missing. One was Sprague.

How they got the Major no one knows exactly. Stauter reported by radio: "The Major didn't have a chance," and someone else was supposed to have said—they thought it was Gallienne—"I can see him going in."

On the raid before, Sprague's mechanic—a staff sergeant from Seattle named Robert Jung—had complained about the redheaded commander buzzing the field too low when he came in. "You shouldn't do that; I got a weak heart," he said. He had already painted the name *Hell Diver* on Sprague's plane; the day just preceding the Bali landing Sprague asked him to put the name of his wife, Lillian, on the ship.

How the nineteen-year-old Perry felt at Sprague's fall is somewhat how all the members of the Seventeenth felt: "All of us liked Major Sprague and considered him the best C.O. we ever had. He flew for the love of flying, he fought for the love of fighting and to avenge the deaths of his partners in the Philippines. He instilled his courage and fighting spirit into all the pilots and men and there was no one who did not admire him. He was a square-shooter and hell on wings for the Japs. When he buzzed the field he came lower than anyone else, and that was low. Prop blades chopped the grass as he soared over the field at 300 miles an hour. We had to clean his coolers a couple of times a week because of the collection of leaves and grass inside. He was usually first to take off on an alert and never asked his pilots to do something he could not do himself. The Seventeenth will long remember him."

Lieutenant Gallienne, the San Franciscan, was not heard from again.

Thomas Hayes of Brooks, Oregon, who had his elevators virtually shot away by the 20-mm cannon in the Zero's noses, was nevertheless just able to make the home field alive and walk away from his fighter's wreckage. He was saved largely by the circumstance that ordinary rubber bath sponges, which the ground men had tied onto the gunsights frame in lieu of the regular cushions, held the snap of his forehead as he fell on the runway. As soon as his tailskid caught the weeds, Colbert peeled back his canopy and dragged him out, bleeding.

Three Zeros had been shot down, and one destroyed on the field at Den Pasar.

Two of the four missing pilots, Stauter and Johnson, made emergency landings in out-of-the-way places on the beach.

Stauter crash-landed, pulled himself out and found that he was wounded and his plane was ruined. He walked, losing blood rapidly, until he came on a native pedalling along a path on a bicycle. He bade the native get on the handlebars and began pedalling himself. Then he passed out from loss of blood. When he came to he found himself in the hands of the Javanese police. They had taken away his gun, and for some reason his shoes—perhaps standard practice to keep a tenderfooted white man from running away. They brought him, shoeless and disarmed, to the hospital at Malang where he, Hayes and Foy were nursed, along with wounded Fortress pilots and gunners, by a Celebes-Javanese nurse who refused to get under the bed with Americans during air raids because she anticipated amorous advances.

Johnson, of Mesa, Arizona, had the most peculiar experience of all in that he was rescued by the baby ship of the Asiatic fleet, the little schooner *Lanakai*.

The *Lanakai* was the schooner that had been used in the movie *The Hurricane* and sold to the navy as a patrol schooner three days before war broke out. In an extraordinary series of escapes from Japanese bombings she had made her way through the straits of Macassar to Soerabaya, and later around through Bali Strait, always just one jump ahead of the Japanese coming the other way.

The *Lanakai* had seen Johnson hunting up and down the coves of southern Java for a landing and watched him come in on the tight little beach. They sent a boat ashore, tried to help him get the P-40 off, failed, and helped him dismantle his guns and remove his ammunition before touching off the plane. In his first flight Johnson, unused to the new belly tanks upon which the Americans depended to give them time over Bali, had used the gas in his regular tank above the belly tank. When he was attacked by Zeros and had to drop his belly tank, he quickly ran dry.

The coverage to the bombing attack furnished by the P-40s made it possible for the Dutch mixed force of cruisers and torpedo boats, together with American destroyers, to creep up on the Japs before the convoy could get away. The battle of Bali Strait resulted in the probable sinking of several Japanese ships. Two of the seven dive bombers did not come back, but the Fortresses did well; when the writer spoke to the returned pilots on the field at Malang, they were jubilant.

Almost a week later, after returning to Bandoeng and coming back for the last hours to Soerabaya, the writer was able to talk with the crew of one A-24 who had dropped their 600-pounder on a cruiser. They were Lieutenant Richard Launder and Sergeant I. A. Lnenicka, both barely twenty.

They said: "We started up under the umbrella of P-40s and dived straight from 14,000 feet. Our 600-pounder hit exactly on the cruiser's bow, and our two little bombs, just to make no mistake, hit on both sides, showing a direct straddle.

"We came out of our dive, but then our oil line burst. Black oil covered our windshield and we could see nothing. With the motor getting hotter every minute we scooted across the Den Pasar field—the Japs must have thought we were finished. We skimmed over the surf, aiming to put her down where the breakers were not too big. Finally we hit the water about 15 miles west. Somehow we got through the surf.

"We climbed up into the jungle, still carrying our Colts—useless because the ammunition was wet. The Japs were looking for us, but suddenly a Balinese chief turned up. One boy asked us 100 guilders (50 dollars) to take us to Banjoewangi on the Java side. This chief gave us two coolie hats to wear for camouflage and the equivalent of 35 cents for food, and told the boy to take us across for nothing. After thirteen hours paddling through the cross currents of the Strait in this little *prau* we reached Banjoewangi. I guess we were the last American tourists to leave Bali."

It is possible they were not. Months later, as we sat together on an Australian beach facing the sunset, Lieutenant-Commander Frederick Warder, one of the most successful American submarine commanders, told the writer how, just about at the hour of the air battle, he had seen the white canopy of a parachute break out over Bali and a man come floating down on Nusa Besar Island. Was this Bud Sprague?

Everyone who knew the commander of the Seventeenth hopes that it was.

The next day at 9:30, four flights of the squadron went up to meet a force of eighteen bombers at 20,000 feet directly over Soerabaya. Just as they started in on the bombers, waddling badly in the thin air, the Kittyhawks saw a cloud of Zeros coming upon them. The attack was broken up. Lieutenant George Hynes—a quiet boy from San Antonio who always carried rosary beads—was caught by Zeros and killed before Mahony (leading his flight), Hennon and Fuchs could go to his rescue. The third and fourth flights were able to get through to the bombers; Frank Adkins, a dark-haired, usually unshaven pilot from Tennessee, got his first Zero.

Walt Coss led in Oliver, Reynolds and Wally Hoskyn. This flight had the most success; the air directional control, watching through binoculars, saw two bombers go down and crash. There were twelve Zeros in all and they outnumbered each flight of Kittyhawks. But Hoskyn, even after the Zeros were on his tail, kept coming back to the bombers; he got at least one, and probably a Zero. (When they gave "Hosk" the posthumous Silver Star months later, they wrote: "His tenacity of purpose, coolness under fire and outstanding courage were instrumental in much of the success enjoyed by the squadron and an inspiration to all of the men.")

The day before Hosk's last flight, Perry and Deyo, his pals, had painted, at the pilot's direction, the name *Stub and Lou* on his plane. Whenever he took off, Hoskyn always used to give the rounded thumb and forefinger signal, the American signal of okay, to his line chief. On his last flight he forgot to give it.

When both Sprague and Hoskyn fell immediately after putting names on their ships, no more names were given. Christening seemed a prelude to death. Both Jackson and Kiser, the more reserved members of the squadron, had never painted anything on their ships anyway. Egenes, given ship #13, re-named it *Eight-Ball,* and got behind it. Gilmore, who got his first Jap in the Philippines, and two in Java, had *Drummer Boy* and *Michigan Kid* on his ship. Fliers like Morehead and Adkins, however, flew any plane they were given, even the over-decorated shark on whose guns twang-voiced Benjamin Culpepper, of Pine Bluff, Arkansas, had inscribed *Tom, Dick and Harry,* and on the other wing vents *Sally, Irene and Mary.*

The squadron was now leaderless, having lost two of its best-liked pilots. But it was getting recognition from the Japs, the low hissing obeisance of ever more Zeros.

The surviving seventeen P-40s were all flyable. The next day the signal came from Brereton in Bandoeng that Mahony was to take Bud Sprague's empty place.

The Japs were now closing upon Java in earnest. Things began cooking immediately. Just before ten o'clock the Soerabaya air control signified that trouble was coming over from Kendari. The Seventeenth found them up at 22,000 feet.

The battle split unequally from the beginning. The Japs had sent over nine bombers with nine Zeros as guardian angels. The two first flights to take off put their cannon shells into three bombers and chopped up three pursuit ships. Two smoking birds were a Zero that Ray Thompson caught over Malang and a bomber Bill Turner brought down over Soerabaya. But things were too hot and the air too full of loose things to watch everything, and none of these crashes were confirmed. Throughout the time in Java the totals of Dutch air controls systems of how many ships were shot down was about twice those which the Seventeenth claimed. The pilots paid scant heed to tallies when Zeros were around; they wound their heads around, not down.

This day Cy Blanton's gang drew one of the combinations that nobody likes: nine bombers with no less than fifteen Zeros over them. Besides Cy ("Baldy" to the gang when they wanted to tease him) there was Dockstader, the boy from Long Beach, Irvin and "Jack" Jackson to help him. Cy got his bomber and everybody else took his pass and away safely from this hot alley of overhead thugs. Fifteen Zeros upstairs was too many for four P-40s to tackle, especially when they knew they could not strike the bombers again. They dived off and away.

The squadron now had many more pilots than planes, and some were ordered away immediately by Major Fisher to pick up Kittyhawks elsewhere. A number of boxed P-40s had been landed at Tjilatjap in southern

Java, and the *Langley* was coming out with more. Twenty officers and twenty men left on February 23, and another sixteen men the next day.

The men who left had not the slightest idea of where they were going, and little apprehension what was happening to Java. The order came suddenly; actually when Mahony called those departing together for the last time it was for a checkup on their work. "What I called you in for was to bawl you out," he said. "That's no use now. Where you boys are going, you'll get a good deal. I'd like to be going with you. You'll go into Blimbing, gather your belongings and leave for Soerabaya."

Winding across the old temple-laden hills of central Java, where Buddhism once came and went, and where the beetle-browed Java man stalked strange animals before time was, they discussed in the sleepy train all night long the question of where they were going. Most thought it was merely a routine transfer to India. But it was Mahony, not they, who was to go to India. They were still to cross the Indian Ocean, the great Australian desert, the coastal rim of parasitic cities; and they were to go north to the tropics again to strike the Japanese in the humid skies of Papua.

None of them had dreamed anything like this would happen to them.

The Japs kept coming. The handful of P-40s rose and fell, day after day.

On the 24th the largest swarm of Japs yet seen came over. The naval PBYs wrote succinctly in their log: "There were 44 to 54 bombers over the navy yard today. Able damage was done." The Americans met them this time at 21,000 feet with four flights of fighters. "Kay" Kiser caused one big bomber to bend its flight until it touched the ground—in flames. Dockstader shot up another badly and the sharp eyes of the air control saw it fall into the sea. All the others came back safely, but some were severely shot up, and others were worn out with this heavy daily use.

The young armorer Perry heard something in Soerabaya that drew him closer to the Dutch: "When I was walking down the street, after dinner at the Café Royal, I met my friend, the father of the Dutch girl. I called twice before he recognized me, then came over. The following conversation resulted in one of the deepest personal tragedies I have ever had. 'How is Doreen, and her mother?' I asked.

"He looked away for a moment and then, straightening up, he said in almost a trembling voice, 'Doreen is gone. She was taken from us a few days ago . . . when they hit the Tip Top Café.'

"Doreen, the fairhaired girl I had spoken to and laughed with only a few days before! I turned away, but I kept thinking of it all day. The beautiful daughter of the first friends I'd made in Java had been killed by the Japs. An innocent civilian who, only a little before, had been joking about the war. If coming too close to bombs myself and being shot at by strafers hadn't brought the full meaning of war to me, this did. I knew I would never be satisfied until I killed at least one of them myself."

There were only ten Kittyhawks left to defend Java, and this was the day when the Japanese invasion force was beginning to mass itself in Sumatra, at Balikpapan, and in Macassar Strait. The navy, having at this time only three serviceable PBY Catalinas, was to have none at all the day before the Japs landed.

General Brereton in Bandoeng, knowing that he would need a fighter force in Burma to save India, crooked his finger to Mahony and once again the Seventeenth lost a commander. When Brereton took off in a Fortress for Colombo, Mahony was ordered to go with him.

The last time anyone met the second commander of the Seventeenth was in Jokjakarta, where McNeil, Caldwell's armorer, saw him across the street. The ace and the armorer had both been reading a western novel about a wild and untameable mustang, California Red.

"Hey, McNeil, did they ever catch that California Red?" Mahony asked.

"No, sir, they never did get close enough," answered the sergeant.

Mahony shook his head and walked away, never to be seen by his squadron again. They said of him afterward, *He had the darkest, tiredest eyes, with deep rings under them, you ever saw.*

The night after Mahony flew with Brereton to India, the writer had dinner in a mountain inn with three ground mechanics of the Seventeenth. They resembled high school kids; one wore a sweatshirt with an Indian's head. They looked strange in the middle of Java, suspended at the far end of the thread of American retreat.

But there was no question of leaving. "You can't run a war out of your pants pockets," they said. "But as long as the pilots stay with the Dutch, we stay. Until we have nothing flyable left, until we're just as hard up as the navy, we'll stay."

Japan, having wrecked Darwin, was throwing her full force at Soerabaya. What they sent the next day can only be compared with what the

Luftwaffe sent over the British Channel when the sun was obscured with German planes. They had bombers and fighters; they had height. The bombers were stepped up from 27,000 to 30,000 feet. After every 9 bombers came 6 Zeros, totalling 54 bombers and 36 Zeros against 12 American lone wolves. (Two more Kittys had been tinkered into operation by the grease-balls in sweatshirts.) This was meant for the knockout blow.

Jerry McCallum, the Louisianan picked to succeed Mahony as squadron head, led his first command into action—Marion Puchs of Big Springs, Texas, Williams, and Irvin. At the same time Dale, Johnson, Paul Gam-bonini of Petaluma, California, and Bernard Oliver of Prescott, Arizona, tried to climb to the lowest level of bombers. A thousand feet below those red-balled wings, the hive of Zeros opened on them.

At such a height it was foolhardy to try outmaneuvering the butterfly Japs, and the eight went into their dive. But the other four Americans— Adkins, Hennon and Reynolds, with Kiser giving them signals—were able to dive upon the Zeros' tails after the leader followed the first two flights down far enough.

Irvin saw a Zero about to attack, dropped back and got him.

Hennon and Reynolds each got a Zero in their sights and burst him open from the rear; in a diving match a heavy P-40 could beat a Zero any day. But McCallum, feeling his responsibility to cover the tails of his companions in the escaping dive, was reached by one of the leading Zeros.

His plane faltered, his engine smoked. When the Japanese saw his canopy open they left their dive and twisted away after it. McCallum was machine-gunned in his parachute as he fell. He had bailed out like "Chief" Fields, and his bushido-loving, chivalrous enemy followed him down. Death was mercifully quick. There were thirty holes in his chute—he had been hit twice each in his head and heart.

When Jerry McCallum went, the officer who had tried to run their rude little engineering shack, to hold airplanes together by gum and by God, was gone. You could feel Java creaking and cracking around you, getting ready to break up. This was the day Wavell and his staff turned the defense of Java over to the Dutch and followed Brereton to Colombo. That afternoon there was a report that a big Jap fleet had already been sighted north of Bawean Island, off Soerabaya.

The invasion of Java had begun.

Fighters had more chance to get away from the cruiser-based seaplanes, that were playing the role of sheepdogs of the Jap invasion, than the single navy Catalina remaining in Soerabaya. Kiser and Hennon were sent off as the sun was descending to hunt for the Japanese convoy. They hunted for two hours, but never saw it.

There were now more Zeros because the new Japanese fighter base at Den Pasar in Bali was in full operation. Java was being hit in the face with bombers and stabbed in the ribs with fighters, simultaneously.

The next day [February 26] 26 bombers unloaded everything they had upon the Soerabaya navy yard from 30,000 feet. Their protective cover of Zeros flew at 27,000 and attacked the rising handful of P-40s, which could only dive away.

Hennon, more persistent than the others, followed the bombers and fighters until they parted company, then intercepted all by himself two Zeros that were flying low on their way home. He sent one of them down aflame into the wet ricefield and was back at his little field shortly after eleven o'clock.

The Fortresses were leaving Malang, having been badly shot up by strafing Zeros. They asked for protection, but the air direction control could not give it to them. There was enough work for 120 fighters, and there were only a dozen.

Around lunchtime word came that six Brewster Buffaloes with Dutch pilots—some rescued from Singapore—would arrive at Blimbing and lend a hand as well as they could, with their 16,000-foot operating ceiling and 160-mile-an-hour speed.

The Dutchmen landed at two in the afternoon. Next arrived six Hurricanes piloted by Dutchmen averaging of two or three hours' experience only. This was not so bad as it sounded; some American fliers had left Australia with only two fast fighter hours on their logbook. The Hurricanes took the air only the day after the Japs landed, because at the American field the hydraulic fluid and ammunition were unsuitable for British motors. Little Lester Johnsen wrote in his notebook: "These Dutchmen were very courageous and excellent pilots. Lieutenant Anamott was their commanding officer, a half-caste Dutch Javanese, a smart man and well-liked."

The relations of the Americans with all tints in Java had been good, right from the pure Dutch through half-castes to the full-blooded Javanese.

Staff Sergeant Jung, who spoke no Malay, had been teaching a class of Javanese mechanics, who spoke no English, the guns and vitals of the 1150-horsepower Allison engine. Though lectures consisted mostly of dumb show by the professor and grunts of comprehension by the class, the visiting pedagogue said his pupils "caught on in no time at all."

Now the Japanese convoys were on the way across the Java Sea and the invasion of the last fort in the Indies was in full progress. By working hard on each gasping and weary engine, and repairing every bullet hole, the ground crew had managed to keep a dozen P-40s still in flying condition. The Jap fleet was coming in not straight for Soerabaya but to the west. It was only one of three fleets trisecting Java.

The one remaining navy PBY Catalina counted eighty Japanese transports. It took this last battered "Cat" ten minutes to fly the convoy's length, with every anti-aircraft gun in the enemy fleet sending up hot needles.

The three remaining A-24 dive bombers were still anxious to do their part in making invasion costly. That afternoon, with the Japs just off Bawean, they set off to attack. They were protected by four Kittys in the first flight, and six in the second.

This attack was almost simultaneous with the first joining of the battle of the Java Sea, from whose final phase not one of five Allied cruisers escaped. The dive bombers put their loads directly on the deck of a 14,000-ton transport. It burned beautifully before their eyes. It was only a pinprick among the eighty transports but there was one delight: everybody got home.

Here's what little Lester Johnsen, the Stanford relay runner, wrote in the notebook he was saving to show his wife: "We encountered no enemy planes. The Jap fleet was composed of forty-five transports and twelve warships: subs, corvettes and cruisers. One could not see from [one] end of the convoy to the other. . . . On this day our operations staff consisted of one clerk and one Dutch army lieutenant."

The last day of February was Java's black day. Six more Fortresses had been sent away to the final American base at Jokjakarta to be evacuated. The remaining members of the Seventeenth were beginning to feel like the last tenants in a house that is being demolished.

By nine in the morning, the first gong of enemy aircraft approaching sounded in the village, and the twelve P-40s with four Brewsters took off. They missed them.

It was pretty hard that day to hold a breakfast down; you could not tell whether you would live until sunset. The next warning came at ten past two and the P-40s and Brewsters went up. The P-40s led the way—the Japs had sent a dozen bombers and nine Zeros up about five miles but the P-40s could not get there in time.

Zeros, recognizing cold turkey in the Brewsters, went into their dive, but the little barrels on wings could match rates of fall with anybody, and they got away. One Brewster motor stopped, and the Dutchmen bailed out safely. The Americans struggled to get up at the bombers, but the Japs stayed too high.

By this time interceptions were being broken off repeatedly on account of motor trouble. The engines had been fighting full throttle for over 150 hours. They could not be repaired or overhauled; they were too few. All had to remain on alert all the time. One flyer took a sad inventory of the P-40 that had brought him all the way from Australia and kept him alive in the face of all the Zeros, and he wrote: "My plane has two tires that have huge blisters in them. It has no brakes and no generator and hydraulic fluid is leaking into the cockpit."

Meantime the Japanese were landing at Rembang, about seventy miles west of Soerabaya. The Dutch motor torpedo boats were to attack the Jap destroyers under the leadership of the Dutch Lieutenant Henry Jorissen. (Jorissen, incidentally, is one of the leading young Dutch poets, a tall, blond and delightful Hollander.) They were to hit the beach at dawn, as soon as they could see.

The Japs used the perfectly moonlit night for unloading. Nearly everything was on the beach the next morning.

The little fighter force took off. It was to be the last blow struck for Java; already the Allied fleet was scattered and the Japs were picking off the cruisers one by one. Only nine Americans had P-40s that could fly, so they were broken down in flights of three each. They knew it was to be the last time.

So did the Dutchmen, who desperately forced the engines and guns of their Hurricanes into shape; all seven took off together with their five flyable Brewsters.

As they came down over the paddy fields outside Rembang they could see the line of transports parallel to the coast. It was a peaceful sight; the landing barges were shuttling back and forth in the usual systematic fashion of the Nipponese grab.

The Japs had already landed aircraft on the shore. These guns and the ack-ack on the destroyers and cruisers opened up a terrible fire. The orange dawn was seared with grey smoke tracers, and scarred with gleaming incendiaries.

Kiser led the flight around in a broad curve to approach the bay out of the sun for possible protection. The orders were that the P-40s should lead the way in, and the Dutchmen and Hurricanes, flying in two strings, should follow. But the Japanese crisscrossed their fire closely. Jock Caldwell went down with a crash into the water.

Reagan's plane caught on fire, and only a glimpse was seen of him as he tried to land. McWherter signalled Reagan, whose motor was spitting flames, to fly with him to the beach and bail out. Reagan understood and waved back. Possibly he was shot or his parachute was holed. Whatever the reason, he did something McWherter never forgot. He plucked himself a cigarette, rolled back the canopy, reached forward, lighted the cigarette on the burning motor, and put it in his mouth to await the end. When the plane fell McWherter followed him down, but was met with more fire from the ground and ships, and turned away before Reagan struck the ground.

Kruzel received a cannon shell in his tank and oil line. Hot black oil spewed back as he fled for Blimbing. He landed covered with hot black oil himself, in a ship black with oil from nose to empennage, with an inch of oil in the cockpit.

Adkins was shot down, too, and was thought lost.

The enemy anti-aircraft from the beach and ships was chewed to pieces by the strafing American fighters, making the way for the Dutch somewhat safer. The enemy barges and small boats were shot up and sunk. They were strung seven or eight deep in long columns, indicative of the confidence the Japanese felt that their landing was safe. Several burned and sank.

They never saw Caldwell or Reagan again, although Reagan may have lived.

Jock Caldwell was interwoven in the lives of all at Blimbing. It was he who handled the uncrating in the critical first days in Australia, when they realized once they began to negotiate about unloading the ship that they stood alone. It was Little Tarzan who made the Japanese real to them, worthy of the sacrifice of their lives—a creeping disease that would spread far unless lanced with an American sword. "You can tell Chinese and Japs apart," he told them, "because the Chinese are lighter and fleshier than the Japs." He was their kindergarten master in the politics of Asia—so vital to their country, so neglected in their educations, so intimate with his.

Adkins had an incredible experience. He landed on the beach and bounced off the water after pulling out of his power dive. He made two attacks in all, and finally bailed out over the beach, only about three hundred yards from the Japs.

A Javanese, frightened by the exchange of fire, was pedalling by along the beach road on a bicycle. Adkins was still full of the will to live and commanded the Javanese to stop, jumped on the handlebars, and yelled to his chauffeur: "Come on, let's go!" The legs of the terrified Javanese soon grew weak. Adkins, with the Japs close after him, ditched the owner of the bicycle, and pedalled away at top speed.

The remaining planes got back to the field at twenty to eight, tragically shot up. Skimming after the landing barges with everything blazing, one fighter had gone so low that the concussion of the wave tops bent back the supports for his belly tank against the body of the plane. The waves also bent in the combing of his under plane radiator. Only six P-40s could still fly. But none could fight.

By nine o'clock not one of them could fly. The Japs sent over two Zeros, and strafed the entire field back and forth, wiping out every one of the six. It was over.

For once the enemy had done the earth-scorching of the Americans for them at the last moment. Just to make sure—the Dutch are great people for making *sure* of things—the Dutch native soldiers burned the perforated Forties. The Kittyhawks died like phoenixes in fire and ashes, and the army fighters, like the navy patrol bombers, left Java only when they had nothing left that was fightable.

It was the end, too, of the Seventeenth Pursuit, Provisional. Provisional they had been, indeed. But their wings were broken.

One staff car and two trucks remained, and they loaded themselves aboard, deeding what was left to the Dutch. They paid their last bills, down to the *groschen,* as a departing Dutchman would have done. Their papers were torn up and burned.

Shaking hands for the last time with the Dutch family that had cooked and cared for them, looking around the debris and ashes-strewn quarters for the last time, the men of the Seventeenth heard a sound like weeping. It was the coolie-boy, Judy, and he was crying, a line chief said, "fit to break your heart."

Judy was just a brown mite from the swarm of Java's forty millions, twelve years old some said, while others thought he was twenty. He seemed to love to work for the Americans, so they made him a staff sergeant. They painted the herringbone chevrons on his skinny brown arm with white-wash, renewing them each day. They gave him metal parts of the Forties to polish, and got him an artilleryman's hat from one of the dozen Texans that Sprague had shanghaied from the camp at Malang.

They had taught Judy to call the camp roll, while all hands stood gravely at attention before the slim brown boy-man. "'E Jung, 'e Little, 'e Merriman, 'e Schott," the little top kick would say.

Now that he was weeping, so clearly wanting to go away with them, they did not know what to do. They filled his hands with all the gliders they had left, more than he would earn the next ten years of his life. Still he could not stop weeping. So they took him out to the shattered workshop, put tools in his hands, and gave him an old cartridge case to clean. "Have it ready by the time we come back," they told him.

Judy nodded through his tears and began to polish earnestly.

Under the orders of Major Fisher, the whole party, pilots and men, started for Jokjakarta, now the last Fortress base since Malang and Madioen were abandoned. En route the trucks got separated from the staff car, and ran into some Dutch troops whose officer told Washburn, whose linguistic talents later made him a lieutenant, that the Japs were only a half mile away. They saw the Dutch blowing up their sugar mills, and through helping a fleeing Dutchman fix his broken cart, they missed being bombed on Jokjakarta field.

Johnsen wrote: "We drove to Jokja by car and had to go very near the enemy. We could see the fires of the towns that were being burned. The Nips bombed the field, destroying the B-24s. The Zeros came down and strafed us, afterward."

They spent their last day in Java on the field at Jokjakarta, from which every coolie had fled, rolling gasoline drums out to the last Fortresses that escaped the 2 p.m. raid by Zeros. The ebullient Adkins, who had missed them at Blimbing, arrived in a carful of Dutch officers. Their roster was complete except for one corporal whom no one was able to find.

After supper Captain Lane, having consulted the bombers, said that fifteen men under Lieutenant McCartney would have to be left behind for safety of load. Sergeant Evans offered to stay. Rickmar and other enlisted men went to the bomber crews and asked them to take all. All were taken.

That Sunday night, March 1, with the Japs fifty hours landed on the teeming island, the last of the Seventeenth took off at 11:20 p.m. In dawn light they landed at Broome, halfway down the coast of western Australia. They had been raided at Jokjakarta the day of their departure; the day after their arrival a raid by Japanese long range fighters—the most costly in human life after that of Darwin two weeks before—left the waters of the harbor best known to the Japanese pearlers filled with the bodies of Dutch women and children, together with five members of the Seventeenth. Fifty-nine came out by plane, thanks to the bombers.

Forty-six had already left on the battered but still reasonably fast-footed Dutch freighter *Abbekerk*. After leaving Tjilatjap, Java's only port on the Indian Ocean, on the last day of February, the strong-minded captain broke convoy and—ignoring naval orders—took a course of his own. Several other members of the convoy were sunk. (This was the day before the Japanese trapped the aircraft tender *Langley*, with 32 more P-40s and pilots aboard, in these same waters.) Armorers and crew chiefs, pilots and men, slept on the cold decks in the rain, one blanket per man. The ship was full of dirty, bearded British and Australian troops who had evacuated both Malaya and Java. Water was rationed on the crowded decks to one canteen a man. There were two identical meals daily: canned willy, hardtack, and sour coffee.

The *Abbekerk* reached Fremantle on March 4, nine days ahead of an even smaller Dutch freighter of six-knot speed, the last vessel larger than a trawler to escape from Java, aboard which the writer arrived after being strafed by Zeros.

When the Fortresses from Jokjakarta came in one by one to Broome, in northwestern Australia, groaning with their extra load and riddled with the holes of eight weeks of fighting off Zeros, there were no facilities to fuel them rapidly. Moreover, the harbor was full of Dutch flying boats filled with women and children.

A big B-24 Liberator flew to Java the night of March 2 to take off the remaining air force personnel, who were to have given a pre-arranged signal from the field at Jokjakarta. The B-24 circled in darkness, saw no signal, and returned to Broome the morning of March 3. Java's wounded were loaded into it, and from the Seventeenth, as passengers, Beatty, Donoho, Foster, Rex, Sheetz, Steinmetz and Taylor. The B-24 took off, and minutes later the second worst air raid in Australian history began. Broome had neither radar, anti-aircraft guns, nor fighters. It was a defenseless bay and air field, both crammed with aircraft, both completely helpless.

Nine Zeros came in from the sea. Six began strafing the harbor, making one leisurely pass after another until flying boats and bombers, the former loaded with the wives and children of Dutch officers wanted by the Japs, puffed into flame and exploded. Three Zeros went after the B-24, which was carrying fifty passengers beside its crew, and had attained about 600 feet.

Donoho, a stockily-built armorer who in Java had taken care of Blanton's plane, was lying at the bottom of the bomb bay. "I looked up and saw what looked like an arc of electricity come into the plane. It came once, then it came again."

The gas tanks caught fire. The passengers on top of Donoho crawled out of the bomb bay to the rear of the plane in a squirming mass, trying to escape. As the flames found more gasoline, the fire pursued them. The plane was falling.

"I figured it was all over anyway, so I lay down on the catwalk and just waited." The next thing Donoho knew he was below the surface of the water, where the plane had landed with a crack that broke it in two, and was looking up through greenish light. He came up. The two parts of the plane were well apart, the tail sticking up vertically, the nose still afloat with men jumping out of it. There was no one discernible alive where the flames had been, in the tail, but there were fifteen or sixteen men, doctors pulling out their already wounded patients, around the nose.

Donoho found Beatty, who seemed the only one alive from the Seventeenth. They could see smoke on the horizon, but were not sure it was land. Actually, it was the planes burning at Broome. They began to swim. In twelve hours they were a quarter mile from shore. Then it was night and the heavy tide of Broome, which falls over thirty feet and leaves freighters stranded on the mud at their piers, took them out to sea. They swam all night, on their backs as much as they could, keeping together in the darkness—Beatty, the weaker, swimming between Donoho's legs. Beatty kept urging Donoho to go ashore and bring help. He complained of being cold, too. Finally, about noon next day they saw a lighthouse, with docks and fishing vessels. "Go on in, leave me," Beatty said.

Donoho, who was twenty-nine and had worked in oilfields, still had more reserve than Beatty, who at twenty-six had spent seven years in the army. He struck on ahead. Within 200 yards of shore, the rushing tide carried him out again. "Hell, I thought I'd quit." Then he decided to go down the coast from the lighthouse.

The next thing he heard was a slapping noise. It was waves striking rocks. He reached them, climbed up, and collapsed. Shore was fifty yards away across a channel. He made it and started walking back up the beach toward the lighthouse. It was five miles away. When he got there it was deserted and there were no docks or boats. They had been a mirage. He found water in a cistern, staggered through the reeds for hours, and finally walked into a major's arms on the air field he had left 36 hours before, a naked, sunburned and exhausted man.

By daylight Beatty was found on the beach, delirious. Flown to Perth, the nearest city, 1400 miles away, he died in hospital without returning to his senses.

The evacuees from Java, though hardly a trickle of its millions of Javanese and thousands of Dutch, were an overwhelming torrent when they touched the northwest coast of Australia, isolated by the wet season among its meager foodstuffs shipped from Perth. They remained only a day or two; yet it was enough to eat the one or two aboriginal missions and the scattering of settlers out of the little they had left. It was impossible, even after the evacuees meandered south to Perth, to send food by ship to northwestern Australia because the Japs sank the ships.

An Arkansas private by the name of Ewart managed to hold on, all the way to Perth, to a Javanese monkey. He seemed to be trying, in this way, to express the very strong attachment for Java, the Javanese and the Dutch, that almost everyone of the Seventeenth felt, the most extraordinary six weeks in the lives of any of them.

They had much to remember.

They remembered the day Morehead came burning in over the field, did a victory roll straight down the middle of the runway, then another. They remembered how he landed—he had run into nine bombers over Malang and shot down two—how he threw back his canopy before his wheels stopped rolling, stood up with two fingers in the air and shook them, grinning, and how he yelled: "Hell, you guys are crazy! Those Japs can't shoot. . . ." That day a Zero was on his tail as he pursued the bombers, but he just seesawed his plane up and down like a bucking horse to spoil the Jap's aim, and kept on boring in. All he got was a bullet hole in his stabilizer.

They remembered the day Egenes and Parker mistook tall cane for young rice, landed in the high green stalks, were surrounded by natives with spears who took them for Japs, saved themselves with the Javanese words Geurtz had taught them, and finally took off on a curved tar highway, everybody happy and waving.

They remembered the day when Coss, their last commander, got his first Jap, how he could not speak but just kept smiling and smiling to himself.

They remembered combing the jungle after the Seventeenth itself lost a plane, trying to get enough parts from the wreckage to keep some other pilot's ship flying.

They remembered Sprague on their first payday in Java, when he said, "We haven't any records or finance officer yet, so you just tell me what the government owes you, and I'll pay you, only remember to be honest because I'm responsible for this," and how he did pay them, out of the pockets of his flying suit.

They remembered the silver loving cup that the Dutch couple who took care of them had bought, inscribing with care the name of every pilot who brought down a Japanese. There had been five names on the cup, then things began to happen too fast to keep up with inscriptions. Whatever happened to the loving cup, anyway?

They remembered Kiser, one of the most cunning pilots in battle, whose strongest cussword was "by damn," and they remembered "Stonewall" Jackson, his crew chief, an old Regular Army hand who tinkered constantly through his waking hours and chewed cigarettes because Java had no cutplug.

They remembered the Dutch pilot of a B-10, seeing his bomber as vulnerable as the early B-17 Fortress because it had no tail gunner, who painted the point of his tail black, put in a flashlight attached by switch to his cockpit, and used to wink the light at any Jap diving on his tail to simulate machine-gun fire.

They remembered the day when the three little sergeants Austin, Killian and Merriman, who looked as alike as Javanese and always went around together, found themselves on the runway at Soerabaya in the middle of a raid. A burning Dutchman came down with his landing wheels retracted and bellywhumped along the strip, a doctor ran out to help him, the pursuing Jap strafed him, the doctor ran back, the Dutchman tried to climb out, the doctor ran, brought him in, the Jap came down with his machine guns going, another Dutchman came in and crashed with his wheels down. Austin saw an unused P-40, started to run for it, angry for revenge. Killian and Merriman held him down as the Japs came in, and Austin cast them aside long enough to get his helmet off and throw it passionately after the Jap as he went by.

They remembered "Toughey" Hague who said, "The first time I saw a Nip I was so excited to get at him I wobbled my fire all over the sky."

They remembered the rare nights of Soerabaya, at the Shanghai and the Tip Top—the officers went to the Oranje—and they remembered the look in the wet red dawn at Blimbing, of the palms and the red, yellow, blue and green sharks and dragons of the impatient planes.

Perry, with a young man's sense of what he will remember, said: "With forty millions populating Java, one could not walk more than two hundred yards through the jungle without seeing at least five native huts, or a whole village. You saw the Javanese everywhere, washing clothes on the stones in the river, dressed in their Sunday best on a day off in town, squatting along the streets and crowding around to sell you something. From a soldier's viewpoint, with the idea of returning with lots of time and money, it was a place where the best drunk, the most fun and the best chance of having the time of a lifetime were to be had. We loved it. The tropics, the romantic South Sea isles, the cities and tangled jungles filled with strange people. We liked seeing half-primitive modes of living, hearing strange words and guessing at their meaning, being able to visit exclusive bars and cafés and exert a certain amount of influence where it meant most."

Such was the close of the work of the Seventeenth Pursuit. All their planes were lost, but for these battle-weary Kittyhawks the Americans exacted a price of at least fifty Japanese planes, nearly half of them heavy bombers and most of the rest Zeros. (The Dutch said they were certain of at least sixty-five, positively seen to crash.) And this destruction, amounting to the loss to Japan of at least two hundred trained airmen, was caused by a squadron which had only thirty-nine planes—flyable and faulty included—but which yet lost only eleven men in all, and only nine in combat with the Japanese in Java, in a period of four weeks' single-handed fighting.

And all this was accomplished without a radio warning system.

Had there been an adequate air warning system at Soerabaya and four times as many P-40s, Java might never have been taken.

As the Seventeenth was disbanded and scattered, their fortunes changed. Andy Reynolds and Jim Morehead became two of the finest fighter pilots in Darwin, where the pickings were poor because the Zeros didn't like to fight after the long fuel-exhausting run from Koepang. Robert "Big" Johnson crashed in Moresby and "Toughey" Hague was lost in August on a raid in northern Papua. Many, like little Les Johnsen, went hotfoot after the records of those like Kiser, who had come back from Java laden with scalps. Dutton went to the Solomons and collected two Zeros and three medals, filling with pride a father who was an adjutant in the bomber command. Adkins and his irrepressible sidekick, the bushy-bearded Wahl, did well out of Moresby, and Turner topped all others for honors in New Guinea; while McWherter and Egenes held their own.

In far-off Washington, Princess Juliana called Willard Reed's widow and thanked her for what "Jess" had offered Java.

Many of the enlisted men who fought in Java were still carrying the battle a year later in New Guinea. Sergeant Jack Evans, the one who offered to stay behind in Java, became a Fortress bomber, won his Silver Star and Purple Heart, and joined Paul "Pappy" Gunn, the daredevil middle-aged bellwether of the Beechcraft, in low-level strafing jobs in A-20s and super-gunned B-25s.

Corporal Ollie Hale, the World War I veteran who could make a radio talk any language, was handling the earphones in General MacArthur's private plane.

Langjahr, a private in the rear rank in Java, became a Fortress bombardier, went to the Buin-Faisi retreat in the Solomons, and put two 500-
pounders on the decks and two nearby a Japanese monitor battleship, one
of those new high-speed, heavy firepower creatures that specialized in
night bombardments of Guadalcanal.

When the Seventeenth's enlisted men crossed Australia they found
newly arrived officers from the States who said there'd never been any
American fighter planes in Java. Hadn't there? So they did what the army
calls "a snow job" and told the Australian girls they had all been "tail gunners in P-40s."

The story of the Seventeenth is one of the necessity of permanent
American air and naval bases in Asia and Australia, like those in the Atlantic, in order that the unpreparedness they fought to remedy may never
be ours or that of our Allies again.

Today the American wings over Java are folded. But someday they will be
spread again. Until then, as the Dutch used to say: "Luck to the fighters!"

AMALGAMATED WIRELESS (AUSTRALASIA) LIMITED
(Incorporated in New South Wales)
TELEGRAPH OFFICE
47 YORK ST., SYDNEY   163-173 QUEEN ST., MELBOURNE
Telephone: B 0522 Extns. 286, 287, 288 (3 lines)   Telephone: M 4161 (12 lines)
Direct Wireless Service to England, Canada, Pacific Islands and ships at sea
In any enquiry respecting this message please quote Reference No.

OFFICE STAMP

4-MAY 1943

'Via Beam'

The first line of this telegram contains the following particulars in order named :—

No.	Office of Origin	No. of Words	Date	Time	Official Instructions
MS16	CHICAGO ILLS	33	3RD	4 55PM	

LC GEORGE WELLER

AMERICAN ARMY HEADQUARTERS SYDNEY

WARMEST CONGRATULATIONS RICHLY DESERVED PULITZER AWARD

REPORTERS WORK SPECIFICALLY APPENDECTOMY STORY ACTUALLY

RECOGNITION THREE YEARS ABLE COURAGEOUS REPORTING WHICH

NEWS AND EYE PROUD CORDIALLY

CARROLL BINDER

12 40PM ZJT

XI

The Defense of Australia

By his own admission, Weller arrived in Australia scared and filled with "guilt about the people left behind." (At least one colleague "escaped and went home to suicide.") From mid-March 1942 until the end of November 1943, Australia was his base of operations, even though he was in New Guinea for much of that time and traveled extensively through the Pacific islands. Thus for the next three chapters this book leaps around within those twenty months.

Weller seems to have produced *Singapore Is Silent* by August, before his first assignments in New Guinea. His 1942 datelines show that he made a long journey—almost fifteen thousand miles—around the circumference of Australia, writing all the way. "I've tried to cover more ground, both tactically and physically, than any other correspondent in Australia," he wrote in a September letter to a friend. "This trip made me the first to make the full swing around the continent, just as I was the first to visit New Guinea's Milne Bay."

For the Allies, Australia was the final fortress that had to be held at all costs, and the Americans poured everything they could into its defense. "A chaos that had to be experienced to be believed and even then could not be understood," Weller characterized it at the time. Shortly after he arrived, he was able to send in the earliest meaningful reports of the dramatic Battle of the Java Sea, which saw the *Houston* and thousands of tons of other Allied ships sunk in the first all-out naval action of the war in the Pacific.

This chapter concludes with the story that earned Weller a 1943 Pulitzer Prize for foreign reporting: the account of an emergency appendectomy performed by a pharmacist's mate on a U.S. submarine, the *Seadragon,* while in enemy waters. In those days, submarines routinely did not have a doctor on board and might be at sea for a couple of months. (Much to Weller's dismay, the episode, along with his dialogue, was used without payment or even acknowledgment in a Hollywood feature film, *Destination Tokyo* [1943]. There was also a TV adaptation by Budd Schulberg.) The operation took place in September 1942; the award-winning article was published three months later. Weller, in Perth, heard about the story from a Navy commander, and was led to the captain and the crew, whom he had reenact the surgery several times over so he could get all the details right.

When he learned, a few months later, that he had been awarded the Pulitzer, he didn't feel triumphant—thousands of miles away, in the midst of war, it didn't feel like a victory. But one lesson of getting the story in port in Australia was that the best "adventure" he could've found had found him, in a most unlikely way.

—

EXCLUSIVE EYEWITNESS STORY—STORY OF EPIC JAVA SEA BATTLE

Fight to Finish Told by Weller

Somewhere in Australia—March 19, 1942

A regulation American Navy life belt, with the Holmes floating light attached, tossed overboard from the cruiser *Houston* in the latter stages of the Battle of the Java Sea, not only saved the lives of 116 men but has brought back in the words of a Dutch destroyer commander the first comprehensive story of that naval combat.

Struggling for their lives in the oil-burned waters after their destroyer *Kortenaer* was torpedoed, the 116 men clung to their rafts as the Allied battle fleet steamed past through the moonlit night. Their cries were answered by return cries from the cruisers *De Ruyter, Perth* and *Java,* but only some unknown, friendly hand aboard the *Houston* had the quick wit to throw them the illuminated life preserver. Hours later the Holmes light, in a battle which virtually wiped out the Netherlands East Indies fleet, guided a British destroyer to their rescue, although not before their radio operator suffocated on heavy fuel oil clogging his nose and throat.

Thirty-seven of the *Kortenaer*'s crew perished when a Jap torpedo, fired probably from a submarine, hit her near the engine room, destroying the munitions magazines. The *Kortenaer* split amidship, sinking perpendicularly, "like stakes driven into the sea," within two minutes.

The Allied and Jap fleets were ill met by the moonlight. Knowing that the battle odds made clean-cut victory impossible, Vice-Admiral Helfrich of the N.E.I. fleet based his strategy on dark nights and bad weather, striking when enemy visual communications were upset. But the Japs invaded when the day was unclouded blue and the sea smooth, followed by a star-hung night with the moon barely past full. Under revealing conditions, the inequality of forces was heightened by the Jap force having two seaplanes to each cruiser. The Allied cruisers had none.

Several weeks of attacks by Zeros on American and Dutch Catalina flying boats patrolling the coast caused an underestimate of enemy forces.

Invasion convoys were seen gathering in Macassar Strait two days before. As a defensive force, the Allies, under the immediate command of Admiral Karel W. F. M. Doorman, had to accept battle under whatever conditions the Japanese imposed.

The Allied fleet (including the destroyers *Electra, Jupiter, Witte de With, Encounter* and a number of American destroyers) was deployed around the cruisers *De Ruyter, Exeter, Houston, Perth* and *Java.* The fleet had left Soerabaya on Thursday night [February 26] for an eastern sweep along the north coast of Madura island, thence westward beyond Rembang, seeking to intercept the convoy.

The crews were tired to the point of exhaustion, having spent the night of Feb. 25 at battle stations on a similar sweep. About 10 a.m. on the 27th, about ten miles off the headland west from Rembang, the Allied fleet was attacked by three bombers probably destined originally for the Java coast. No bombs hit, but a Jap seaplane immediately appeared astern and there-after trailed Admiral Doorman's fleet, keeping barely beyond gunshot. After 37 hours of continuous battle stations, the Allied "exhaustion point far exceeded" (as Doorman wirelessed Helfrich), he proposed breaking off the sweep and returning to Soerabaya.

The fleet turned east again, planning to make base about sundown. But Friday afternoon, when the fleet was midway between Soerabaya and the island of Bawean, the signal came that a Catalina had observed a squadron of "two cruisers, four destroyers and many transporters" (apparently the forty seen in Macassar Strait). This squadron was but fifty miles away, al-most directly north.

Helfrich's order came from his Bandoeng mountain headquarters to "attack immediately." The ships swung north. Doorman arranged his for-mation with the British destroyers, *Electra* and *Jupiter*, heavier armed than the Americans, leading a column of cruisers with a mile of open water between. Next came Doorman's 6500-ton flagship, the *De Ruyter*, followed at five-hundred-yard intervals by the 8400-ton *Exeter*, the 9050-ton *Hous-ton*, the 7000-ton *Perth* and the 6670-ton *Java*.

The plan was to engage the Japs to starboard. The *Houston*'s comman-der requested a place midway in the cruiser line, because only the two for-ward turrets' eight-inch guns were serviceable, the single stern turret being put out of action by Jap bombers four weeks before. Two Dutch de-stroyers, the *Kortenaer* and the *Witte de With*, steamed parallel to the line, two miles to port, with orders to escort any cruiser disabled through enemy fire. The British destroyer *Encounter* was to port of the column's end, a mile away. American destroyers reserved for torpedo attacks brought up the rear, their lighter armament more suitable as an anti-submarine screen. The entire column was making 25 knots when it entered battle.

When action was joined, the Jap force—reported as far smaller—proved to consist of at least eight cruisers—at least two in the 10,000-ton Nati class, with probably most of the others the 8500-ton *Mogami* class, plus at least thirteen destroyers. Thirty-odd transports fled north. Firing began at 25,000 yards, and a *Mogami*-class cruiser, hit by the *Houston* or *Exeter*, began laying a smoke screen.

But after five minutes of finding themselves at a disadvantage through the enemy's heavier fire power, the Allies moved closer—to 20,000 yards [eleven-plus miles].

Now the battle was at its hottest, and the Jap destroyers moved in. Columns of water arose around the Allied vessels which, counting fifteen greenish white spires after single Jap broadsides, knew the cruisers were in range of fifteen six-inch guns carried by the Mogami class. The *Perth* scored a hit on a Jap destroyer and the *De Ruyter* demolished another warship, believed to be a cruiser.

After a black puff of smoke silhouetted a sinking Jap, the *De Ruyter*'s big guns slowly swung around and began firing hungrily against the next destroyer. The enemy's attack was frustrated barely in time, because four spent Jap torpedoes blew up harmlessly in the water.

Even though Jap firepower exceeded Allied by two to one, and Jap spotter planes were undisputed overhead, the battle went favorably for Doorman's force until a Jap shell hit the British *Exeter*'s engine room. Its speed faltered and the cruiser fell away. As the following *Houston* pounded down upon him, the *Exeter*'s commander made a full 90 degrees portside turn, breaking out of line to not impede the other vessel's movements. However, the *Houston,* the *Perth,* and the *Java,* seeing the new maneuver, likewise turned to port. The *De Ruyter* followed and so did three British, two Dutch and several American destroyers.

The battle had been opened at 4:14 p.m. The *Exeter* was hit at about 5:10. The Dutch destroyer *Kortenaer,* ordered to escort whichever cruiser was first damaged, changed course to accompany the stricken *Exeter.* The Allied fleet, which had been proceeding Indian file, was teaming abreast and away from the enemy. But even as its helm swung over, the *Kortenaer* received a torpedo on the starboard side. The nearest Jap warship was 25,000 yards away, an impossible range for a torpedo; therefore Jap submarines must have stolen in during the surface engagement.

The *Kortenaer* went down in halves in about two minutes. The destroyer's surgeon, defying the laws of suction, stood upon the stern as it sank, yet managed to dive clear from the whirlpool and join 115 survivors in water sticky with oil.

The sun was nearly down and the first stars emerging as the blackened sailors saw the Allied and Jap fleets disappear over the horizon. But half an hour later, while counting heads aboard the waves, the survivors saw a flotilla of destroyers speeding straight toward them. Suddenly a sailor on the nearest raft saw they had only a single funnel and yelled: "Japs!" He dived under the sticky, black waves and others followed. The Jap column went foaming by half a mile away. It was 5:45, and the shadow of the coming night protected the swimming sailors.

But a surprise struck the Japs, too, for as the line passed, the destroyer immediately following the leader suddenly blew up before the swimmers' eyes.

"There was just a big cloud of smoke, very dense and black and nothing more," Lieutenant Benjamin Reiche told this correspondent. "All hands must have been lost because, though we were very near, we never saw or heard any survivors. And the following seven destroyers neither stopped nor made any attempt at rescue that we could see. They simply went speeding past the wreckage."

Since the Allied ships were already far away, it is probable that the Jap hit a spent torpedo, as had possibly the *Kortenaer* itself.

The Japs launched an attack upon the *Electra,* which reported sighting three enemy destroyers at approximately 5:45 and said it scored hits upon the leader. But the *Electra* was hit again in the engine room. It stopped and listed to port. A single Jap destroyer closed in for the kill, silencing the wounded ship's guns with raking salvos, eventually using pompoms at short range. The *Electra* sank shortly after sunset and 54 survivors remained in the water until 3:15 a.m. Saturday [February 28], when they were picked up by an American submarine which reached Soerabaya Sunday morning after undergoing seventeen depth-charge attacks by Jap destroyers.

After the *Electra*'s sinking, the *Kortenaer* survivors saw the same flotilla of Japs returning from the engagement at 6:15 p.m. Two more were missing, reducing the original nine to six.

The crippled *Exeter* had now turned back to Soerabaya, with the *Kortenaer* (its intended escort) already sunk. Her task was taken over by the *Witte de With.* Except for the 1690-ton *Jupiter* and the 1375-ton *Encounter,* Doorman's four cruisers were virtually without protection—the lesser-armed, 1200-ton Americans were inadequate. Should such exposed cruisers, with weary crews, attempt to pierce the heavy Jap fleet in mercilessly bright moonlight without destroyers?

Somewhere beyond was the Jap transport convoy, still intact. The original plan had been to imitate the technique American destroyers used with such success against overwhelming Jap forces at Balikpapan, when they ran directly through the middle of the clustered transports and fired torpedoes from both port and starboard like firecrackers, creating complete disorder and havoc.

Admiral Doorman, furthermore, knew his cruisers virtually stood alone and the likelihood of reinforcements was remote. He gave to his little fleet the signal, which he repeated twice more before the two Dutch cruisers *De Ruyter* and *Java* went to their doom: "I am attacking, follow me."

Doorman was the most offensive-minded of the entire N.E.I. fleet. But at about 9:30 the biggest remaining destroyer, the *Jupiter*, received a torpedo and began to sink. It must have been close to shore between Soerabaya and Rembang because the few survivors upon the Carley float managed to paddle ashore, attaining the beach shortly before midnight Saturday after 26 hours in the water.

The British *Encounter* was now the only first-line destroyer left to Doorman but the Dutch admiral was soon to lose even her, though not through enemy action. The plan was to make a final attempt to penetrate the Japs. Then all ships were to scatter and proceed separately to Tanjong Priok, the port of Batavia in western Java. There they would attempt to rest briefly before attacking the other two big armadas and transports approaching both central and western Java.

But the *Encounter*'s bunkers were down to less than 100 tons of fuel oil due to the protracted sweep before the battle, and it asked Admiral Doorman for orders to return to Soerabaya because Tanjong Priok was too far. Though this deprived the cruisers of their last protection, it saved the *Kortenaer*'s men.

The night was continuously illuminated by star shells. The four Allied cruisers, turning their course at new orders to attack, crossed directly through the *Kortenaer*'s wreckage. The floating men shouted for help. Warships were hardly fifty yards away and the waves created in their wake washed men from the float into the water. Then someone aboard the *Houston* threw out a life belt with the Holmes light attached. At about 11:15 the *Encounter*, bound for Soerabaya, saw the floating light and drew cautiously near. Finding that it was not a Jap ruse, the commander picked up all remaining men till every raft was cleared despite the submarine peril.

Shortly before midnight, the *Java* and Doorman's flagship the *De Ruyter* ran into a barrage of torpedoes, probably from destroyers, and sank, apparently with few if any survivors. Doorman's orders for the return to Tanjong Priok then came into effect, and the *Houston* and *Perth* steamed there as well as the American destroyers.

The Japs were, meantime, busy bottling up the Lombok and Bali Straits—the eastern exit from the Java Sea box—and the Sunda Strait, the western doorway.

American destroyers and submarines escaped through each, but when the American *Pope* and the British *Encounter* tried to take the crippled *Exeter* east, past the northern coast of the island of Madura, all were lost. Survivors, if any, must have landed on the wild western coast of Java which will be the last part of the island to be cleaned up by the Japanese forces. It is possible some may have been able to join Dutch guerrillas reportedly operating in the mountains.

Admiral Doorman went down with his ships.

The *Exeter* sank one destroyer, the *Witte de With* another. The hospital ship *Op ten Noort* left Soerabaya about 9 p.m. Friday to search for survivors and managed to find 137 of the *De Ruyter*'s and *Java*'s crews, originally about 500.

Dutch officers are—and this is no propaganda—more eager than ever to get new destroyers from America to fight the Japanese and avenge their lost comrades. They pray America can give them a cruiser, even an old one. Their fleet is gone, their families are prisoners, their homes the domiciles of Japs. Few have anything more than a pair of shorts, a shirt and a water-soaked picture of wife and children.

All they want is a chance to fight. It seems little enough to ask.

The tragedy in the Java Sea may be classified like other Allied defeats in the "always too little, always too late" category. As long as Britain and America continue to be mastered by the invasion tailored for them, their enemies will widen the field of domination, and exploit the resources of the conquered areas.

For America, the southwest Pacific is characterized by the complete lack of a political pattern which would give its forces something real, in territorial terms, to battle for instead of selfless sacrifice against heavy odds. Few of its fighting men can be satisfied with an unrealistic political plan to restore those lost areas to the flabby status which caused America to be confronted with this dilemma.

—

AVIATORS ABOARD *HOUSTON* SAVED SHIP WHEN TURRET WAS AFLAME

Heroes Are Missing and Still Unavenged

Perth, Australia—April 14, 1942

A 22-year-old aviation machinist's mate, with a handful of other flying personnel headed by two pilot officers, saved the U.S. cruiser *Houston* from blowing up when, with her stern eight-inch turrets aflame and repair crews already killed, a Japanese bombing squadron rained explosives around her. Almost all the men concerned are now listed as missing because the *Houston* was later lost after the Java Sea battle, somewhere in Sunda Straits, attempting to go to the rescue of the disabled Dutch destroyer *Evertsen*.

But a corner of the veil of naval secrecy has now been lifted, making it possible to tell in part the story of the February 4 attack upon two U.S. warships sixty miles north of Madura island, near Bawean off the north coast of Java.

The *Houston*'s companion warship, although suffering damage, escaped and the *Houston* herself missed becoming the victim of Japanese air superiority only through the heroism of the flying personnel in mastering the turret fire.

Fighting fire inside and with the armored hood of the turret strewn with bodies and piled with shells so hot the grease on them sizzled, the aviators managed, by twenty minutes of hard work, to stifle the fire sufficiently so that the shells failed to explode. Since the report commending them perished with the *Houston,* what they did has only now become known and confirmed by eyewitnesses' statements.

The man who saved the *Houston* was John William Ranger of Gillespie, Illinois. He was the husky son of an immigrant Polish miner and had hardened his fists in many a labor scrap. Two years in junior college was his education and he altered his original difficult Polish name before enlisting. Ranger was working under the command of Lieutenant Jack Lamade of Williamsport, Pennsylvania, a 1932 Annapolis graduate, when the alarm "enemy aircraft in vicinity" sounded.

First aloft was Lieutenant Thomas Paine, who stepped into a catapult monoplane, goggled and helmeted. Paine, an Annapolis man with a wife and child in Corondado, California, was one of the fleet's aviators. He was known among his friends as the man who, while driving a motorcar at top speed, climbed suddenly into the back seat with the passengers, leaving the front seat empty, and who once dialed his mother's phone number on the *Houston*'s switchboard, while 200 miles at sea, and complained about getting no service.

Once Paine had shot away, Lamade, second-in-command, jumped into the cockpit of the second plane and his prop began to spin. Before he could clear, 46 twin-engined Jap bombers, humming through the blue sky, released their first load.

Lamade sat stiffened in his plane as the gathering squeal of falling death came down upon the *Houston*. Columns of green water jumped skyward and flickering fragments flew clanging all over the decks. They were big armor-piercing bombs intended first to penetrate and then explode. The nearest fell five feet from the *Houston*'s speeding grey flank.

Most of this bomb's power, intended to blow out the ship's vitals, was expended in water. But fragments flying up stripped all the fabric from Lamade's plane, leaving him with a tattered skeleton. Tearing off his flying togs, Lamade ordered the two remaining planes below decks housed in deck hangars. While the men worked, led by Lieutenant Walter Winslow of New York City, the Jap bombers wheeled leisurely and began a second run.

The *Houston* sent up puff after puff of anti-aircraft fire, pocking the sky with cottony meatballs. But because the anti-aircraft directors were hit, the *Houston*'s fire was by guess and by God, and little calculated to discourage the Jap wings. The Japs were flying in an open U about 600 feet across, dropping sticks, when the leader came over the target. By this method they consistently achieved close, neat brackets over the zigzagging warships.

Three more runs were made. During the third, hits were scored on the *Houston*'s companion warship. The ack-ack was getting hotter. A Jap bomber was hit and zoomed down in a succession of sideslips, trying to fall upon the deck of the other warship, but missed and splashed into the sea. The first two runs were made with medium-heavy bombs but on the fourth and fifth the Jap planes released bombs of the heaviest possible caliber, 840 pounders. For the fifth time the *Houston* was relatively unscathed.

Then came a whistle and an enormous concussion. A projectile landed on the main deck between the stern turret, whose guns were then pointing to port, and the mainmast. Almost immediately there broke out the most terrible cry that can be heard aboard a warship, "Fire in turret number three." A bomb had made virtually a direct hit and been detonated by hitting the mainmast in the fall. Old Glory, which had waved from the mainmast crosstrees, was torn away and the fourteen-inch searchlight on the high platform smashed. Perforated with 196 holes, the turret was a mass of flames with bodies inside. All the pointers, trainers and loaders were killed, only the hoist men beneath the turret having escaped. In the smoke-filled darkness flames could be seen beside the shells.

There were a few moments of shock while the arrival of the repair party, always delegated to such jobs in a battle, was awaited. Then it was discovered that the repair party too had been killed.

It was about 100 feet from the hangar on the main deck, where the fliers had been putting away the planes, to the smoking turret. The flying personnel came at a dead run. Winslow broke out the hoses below, while Lamade took command of the turret whose starboard door was open, venting power fumes. Ranger glanced up. He saw that the Stars and Stripes had been blown away. Running to a motor launch affixed at the stern he snatched up the flag, which flies upon the stern poop when liberty parties are going ashore. The former miner was determined that if an explosion should occur, the *Houston* should sink with her colors flying.

Ranger lashed the flag to the *Houston*'s stern stanchion where Jap spotters, 15,000 feet overhead, could see that the *Houston* was still fighting. With an explosion expected any second, Warrant Officers Louis Emil Diechlem, a carpenter, and James Elmore Hogan, a gunner, joined the party below tugging up hoses. Chinese mess boys from the officers' quarters also lent a hand.

The boots of an officer beside the turret had been blown away. Ranger leaped into the turret door. Lamade began handing him bottles of carbon dioxide fire suffocatory. Shells with gun grease on them were bubbling with heat. Ranger went inside without an asbestos suit or other protection, and broke the bottles upon the flames. Thereafter he reappeared only for more bottles or a single deep whiff of fresh air. Most times he stepped only half outside the turret, enough to extend an arm and get a lungful of air.

Lamade managed to get the hose up to Ranger, then ordered him: "Get out of there."

"I'm all right," was Ranger's answer. He went in alone, tugging the heavy nozzle. The smokeless powder was actually burning; the oil-smear upon the shells could be heard hissing. It was simply a question of how long the heat would take to penetrate the metal shell and detonate the cap connected inside to the powder. Then, suddenly, water gushed forth. The turret was saved.

The first thing Winslow, who led the removal of the bodies, handed out was a single white sneaker of a dead gunner so perforated with holes that it resembled lace. Ranger staggered forth into clear air, his work done.

The next day, her fantail piled with coffins, the *Houston* entered Tjilatjap. There were buried the *Houston*'s dead with walnut-brown crosses overhead. The funeral was held in early morning when the people of the little southern Java town—destroyed by Jap bombers exactly a month later—were going to work.

Americans present there will never forget how two Dutch working women came alone to the service read by Chaplain Rentz of the Asiatic Fleet and a Dutch priest. In their tears was the grief of America's faraway womanhood. Uninvited and unknown to either the dead or living, they remained weeping in the cemetery alone, hours after the hard-eyed men went back to their ships.

In the front row was buried Boatswain Joseph Bienert, who had pleaded with the ship's surgeon to end his suffering. Paine, Winslow and Lamade bore to its grave the body of their fellow flier, Lieutenant Edward Blessman, who died aboard the other warship.

Thus were laid to rest the *Houston*'s unrevenged heroes. Of all the above living, everyone is missing except Lamade, who about ten days later was ordered to fly his plane to the coast.

Perhaps they are all Jap prisoners, perhaps they are gone to join the great corps of unavenged of Pearl Harbor, Manila and Bataan. And nobody knows who were the two Dutch mothers who wept in the cemetery at Tjilatjap.

—

ATTACK ON AUSTRALIA NEAR

Japs Ignore Nazis

Somewhere in Australia—April 30, 1942

The prospect of an attempted invasion by Japan seems to have risen. Due partly to British losses in Burma, the pressure is increasing along the northern Australia coast. Naturally, nothing can be said regarding preparations for the onslaught. The Japanese trick of masquerading as natives will meet with obstacles because the aborigines are almost as few as the red Indians in North America relative to whites. Should invasion reach these shores, guerrilla fighting would be in an arid country different from jungle-shrouded Malaya, Sumatra and Java, for west Australia is divided from the east by desert.

What tempts the Japanese is their ambition to close tight the naval portcullis they have already dropped from Vladivostok to Australia. In Japan's military plans for expelling the United States from Asia, an invasion of Australia is probably inevitable, a natural denouement to victories in the Indian Ocean. Furthermore, Japan anticipates more attacks upon her home islands, possibly from Alaska, and will do her utmost to spread the American Asiatic naval forces.

Germany wants Japan either to strike across India or cut the lifeline of American supplies up the East African coast to the Suez Canal. But in recent military talks in Berlin, Germany apparently failed to convince Japan that her destiny lay in the Middle East.

Everything points once more to Japan's strategical domination over

Germany in the worldwide Axis pattern. By attacking Australia instead of pushing toward India, Japan is playing the canny game of ensuring that Germany is saddled with both Russian and British antagonists for 1942. If Hitler strikes Russia, Egypt is left unliquidated. If Hitler strikes Egypt, Russia remains.

Heavy British defeats in India, with its unsettled politics, protect Japan against the Allies seriously exploiting her long communication lines across Burma.

Should Japan invade Australia—virtually a necessity with American supplies flowing here—this would provide an excellent excuse for not attacking Russia.

Thus, Germany's apparent uncertainty about where her spring drive should be directed may be due to Japan's having decided to attempt a diversion southward, rather than rescue Germany from either the British or Russians.

Distant observers should keep in mind that the Japanese, exactly like the Germans, are planning to conquer the world.

—

FLIERS FOOL SUB AND WHALE TO SURVIVE 48 DAYS AT SEA

Somewhere in Australia—May 5, 1942 (Delayed)

Inspected successively by a Japanese submarine and by a giant humpback whale but harmed by neither, twelve Australian and British aviators have reached a port in southwestern Australia after a 48-day voyage from Java in a 28-foot sailboat. They were the last known of that force which defended Kalidjati airdrome when the Japs, bent upon obtaining a fighter base near Bandoeng, overwhelmed them with 100 infantrymen and three small tanks the day after landing upon Java.

The fliers, arriving in the southern Java port of Tjilatjap on March 6, managed to find a sailboat which they filled with any provisions available. They sailed by night from the harbor, whose entire waterfront was a mass of flames from successive bombings by the same planes which, coming from

Bali, flew over the little Dutch steamer in which this correspondent escaped from Java two days earlier.

The officer who steered the craft to safety told this correspondent today that he had been frightened for the first time two days south from Tjilatjap. "A Japanese sub arose almost without a sound twenty yards away. We could see his number and the lettering near his waterline. An officer appeared upon the conning tower and calmly looked us over. He wore glasses. He never said a word, or even raised his hand in signal. It was the longest silence I ever experienced, waiting for him to make up his mind. Then, suddenly, he disappeared inside the tower and submerged."

The fliers fought direct headwinds almost continuously. Once the wind blew contrariwise for almost a week and, being without sea anchor, they lost 200 miles. Attempting to compute their position by dead reckoning, using a tiny illustration as a map, they at first neglected to allow for the time error and were baffled to find themselves, theoretically, in the middle of the central Australian desert.

Their food was chiefly corned beef and rice but they marked Sundays by opening cans of spaghetti and beans. Thirst never became a problem because, while water was doled at a quarter of a pint daily, no less than 76 dozen cans of beer had been found before their departure from the ruined Javanese city.

"We thought another submarine was attacking us when, on the thirtieth day, a great black bulk appeared forward and began circling our boat. As it drew near we saw it was an enormous whale. We were afraid the whale would mistake us for a brother whale and attempt to get chummy . . . or aggressive. He came so close that we could see a single big eye looking us over. Then, fortunately, he lost interest and dived, just like the submarine."

The aviators made a first landfall, after sailing 1300 miles, when they reached uninhabited Frazier Island in the Dampiers. They continued on and were eventually picked up by flying boats. The last flier practically hated to be hauled in. "I could've made the last ten miles to the Australian coast in another afternoon," he declared.

One flying boat landed a bearded castaway only 200 yards from the modest cottage where he lives. Five minutes after setting foot upon Australia, the flier was in his own home in the arms of his wife, who had long given him up for lost.

SHELLS, BOMBS GOT 'THE ROCK' IN VISE OF FIRE:

Sledge Hammer Needed to Crack Fort, and Japs Rolled One Up

Somewhere in Australia—May 8, 1942

"The Rock" is gone. Only after the people got out did they commence calling it Corregidor. While you were there it was always "the Rock." You need a sledgehammer to break rock. The Japs needed scores of sledgehammers before Corregidor's tortoise back was broken. Nothing like Corregidor has happened in American history since the Alamo.

Corregidor's pounding cannot fairly be compared with Singapore or Malta. The latter islands have far greater surface area and were equipped with airdromes and fighters for protection. The Rock succumbed to aerial bombardment—every known method for hurling explosives through the air was used. Corregidor was high-level bombed, low-level bombed and strafed. Its defenders were subjected to fire from every caliber missile, from machine-gun bullets to fourteen-inch shells.

Against this picture of Corregidor's end, the American people may well keep another sharply in their minds. The year is 1925. A small harbor vessel emerges from Manila Bay, comes to Corregidor's quay and discharges several passengers. They are bright-eyed, intelligent Japanese, full of breath-sucking politeness. Their errand is to check on America's honesty; it has been reported to Japan that America violated her Pacific treaty obligations by illegally fortifying Corregidor. (The Japanese, however, refused to permit League of Nations' representatives to inspect their illegal fortifications on the Marshall and Caroline Islands.)

Today must be a happy one for the investigation committee. Now they can examine Corregidor's fortifications at will with the Americans accompanying them, not as hosts, but prisoners.

The Japanese broke Corregidor as they have broken the Allies elsewhere, by overwhelming power. Even before Bataan fell, Corregidor was under regular fire from the opposite peninsula closing Manila Bay. There, at Ternati, the Japs placed fourteen-inch batteries which daily pounded Corregidor's back. The tortoise's tail was being hammered. In the opposite direction, the head was under fire long before the April 8 surrender. There the Japs had 105-mm artillery, moved by a circular road around Bataan to almost pointblank range across the two-mile stretch of bay.

For dive-bombing the Japanese had one chief target—a power plant. Their other targets were the coast defense guns and anti-aircraft. All were fully exposed. The first three bombers went straight for the power plant, literally at Corregidor's heart, which pumped air into the tunnels upon which depended the safety of every living thing in Corregidor. Life in these tunnels was almost one continuous air raid. There were people who emerged from the fanned air and electric light only by night; like a submarine crew, they never saw sunlight. Some suffered from "tun-nelitis," a condition under which a human being becomes so stultified that he is unable to go outdoors. Heavy Jap bombs could be heard rever-berating inside the tunnel.

The Rock was never starved out. When Bataan fell there was abundant food, nearly enough for 80,000 persons for eighteen days. This could feed approximately 12,000, living the life of moles, for a minimum of four months. The besieged, like all hard-pressed people, often attributed to the enemy more intelligence than they possessed. During a six-week lull in the campaign, they said: "The Jap idea is simply to let Corregidor alone so the defenders will be forced to eat at U.S. instead of Japanese expense. They consider Corregidor a big concentration camp."

But the Japanese thought far more of Corregidor than that. They had carefully plotted the currents around the shores. For example, when 57 Philippine scouts, aided by sailors and Marines, forced some Japanese, flanked by the sea, to commit suicide by jumping from the cliffs, the Japs sent over an airplane which dropped a message of guidance for those re-maining on the beach. The message said: *Soldiers, you are ordered to find a log or other floating object and swim straight from shore, using the wood as support. Not far out from the beach, you will find a current which will carry you rapidly in the direction of Subic Bay.*

Instead of concentrating on the immediate invasion of Corregidor, however, the Japanese tried several games of deception. Laboriously they fitted hundreds of sea buoys with tiny electric bulbs and towed them around Manila Bay, causing the report upon Corregidor that invasion was imminent. After a while they abandoned this plan. But small Manila ship-yards kept busy building tiny craft to supplement Japan's formidable landing barges, which are lined with one-half-inch steel plate.

The Japanese repeatedly used the psychological weapon. In mid-March, they dropped pamphlets directed to Lt. General Jonathan Wainwright, stating the fortress would fall within two weeks. In early April, they dropped more pamphlets: *The help you are promised will arrive in a fort-night, but you will fall within a week.*

The American anti-aircraft was excellent. The courage of the men who manned the coast artillery guns under dive-bombing was a thing of wonder to those who witnessed it. But neither the anti-aircraft nor artillery could fire without betraying their positions. Had it been merely a duel between Corregidor's batteries and those of the Japs, Corregidor would have held out indefinitely.

Once more, aircraft were decisive. When Japanese shore batteries con-centrated upon the machine guns lining Corregidor's beaches and capping her eminences, the artillery could ordinarily have hit back. But the artillery pieces—in many places, exposed in open pits—were undergoing bombard-ment by planes. Just as the artillery could not defend the machine gun and ack-ack posts from fire from shore, similarly the ack-ack and machine guns under the battering of shore fire could not defend the artillery against dive-bombing and high-level bombing.

Before Bataan fell, Japan was like a man holding a needle three inches before his nose and trying to thread it with only one eye open. Japan kept stabbing with her thread but, because she lacked forward observation posts upon Bataan, was unable to give directions to the gunners in Ternati. Being unable to adjust vision to both eyes, she continually missed thread-ing the needle. Japanese planes did not dare to remain over Corregidor's ack-ack long enough to give sustained directions to the Ternati batteries, and the batteries behind the Bataan lines were firing blind.

Only after Japan secured observation posts on Bataan could she com-mence fire which silenced the anti-aircraft and opened the way for continu-ous dive-bombing directly upon the pits of the coastal guns. Even before the artillery duel of the closing phase, the Japs sent high-speed ground-strafing planes across the water from what they hoped were the blind angles of the island. Coming at over 300 miles an hour, the fighters hedgehopped over the Rock's back or between its two small peaks, machine-gunning and dropping bombs.

When Bataan fell, in a certain sense Corregidor's work was done. It was Corregidor at their back which had sustained Bataan's defenders from January 4, when the first line was drawn across the peninsula from Abucay to Moron.

The hours for the men at "Skinny Wainwright's" headquarters (on Bataan) to eat were determined by when small boats could cross the two miles of water. They ate, therefore, at 8:30 in the evening and 3:30 in the morning and fasted seventeen hours daily. By the first week of April only nineteen cavalry horses were left uneaten upon Bataan, but food was still coming regularly from Corregidor.

Corregidor was for Bataan what the U.S. is for the Americans in Australia—a safe place at one's back, though dangerously far away. When Bataan fell, scores of highly trained pilots of the Air Forces, captured by the Japs but left unguarded on Bataan's beaches—with four months' fighting as ordinary infantrymen in Bataan's hills behind them—swam across to Corregidor. It was like swimming the Pacific to America. Wherever the handful who escaped Corregidor sit today they are praising Wainwright. Whatever has happened to him, he will be known forever among those veterans as a beloved and admired first-class fighting general.

—

WOMEN STORM 'BARRICADES' IN AUSSIE STORES

Somewhere in Australia—May 13, 1942

Urban Australians saw their first barricades yesterday, but they were erected not in the streets against the Japanese but in the department stores against women shoppers.

Thousands of merchandise-hungry women, anxious to buy clothing before rationing tickets were issued, attacked the counters with a fanaticism and indifference to wounds which veterans of the Indonesian campaign pronounce equal to the Japanese at their most suicidal. To halt these Amazons, floorwalkers—unable to stem the rush—threw up benches, making small fortresses within the store where the invaders were compelled to attack by the dozens instead of by hundreds.

Americans are feeling the pinch because some have depended on Australian sources for shirts, underwear, haberdashery and even uniforms. This correspondent, having lost almost all his clothing fleeing Java, failed today in an attempt to increase his number of shirts, which now total three.

—

TAKE RIDE ON U.S. BOMBER, FASTEST OF ALL, IN AUSTRALIA

Somewhere in Australia—June 5, 1942

The world's fastest bomber* is American-built and American-flown. It is an enormous wasp with thousands of horses sucking it forward at a speed that the terrestrially bound human being can hardly understand even while he experiences it.

The wings are so short that the bomber looks like a fledgling. Those wings caused a dispute between young and old as to whether this enormous creature could be flown. Old heads said that, because air fields cannot be lengthened indefinitely for take-offs, the wings would have to be extended. Youngsters said that they themselves could take these big bombers with their terrible power aloft, on fledgling wings alone.

Youth won. They are taking the world's fastest bomber aloft every day not only for combat but also for experimental purposes. Amidst war, the experiment goes on continuously. And it is young men—only one over 22 years old—who have been entrusted with the job of finding out what the giant can do. Far trickier, they are setting her down without burning her huge tires off the wheels.

This has been a war of improvisation. Due to low monsoon clouds, the

---

*A Martin B-26 Marauder. Presumably, the plane was still under wraps, and Weller was not allowed to identify it. The B-26 participated in the Battle of Midway, and flew on just two powerful engines. Its very short wings terrified many pilots and at first earned it the nickname of "Widow Maker."

Flying Fortresses, whose proper altitude is five miles, have been obliged to come down sometimes to less than one mile. So, also, with the world's fastest bomber. What she can do in straightaway speed and climbing ability is well known. But this only begins the discovery of what this creature can accomplish when unchained.

This correspondent got his introduction to the big-timer today and it will be a long time before he forgets the experience. It is one thing to ride a bomber back in the fuselage, with only enough light to find things. The plane's torso is as jammed as a kitchen pantry with everything thinkable on the shelves from navigation drift-finders to a black, compartmented radio set, and with an emergency lifeboat of yellow canvas hung in a tight blanket roll above the aisle. It is quite another thing to ride forward in the bomber's glassed-in nose. If you elect to take a short trip at four miles per minute, which is 360 feet per second, you would not choose your mother's cut-glass bowl as a vehicle for this excursion. But flying in this bomber's nose is precisely like riding in a cut-glass bowl, with free visibility in every direction except behind—where you don't want to look anyway.

The view is excellent. In fact, the view is just a wee bit too good. You can see everywhere, up, down, right, left and center. You are in a great prism of glass, annealed in a kind of glass belt at chest level. You cannot stand up but you can sit down and dangle your feet upon the glassy floor, like a boy on a cliff, while a world of houses, streets, rivers and little boys and girls waving at you zips past underneath.

It was hard, in your leather coat, to push your 195 pounds forward between the two bombing pilots and crawl, as Alice through the keyhole, into this translucent world. But it was worth it. There is nothing you do not see, nothing. Nearby is a pair of headphones and a hand mouthpiece that works by pressing a tiny catch.

It is the low-level runs that take your breath away.

"Don't be afraid that glass will break, George," says the voice of Frank Allen, who, from his co-pilot seat, can watch you through the keyhole as somebody studying a bug under glass. "Crawl over and lie on your belly."

Somehow you flounder to your knees and lie at full length. Suddenly pandemonium is loosed. Your coat tries to jump off your back and icicles fly hissing up your sleeves. Something inside the fishbowl, like the voice of an animal, is shrieking and tearing at your throat. The trouble is that your elbow struck an unnoticed little window in the glass and moved it open about a quarter inch.

With the earphones now dangling around your neck, you shut this tiny letter slot. The uproar ceases instantly. It is silent again. The map of the world unreels faster than ever below you, red-roofed houses yanking away. It is fast, yet nothing is blurred. You can see even the expressions on the faces and tell an airedale from a terrier, a lawn mower from a child's veloci-pede. You see with unforgettable clarity.

Captain Franklin Allen is a former country editor, now 24, whom Major General George designated, shortly before his death, to carry out investiga-tions on the hitting power of this vicious bomber. Allen is slender and blond. He graduated from the University of Oregon in 1939 and used to run a 900-circulation weekly called the *Springfield News*. Allen probably has more hours on this bomber than anyone else. They used to say the bomber was too dangerous for such boys to fly but Allen has put more than 600 hours behind him. There are five other lieutenants, all in their twenties: from Illinois, Michigan, Massachusetts, Iowa, and Texas.

"There is a strange plane over there," says Frank gutturally through the earphones. "Let's go see what it is."

It is a bug transport plane. Despite your speed, nearly twice his, you turn inside him as neatly as a motorcycle inside a brewery wagon. The big transport seems hung upon a thread, motionless in midair. Actually, it is poking along at two miles per minute.

"Come on back now, George," says Allen through the headphones. "We're getting ready to approach the field. It may be bumpy."

You creep and crawl back through Alice's keyhole in your leather coat, like a shedding beetle. It is much noisier back here than up in your slightly overheated fishbowl. It is cooler too, however, and you realize that the sun had given you a topsy-turvy feeling in your stomach. Humbly you crawl on your knees to the doorway, descend the stair and for the first time in an hour stand upright.

Everybody hooks his seat straps before landing, tenses up slightly as hangar roofs nip past, and holds tight as the wheels reach the ground. Then, as bounces begin to nullify each other, one turns to his neighbor and smiles.

George Weller in a *Chicago Daily News* publicity photo; December, 1940.

Shilluk village traversed by Belgian Congolese troops sent to Ethiopia; August, 1941.

Liaison plane for Belgian Congolese troops in Ethiopia; August, 1941.

Belgian Congolese riflemen charging, with bayonets, in Ethiopia; August, 1941.

In Central Africa; probably September, 1941.

Weller before dive-bombing with the British over Italian-held Gondar, Ethiopia; November, 1941.

Interviewing Haile Selassie at his palace in Addis Ababa, Ethiopia; December 11, 1941.

With General Van Oyen, head of the Dutch Air Force, in Bandoeng, a few days before Java's fall; late February, 1942.

Lt. General Bennett and foreign correspondents in Australia; 1942. At Weller's right is Thomas Fairhall, *Sydney Telegraph*.

George Weller in Port Moresby, New Guinea; August, 1942.

Patient and doctor from Pulitzer Prize–winning submarine story, Seaman Rector and Pharmacist's Mate Lipes, in Perth, Australia; December, 1942.

Weller with U.S. officers near Buna, Papua New Guinea; Christmas Day, 1942.

Somewhere in Papua New Guinea; probably April, 1943.

George Weller with fellow CDN correspondent Leland Stowe in Athens; March, 1945. *(Photo by Costa Kouvaras)*

White Horse Camp, Iran, on Persian Corridor route to Russia; May, 1945.

Jingpaw Rangers (guerrillas) behind Japanese lines in Burma; June, 1945.

Just-liberated Allied POWs, probably U.S. servicemen, at Camp #17 in Omuta, Japan; September 12–14, 1945.

—

FLIER EMULATES DUTCH BOY AND HIS DIKE—LIVES

An American Naval Base Somewhere in the South Pacific—June 9, 1942

By popular acclaim, everybody in the fleet concedes an invisible extra bar for understatement to the Navy Cross already scheduled for Lieutenant Joseph Gough of Baltimore. Gough, a member of the naval reconnaissance patrol in Jap-controlled waters north of Australia, was shot down in his big PBY Catalina flying boat. His inflatable life belt was pierced by a Jap bullet. Yet Gough managed to stay afloat twenty-four hours in tropical waters alive with sharks.

"How did you succeed in staying above the waves with a hole in your belt?" rescuers asked him.

"Oh, I just covered the hole with my thumb," said Gough modestly.

"But the whole day and night with your thumb over the hole! How could you keep it up?"

Gough hesitated and his eyes fell modestly.

"Well, to tell the truth, I finally had to use both thumbs," he admitted.

—

JUBILATION OVER MIDWAY VICTORY HELD DANGEROUS

Somewhere in Australia—June 13, 1942

The American press and public comment upon the battle of Midway Island show a tendency to exaggerate the political consequences, a tendency disturbing to military and naval men here. The war is not aimed at sinking the Japanese fleet or even reducing her submarines to impotence. The purpose is to establish lasting peace in Asia, which can be done only by depriving the Japanese permanently of the sinews of war, rubber, oil, and metals that Japan has seized and still possesses.

While victories in individual battles will shorten the war, competent officers believe the public should keep in mind that the war's epicenter is not at Midway but at Singapore, where it will remain strategically until Singapore is recaptured, then shift to Tokyo. American progress toward rendering the Japanese harmless forever can only be estimated by the key naval bases that come into American hands and the resources of war, now in Japanese hands, that are restored to their rightful owners.

Editorial jubilation undoubtedly has its place, but it is extremely premature and may relegate the Far East front to a secondary position. Victories are welcome after the long hard road from Corregidor to Australia, but every inch must be retraced and fought for bitterly, with America carrying the major portion of the burden. The area is twice as large as the United States, with 150 million people still awaiting liberation.

The war is not yet over. The war has just begun.

—

YANK FLIERS FIND BUSHIDO FUNNY CODE

Somewhere in Australia—July 27, 1942

If you can ask the pilots of big American bombers operating over New Guinea what this *bushido* is, they scratch their heads.

"Darned if we know it ourselves," they say.

It is supposed to be the code of Japanese warrior chivalry. But it works out pretty strangely sometimes. Take what happened to the American bomber that was returning to its base and was pursued by a single Zero.

The fast little Jap attacked from forward, rear, below and above so many times that eventually the bomber had exhausted its ammunition. The Jap pressed the attack unsparingly and the bomber narrowly made the periphery of the home anti-aircraft guns, and it was considerably heavier with armor piercing bullets.

The next day, another bomber was chased by the new type Zero whose speed appeared well in excess of 400 miles an hour. The harried plane crew, with ammunition exhausted and fuel gauges low, threw over the machine guns to lighten the craft.

When the Jap saw the guns jettisoned he roared by with lifted hand in salutation and farewell and fired nothing more from his cannons or machine guns. Perhaps he, too, had exhausted his ammunition. Nobody really knows.

You can cut it or you can slice it; it's still *bushido*.

—

Writer Mourns Darnton, Killed in New Guinea

Somewhere in Australia—October 22, 1942

"Barney" Darnton of the *New York Times,* buried yesterday in New Guinea, was among the best-beloved, as well as most respected, of war correspondents in the Pacific area. His plump but debonair figure, his large head with the slightly greying hair of 44 years and his gentle and sensitive voice were the accouterments of a spirit well equipped for his task.

Byron Darnton had the searching eye of the reporter, without being cynical. Making no excuses for himself and working without stint, Barney was nevertheless always the first to excuse shortcomings in others. His principles as a correspondent were high; he was always ready to strip the story to its skeleton in order to keep a strict truth. His work was balanced, flexible and honest without ever being dull.

As assistant editor of the Sunday magazine section of the *New York Times,* Darnton gained a wider and broader view than that of many of his colleagues.

What this correspondent loved best in Barney after knowing him nearly ten years was his slow, dry wit which was completely untainted with Manhattan smartness but had, rather, a warm fatherly quality.

Darnton was the calm rather than high-tension type of correspondent. He was one of the few members of the profession with whom one could be silent and yet know the silence was unwasted. Barney lies today in New Guinea's thick soil. This last silence will be endless.

—

Somewhere Australia,
care: American Consulate,
MELBOURNE. AUSTRALIA,
22nd October, 1942.

Dear Mrs. Darnton,

I want you to know how saddened all the American correspondents were by Barney's death.

He was one of the most delightful and most lovable newspaper men I have ever known. For me, there was a kind of exhilaration in being with him. I had known him about ten years but came to know him better in Australia than in the days when I worked on the Foreign Staff of the *New York Times*.

On one of our last evenings in Brisbane, we went to a movie together. I miscalculated the trolley stop—we were joking about something or other—and we ran clear to the end of the line. Barney was very tired, and almost anyone else would have been disgruntled. It was the last car for half an hour, and we had to walk home in the moonlight. Yet he made fun even of this, tired as he was. It was a minor experience, but for me a pretty good way to remember him.

We all know how devoted he was to you and your children. He used to read and reread your letters and seemed to love to write home more than most newspaper men do. He mentioned, I remember, your having been sought out by the relative of one of the boys he had written about; this was the kind of thing that warmed him very much.

Barney was in good health and high spirits right up to the end, and I think you can probably think of him as having been accomplishing some of the best work of his career when it was broken off.

We shall all miss him very much, and we extend our hands to you in sympathy.

Sincerely,

George Weller.
correspondent: Chicago Daily News

—

NIPPONESE MURDER SLEEP IN FUTILE RAID ON DARWIN

Somewhere in Australia—October 27, 1942

"Roll out, Yank. Here they come," an Australian's voice rang across Darwin's moon-flooded street.

Captain Lewis Turner carefully lifted his white mosquito net. Then the siren went off. "Those Aussies always get their signal about five seconds before the siren," explained Turner.

One Wellington half-boot stuck while being pulled on. "Hurry up. We need every minute to make that shelter," said Turner. It looked for a moment as though this correspondent would be obliged to go like "Deedle Deedle Dumpling" to the shelter but the boot finally gave.

Turner already had the motor of the big American Army car turning over beside the door. It was the first time in dozens of raids over Malaya, Java and New Guinea that this correspondent had driven rather than run to shelter. He felt luxurious but slightly guilty, too—a little too sissy, perhaps.

But as an indication that Darwin was now prepared and would never again experience anything like her black day of February 19, the tolls of which still are unannounced, it was reassuring. Darwin's blocks are about twice as long as America's. Scarred, jagged buildings leer at you by moonlight and after the siren's howl has sunk, as it unwinds to a groan and finally to a sigh, it is uncannily silent.

Everybody else reached shelter about the same time as we did.

Everyone around us was Australian because American fliers and ground crews, who have trounced the Japanese every time they have tried

to raid Darwin, have their own shelters and they are naturally not in battered downtown Darwin.

Turner knew everybody and there was time for introductions as we
stood outside the shelter. The moonlight glimmered on Darwin Bay, which
faces so peculiarly that even though Jap bombers come directly from
Koepang or Dilli in Dutch and Portuguese Timor, they seem always to approach from your back as though based in Daly Waters or Derby.

As the mighty weather of the approaching subequatorial summer descends upon red-dust-caked Darwin, one of the new diversions is listening
to Berlin on the short-wave as it repeats Jap claims of raids on northwestern Australian "cities." These "cities" are single-pier settlements which in
the United States and in Australia itself are called villages and hardly mentioned except on automobile maps. Placed beside the relatively straight-
laced Reichswehr and Luftwaffe communiqués, these Jap fairy tales about
raids which quite simply never occurred are one of the few diversions in
what a war doggerel tersely described as *Bloody, Bloody Darwin.*

"Here they come," said someone casually. Turner drifted toward the
shelter. Others moved inside. Still the humming seemed to grow a little
louder, so your correspondent remained outside watching the dark outlines
of the harbor.

It is always difficult to tell how many Japanese bombers are aloft because the noises seem to mingle. Searchlights shot up, fingering the heavy
monsoon clouds and trying to find their way through the iridescent mist. It
was like directing a flashlight into a bowl of milk. Every glistening, moist
drop in a cloud threw back the rays a dozen times. The searchlights went
on and off, apparently recognizing the Japs could see as little of them as
they could of the Japs.

The droning bombers—"Guess they are at about 25,000 feet"—crossed
the harbor, probably trying to get their bearings. "Looks as though they
dropped their packets somewhere along the road," muttered someone.
Heads appeared in the dugout entrance and men emerged. One man drew
out a packet of cigarettes forgetfully, then realized what he was doing and
replaced them.

Although the bombers had passed over they were still audible. They
made a full swing methodically around the harbor and seemed to be heading homeward. Then abruptly the noise began to increase. The sound of

motors was underpinned with a new firmness. For the first time there was something slightly venomous in it.

Again all hands drifted back into the long shelter tunnel. Turner, who comes from Kansas, said, "I think this is it." As he spoke there came an irregular cracking sound in the air.

There was a momentary pileup at the shelter's entrance, a conventional I-shaped barricade opening into a tunnel. There this correspondent's football training came into good use and he was not the last in jamming through. When women and children are absent from the scene, as in Darwin, and if shelters are ample, there is small ceremony and no Alphonse and Gaston business at the mouths of shelters. The best man is he who has least flesh projecting when the crackling noise begins.

There was a shaking blow, then another, another, another and another. Dirt fell from between the timbered overhead buttresses of the shelter but nobody even ducked. Faces were serious but unworried. That is what fifty feet of solid earth will do for you. In raids men look to heaven for succor, but go as deep as possible into Mother Earth for protection. Paradise is here below, the farther below the better.

"I think they hit the brewery," said Turner, referring to the establishment which the Aussies built to meet Darwin's perpetual thirst.

From the shelter's mouth the lookout said: "Here comes another pack."

Everyone's head went down slightly. They hit quite close this time but there was something different in the impact. The dugouters exchanged meaningful glances. Whatever happened was too obvious for old Darwinians even to mention.

"Landed in the water," whispered Turner. "You can tell by the sound."

Some began to adjust their tin hats to leave the shelter.

There was one outside—there always is—who had braved the bombs, counting on luck and moonlight for protection. "That last bunch landed right out there," he said, pointing to a portion of the bay occupied only by moonlight. "A few more fish for the Abos to eat." (*Abo* is Aussie slang for aborigines.)

Yank Sub Crew, in Action, Stops, Snips Appendix

Saves Life of Stricken Youth as Craft Hides from Jap Ships

Somewhere in Australia—December 14, 1942

"They are giving him ether now," was what they said back in the aft torpedo rooms.

"He's gone under and they're getting ready to cut him open," the crew whispered, sitting on their pipe bunks cramped between torpedoes.

One man went forward and put his arm quietly around the shoulders of another man who was handling the bow diving planes. "Keep her steady, Jake," he said. "They've just made the first cut. They're feeling around for it now."

"They" were a little group of anxious-faced men with their arms thrust into reversed white pajama coats. Gauze bandages hid all their expressions except the intensity in their eyes.

"It" was an acute appendix inside Dean Rector of Chautauqua, Kansas. The stabbing pains had become unendurable the day before, which was Rector's first birthday at sea. He was nineteen.

The big depth gauge that looks like a factory clock and stands beside the "Christmas tree" of red and green gauges regulating the flooding chambers showed where they were. They were below the surface. Above them—and below them, too—were enemy waters crossed and recrossed by whirring propellers of Jap destroyers, transports and submarines.

The nearest naval surgeon competent to operate on the young seaman was thousands of miles and many days away. There was just one way to prevent the appendix from bursting and that was for the crew to operate upon their shipmate themselves. And that's what they did. It was probably one of the largest operations in number of participants that ever occurred.

"He says he's ready to take his chance," the gobs whispered from bulkhead to bulkhead.

"That guy's regular"—the word traveled from bow planes to propeller and back again.

They kept her steady.

The chief surgeon was a twenty-three-year-old pharmacist's mate wearing a blue blouse with white-taped collar and squashy white duck cap. His name was Wheeler B. Lipes. He came from Newcastle near Roanoke, Virginia, and had taken the Navy hospital course in San Diego, thereafter serving three years in the Naval Hospital in Philadelphia, where his wife lives.

As a laboratory technician, Lipes' specialty was operating a machine that registers heartbeats. He was classified as an electrocardiographer. But he had seen Navy doctors take out one or two appendixes and thought he could do it. Under the sea he was given his first chance to operate.

There was difficulty about the ether. When below the surface, the pressure inside a boat is above the atmospheric pressure. More ether is absorbed under pressure. The submariners did not know how long their operation would last. They did not know how long it would take to find the appendix. They did not know whether there would be enough ether to keep the patient under throughout the operation.

They didn't want the patient waking up before they were finished.

They decided to operate on the table in the officers' ward. In the newest and roomiest American submarines the wardroom is approximately the size of a Pullman car drawing room. It is flanked by bench seats attached to the wall, and a table occupies the whole room—you enter with knees already crooked to sit down. The only way anyone can be upright in the wardroom is by kneeling. The operating table was just long enough so that the patient's head and feet reached the two ends without hanging over.

First they got out a medical book and read up on the appendix while Rector, his face pale with pain, lay in the narrow bunk. It was probably the most democratic surgical operation ever performed. Everybody from box plane man to cook in the galley knew his role.

The cook provided the ether mask. It was an inverted tea-strainer. He covered it with gauze.

The young surgeon had as his staff of fellow physicians men all his senior in age and rank. His anesthetist was Lieutenant Franz Hoskins, communications officer of Tacoma, Washington.

Before they carried Rector to the wardroom, the submarine captain, Lieutenant Commander W. P. Ferrall of Pittsburgh, asked Lipes as the surgeon to have a talk with the patient.

"Look, Dean, I never did anything like this before," Lipes said. "You don't have much chance to pull through anyhow. What do you say?"

"I know just how it is, doc," said Rector. "Let's get going."

It was the first time in his life that anybody had called Lipes "doc." But there was in him, added to the steadiness that goes with the submariner's profession, a new calmness worthy of an Aesculapius.

The operating staff adjusted gauze masks while members of the engine room crew pulled tight reversed pajama coats tight over their extended arms. The tools were laid out. They were far from perfect or complete for a major operation. The scalpel had no handle. But submariners are used to "rigging" things. The medicine chest had plenty of hemostats, which are small pincers used for closing blood vessels. The machinist rigged a handle for the scalpel from a hemostat.

When you are going to have an operation, you must have some kind of antiseptic agent. Rummaging in the medicine chest, they found sulfanilamide tablets and ground them to powder.

One thing was lacking: there was no means to hold open the wound after the incision had been made. Surgical tools used for this are called "muscular retractors." What could they use for retractors? There was nothing in the medicine chest that gave the answer, so they went as usual to the cook's galley.

In the galley they found tablespoons made of monel metal. They bent these at right angles and had their retractors.

Sterilizers? They went to one of the greasy copper-colored torpedoes waiting beside the tubes. They milked alcohol from the torpedo mechanism, and used it as well as boiling water.

The light in the wardroom seemed insufficient: operating rooms always have big lamps. So they brought one of the big floods used for night loadings and rigged it inside the wardroom's sloping ceiling.

The moment for the operation had come. Rector, very pale and stripped, stretched himself out on the wardroom table under the glare of the lamps.

Rubber gloves dipped in torpedo alcohol were drawn upon the youthful "doc's" hands. The fingers were too long. The rubber ends dribbled limply over.

"You look like Mickey Mouse, doc," said one onlooker.

Lipes grinned behind the gauze.

Rector on the wardroom table wet his lips, glancing a sidelook at the tea-strainer ether mask.

With his superior officers as his subordinates, Lipes looked into their eyes, nodded and Hoskins put the tea mask down over Rector's face. No words were spoken; Hoskins already knew from the book that he should watch Rector's eye pupils dilate.

The surgeon, following the ancient hand rule, put his little finger on Rector's subsiding umbilicus, his thumb on the point of the hip bone and, by dropping his index finger straight down, found the point where he intended to cut. At his side stood Lieutenant Norvell Ward, of Indianhead, Maryland, who was his assistant surgeon.

"I chose him for his coolness and dependability," said the doc afterward of his superior officer. "He acted as my third and fourth hands."

Ward's job was to place tablespoons in Rector's side as Lipes cut through successive layers of muscles.

Engineering officer Lieutenant Charles Manning of Cheraw, South Carolina, took the job which in a formal operating room is known as "circulating nurse." His job was to see that packets of sterile carlisle dressing kept coming and that the torpedo alcohol and boiling water arrived regularly from the galley.

They had what is called an "instrument passer" in Chief Yeoman H. F. Wieg of Sheldon, North Dakota, whose job was to keep the tablespoons coming and coming clean.

Submarine Skipper Ferrall too had his part. They made him "recorder." It was his job to keep count of the sponges that went into Rector. A double count of the tablespoons used as retractors was kept; one by the skipper and one by the cook who was himself passing them out from the galley.

It took Lipes in his flapfinger rubber gloves nearly twenty minutes to find the appendix.

"I tried one side of the caecum," he whispered after the first minutes. "Now, I'm trying the other."

Whispered bulletins seeped back into the engine room and crews' quarters.

"The doc has tried one side of something and now is trying the other."

After more search, Lipes finally whispered, "I think I've got it. It's curled way into the blind gut."

Lipes was using the classical McBurney's incision. Now was the time when his shipmate's life was completely in his hands.

"Two more spoons." They passed the word to Lieutenant Ward.

"Two spoons at 14.45 hrs," wrote Skipper Farrell on his notepad.

"More flashlights. And another battle lantern," demanded Lipes.

The patient's face, lathered with white petrolatum, began to grimace.

"Give him more ether," ordered the doc.

Hoskins looked doubtfully at the original five pounds of ether now sunken to hardly three-quarters of a can, but once again the tea-strainer was soaked in ether. The fumes mounted, thickening the wardroom air and making the operating staff giddy.

"Want those blowers speeded up?" the captain asked the doc.

The blowers began to whirr louder.

Suddenly came the moment when the doc reached out his hand, pointing toward the needle threaded with 20-day chromic catgut.

One by one the sponges came out. One by one the tablespoons bent into right angles were withdrawn and returned to the galley. At the end it was the skipper who nudged Lipes and pointed to the tally of bent tablespoons. One was missing. Lipes reached into the incision for the last time and withdrew the wishboned spoon and closed the incision.

They even had the tool ready to cut off the thread. It was a pair of fingernail scissors, well scalded in water and torpedo juice.

At that moment the last can of ether went dry. They lifted up Rector and carried him into the bunk of Lieutenant Charles Miller of Williamsport, Pennsylvania. Miller alone had had control of the ship as diving officer during the operation.

It was half an hour after the last tablespoon had been withdrawn that Rector opened his eyes. His first words were: "I'm still in there pitching."

By that time the sweat-drenched officers were hanging up their pajamas to dry. It had taken the amateurs about 2½ hours for an operation ordinarily requiring 45 minutes.

"It was not one of those 'snappy valve' appendices," murmured Lipes apologetically as he felt the first handclaps upon his shoulder.

Within a few hours the bow and stern planesmen who, under Miller's direction, had kept the submarine from varying more than half a degree vertically in 150 minutes below the stormy sea, came around to receive Rector's winks of thanks.

His only remark was "Gee, I wish Earl were here to see this job." His brother Earl, a seaman on the Navy submarine tender *Pigeon,* is among the list of missing at Corregidor, probably captured.

"I'd like to show that cut to Captain Voge," said Lipes. "I used to tell him how I got my first experience at a morgue and never missed a patient coming or going. I had just as soon try a colostomy on one of that gang. But I could get away with brain surgery if I had to." Lipes formerly served under a Chicagoan, Lieutenant Commander Richard Voge, until the pharmacist of his present submarine was wounded in the Cavite bombing. Although Lipes' arm was steady in operating on his shipmate, he had suffered four shrapnel wounds when the Japs bombed Cavite.

When the submarine surfaced that night, all hands who had been near the wardroom found themselves frequently grabbing the sides of the conning tower and slightly unsteady on the black, vertical ladders. It was because of the ether they had breathed, which came out again at the lessening of surface pressure.

But all their intoxication was not ether; some was joy.

The submarine again began "patrolling as usual." Thirteen days later Rector was manning the battle phones.* And the submarine was again launching her torpedoes.

And in one of the bottles vibrating on the submarine's shelves swayed the first appendix ever known to have been removed below enemy waters.

---

*Lipes died in 2005, age eighty-four, as a lieutenant commander and one-time surgeon who became a hospital executive. He received the Navy Commendation Medal in old age. Hoskins, who eventually captained a submarine, died in 2001, age eighty-six, having been a family doctor for forty years. Rector died in October 1944 off Formosa, age twenty-one, when his sub's torpedo, fired at a Japanese ship, turned around.

A.P.O. 500,
San Francisco.

July 9th, 1943.

Mrs Odessa J. Horton Jr.
906 Talma St.,
Aurora,
ILLINOIS.

Dear Mrs Horton,

I received your letters of January 30th and
your card of March 20th addressed to Mr. Carroll Binder, and also
your letter of February 3rd addressed to me with its carbon copy.

You will have wondered why I did not reply to you
sooner. At the time your letters came I was out of action with
malaria and I did not want to reply to you until I was absolutely
sure of the facts about your son.

It is painful for me to have to do so, but I must
with regret say to you that there is no basis for hope that your son
will return. I have visited his grave and established some of the
facts concerning his death.

Your son was one of the first to be killed in the
effort to establish the road block which I have described in the
history of Sanananda's "Lost Company". Communications from where we
were, were so difficult that it was impossible to inform relatives
promptly of individual deaths. When I wrote on December 18th of
what your son had done, without specifying that he had been killed,
it was because correspondents are not allowed to state that men have
been killed until it is positive that word of the mans' death has
gone through channels to reach his relatives. The War Department
naturally does not wish relatives to be notified first of their loss
through newspaper publication; they feel that the families should
be notified first officially.

For that reason I was able to mention your son's
gallantry, without mentioning his death. If I had mentioned his
death it would not have been possible to do honor to his heroism
because both my pieces about him were written before word had been
sent to you, although one of them appeared (on January 26th) two days
after the sad news had reached you.

Your son had in fact been killed about five days
before I reached the Sanananda front, but had not been mentioned
before because there was no other American correspondent there.

I presume you know your son was recognised as a fin
officer and a spiritual man. The sacrifice of such men is not wholl
a loss, because their memory remains with the men who fought at the
side.

I have visited your son's grave. You asked me

XII

Somewhere in New Guinea

The battle for New Guinea was really the battle for Australia, which it overhangs like a protective bulwark only a few hundred miles to the north. The enormously difficult Allied campaign to hold Papua (New Guinea's eastern half) against the Japanese, under horrible conditions, saw some of the worst combat of the Pacific war and inspired some of Weller's toughest reporting. He covered Papua for over a year—with its new demands of learning to fight jungle snipers—and was the only correspondent to witness all its major struggles.

After a brief first visit, once he returned to the vast island late in 1942, he contracted malaria but kept working and grew ever sicker there for nearly seven months straight. In April 1943 he informed his editor:

I am confined in an advanced portable hospital in Papua with what doctors describe as "benign and malignant malaria in heavy concentrations." This is not the first time I've had fever, though it is the first time I've mentioned it. I was up and down all through the Buna and early Sanananda campaigns, but kept going by heavier and heavier dosages of quinine. Then I came back to Sanananda for the final campaign here, and still was able to keep going by repressive measures, which did not change the fact that I was full of the disease. This covers the period of December and January, into early February. I finished the Gona-Buna-Sanananda campaign with a complete tour of our troops.

On returning to Moresby, extremely underweight, I cropped out with tropical sores, which I had avoided somehow in northern

Papua, and (the doctors said) took nearly a month to heal them because of my generally rundown condition. At this time all the troops
with whom I served the earlier three-quarters of the Buna campaign had long been withdrawn. The AP correspondents Spencer
and Boni both went to Australia with malaria, and so did UP's
Frank Hewlett, the only correspondent of the American press who
served as long as I did with the front line troops. At length I was left
with AP's Tom Yarborough who arrived in February as one of the
two Americans surviving here. I at first made gains in Moresby,
where there is more and different canned ersatz [i.e., lousy food—
ed.], but rapidly lost ground after the Bismarck Sea battle. All this
time the doctors said I had to have a very extended period of rest
and several months of fresh food to buy back lost ground.

You may wonder why, with these explicit warnings, I tackled
the 41st Division story. It is because we have by far the most complete account of the campaign and I wanted to keep the record. But
the doctors say I have very seriously overextended myself, and I
must heed them.

He did not, however, and in June 1943 he was allowed by
MacArthur to train as a paratrooper, to better understand the
kind of warfare he was not allowed to write about. (These dispatches appeared in late November and early December, as he
was finally leaving the southwest Pacific for the United States.)

There were other stories he was not permitted to touch, of
course. In April 1964, on MacArthur's death, his remembrance of
the general began:

In the prickly heat of the New Guinea jungle a lieutenant general
stood up in the stifling mess tent, pushed aside his coffee cup and
rapped it with a spoon. "I have received a message from the general," he said. The sweating officers loosened the open throats of
their shirts and looked sideways at each other.

"The general" could mean only MacArthur, 1000 miles to the
south in his office in downtown Brisbane. It was almost Christmas,

1942. MacArthur had announced that his troops had captured Buna, a gift for Roosevelt to offer the American people. The trouble was that the Americans hadn't taken Buna. They were still trying to solve the tangle of swamps, snipers and crossfire. What would be MacArthur's Christmas message?

Lt. General Robert Eichelberger, a tall, balding man who like MacArthur had been superintendent of West Point, held up a handwritten flimsy under the hissing lantern. "The general says," he paused and his hand seemed to tremble, "he says, 'I want to hear that you have captured Buna or I want to hear that you are dead.' "

The tent was so still that only the razor strop sound of giant bats in the palms could be heard. Every infantry officer there knew that the message didn't mean death for Eichelberger. But it meant that Eichelberger was ordered to push forward regardless of cost to the Wisconsin-Michigan 32nd Division and the Northwest's 41st Division. MacArthur's message meant death first for young lieutenants and sergeants whose jungle tactics had never been revised. MacArthur did not get Buna for Christmas, but he got it later—through a starving deserter stumbling into an American camp and giving away a path through the hip-deep swamps, the barbed wire and trip mines and the tree snipers.

MacArthur perceived that publicity was the lever of American power and he used it openly. His censors, by suppressing almost everything political and meaningful from the Southwest Pacific, reduced the war to a series of banal hero stories costing the American people a generation of political education in Southeast Asia. To MacArthur ruthless censorship was a means not to deceive the Japanese enemy but to keep his material supplies increasing in an uncritical atmosphere. When I tried to cost-analyze the sending of 25 bombers to destroy a single Japanese Zero parked on a field, the story was instantly killed. To MacArthur this was the way to keep the public happy and tractable.

**Late in life, he characterized MacArthur even more bluntly:
"He cowed the entire American press into suppressing the fact
that his battle of malaria-ridden New Guinea was directed from**

the hotel apartment in Brisbane where he lived with his wife and son. Bataan it wasn't."

This chapter also contains a short story, "By the Light of a Mushroom," published in the Autumn 1945 *Yale Review*, which describes the special fellowship in New Guinea of enlisted men, correspondents, and officers.

In July 1943, Weller wrote again to his editor, Carroll Binder:

My health is improving as I get fresh milk and sleep. Some people have very severe malaria recurrences; I wanted to get fresh food in me and my corpuscles back, and to get my affairs together before leaving. The jungle breaks everything down, typewriter, camera, papers. I lived for months in one set of jungle greens with a notebook in the pocket. My glasses gave way this morning; it takes days to get things done that take hours under ordinary circumstances. And my conscience is troubled by letters from parents of men who are dead, whose outfits are scattered, but who must (I feel) be answered. My pile of them is three months old.

To preserve his health, Weller had to leave New Guinea a year before the campaign for Papua ended. He was replaced there for the *CDN* by Hal O'Flaherty, who near the end of the war would take over as foreign editor back in Chicago from Carroll Binder. Binder, a veteran correspondent himself, had lost his eldest son over France, and never recovered from it.

—

MOSQUITOES, JUNGLE TOUGHER THAN JAPS IN NEW GUINEA

At an Advanced Allied Base in the Southwest Pacific—August 5, 1942

Until you have been bitten by your first New Guinea mosquito and seen your first raid against Port Moresby you cannot say you belong on the island that blocks Nippon's progress southward. (With the Japanese pressing toward the Owen Stanley Range and their plan undisclosed, little can be written outside the communiqués.)

Up in the mountains, where the monsoon deposits its burden of rain-heavy clouds, everything is green, thick and tangled. Troops, as one officer said, are "fighting the country ninety per cent of the time and the Japs ten per cent." But Port Moresby is not part of that steaming hell tied together with vines and creepers and infested by hundreds of wild animals and savages. The town stands on a small promontory jutting into the Coral Sea. The thirty-mile semicircle has been dried by the South Pacific autumn until the hilly countryside is withered and brown.

Across this relatively open country, MacArthur's Australians and Americans have disposed themselves in a manner calculated to puzzle Japanese bombardiers, who are still trying to find out what is significant upon this parched panorama.

It might be the Sudan or Libya, as far as personal appearance is concerned—shorts, shirt, boots and socks. One sees even dispatch riders on motorcycles wearing only shorts, their faces creased into lines of dust.

The climate now is clear and healthy with the southeast monsoon blowing in from the Coral Sea. But there are mosquitoes. Malaria must be consistently fought and quinine taken for six weeks after leaving to prevent hot and cold chills.

—

HUSH-HUSH BASE READY FOR JAPS' MILNE BAY STAB

Soldier-Workers Spend Long Days Preparing Surprise for Foe

Somewhere in Australia—September 1 & 4, 1942

"What are you doing here? We never expected a war correspondent in this neck of the woods. Who told you we had a base at Milne Bay?"

With those words this correspondent was greeted several days ago when he succeeded in reaching the secluded, secret base at the extreme end of southeastern New Guinea, the scene of the crushing Allied victory over invasion forces and now the center of a jungle hunt for Japanese who escaped the Allied trap.

The Americans' surprise was understandable. Although dozens of correspondents have been able, during the last nine months, to reach Port Moresby and describe the Allied situation there, none—either American, English or Australian—had been able to get from there to the hush-hush base at Milne Bay.

How well the secret was kept may be judged by the fact that many troops in Port Moresby never knew of the base.

Even high officers who had visited could be counted on one hand. This correspondent's trip, made with a general of engineers, naturally could not be the subject of dispatches. However, the direct attack by the Japanese upon the base itself makes possible some relaxation of the double secrecy, though naturally many facts useful to the enemy must be withheld.

This correspondent reached Milne Bay aboard an aircraft with guns ready against patrolling Zeros. Australian gunners, naked to the waist and wearing only shorts and half-length boots, sat vigilantly at their positions. Every person aboard, including the American general, scanned the skies unceasingly. Zeros have been seen repeatedly over this lonely tongue of land.

Going to Milne Bay was mighty different from going to Port Moresby, which seemed a haven by comparison. In other words, this correspondent—as many other times in the war—was just plain scared. You cajole and plead to get a peek at places like Milne Bay without any hope of being able to write about them for months. Then, en route, straining your eyes at the lookout windows, with phones strapped over your head, you listen to an inner voice saying: "Well, you asked for this, didn't you?" It must be nice to be a Japanese correspondent and be able to take a short snifter of *bushido* whenever it is needed.

Milne Bay is a horseshoe twenty miles long and two to four miles wide. Its prongs point at the reefs and coral islets that form a natural barrier against Japanese naval incursions southward. Strategically this means that if the Japs take Milne Bay, they have still not penetrated the barrier by sea, but can easily do so overland.

The Japanese calculatedly avoided taking any particular notice of Milne Bay before their attack. When this correspondent walked ashore, his first question was when the last red-balled reconnaissance plane had flown overhead. An American officer's reply was that it had been nearly three weeks since humming, heard through the overhanging palms and coconuts, had betrayed Japanese interest.

Prior to the attack the base had never been bombed or even strafed. It seemed as though the Japs were prepared to ignore the work going on there.

In Milne Bay, Americans and Australians shared something between rough plantation life and the muddier existence of Australian Commando troops. Men from all parts of the States were there, mostly living in the plain, square plantation houses characteristic of this coconut-growing area. Some privates, white and Negro, lived in tents. Both officers and men slept under long mosquito nets.

What happened when it first became known that a Jap force, despite attacks of Australian bomber-fighters, was actually landing can only be conjectured. But certainly it was not a case of being wholly taken by surprise. Submachine guns, loaded and oiled, were ready. Guards against Jap parachutists were maintained. Two American sergeants echoed the general sentiment when they said: "If the Japs strike here they'll know, even though we may only be pencil pushers, that now we're able to fight if necessary."

Milne Bay is covered by two canopies, one permanent. The semipermanent is a thick layer of wet mist which fills the enclosure between the horseshoe's sides sometimes down to the level of the palm tops. This layer effectively concealed the base's preparations from enemy eyes, but played the Allies false by making it difficult for our fighter-bombers to hit enemy landing forces. Once the invader knew what was going on under the clouds, the weather was with him.

The other canopy is that of green, feather-duster palms planted systematically close, so only half-light falls into the glades beneath. Both large coconut plantations are controlled by Lever Brothers' soap interests, but not a single company employee—only officers—occupy the square bungalows with bare colonial furniture. While Kittyhawks snarled overhead on patrols, Milne Bay prepared for the Jap onslaughts which the men believed were certain.

This correspondent spent a 21-hour day, from 5 a.m. until 2 a.m. the next night, with an Army captain who had been his friend as a businessman in

Singapore. These Americans were unquestionably working harder at the job of creating this New Guinea base than any other officers or men elsewhere in the Far East.

Where the Japs landed, before the Allies annihilated them in a trap, was "a tiny narrow strip of black-sanded beach, with palms dipping over the waves." Here the Allies built a short primitive road. All day and night, sighing trucks bumped along. Far from being a soggy swamp, it was nearly as deep in dust by day as Port Moresby. But when night mists fell, all turned to mud.

It was characteristic that when the Allies, in the mosquito-infested night, discovered a truck with a broken axle lying across the road, the officers, the men, and also this correspondent fell to and somehow hefted the big fellow over to one side on the beach so that more important caravans might pass.

These men were proud that in many cases their jobs of uploading had been accomplished faster under the rawest tropical conditions, with hearty, spirited labor, than by professional stevedores working in safety thousands of miles away. They made the boast that every ship was unloaded with their crude means faster than they had been loaded by modern means elsewhere.

Nowhere so much as at Milne Bay has this correspondent wanted honor for the unknown soldier-worker who sweats alone unrecognized. Among the perspiring officers were three doctors, from New York, Cleveland, and Chicago. Dawn would find them already at work. They were living on canned food, with occasional banana leaves and papayas. They taught this correspondent how to select the best coconut for drinking, shave off the end to a point and clip it off. They are already jungle troops. They are fighting a war of roads, of concealment, of disposal and never without pistol in readiness. It was symbolic that they kept their screen doors shut by the weight of a spade suspended on a pulley by a heavy window cord. Continually wet with sweat, they never could bathe in the ocean, which sharks frequent. Instead, they used a small creek with signs: *No swimming above this point. No washing above this point. No drinking water above this point.*

"We need more newspapers at Milne," said a sergeant who used to be a factory foreman in Michigan. "The natives make cigarettes by rolling tobacco in old American newspapers. They don't seem to mind the taste of newsprint."

A private, another of those who defended Australia by defending Milne Bay, said: "One thing we watch for is spiders getting in our boots. Every morning I always shake out my shoes. In Papua it's the tiniest spiders that are the deadliest."

Pointing through the dark glades of coconut palms, where his Kittyhawks were hidden, an Australian squadron leader picked out for this correspondent the names the pilots had painted upon their American-built fighters.

Instead of girls' names, which American pilots frequently use, one grinning shark-faced plane was sarcastically titled *U-bite.* At the runway's end was another bearing a title evidently adopted from James Joyce: *Opityerbich.*

Australian fliers are readers of comic strips imported from America, too. One toothy Kittyhawk is called *Mandrake,* after "Mandrake the Magician."

Milne Bay has undergone German, American, and Australian influences during its period as a tiny coconut port. The Germans, left over from the days when New Guinea was their possession, put the mark of Adolf Hitler upon their bags of copra. (American officers uncovered a cache of bags with swastikas, but they were put to anti-swastika use.)

The Japs first tipped off the Allies that they knew what was going on at Milne Bay by sending over a small handful of Zeros, which shelled and machine-gunned the airdrome, smashing one Australian-piloted Kittyhawk and partly damaging two others. Thereafter they left Milne in peace for three weeks, only about half their forces returning from this raid.

Their plan of conquest at the entrance to the Coral Sea was delayed by the destruction of their fighters on the ground at Buna—then destroyed completely. While the Airacobra pilots operating over New Guinea have a lower record of downing bombers than their colleagues in Kittyhawks around Darwin, their strafing efforts have been murderous to parked aircraft. Whether the Japanese use dummies or the real thing, it doesn't matter; the Airacobras tear them apart.

Like Port Moresby and Darwin, Milne is a womanless Eden, for all the dark-skinned females, except for one pudgy creature in a grass skirt, have moved out to the hills. The dark-skinned men who remain wear light powder in their stiff hair. This makes their coiffure look like a dandelion gone to seed. With high-girted calicos bound around their waists by leather belts and legs tightly bound below the knees, they walk along, tasting that combination of betel nut rubbed in dust of lime which is their mild intoxicant.

"But don't make the mistake of thinking they're dumb or anything," warned a captain. "Remember what happened to Lee when he first came to Milne Bay."

Lee, a husky, square-built officer, was trying to get some biscuits made for a luncheon in honor of a captain-physician in charge of Milne Bay's hospital.

Addressing a puff-haired, tattooed native who had just applied for the job, he said in pidgin: "Rastus, blackfellow, you savvy, gettum flour, milk, mixum plenty good, makum crumpets?"

Rastus drew himself up and replied: "I'm deeply sorry, sir, but I don't believe I shall be able to secure sufficient baking powder."

Rastus learned English from Miss Doris Passel of the London Missionary School, a young New York woman who taught the natives not only respect for God but also an American attitude toward native populations. Troops here owe her a debt of gratitude. These splay-footed brown men remember her. One named Kwato, about eleven, did arithmetic sums for me and printed his name perfectly. All wanted to know when Miss Doris Passell was coming back from New York. Yes, they get their pound of rice daily and their two sticks of nearly black trade tobacco. And yes, American fighters whine overhead. But where is Miss Doris Passell?

—

'Battle of Lungs' in Guinea Mountains

Somewhere in Australia—September 12, 1942

In lonely forests of perpetual rain, 6000 feet above the seas that flank New Guinea's eastern peninsula, Australian and Japanese troops carry on a deadly struggle for tactical position on several gully-rippled dorsal fins of the Owen Stanley Range. For the first time in this war the great equatorial rain forest which girdles the entire world's circumference, crossing Africa, South America, Borneo and Sumatra, is a sustained battleground. It is a strange region anywhere, but here it is lonely, wet and terrifying.

Great tree ferns, their leaves forever bright with mist, thrust their arms from the black walls of precipitous rock and the disordered pell-mell of enormous slate boulders. The atmosphere is clammy-cold, and hands upon a rifle grow damp with the chill. Animals are few because the sun is little seen.

Isolated rifle cracks speak across misty gullies as scouts try to pick off sentries. Through the gloomy clouds that hang overhead or scud across intervening ramparts of black rock, a shaft of light comes only occasionally. It is gone before the men, crouching behind rocks, can emerge to dry out their muggy clothing.

Even at 14,000 feet, the uttermost peaks rarely get sun and never snow. The trickle of water whispering among the rocks is the only constant sound.

Altitude itself is a bitter antagonist amid a 6000-foot network of interlacing ravines on the broad back of the mountain chain. Australian fighters now meeting Japs are, like their antagonists, undergoing a struggle for breath as well as mastery. The air is thin as well as wet. At such an altitude the necessity to leap and climb swiftly among boulders as big as a house, without exposing a single movement to well-camouflaged Jap scouts, is a test of endurance.

When one considers that heavy mortars, with their cumbersome base plates, must be tugged by hand or carried on sweating backs from one position to another, with changes being as often vertical as horizontal, the effort in merely keeping the breath or even the heart action unstrained is formidable. No human beings, native or Australian, have ever attempted tropical fighting at such an altitude or under these rigorous circumstances. Australians are by nature a people of dry plains and hot desert; their factories and cities and their tendency to move to the seacoast have made pioneers rare and mountaineers almost nonexistent.

Native Papuans, with their puffball black heads and loincloths, have always shunned the mountains because of the insupportable climate and the necessity to have clothes there which they do not possess—and because of the eerie, sunless, haunted atmosphere. Lowland carriers in the mountains suffer sometimes more from the altitude than white men, and frequently die. Two, for example, who bore cameras for newsreel photographers in a recent film being shown in Australia, died of pneumonia en route even though their aggregate period at high altitude was only three days. It was to avoid the black reaches of New Guinea's mountains that the famous gold-carrying air transport system was developed.

Australia, counting upon Singapore and the Dutch East Indies to hold, had no way of anticipating that Port Moresby would become her Singapore, and that a battle in the mountains would be necessary to defend Port Moresby from an attack by land. Australians, who consider themselves able to fight anywhere they have to—like Americans—have never developed a specialist corps resembling Germany's *Jäger-truppen* or her Italian ally's Alpinists.

Japanese troops feeling their way through the mountain mists some sixty miles from Port Moresby were trained for altitude fighting as part of a thorough plan for Far Eastern conquest. While American Marines were hewing their way through Nicaragua's lofty jungles, their Japanese proto-types were hardening themselves in Formosa for a battle that would one day be fought in the Owen Stanley Range. Had the American combat troops now in Australia ever foreseen a worldwide role, their training might have been similar. As it is, the New Guinea situation must be faced in terms of the axiom that only experience makes a soldier. The Japanese, by schooling, learned what the Australians rapidly are learning under fire and what Americans still have to learn.

It is not only a battle of lungs and hearts, but of bellies. The bigger, looser frames of Australians are used to nourishing food, and require more per man than the rice- and yam-eating Japanese. More food poundage brought up from Allied advance bases means less ammunition. Along the several days' journey through the slippery, clammy path, the carrier must also carry food for himself. Thus, in one of the world's most sparsely populated tropical regions, a labor problem is created.

One white man cannot serve as a food carrier for another, however willing he may be to sweat his way upward along the trail front by Mount Victoria. By the time he reached the "roof" he would have consumed the whole poundage on his back. It is wrong to think of Australian troops requiring a porter each, just as it is exaggerated to picture the Japanese as some miracle fighter living like an animal off his own fat. But how can General MacArthur's Australian commanders bring together sufficient Papuans to keep the mountain troops fed and nourished? This question is being answered with energy and thoroughness.

The Japs have bearers, too—many being natives pressed into service and brought over from New Britain and the Rabaul region—but their dependence is considerably less and most bearers carry war materiel. The Japanese Institute of Tropical Warfare has made a study of edible wild plants throughout their intended empire, and the Jap's little bags of rice and meat are savories rather than staples. Instructions are to live off the country as quickly as possible. Wherever the Rising Sun flag is planted, a vegetable garden follows soon afterward as part of the Jap soldier's regular 16-hour fighting day. Where rear troops grow their own food it means less transport devoted to their sustenance and hence more advancing forces engaged in the forward areas. Less food means more and bigger guns in the mountains, and more and bigger caliber munition. Or it means, as today in New Guinea, that the Japanese are able to sustain a bigger force in an inaccessible area and make outflanking movements.

Given the long record of air exploitation of New Guinea, the first inquiry of a visitor to Port Moresby is always whether our troops, like the gold miners, are being supplied from the air. But the difficulties among mountains forever hooded in clouds must be seen in order to be appreciated. It requires more than exceptional courage for a pilot to fly two miles a minute through narrow misty valleys walled with black slate while seeking a tiny ground signal. It also requires plenty of reserve transport aircraft, for there are losses.

Even by using air supply to the utmost, Allied generals are still leaving themselves a fundamental problem: Anglo-Saxon troops under tropical battle conditions simply require more than Japanese, and somehow that must reach them. Wherever the inured and imperial-minded Japanese make up their minds to hide in the jungle, the Allied capacity to seek them out and destroy them depends not alone on cutting off their slender and relatively unimportant line of supplies but on becoming troops capable of enduring greater hardship.

The Allies are feeling their way toward the development of a corps of elite jungle fighters who can endure any altitude and any heat and cold that a Jap can, without making greater demands upon bases for sustenance or support. That idea is likely to take root before long, as the Japs push toward Port Moresby in their surge to snatch an empire.

—

MORESBY DONS LONG PANTS, GROWS
INTO MAJOR FORTRESS

Somewhere in New Guinea—December 5, 1942

Only when you return to Port Moresby after a few weeks' absence can you see what has been accomplished. In this scattered stronghold of closely woven hills and air fields, sweating under the grey clouds of the still-unbroken monsoon, you find how powerful Port Moresby has become: a fortress whose walls are mountains and the blue waters of the Coral Sea, and whose eyes are far-striking aircraft. What is here now is here to stay, come fever or air raid. Port Moresby will stand, for her invulnerability has been hewn by the sweating arms of her defenders, white, brown, and black, American, Australian and Papuan.

At first a visitor is lost in the developments. New roads send clouds of dust up over a jeep, encrusting your body in tan dust, caking it with perspiration. The new roads are named Pitts Street for Sydney, and Broadway or Michigan Boulevard. Mosquitoes still hover around a typewriter. There is the wracking noise of machine guns over one of many fields. New aircraft, new faces, new gossip are everywhere.

Somebody has taken away the worried Port Moresby. Here is this new one, where paths to showers and latrines are laid out in crushed stone with boulders for borders. Drinking fountains are still created by twisting brass faucets upside down.

When the Jap bombers come over, the anti-aircraft fire goes stabbing up but there is more of it, much more. (A helmet still hangs by each cot.) When it patters down on the grass roof, it sounds like hail. In the bad old days, it sounded like rain.

There is still the brown bottle of quinine tablets and the blue bottle of salt tablets on the mess table. Butter still drips soupily yellow from the knife and all drinks are warm. But fighters now have vitamin tablets and there are wounded, too.

Here the Japs' wounded and our own wounded are in the hands of American nurses, the first women to return to Port Moresby. Already they have their own hospital. This touch of feminism is the hallmark of a new stability, but it imposes sacrifices, too. No more bathing of sweaty bodies in the open; baths have shoulder-high palisades of thick bamboo. Grass skirts hang from roofs, or are draped across tied-up mosquito nets. Their original wearers are on the other side of the Owen Stanley Range, upon the cloud-wrapped peaks undergoing almost continuous rain.

Across these hills, with their short green trees and dead brown grass, moves an endless crisscross procession of why Port Moresby is strong: Fortresses, Havocs, Liberators, Kittyhawks, Airacobras. Port Moresby had nothing six months ago, not even geographical advantage. The battle of Milne Bay saved it, to stand beside Guadalcanal as long as American wings are spread over its boomtown defenses.

When we came in aboard Major General George Kenney's big B-17 Fortress, there was a "quarrel of nature" over the hills: rainbow, sunlit clouds, bursts of rain falling on perspiring bodies. We manned our machine guns as our giant wings dipped and our pilot chose his airdrome. An alert was on and the runways suddenly deserted. But nothing happened. And then we knew that, in this new system of American defenses upon Australian soil, Port Moresby would become—until better bases took its place—a true Singapore, not too confident but self-reliant, sure that its labors would endure.

—

JAPS AT BUNA TESTING ALLIES' ABILITY TO DIE

Somewhere in New Guinea—December 6, 1942 (Delayed)

Sitting in a thatched grass hut as the guest of an American fighter squadron, this correspondent is one of many observers awaiting Buna's fall, in MacArthur's first offensive in this war to capture Papua. Tomorrow I will cross the grey-veiled Owen Stanleys to join troops in the field, having at last found a seat aboard one of the transport planes that helped accomplish this great airborne invasion. Crossing the range and descending into the field with the troops will necessarily limit the writer's vision, for the three principal sectors are remote from each other.

The Japs lost the battle for Port Moresby last September when stiff air attacks drove them back across the range. Buna will be a baptism of fire for American soldiers fighting offensively against the Jap infantry.

Progress has at times appeared slow. Buna has seemed repeatedly upon the point of falling. But Japan is deliberately spinning out this battle. Her slow pusher planes, slipping in under tremendous clouds—piled 40,000 feet high each afternoon in swirling arabesques that are deadly to pursuit aircraft—have successfully dropped parachute supplies upon a small rectangle along Buna beach. Jap machine-gunners with their protected positions among the marshes and creeks, and with the grass before their posts cut down to afford a full sweep, still are being eliminated only a single gun at a time. And the price of this elimination is not cheap.

To some, it has seemed that the inability of Allied airmen to shake Japanese soldiers' positions on the ground—though causing heavy losses—was proof that until the ground was gained by our infantry, victory could not be considered won.

The Japanese are ingenious in devising means of undergoing Allied air attacks and at the same time holding positions that still can repel infantry. The best device they have developed is the natural pillbox created within the roots of trees along the marshes from Cape Endaiadere to Gona. This tree—not even old New Guinea hands have been able to furnish the writer its name—has thick roots that meet six to ten feet above the ground, forming a cone structure something like the poles of an American Indian tepee. The Japs mount machine guns within to sweep every direction. They can be taken only at the point of a bayonet. Sunk so low that they are almost undisturbed by aircraft attacks, difficult to see beneath the foliage, their woven form protects them from mortar fire.

A striking paradox of the Papuan campaign is that, after being fought so recently among the rain-drenched tree ferns of the "Roof of the World," it is now entering its final phase in the marshy, foul and steaming flatland. What was supremely right in the mountains has become inapplicable.

The Japs, being attacked only by land, therefore have a ten-mile front on one side only. Although many rivers and creeks must be crossed with our supplies, and muddy marshes traversed in attacks, the Japs cannot counter-attack us this way because our destructive raids upon their supply barges have made it impossible.

Our air umbrella has been used offensively over land, and used defensively over the sea to prevent the Japs from landing any reinforcements or vacating those already there. Yet the primary idea of amphibious war—using water to skirt the enemy for a rear attack—remains unexploited at Buna and Gona.

The battle for Buna is plainly what faces us in the many months that lie ahead. Japan is betting on scores or hundreds of Bunas. She means to curdle the blood of her enemies by causing her peasant infantrymen to fight so suicidally—and inflict maximum losses—that the Christian nations will be repelled and negotiate a peace that will leave her part of what she so adroitly snatched. With Japan on the defensive, it is clear she never intended an equal relationship as one of many partners in the Pacific peace. What Japan wants is to be master, or die.

This, at least, is the aim of the military caste behind such doomed resistance as that of the Jap marines and army at Buna. To uphold that idea, the Japanese navy squandered destroyer after destroyer while knowing Buna was strategically only an anachronism of the misbegotten plan to take Port Moresby.

Their Milne Bay defeat lost them the China Strait. By spending blood lavishly to delay the Buna surrender she cannot prevent, Japan means to test the capacity of American and Australian troops to carry the battle to Tokyo. Her answer is coming slowly but with it the first light that the western nations are resolute may possibly touch Jap leaders, though it will never be permitted to reach their people.

That is what actually is being decided by our men under the hot suns and steaming rains of Buna's swamps and beaches.

—

CRAWLING THROUGH JUNGLE TO KILL, OR DIE, IN GUINEA

With the American Forces in Papua—December 11, 1942

Not a bird chirps, not a leaf stirs. A cricket somewhere in the high, green kunai grass begins a faint song, then, oppressed by the sun, fades away. It is silent again. Suddenly the earth seems to rise and a soft blow of air, like a hand pat, strikes your face. Every tree trembles with the shock of shells.

"Still looking," says the corporal leading you to the advance post. "Landed about there. Those Jap 75s only have a fragmentation arc of thirty yards. They'll have to get better observation posts. Unless they see us, how can they hit us?"

He has hardly finished speaking when another blow and concussion make the earth rise, as though outraged, beneath your feet. There is no whistle of warning because you are right under the shells, aimed at our line of communication. In these leafy tunnels we are as safe as rabbits scurrying through tiny paths in deep grass.

Abruptly a tommy gun sounds its hard punch gruffly just ahead; again, then once again. That's ours. A single biting rifle crack. That's a Jap sniper trying to get our tommy-gunner. Whoever sees the other best, whoever waits the longest without being seen and fires the surest, will live. The other man will die. On both sides, there are plenty of quick and plenty of dead.

Now the humming of aircraft. Scanning the treetops, you try to see whose planes are coming. In this overhanging green you've as much chance as looking through a chimney; you can only tell by the engine sounds. Our plug-ugly infantry doesn't pretend to be sure of the difference between a Nakajima and an Airacobra.

The sniper snaps his whip again and a big leaf comes floating down. But the leaf is old and yellow, not fresh green. It was just a dead leaf, nothing hit it.

There is a singing whine. Almost simultaneously a shell crashes ahead and behind. That is our artillery. Another snarl, then again *wham-wham*. You hear it and the fall of the shell nearly together, close overhead, because the range is short.

Off to the left two machine guns have begun to argue. One accuses, the other answers, then both talk at once.

Here on the front between our Gona and Buna drives—sometimes called our Sanananda push, midmost of our three drives to the sea—the Jap lines and ours are stretched across a ten-foot-wide road that bends east toward Buna. Two miles more and we'll see those blue waters again. But in those two miles lies an indeterminable number of Jap machine-gun posts not yet uprooted. There are grenade-throwing rifles. There are clip-haired, bearded Japs in two-foot foxholes, covered over with matted foliage so that only muzzles of machine guns protrude. There are others in huge protective roots of the peculiar giant eucalyptus which no one seems able to name. Its roots are interwebbed like ducks' feet, making separate polygonous chambers. The Jap gunner simply crawls from one chamber to the next, protected on three sides. Could we do the same thing? Of course we could—defensively. But this time we are advancing, not the Japs. And it is for us to dig them out.

War is never very clean or quick on the ground. But for slowness, heat and mud, this has most wars bettered. The Australian Imperials say that Papua is worse than anything Libya, Syria or Palestine ever offered.

Two majors sit before hip-high shelter tents scraping bullybeef (meatball style) and rice from their plates. Both their overall uniforms, like our own, were originally light green, but are now stained and mottled almost black by dirt and 24-hour sweating. Baetcke has a bead of sweat on the brow under his helmet. He is tall, sandy blond, spare. His junior, Boerem, is dark, plump and deadly earnest. Both are true infantrymen. Both have led attack after attack through this labyrinth and so have their lieutenants. Both know what it is to fight day and night, to lie in the lines for fourteen days straight, fighting for every gain by yards and paying for it in men as parsimoniously as possible.

With their men, both officers are learning to kill Japs in the Japanese way.

"See that thing," says Baetcke, pointing to a shapeless, dark green cloth mass. He lifts it up, still stinking wet.

"I wore that fifteen days continuously. It belonged to another officer; we don't have any valets in this colonial war. When we reach a river we wash. Until then we just fight."

—

MIRACLE PILOTS CARRY A WAR OVER THE GUINEA MOUNTAINS

With the American Forces in Papua—December 12, 1942

Now that you're here and your conversation pauses to guess which gun is firing and who has cleaned out what machine-gun nest, you are liable to

forget how you got here. But you'd better not because that's how your food
and your ammunition get here, too.

Just now you're down in this little clearing flanked by high jungle trees.
Brown "boongs," native carriers, with long, three-pronged pitchfork combs
thrust in their chocolate-colored hair, walk loose-jointedly past. Few typewriters have crossed the range and some pause to listen and wonder at this
strange new thing.

What you must try not to forget is the fellows responsible for you being
here—you and all the hundreds who have flown across one of the world's
most terrible ranges and been set down on the muddy landing crevice (it
cannot be called either a landing field or strip) amid these great trees.

Seeing another transport coming in, looking again for that crevice in a
green sea of danger, you remember things that a Japanese shell landing
nearby caused you to forget. Who is bringing her in this morning? How will
he ever slip her down? How many razor blades could you throw free-hand
through the crack in her deck?

Looking out the left-hand window in the big flying corridor of a transport plane, seeing the rim of trees rising five feet from the wing, then
looking out the right-hand window and seeing branches practically poking in, makes you feel you are participating in a new form of aerial acro-
batics. As an assistant radioman says: "Where there is land, we can put
this big baby down."

The far side of New Guinea's backbone, the Owen Stanley Range, was
first crossed by gold-eager Australians shortly after the area was obtained
from Germany through peace treaties. They flew everything: German
Junkers, American tri-motor "tin goose" Fords and British Puss Moths.

Today great American transports cross this range—whose castellated,
cloudy crests are even more dangerous than its swirling precipitous currents—more times on some days than the gold service did in six months.
They carry the entire war by air across these cloud-walled peaks in the face
of attacks by Zeros.

En route you unroll again all the bloody places over which the Australians pursued the Japs after the failure of their double-edge coup to grab
Milne Bay and China Strait while attacking Port Moresby by land. The
course is a secret, but here is Wairopi Bridge, which our P-39 Airacobras
used to strafe and dive-bomb as fast as the Japs repaired it. Ahead you set

the whole panorama—Cape Endaiadere, where Japs and Americans are struggling for airstrips, and Sanananda Point, where Australians and Americans are fighting together.

A radioman brings you a letter of commendation these crews just received from the American general. This compensates for the daily risk of losing themselves amid the woolly walls that build up within a minute over these passes. The crew chief does not want any misunderstandings; indicating his plane's window, he says: "I don't want you to think we're too lazy to wash them. We keep the windows dirty because it stops them from glinting and attracting the attention of the Zeros."

And when they finally slip her into that crevice—she who was made for airdromes measured in thousands of yards—and you jump from the loading platform, you see scores of muddy-booted Aussies and Americans with shirts plastered to their bodies. There is a jeep, the only powered creature in sight. Bushy-headed carriers eye you. It is hot. It is wet. Ahead lies the passage through the jungle, dark as a cathedral aisle. Men with tommy guns are splashing through mud up to their ankles, dim in the wet darkness, and cursing.

"That way, buddy," they say, pointing across the lagoons, and grin muddily as you start.

—

GONA FALLS THE HARD WAY, BECOMES A BEACH OF DEATH

With the American Forces in Papua—December 14, 1942

Gona fell because the Japs could not stand two hundred and fifty 25-pound shells thrown into a position about three hundred yards by fifty. They attempted to escape both east and went along the black sand strip on which they were trapped. They were hemmed in by four big, low trees, something like American river willows, ranged along the beach at intervals of fifty yards. Their enormous trunk roots turn the beach sand to black turf. The trunks are at least twelve feet in diameter and the roots and lowest branches can be formed into a wall with rice bags.

Among these thick, squatty trees the thick squatty Japs made their last stand. They had plenty of ammunition, food and water and also possessed shells for a 75-mm gun—but no gun. Their uniforms were clean and new.

Meanwhile, Australians—tall, mud-drenched, bearded and tatterdemalion—closed in on them, crawling from one flooded foxhole to the next while their own 25-pounders threw shells over their heads at almost point-blank range.

After the bombardment the stench of dead bodies was so powerful that the Japs donned gas masks. By night the enemy pushed east along the beach, possibly intending to join the force fighting the Americans and Australians about five miles away inside Sanananda Point. Ninety-five Japs were killed.

Another small party went west. How many Japs were killed there is still not known but the official total of buried dead at this unfinished stage is between 500 and 600. A number of Australians gave their lives for this seabound position.

Gona has now become a beach of death. The great palms are bitten and chewed with fire from everything in modern war that explodes and kills. Some palms are headless torsos, their torsos nicked and frayed.

The water is as still as a pond; there is no surf. The grass walls of the tiny mission whose entrance path runs down through an aisle of smashed palms to a torn-up rowboat pier—the only landing facility—are in ruins. An enemy barge is stranded like a turtle under one of the heavily armed trees overlooking the beach. A mile offshore, a big Jap freighter lies on its side. Fugitives from the beach are still there. You can see them with binoculars.

It is a Japanese Dunkirk, but there was no evacuation. Bandages, pot-shaped helmets, rifles, unopened bottles of vitamin pills, undischarged grenades and bullet clips lie in the mud. This is one end of the road that began outside Port Moresby.

Beside an Australian officer's tent stands a Jap officer's curved sword in leather field case, sharper than an officer's razor.

The bodies of enemy soldiers who made their final stand here are in various stages of decomposition, and make breathing objectionable.

The sea, impassively calm, touches the black and even clouds that lie quiet upon the promontory toward Lae and Salamaua.

Although the Americans are nearby, the country where they are fighting—in deep shadows and flooded jungle, with little low paths made by crawling men—belongs on another continent. Here at Gona, it is relatively open country with the intervening meadows of green kunai grass six feet high and rapier-sharp.

Arising this morning after a night on the ground in a thunderstorm, during which firing continued, the writer, going to the beach, found a group of Australians standing in an open patch of kunai. A Jap had been stealing across the road a few minutes before; the sentry got him.

"He's planted right there," said one, pointing at a mound. Another man was scraping wet earth from a short shovel, another fitting a new clip to his gun.

Six American fighters moaned faintly against the woolly wet clouds.

The heat in Papua is oppression itself. When the sun comes out you feel your body is an anvil being hammered. When it disappears behind low monsoon clouds your whole torso bursts out with a thick black film of perspiration. Stinging sweat seeps into your eyes. Your nose and naked shoulders are streaking. You wipe your body with the plane mechanic's baseball cap and replace it on your head to dry.

On the beach is a starling-yellow blob of canvas—the new life raft for an airplane, half-deflated and misshapen. Its trademark says it was made in Clifton, N.J. And this beach was Japanese.

Your kinky-headed native carrier, with sweatband, grass armlets, frayed girdle and bushknife, is hunting around the beach. Amid this baggage of warfare worth thousands of dollars all he wants is a blackened saucepan. And coconuts. Smashed trees have been razed by the filter of fire and everywhere in gunpits lie tawny coconuts. Coconuts, and heads of the dead.

The Gona Mission, which is all there was to the beach of death before war came, consists of two small buildings upon stilts about a hundred yards from the body-littered beach, with tall roofs of brown grass. Shells went through both grassy arches, leaving a hole big enough for pterodactyls to nest in the entrance. Before both buildings are round craters the size of swimming pools, filled with water. Water is everywhere and turns any cavity more than a foot deep into a basin.

These craters, which are Flying Fortress bombprints, lie among the topless palms like some macabre effort at landscaping. Any platoon of soldiers could swim in them. But none does for the reason unnecessary to explain.

For these now nauseating dead who, hours ago, were quick with life, there was a single means of nourishment—big, woven raffia bags of rice scattered along the black sand and dragged in under fire. Neither rain, sun nor shells spoil Jap army rice, a mixture of nourishing whole grains and our kind of polished grains. They ate from bags that Australian bullets and American bombers split and shattered. The Japs fought alongside the bodies of their dead; some were nearly skeletonized.

"See how they lay right down among their first corpses," said one tommy-gunner puzzledly, pointing with his muzzle. "The Japs are different from us."

Burial may mean little to them, but form means much. Little bags of hair cuttings and nail parings were found in several places, which the soldiers took from the fallen to send to relatives in Japan.

"They're opposite to us in every way. They save what we throw away."

Now grenades are bursting on the left, up the beach farther off. American guns to the right are silent. Several American-built trucks lie nearby, blown in on the sides by the concussion of bombs. One rusty officer's car, probably brought from Java, is down to the hubs in muck and as full of holes as a colander.

The strip of black sand is pocked with machine-gun and mortar holes. Lifting slowly upon the tide, the body of a mustached Jap infantryman drifts idly. Between the rended, wispy palms winds a burial party led by an English chaplain of a unit from the remotest quarter of Australia. The freckled chaplain, straw-colored hair exposed—everyone else is wearing a helmet with camouflage net—is fingering a sodden bunch of letters.

Gona is the westernmost salient of the Allied three-prong drive to the sea. Sanananda, where both Americans and Australians are fighting, is the central salient and Buna, with its pair of prized airdromes, is the American.

For several minutes the only sound is the squelch of passing boots sucking up mud as a helmeted Australian goes by, tommy gun in the crook of his arm, peering into slit trenches for snipers who are known to be still about.

Then, suddenly, down the beach toward Sanananda and Buna there are several bursts of machine-gun fire, followed by a mortar's deep, hollow boom. Somewhere back there the Americans and Australians are thrusting their way through one machine-gun nest after another, sometimes taking three days to clear up a single post and living meanwhile on half-flooded islands in a morass of hip-deep, fever-infested mud.

"Don't miss any hole merely because it contains a body," says a sergeant major. "Use your muzzle to look underneath. Round potholes are Jap. Rectangular ones are ours."

———

ALLIED TROOPS RISE FROM SHELL HOLES TO SWEEP FULL LENGTH OF CAPE ENDAIADERE

With the American-Australian Troops in New Guinea— December 21, 1942

Breaking the deadlock amid swamps and machine-gunned coconut groves east of Buna, Allied forces have sent a sweep of troops along the outer length of this strategic cape. Jap possession of Buna's pair of fighter strips was threatened, but not yet shaken.

By a circuitous route involving travel by aircraft, bumping jeep, and on foot, this correspondent arrived at the best-known of Buna's three fronts. The atmosphere is one of chastened resolve—chastened because the American infantry is learning how stern is the task ahead.

While the Jap trenches overrun yesterday were simpler than those elsewhere—which this correspondent saw after dawn from his treetop observation post—the trenches, at right angles to the beach and protecting both airdromes to the rear, had already resisted the efforts of Australian artillery and American dive-bombing.

In this stiff battle probably 300 or 400 Japs lost their lives. Many who fled through the underbrush to heavier pillboxes ranged along the two airdromes were presumably wounded. Some even tried to swim away from the palm-fringed beach, where the impassive sea flanked their bloody engagement.

While the Allied step toward hemming the Japs from the sea was a tactical success, the brunt of losses was borne by Australians. (The Americans, who have fought doggedly in this sector under heavy Jap mortar and artillery fire, this time were sent in to follow.)

Going up with the American troops into trenches still occupied by occasional enemy shamming death, this correspondent, with the others, had an ugly half-hour when a Jap fifteen yards away opened up with grenades while his mate, hidden high in the coconut palms, began trying to pick off individuals crouched in holes. His rifle's whipcrack reports sent bullets singing near.

The biting chatter of tommy guns was almost continuous; fighting went on long after the forward troops made their sweep. The Japs used one flamethrower and this was captured. Not until the entire ground had been gone over three or four times and every interlaced trench emptied—several had bays enabling fire to any point of the compass, and loopholes hung over with dissembling grass—was it possible to move except by dashing from shellhole to shellhole.

Frank Hewlett of the UP and Merlin Spencer of the AP occupied adjacent shellholes to me when the Japs crawled from hiding to resume their fire after the forward troops had passed, but two photographers had the narrowest shaves. George Strock of *Life* magazine photographed a dead Jap who came to life when Strock's back was turned.

"He sat up and blinked, he did," said the Aussie who shot him.

Another Jap came toward George Wilk, the Australian photographer, with his hands above his head as though in surrender. Abruptly he rapped his head with his left hand, which infantrymen near Wilk fortunately observed was holding a grenade. The Jap was disposed of before the grenade could be cast.

For at least an hour before the battle, American Mitchells and Australian Beaufighters swept low over enemy positions, bombing them from little more than treetop-level. The Japs who raided our rear heavily on Saturday night had withheld all anti-aircraft fire Saturday, concealing their positions even in the face of bombing. But yesterday they cut loose with everything.

Promptly at seven in the evening, following their artillery barrage, a prisoner was taken alive. Getting him was difficult because as soon as his surrender was perceived by others in nearby trenches, their fire was directed against that spot and the Jap, with whom I rode partway into our lines, was hit in the head. Like others, this Jap seemed well fed and in good spirits.

Sergeant Robert Almonds of Wisconsin, who was near me when firing broke out, led his men in ferreting for Japs. "I never saw them dug in so deep. I threw one grenade in that hole, then had to come back and put down two more," he said.

When the scene seemed peaceful—disturbed only by the chopping of tommy guns and the occasional boom of grenades a hundred fifty yards away as trenches were cleaned up—a walloping crash sent this correspondent first flat, then crawling. The Japs opened with a mountain gun concealed somewhere in the jungle. Three Chicagoans beckoned the writer to cover just as another shell hit. Two others took refuge nearby. Their corporal was farther back.

The Japs' peculiar airburst shell sometimes goes off instantly, sometimes in three bursts. One shell landed in the sea near shore; another short, in the bush.

"We've made seven attempts to get this position before," said a lieutenant, "and now we're going to keep it." His well-armed eight-man patrol appeared adequate to the task. I shared a shellhole with a railway mail clerk for the Chicago-Carbondale train run.

At the most advanced hospital, I saw a transfusion given to the first victim of this shelling.

Americans yesterday marked one month's anniversary of their efforts to drive the Japs into the sea on the north coast and to annihilate them where they stand. The Australians cinched their belts tighter, too, as they returned after the lull that has followed the fall of Gona and Buna Village to watchful probing of the enemy's deeply dug-in positions.

Here is the same bumping jolt of artillery; the shock of mortars can be heard sharply above the chatter of these typewriter keys. Here are the same begrimed, sweaty men. The only discernible difference between the fighters at Buna and those at Sanananda is the latter's thicker beards.

The fight for the two airdromes has pushed slightly farther, but it is the same everywhere. Japs are literally picked from their positions with bayonets. Fliers and seamen, meeting the enemy, can decide an issue in seconds; for the infantry it is a long, dirty, costly, wearisome and little-gloried task in this vine-entangled, choking jungle. It has already run one month and could run another. Anything done fast here is done badly and usually dangerously. It is dangerous however you do it.

—

BATTLE OF BUNA: A DAY AT THE FRONT

With American Forces in New Guinea—December 24, 1942 (Delayed)

The bitter battle of Buna grows harsher as it progresses. Today on the right flank, where the prize is a mud-slogged airdrome with two wrecked Jap fighters on it, tanks again pushed our line farther up the field in what resembled a bloody gain for yardage upon some incredible football stadium of enormous size.

Meanwhile, on the left flank, American troops—with Australians on their way from the "island" in the mouth of Entrance Creek—succeeded in reaching the sea with a gallant effort which your correspondent witnessed under fire. By this hazardous, courageous charge the American infantry, in alternating rain and spasms of sunlight that left the ground steaming, once more fought their way to the borders of the black beach while Jap snipers in trees plied their carbines.

"Spray trees" has been the order of the still-unnameable American general commanding both countries' forces here, an order punctiliously observed.

Twice today your correspondent crossed that 60-foot mud-choked malarial stream which surrounded the island, once in a squashy, mud-smeared rubber boat run upon wires by an infantryman crouching in the lee of a coconut log, once over the crazyquilt bridge built under fire. Another bridge was needed to approach the labyrinth of entrenched Japs on this marshy tongue of land and coconut palms which occupies the west of the outthrust campo between Buna Village and Buna Mission. Called Government Gardens, it is simply more stinking Papuan swamp.

From lying half-crouched in the palpitating rubber boat's mud-filled interior, the writer then followed the men as they methodically darted from tree to tree. Every man nearby lay in a mudhole behind a log or thick-veined tree while the rain pattered on green shirts sour with sweat. As machine guns clattered, the smell of the first bodies came to us across Government Gardens.

Captain Byron Bradford, whose group of men are advancing through this difficult, steaming marsh, today talked with this correspondent in a grassy hole behind the firing line while heavy weapons crashed in the trees. He pointed out that his runners and his lieutenants have been outstanding.

"Were it not for Lieutenant Kleinschmidt silencing a machine gun that was sweeping this creek, our advance today would have been impossible," he said. "And that is the best jungle fighter here," he said, pointing to Lieutenant Roger Upton, a narrow-faced, sharp-eyed officer of about twenty-six. Upton explained: "We simply use the Jap trick of giving them bait at the side, then slipping around and attacking from the rear. Anybody can work these things if he has training."

The time was nearly ripe for the main attack toward the beach, shortly before noon. After talking quietly in the trench, we crawled out and everyone took cover behind piles of captured Jap stuff including beautifully chromed radio receivers.

—

Intrepid Yanks Turn Pillboxes into Jap Tombs

Daring Maneuver Destroys Defenses at Buna
After Frontal Attack Fails

With American Forces in New Guinea—December 29, 1942 (Delayed by Censor)

The bloody triangle of Buna broke today amid the thunder of mortar fire and the song of shells whamming into retreating Japs. With his head lowered like the infantrymen in front and behind, your correspondent ran through sniper fire across this pillbox-pockmarked triangle to reach the advanced post where lay, under fire, three of the men responsible for this achievement.

A few yards ahead was a continual mighty threshing of undulant foliage as crawling tommy-gunners hosed them endlessly with .45 slugs. I lay at the foot of a tree spattered with blood where one sniper had just been shot down. In another's branches dangled the silvery wing-panel of a Zero. Concealed in foliage under the motherly protection of a thick-rooted tree, I heard the story of this taking of the bloody triangle directly from the soldiers who accomplished this costly task.

I reached the outpost, on a field dominated by Jap fire, by a twisting course around another field. On my back I wore the knapsack of a runner who had been sent for water. The runner carried filled flasks, strung by chains upon a stick. Two tommy-gunners covered us as we ran across the field. At the bridge a fusillade burst out and I flung myself flat. The others crossed amid the enemy fire, which then stopped. When I began my dash across the final fifty yards, the Japs opened up again. But in the last dash I reached the company that had broken the triangle.

The triangle is that scarred swamp of pandanus and betel nut trees, and thick grass, where the roads to Buna Village and Buna Mission diverge left (west) and right (east). "Road" means a trail big enough for a bicycle, not for a four-wheel vehicle such as a peep. It is a partly dry lane, lifted above the surrounding morass.

To take Buna Village two weeks ago the Americans hewed a jungle path to the left of the westward road. They desired to go straight through simultaneously on both roads, but were prevented on the right by a Jap pillbox—heavy palmetto logs filled in with earth—lying athwart the trail. Deep quagmire flanked both sides.

For nearly a fortnight Americans launched every conceivable infantry attack against the right-hand fork, to Buna Mission. Our first heavy attack came ten days ago, preceded by a 25-pounder barrage. These shells, however, bounded off the tops of the dugouts. Japs could be heard calling, "Hello, boy," in apparent derision.

After the failure of a first attack, the commanding general said he would give high honors to any group of men who reached the pillboxes.

Last Thursday (December 24) a second attack pressed with great courage but was unable to penetrate Jap fire. When the American general reiterated that this fork was the key to Buna Mission and must be conquered, his own aide volunteered. The aide led a new attack, but losses obliged him to withdraw like his predecessors.

When all efforts to circumvent the pillboxes failed, Sergeant Harold

Huyck led an assault straight down the ditches flanking the foot-wide path. This four-man party managed to make it forty yards from the foremost pill-box before the bullfrog-like mouth belched machine-gun fire. (These men described their attack to the writer after emerging from the swamp with faces blackened with mud, mired to the hips.)

The thankless task now fell to Captain James Alford, a dark-haired, friendly Mississippian, thin and modest, and usually helmetless.

"First, we decided to go through the swamp and see how the pillboxes looked from the rear," said Alford, as though this day-long pull through shoulder-deep, sniper-filled swamp were a Sunday stroll. Alford established a small sniper-free area in the jungle bordering upon the creek and coconut grove at the enemy rear.

"We began by killing tree snipers. Our best shot got two."

"And you got three yourself," prompted a sergeant.

Having cleaned out the snipers, and learned the Jap trick of suspending a straw-filled dummy in the same tree with a sniper to reveal the sources of fire, Alford's company then established a treetop lookout, Jap-style. Their first important discovery from this vantage point—within enemy lines, it should be remembered—was that they were confronted not with three, but fourteen pillboxes. The Japs had spent weeks preparing this system against either rear or frontal attacks.

Alford's next attempt was to start a bushfire, hoping to burn off the fo-liage cover. It was partly successful, revealing some pillboxes, but the Japs put an end to it. Alford now called for mortars. Even though the palmettos threw them off, the projectiles made it possible to harry the Japs in their holes. But their fire continued.

The turning point came today.

Without telling Alford, a sergeant with a revolver and a weaponless run-ner started for the pillboxes. This duo made a series of daring, circuitous approaches. Finally they got to within ten yards of one heavy-lidded pill-box. The question arose how to make the test. They lacked sufficient arms. Finally, Sergeant Wagner exposed himself slightly and, getting no action, stood up. There was sniper fire from above but, again, nothing from within. Wagner sat down. Green, the runner, stood up. Again nothing from the silent pillboxes.

They crawled back—the journey taking almost an hour—to Alford and confessed their trip. They asked permission to take out a party. This time Charles Logsdon, a thin-faced chap with a small mustache, asked to be in the advance with them. A group of sixteen volunteers formed a larger rear party.

The group was broken up into three parties with Wagner, Green and Logsdon in the lead. They crept from shellhole to shellhole and finally got within five yards. Each was carrying a torpedo. They made the last rush, threw the torpedos inside and ran. The pillbox blew up. Then the whole party rushed the pillboxes, one by one.

Hours were spent burying the dead from both sides in pits full of blankets, wornout snipers' sandals and unfired ammunition.

The writer doubled back through the blackened pillboxes between spurts caused by a sniper to the east. Every so often the sniper would use a "firecracker bullet." These explode with such a sharp noise—part of the Jap game of unsettling nerves—that one imagines the sniper is near. These firecrackers are safe enough so long as they hit the tree above you.

And then began, over this fought-for ground, a long, long walk to the peep-head.

—

JAPANESE IGNORE RED CROSS, BOMB NEW GUINEA HOSPITAL

With American Forces in New Guinea—December 31, 1942

With your water bottle spanking your sweat-soaked shorts and your knife case soaked black with perspiration, you stop at the intersection of a dozen little rabbit paths, all unmarked and all leading in different directions into the vine-netted screen. All are ankle-deep in the slipperiest, skiddiest mud in the world. Some lead into Japanese lines, some into yours.

American machine guns are chopping their way to the sea through Buna Mission nearby. The sun is hot and high. Every time you doff your helmet to clean the rivulets from your brow, you feel the sun trying to bring your brains to a thirty-second boil.

It has only been a few minutes since that three-man tommy-gun patrol you accompanied struck off into the jungle. That was back by those many-legged pandanus trees. You have no compass, because compasses here are rare.

You can hear shells from the 25-pounders going over and bursting almost immediately ahead. It is sensible to turn away. But your eyes keep watching the jungle on that side; you are unarmed, as regulations require. It would be pleasant to have that tommy-gun patrol nearby. And then a voice speaks from the shadows at your side: "Well, how did that operation turn out? How are you feeling now?"

These doctors never forget. It's Major Neil Swinton, of Boston. The last time you heard him say something like that was exactly two years ago when you came out from under his ether cone in a Boston hospital. Then it was plain Dr. Swinton. Now, standing by the trail waiting for the black boys to bring the litters of wounded from the front, Swinton speaks to you from the shadows once more.

This time, instead of the swirl of an ether dream, it's from the barely discernible path through the muddy lane leading to his hospital.

The hospital is hardly identifiable as such. It is a cluster of five huts, each about as big as a large drawing room. Its floors are not some polished urban surface but a grassy jungle floor. The supports are slender poles of grey betel nut, held together with vines. Overhead are tiers of grass, laced together, packed in rows like bunches of celery. Above are interwoven branches of thick trees. The hospital was placed in a clearing but got bombed despite its Geneva cross markings.

As you stand there, four black boongs carry in an American with shrapnel in his leg. Enemy artillery is still not wholly silenced. Two other boongs trot behind, watching carefully to see that the big banana leaf which covers the soldier's face does not slip aside. The other relieves if one bearer flags with fatigue.

Major Swinton gets busy immediately.

Swinton's hospital is one of several such portables flown across the Owen Stanleys. Although Swinton is not a Harvard man, two of the three other doctors are, and this is one of the portables which have been called Harvard units. Here in the front lines, all the nurses are helmeted soldiers. The nearest nurse in skirts is on the other side of the mountains, in Port Moresby.

At the other Harvard hospital, a couple of hundred yards deeper in the jungle, crisscrossed with the boots of three armies, you find gallant officers recuperating from the attack on Buna Mission. Here the doctors are headed by Major George Marks of Massachusetts General Hospital, a busy man with blondish hair, in shorts and naked to the waist. In a straight line, his cluster of grass roofs is probably slightly nearer to the Jap lines than Swinton's. Amputations have been carried out with the surgeon's flashlight drawing sniper bullets through the roofs.

Here young Captain Lawrence, a graduate from the University of Chicago, is just getting some rest under the mosquito net on his canvas cot. You leave the trail to fill your canteen at the bulging green udder of the hospital water bag. Mortars are belching into the enemy lines.

"The Japs raided us the second day," Lawrence says. His hair is clipped short, crew-cut style. "The first day the Japs sent over reccies, presumably to take photos. The next day what looked like navy-type dive bombers dropped both wing bombs on us. They are light but they were accurate. We had five personnel killed even before we started working. We make no atrocity claim, because we had not yet even had time to get our cross spread on the ground. But we believe the deep, dark bush better protection than any cross."

Captain Lawrence added that though the Japs generally shoot men going out to rescue the wounded, once on this front the litter-bearers brought in a man without being fired upon. But in the same spot the next day, rescuers were shot. "So you cannot make a rule even for a given patch of ground," he concluded.

The creek behind this hospital sometimes rises eight feet in a single rain and floods the wards. It took fifteen days of climbing slippery rocks in the continuous rain and mud of the "Roof of the World" for this portable to reach the Buna plain.

—

LESSONS LEARNED AT BUNA WILL PAY OFF FROM NOW ON

With the Allied Forces in New Guinea—January 2, 1943 (Delayed by Censor)

With Buna Mission fallen into our hands and Giropa Point swept clean by Australian tanks, the Allied command made clear today that the Sanananda front of Papua's triple beachheads remains high on the list of unsettled affairs. Gona is taken on the left, Buna on the right, but Sanananda in the middle remains.

Even as Old Glory rose over the handful of smoking shacks on stilts that had been Buna Mission, and snipers who had slipped through our lines in a desperate effort to escape were tumbling from their treetops to the rattle of tommy guns, the lessons of this bitter prolonged campaign were being discussed among Americans and Australians in many foxholes and on the hard steel seat of many a jeep as it bounced over the corduroy trails.

Papua cannot be ours until the hundreds of Japs dug in along the Sanananda trail are uprooted by the same combination of air attacks, tanks and heavy weapons as eventually broke Buna to the east. The last heavy Jap bombings on Christmas Eve were made by full moon and the Buna victory came in the dark of the moon, just before the regular rainy season. In this sodden, mud-slogged country, weather is everything—one element that modern warfare has left unchanged.

Smoke ascending from the last pillbox on the old air field announced that the Australians had literally smoked out the last Japs. The pillbox, which contains the bodies of over a hundred Japs, resisted for seventy minutes against the assault of three Australian-manned tanks, which delivered 150 shells at point-blank range. The tanks bored through the logs by concentrating their fire on a single spot.

Tonight our artillery was silent for the first time, but the Japs had offered no mortar fire for about ten days. Their sole defense has been a network of snipers in the highest, densest trees, combined with deeply dug trenches venting continuous automatic-weapon fire. The narrow defiles, flanked by armpit-deep quagmire and backed by the sea, compensated for the fact that they were at all times outnumbered.

Our mortars carried off the honors as an offensive weapon. Their high projectiles, beautifully controlled from forward command posts, gave confidence to the troops, unaccustomed to seeing high explosives from their own lines fall less than thirty yards away.

In the jungles, where it is commonplace for patrols to approach within twenty yards of each other's lines, the mortar becomes more and more the ace played close to the fighter's belt—sometimes so close that it is terrifying. Mortar crews, often exposed to enemy counter-fire and sniper attack, are among the coolest, most admirable, least-known soldiers we possess. When a fuse cut by fractions of an inch may determine whether shells fall within their lines or ours, the mortarist becomes the William Tell of forest war.

Ask any heat-weary, black-bearded fighter with mud impregnated in every pore as he lies in Buna's bypaths—tommy gun at his side, still scanning the trees for snipers—whether this has been an amphibious war. He will part his mud-caked lips slightly, lift his mud-heavy eyelids and answer, "Don't I look it?"

Yet this has been an amphibious war in only a narrow sense. All attacks, both American and Australian, including Gona, Buna and Cape Endaiadere, have been delivered from land. There has been none of the leap-frogging from beach to beach, from river-mouth to inlet, that characterized the Jap offensive in Malaya. But many Middle Westerners have been forced to swim through mud-clogged streams under fire, alone, sometimes knocking aside others. And in the break-up of both Buna and Cape Endaiadere, many Japs swam ineffectually seaward for their lives.

Kitchener's saying, "You can attempt anything with an enemy who does not move," was modified here by the discovery that there is much you can do which costs you more than it costs the enemy.

The unaccustomed jungle fighting has kept alive the American genius for improvisation. What everyone, from the blackest dogface to the commanding general himself, seems to agree on is that the American spirit lacks nothing for this foul, energy-sapping and tricky war against unfriendly nature, canned food, diarrhetic water, malarial swamps, suffocating heat and a merciless, extremely cunning enemy, who believes he becomes a god by dying on the field of battle.

Our wounded have had treatment from surgeons better, as one doctor said, "than if hit by a car in Fifth Avenue and carried by ambulance to a hospital."

The Allied soldier, knowing the tommy gun is his best friend, has learned, although city-bred and pavement-raised, to give meaning to every tremble of a leaf and to resist premature fire. The hardest decision in the jungle is when a trigger should be pressed.

GET OUT THAT SQUIRREL GUN; NEED DAN'L BOONES IN GUINEA

With the Advanced American Forces near Sanananda— January 8, 1943

Sons of Daniel Boone and Davy Crockett, where are you? You Tom Sawyers and Huck Finns of America, you squirrel hunters and turkey shooters, stand by us! We need minutemen like Lexington's. We need crack shots. We need woodsmen.

Such is the refrain, less lyrically expressed, that goes up from campfires on the steaming, swampy Sanananda front.

Tanks, the 13-ton General Stuarts, broke Japan's network of marsh-flanked coconut groves at Buna. But for the most unusual phenomenon of this campaign, one must look to the Jap fighting defensively against the American Army for the first time in history. And the enemy's strongest threat is her jungle sniper.

The great lesson of the campaign, when we have still not fully countered the enemy landing on July 21 [1942], is that a Jap woodsman cannot be beaten by the fact that our Garand is a superior rifle to their .25 caliber. Only when our infantryman is more cunning in jungle guile can the sniper menace be eradicated.

This calls for a new kind of soldier similar to the frontiersman. Clay-pigeon champions and professional marksmen, with their stances and quantitative records, are about as useful here as a racing driver bringing wounded on a peep through seas of mud. Sniping and counter-sniping are arts which go back to the last Indian wars, but America's rural tradition has been pushed to the rear by industrialization. Here in Papua, it is a couple of shoeless boys from Kentucky, Tennessee, or the Arkansas hills who feel at home stalking the Japs. Only reluctantly are city-bred boys coming to realize that their deficiency—"if we could only see where the little so-and-sos are"—is one they alone can correct, by acquiring woodsmen's eyes.

Pleasant though it is to imagine that Japan can be beaten by sinking aircraft carriers and massacring by the thousands, it is clear to all who grapple the enemy here that cleaning up the vast tropical wilderness through the Indies, Malaya, Indo-China and the Philippines will not be accomplished easily. Some army is going to have to walk in on the Japs' fortifications, which resist both artillery fire and bombing because they are underground, dig every Jap out at bayonet point and kill him. To do that, someone must deal with that ornery creature, the sniper. Every position has a complement commanding a view in several directions. Most are lashed in trees.

In Jap warfare, the idea is always to divide the enemy's attention. In an offensive, the effort is to get him to look over his shoulder and imagine himself surrounded. In defensive war the effort is to pin down the attackers with a machine gun, then pick them off with fire from the trees. If the attackers advance, automatic fire gets them; if they flatten, the snipers go to work. The key to every Jap position is not the position itself, but the snipers concealed against the sky all around.

The trouble about cleaning out snipers is the same old thing: where are they? Their small bodies, like those of Filipinos, lend themselves to concealment. Their powder is smokeless and some rifles have silencers. This means that a bullet's whisper is often the first intimation a patrol gets that it is under observation.

Japs on the defensive often withhold fire in order to encourage advance by a larger force. Or only one sniper will fire when four or five are in the trees.

The American forces with fewest sniper casualties achieve this by systematic "hosing" of treetops—heavier firepower rather than superior woodsmanship. It requires great expenditure of tommy gun ammunition and slows up a main attack against palmetto bunkers. Besides spoiling any surprise by chewing up the foliage with fire, it lets some snipers remain concealed behind these sometimes 100-foot trees. Using vine slings, the Japs swing themselves around, keeping the trunk as a protection, squirrel-wise. Therefore it is never certain that mere volume of fire, as a substitute for hitting the sniper with a single aimed bullet, is the answer.

The Japs also use straw-filled dummies on cords which, when shot down, invite an advance, offering prey for live snipers who act as lookouts and carry signal whistles. When hit they rarely fall, and are replaced. Snipers work in teams, climb with splay-toed tabitabi sandals, and hoist ammunition and food with vines.

Primitive war reverses the industrial order. In the jungle, a city boy is a hick. Army rifle training calls for targets on a painted background, and combat firing teaches shooting while advancing. But nobody can hit what he cannot see.

Can our infantrymen make their eyes as sharp as the pioneers'? Can our scouts conceal their bodies better than Japs? Can they move more silently, climb more surely, wait more patiently? Corps of man-hunters, trained in woodland wisdom, would today be more valuable in the western Pacific than millions of marksmen who need stalking rather than killing practice. This is history's first true jungle war with modern weapons. More surprises are coming.

—

HYMIE EPSTEIN WOULDN'T QUIT, HERO IN GUINEA

With the American Troops near Sanananda—January 18, 1943

"He was one swell little guy, that Hymie."

That's all his company will say about Hyman Epstein. They are still living in drowned mudholes amid sniping, fighting off fever. But when they mention his name among those who have gone, there is a special tightening around the mouth and a vagueness of the eyes as they look away.

"In war I guess the best go first," says Major Bert Zeeff of Grand Rapids, who has fought in two wars. "That kid was the best."

This is the last twelve hours of Hymie Epstein's life as Zeeff tells it.

"We were sent out to carry rations to a unit cut off in the forest. They had several dead and a number of wounded. Epstein was a medical aide. Medical aides are forbidden by the Geneva Convention to bear arms. Casualties among their ranks have been as high or higher than among fighting troops because when the Japs wound a man with sniping, they do not finish him off but wait for the company aide, and get both. This is accepted practice in this jungle game where the Japs' one aim is take a maximum number of American lives before being wiped out.

"The Japs must have heard us creeping along because they moved a machine gun across our line of crawl. They got another gun and had two converging lanes of fire directed upon our mudholes. Then they sent snipers around the sides so they could pick us where we were if we stopped moving. We had to stop because it was getting dark and we could not see where we were going. Then they opened fire."

Epstein, a small, slight youngster from Omaha, was lying at the major's side about three feet away to the right. Suddenly, a man about eight feet ahead was hit in the neck by a machine-gun bullet.

"Both Epstein and myself saw him get it. But the Japs knew we were there and kept their fire right in that spot. You could see bullets hitting all around. I would not order anyone to go out into that fire to get that man. I could not. It was just throwing one life after another. But this little kid, he crawls right from the mud to the wounded man who lies on his back. Epstein gets out his sulfanilamide powder and bandages and, lying on his back, binds the wounded man's neck. Then he crawls back with bullets all around him.

"Just before darkness came down—with Jap snipers firing from the sides and working around behind, while the machine guns continued in front trying to probe out the Americans in the mudholes—another man was hit in the head. Without any hesitation out crawls that kid again with his packet, gets to the man, rolls over and, lying on his back, binds up his head and gives the man sulfanilamide. I could not understand how he ever got back that time. They simply poured fire around him. But he did get back."

Through the night the men hugged the mud as low as possible while Japanese machine-gunners and snipers systematically worked over the muddy layers of fallen foliage where they lay. Then dawn began to lighten the sky toward Buna.

"You could hear the men talking all night. 'Did you see what little Epstein did?' they would say. Word had gone the whole length of the line in whispers. At dawn the Japs began to get more accurate with their fire. A man over on the left was hit and word came a medic was needed. Epstein crawled down the line. Five minutes later, word passed up the line that he was dead. How they finally got him was this: a badly wounded guy was out there with fire all around. Epstein went out and just got him fixed. Then the Japs put in everything they had. Epstein could have crawled back, but he chose to stick until he finished the job. He stayed a little too long.

"What I will always remember was that wounded man when he dragged himself in. It's not often you hear a soldier crying and he was a tough baby himself, but he was crying, crying like anything as he reached us. He kept saying between sobs, 'Somebody's gotta go out there and take care of Epstein. Epstein's bleeding to death. Somebody's quick gotta go out and get Epstein.' Of course he was delirious. We could see Epstein was already dead. But even in delirium and with his severe wound, that guy felt worse about Epstein than himself.

"I've seen a lot of men do things out there in the swamp that never would be believed. We buried the man he tried to save by moonlight the next night, and we buried Epstein by day as we pulled back through the forest. You never know who is going to be a good soldier and who isn't. But when they are handing honors around, you can give mine to that little Hymie Epstein. And that goes for all of us."

—

THE SAGA OF THE "LOST COMPANY"

(Attention has been drawn to the Sanananda front only since the fall of the Buna area permitted an Allied concentration of forces. Fighting was continuous at Sanananda for seven weeks before that, with American troops of the 32d Division and Australians. The present situation makes possible the release of the story of the "Lost Company" of the 32d Division which held out for three weeks in a roadblock on the Sanananda road, entirely surrounded. The story is told by George Weller, whose dispatches five weeks ago from Sanananda were the only American accounts from that front prior to Buna's fall.)

With Advanced American Troops at Sanananda—January 21–24, 1943 (Delayed)

Japan's most prized weapon is a stab in the back. But the thrust from the rear has even a more honored place in the Nipponese lexicon of military tactics than in diplomacy. Army commanders will do anything possible to get a harassing force in their enemy's rear. If they cannot give the fatal stab, the Japs try to cause the enemy to yield that "look over the shoulder," which can begin the disintegration of forces.

The story of Sanananda's "Lost Company" is that of the American use of this weapon of trickery. A small but sternly resolved American force, entirely encircled by Jap troops whose entrenchments were superior, was able to cut the Sanananda road and hold a dagger at the back of the Japanese front line troops. These men, who fought and died to maintain that "island" amid Jap forces until Buna's fall, released the main American and Australian troops for Sanananda.

The plan to strike the Japs' rear and cut off their forward lines from using the Sanananda road, which was 3½ miles from their beachhead to our front lines, was led by Major George Bond. Two companies of American infantry, plus another equipped with machine guns and rifles, comprised the force selected for the daring operation. I and K Companies were under Bond's direct leadership, while their support—where combined American and Australian forces already faced the Japs across the ten-foot wide muddy road—was in the hands of Major Bernt Baetcke.

Company K set forth on November 23 to establish a command post deep in the jungle on the left of the road between Soputa and Sanananda. The mud varied from ankle to waist depth. Often they tripped on giant buried roots and fell. Finally they discovered a place behind enemy lines, parallel with Jap artillery positions a theoretical mile distant across the jungle, but three hours' floundering from the road.

In bypassing enemy lines in this sweeping curve westward, Company K felt only desultory sniper fire. But that showed the Japs knew something was coming.

Company I—leaving a third of the company and K to protect the thin rampart of earth around the new command post—started out to cut the road, accompanied by a force with machine guns. The party's 367 men were commanded by Bond.

"Follow the sun," were the orders. The only maps were inaccurate but it was certain that by heading east they would cross the road somewhere. From 7:30 to 11:30 they crept through the swamp. The sniping had fallen off in a deadly lull.

They reached a dry patch of kunai grass; in the middle was a huge fallen log, five feet thick. When the point men, creeping low, rounded this log, terrific fire opened up from a machine gun on the left and snipers in the trees. There was mortar fire, too—not of a "Charlie McCarthy" mortar, with a saddle so a Jap infantryman can place it on his knee like a ventriloquist's dummy—but heavy mortars.

The Americans had crossed the Jap trail through which the enemy front lines were supplied. It was an ambush.

During the terrible days to follow, the Japs stubbornly held this bottle-neck on the American line of communications. It came to be known simply as "the log." Where the Japs would lay ambushes for food and ammunition columns was never certain. But whenever the Americans passed this log they were fired upon.

"As we lost men we filled columns with new ones," said one officer. "We came to know it was necessary to crawl the full length of the log, go around the end, then double back. The Jap fire went straight along the log's top. But always there would be some wise guy who would hear voices of our point men on the other side and decide to take a short cut by crawling over. Almost invariably they got him."

Why, during the weeks that the Lost Company was supplied along this slender swamp path, was nothing done to eliminate the pillbox? The reason was that because the men were looping around enemy supply lines, it was inevitable that Jap and American paths should intersect. The log furnished protection against machine guns, whereas any new crossroads might have proved even hotter.

The Americans, having established a supply dump and advanced battalion headquarters, continued following the sun, seeking the narrow jungle road in an effort to cut the Japs' motorized supply from Sanananda. They knew by pressing east they must strike the road somewhere. The Japs evidently phoned back word that a large American party was fighting its way through.

When the Americans, mudded to the hips, laden with ammunition and food, and sweating streams in the humid, breathless shadows of the swamp, reached a point afterward determined as 200 yards from the road, machine-gun fire bit the open green quagmire ahead. As the Yanks flattened, Jap snipers in the trees opened fire. It was the regular Jap sequence of pinning down with a machine-gun barrage, then picking off with snipers.

The party took cover behind giant-roofed mangroves while bullets hissed among them.

The sun was low and soon darkness would overtake them. Isolated deep within the Jap lines, they would be easy prey for raiding snipers. Ignorant of their own whereabouts, they were uncertain whether they could find the road before night. The officers decided to send out patrols. The patrols paddled through the encircling muck awhile without drawing Jap fire, but they had hardly gone 75 yards through the swamp when machine guns challenged them again. They felt they must be getting near the road. Captain John Shirley of Grand Rapids decided the issue. "Let's get these so-and so's," he said. "Put your bayonets on your rifles."

Shirley led the charge himself. It was not a charge such as history books describe, at full run. It was half-wading, half-swimming, with enemy fire flickering all around. Knee-deep mud made the charge at once gallant and clumsy. Hidden roots threw the men on their faces; they struggled up and went on. Finally Shirley and some men reached the jagged line of trenches where the Japs kept swinging their machine guns to bear, then half-dived, half-floundered, upon the enemy.

The trenches were cleared.

Within minutes the Americans burst from the swamp onto the road. They had no choice and did not dare push forward or back to a better location. They had to take whatever strip of road they happened to blunder on first.

Today, standing where mud-blinded tommy-gunners, followed by sweating carriers with the wounded on litters behind, saw a deserted, muddy road amid the hostile jungle, the writer could appreciate how lucky they had been.

Frequently flooded, the road was sand mixed with mud. The men dug holes for shelter immediately, and cut shallow trenches for machine guns as well as heavier guns pointing both ways.

The Japs apparently knew they had been outmaneuvered. Where the Americans hit the road was a small enemy supply dump and repair shops. What the men began to call "our 5 o'clock rush" had yielded modest prizes. There were two big supply trucks fitted with maintenance equipment, lathes, dies, and clutch disks. There were two shacks full of motor supplies. Best of all were several tin cracker boxes and bags of fresh onions, an unbelievable treasure in can-fed Papua.

This find—symbolic of the difference between being supplied by sea, as the Japs were, and by transport plane and parachute, like the Americans—delighted Lieutenant John Filarski, supply officer of the Lost Company. As he told the writer, "Those onions were swell, but the beginning was also the end of that kind of food."

As dusk fell the officers marked out an area running 350 yards along the road and extending 125 yards into the jungle as the "perimeter."

The word, in jungle fighting, means any area where you can dig an encircling line of foxholes around a command post and maintain fire directed out. It is the jungle equivalent of the pioneers' wagon train circle to repel Indians. Within such a perimeter one is always exposed to sniper fire from the outside.

Digging their foxholes with short shovels, the Americans were under the impression they were only 600 yards beyond their own lines. In fact, as aerial photos later revealed, they were cut off 1800 yards—more than a mile—*behind* the Jap front lines, just 2½ miles along the road from the Jap beachhead, and they could hear the enemy's single precious anti-aircraft gun belching.

The Lost Company was now cut off from Baetcke, their commanding officer. The phone line running through quagmire, giant fern, kunai grass, clearing and more quagmire was immediately severed by the Japs. Walkie-talkies were unworkable.

This meant the force could communicate only by runner. It required one whole day for a runner to get to the front lines and the next to return, with excellent prospects of being ambushed. So it was necessary to repair the phone lines and get messages across before the Japs severed them, as they did sometimes twice daily.

The two phone men for the Lost Company who attempted to keep the line working back to the advanced battalion command post established in the jungle were Marcellus Nye and Gerwin Dollinger. Nye, a short, stocky 28-year-old, used to work for a phone company, but gave up the work because he preferred driving a cab. Nye says: "Mostly we worked in water to our knees. Those Jap clippers tried cute tricks. They would nearly always remove the wire, sixty or a hundred feet, increasing each time to more than I could carry. Their idea was to make me go back for wire and lose another day. Once they cut out the longest piece yet. The gap was a full 120 yards. But they left a piece coiled up, as though accidentally. When I began working to join the ends across the swamp I got pretty well along before I discovered they'd cut off just enough so the ends would not quite meet."

According to orders, Nye at first went out only with the columns trains which carried food and ammo up and wounded or feverish back. But the trains could not wait while Nye searched for breaks; besides, the wire was sometimes cut three-quarters of an hour after being spliced. At one time Captain Peter Dalponte ordered him to remain within the perimeter two days, Jap fire being especially heavy.

The roadblock party was completely cut off during this time. Nye, restless, asked for two tommy-gunners but led them himself, carrying a tommy gun. Fingering the wire backward, he reached the famous log.

"I noticed something funny. There was a bush growing. I had crawled by the other end often and never remembered seeing the bush. I signaled the other guys to keep quiet. Pretty soon the bush moved a little. I saw a Jap's legs and arms behind. The bush was tied around his waist and he had more bush on his helmet. I was pretty far off but I took aim and squeezed out a short burst. That bush got up from the end of the log and ran into the jungle."

The Japs kept a phone line on the other side of the road, and once Nye found an experimental wire made from American splicings, which he gleefully rendered unworkable. Nye failed to splice our wire only four days.

The Americans' first decision after finding they were isolated by phone cuts was to attack. For three days the enemy had been throwing explosive mortars at the Americans lying in water in their foxholes. There was a Japanese encampment southeast of the roadblock; an attack on it turned into another bayonet assault where one of the bravest was Sergeant Robert Devereaux, who had already contracted malaria. Not until his temperature touched 106° could Devereaux be evacuated over the perilous trail back through the jungle to recover.

Everything about this campaign is incredible, and probably fevers this high are unbelievable. They mean somewhat less in Papua where fatigue brings out fevers latent in nearly everyone. The writer has often worked for considerable periods with a temperature over 100°. He has seen men still

fighting with their temperature at 102°. On the Sanananda front he saw
five men with temperatures 104° and above pull themselves from foxholes
and reach a hospital on foot. Many men with temperatures of over 106°
have been evacuated by air and lived. At the American roadblock in the Jap
rear, litters were few and evacuation through snipers dangerous and long,
but when fevers reached 104°, the men went back, sometimes protestingly,
carried by men with temperatures of 102°.

Today, when the American roadblock is no longer isolated, disturbed only
by furtive shots from the last remaining snipers in the trees, it is no longer
known as the Lost Company, but as Huggins—as it doubtless will be
marked on historical maps.

Captain Meredith Huggins, of Salem, Oregon, was one of two officers
who led the island on the Jap road for eight days. He became commander
when, after taking a ration party across the jungle to a tiny encampment,
on starting back he learned from Baetcke that enemy fire had thinned the
officers in the outpost.

Asked whether he could hold the Japs, he replied: "I'll hold that place
until hell freezes over," and returned to the inferno of mortar fire and
sniping.

It was appropriate that the Huggins roadblock should be named after
the man who, ordinarily an operational officer, should go in a single day
from being leader of a ration train harassed by snipers to the commander of
the "lost" garrison. For the supply trains kept the Americans in the jungle
alive. Even Dalponte, his successor after Huggins was wounded, came in as
supply column leader and found himself commanding the garrison.
Columns were frequently full of men who throbbed with fever, loaded down
with ammunition and food. Supply trains went if possible every two days
from the command post—itself deep in the jungle behind the Jap lines—to
Huggins. Anyone who made the eight-hour journey through the ambush-
ridden swamp was a hero.

The most frequent leader of such trains was Lieutenant Zina Carter,
now Captain. Very much alive today, he says quietly: "The trail was just a
death trap from one end to the other. You hated to start out. You knew the
Japs were always waiting and you had to run their fire in at least two
places—at the log, and at another place where their machine guns had a

fire lane under which we crawled through the grass. But when you got there and saw how those guys were living and saw their expressions when you came through the jungle, that paid for everything. Their faces were thinner than ours, but the way they lighted up when they saw we'd got through again was worth everything. They knew then that we hadn't let them down. It was like a little Bataan, but harder for them in a way because they knew they could sneak out any time they wanted. It was only their willpower that kept them together, and the fact they knew that if it was possible to fight through the Jap lines we'd get there."

The Lost Company drew four full-scale attacks from different directions. Two occurred while Shirley was in command, and two more while Huggins headed the sniper-surrounded garrison. Usually the enemy were divided into squads of ten or twelve men, trying to find a loophole in the American rectangle of machine-gun flanked potholes. When these attacks all failed, the Japs tried to make Huggins useless by building more pillboxes on both sides of the road. (The writer has seen these pillboxes bombarded day after day with mortar fire. One, taken this afternoon, revealed 150 bodies. Three other such strongpoints in the jungle remain but will probably have been hammered into muddy death by the time these words are read.)

The American response was to send harassing patrols. The enemy response was to put their mountain gun, in addition to mortars, on Huggins. If a man lived past the morning shelling at 5:30 a.m., he was certain of life—except for mortars and snipers—until the 6 p.m. evening shelling. Japs continually wandered into the perimeter of roadside foxholes stretching along the jungle's edge. Some were dazed, and half starved, some only in shorts; many past recovery, full of malaria or dysentery. Behind them were plenty of well-fed Japs with plenty of ammunition.

Volunteer patrols often ran into snipers. Frequent rains held the Americans to their inundated foxholes. Once Dalponte (in command from December 9 until Christmas Day) had a whole party pinned down en route to Huggins with food and ammunition. The point members ran into a figure dressed in an American uniform in a kunai field. His skin looked white and they said, reassuringly, "It's alright, fella; this is only a ration party going through." As the man fled into the jungle, they saw it was a Jap.

Among the more successful patrol leaders was Sergeant George Zietlow, who authored the famous "Zietlow system" for keeping down itchy fingers when the enemy were fishing for machine-gun locations. The Japs have many tricks for this, from throwing chains of firecrackers (to simulate an automatic weapon) to exposing a single soldier as a target. Zietlow also tried the Jap trick of moving the machine guns' location frequently, and found it worked.

Meanwhile the swamp trail was getting constantly more dangerous.

For seven days, from December 9 to 15, the Lost Company was literally lost in its roadblock behind Japanese lines. Dysentery, malaria and ringworm infected some men in the water-filled foxholes and the cases increased faster than they could be evacuated. Food ran lower and lower. Discouragement, too, made inroads in the weakening men under Dalponte, a tall, thin, resilient young commander. To keep the garrison well deployed along the 350 yards of sniper-surrounded road, it was ordered that no more than two or three men should ever gather.

Dalponte, who knew the jungle trail better than anyone, assured his men that even though the phone was cut, food would come through. It was impossible to drop supplies from aircraft because the Japs dominated the air with their machine guns. Sometimes supply trains were halted by the besieged and needy themselves. At least one time the train was stopped midway by telephoneman Joseph Kramarz—one of the men who proved their courage dozens of times—who said: "Don't come in today. We just had a counter-attack from the Japs. It's too tough for you to make."

Then came the afternoon of the 15th, when Lieutenant Zina Carter broke through the jungle with a long line of green-clad perspiring men plugging along behind him. They had shot their way through two lanes of fire. Dirty, hungry men dragged themselves from foxholes and met the newcomers with hope in their eyes.

The "guys back there" had kept faith and not abandoned them. There were belts of gleaming cartridges for their guns, cans of beef and beans, quinine to batter down their fever, more bars of chocolate and more crackers. Best of all, there was something incredibly wonderful in the sacks on the backs of the men drenched to the waist. There was canned heat.

For days, unable to light fires to heat water, they had lain in the coffin-shaped foxholes in rainwater, under the whispering bullets of snipers. Not once had a warm drink brought life to their diarrhetic insides. Now there was heat—heat that was safe, heat without smoke. At their first drink of tea, for which the men tottered from their holes, life began to come back. Their deeply-lined, bearded, mud-marked faces relaxed as the first warmth in days made itself felt deep in their cold stomachs.

The original plan was a line of communications both to left and right of the road, where enemy fortifications were stiffest, but Buna had drained the manpower necessary for the double-pincer operations. More than three weeks of fighting under Major Bert Zeeff were required before the line of dugouts could be pierced.

The attack was launched from the banana plantation held by Captain John Blamey, nephew of the Allied ground force commander. The Japs were dug in across the stream bisecting the plantation.

In the first fight, from a kunai grass patch, this force ambushed a marching column of thirty Japs by early moonlight. The grass was seven feet tall and this American use of their own tactics surprised the enemy. Their machine guns aimed too high but when they used firecrackers to draw fire the trick was partly successful.

The small Jap counter-attack was eerie. They crossed the road in four waves of four men each, crouched over. They wore leggings and helmets and kept saying "Good day, good day." Every Jap was killed or wounded.

The force under Zeeff, however, found itself under heavy sniper fire during five days' isolation—three on the right side of the road, two on the left. But the phone wire back to Blamey's was never cut.

After passing through the banana plantation, the Japs' main force held the west and 150 Americans and 60 Aussies the east. Daily rations at Blamey's were one can of meat and beans, four crackers, and a chocolate bar, until the Aussies captured three tons of Jap rice with canned cabbage and onions, lifting the crisis.

The Americans attacked across the creek and captured two machine guns. In this attack Captain Blamey was killed, but the Japs were cleaned out.

Zeeff's two and a half platoons, ignorant exactly where the isolated Huggins-Dalponte roadblock was, had bogged down in the swamp and itself become cut off. But now the Japs had their only path of motor transport from the beachhead to their front line stopped in two places by American forces. The Japs attacked viciously.

Zeeff, to whom your correspondent talked, like other Sanananda leaders said immediately on emerging from the jungle that he asked by phone for reinforcements but they were unavailable. In the words of Private Eddie Eben, "We simply dug in with everything we had. We hacked into the mud with mess kits, spoons, bayonets, as well as short shovels and axes, and got six inches of earth around us—enough to protect us from Jap machine-gun fire sweeping the road."

Finally rain, through the noise on millions of leaves, made escape possible though it made the swamp deeper. Zeeff led them out in utter darkness, lighted only by the storm's flashes. The fact that the Japs did not cut the phone line made it possible for Zeeff to retrace the wire through his fingers after days of isolation.

Another attack on enemy lines from Blamey's banana grove started early on December 5—machine-gun fire preceded by a creeping barrage of artillery. Mortar shells hit a Jap dugout of seven ground snipers; only three came out alive.

The Americans advanced fifty yards but were soon halted by machine-gun fire and snipers. James Kelly described his experience: "Another fellow and I were lying twenty yards from a Jap pillbox. We got about eight Japs before being pinned down. We lay in the sun, not moving, for three and a half hours. The kunai grass was short, we knew the Japs were watching. I suggested we run. He said, 'You go first.' I agreed but said he should wait fifteen minutes, then run, not crawl. I ran, but he decided to crawl. They got him through the spine."

In these attacks, the Americans under Lieutenant William Johnson, a young Grand Rapids lawyer, followed the practice established by Boerem and Baetcke of talking over attacks beforehand. Chances were weighed, suggestions invited, and the purpose of relieving the isolated Huggins force kept always in view.

The roadblock under Dalponte made efforts to meet Johnson's force by sending out patrols, but the jungle was getting more dangerous. Neither the Japs nor the Americans were certain of their location. All that was certain was how the two forces lay in stripes across the road. At the south were the American lines, then opposing Japs. Next came Zeeff's roadblock, then more Japs. Next came the isolated Huggins-Dalponte roadblock, and finally the solid force of hundreds of Japs stretching to Sanananda Beach-head, three miles away.

Dalponte, after numerous Jap harassing attacks, sent a patrol on December 20 to reach the Johnson force, striving to create a communications line to right of the road. The patrol lost two men out of eight and returned without finding Johnson.

Three days later, determined that the Lost Company should somehow be relieved before Christmas, Johnson talked over the possibility of staking everything on a final thrust. (Modest to the point of self-effacement, Johnson says: "I myself was reluctant but my men virtually pushed me into the thing.")

The Japs arranged the usual alarm system of vine fences but when their fire opened Sergeant Ray Evans took his men in, plastering the enemy with grenades. "Then we went *brr—brr—brr* with our tommy guns and they tried to get away."

All night the battle of grenades went on between the creeping Americans and Jap rear-line dugouts. Dalponte's force could hear the battle and sent out a force at Johnson's request. They ran through the Jap line of fire, losing two men, but made contact. With the help of Aussies who intended to relieve Dalponte, a trench was dug to ensure communication. In a final attack the Americans smashed through, and with the Australians on December 23 they reached the Lost Company who had endured fever, hunger and enemy fire for twenty-three days, surviving athwart the road 1800 yards behind the Jap lines.

Dalponte says: "When we saw those Aussies and Americans break through, at first we could not believe we were actually going to be relieved. What with snipers and being shelled and getting counter-attacks, we had got so we believed it would never end. The Aussie commander was surprised when I said, 'Until I see your men get down there in our foxholes, I won't be able to believe we can really go.' Then they got down and we saw it was true."

A Chicagoan, Lawrence Ghilardi, said, "It seemed kind of hard to believe that we would ever get out of there. And when they reached us and told us we could go, I can't describe how I felt."

Jerome Stoffel said: "What I thought was, now maybe we'll be able to go somewhere and forget Sanananda."

The Aussies did not come empty-handed. They had stolen two loaves of bread, shipped them across the mountains by air, and brought them to the Yanks as a Christmas gift.

—

[probably somewhere in Australia]
July 9th, 1943.

MISS ARLENE SHIRLEY,
DETROIT, <u>MICHIGAN</u>

Dear Miss Shirley,

I have delayed replying to your letter about your brother until I could, as you asked me to do, positively confirm the news of his death which you received some six months ago.

It grieves me to say to you and Captain Shirley's Mother that it is true that he is dead.

You know already from my dispatches the gallant circumstances of his sacrifice.

To this I can only add that I have visited the new grave in the formal American cemetery where he now lies. His body has been transferred from the temporary cemetery near the front to this more formal and possibly permanent resting place. The grave is clearly marked and the cemetery carefully cared for. His identification tag is bound on the cross on the grave.

Declaration of the individual graves is not allowed, for reasons you will be quick to understand. I therefore took only the liberty of saying a short prayer on behalf of you and your family, as I felt perhaps you might have wished me to do.

Sincerely yours,

George Weller
Correspondent: Chicago Daily News.

Chicago Boys Trample Japs in Jungle Mud

With the American Troops Before
Sanananda—January 22, 1943 (Delayed)

As shells from our artillery whined their keening chant overhead and mortars bumped the earth underfoot, a green-clad man, wet to the armpits and dripping from the knees down, stepped from the swamp beside the Sanananda road where this correspondent stood. His face, sunk deep in his mired helmet, was sweaty, dirty and bearded. Two of the four grenade pouches slung sideways across his chest were empty. His fingers still were locked around his tommy gun, his left hand forward and his right hand back on the trigger. His expression was hard and challenging.

"The road is clear," I said. "They just started running from that last pillbox on the right."

A sniper hinged toward us. A fusillade of tommy guns overwhelmed him and only then did the American soldier's expression—duplicated by dozens of men ahead and behind who were soaking wet and caked with several days' layers of mud, and stepping similarly from the swamp to the only road—relax slightly.

This is the new American soldier. He is a killer. He has seen friends shot beside him. He has buried his friends. He has learned what it is to be hunted by Japs without mercy and to hunt them back and kill them coldly and absolutely—twice and three times over if necessary.

Before the war Bernard Zidrich, 22, of Chicago, was employed in a canned soup factory. Now he is a killer and sleeps beside the dead. From the pot-shaped helmet in which he carries water and sometimes washes himself, to his feet, swollen inside mud-impregnated shoes, he is a jungle fighter. Every day I talk with scores of these men who live under fire.

Today was the last day's hard fighting to the accompaniment of artillery and mortars. Zidrich said: "We had been in there four days and made three attacks without much progress. Today they cracked. Anyone we saw, up or down, we shot full of holes. My company passed the last forty minutes sweeping through pillboxes. I caught one Jap trying to fake dead, but I saw his chest rise and finished him off."

Toward evening, while I was investigating Jap regimental headquarters—filled with bodies agape as though yawning and hands thrown carelessly in stiffened attitudes of death—a spurt of shots broke out fifteen yards away. A man who had been checking inside the dugout on the opposite side of the road toppled over, shot through the throat.

My day at the front began at the hospital, with patients being hastily dragged from their grass huts as snipers opened fire. Where the patients lay a moment before, riflemen crouched, peering into the tops of mighty trees against the sky. It is hardly necessary to get any more instruction in the tremendous difficulties hidden in that phrase "mopping up." Thirty-five more Japs escaped from the perimeter and slipped through the jungle, headed south. As darkness fell and the moon rose tonight, they were being engaged by our patrols.

There is nothing more disagreeable than a long hot day of being shot at, unless it is sleeping in a leaky broken-down hut where the preceding night's rainfall exceeded ten inches and everything you own including your body is partly broken, rusty, moss-covered, insect-infected, diarrhetic, fevered, dirty, diseased, wet and muddy, or smells of putrefying Japs. Some idea of much of this country is conveyed by an official description: "Small islands in a flowing inland sea."

The Sanananda road, opened by the Americans' taking pillboxes some 2½ miles from the coast, was marked with sagging skeletons flattened in their uniforms. The dugouts were dotted with newly dead, some still in blue navy trousers and undershirts, others in the Japanese Army's peaked, starred cap. The first mine left behind by the enemy, which I passed, was cleverly hidden. Someone had scrawled the word *"mine"* in the mud and I surrounded the place with palm leaves and branches to make it conspicuous for coming troops.

Tonight the commander of the Australian forces in Sanananda, Major General G. A. Vassey, told correspondents that American troops had held up well and been "several hundred percent improved" by their first experience in battle. He said that our pleasure with the campaign's being ended six months after the Japs landed in Buna should be moderated by the knowledge that the enemy in the final stages possessed neither aircraft, artillery, nor mortars.

The tommy guns continue stammering in the moonlit jungle nearby as this is written. Cannons are thumping energetically and Jap bombers cross overhead. Of approximately a hundred Japs killed today, thirty-three blundered about 5:30 this morning into an encampment of forty Americans commanded by Captain Edward Reams, a young farmer from Montana. We spoke shortly afterward deep in the jungle. "Our sentries woke those not already on their feet but two men had close calls. Frank Navoli was awakened by getting a bayonet poked in his stomach but managed to kick the Jap in the jaw, grab his gun and shoot him. Bill Huff got pricked in the shoulder but grabbed his tommy gun and got his man."

Another party from this same company gave the details of storming the Jap regimental headquarters, surrounded by dugouts and a dozen camouflaged trucks stacked with supplies. As I listened to the narrative, our men cleaned their mottled feet in mudholes in the shadow of trees, with bullet-riddled trucks all around. Two dead Japs sprawled within touching distance.

"We not only have dishwater hands but dishwater feet," said Sergeant Dean Poole. A tall, boyish tommy-gunner, Lawrence Burton, said: "Last night before this attack, I said nothing when Japs walked past me. But when one tried to climb down into my slit trench in the dark, it was too much." Burton shot four Japs today.

Brothers Joe and Clifton Deason, who have been fighting side by side, said: "We pulled around the Jap left until we could see their fire. One came up to Naryka, looked at him and walked away. He was wearing one of our helmets and full G.I. equipment. You could tell in the moonlight he was a Jap by the square pack on his back. After we shot at three only one crawled away. Then their fire wounded one of our best men. He lay there hollering for someone to come get him. We told him to crawl toward our voices. He crawled to the creek and we dragged him back."

—

YANKS BLAZE AWAY, ADVANCE IN GUINEA

With the American Forces on Sanananda—January 25, 1943 (Delayed)

Here, deep in the Sanananda swamp, men are taking off their mud-clogged boots, hanging up their wet socks in the shafts of sunlight that penetrate the brush, and breaking down their tommy guns for the first thorough oiling in ten days.

Christmas mail is getting through to the outlying posts in the green-hung quagmire. The bearded barefoot men pick their way across, between mudholes, and extend their dirty hands for their first news from the outer world. As the mud-bedaubed runner reads the names he sometimes pauses, waits and gets no answer. Without a word he puts these letters, which will never be claimed, back in his haversack.

Yesterday there were several bursts of fire at odd places nearby. Today there were only two and nobody pays any attention. A captain and his bespectacled aide are working under a shelter half-open to the sun, dictating citations for bravery.

Two Australian war correspondents in a jeep were blown up by a mine a few feet from another mine this correspondent had marked two days ago, and one was wounded, making two killed and two wounded since the Buna campaign began.

It is quiet except for the occasional lone bombers on moonlit nuisance raids. Our own fighters drone with a comforting monotony. That fellow shot by a sniper across the road from me died today. But in general, it is tranquil. Clean-khakied men are beginning to arrive from over the Owen Stanleys on official errands. They want to hear what happened and would not refuse a Jap officer's sword if you could suggest where it could be obtained. The clock on this campaign has run down.

—

GUNNERS DRIVE JAPS OFF; WANT TO SHOOT AGAIN

With the American Troops in
New Guinea—February 23, 1943

Having driven off a bevy of Zeros that tried a hit-and-run raid by daylight against American positions in northern Papua, a force of anti-aircraft gunners with whetted appetites are awaiting Tojo's return.

"It was a pity our guests stayed such a short time," said Major Earl Marsha, a former insurance agent. At the moment of this hospitable statement, Marsha was sitting on a stool under a palm, having his hair cut. As the major told his story, a Zero with his landing gear down as a sign that he was friendly came in low and dropped bombs in the area. Two others that followed met a fusillade from a gun tucked away in a well-prepared position. Although none of the Jap planes was hit grievously enough to fall, after the run by the leading Zero caused no damage, the others sheered off. Six bombs were dropped, but ineffectively.

As these three Jap planes took their departure another three came over the trees, making their circuitous approach by land in order to avoid American-held beaches like Sanananda and Buna. Met by guns, the Zeros took one look at this upraised wall of fire and with what is variously interpreted as a sneering or terrified note in their engine throbs, turned to sea and dropped their bombs offshore.

Other things happen around this tropical outpost that call for emergency action. During two visits by this writer at a fortnight's interval, dirt piles fell in on a backed-up truck. The second time the Australian driver was pinned inside the cab, his left temple split open, his head forced completely through the wheel.

The first to reach the still conscious and bleeding Digger was Captain Joseph Gross of Brooklyn, whose medical aide station was nearby. Leaning through the shattered window, Gross—an energetic, chunky doctor—gave the Aussie an injection. Afterward sixty Americans worked an hour before the now-unconscious man could be released. (This correspondent plied a shovel atop the truck.)

Gross has an intuitive eye for malaria symptoms and twice has knocked this writer's malaria back far enough to permit him to keep going a while longer.

When a raid comes, everyone anywhere near the Japs tries to help with the guns. In the last low-level raid John Staron, unable to get any weapon, lost his temper and began throwing rocks. His unit is proud of his zeal but claims no hits.

As everywhere in New Guinea, the Americans' relations with the natives are excellent, although some anti-aircraftsmen underestimate the intelligence of the boongs. An armorer, for example, marshaling his best pidgin, addressed one: "You, boy, climb plenty high bit tree, catchum one coconut, savvy?"

"I beg your pardon but just exactly what do you want?" responded the native.

When the armorer explained that he was offering a cigarette for coconut service, the native retorted: "I don't have to climb trees for cigarettes. I am in the native constabulary and get mine on issue."

Newcomers are often bewildered by the tastes of the more primitive tribes coming down from the hills. Some wear the shredded papers in which perishables are shipped from the States, plaited in their hair and wound around their ears. This style is said to be irresistible to the Kikinis' girls, who remain hidden in the forest.

The style that really breaks dusky hearts, according to the local American dentist, is bridge paint. It seems that Americans, erecting permanent structures while building roads in undeveloped parts of Papua, are using lead paint as a metal preservative. The natives find that this red paint smeared on foreheads and even in bushy hair adds just the right *je ne sais quoi* to a warrior's appearance.

This is also a lovely outpost of the tyranny of paperwork. Gross still treasures one document which just arrived from the United States.

"Are you doing your duty?" the circular demands. *"Are you serving as one of these: air raid warden, block salvage captain, fire warden, blood donor, police messenger, plane spotter?"*

"If I'd been a plane spotter," said Gross, "I could have stayed in Brooklyn."

Gross is sitting tight among ack-ack guns manned by former insurance men, and waiting for breaks.

—

By the Light of a Mushroom

A Short Story

In the coconut grove at Senemi, which had a floor as hard and level as a ballroom, we used to gather, around eight o'clock, outside the barber shop. Even when there was a moon shining down through the aisles of palms, whose poles were straight and round as the pillars of a temple, you had to be careful where you walked because there were slit trenches everywhere. We gathered outside the barber shop because the barber had a portable radio. It was not a tropical radio, but a cream-colored picnic portable with Mickey Mouse's figure done on it in red and black.

Though the Sydney-made "tropical" radios distributed by the Red Cross to some outfits after the fighting ended all broke down after three days in the kunai grass, this little job in picnic ivory kept right on giving out the news.

Every evening the barber, a corporal from East Chicago, put his radio out on the narrow, shelf-like verandah of his native hut, which was so raised above the ground that he entered it by a ladder. We stood around or squatted on the hard ground of the palm grove. The barber in his stained, green jungle dress lay out at full length on his verandah at the level of the eyes of standees, and then began to work the dials. The air smelled of sweat, crushed insects, mosquito lotion, blossoms, rotting coconuts, and smoke of cookfires. Because of the blackout, no cigarettes were allowed.

In this colonnaded grove the only sounds beside the nasal voice of the radio, frequently half-intelligible between bursts of static, were the sounds of things flying. There were mosquitoes beside one's ear, or working on one's wrists and ankles. There was the synchronized grinding of the nightly nuisance raider from Rabaul, which patrolled the coast two miles away dropping an occasional small bomb like a man playing a long line of gambling machines with a pocketful of nickels. And there was the sound of the big fruit bats overhead. Disturbed by the radio's penetrating stridency, the bats would take off with claps of their wings, making a squeaky flapping, as they paddled back and forth among the palms, exactly like the stropping of a razor. One night Roy Hodgkinson, the Australian army's official painter, pointed his finger up into the darkness as a pair of dark wings went plopping creakily by and roared: "God, would you mind having that big 'un oiled?"

Although the radio program was Australian in origin, the station had an American announcer for American news. One had the illusion that one was hearing the United States. This illusion was strengthened by the fact that, after the program was over, there were often re-broadcasts of old American comedy programs made from records. A Bob Hope show, full of cracks about turkeys and stuffing and Pilgrims and Indians, was heard around St. Patrick's Day. But this tardiness and remoteness were in key with the way we felt. Men who had walked by twos and threes to the grove stood alone and apart from each other when the radio was on, listening singly because they were listening to home. While movies, when shown on the Moresby side of the Hump, always drew wisecracks and ironical cheering, not a sound was made on the fighting side of the Owen Stanleys as long as the little ivory box was on. At the last syllable of the sign-off the barber would extinguish the tiny light, saying, "That's all, gang. Only battery we've got." Then we would all drift away, back to our mosquito nets, our cots, and our lean-tos.

One evening I was walking away with two war correspondents, Bill Terriss and Frank Hallett, when Bill stopped abruptly and said, "What's that?" He was looking off the side of the path toward the underbrush slashed by the machetes of the engineers, from which a sour, rotting smell still came. What we saw was a pair of green eyes.

We glanced back to make sure that the M.P.s enforcing the blackout had already gone, and then gave the thing a quick dart with the beam of a flashlight. It did not move. We went closer. The creature's green eyes shone right at us without fright, unperturbed. We came up ten feet from it, listening for an animal sound. None came. Perhaps it's scared, or blinded by the flashlight, we thought. We held off until we were all but over it then let it have full flash and held it in the beam.

It was not an animal. It was two mushrooms. They were growing on the rotted stuff cut down by the engineers. One was about an inch in diameter, the other, which looked like its mate, a little less. Illumined in the beam the two growths appeared white, vegetable, and static. In the darkness, however, they were a bright milky green, a green that seemed alive.

With some hesitation we picked them up, careful not to separate them from the putrefying slabs of bark on which they lived. They shone persistently and cheerfully at us. Quite unsinister, they had a kind of gay green vivacity about them. Frank held one a couple of inches under his hand. "That light is strong," said Bill. "I can see every finger you have."

The mushrooms, we observed, were not simply coated with phosphorescent fungus; they were luminous through and through. The underside of each little umbrella was as bright as the top; the tiny green parasol illumined the bark on which it stood. Even the sturdy little stem was a column of cool, crisp green. Unlike artificial tools of light-making, the mushrooms had no blind spots or handles. They were completely effulgent, gently luminous all over.

We stood there a while, passing the chips of bark like candleholders from hand to hand. "Let's take them back to the intelligence tent and see if they'll put them in the communiqué," said Frank.

"No," said Bill, "let's put them back where we found them. They're better off there." So the mushroom couple went back where they had been. Until we reached the head of the path we could see the two of them gleaming greenly at us, the way you can still see the riding lights of a plane long after a night take-off.

"I wonder if anyone ever measured the light those things give out," murmured Frank.

"I bet it's a half of one candlepower, at least."

"Half, hell. I could read by that bigger one. It was as good as any bed lamp. Better light, too. Natural light."

Bill, who had a case of malaria that was being held down by atabrine like a fire by a wet rag, had been trying to get himself transferred back south where he could get rest and treatment. His several messages requesting a change had been ignored. Suddenly he took Frank and me by our sweat-slippery arms. "Hey, listen," he said, "I think those mushrooms are the answer for me. They can get me back to Australia."

"I doubt if they're poisonous," I said.

"I'm not going to eat them," said Bill. "I'll just take them to my lean-to, get out my machine and write a story."

"What about?" said Frank dourly. The censorship had not been easy on us.

"It doesn't matter what it's about," said Bill. "It's the lead that will get them. The minute New York reads my lead, they'll understand it's no use keeping me this side the Hump any longer. They'll realize I'm off the beam, but good. The first words they see will be better than a certificate of cerebral malaria. They can't miss that I'm troppo and have to be taken out."

"What'll you say, then?"

It seemed now almost as if Bill's face must give out a glow, so intense and confident was his voice. "Listen, now," he said, "here's my lead: *Somewhere in New Guinea.*" He took a breath and held our arms tighter. *"I am writing this story at the front by the light of a mushroom."*

We thought it over a little. Frank and I had been at Buna just long enough so that neither of us was very sure of his judgment. "Might work," said Frank at length. "Worth trying," I agreed. It seemed a rather plausible device to us, perhaps because we were on our second and third recurrences ourselves.

As soon as we got back to the intelligence tent, we were told that a courier had landed at Dobodura just before sunset with a bag of mail. There was a letter waiting that said a replacement would arrive next morning to relieve Bill.

The next night during the radio hour, an M.P. noticed the two mushrooms violating the blackout and picked them. He took them to the cooking enclosure, where there was an argument as to whether they were edible, and if they were, whether they would give out a light through your stomach. I went away before the argument was settled, and the next morning no one in camp knew what had become of the illuminated mushrooms.

Eventually Frank and I decided to go to Milne Bay. We caught a jeep to Buna Mission, where there was a colonel who was an old friend of ours. At one time this colonel had been known as "the mayor of Dobodura," because he gave directions to all who tumbled into that nexus of Kenney's early airborne operations. He was a middle-aged colonel of supply from a college town, and he spoke with a careful enunciation that seemed out of place in the jungle. He was helpful and courteous, and we knew he would get us aboard some kind of coastal lugger to reach Milne Bay.

It was already night when we reached the place on the beach where the colonel and his outfit were camped. Once there had been a time when he was in charge of all the supplies that came over the range, and the campaign had depended on him. But Buna was over, the dead were buried, and the supplies which had once been flown in by transport, skimpily and irregularly, were now arriving less dramatically but much more frequently by sea. So the colonel now had a grimier and less attractive job than supply: salvage. His men were camped in the thick squatty trees by the black sand beach, and they were sorting out the lost rubbish of war, the misshapen shoes, the discarded jungle jackets foul with odors, the guns that had been buried in the muck by mortar bursts (their former owners now lying under crosses in the little cemetery with the drivers of the Australian Bren gun carriers)—all the lost parts of two armies that had fought and passed into time. It was a sour job, like washing up the dishes after a party. Tied down to such tasks, with the real job already finished, soldiers and officers feel themselves forgotten.

In answer to his questions we told the colonel that the commanding general, his G-2, and his G-3 had flown back together to Australia, presumably to talk with General MacArthur. "Anybody say anything back there about orders to take us out?" he asked. We shook our heads apologetically. Supply and salvage, the housekeepers of the army, go on forever. "I didn't expect so," he said. "Well, I'll put you aboard a Tazzy boat leaving about two in the morning."

In the middle of the evening we were taking a walk up the beach with the colonel when the bomber from Rabaul came grinding in over the sea. It was hot and still, and the little waves made a delicate fussing sound as they patted the beach. The Japanese turned at sea and started east toward Oro Bay, where he usually began his nuisance patrol. We had settled down in a slit trench and were waiting for the raider to come back, pass overhead, and go on toward Morobe, when the colonel stood up with a start, and staring into the darkness demanded: "What are those eyes looking at us there?"

It was a cluster of small lights, green and cool, shining out of the jungle. "It's not animals, Colonel," said Frank. "It's mushrooms."

"Mushrooms?"

"Yes. We have luminous mushrooms in New Guinea."

"I never heard of such a thing," said the colonel. "It's some sort of animal."

"Wait, I'll get them for you," said Frank, getting out of the trench.

"Don't show a light," said the colonel. "That Jap is smart."

"You don't need any light," said Frank. "These mushrooms give out a light of their own." He was already twenty feet away, climbing over rotten logs.

The colonel leaned nearer until his shoulder touched mine. "I don't mind Frank having his little joke," he whispered. "But personally it sounds to me as though he's been on this side of the range too long. Malaria can affect a man to the point where he's not responsible for himself. Sometimes I have to keep a tight grip on myself. I hope you'll put Frank on the first plane you can get out of Milne Bay. He needs a good rest to clear his mind."

Then Frank came back. He had a long dead branch, which he was carrying carefully. There was a row of five luminous mushrooms on it, as even and similar as green buttons on the wall of an elevator. "There, Colonel!" he said, handing it down.

The colonel took the branch as if he thought it electrified. "Well, I never—certainly never in my life—never saw anything to match this." He held the mushrooms out as a child does buttercups, under my chin. "You look supernatural," he said. "Well, I never. I certainly never."

"Take them to your tent," suggested Frank. "Plant them back of the guy rope, where the sentry can't step on them. Kind of mark of rank, see?"

"But aren't they visible to aircraft?" asked the colonel.

"If they are, then that Jap must be seeing nothing but green buttons all over New Guinea," said Frank.

"That's true, that's true," agreed the colonel. He held the branch delicately in long, thin fingers. "Well, I never, I certainly never." He carried it back to his quarters.

Uncertain what kind of accommodations there would be on the Tazzy boat, we turned in for a nap on the floor of the warehouse. When the sentry wakened us at one, we went over to say goodbye to the colonel. His tent was dark, and I parted the flaps hesitantly. "Come in, come in," said the colonel loudly and warmly. We pushed in.

The colonel was sitting at an improvised desk. In the position before him where a pen set would be was the branch with the little green creatures on it. They shed a faint, gentle light on his intent face.

"You won't guess what I'm doing," he said. *"I'm writing."*

"What are you writing, Colonel?" said Frank.

"I'm writing a letter for you to take back to the base censor," said the colonel. "A letter to my wife."

"Not much you can say, is there?" I said politely.

"There's never much," said the colonel. "That's why I don't write very often. But this time is different. This time I've got an opening sentence here that is going to make her sit right up. You're reporters; you ought to be good judges of how to hold a woman's interest. What do you think of this?—here's how I begin: *'Darling, I am writing you tonight by the light of five mushrooms.'* How about that for a salutation?"

Before I found words, Frank was able to reply. "It certainly ought to interest anyone, Colonel," he said. "Why, a lead like that would make anyone wonder whether you oughtn't to be relieved."

Rich Food? That's Rich—Can Opener Tires Yanks

With Advanced American Troops in New Guinea—April 6, 1943 (Delayed)

One American airman was killed and another wounded last week by stray Japanese soldiers living a vagabond existence in dugouts near the portable hospital with forward American troops where this writer is confined under treatment. But the most disturbing phenomenon during convalescence under a torrid tent in northern Papua is not the possibility that Japs may emerge from the surrounding jungle seeking food, and knock off this correspondent on his canvas cot. It is, rather, the plain American "G.I. Dogfaces," obsessed with their own food problems, who surround the writer's cot, can openers in hand, and peer through the mosquito net, demanding: "Are you that jerk correspondent who wrote all the so-and-so about the rich French food we are supposed to be getting here? We're looking for that liar."

Everybody in New Guinea, especially on the northern, uglier side of the Hump, understands that canned, dehydrated, denatured foods are unavoidable circumstances of war—like bullets, ants, dogtags, and blood tests. When tommy guns have denuded the last trees of coconuts, and native gardens remain deserted by their dusky keepers—who have either been pressed into labor corps or fled to the hills—it is more than we could expect to be living in a paradise of tropical fruits and fresh fish as imagined by steak-and-orange-juice-fed cartoonists 12,000 miles away.

Broken crackers or water flavored with orange extract are accepted as part of the war scene. What gripes the slouch-shouldered dogfaces fighting off malaria, bush typhus, anemia and hookworm is being told by letter from relatives in the United States, or thinkers in Washington, or trenchermen covering the Papuan war from "somewhere in Australia" (American correspondents in New Guinea now total two) how luxuriously he is living in the jungle and what sacrifices are being made by the public to keep him fat and jolly. Meat may be scarce and expensive in America, but not because the Army in Papua is living off it. Fruits and vegetables may have risen in price in Australia, but not because the soldier here is eating them.

What really gets the hairy infantrymen down is reading eulogies about how much shipping space has been saved by dehydrating eggs, drying milk into dust, and canning everything. Did anyone of these dietary lyricists ever try fighting on inert foods after being accustomed to fresh meat, salads, vegetables, cow's milk, fruit? It is recognized that these shipping savings are unavoidable. Nobody in the swamp expects an official announcement of the obvious fact that compressed foods taste like hell. That is war. But it is peculiarly maddening to be told that war is a feast.

The catalogue of fresh food that has reached this correspondent during the last fortnight may be interesting to those who think the American soldier is eating them out of house and home. In thirteen days this correspondent has gluttonized on the following uncanned provender: one piece of meat, one egg, one pear, one beet, one dish of cabbage, two split plums, twelve individual grapes. Two apples, one of which was obtained dishonestly. Everything else was canned.

Today a man in the next thatched hut received a letter from his girl, saying: *"Tenderloins have disappeared in America, but we are glad to make this small sacrifice for you to have them."* When he read this passage to fever patients they were impelled to do something violent. But only their temperatures were able to rise.

—

CHICAGO MEN IN NEW GUINEA TALK OF HOME

With Advanced Forces in Australia-mandated New Guinea—May 14, 1943

You slip over Huon Gulf with gasoline fumes in your nose. You slept on an uncushioned deck last night and will tonight. But leave it to Sergeant Eugene Sullivan, Chicago's junglewise policeman, to say something relaxing.

The lean, dark former pavement-pounder points to a long, green island—one of scores stretching along this coast to Salamaua—shifts his revolver and says: "Me and Madeleine Carroll on that island." Sullivan is twenty-eight and unmarried, but the only time he has ever been near this island was when searching for Jap survivors from the Bismarck Sea battle.

Your putt-putt approaches the beach. You and Sullivan undress, pile

your clothes on deck and jump overboard in the neck-deep water. A lieutenant hands your clothes down and you stack them on your head. No
sharks' fins can be seen, so you leave the boat's cool shadow for shore.
Halfway in, clouds of sandflies attack. As you step on the deserted beach,
flanked with tumble-down brown native huts, you struggle into your
clothes without pausing to dry.

Sullivan says: "You'll think you're not bitten for about two days. But
just wait and see."

As usual he's right. Within forty hours you develop hard-cored red pim-
ples—an average of fifty to seventy bites per square foot of flesh—and
scratch all day and night for the next five days.

The only sign of war in the stilt-supported village is a Jap belly tank
that some native suspended under his hut as a water tank before he decided to flee. Everything has gone. Pots and pans have been carried into the
jungle pending decision as to whether the Japs will be expelled from Salamaua. A sandy circle on the bamboo floor, like the hearth in an American
home, is empty. A ceremonial mask for dances lies broken nearby, grimac-
ing its white-striped palm-husk cheeks.

But the village isn't wholly deserted. Two sad sacks in green come down
the beach, shoeless and with pulled-down fatigue caps and rifles. Soon
there appears a sarong-clad member of the Australian native constabulary.

Under the beating sun, which makes you giddy reflecting from the sand,
you wander through the empty village to the graveyard. Behind some
stilted houses are doghouses, also on stilts. That is where the family's tame
parrot lived, but he has gone too. A tiny chapel's benches have been over-
turned by the Japs; during their occupations, Christian religious literature
is used as scrap paper. Even the Bible is not respected, and pages of St.
Mark are scattered about.

Here is a broken-down hut where, as the native cop tells the Chicago
cop, "Bebbies go mission school, sleep here, kiki here." *Kiki* is food.

The graveyard's sleeping forms are outlined ovally in pebbles, the tall
wooden crosses with peculiarly short arms marking Christians. Shifting his
musket, this No. 1 police boy shows how they are buried, not by families
but by status, in three rows: "Here man fella, here Mary and her pick-
aninny bebby." He also shows, with shadowed face, the grave of his predecessor killed by Jap strafing. "One fella, balus [pigeon] belong Japan shoot
him. This fella police boy; he die."

As all along the coast, there are Jap entrenchments meant to hold off landing parties. You wander through an endless line of huts, some merely mangers for common soldiers and coolies. The officers' quarters are more elaborate. Finally, you come upon the full-size hut of the commander with adroitly concealed chair for sitting alone watching the sea. His chair of meditation faces the dimly seen shore of New Britain—and Tokyo.

These shore defenses, evacuated without a fight by Japs withdrawing toward Salamaua and Lae, are quiet, unlike the marshy glades around Sanananda. There, a few days earlier, the writer wandered among hundreds of Jap skulls and forgotten equipment deep in forest. Here everything is policed as carefully as a picnic ground. In an hour's search, you sweatingly find one broken water filter, one pair of shorts patched with a piece from a blanket, and a large sea turtle's shell used for washing. You discover a single corpse on the beach with pelvis bones and white ribs sticking out from the sand. At first you think it must be from Huon Gulf, but the police boy hands Sullivan a Jap sun helmet found in the coarse witchgrass, points to the bones and says: "Plenty too much sick—he die."

After a march of some distance on the blinding sand, you reach one of those innumerable green rivers that emerge from this mountainous shore. Manned by native boys, there are two outrigger canoes, each with a tiny deck five feet by eighteen inches. You and Sullivan sit down on these precarious platforms, the boys dip rounded paddles, and you move upstream, losing the ocean immediately.

Presently, by means improper to reveal, you reach the farthest forward Allied outpost, quite unlike those crashing battleposts with shells always overhead and mortars pumping. It commands a good view in a certain direction. It is quiet. And in this outpost occurs the Stanley-Livingstone meeting you have been planning.

You approach a dark-haired, slightly bearded young man and say, "John Justin Smith, former assistant music critic of the *Chicago Daily News,* I presume."

Taken aback in quite un-Livingstone fashion, Smith responds, "Yes, but who in the heck are you, and what are you doing here?"

At first Smitty is dumbfounded. We try to pass off this meeting at the end of MacArthur's uttermost tentacle as nothing. After all, aren't Chicago newsmen always running into each other in these jungles? One must remember that the world is getting smaller. The war correspondent starts to thumb through Smitty's copies of the *Daily News,* not having seen any in six months.

"Read them but don't take any," says Smitty. "The natives buy them for cigarette paper." The favorite dish here is C-ration with onions, purchased with old *Chicago Daily News*es. "They taste fantastic," Smith says.

The natives show impatience, and Smitty says, "You stop all right along canoe, pretty soon me come."

The paddlers obediently leave. As we plunge through the thirty-foot jungle of brown, fernlike sago palms, he tells how he went swimming in the river until the natives warned of poopook, or crocodiles. When eventually we reach the two outrigger canoes, the music critic himself takes the paddle while the displaced boy sits in the bottom of one hollow log. As he dips in the limpid green water, Sullivan remarks, "Bet you wish you could paddle this job right down the Chicago River."

We round the green bend in the river to the ocean and motorboat. We begin slowly to undress on the beach and more rapidly as the flies began biting—racing into the water and resuming conversation when the naked neck-deep critic and the naked neck-deep correspondent are deep enough so the flies can bite only our heads.

When the writer clambers into the launch, Smitty adds: "And say hello to Paul Mowrer, Hal O'Flaherty and Carroll Binder"—not realizing he has seen these *Daily News* powers more recently than your correspondent.

Smitty reaches the beach again and the launch's motor begins to flutter. The critic can be seen jumping into his clothes, surrounded by clouds of eager sandflies. As the boat turns for the open sea, Smitty comes down to the water's edge, cups his hands and yells something. You cup a hand to your ear. This time Smitty yells louder and points up the coast to where Lae and Salamaua and Jap-held Finschafen Head can be dimly seen.

"Land of milk and honey," he shouts.

You raise both clenched hands in the boxer's salute.

After a cheerful wave, Smitty goes running up through the tumbled houses of the native village, dodging like a halfback as the midges pursue him.

"Here we are in New Guinea, two fellows from Chicago," murmurs Sullivan as the little figure disappears among giant palms, "and the Japs are right over there."

The former policeman pauses at spray from the gunwale, then adds mildly, "Sometimes I can hardly believe what is going on in this world."

Simultaneously, we begin the first gentle scratching of our emergent bites.

—

NATURE CONCEALS MOROBE FROM BAFFLED JAP PILOTS

With Advanced Troops in Australian-Mandated New Guinea—May 17–18, 1943

Morobe would, in one sense, be a lovely place to fight a war. It is the complete antithesis of the swamps around Buna and Sanananda, scourged with malaria, scrub typhus and hookworm. It is cool and the Japs restrict their activities to harassing raids by single or pairs of bombers, by dark. Since the coast is a small-scale Norway, with deeply-cut bays, navigable streams and involuted deep harbors, these Jap aircraft—sometimes with navigation lights temptingly aglow—cruise up and down the coast all night looking for ships and for Morobe.

It is not easy for the Japs to find the target. The coastline's indentations are all similar. In the old days, when the writer was camped in the swamps of Buna at Christmas, one could hear Jap bombers approaching the coastline often at the wrecked Jap freighter which lies on the reef at Gona. This furnished a good marker.

But Morobe is harder because dozens of coastal inlets all have islands at their mouths and from the air all the islands look alike at night. Pity the poor Jap pilot. He cannot come over by day because he may be shot down, so he comes over by night and begs pathetically for someone to fire at him and give him some guidance.

Food is coarse and pretty simple here. Most natives have been frightened away by the Japanese, who, although losing Morobe with hardly a shot fired, had a perimeter nearly two miles long beautifully concealed along the fringe of beach.

In private life Sergeant Eugene Sullivan is a Chicago policeman, but among Morobe's green hills he is recognized as the man who knows more about trailing through the jungle than anybody else. His job is silently tracking down Japs still lurking along the coast and trying to harass our communications lines. His patrols operate in some country where less than half a dozen white men have ever been before—chiefly during Germany's pre-war possession of New Guinea. It is now well known to the Americans even though it is not listed on most of the crude and disjointed maps available. Sullivan can talk pidgin as rapidly as a coconut planter, missionary or district officer of less remote districts, and so can his men. They have learned to deal with the natives with courtesy, honesty and dignity.

When you sit on the hill with the Sullivan bunch and look toward the faint shores of New Britain it seems natural enough that these Americans should become explorers in a region of unvisited vastness. The gold-bearing valleys behind Lae and Salamaua are known, but the Morobe district is not. Before the Americans it had one house, built by Germans, and deserted.

Sullivan says in his slow reasonable way: "We try to avoid trading with the natives and attempt to live on canned food. Once when we were very hungry we traded a razor blade and a can of beans for one chicken and two dozen yams, a dozen pawpaws, one watermelon, and a single stalk of about two hundred bananas."

Sullivan's territory includes places where dogfights have occurred with Jap fighters. Searching for traces, Sullivan uses "balus," meaning pigeon, and says to a native, "You see this fella, balusey, he walkabout on top, you come lick, lick, tell number one white fella." Sullivan belongs to the persuasive Irish and gets results.

Living the true life of amphibian war, half the time in canoes or small boats and the rest on trails, these scouts subtly change. Frank Szczpanski, blond former machinist of Chicago, says, "When doing long patrols we generally give the native boys names of our choosing. They like it. One, who always wears a red courtship flower in his hair, we call Rose. A smart but lazy one we call Goldbrick, to remind us of his shirking without his knowing. They are often saucy, even when friendly, because they really need nothing from us and need not work if they do not wish. They call the Germans Hamburgers. One boy called me in mixed Australian and German, 'You bloody Hamburger.' We called him Hamburger always after that."

It rains often throughout this country. You get the same plain Army cot with single blanket and mosquito bar as has been yours in most camps for twenty-two weeks. At night everything is blacked out; it is impossible to move without a flashlight even though the walks between tents are marked with stakes and hung with connecting lawyer vines. One night soon after your arrival—flashlight left in your tent as part of your self-training to move in the dark, Jap-fashion—you blunder along the walks. Then begins twenty minutes of wandering: falling into slit trenches, stubbing toes on coconuts, jumping when another falls nearby, walking up promising sidepaths, feeling the way toe-first, then stubbing violently against the crackerbox latrine. Falling, picking yourself up, you find the tent of a surgeon who has patched the broken rim of his eyeglasses with adhesive. The nearest optician is eighty days' journey away, by the fastest connections. It is a rather lonely war.

It always rains mornings and perhaps that is why the cricket's song before dawn means only that daylight is on the way. You fold back your blanket on your bare cot and fumble for your shoes. Some officers smoke thoughtful cigarettes in bed while their minds are still warm for the preparations of the day's wet duties.

Then you get back into the same stinking jungle suit and walk along the path to the mess tent. The officer knows you carried no pack except a pencil and pad, so you get your mess kit here. Breakfast consists of one pancake and one cup of coffee.

You keep wondering why the infantry, which has everything the hardest, including food and losses, is so consistently cheerful. One officer had a single egg, obtained from a native. They passed it gingerly from hand to hand and kidded him endlessly before watching him eat it.

—

'FOULEST SPOT' IN EAST INDIES HOLDS HOPE OF FREE HOLLAND

Somewhere in New Guinea—June 1, 1943 (Delayed)

Twenty times bombed by Japanese planes but still courageously holding on, little Merauke, mudbound rivermouth port of New Guinea's mosquitobitten swampland, still proudly flies the red, white and blue of Queen Wilhelmina's lost Indies. Merauke alone is still unlost.

And beside Holland's lonely flag, that swamp-surrounded port flies today another red, white and blue flag, symbol of the fact that America has pledged itself to recover Holland's Indies.

Australia too, is there, with its brown, slouch-hatted Diggers, naked to the waist, laboring alongside Americans and Holland's own Javanese troops.

Uglier even than the swamps of Gona, Sanananda and Buna is this little port where exiled felons were once unloaded but which has now, by a twist of this conflict, become the residence of all Holland's hopes.

To those who, like this correspondent, left part of their hearts with those brave Dutchmen of Java who stayed at their posts with the natives—stayed to shovel excrement and pull rickshaws at the command of their Jap conquerors, but stayed anyway—there is something touching about Merauke. As England was Germany's Achilles' heel, so Merauke, with its clouds of mosquitoes and fetid swamp odors, its circling white pelicans and foul beach of yellow mud, is destined to become a place which, never taken by an enemy, will be the cornerstone of recovery.

Japan is the world's second imperial power, but the answer to its aspirations is being prepared which will cut it down to measure. Like de Gaulle's Brazzaville in French Equatorial Africa, symbolically Merauke is a place of beginnings. Japan never fully conquered the Dutch Indies and now is too late for it to do so.

Jap bombers, coming probably from Babo and Fakfak—fine, readymade bases which the Allied retreat presented to the Japs eighteen months ago—have done their dirtiest to smash little Merauke. As you wander through shattered "tokos," or native shops, it is as though you were in Soerabaya again when Japan's first bombers came over from Kendari with only a handful of outworn American P-40s opposing them.

Whether you approach Merauke by air or by sea—and so foul are the vast swamps stretching hundreds of miles back to New Guinea's mighty range that you cannot approach by land—you cannot fail to be impressed that in Merauke, freedom has chosen a strange vessel to endure in. It is as though Quasimodo should replace the Statue of Liberty.

As one passes through Torres Strait, flanked by the greenish waters around Horn and Thursday islands, and enters the Arafura Sea whose domination Jap, American and Australian airmen are still disputing, one is at the threshold of that old and cultured archipelago of Javanese influence. Yet here in Dutch New Guinea is a vast wilderness beside which Papua—no longer raw since America has poured in millions of dollars in highways and air fields—is as civilized as a downtown American city.

Dutch New Guinea's doorstep is, instead of the glittering green, blues and purples of Australian Papua's reefs, a twenty-to-thirty-mile apron of pestilential mudflats running far into the ocean. Behind them hundreds of miles of dank rivers crinkle the surface of the swamps. Trees grow in the ocean and sharks swim into swamps. You cannot tell where sea ends and land begins.

Such is Merauke, that former colony of political prisoners—unconfined and working their small land holdings—chosen as the end point of the Japanese advance southward in 1943.

Mosquitoes! This correspondent thought he had been bitten in every way a mosquito could bite until he met Merauke. Around that area of General Douglas MacArthur's four Ms (Morobe, Milne Bay, Moresby, and Merauke), there is every kind of malaria from benign, which leaves you shaky, to cerebral, which leaves you insane, and there is a mosquito to fit each. But Merauke's are something special.

When these malaria-transmitters light on your arm, they tilt their thick black bodies vertically for a straight downward dive. Instead of merely tapping you, they stab you with a deliberate, muscular thrust. They fly far out over the yellow mud waves and enter boats' portholes. Ashore it takes ten minutes with a flashlight to clean them from the inside of your hammock net before you can sleep. They patrol outside, singing in nasal fury at the appetizing odors coming from your naked, sweating body. If, stirring in sleep, you touch your elbow to the mesh of net, they cluster instantly at the opening and pebble you with stings. Droning in several tones, they go to sea with you and are still making final efforts to sting when the first cool night sea breeze sends them into drowsy death.

—

GUINEA'S PEACEFUL KOKODA REMINDER OF TASK AHEAD

Somewhere in New Guinea—June 18, 1943 (Delayed)

If you feel overread and overstudied on the Pacific war and have thought too long about America's future political role in the Southwest Pacific, you can go to Kokoda, if you want to see the real ground itself. Not Buna or Gona; not Sanananda or Milne Bay. Not even the empty waters off Misima Island, where thirteen months ago, in the Coral Sea battle, America's fleet first helped save Australia.

It is hard even to get to these places. You have to wait around for several days until you can get a tiny Puss Moth with a Royal Australian Air Force pilot to fly you back from Dobodura along the once Jap-held trail from Buna to the edge of the Owen Stanley Mountains. After so many hours in bombers and transports it is like riding in a baby carriage through the skies. The cloud-hung Owen Stanleys rise like a rampart behind Kokoda. Kokoda's tiny airdrome, on which Australia's fate once depended, is now quiet. Far overhead streams the endless, year-old shuttle of big American transports.

Only a few blacks are working negligently at one side. The drome is worn like an old croquet ground, because Papua's autumn is upon it, and the once-green carpet of the runway is old.

Kokoda is an important warning that our greatest battles against Japan still lie before us. Japan has been met and beaten in the Southwest Pacific, at Misma, Milne Bay, Ioraibaiwa and at Buna. It has lost much shipping, some men and considerable aircraft, but still holds the chief places of New Guinea that it seized. Tiny Kokoda, little more than a cluster of mission buildings beside a rubber plantation, with a scattering of three or four European-style houses, is the biggest place we have recaptured. It is slightly bigger than Buna and Milne Bay were before we retook them. Yet Kokoda is a reminder that we have retaken nothing much territorially. Lae and Salamaua are one task; then there are Wewak and Rabaul.

This is in New Guinea alone. The islands of the Indies, lost in one overwhelming twinkling, await us. It is humbling in a healthy sort of way to look at Kokoda, this small, white chip, the biggest we have recovered after so much brilliant and heroic fighting. Thus we can measure the magnitude of the task lying before our ground troops, whatever the setbacks dealt Japan by sea and air.

Beneath big old rubber trees, where was slain the first Australian decorated with the Distinguished Service Cross by MacArthur—Lt. Colonel William Owen, who died hurling grenades at the Japs—you can stop in meditation appropriate to this place. You are on a tongue of land about 300 yards long by 200 yards wide. Your view dominates a valley lying about 150 yards below. Down there are new white crosses, for the Australian Graves Commission is hard at work. Those bayonet-stabbed bodies from Templeton's Crossing are not here; they lie still in the mountains. Only one American fighter pilot, Lieutenant N. E. Brownell, who fell on November 6, lies here among his Australian comrades of all those who fought and won control of the skies above them. Many of our most gallant fliers lie unfound and unfindable in the impassable clenches of the Stanleys.

Walking along with brown-mustached Captain Alfred Watson and District Officer John Galvin, you see underfoot the leaves of these rubber trees far bigger and older than Japan's new industrialized plantations captured from the British in Malaya. There is a quiet "pop-pop" then a slight whispering—seeds falling from the trees. Life is resuming at Kokoda.

You seek out Captain Allen Champion, who with his brother Claude is among the best district officers of Papua. Allen, who is deaf, is the same slight, lithe brown man with whom you talked last August in Port Moresby at the end of the long trail across the Stanleys. It was then that he told your correspondent the first story of what happened at the Jap landing in Buna and at the first fight in Kokoda. Now he looks more rested. He has resumed work and even has a small hearing aid on his lapel, which makes it easier to talk with him.

America, recently tied up with the world-wide food conference and the problems of liberty of the press connected with it, might well look to Kokoda for a principle of treatment of rehabilitated countries. After Kokoda was reconquered, American Army transports flew dozens of loads of food there to help the Australians get native life going again. But it became apparent the natives would not work well so long as they were fed at Australo-American expense. While food itself (like wheat meal and rice) was sent, seeds for planting also were distributed. At the same time Champion and other district officers planted those gardens with the same seeds, especially corn, pumpkin and banana shoots.

"When our garden is ripe and we eat from it, you should be able to do the same without depending on the government," they told the natives.

Food relief at Kokoda now has ended and the natives' own gardens flourish.

Kokoda's natives have sharp memories of Rabaul's natives, alongside whom the Japs forced Kokoda men to carry burdens over the mountains and upon whom they spat. Contrasting the Japanese with the Australians and Americans, their summary was: "White Tabauda (master) make two boys carry one box. Jappo make one boy carry two box. If boy no carry, stickum along knife." Meaning that Jap soldiers used the bayonet as a persuader.

At Oivi—which Diggers pronounce stubbornly "Wyvee" instead of the correct "Oeevee"—the Japs felled coconuts and betel nuts, thus wiping out food and narcotic at once. They finished uprooting native life by killing pigs. (Pigs are so precious in Papua that they are always the main part of a bride's dowry.)

Having destroyed all provender, the Japs caught dogs and ate them. This upset native currency, because dogs' teeth are the coins of the Owen Stanleys just as the conch shell is for the coastal tribes.

But today the small, wild red tomatoes growing at the edge of Kokoda's rubber patch taste as sweet as though they had not been grown on bloody ground.

Seeing the greensward before the mission house, you remember bringing from Perth, in western Australia, a letter from the wife of Captain Noel Symington, who at that moment was fighting a four-day battle for this Acropolis-like plateau of Kokoda. Every night Japs crawled up over the edge of the plateau past Lt. Colonel Owen's dead body and every morning Symington's men threw them down again. One day an American Airacobra flew low and saw black-haired, twenty-five-year-old Symington waving from the split trench in which he lay flat on his back under Japanese fire. From that view came the worldwide report: "Kokoda recaptured."

The Japs next attacked the plateau with overwhelming force. All this went unrecorded in the newspapers of those days.

Yet Symington, whom your correspondent saw again at bloody Gona, is today one of the few alive out of that campaign and the bride with whom he spent only five days is now the mother of a son. Sometimes these things turn out right.

Captain Vernon, also deaf, operated on the dying Owen in this mission house when the Japs, crawling over the lip of the plateau, opened machine-gun fire. Owen had been hit halfway up the plateau and been carried here to the top.

"The Japs are machine-gunning us," said Vernon's assistant, Warrant Officer Wilkinson.

"You say rats are bad here?" said the doctor, working patiently on the expiring hero. Then the Japs attacked and soon the gallant Owen succumbed. His body was found by Captain Peter Brewer, one-time district officer of Misima Island. The body had been shoved under the earth, but it was recognized by the epaulets and the dog tags of another Australian known to have fallen with him on July 29.

The Japs have erected fourteen of their grey, wooden stavelike markers on the plateau, and these are left undisturbed.

We visited a hut raised from the ground where the graves registration workers are painting crosses below and the district officers live above. Its floor is scarred with American machine-gun fire from the days when Airacobras persecuted the Japs within. What is remarkable is that the scratches of bullets are horizontally long, showing that the American pilots must have approached at a daringly low level before thumbing their buttons of fire.

It is somewhat disorganized, like most such places. A few scrawny pineapples and bunches of bananas hang on the wall. On a table are scattered copies of Australia's *Women's Weekly*, which their well-meaning mothers and wives seem to think is exactly the thing to send to grizzled Diggers in the jungle, together with a layer of copies of *Life, Time, Saturday Evening Post, Collier's* and the *New Yorker*, which your correspondent flew in with from the nearest American camp. There is a Thompson submachine gun against the wall, just in case anything should happen.

In a corner under the table you find an old diary. A note dated November 15 reads: *American transports today evacuated four litter cases, ninety-five walking wounded, eight prisoners of war, three provost guards and three miscellaneous passengers.*

Just one stray footnote of history.

Kokoda received the wounded who had been carried three days down the mountains from Myola. It got other peculiar travelers, too. There was a B-25 Mitchell over Myola whose motor began backfiring. The plane fell 1500 feet, with its pilot telling the crew, "Get out." They did and even took the door with them as they hurtled with their parachutes into the jungle.

The plane's motor came to life and they got back to Port Moresby two weeks after the pilot who had summarily ordered them overboard. But they had been among Kokoda's honorary citizens.

Today on Kokoda's green common you can see a native making a soccer goal. Why does he hang leaves on it? Because he believes that by undulating, the leaves make a wind which will blow the oncoming ball away.

On the cross of one Digger's grave—an A.I.F. [Australian Imperial Force] named "Corp. R.A. Williams"—is written in pencil a pathetic memorandum of another, the elder Williams, who came through Kokoda with the militia. The scrawl reads: *Should be A.R. Williams, his dad.* Only two weeks separate the dates of the younger Williams' death and the note.

Kokoda is already a place of memories.

—

YANKS IN GUINEA BLESS ENGINEER SWAMP TAMERS
Somewhere in New Guinea—June 26, 1943 (Delayed)

Troops who fight in New Guinea are always conscious of the labors of U.S. Army engineers. As they lie in their foxholes before a dawn attack, sleeplessly awaiting the order to go forward, they hear footsteps splashing past in the swamp. Then the footsteps pause and the crouched soldiers overhear engineer officers talking to their men.

Everything is carefully explained.

"If we can get this stretch of corduroy built across the swamp today, food can come to the troops from the beachhead instead of the air field," they say.

That means that line companies will get bread instead of broken crackers and maybe a fistful of dried apricots per man each week. That means they will get all the ammunition they need instead of just air-transported handfuls.

And the infantryman, waiting for battle, looks at the luminous dial of his wristwatch in the dark. It is 3:30 in the morning. The engineers will already have been working for three hours when he goes into action.

Today, with northern Papua transformed from a swampy wilderness into a strong secondary line of defense against Japan—the first line is our war-ranging heavy bombers—the routes once marked out by American engineers under stress of battle are now being extended and developed by other American engineers.

The Tokyo radio prophesies confidently that Japan someday will use these extensive improvements to New Guinea's hitherto untouched real estate for its own.

However that may be, the time is certainly ripe to honor those first American engineers under two brothers of Medford, Massachusetts—husky, ruddy Colonel John Carew, decorated by MacArthur with the D.S.C., and his physically slighter brother, Major Lawrence Carew. The first bridges built under fire by Americans in this war, so far as is known, were the handiwork of their outfits.

Sometimes people think of engineers as just grubby, hairy "dogfaces" doing the dirty work for the Army's progress. They do the dirty work, all right. Before they marched across the Owen Stanley Mountains—the only engineer outfit to accomplish this—they were constructing mountain bridges which Papua otherwise never would have had. They built probably the highest span in New Guinea, 150 feet above a tropical torrent and 180 feet long—all from giant trees lying nearby.

—

[probably somewhere in Australia]
July 9th, 1943.

MR. AND MRS. EDWARD & EVA SHERMAN,
NEW YORK CITY.

Dear Mr. and Mrs. Sherman,

My reply to your letter of March 27th has been delayed first by a period of extended illness in New Guinea, and then by inability to find immediately the full circumstances of the sad passing of your son on February 7th.

It was not possible for me to go directly to the place where your son was killed, because regulations have long forbidden War Correspondents to go there.

What I tell you, therefore, is the account of a superior officer of your son's organization and not due to my own first-hand observation.

One of the most essential and at the same time dangerous jobs of the war in New Guinea has been the transport of troops and supplies across the Owen Stanley Range. You have doubtless read how fighter cover is provided for all transports, but nevertheless this system is not perfect and there are occasional loopholes when Japanese fighters creep through.

In the case of your son, as I am told, he was one of the pilots taking essential materials to Wau, an Australian and American base in the mountains behind Salamaua. At that time Wau airstrip was being closely attacked by Japanese ground troops and it was most essential that help got there.

From the Japanese point of view it was essential that the air field be captured and the transports cut off.

On the day that your son was reported missing a force of Japanese planes raided Wau and tried to chop up the transports. And as I am told, your son's plane took off from Wau and was last seen heading up one of the very wild and savage valleys that surround the air field, and was being pursued by Japanese fighters.

Since then, natives have come in from this extremely difficult country, which is largely uninhabited even by natives, and reported that they knew where the wreckage is of the missing plane. There was a close search of the whole area for several days before hope for the plane was given up.

According to the natives, as I am told, the plane crashed and burned and there is little doubt but that all in it were lost.

While the plane lies in country that makes it difficult to find, it is only about twenty-five miles from Wau, according to the natives.

At the time I left New Guinea, about a month ago, the plane had still not been found but search parties were again going out to look for it.

I can assure you of one thing and that is that if it is true that your son has been killed, and his body can be found, it certainly will be found by the efficient and conscientious Graves' Registration which handles these things. But the country is extremely difficult, the area is still very much in the combat zone and it is necessary to be patient about carrying out these things.

I suggest that you write in a short while again to the Commanding Officer of your son's squadron, and a fortnight after that to its Chaplain as well.

You have my full sympathy in your loss.

George Weller
Correspondent: Chicago Daily News.

—

Dodge Bullets in Jungle and Bury Yank Dead
Somewhere in New Guinea—July 15, 1943 (Delayed)

When the sun lies on the tops of the palms and betel gums and the green shadows of evening steal through the forest, you go down to the river to wash your green jungle fatigues and meet there the same handful of quiet young men you met last night.

Every night they are there, washing the sweat off, standing knee-deep in the brown running river and soaping each other's backs. For young men their behavior seems exceptionally composed. They never splash each other. Everything they do is a little subdued. They never sing. They never raise their voices.

The war has passed this point six months ago. These men have rifles outside their tents and take them with them whenever they leave their

small isolated camp. But the rifles are never used. Even the last Jap stragglers perished long ago in this jungle.

When the evening's first cool breath comes down the river and the mosquitoes are getting thicker and the water seems for the first time warmer
than the air, these quiet young men emerge from the river, dry themselves
on the bank and go by the muddy zigzag path across the sagging jungle to
their camp.

The oil lamp is already lit in one of their two tents and they are at home
here. In the background stand their two broken-down jeeps, with spades
and brush-cutting tools sticking out.

Someone lights a cigarette over the hissing, bright gasoline lamp, and
these unhurried young men gather around the table. Twenty-four-year-old
Sergeant Walter McGrane, of Chicago, slowly unrolls a map. It's a map of
battle. Yet no thud of mortar or keening message of shell can be heard. For
this is a map of a battle now ended, and these quiet young men are those
who care for our dead.

When the War Department informs his parents than an infantryman is
missing, this does not mean that hope of finding him has been lost. It
means that he is still being searched for. The first hope of the searchers is
to find him alive. But when weeks pass and the man still has not been
found, new parties set forth after him. The Army's determination to find
his body, if he is dead, is no less than its first effort to find him alive.

That is the work of these quiet young men. The writer has been living
near them and witnessing their work. It is impossible to know them without
being impressed with the extraordinary conscience and resolution these
little-appreciated soldiers bring to duties which few would like to undertake.

After such fighting as occurred in Northern Papua the jungle is one
great conglomerate of marked and unmarked graves. Most are marked. Individual graves are near the fighting scene. Clumps of twos and threes are
found near first-aid stations or machine-gun posts. Then, farther back, are
small graveyards—often near portable hospitals—where lie those men who
survived the battle against the enemy but nevertheless yielded their lives,
eventually, to their wounds.

All around stands the mammoth kunai grass, six to ten feet high, and
behind that jungle and more jungle. The tiny temporary crosses are
dwarfed and hidden in the long green spines. Where are the bodies? Only
the maps of battle can tell that.

These quiet young men—members of what is officially called the Graves' Registration Service—also go into battle behind the troops and the medical aid men. The jungle is not like the desert, where every fallen soldier can be seen. Here it is almost as important to mark the bodies of the killed as of the wounded. The battle line in the jungle is not a line at all. It is composed of many-branched stems like coral, placed beside each other, with patrols constantly coming forth from each notch, and brook, and turning. It is impossible for these quiet young men to follow every party since many patrols take place simultaneously. When patrols are ambushed, they sometimes cannot return for hours to claim the bodies. Often they get lost trying to find the way back to their starting place. That is what sometimes lies behind the word "missing" so far as an infantryman is concerned.

When men fall fighting in the jungle, a Graves' Registration soldier attempts to creep forward, often under fire. He tries to reach the body and get one of the two dog tags around the neck. Using a short-handled shovel, he labors to get his comrade underground in a shallow temporary grave, which means protection against the Jap looters roving the glades by night.

Just as medical aid men frequently lose their lives crawling into fire to help the wounded, so the Graves' Registration man must often choose between exposing himself and protecting his fallen comrade's body from desecration.

This Graves' Registration operates in the jungle in a manner unlike any other outfit. All the men, including the officers, are licensed morticians. All have staff sergeant rating. The two lieutenants must keep constantly moving.

For this observer, it was particularly remarkable that these men treated what they found with much more care and attention than might have been expected.

Often your correspondent has passed beside the grave of one Chicagoan, John Nelson, which lay in deep kunai off the trail between Senemi village and Buna air field, with Eugene Lockard of Three Rivers, Michigan, sleeping at his left, and Ira South of Decatur, Iowa, at his right. He could not help wondering whether the Graves' Registration boys would find this tiny clump of three mounds. They did. The heroes have been taken to one of our three principal forward cemeteries; at Giropa Point, Buna Village and Soputa.

"We try," said McGrane, without cataloguing any of the difficulties, "to treat every man with the same respect he would get if he were with his own people at home. That is the real reason behind all this business of coordinates in the jungle. Our own maps are the only ones we fully trust."

—

HOW A CHUTIST FEELS—DREAD, DROP, ELATION

(With seven parachute jumps—two more than the qualifying count of five—George Weller became, by special permission of General Mac-Arthur, the first war correspondent to pass the regulation tests for a paratrooper in the Pacific.)

Somewhere in New Guinea—November 26, 1943

"Stand in the door!" That is the order which rings in paratroopers' ears even in their dreams. That is the last order they hear before the final command, "Go."

If your legs could relax, they would tremble. If your heart were not commanding all your blood, it would climb in your throat. But every sense, every tension, every resource is concentrated on this final second.

"Stand in the door" is a command nobody hears with indifference. Here is the essence of war. It is what that lost word "charge"—never heard in the jungle—once was to infantry. The men get $50 and officers $100 a month extra as "jump pay," but few volunteer because of the money. As one paratrooper said: "Nothing could pay you for that moment when you are standing in the door for your first jump. You're just numb." Paratroopers think that any congressional committee which looks askance at their extra pay ought to stand in that door sometime.

Perhaps you have time to look down at the left of the door through whose windblown emptiness you are about to launch yourself—or be launched, for your comrades will carry you through it in their plunges, should you hesitate.

If you look down by the door you see the helmeted jump master, crouched in the ripping wind of the propeller blast. His cheeks are distorted, pulled out by the wind. He peers with terrible intentness along the grey flank of the plane, watching for the tiny patch of land to which you must float. Two lights on a tiny switchboard labeled *Jumpers' Signal* are against the inner wall of the plane, about head-high and operated by the pilot. Red is warning, green means jump. But it is not the pilot who has the job of starting you down toward the field. His responsibility is the approach. It is that peering officer—sometimes a sergeant, sometimes a lieutenant, sometimes of higher rating—who will send you through the door. His eyes are wind-clouded. Tears creep down his face but are blurred on his cheeks and dry almost instantly.

The propeller noise whips your ears to deafness. They are dulled anyway, for that vacant door has been staring you in the face ever since you hobbled aboard with your back laden with ammunition, food, gear, rifle and sometimes a telephone.

The whole plane has been vibrating tinnily. Unexpectedly the propeller roar is curbed. The pandemonium of wind dies, and more tinnily than ever you hear the stamping of those high boots which will soon—whatever happens—bite the soil.

Softer and softer grows the sound of the wind. The pilot is throttling the motors down. It is like that moment when the plane is coming in for a landing and you are uncertain how things will turn out. It seems incredibly quiet.

"Well, this is it," says the man behind you. A few seconds before, he checked those grocery-store strings that bind the upper cone of the parachute to a static line.

You look past the helmet of the man ahead as he stamps. You see a row of upraised left hands, each grasping a silvery hook that runs like a trolley on a cable lengthwise through the plane's cabin. Every broad, white linen static line, you observe, is looped over the paratrooper's wrist and over his left shoulder to the center opening of the chute pack. None is wrongly under his wrist. At least nobody ahead will get fouled and have to be propelled through the door football-wise.

Now it seems almost silent, for the motors' thick voices have lowered to the gentlest whisperings. This is the instant for which everything has been planned—all the days of roadwork, the weary exercise, the maddening rehearsals on mocked-up platforms, the monstrous packing of fighting, eating and communicating equipment.

The jump master's wind-torn face becomes set behind its twisted, jowly expression. "Jump!" he shouts in a loud voice, as though the plane's motors were not stilled.

From the uplined men there bursts a wild shout in which the jumping cry, "Geronimo!" is mingled with other raw-meat gutturals more expressive than the wary cry of an Indian chief's name.

You catch a glimpse of the first men leaping and vanishing into space. The line is melting away. The noisy cabin is getting emptier and lonelier.

You feel yourself pushed from behind. You push, too, hugging up close against the pack of the swollen man ahead. There is no time for any calculation in the doorway. There is no time to get set and make again that same kind of jump which, on your baptismal plunge a few days ago, earned you the simple but golden praise of "Good exit" from the officers watching below.

No, this time it seems more as though the door came up to you than you to the door. One second you're between those two conspicuously vacant rows of seats with your fists tightened around your hook. You're thinking about space—how empty it is and what a lot of it there is underneath. So much of nothing to jump into. You can see clouds on the horizon, and you're so low that the green rims of the mountains show through the window.

You are in the door, and because you are near the end of the line, the jump master himself is now standing, ready to follow the last jumper into space. His is the only face you have seen since standing up and it is tense, anticipating his jump.

Then you are on the threshold, with a cold wind in your face and the grey tail of the plane in the left corner of your eye. An upside-down tumbling blob is falling about fifteen feet below. Your predecessor is still attached by the static lines of the umbilical cord to the plane as you cross the threshold.

And then you are in space, you are out in the great vastness of the world and falling. Like an animal you close your eyes. You have been taught to count "one thousand, two thousand, three thousand," as loudly as you did so well when jumping off the mocked-up platform. But there are no words in you. You are counting farther in the vast pulse of the new outdoors. Your eyes are shut. You are seeing with sensation only. It is totally silent out here in space. You are completely alone, tucked in a half-ball, arms crossed mandarin-style. Your right hand, biting into the left side of your emergency chute, is ready to draw across and pull its red metal ring at what would be the "four thousand" count.

Suddenly hands seem to place themselves around your shoulders and waist. You get yanked back. Your fall is stopped with a jerk, like being tackled in football from behind. Your head is snapped back, and that foetal curve in which your body protectively coiled itself is abruptly opened. Your legs dangle straight, and you become conscious of having heavy feet. Your eyes open, and everything is blue and airy and silent all around except for one long disorderly choppy carpet called the world, which happens to be slanted up beside your ear but takes the position where it is lying just under you.

You've stopped falling. The earth—yes, that's what it is down there—is far away. Its patchy rug stretches all the way to the horizon ahead.

The air is beautifully quiet. Ahead, dangling and twisting, reaching up arms to their suspension cords or grabbing helmets knocked askew by their opening shock, is a long line of your comrades. Everybody is falling together, lined up just as they were in that noisy cabin with its ugly open door but with the difference that they are suddenly spaced much wider apart, stepped down like a staircase—the man ahead seemingly on your level, but the lead man so much lower you realize that all are actually sloping in an inclined row of white chutes.

You look up and see the most lovely sight of all, lovelier than an outspread landscape. It is the white silk canopy of your chute overhead. It has recovered from its opening shock before you have. The edge of the white panel still is palpitating—more gently than your heart—breathing with a slight give-and-suck motion as it feels the cushion of air. It looks like a big white sea anemone, breathing underwater, calm and regular. You are falling, but you are falling safely.

After glancing up, you raise your arms to the "risers," the four webbed straps by which you dangle. A pair vee upward from each shoulder. To get a good look at the 28-foot white silk billowing so beautifully, you grab each pair of risers and spread them. If light shines through rifts in the chute, you have "blown" the panel. Then you can pull the red handle of the emergency chute, strapped to your chest. With both chutes open you get nearly the same rate of descent, because pushing against each other the two big silken mushrooms partially deflate.

Usually after your chute snaps open, you oscillate like a pendulum in space. It is agreeable to know you are safe, but this motion is the most dangerous element in jumping. It is not vertical fall at a gentle rate of 14 to 20 feet a second that is perilous, but a sidewise swing on the ground. No soldier is so vulnerable as a paratrooper lying with a broken leg on a field, trussed in equipment from which he cannot free himself.

At this moment, when the white static line which opens the chute is left behind, pasted by the wind to the plane's fuselage, each paratrooper ceases to be a jumper and prepares to fight.

The deadly metronomic oscillation, which every puff of wind accentuates, can be stopped only by another stunt with the risers. Having grasped both pairs and examined the inside of the canopy, the swinging paratrooper shifts his hands and grabs the risers diagonally—either the front left and rear right, or the front right and rear left. Then he starts "climbing," or pulling down on the thick webbing. This flattens the parachute into an oval like a meat-dish cover. The wind causing the oscillation slips by, and the swings become shorter.

Parachutists share one thing with aviators; the higher they are, the safer they feel. Yet safety is denied in all directions: if the jump is high they present a target to the enemy for a dangerously long time, while if dropped from low altitude they may be unable to check their pendulum swings in time to prevent broken legs.

U.S. Army jumpers have been dropped in combat from 400 feet or lower.

While halting his oscillation, the infantryman studies the ground. On a small sandtable in a corner of the parachute repair shed, he has often seen this land pattern in miniature, with trees indicated by pinches of moss on sticks, and rivers by torn strips from chute panels. Now here is the real thing below him.

Contrary to the general view, trees are not dangerous in themselves. Though canopies entangled in branches can cause costly delays, injuries in trees are no more numerous than injuries suffered in landing on the ground. What the chutist fears is rocks and, above all, water.

Parachutists struggle with their risers because they are trying to steer. The main problem is to land with the wind either from the rear or from the front. If the chutist hits the ground while sweeping sideways, the crash can knock him out or cripple him. Landing "squared away" downwind, the paratrooper knows that he can take up the landing shock by tumbling forward. Or if the wind is blowing in his face, the ground carpet unrolling at his feet instead of being hauled away behind him, the paratrooper gets ready with a backward tumble.

In the last few feet, the ground rushes up swiftly. The chutist's last act before hitting is to take a deep breath and give a simultaneous pull downward on both pairs of risers, using all the strength he possesses. The vicious pull lessens the landing shock by increasing the pressure of air imprisoned in the canopy, hence slowing his falling speed.

Rolling as he lands, the chutist comes to his feet, sometimes amid the silken mesh of suspension lines. Throwing them off, he jumps to his feet, unlimbers his short carbine and begins unsnapping the chute harness. If the billowing chute is pulling him over the ground, he outdistances it by running in a half circle downwind until he gets on the other side of the chute. As the chute turns, it is deflated.

Sometimes the paratrooper is under fire. Without stopping in the exposed middle of the field, he dogtrots as fast as his overloaded pack will let him to the "assembly point." The deflated chute lies on the ground. Parachutes are expendable and so, too, in the grim way of war, are paratroopers; it will be recovered by us if we win, by the enemy if we lose.

And that's what it's like to jump as a paratrooper.

—

THE SERVICEABLE WRECKS OF NEW GUINEA

1944

The battle for New Guinea was a war between two shipwrecks. No historian will ever tell it that way. Yet without those two rusty, bomb-distorted hulks, one Japanese, one Allied, the duel for air dominance over the ex-German mandate of New Guinea and the Australian territory of Papua might have gone far differently.

Like felled lighthouses, immutable to tides and weather, the two wrecks lie on the northern and southern coasts that slope up to the 16,000-foot wet green roof of the Owen Stanley Range. They lie almost opposite each other, the Allied victim on a bluish-green top branch of Australia's Great Barrier Reef in the Coral Sea just outside Port Moresby, and the Japanese corpse off Gona on a submarine appendage of the manifold coral labyrinths of the Bismarck Sea. These two wrecks were the pylons of the race for air power over New Guinea.

Flattened on the darkened foredeck of a prowling PT boat, the writer drifted one night past the Japanese wreck. An enemy bomber, hunting for coastal creeping LSTs and LCIs, hummed through the stars. Sagging overhead like a building ready to fall, fishes swimming in phosphorescence through her bulkheads, the Japanese merchantman seemed forever bound for that nearby beach she would never attain.

Escaping Japanese often made their way out in native outrigger *lakatois* over three miles of tepid, tropical sea to their wreck. They would hide in the slanting, shattered cabins, ransack the sea-soaked stores for rice and small cans of infantry tunafish, and hope for rescue. When they had an officer to give them orders, they would build machine-gun nests on the starboard side, away from the binoculars of our beach patrols. From these nests they shot up covert fusillades, in the half light of dawn or sunset, at low-flying attack bombers on their way north to strafe Rabaul.

Often search parties were sent to the wreck with hand grenades and dynamite and orders to give the cadaver a thorough de-lousing. Scraps of rice and fish would be found behind the flaky brown lifeboat davits, and fresh .50-caliber jackets in the scuppers. But the stowaways were deep in the half-flooded, labyrinthine depths. It is never easy to dig the Japanese from his dugout; in this weird wreck, where anemone and coral clung and glowed in the Venetian corridors, it was impossible.

On a brilliant day, crammed piggyback in a single-seater P-38 photographic plane, head jammed against the shoulder of Lieutenant Fred Hargesheimer, the writer took a buzzing look at the other shipwreck: our own freighter that lies on the reef off Moresby. Even from the air, and over two miles up, one could see it was scribbled over by fifty-calibers. Unlike the slanting Nipponese merchantman, this wreck sat squarely upright on its reef, like a battered drunkard proving a doubtful sobriety. Had the freighter been pierced in those repeated bombings of Moresby in the first year of war, when our Kittyhawks, American- and Australian-flown, were far outnumbered by Zeros? Or did some Japanese sub, patrolling the mouth of the glaring Torres Strait, nail her in those evil, difficult first days as the freighter slipped outside the heavy net at Moresby? Nobody was certain.

Hargesheimer circled at 10,000 feet, then stabbed a finger. The twin tails of the P-38 arose and we went down in an ear-stopping dive. The water came up fast, as though the sea were a blue enameled basin, daubed with the off-green and white of the coral reefs. Just when it seemed our nose would dip the waves, Hargesheimer pulled back the stick and we were off in a flat glide, roaring over the wavecrests, scattering schools of flying fish to veer away. The wreck was ahead.

She must have once been black. Now she was sourly rusty, burned, chewed by bullets and cannon shells like an old shoe worried at by dogs— the eyelets of her portholes torn apart, the heel of her fantail half ripped away and sagging. Whatever skipper had beached her on that reef had beached her well. Great bomb holes had torn her sides. The Coral Sea lapped her vitals. Her stack seemed made of bronze lace. Her bridge and superstructure, the brow and visage of a ship, looked like the punch-bitten face of a hobo prizefighter. Yet for all her mutilations, she still rode astride her reef. And her wounds were honorable; those marks in her side were made by friendly bombs, if there is such a thing. For this anonymous freighter was the true victor of the battle of the Bismarck Sea. Here, lagging on a reef outside Moresby, lay the tackling dummy of Pacific air power. The stuffing was leaking out, the uprights were sagging; even the dummy's name had been stricken from Lloyd's. Yet this dummy had taught tackling to the squad that saved New Guinea.

New Guinea, and Australia with her, was twice rescued by U.S. air power. The first time was the Battle of the Coral Sea when two American aircraft carriers, the *Lexington* and the *Yorktown,* halted a combined Japanese task and invasion force attempting to round the corner of New Guinea southbound—a critical and desperate encounter in which much went wrong, a wild act of defense for navyless Australia by an ally which had lost most of its force at Pearl Harbor. When the Battle of the Coral Sea was over, the remnants and bodies of the *Lexington* were scattered across the sea approaches to Port Moresby, from gold-veined Misima Island to

where the Mud People at the mouth of the Fly River grub out their insect-
tormented existence.

Ten months later there took place off New Guinea another far different
battle of air power against sea power for the salvation of Australia. Re-
hearsed, practiced, and methodically executed, the Battle of the Bismarck
Sea was the turning point of MacArthur's campaign. A reported 22 Japanese vessels left Rabaul and crept down western New Britain through the
Bismarck Sea into the Huon Gulf. Their task was to relieve the Emperor's
fading garrison at Lae, whose supply barges had been lacerated by PT
boats. Not one vessel arrived. For three days that convoy underwent the
bitterest, most systematic lashing of air power any seaborne force encountered. Fortresses, Liberators, Mitchells, Bostons, Lightnings, Kittyhawks,
Airacobras and Australian-flown Hudsons cut the Japanese force into
smoking hulks and oily eddies. Most of the Japanese troops stayed below
decks and went down with their transports. Bodies were scattered over
miles of water. The sharks feasted.

How was the convoy's annihilation made possible? Only by the tackling
dummy on the reef outside Moresby. For it was here that skip-bombing,
deck-level bombing, and masthead bombing were first tested in the Pacific.

Where should you drop your bomb: fifty feet from the side of the *What-
sis Maru,* or twenty? Should the bomb be skipped in, like a flat stone making one hop before it strikes? Or should it be slugged in close to the
waterline in a shoestring tackle? What are your chances of a hole-in-one in
the smokestack? . . . In many long hours of rehearsal on the old wreck such
questions were answered.

When should the high-level bombers loose their falling patterns of
death, when the mediums, and when should the Water Level Limited go in?
What is the right moment for strafing, the specialty of the Australian Beaufighters and the American A-20s? What should be the cue of torpedo-
carrying specialists like the Hudsons?

All these delicate timings, aimed to exploit every weakness of a convoy,
had been reckoned in the hilltop headquarters of the Fifth Air Force long
before the Japanese admiral led his doomed column past the fuming volcano of Rabaul. We decided, in those months, how the Battle of the Bismarck Sea was to be fought. As Lieutenant General George Kenney, the
little ex-fighter pilot who commands the Fifth, might say, we planned it

that way. The wreck on the reef outside Moresby made it possible to re-hearse, at the very edge of the aerial front, these new tactics.

There were casualties. No bombing range, even back home in the United States, is without them. More than one B-25 picked himself up from deck level too late, caught the freighter's goalposts with a wing, and went in to death. Sometimes a bomb skipped too far out would jump the riddled torso and explode on the other side. More than one P-39 was lost determin-ing how close, for a fighter, is too close.

But the old wreck was always there. Whatever new stunt they thought up to test on it, however big the bomb and terrible the impetus, the old freighter absorbed the punishment. She was the Durable Malloy of all the Pacific, and like that famous stumblebum who absorbed poison, was run over, frozen, beaten and thrown into the East River, the ancient hulk took everything slung at her, without dishing any out.

The Japanese wreck, on the other side of the Hump, had a double role in the battle for New Guinea. First, it was a memorial.

When the Japanese were halted at the China Strait by the *Lexington* and *Yorktown,* they drew back just long enough to prepare at Rabaul an-other invasion force for New Guinea. Seven American A-24 Dauntless dive bombers, remnants of that same outfit which had tried to stop the Japa-nese at Bali, went out to meet them. The war was eight months old; our ex-perience was thin. Something went wrong about the rendezvous with the top cover of Airacobras—the lone P-38 in New Guinea in those days was a gunless photographic job—and only two crews of the A-24s got back. But one of the crews that was missing, before they died, launched the bomb that put that Japanese merchantman on the reef between Buna and Gona. They died, but provided themselves and their comrades with a tombstone.

Besides being a memorial to the last dive bomber outfit in New Guinea, the Japanese wreck became a kindergarten. It taught fliers—not the vet-erans preparing the Battle of the Bismarck Sea, but novices fresh from the States.

The B-26s, a lonely and little-known bunch of specialists who did not even get into the famous battle, used to dry the ears of their fledglings on this wreck. Time after time an excited crew fresh from the States, not too certain of what was where on the deceptively rippled, imperfectly mapped coast of northern Guinea, would come back to Sloppy Joe's at the end of

Seven Mile Drome in Moresby to report: "Boy, we got a big 8,000-ton merchantman! Where? Oh, about three or four miles off Soputa or Sanananda or one of those places. We could see the wake—she was steaming along at about quarter-speed. Our bombardier let her have two 500-pounders and then I did a vertical bank and went right down close and she was listing and her crew had abandoned her guns and there wasn't a sign of life aboard! Boy, is that a thrill!"

The intelligence officer would take the exultant newcomer by the hand and lead him into the photographic tent. "Close your eyes, my friend," he would say kindly. He would put a photograph in the trembling hands of the novice. "Now open. Did your victim happen to look anything like that?"

"Uh-huh," the novice would say. "How'd you get the picture so quick?"

Then, watching the flush rise rosily into his hair, they would tell him. Once he had been told, he was a different pilot. Scratch one set of illusions. Log up a new kit of skepticisms. . . . The next Japanese merchantman the newcomers bombed would not be a reefbound cripple.

At one time MacArthur ordered the *Motionless Maru* to be blown up and destroyed. He did not claim she was a menace to navigation; indeed, she was an aid. Anything that stuck its head above the labyrinth of reefs was an asset to the uncelebrated mariners of small ships who spent their time listening for the crunch of a stove-in bottom as they tried to keep open the lines of coastal supply. The trouble was this: after enemy bombers were driven from daylight skies by our fighters, they came back at night, when harassing is cheaper in losses though bombing is less accurate. From above at night our bases like Oro Bay and Morobe appeared almost alike, because the coast here is scalloped with identical-looking harbors and pseudo-harbors. MacArthur believed that the Japanese bombers, which were attacking our coastal supply LSTs and vagabond schooners, were orienting themselves by the prostrate merchantman. The current at her stern was often so strong that it showed a white fishtail of phosphorescent water visible at night three miles in the air.

But soon Lae, Gasmata and Finschafen were taken. We jumped to Cape Gloucester and pushed toward Rabaul. New American night fighters began to make harassing raids unhappy affairs for the Japanese night bombers. If the Japanese pilot tried to beat a course from Rabaul for his old friend the *Motionless,* he was as likely as not to find a night fighter there in the dark waiting at his altitude for him—with guns primed. So the order to wreck the wreck was not carried out.

They still squat in mutilated magnificence on their home reefs on the opposite shores of New Guinea, those two old reprobates of wrecks. They will squat there, probably, until the war ends, or at least until the salvage phase hits New Guinea. Then the hairy salvage men, civilian scavengers as rusty as themselves, will go out in stubby Tazzy boats and cut them up into iron. In lighter after lighterful of scrap they will be hauled away in fragments. In some drab foundry in Townsville or Brisbane they will return to the anonymity of melted iron. And once more the waves of the Coral Sea and the Bismarck Sea will suck and draw rhythmically on the two vacated reefs. The bright fishes will move in and out; the submarine weeds will wave, graceful in their dance; and all that happened on the two reefs will be forgotten.

<u>CERTIFICAT ADMINISTRATIF</u>

Je soussigné, PASSARD, Charles, Chef de la Circonscription administrative des Iles-Sous-Le-Vent, certifie que M. Georges WELLER, correspondant de guerre auprès des Forces navales américaines dans le Pacifique Sud est autorisé par le commandement américain à se rendre en mission spéciale à Papeete.

M. WELLER est prié de bien vouloir se présenter au Commissariat de Police du Chef-lieu.

Uturoa le 13 aout 1943

XIII

The Struggle for the Islands

To escape the malarial zone and recover his health, Weller left New Guinea briefly for Australia in June 1943 and set out for five months of incessant wanderings among island groups: the Solomons, site of some of the fiercest fighting in the region; the Ellice Islands; the Fijis; the Tonga Islands; the Society Islands (Tahiti, Bora-Bora); and the Cooks (Rarotonga, Aitutaki). There may have been more, but Weller published fewer dispatches in this period than usual and went silent for weeks at a time. Not all his journeys are documented.

His work in the Solomons—he just missed the struggle for Guadalcanal—makes up many of his island stories. He was fascinated by the new questions of terrain, strategy, and supply that island warfare was presenting to the Allies. I have chosen to provide a diverse sense of the dispatches, including a surprising piece from Tahiti on acupuncture. Sadly, there are no portraits of two great literary figures of the South Seas who became his friends: James Norman Hall (1887–1951), longtime resident of Tahiti and coauthor of the *Mutiny on the Bounty* trilogy; and Robert Dean Frisbie (1896–1948), author of *The Book of Puka-Puka*, whom Weller met on Rarotonga.

Notable among the stories is a portrait of Tonga, a resolute Polynesian society that maintained its equilibrium through two centuries of foreign designs in the region; and an exploration of the problems of warfare on a naked atoll, with nowhere to hide— the antithesis of a New Guinea jungle.

Bombs Hit Rabaul Target Squarely in Raid in Pacific Dawn

An Advanced Allied Operational Base in the Southwest Pacific—August 11, 1942

There was something unforgettable about this heaviest raid upon Rabaul. Sleeping under the stars in a dust-covered truck with an old potato bag over your knees, hearing the quiet breathing of the ground control men on the canvas cots in the control hut, you had no way of knowing that great events were impending.

Somewhere far off across the sea, as would be learned two days later, Americans were striking at the southeastern Solomons. But the target was still secret and none of the pilots offered a clue.

The headlight beams of the bomb trucks poked through rolling clouds of dust as the first planes arrived and departed. The ground control men still slept, for their hour was not here yet. In the darkness a dusty jeep came up and men jumped out and others jumped in and drove away. A shady light was on in "Sloppy Joe's," where there was lukewarm coffee, crackers and cheese with the pilots.

The bombers, propellers at rest and their bodies made more massive by the darkness, stood awaiting their crews with that curious nimbleness of great machines when man is absent. Then we saw the first truck loaded with swaying men come out as dawn came up over New Guinea. The covered-wagon-style truck, that saves the men a long weary walk through the ever-rolling dust clouds along the take-off run, appeared at the end of the field and began dropping men.

The slender waning moon was also fading and the first rim of the sun lifting above the horizon. This was the moment of briefing; the crews gathered in clusters. Their voices were low in response to the majors heading the various groups.

You went about trying to get some names of those about to launch themselves into the infinite. Names bring you quickly down to earth, and put you instantly in the United States which somehow is more real than the presence of all these boys in the far Southwest Pacific battling for Japan.

The palms now stood out in sharp silhouette along the rim of the surrounding hills. Men were heading out to meet the most maneuverable high-altitude plane of the war, going over the sea a distance so long that it denied them fighter protection. The bombers were once more depending only on their machine guns, and would attempt to blast their way through to Japan's biggest eastern base in the Pacific.

One motor far down the line sputtered and you saw it would be impossible to meet them all. It was a matter of running to the next monster ship as the first prop began to throw dust. Another big bomber was already whirring at the runway's end with the last member of the crew jumping aboard as the runway was cleared from the last dust cloud. Men wore yellow swim jackets or simply furred flying jackets.

By looking down the runway they could see that the raid they were going on was historic. Now briefing instructions were ended, even for the crews scheduled to take off last, and the men were breaking away, walking slowly in their heavy flying boots toward their machines.

When the bombers left, looking like a musical scale placed against the sky, there began the longest wait in the world. They were not informed until they left, and only afterward did their destination become known to us.

They were to smash the runway of Vunakananau Field near Rabaul, in the Solomons—smash it, if possible, beyond immediate repair. How important that smashing was we still were not told.

While a raid is in progress you might as well not ask Intelligence or Operations how things are going. They ladle out silence in bucketfuls—deep, rich, calm silence. They are thinking of the raid as a whole. But you cannot help thinking of the crews as people. Your palm is still warm with their handclasps.

"The bombers are out," you comment laconically.

"Oh," they say, and sit down.

Then you hear the first motor. It is over the mountains. You can count the motors—four. But as the plane moves overhead not all her propellers are invisible, as they should be. One is motionless.

"Oh, oh, Japs at work," says a gasoline truck driver.

The big craft swings around the field and before she has squared away and is sloping toward the runway, another roars over, and another. Each brings its separate joy at the return. They begin coming in, riding proudly in the terrific dust.

Everywhere are crews that have shot down at least one Jap. Now we have two, three, five. Here come more men clapping each other upon the back. "There must have been twenty Zeros at once," says a bombardier. Then, using the flier's indication for where he saw them, he says: "I saw two coming in at 11 o'clock and two coming up at 6 o'clock, with a whole bunch coming down at 12 o'clock."

What happened begins to assume form.

"Boy, I'd like to sock anybody who says anything against our bombing after this," says one officer. "I never saw a better bombing anywhere. We laid three absolutely perfect strings down that concrete runway, one to the right, one to the left, and one in the middle."

The door first open, you will later recall, is that of the plane piloted by a lieutenant colonel from Texas, seemingly too young to be a colonel, with a fresh, smiling face and white teeth. Their wings have been severely hit by a Jap Zero's shellfire but the Zero has paid with its life. Lieutenant F. A. Norwood shot him down—a dark-complexioned Southern boy, handsome and lively. His hands are small and his body, too, and he is still trembling with excitement.

"I saw him coming down with all his guns talkin' and he came right into mine," said Norwood. " 'Keep a-comin',' I says, 'and long's you keep a-comin' I'll keep a-shootin'.' And just when he passes under us he does a belly roll. That's when I got him."

But on the plane's floor there is one good comrade, who must be nameless, who fired his gun until the end and now will fight no more.

—

Long Struggle Ahead for U.S. in Southwest Pacific

Somewhere in Australia—October 22, 1942 (Via Honolulu—Delayed by Censor)

America's struggle to regain the British Solomons is teaching the public of the United States and Australia how long and hard is the task of our Navy and Air Forces in leading the way west to Singapore and north to Tokyo.

Among the latest announced losses are the U.S. cruisers *Quincy, Astoria,* and *Vincennes,* and while personnel losses are still undisclosed, it is possible to examine our sacrifices, together with Australia's loss of the cruiser *Canberra,* and gauge the eventual cost of mastering Japan. Land forces engaged in skirmishes in the Owen Stanley Range of New Guinea are only fractional as compared with those on the plains of Guadalcanal.

Several major American naval battles in the Southwest and South Pacific area have been fought in various straits, from Sumatra to the Solomons farther east—the Macassar battle, the Bali Strait battle, the battles of the Java Sea and of the Coral Sea. Now come two bills for the recovery of about a third of the Solomons, the archipelago which the Japs took from the British without resistance. The bills for these successes are not small. Japan's, however, seem greater.

It is significant that a Navy communiqué states that these losses were incurred partly to protect Darwin, nearly two thousand miles away on the Australian coast. Darwin may be classified as yet another outpost of empire whose strength, when war was declared, was purely potential and hypothetical.

When it is realized that the American crew of any one of the three cruisers sunk was the equivalent of the total white population of the whole Solomon Islands, some idea can be derived of what disproportions the U.S. Navy is now correcting. The only British force there consisted of the police plus two tiny gunboats used to enforce peace and collect taxes from the headhunters.

When the Marines plunged through the surf by the hundreds in the face of enemy fire, they were taking back Tulagi, a town with only one 67-foot wharf, and an area where the white population never reached two hundred. In repairing these long-vacant gaps, the American people must be prepared to make even greater sacrifices. Our Navy is essentially creating a system of air and naval bases to replace those forsaken in the retreat before the Pacific fleet arrived upon the scene.

In this conflict figures tiny Savo, in the Solomons between the northwest extremities of Guadalcanal and Florida Island and within sight of Cape Esperance, where Japanese cruiser and destroyer convoys have been landing reinforcements.

Unlike the cannibals of the other Solomons the Savo natives are peaceable. Their midway location made their islet a frequent calling post for trade schooners.

At Savo's northwest, facing Cape Esperance, a Roman Catholic mission has long been situated. Two Catholic priests and one sister identified with these missions were found dead, bayoneted in the throat; another sister escaped. There was another Catholic mission on the slopes of Mt. Veisali until the Japanese landed.

This part of the Solomons is swept year-round by southeast trade winds, but when these begin to clash around Christmas with northeast winds, the general weather conditions become worse, with rain falling half an inch daily.

As at Milne Bay at the southeast corner of New Guinea, MacArthur's strong point guarding China Strait's coconut-covered islands, the principal exploiting agency is the Lever Brothers Pacific Plantations Proprietary Ltd. which, until the Japs came, maintained an engine and boat repair shop.

It is noticeable that when American Flying Fortresses drive across Buka and Bougainville (where the Japanese have built bases and airdromes), they are hitting two islands which, though geographically part of the Solomons, were mandated to Australia as part of New Guinea. This was done under the Versailles Peace Treaty, the Pacific lines of which were arranged at the imperial conference of June, 1918, six months before World War I ended.

—

AUSSIE OFFICER DETESTS NOISE, BUT GRENADES ARE SWEET MUSIC

Somewhere in Australia—November 21, 1942

How fantastic a figure—compounded of daring, resourcefulness and hair-trigger sensitivity—an Australian guerrilla leader can be is illustrated by a story about one of these officers in Timor.

A Digger who accompanied a guerrilla officer on patrol through a Japanese-occupied town related this tale:

The officer had his finger inserted through the ring in a Mills hand grenade and kept twirling it carelessly around. The Digger kept wondering whether the grenade might not explode accidentally.

As the scouting party moved through the streets of the town, the officials of which had been banished and replaced by the Japanese military, the Australian officer suddenly whirled upon his companion and exclaimed: "Will you stop that bloody racket?"

The Digger discovered that the "bloody racket" so offensive to the keen leader was nothing but the gurgling of the water in the Digger's army flask.

"But he made more noise than I at the next corner," said the Digger. "A Jap sentry challenged us. And my commander said, 'There you are,' and gently tossed him the grenade."

—

ISLANDERS TAKE UNWARY IN WITH SQUARE HERRING
Somewhere in Australia—December 2, 1942

Horn Island in the northeastern corner of Australia, occasionally mentioned in Allied communiqués when the Japs attempt bombing raids there, is now known as a place of "square fish and mustache wax."

Americans and Australians, who have been quartered on Horn Island for several months, have set themselves the task of "selling Horn" to the rest of the Allied forces. Their favorite method of accomplishing this is by returning to the Australian mainland on leave and persuading the ignorant continental yokels to bet that there is no such thing as a fish that is square in shape.

After the money is deposited with neutral parties, the Horn Islander returns to camp and then sends to the referee a peculiar fish found there, which is actually square in form.

Through long semi-isolation, Americans and Australians on Horn Island have achieved what amounts to a new insular consciousness. The other day the supply department was puzzled to find an order for several cases of mustache wax. The Horn Islanders had passed a new law whereby all residents, whether American or Australian, must grow mustaches and wax them daily.

Life on Horn gets queerer and queerer as the weather gets hotter.

—

YANKS PIERCE JAP RING TO RIP MACASSAR

Somewhere in Australia—June 24, 1943

Yawning crews of American heavy bombers awoke in their frosty camps in northern Australia this morning to find that yesterday's raid against Macassar at high noon had broken every long-distance record of the war for land-based planes, save the single stroke dealt some months ago from Hawaii against Wake Island.

As the news that Macassar had been struck flashed across Australia, it electrified not only experts who know the intricate charts of enemy bases in the Indies but especially Dutchmen whose hope of recovering their lost empire lies in such super long-range stabs of surprise.

Thirty-eight tons of high explosives and fire bombs fell on this Japanese rear base. But the force of the raid cannot be measured even by the fact that its fires could be seen seventy miles away, or that the round-trip distance flown to this former Dutch port was probably well over 2000 miles.

What is causing uplifted hearts is that for once we have struck deep into Japan's "dead hollow" system of defense. For the first time its triangulated plan for protecting its greatest resources—Tokyo, the Solomons, and Batavia—was pierced. This Macassar raid penetrated the airdrome bases forming their triangle defense along the Indies island chain (from Fakfak and Babo in New Guinea to Somebawa and Kendari in the Celebes) and knifed the Japs in their central area of support.

In distance alone it equaled the Royal Air Force raids from London to Naples and Warsaw, but it was accomplished not under cover of darkness but by daylight. In other words, the fliers of General MacArthur and Lt. General Kenney deliberately informed the Japanese they were coming in, being obliged to fly directly over the islands' chain of listening and watching posts, and challenged the Jap fighter defenses to do their worst against our B-24s' biting .50-calibers.

The Japs accepted the challenge by putting up formidable anti-aircraft fire from batteries dug in along the shore and from warships' guns. Apparently this took little effect, despite the advantage of daylight, for the only

bomber lost fell due to a collision—possibly suicidal—with the single perforated Jap fighter which tried to repel this heavy American force.

These Liberator bombers are already known as superlative merchant
raiders, their armed reconnaissance having taken over the role that cruisers once held in other wars. But that they could lug bombs this far into
Japanese defenses—notably beyond the rear door of Kendari, the air base
from which the Japs hammered Soerabaya into submission—is remarkable. It was a demonstration that when General Keene went to Washington, as the last Jap destroyer was sinking in the Bismarck Sea battle, and
said, "Give me more aircraft and I will show you more targets," this energetic stubble-haired little general was ready to fulfill his promises.

Though Macassar's biggest docks were soundly pummeled, it is clear
that bombing these places harasses rather than defeats the foe. Nothing
important is manufactured there. But this raid proved our bombers can
penetrate more deeply into the Jap defenses than had been expected.

—

The Pin-up Doctors of Tahiti

South Sea Medics Find Strange New Cure

Papeete, Tahiti, Society Islands—August 30, 1943

The great mid-Pacific campaign of the United States Navy, the mightiest
air and naval symphony the world has ever seen, did not open with a crash
of great guns. It began with the occupation in early 1942 of a small French
possession in the heart of the Pacific: Wallis Island. Nothing could seem
more unlikely than that this landing should affect the history of medicine.
Yet a series of circumstances was started which has given the Western
world the first systematic experience of curing the sick by acupuncture.

Wallis is the lowermost of the islands and archipelagoes leading up
through the Ellices to the Gilberts, and from the Gilberts westward into
the Marshalls and Carolines. When the Navy gently arrived it freed a
French colonial physician who is one of the most extraordinary figures of
the South Seas.

Doctor Leon Vrignaud, who lives and practices medicine in an obscure corner of Tahiti, is a blue-eyed, bald, stocky thirty-nine. He has accomplished a remarkable series of cures by the unheard-of method of pricking the afflicted with gold and silver needles.

"I am not a charlatan or a sorcerer," says Vrignaud. "All I know about acupuncture I learned out of a book. Anybody else could learn it and with practice apply it in the same way."

As long as he lived on Wallis in the middle of the Pacific, receiving orders by radio from the Vichyist governor of French Indo-China in Saigon, his work as an acupuncturist was unsung. With his wife, his child and a single radio operator as the only white residents of the island, he was little known to the outside world.

Taravao, where Vrignaud quietly practices acupuncture today, is at the extreme eastern end of Tahiti. Although only walking distance from Stevenson's one-time villa, it is difficult of access from Papeete except by a single Polynesian-packed autobus. To call on Vrignaud, the writer formed a small bicycle party consisting of James Norman Hall—the kindly and generous-hearted Iowan who has become a kind of American mayor of the South Seas—an Australian friend of Hall's, and the U.S. consul in Papeete. It required a full day, bicycling the long way around the island's road from west to east, to reach Taravao.

The doctor, a man of almost shy deportment, lives with his small son in a modernized native home lifted several feet above the ground. His spotless clinic, a modest one-story white structure, is equipped with a full complement of surgical instruments and medicines like the much larger government clinic at Papeete.

Almost from the time Vrignaud arrived from Wallis, a trickle of both Polynesians and Americans and Europeans began to make their way over the approximate fifty miles of highway from congested Papeete to the tiny rural clinic. Taravao became a kind of Tahitian Lourdes. Because he could not singlehandedly cope with all the ailing who came to him to be needled, Vrignaud eventually had to refuse treatments to patients from outside his own country doctor's district.

The feet of this writer had been operated on in an American army clinic at Aitutaki in the Cook Islands, and the long bicycle ride from Papeete had affected the bandages. It was necessary for Vrignaud and his Polynesian assistant to change the dressing. As he did, Vrignaud remarked: "Perhaps you have heard I use acupuncture to cure all cases. Nothing of the kind. I have seen what it can accomplish, but I never use the needles if I know more conservative methods will give sure results. It is only when the conventional methods have failed that I employ needles. Even if they fail to effect an improvement or a cure, a simple prick cannot harm the patient, and most of the time does not even draw blood. It pierces the skin only for a few seconds."

Vrignaud's clinic, of course, was stormed by patients who expected him to cure everything from leprosy to lockjaw. The reason was not in his cures alone. By a totally unreasonable combination of chances the U.S. Navy, when it politely dislodged Vrignaud from the residency at Wallis, was sending him to the only other South Seas island which possessed an acupuncture pioneer.

As a Cagliostro* of medicine—the reputation which saddles both doctors—Albert LeBoucher, fifty-five, a portly, retired businessman of Papeete, is more improbable than Vrignaud. As a physician he is strictly an amateur. The role of wizard had been thrust on him by his accidental discovery of the art from an American friend. That was a decade ago, about when LeBoucher sold off the department store he had long operated in Papeete. Although it has brought him no financial revenue—French law making gainful practice illegal for a physician without diploma—acupuncture has left LeBoucher little time to himself. (Those physicians who considered him a public danger could not take steps against him, because only the profit motive makes such cures culpable.)

Vrignaud, through the chronic gasoline crisis which has stripped Tahiti's roads of all but an occasional bus, has been able to keep from being overwhelmed by his clientele. Not so the affable LeBoucher. He works from eight in the morning to eight at night, sticking his indefatigable needles into patients. He never accepts a *sou* for his labors. This dedicated service has been going on for over ten years. It has survived derision and attack from every side.

Acupuncture broke in unasked on LeBoucher's contented retirement.

---

*Count Cagliostro, an eighteenth-century Sicilian magician, occultist, and swindler.

The tiny office he keeps in the rear of a café-saloon on a side street of Papeete, a clinic hardly bigger than two telephone booths, is nearly always occupied by a client. A characteristic of both acupuncturists is their unpretentious attitude. Vrignaud's fees are the standard clinical ones whether he does acupuncture or not, and LeBoucher's fees are nothing at all. Both say: "What we have done, you or anyone else could do. It is only a matter of practice."

Their methods of curing patients, most of whom are educated, fully literate Polynesian natives, cause curiosity among the U.S. Navy officers and occasional airmen who visit Tahiti. According to both men, a difference of a few millimeters between the points pricked may be the difference between cure and failure.

How valuable is acupuncture? How many cures has it accomplished?

LeBoucher has been pricking people for ten years, but has no records of his patients. Vrignaud keeps records in his clinic, just as in his previous posts in Dakar and at Lao Kay in French Indo-China. Such records, if shared, might imperil his position with his superiors, who regard his experiments with differing degrees of tolerance. To make a firsthand survey of all the scattered Tahitians treated by the two men would be the work of six months at least (which this writer was unable to do before the next Air Transport Command plane left Bora-Bora).

"I started this acupuncture very slowly and skeptically," Vrignaud assured me in Taravao. Although many patients come in the spirit that impels Tahitians to close their windows at night lest a *tupapau* (ghost) creep in, the majority have the same tentative spirit as the doctor. A good example is Lewis Hirshon, an American family man of means and one of the most stable figures of Tahiti.

During the years of LeBoucher's practice, Hirshon, a New Yorker who owns a Tahiti canning factory, a dairy, and an inter-island steamer, was unimpressed. He regarded these cures, as did nearly all European residents, as a kind of unconscious quackery. He knew LeBoucher as a businessman, and could not think him a charlatan, but felt there was mutual self-deception going on between "doctor" and patients that persuaded these people they were cured.

When Vrignaud, with a degree granted by the University of Bordeaux in

1930, arrived from Wallis and began to practice acupuncture, *le tout Tahiti*, including Hirshon, were upset. Those who made fun of the genial merchant LeBoucher had to consider their attitude afresh in light of the bothersome presence of the experienced colonial physician, whose official medical record was second to none and who had been using the needle longer even than LeBoucher.

Hirshon, who is in his early forties, over six feet tall and brawny, had been troubled for some time with a pronounced stiffness in his back. The condition grew worse, and he became unable to sit, or stand upright. He tried massages, oils and ointments; all failed.

In a mood to risk anything, but feeling ridiculous, he motored to Taravao in his big car. He stood in line like all the Polynesian patients. When his turn came, Vrignaud gave him a regular checkup, asked a few questions, then opened his box of gold and silver needles. He pricked Hirshon in the trunk and in the leg. "Do you feel any better?" he asked. "Not at all," said Hirshon. "If you feel no better in two weeks, come back again," said Vrignaud.

Two weeks passed and Hirshon's condition was unimproved. He was as bent over as ever. He reproached himself for acquiescing to a superstition. His gas rationing was low, the distance to the end of Tahiti was long, and he resolved not to go back. At the last moment, acting on impulse, he drove to Taravao and waited in line again, "feeling more foolish than ever." Vrignaud pricked him again, in almost the same places. Hirshon felt no better, and flatly said so. He left the bottle-lined office and went into the corridor, as painfully hunched as ever.

"I was kicking myself," he says, "for having spent the gas to see this phony doctor a second time. I stood reading some document framed on the wall. The print was small and I had difficulty. One minute I was bent over the way I had been for weeks. And the next minute *I found I was standing up straight.* Don't ask me how it happened; I don't know. And I haven't had another attack since."

On this point Hirshon is unshakeable: Vrignaud used the needle on him twice, and his crooked, painful back was straightened and relieved. "They can say all the rest is old wives' tales, if they want to. But not my case. It happened to *me.*"

When the writer asked Dr. Vrignaud which cure astonished him most, the acupuncturist said, "They sent me a carpenter who had not been able to lift anything for two years. I cured him. I can't explain it myself. He works, now."

LeBoucher preserves even more original wonder than Vrignaud. "I had an American friend," he says. "He came to the island as a tourist. He had many books. He knew that I used to read a great deal since I retired. When he went away he left me this book which changed the course of my life."

The volume which LeBoucher refers to as "the book" is a paper-covered summary of acupuncture, a short popularization of a longer work translated from Chinese—the only such in a Western language—brought out by George Soulé de Morant, at one time French consul general in Shanghai. De Morant is responsible for bringing acupuncture from China, where it originated, to the Occident.

LeBoucher read this book idly, thought it somewhat occult, but kept it. Not long afterward the youngest of his four sons, then in his teens, fell ill. He lost weight, grew weaker and seemed to waste away, as through tuberculosis. Regular physicians were unable to help. LeBoucher turned to the book.

Diagnosis for acupuncture is similar to an ordinary medical checkup of temperature, tongue, bowels and symptoms of pain. It has one important difference: acupuncturists consider the master key in the pulse. According to their theory, in each wrist there are not merely a single pulse but six. Three are on the surface, three below. An ordinary doctor is actually taking six pulses at once, though he does not know it.

Each pulse connects with an organ or a function, one with the heart, another with the kidneys, another with the liver, and so on. By trying each pulse, not for its tempo but for the strength or weakness of its beat, the acupuncturist determines which organ has been affected. If the organ needs stimulation, as shown by a weak pulse, certain points on the body must be pricked. If the pulse is hammering too hard and needs soothing, other points must be touched with the needle.

LeBoucher studied his son's pulse for the first time. The directions in the book indicated that his son's ailment lay in the bladder and the needle should be applied gently to his knee. Month after month LeBoucher persistently followed the method. At first three times a week, then every day, he placed a needle against his son's knee, penetrated the flesh a fraction of an inch—never enough to draw blood—held it there a moment, then withdrew it. There was no improvement. Feeling a fool, he cautioned the boy to say nothing of the treatment.

After carrying on this method for more than half a year, discouraged, he chanced to study the diagram more closely. He found he had not read the anatomy correctly. He had been pricking just off the point indicated by de Morant. He changed his attack slightly. "My boy's eyes cleared," he says. "He sat up. He said he felt better." The next day LeBoucher renewed the treatment in the new place. The boy continued to improve. Today he is large and healthy, not quite so big as LeBoucher's handsome eldest son Toti, a French officer whom the writer met at a Tahitian wedding, but strong and robust.

From the day LeBoucher cured his son he had no peace. The public sits in his barroom-anteroom day and night, awaiting free treatments. His bewilderment at the cures has changed slowly into a stubborn faith. "When Vrignaud came here," he says, "it was not so much that people stopped making fun of me. It was that I had a colleague who really knew his way around in medicine as well as acupuncture, one whom I could lean on."

One of LeBoucher's difficulties before Vrignaud arrived was that the Tahitians came to believe he has supernatural powers, since on one occasion he did bring a corpse back to life.

"I had gone to bed," he says, "when a phone call came from a village several miles from Papeete. They said a baby there was very ill. I drove out and found they were lying. The baby was already dead, but they did not say so because they knew I would not come. Everyone in the village was around the house, waiting for me. I said to them, 'I am not Christ, I cannot raise the dead. I am leaving.' They held me by force. They pulled me away from the car and into the house again. It was impossible. There was no pulse. 'I am sorry,' I said to the parents, 'but your baby's body is already growing cold.' Still they would not let me go. So finally I gave in. I got out the needles. I did not know where to begin. I am not a physician. I had no idea what the baby had died of, and there was no pulse to guide me. Not being a doctor like Vrignaud, without a pulse I am lost.

"Anyway, for fifteen minutes I pricked as I would if the heart were affected. There was no change whatever. It was hopeless. I tried to leave, but the bedroom was filled with villagers and they would not let me. 'Your baby is dead,' I told the weeping mother brutally. 'Let me go home. I cannot cure death.'

"Still they forced me back. So I got out the needle and began pricking again. The little body was completely icy and white. It was idiotic. At the end of an hour I got up and beat my way out to the door. They tried to hold me, but I managed to reach my car. There I found that the father had let the air out of my tires. It is a Tahitian trick to keep guests. The car was flat on its rims. 'Go back and try once more,' said the family. 'Meantime we shall pump up your tires.'

"Almost beside myself with anger, I went back. With my hand on the little cold pulse, I began pricking to stimulate the heart the same as before. Suddenly I thought I felt a tremor. I pricked again; again the same flutter. I waited a little. I thought it might be my own nerves. I continued pricking; I got the same tiny reaction. Soon you could see the heart beat. Warmth began to come into the body.

"I worked until dawn. I was drenched in sweat. I could not believe what I had done. I told those villagers they must not mention it to anyone. They promised, but they did not keep their promise. Never since have I been able to shake off a reputation of sorcery. And until Vrignaud came, the undertakers, my old friends in business life, were looking angularly at me, just like the physicians. They saw in me a competitor. Now I absolutely refuse to touch the dead. Dead is dead."

Vrignaud's arrival enabled LeBoucher to turn over all doubtful cases to the authorized physician. I asked Vrignaud how he felt toward the amateur; as fifty miles of road separates them, they see each other only rarely. "We are both learning at the same time," said Vrignaud carefully. "He does not have a medical education, and his text is a vulgarization of the theory. But he is an intelligent and cautious man, who recognizes his limitations and sends me any borderline cases. We do not pretend anything like perfect results, and in this way we avoid giving scandal to acupuncture until we are both better learned."

Vrignaud's own guide is Volume I of a set of three books on acupuncture by de Morant in Paris. This volume, bigger and more abundantly illustrated than LeBoucher's minor guide, has full drawings of the human body with the Chinese names for the pulses and organs and the points to be

pricked. It came out in April, 1940; its two successors were awaiting publication when France fell.

While LeBoucher has only two plain, double-ended gold needles, carefully cauterized after each use, Vrignaud has a boxful of needles, long and
short, thick and thin. The needles have no eyes; some have points on each
end. Otherwise I could see nothing remarkable about them. Both acupuncturists showed them freely and casually, and allowed me to handle them
without inhibition.

Besides the theory of pulses, acupuncture depends on *meridians*. It is
conceived that the body is vertically encircled by girdles of energy, each af-
fecting a given organ, just below the surface of the skin. The apparently ar-
bitrary points at which the needle touches the body are on these meridians.

These points of vulnerability seem wholly irrational, even to Vrignaud
and LeBoucher. For an ailment apparently located in the stomach the needle may be applied to the instep of the left foot, or perhaps a point behind
the lobe of the right ear. There is no pretense on the part of either doctor
that this singular treatment should appear other than cabalistic to one attempting to find its meaning. "We do not pretend to understand it ourselves," both say. "We are beginners. Each year we know better how to read
the pulses. It works; that is all we know."

Before the war, LeBoucher had some correspondence with de Morant to
find out whether acupuncture would cure filiariasis—the first form of ele-
phantiasis—and also malaria. The father-translator of acupuncture replied
from Paris saying that he had been unable to make any experiments, because South Sea diseases were rare in Europe. But he suggested certain
places that LeBoucher might prick, and asked for an account of results.
The war interrupted this correspondence, but LeBoucher looks forward to
resuming it. At his age, his studies are inevitably limited. Vrignaud, on the
other hand, intends to return to Paris on his first leave and study acupuncture at Saint-Louis hospital, where he first heard of it.

I asked Vrignaud his ratio of cures to treatments. (LeBoucher had said
that he found liver and kidney cases most often curable.) Vrignaud's particu-
larized list, in his slanting hand, read: "Female illnesses, neuralgia, sciatica,
intercostals pains, headaches—90% successful treatments. Asthma, diges-
tive troubles, disturbances of the liver, illnesses of the mouth and throat—
80% successful. Dental pyorrhea, functional heart troubles, and pulmonary

diseases—70% successful. Much less successful results were achieved on skin diseases and lockjaw."

With his small boy nestled in his arm, Vrignaud sat in an armchair of the tiny clinic at Taravao, and gave one last bit of advice. "There is much to be studied," he said. "Only one thing I have learned. You must never start from a fixed idea. First you give the patient a full analysis. Then you try all the pulses. Keep your mind open. Be willing to learn. Once I even cured a drunkard. One uses the needle gently. Yet there are surprises, there are many bold surprises. I am very much interested in acupuncture and I intend to follow wherever it leads."

—

YANK TOEHOLD IN NORTHERN ELLICES THORN TO JAPS

Goads Tojo into Hitting Back by Air—Marines and Sailors Cling to Nanumea Under Heavy Bombing

Funafuti, Ellice Islands—September 8, 1943 (Delayed)

In a whirl of yellow sand and powdery coral dust, two jeeps spun along the bright, greenish-blue edge of the coral lagoon and pulled up to the waterside with inches to spare.

Lt. Commander H. A. Sommer, an able young pilot, his flying boat jacket already strapped on, led us into a small launch. Minutes later we were climbing through the PBY's machine-gun blister and fitting on yellow float vests. Our destination, still mentioned, from habitual secrecy, as "up north," was Nanumea, or St. Augustine Island, America's newest thorn in the Jap-held Gilberts, 250 miles north from Funafuti, which we had held nearly a year without other progress.

"We may be able to land and may not," said one member of the crew. "It just depends on whether we can skirt our way among those coral heads. Every lagoon and every atoll is different."

Then the fitted cord, like that of an outboard motor, whirled the wheel of the flying boat's generator. The cabin filled with stinging gas. One motor caught and ran awhile. Then the flight engineer in his little perch reported that the two big motors had caught and turned over. A moment later the pilot ordered the whole pioneer party forward to lighten the tail. The blister windows were closed after the machine guns were swung in, and we took off in spuming spray.

Constant vigilance was maintained over the guns en route. Jap photo planes which had already been over Nanumea were sufficiently well-armed to strafe the ground, and they might find our far-ranging but slow PBY welcome meat.

With the engines' noise through the warily opened blisters filling first our ears, then all our senses, we droned on northward and Japanward over the sparkling blue sea. The slowly penciled lines on the navigator's chart lengthened as he marked, by minutes, our advance. Some officers loosened their pistols, knives and canteens—drinkable water is very rare on these atolls—dozed, or made notes.

Then came the moment when one of the machine-gunners, his headphones connecting him with Sommer, turned and peered ahead along his blister.

"The pilot says Nanumea is ahead," he reported.

Soon we came in over what seemed a broken fragment of watermelon rind lying on the azure water. Within the curving lagoon the water was light green, speckled with coral heads.

Four times we circled, trying to land. Sommer brought our big belly down, we touched, and upsurging water obscured the closed blisters as we raced along. The expression of a young Marine captain peering through a blister grew taut.

Then Sommer gunned the motors and the plane lifted suddenly, water drops beating a tattoo on the hull. Almost instantly the green fronds passed beneath, and we barely cleared the palm-fringed end of the closed lagoon.

Again we came down and raced over the yellowish flooded reef, touched experimentally and slowly settled while water churned past the blisters. Before long, two outrigger canoes with three paddlers each came from the beach where the red-roofed cupola of a mission church peeped over the palms. Each *paupau*, or canoe, had a native paddler fore and aft. One *paupau* had a tall, blond British lieutenant in Australian field hat, the other a husky Marine lieutenant.

"We've been just about photographed to death by those damned Japs," said the first Navy man we met as our canoe outriggers grounded on the coral beach. "Yesterday they strafed one of our small craft. I wouldn't be surprised if they were cooking up something."

Wiping his sweaty sunglasses, this correspondent walked down the palm-sheltered trail and was given a bar of chocolate as a gift.

There was no ceremony to mark the occasion of the first aircraft landing at our farthest point north in the mid-Pacific; everyone was too busy working. Most of the marines and sailors already had foxholes built. One said: "This is better than Funafuti, because you can go down six feet without getting flooded out by the sea."

This man little knew that within a few minutes he would be huddled in the very slit trench to which he now pointed with pride, as the Japs thundered down with twelve heavy bombers full of explosives.

When our pioneering PBY landed on another lagoon farther south as the sun was setting, the first beach officer who greeted us said: "You fellows had a narrow escape. Nanumea was raided by bombers just a few minutes after you left."

Anxious for those with whom we had just been talking, we pieced together the meager details coming through. Nanumea's guns had opened up bitter fire on the Japs, who, with unusual boldness, came over apparently unprotected by fighter escort. Most significant was that the Japs spent ninety minutes over the atoll, making a dozen separate runs. Though they were at least 450 miles from their nearest air base, this methodical examination of their target, with their fuel reserve constantly diminishing, indicates the body blows being exchanged between the Jap-held Gilberts and the American-held Ellices. For the moment, the Americans hold the offensive upper hand on the island chain but the Japs are retaliating in the air.

While the Japs caused little essential damage, both the Navy and Marines suffered casualties. At the crack of dawn, another flying boat was en route to Nanumea. Our dead were laid to rest, with the coral giving them final protection.

This correspondent had an opportunity to see with what expediency our wounded were handled. Not one injured man was left on Nanumea. Loaded into the big flying boat, they flew a total of 1100 miles, making the last edge to safety in an emergency-rigged transport plane under the care of a short, red-haired doctor. Lieutenant Meyer Zelics is a psychiatrist and an expert on treating battle shock, as well as a g.p. In the transport's chilly cabin two serious stretcher cases, like the blanketed, walking wounded, shared green lime lozenges with this correspondent.

One man, somewhat bomb-shocked, stared straight ahead. The others never failed to respond when spoken to or smiled at. Both serious stretcher cases were operated on minutes after the plane's wheels touched American soil. The one who had lain on the port stretcher lived, the one who rested on the starboard side died.

This correspondent will not soon forget how the shellshocked man looked bound up in a big leather jacket, staring straight ahead.

—

BRAVES DEATH TO SAVE BUDDY IN JAP BOMBING

Funafuti, Ellice Islands—September 11, 1943
(Via air mail)

When Japanese bombs, aimed for our Army B-24s based on the air field, screamed down over this palm-bordered atoll through skies bathed with moonlight, a tall, 22-year-old marine, Howard Barling, dived from his foxhole. Barling, a well-spoken former General Motors timekeeper in Pontiac, Michigan, had dug the foxhole, with his fellow marines, into hard-as-shale coral.

Somebody yelled: "Here they come."

One bomb hit Barling's *fale,* which is Samoan for hut. Another hit the M-shaped foxhole directly.

"I felt the concussion," says Barling. "Then dirt poured over me."

Even as he struggled from the dirt, Barling remembered seeing Sergeant Chester Woodward, of Springfield, Massachusetts, beside him in the trench. Nothing was visible of Woodward now but his helmet.

"I dug his face free so Woodie could see and breathe. His poncho still held him down. I dug away on that until it came free."

Barling remembered having seen another member of their squad lying face up in the dirt and started in his direction. Then an Army bomber loaded with bombs and gasoline, which had been burning, fizzed warningly.

Woodward dropped to the ground. The bomber blew up, wiping out everything in sight.

Both men plunged into a tiny swamp in the middle of the atoll and cooled their burning bodies. Then they started back. They found the man they had been looking for, who was crying: "Get me out of here." They hauled him free and threw three pails of water on him, but he kept on crying: "Get me out of here."

A sergeant led the shocked marine to an aid station. Next the two found Calvin Kilpatrick, who had been engaged in distilling drinking water from the sea when the blast came and buried him to the knees. They helped him free himself.

Three *fales* were burning and crackling around them, furnishing light for Jap bombardiers still cruising overhead.

With the earlier bomb burst, Kilpatrick had pulled William Sleider, gravely wounded, from one burning hut. "They got me," he said. Now three men hauled him down behind sandbags.

From the burning airplane, .50-caliber machine-gun shells were thudding and spitting against the sandbags. Suddenly another *fale* blew up and turned into a bonfire. Barling says: "Woodie decided it was too hot to continue there. He changed his mind about bandaging Sleider and loaded him on his back. I got a flat board—I think it was a door blown off a *fale*—and we put Sleider on that."

Sleider had been a circus freak specializing in grotesque expressions, and also a fire eater and a human pin cushion. He struggled for a long time in the hospital against his wounds, but finally died.

Barling was recently decorated with the Silver Star and Woodward was strongly commended.

—

YANKS ON ARUNDEL PROFIT BY POORER TACTICS OF JAPS

With Advanced American Troops on Arundel, Solomon Islands—October 7, 1943 (Delayed)

The American forces that attacked Arundel Island profited by a marked decline in the quality of Jap infantry tactics in the Solomons. American casualties were relatively few, though the engagement was extended.

Comparing terrains, this correspondent finds that the coral surfaces of the central Solomons group present problems of digging in and use of tanks about equal to those imposed by Papua's and New Guinea's fetid marsh-lands. As far as malaria in the Solomons is concerned, Arundel, New Georgia, Vella Lavella and Rendova islands are far less frequented by anopheles mosquitoes than is Guadalcanal.

The Japs split up their forces on the northern edge of Arundel and allowed themselves to be killed off separately, like segments of a severed snake. A few high officers remain to tell the tale of their debacle to the Son of Heaven, to whom they are directly subordinated. Many doubtless were killed in the several score barges blasted by the five-inch guns of American destroyers. But before they could leave Arundel—whose terrain only this correspondent has covered afoot—the colonel of this crack 13th Infantry Regiment was killed, as were two battalion commanders.

One regiment of our 25th Division, after walking 50 miles in 13½ hours, has all its officers intact. Although this division will have been outside the continental United States for three years this month, its morale remains good. Their attached artillery, which had faced more than 300 air raids in New Georgia and Guadalcanal, once saved all its supplies and ammunition when a determined horde of six Jap dive bombers and five Zeros raided our landing craft near Kokorana Island, southeast of Munda. So accurate was our defensive fire that the enemy bombs were ineffectual.

The Japs dragged a 77-mm field gun through twelve miles of jungle and began shelling the bivouac point-blank. Heading forth with a Browning automatic rifle, Hollis Johnson of Alabama alone killed five Japs and silenced the field gun.

This division is a typical American melting pot, with many Indian members and a considerable number of real or transplanted Hawaiians—like Lt. Colonel Robert Louis Stevenson of Honolulu. Thin, alert Major John Burden, who was a practicing physician in Honolulu and speaks Japanese well, taught the division to prepare and eat Japanese food. When the last Jap barges left Bairoko for Arundel, Burden was close enough to hear a defiant Jap commander give three *banzais* aloud as a pledge he would someday return in the Emperor's name. Later this challenge was found nailed to a tree and written in English, saying that while Americans might never forget Pearl Harbor, the Japs would concentrate on winning the next American-Japanese war if not this one.

When the 25th Division commander, Major General Joseph Lawton Collins of New Orleans, talks to his men, he says: "The Jap is a tenacious soldier but he's not so big and so strong and smart as you, and his equipment is not so good."

They have found this to be true. Collins also banned the use of the word "sniper" which has a foolish, panicky sound. He allows only "rifleman."

One decorated soldier summarized his battle with a Jap: "He missed. I didn't miss."

—

TINY, DEMOCRATIC TONGA SALTS AWAY DOLLARS, AND WAITS TO SEE THE ADS

Tongatapu, Tonga Group—October 11, 1943 (Via air mail)

Tiniest and least-known democracy of the United Nations, ruled with a gentle hand by a queen of giant proportions, the Kingdom of Tonga has withstood the distortions of war better than anyone ever expected.

Queen Salote (or Charlotte) Tupou, who celebrates this month the quarter-centennial of her reign, has been able to bring together her cabinet, her parliament, her British advisers and her American visiting commanders in a way that augurs well for the stability of the sole surviving house among the great fallen Polynesian dynasties. With the battle fleet and armies of the United States standing between it and Japan, and its political help confined to the British, this last remaining queen of the South Seas island empires can look forward to another two years of serene reign.

Queen Salote is 6 feet 2 inches tall and weighs more than 300 pounds. She is 43, a Methodist by faith, and the mother of two princes. A serious, dignified and intelligent ruler (contrary to the occasional thoughtless caricature to which her unusual physical dimensions have exposed her), Tonga's third sovereign in a hundred years has busied herself making easier the lot of those Americans and British who have been her guests since Pearl Harbor. In Tonga, the smallest of the powers at war with the Axis, the United Nations have an intelligent, politically alert, democratic ally, who has kept its own house in good order.

The independent Kingdom of Tonga—and very insistent is Queen Charlotte on its independence—lies on a line roughly between Fiji and New Zealand. It is a chain of islands, wholly Polynesian, equable in climate and healthy, and lying on the outer periphery of archipelagoes whose disposition has become extremely important to American interests in Australasia.

Compared to Luxembourg, its European prototype, Tonga stands high both for economic sanity and prospects for ultimate happiness. It is 97 percent literate, even though some outlying islands receive visitors only two or three times a year. Typical of these is doughnut-shaped Niufaou, over which the writer flew, about halfway between the capital of Tongatapu and Fiji's Suva. "Tincan Island" has no protective outer reef, being a volcanic mountain peak with a flooded crater inside. Passing ships having to anchor outside throw mail and papers overboard in tin cans to be swept ashore on the ceaselessly pounded rocks.

Tonga is what Washingtonians might call intensely socially conscious. It may not be a republic, but it is certainly a democracy. At sixteen every youth receives eight and one-fourth acres of land as his own freehold and homestead. By this equitable land distribution, Tongatapu—"Forbidden Tonga," the island of the capital—has been able to comfortably feed a population that since 1925 has jumped from 26,000 to 38,000. The means of production is in every family's hands.

Even bats, the flying squirrels of Tonga, are protected. At Kolovai, in Tongatapu, the writer saw them hanging by claw and wing, upside down and asleep, in a small grove in a village. Their yellowish rumps showing, they looked like so many tiny trussed-up packages on a holiday tree. The villagers went around almost on tiptoe while their guests slept, hanging by thousands from their favorite branches.

With its protection against Japan subsidized by the American people and its political direction under British control, Tonga is able to show a neatly balanced budget of about $300,000. Nor has the influx of free-spending American forces upset the economy. Such precautions as the establishment of a fixed-price market for fruit, and limitation of the money allotments to our men, have checked the natural American tendency to pay the highest possible prices for everything and cram every native hand as full as possible with folding money.

This money, in Tongatapu as elsewhere, is mostly being laid away for the day when it can be spent for radios, sewing machines, and other items of the aerodynamic age. Most of this American money, put away under a loose board, will probably find its way into the hands of British exporters. The import duty to Tonga on British imperial products is 12½ per cent.

Easy American money had one immediate social effect. It increased the number of divorces. Formerly the marriage tie's duration had been ensured by a divorce fee of £10. The kingdom has, however, sacrificed its possible profits by cutting the price to £6, still equivalent to four years' land fee for an eight-acre homestead. (The Australian pound is worth about $3.25, the British about $4.)

About the only upset this year in Tongatapu occurred when the police chief, a Fijian, had his car stolen. Search for the culprit was ineffectual, so fingerprinting was introduced. This method revealed that the thief was the lone occupant of the jail. Seized with car fever from seeing American jeeps, he had worked loose a board on the floor of the jail and gone joyriding.

Such minor matters do not greatly disturb the Queen's Methodist chaplain, Rodger Page. He is convinced that the kingdom's earnestly churchgoing people, who include Catholics, Mormons, Seventh Day Adventists and Episcopalians, will save Tonga from corruption.

One surviving custom is the ceremonial apron. This sign of simplicity and toil looks like a plain potato bag loosely tied with old rope around the waist, giving a plain household look to the dress. Men and women wear it, and the Queen and the premier, Salamone Ata, are rarely seen without it, as some American nurses who had tea with the Queen observed.

Salote has two sons, tall and quiet Tupou Toa, 26 years old, an expert marksman who took an honors degree in history and law at the University of Sydney, and 22-year-old Sione Gnu, who studied farming at Gratton Agricultural College in Brisbane. Her majesty is retiring more and more often to her country place on Tongatapu—an island as flat as Holland, and lacking in water—and putting more of her affairs in the hands of Tupou Toa.

The Kingdom of Tonga resembles Ethiopia, another small power with a profoundly spiritual Christian sovereign, in that it began by having considerable bargaining leeway among several great powers, and has now put its principal controls in the hands of the British government, which has shown a tendency to gain more and more sway over Tonga. In 1879 the Foreign

Office made a regular "most-favored nation" treaty with Tonga, whose ample harbors and key position on the Pacific routes made her a desirable ally. In 1900 Tonga agreed to have no relations with any foreign power without London's approval, and Charlotte's father, George II, agreed to give Britain a coaling base and the right to fortify.

The kingdom under Charlotte has adhered faithfully to the agreement made by her father, which was predicated on British naval control of the Pacific. Unlike Ethiopia, whose government London has subsidized financially, Tonga has no debts and has not accepted any monetary aid.

Next to the Queen, the British consul in the large white mansion of the consulate is the most important officer in Tonga. Despite the importance of these islands to us in a strategic sense, the United States is unrepresented politically. Although American forces, in dimensions which can be revealed only when peace comes, have stayed in Tonga, the United States has here, as nearly everywhere in the Pacific, given no attention to acquiring permanent political understanding commensurate with its heavy war burdens. The Americans with whom the writer talked, from low rank to high, spoke of Queen Charlotte with respect as "every inch a queen" but did not seem concerned at having to act individually as their own representative at her court.

Tonga has its own cabinet, and a parliament. The only non-native member of the cabinet is the minister of finance, a New Zealander. A common sight here is the prime minister, the Honorable Salamone Ata, a dignified middle-aged gentleman attired in a blue *vala* (Tongan for sarong), brown sandals, white shirt, grey felt hat and tortoise-shell glasses, entering the saltbox-style building on the main square to confer with the Queen's own affable counselor, 33-year-old John Brownlees, a plump college graduate who served several years as resident on Malaita, most savage of the Solomons, before coming to this tranquil post.

Across the dusty but magnificent broad street, past the post office which resembles a Middle Western railroad station, the ancient turtle Tu'Imalila, presented to the kingdom by Captain Cook at the time of Washington and Jefferson, waddles with dignity toward the refreshing, cool green palace grounds. The palace is a big white dwelling, with several odds and ends of outbuildings all built in the style of an American summer hotel of the 1890s, and exhaling the same general atmosphere of croquet, rocking chairs and peace. Tu'Imalila, the oldest thing in Tongatapu, wanders with the slow step of age through the palace's rail fence and meanders abstractedly past the Chautauqua-style chapel where Queen Charlotte makes her Methodist devotions.

—

ATOLLS ARE MOST SINISTER BATTLEFIELDS YET TRIED BY U.S. FORCES

Somewhere in Australia—November 23, 1943

Those lovely, ring-shaped atolls, with their lapis lazuli lagoons and feather-boa palms continually bent before the trade winds, and thin outer beaches swept with terrific surf for which Americans are now fighting and dying in the Gilbert Islands, are among the most sinister battlefields the world has ever known.

Americans have fought this war on the bare stones of Alaska's snowy ancient mountains, on the open sweeps of Africa's desert, in the New Guinea and Solomon jungles, and on the cliffs of Italy's rainy and wintery hills, but never before have they staked their lives against an atoll, the most complicated form of land structure which the earth knows. Its insect-built, wave-shaped ring is like nothing else.

The difficulties of our "unknown front" in the Central Pacific—where this correspondent, during his stay at Funafuti, was the first newspaper-man to live among forces preparing for the blow now in progress—are little understood. We Americans have been struggling alone for eighteen months to get the upper hand on what was lost after Pearl Harbor. War on this unknown front outdoes all others in demands on pioneering ingenuity.

These British-owned Gilbert and Ellice groups are totally unlike the Solomons or New Guinea. In the latter, Army and Marine landing parties have been able to take sizable ships directly into small, well-protected bays, so difficult for Jap night bombers to pick out that, once taken, they are virtually secure. And if our reinvading forces find strong gunfire from the beaches at one bay, there is always another farther up the coast.

Far different is the atoll, which lies in naked beauty blindingly unmistakable by day, and gives back moonlight and starlight almost as plainly by night. Nobody can conceal that staring white ringlet of coral. Here, anti-aircraft gunners find no thick green hills up which Bofors guns may be tugged to erect a ceiling of fire over beaches where men are toiling to haul ashore shells, food, tanks, and guns, and ever more guns. Sweating engineers and Seabees,* infantry and artillerymen wear sunglasses against the raging blindness that leaps from the coral surface. So bitter bright is the coral that they turn away to look at the greenish blue of the lagoon, which, though sparkling too in the sun, lessens their headaches and dizziness.

From a military standpoint, the essential thing about the atoll is that concealment is impossible. On one side are smashing breakers, swept by trade winds; on the other, sharks home in the lagoon. Between is what you live on: a curving strip of coral, penetrable only to pickaxes and dynamite—and from 300 yards to three feet in width. For the enemy bombardier peering through his sights, there is no doubt whether your camps are back in the hills or tucked along rivers overhung with branches. There is only one place you can be, for there are no hills or rivers. Under the immutable laws of the sea and the atoll, your ships can only be in the lagoon, and there is no chain of lagoons like the pearly bays along New Georgia or the Papuan coast but just a single naked anchorage with just one narrow entrance.

As a military form, the atoll is to the strategist what the sonnet is to the poet. What you can do is ferociously limited. What you dare try is sternly circumscribed by the fact that if you are defending, the enemy knows exactly where you are and if you are attacking, he knows with equal precision where that coral ring binds you to go if you want to dislodge him. This form of warfare, new even to the Pacific, is doubly new in that nobody has ever forced on the holders of these islands the power of mechanized warfare, with its aircraft carriers and shore listening posts, its long-range heavy guns and dive bombers. Never did tanks tread and bite atoll surfaces before the Americans brought them there.

Until today the political pattern of the Pacific has been determined by

---

*The Navy's construction battalion, whose name derives from the initial letters C and B.

peaceful means. From the days of Britain's Captain Cook, France's Captain Bougainville and our own whalers, Americans were unique in claiming virtually nothing of what they found, being too preoccupied in domestic frontiers. Then came another period of peaceful interchange when diplomats at Europe's council tables determined the Pacific pattern, incidentally giving Japan the four great atoll groups that still separate us from our own Philippines. This means that atoll warfare, with all its hazards and peculiarities, has now entered our fighting men's tactical books. Exploration of the possibilities will be paid for not in treaties but in blood.

Until now it has always been the occupation of atolls that the Japs did not quite dare take—like Nanumea, northernmost of the Ellices and nearest to the Gilberts, where the writer flew recently with the first flying boat ever landed there. It is true we are still fighting for British territory, for the Gilberts, like the Ellices, are British possessions. That way lies Japan and that way we must go.

In this unknown form of atoll warfare in the Pacific's unknown front, America's abilities are still fundamentally untested. When strategists talk of island-to-island hopping, it makes all the islands sound alike. But Tarawa and Makin are as different from Kolombanga and Goodenough as the desert is from the Arctic.

To an atoll you must bring everything, even drinking water. Water is measured out as jealously as aboard a transport, but on an atoll it is not just for a voyage but for good. Water distillation equipment, with its long hose in the sea, pumps all day and God help you if the motor breaks down or the fuel runs out.

The atoll itself only looks like a continuous ring from above: actually, it is more often a chain of islets across which bridges or ferries must be placed if your guns are to be dispersed properly. You must fight against the tendency to congest everything at the windward side of the atoll, away from the lagoon's mouth. Yet because that is the only wide place, your air field must almost unavoidably be there.

How can you get the coral filled smooth for your delicate undercarriages? Only by digging up the very coral which is already supporting you in this vast ocean. For that you need everything from dynamite to steam shovels—all vulnerable targets themselves. And wherever you dig, seawater comes in. More holes to fill and nothing obtainable to fill them with except by digging more holes.

Atolls seemed valueless to our World War I diplomats. We shall see what taking them by storm—whose techniques the writer cannot discuss because Gilbert operations are still unfinished—cost us. It will be more than pen flourishes on the green table of a European chancellery, as any officer from Admiral Nimitz down to the lowest dogface could tell you if they could talk across the ocean. Atolls are easy to lose, tough to retake and invaluable in the permanent pattern of the Pacific.

BASES OVERSEAS

GEORGE WELLER

XIV

Bases Overseas

For
Russell T. Churchill

It is often more easy to prevent the capture of a place, than
to retake it.

—THOMAS JEFFERSON

Suffering heavily from malaria and overwork, Weller agreed to take a much-delayed home leave. En route by ship across the Pacific in late 1943, he wrote a draft of *Bases Overseas,* an exploration of military history and strategy proposing a global system of U.S. bases. He spent his early "vacation" revising the book, which contradicted the beliefs of many politicians in the States as well as of his editors—but then again, they had not spent a year and a half slogging across New Guinea and the Solomons, seeing American soldiers sacrificed for what Weller felt should not have been diplomatically conceded in the first place. His sorrow, frustration, and anger are palpable on every page.

The book appeared in November 1944 (by which time Weller was back in Europe) and aroused controversy; Moscow Radio denounced it as "American imperialism." In the *New York Times Book Review,* a history professor from Columbia University called the author "hot-tempered . . . firing off salvos of argument like a heavily engaged battleship" and the argument "expansionism carried to an absurd extreme. He envisages a succession of titanic conflicts . . . He distrusts the future Russia . . . distrusts

China . . . This assumption of a world future of indefinite war-fare . . . amounts to a counsel of despair."

For the present purposes, I have abridged radically, and interpolated a few passages from an article Weller wrote for a magazine.

—

THE REBIRTH OF THE WORLDWIDE AMERICAN

The old American is dead. A new American, with a sense of the world, is being born: humanly wise, technically able, politically uncalculating. Of that soil where he regularly leaves his blood there is not an acre, except below his embassies, that he can call American.

He goes everywhere heavily laden with arms and sustenance. Yet if you ask why he is hurrying to build roads into Assam, and what keeps him busy at Lake Chad, he cannot tell you. He goes because he has been told to do so. The inner voice of war, if he hears any, gives him neither economic limit nor geographical guide.

Techniques of war interest him. But where he journeys, whether he fights for China and the Kuomintang above the Burma Road, or whether he negotiates with Persian and Russian for the passage of locomotives up the servant's entrance of the Soviet Union, it is all one. Politically this new American is not only ignorant; he is indifferent. There is the United States, or Home. And there are all the other places. Milne Bay or Takoradi: they are only other places. He was sent here; that is all.

"I am acting as a guardian on a soil not my own," he will say. "I fight, but I provide, too. I am a sort of grocer to the world of war. To this land I give food, airplanes, fuel, farm machinery. I leave behind air fields, wharves, thousands of miles of road. I pay the natives for the privilege of building or using anything in their defense. This New Guinea, these Solomons, were raw, roadless, defenseless. By my sweat and brains, by the debt of my children and the material of my soil, I am putting places like this in the category of civilized lands for the first time."

A worker and doer, deliberately narcotizing himself with techniques, he is not used to thinking his international politics aloud. "I don't know what

I'll do when we finish," he mutters. "Go home, I guess. If that's what they want." Where *they* will send him the American does not know. "Where there's a job to do" is enough. It is always this remote *they* that determines what men shall do. And in war even the American civilian ceases to query. The future can shell its own peas. He will be glad, some day, to look into the meaning of what he is doing. Today he is too busy.

The American committed himself to war despite fighters that were too heavy and bombers that were too light, the defective old ammunition, the unprotected naval base near the enemy and the carelessly patrolled base near home. In spite of his decision to fight, it was the enemy who selected the moment. The war was three-quarters lost when he entered it. Through all these months after the first help went to Britain, the new American was more acted upon than acting. His political failure he covered up with a moral pose, as false as that of the Nazis, about "being attacked." Having been in the wrong about almost everything in the conduct of his foreign affairs since 1916, he felt an impulse to put himself morally in the right before he got started, with nothing familiar to fight for but his ideals.

To understand his nonacquisitiveness in a hotly acquisitive world, look for a moment at the environment from which he came. Most Americans have never made anything grow with their hands; soil is to them unreal, and land is just a lot of area spread out thin. Many have never owned anything but their clothes and a bank account. When their balance went up, they were rich. When it went down, they were poor. This new American has little idea of the reproductive power of anything but money. Money makes money, he knows that. The only way for America to accept more power is to get more money. By this wholly apolitical standard, all other places the overseas American looks on are poor. Because they are poor he is not interested. If they were richer than the United States, he would want at least to pull even. But they are poor, and he wants nothing of them.

Moreover, the American has been told so often that he is fantastically wealthy that he believes it. So many things are taken from the American soil in defense of allies—so many more millions required to set both friend and enemy up again—that the American has lost all sense of bookkeeping. For a friendly official act, however small, he will award more ships and more money and more food. For a smile he will mark off the debt from his ledger. He translates all values, whether they be the rich oil from his fields or finished airplanes from his engineers, directly into cash—never into political force to his own advantage. And as soon as he has the values translated into cash, he says that it was all for nothing anyway, because cash is valueless, and wipes it off his books.

By providing materials, men, and aircraft he helps to change Britain into the greatest air base in the world. He builds roads even for the Tongan Islands, lest the smallest independent ally be without its gain. Everyone must have protection, and most can have gifts, for the great provider, the Good Guy, is abroad.

The key to the political life of the American is this: he does not care whether he is respected, so long as he is treated with a few forms of respect, but he must be loved, or at least liked, or he withers. His foreign policy represents an attempt to become popular by being benevolent, rather than to be respected by being responsible. He spends his national substance in a vain attempt to buy affection abroad, but at either political advantage or strategic consolidation, he recoils like a spinster from passion.

He is not very astute about his political interests, this new American. He knows he must fight and spend in all parts of the world. He does not like to think what he is spending—how every truck building a highway in Assam represents the value of a home for an American family. It disturbs him, but only a little, to reflect how every palm tree purchased from a British or French copra corporation to build an air field, at one to eight dollars a tree, is tax-earned money poured into an alien land, unprotected strategically or politically however its value is kept on the books. He has little interest in equity, and leaves the politics to someone else. In fact, *all* the Americans leave it to someone else.

To London as to famished Calcutta he bears his own rations of war, and eats, amid surroundings vibrant with history, his lifeless dehydrated eggs— triumph of the industrial mind, chemically full, organically empty, perfect for shipping, impossible for eating—American foreign policy in a spoon.

The first act of the Japanese army on arriving at a new island is to go fishing and start a garden. The first act of the Americans is to try to buy something from the natives. The American is an amasser. The German, the Italian, and the son of the Mikado die in battle to increase the power of their states. The American does so not to increase his own power, but to frustrate the aggressors from adding to theirs. Politically speaking, this is a somewhat aimless sacrifice.

The American is not a sucker; a sucker expects, by winning, to make some gain in power, not to be told simply that he has won. The American has been persuaded to renounce all gain for himself and his country as he moves under orders across this ailing world. A strange Ishmael, this dogface in his G.I. reefer, watching the burnoosed crowd around an African street bar; this mac peering under his downturned cap across the blue waters of the inner bay at Aitutaki in the Cook Islands, hoping to catch sight of a brown girl who was at the engineers' dance last night; this American saving grease in a fighter assembly unit on the Kentish coast and wondering at the reason for his thrift; this other American standing in the sun on the Via Caracciola, watching the boy beggars come running, wondering why they pass by the French and British and hasten directly up to him, avid fingers extended.

—

Defeat in the Pacific

The political defeat of the United States in the Pacific in World War I was only a fragment of its general political defeat. It was a peace in which the nation's ideals, which were immature, were upheld at the cost of the nation's advantage in the peace, which was ignored. Among the European and Asiatic secret treaties the loss to the British and Japanese Empires of key South Pacific island bases, essential now as then to security, is a capsule lesson in American self-betrayal in politics.

The neglect in the Pacific today seems aggravated because of its simple nature. The British and Germans first divided the unattached insular Pacific in 1886. The Americans allowed them to do so. Then the British and Japanese divided Germany's Pacific, in 1915, 1917, and 1919, and America allowed them to do that. The second division was more obviously injurious, for it was made during wartime, under the studied indifference of American statesmen. The German possessions obtained by Britain at Versailles outflanked America's highway to the Philippines. The German possessions taken by Japan wiped it off the map.

Unbelievable as it seems, the secret treaties—the names and numbers of the winners-to-be in the wartime sweepstakes—were divulged while the war was going on. The American government tried to sneer them down, to ignore them, and—trusted by the people—it succeeded. In that war, as in the next, it was difficult to persuade Americans to examine what they were fighting for. The secret treaties were published in Britain by the *Manchester Guardian*. They soon found their way to the *New York Evening Post*, published by Oswald Garrison Villard, a man who was unafraid. There was no one in public life with the courage to say what they meant.

Can a people be excused because its leaders are asleep? Not so long as it has a free press with able minds to perceive what is happening. The guilt of those who do not hold office, who are free to speak, who know truth, and who nevertheless are silent, is more ineradicable than the guilt of those rendered dumb by responsibility.

In the last war we established no fewer than 52 American bases on the Atlantic coast of France alone. We had bases in the Mediterranean and in Siberia. But that was the war that would end war. So we wrote off these bases and came home from Europe, leaving behind only our cemeteries. The result? Another war came, fought for the spoils and mastery of the last, with the sides the same and the forces heavier. And it required more than 2½ years of accumulating men and arms before we could risk our first offensive in France. The war was a year and a half old before we achieved our first continental beachhead in Italy.

This is the second half of the other war. It is bigger, costlier, will last longer, and is worldwide.

In the first half the Pacific was not a battleground. But as soon as Wilson's February 3, 1917 message committed the country's course toward war, the British and Japanese, anticipating an American claim, reserved Germany's strategic Pacific islands all for themselves by a secret treaty signed *two months before Congress actually declared war*. The American people, including the President, were ignorant when they voted for war that their route to the Philippines had been endangered by this secret treaty. And today in the ex-German mandates of New Guinea and the northern Solomons, and in the four Japanese archipelagoes, American cemeteries testify the price of political blindness.

The United States, to correct its diplomatic carelessness, has now built in the third of its overseas wars an overpoweringly large fleet that has broken through the phalanx of mandated British and Japanese islands. There emerges in the American government a tendency to offer its people the satisfaction of victory, without revealing that victory in this case is merely the remedy of a prior political defeat. The jubilation at winning the central Pacific islands in such costly fashion can be tempered by study of how cheaply they were lost.

It is a characteristic of American foreign policy that it often wins by force the points it could have taken in a prior war by right of victory. This defect is most characteristic in the Pacific, perhaps because American policy is Europe-oriented, and Americans east of the Rockies stubbornly decline to understand this ocean.

What are bases overseas worth? Secretary Morganthau, opening the June 1944 bond drive, said it had cost taxpayers $6 billion to overpower the Marshall Islands. The Marshalls are one of the four strategic archipelagoes Japan took by the secret 1917 treaty.

What would American bases in the Mediterranean have been worth, if we had kept any? The Secretary says that to progress from Naples to Rome cost the United States $6.7 billion. Would a base in Corsica or Sardinia have improved that figure, giving us the same aid Malta gives the British?

—

AN AMERICAN SYSTEM OF BASES OVERSEAS

Bases outlive weapons. As cities gather where lines of commerce intersect, bases gather power at the intersection of lines of strategy. The trireme gives way to the galleon; the attack plane takes over some of the functions of the artillery. Yet the defile in the mountains, the strait between the seas, remains decisive. A channel, armed, is mightier than an ocean. Most precious have always been the bases where sea and land meet.

A great base endures whether its walls be wood stakes, granite blocks, or fighters humming overhead. When a base passes away in power, it is either because a civilization has wrapped around it, like the Indian forts of the American West, or the central power has disintegrated. The gun-flanked Straits of Messina must still be taken by him who would cross from Africa to Italy. He who would go from Italy into Germany must still find the key to the Alpine passes.

The wars for possession of natural resources and raw materials go on today, a holdover from the nineteenth century. Beneath them fluctuates the sterner struggle for strategic position. Strong in peace, costing little to uphold, a well-located base can be armed for offensive war in quick order; defensively it is armed already by the advantageous spot where it stands. It menaces only the menacer. Even when almost unarmed, it fixes the attention of the enemy-to-be and diverts his attack. A base is a warning, a reminder against strategic aggression, a memorandum of commitment. Demanding little of the citizen but his consent, of the statesmen little but political foresight and willpower, the outlying base returns to the nation decades of peace as dividend. Like thermometers set in the scattered geysers of the world, the base gives notice that war is coming; it feels the heat and testifies immediately to the pressure.

Any nation which engages in a worldwide war and makes worldwide political commitments without securing permanent worldwide bases is wasting its substance.

It is possible to overwhelm an enemy through excess of production or superior weapons. This shortsighted aim has governed American military action in three overseas wars. The aim was always merely military victory, not its strategic consolidation. The fact that the United States has been successful by massive inundation of the enemy with materials has saddled this people with a pragmatic faith: the cult of production. This cult, which dominates American strategy, believes that nothing is too costly to gain victory; and because burying the enemy under sheer quantity has always met the pragmatic test—it obtains victory—there should be no experiment with any other method. The largest army, the largest navy, and the largest industrial plant in the world: such are the unthinking aims of strategically incurious minds. There is no one to tell them that in war the greatest advantage is position, and that position, if held in peace, is a far cheaper commodity than arms.

In a nation dominated by this cult of production, the *where* of its conflicts are nothing. It will fight anywhere, for anybody. It has no sense of acquisitiveness; it is gawkily grateful for being allowed to "use" bases to attain the shortsighted aim of temporary victory. By lend-leasing power overseas it buys temporary bases at fifty times their cost, and greets victory still strategically empty-handed.

The maintenance of strong bases, on the far side of the world, is a difficult concept for a nation self-hypnotized by the cult of mass production to grasp. But war is the great demonstrator. At the beginning of the war the American people lived in a security upheld by bases. When Crete fell and Malta tottered they were troubled. Yet Malta, down to three fighter planes, held out. Was she helpless? No, for her bombers denied safe passage across the Mediterranean by daylight to Nazi and Italian convoys. Rommel was replenished by night but not by day; Malta halved his supplies. A time came at Cairo's doors when he did not have enough.

Corregidor, if the American people ever understand its meaning, will be a turning point of American foreign policy. When all the famous bases that were not fortresses—Hong Kong, Singapore, Soerabaya—fell to the Japanese, Corregidor held. The Rock held more than twice as long as mighty Singapore, with an equally strong Japanese force against it, and forced the enemy to break up their convoys. They had captured Manila early, but for five months the city was useless to them in a military sense because the guns of sick, starving Corregidor denied them entrance to Manila Bay. This tiny penknife delayed Nippon just enough to save Australia and Pearl Harbor; just enough to prevent Tojo from drawing down from the Aleutians to the Antarctic that iron screen intended to bar America from Asia.

Those priceless months of resistance cost America $49.5 million—less than a single major raid over Berlin. For the cost of *five hours* of climbing war bill, the American people received *six months* of unaided resistance. Does that look as though bases overseas were worth paying for?

—

BASES FOR STABILITY

The Depression—never solved, but plowed under into a new war effort—was the bill for winning bases overseas in World War I. Yet we wrote off the bases.

There have been no reliable studies of the cost of different means of waging war besides comparing manufactured weapons—a torpedo equals so many shells—at the end of the assembly line. But a 20-mm shell in Burma has many times the value of the same shell at the end of the factory belt. An American soldier in good health on the road north from the Persian Gulf is worth a half dozen just out of their dogface days in a training camp. Where weapons are determines their value.

A worldwide system of bases involves placing stores of men, food, weapons, and matériel in locations where their value will be at its highest in the moment of war, being near to the enemy early on. Thus it cuts down the cost and losses of distribution. The overseas base not only guards the peace but shortens the war. It strikes at a rising enemy, and checks him before he is dangerous. Two fighter planes peacefully cruising the coast of a potential enemy beyond the three-mile limit, but in sight, are worth fifteen heavy bombers grounded 600 miles away.

A single base, standing alone, is weak because it can be isolated. A system of bases is strong because it is impossible to isolate. Even cut off from its mother country, it is still able to fight by reason of the power shared among its members.

Any system of bases may be measured by how completely it dominates its area; by whether it is connected with the homeland by the most direct means; and by whether it neutralizes politically any other bases in the same area. Had there been a dozen strong American bases in Mediterranean Africa, had the United States owned a dozen Bataan-Corregidors from the Aleutians to Penang, the American situation would have fallen into a perspective of world dimensions immediately. It would have been clear that though the danger to American outposts was real, no energy should be wasted in the United States on futile alarmism against coastal attacks. Energy could have been directed into holding the bases already under fire, and establishing new ones as long as the outermost were defending themselves.

Cities are cowardly places. All geography comes to their doors, yet their apprehensions of distance are weak and fumbling. When the Japanese were at the gates of Moresby, the press of Melbourne groaned its fear, and in London and New York straphangers trembled in premonition. In Moresby itself all was calm; the Japs had not been able to take tanks or heavy artillery over the Owen Stanleys, and that meant Nippon had lost.

So in any urbanized society like the American, neurotic anxiety over remote dangers is unavoidable. But if, at the far end of the chain of military command, out where the sentry stands peering into the dark, the citizen knows that he possesses a well-built fortress with flanking air fields and mined approaches, and knows this outpost is garrisoned by men strong, intelligent, and practiced in war, he wastes less time worrying over the old political riddle (the only question of international affairs an American ever asks), "How long will it take them to cross the ocean?"

—

AMERICAN INERTIAS

Every man is bound by his allegiances. Only the rare man can see over the wall of his own home, much less over the parapet of the nation. Home is enough.

Why should a man ever go beyond his national wall? Other nations do not seem to want visitors. A million muzzles deny them welcome. Assurances are demanded on a hundred sheets of paper—this being a world ruled half by guns, half by documents, the instruments of quick and slow death—that the stranger will not remain long, and will return home as soon as his purse gets thin. Few men can go abroad and see, and still fewer know the meaning of what they see.

The American is endowed with a statistical sense of other countries. His ideal is a foreign policy rung up on a cash register. The effect of geography on foreign affairs escapes him. He is not capable of standing imaginatively in the political shoes of another people and seeing things momentarily as they do. He does not, even when it would be to his own advantage to do so, spontaneously place himself in Oslo or Ankara and see the world with the eye of a Norwegian or Turk.

One blindness that deprives the American of a political understanding of the world he fights in is this: he allows himself, being a workman of tools at heart, to be seduced into teenage questions of statistics, techniques, and personal ideals. These should have been settled in his mind when he entered manhood, subordinated to a general curiosity as to the duties of being an adult and an American. The defect may lie in the unreal manner in which history is taught to Americans, which seems to commit the making of foreign affairs to other responsibilities than their own.

Today the fighting man overseas is waiting for the statesman at home to do something. The statesman at home is waiting for the people to suggest for him to do something. The people are waiting for the press and radio to suggest what they should ask the statesman to do. The press and radio are waiting for their foreign correspondents and war reporters overseas to suggest to them what they should suggest to the public. And the reporters and correspondents are unable to analyze, much less suggest political action, because the fighting men (officers and censorship, that is) say that politics is the affair of the statesman back home.

The nation, too, feels a right to do what it revealingly calls "getting away from the war." This attitude is natural. Lacking any pattern for being self-interested in gainful war, unsupplied with statesmen capable of building an enduring peace consonant with his own sacrifices, the American turns to an emotional apprehension of war. If you cannot think about the war, can you not at least feel about it? Besides the escapism *away* from the war there is in the United States a unique escapism *into* war, into atrocity stories, magic-weapon stories, hero stories, sex-and-war stories, that defeats the political teacher. Correspondents have observed the impossibility of inducing the American people to make a candid reappraisal of their allies and aims. The will to self-deceive, the determination to be emotional, is almost impenetrable.

The American, moreover, honestly hates war, not for moral reasons— for he can be brutal as well as sentimental—but because he "sees no sense in it." He does not understand international politics nor wish to practice them. Without politics, of course, there is as little "sense" in war as painting on a canvas of air. Why interrupt a sweet life for this dangerous, unintelligible effort? In war he does not want to take political action; in peace he does not even want to think about it. Like a teenager in love he has a sense of moral superiority mixed with an inadequate sense of his interests. The result is alternating international crushes and renunciations.

Besides being held off from international politics by his distaste for war, unable to give war a productive purpose because of his distaste for international politics, and drawn elsewhere by the candied diversions of his amusing culture, the American sees that overseas bases, granting that they are necessary, can only be acquired in two ways: asking for them or taking them. Instantly, misgivings arise. Either method involves plain speaking and vigorous action. In international affairs he shrinks from both. He cuts down his political concept to fit his self-distrust. His allies help. In the end he is empty-headed, empty-handed, strategically and politically disarmed, and silent.

In their first history Americans were the subjects of empire. Eventually they shook off the hateful harness. Not to be part of an empire, to an American, means to be free and happy; therefore not to impose empire on anyone else means only the golden rule. Past empires all fell to pieces; if his nation is careful not to become an empire, it will not fall to pieces.

The temporary duration of empire is another defect, to an American eye, in what many happy imperial subjects consider its grandeur. Looking backward, he can recite the disintegration of empires. But because he looks forward too infrequently and perhaps pessimistically, he misses something more significant than their fall—the never-ending rise of new empires. He perceives the decline of the British raj in India, but may not notice that this is only the bugle of taps soon followed, as history goes, by the reveille of an independent Indian Empire vaster than the original raj.

While the American stands aside, in a sanctimony and virtue that are real only to himself, while he refuses to have anything to do with the control of empire—except subsidize it with his resources and his life—new empires are taking shape within the boundaries of the old. Some will be stillborn, some will reach puberty and die, some will survive. Only the European empires, those the United States has chosen to defend, are on the wane. Other empires are waking to succeed them.

Since France, Holland and Belgium (among empires) all fell, it has remained for Great Britain and the United States to sustain worldwide sea and air power. Britain cannot bear this burden alone. The United States therefore takes over the major responsibility, strengthening her ally by lease-lending 1400 naval vessels.

"Exploitation" is a term the American uses without painstaking search of its meaning applied to himself. It troubles him little that his corporations descend on the countries of Central America, alter their homestead economy into monocultural, industrial farming, modernize their life without getting them any more security, and finally make them completely banana-dependent or sugar-dependent, hence cash-dependent and America-dependent. The American thinks as little of this kind of imperialism, in which he has many willing Latin partners, as the Briton considers the tentacles of the Leverhulme group, which regulates native-collected copra from Funafuti to Stanleyville, buys at its own price, and finally holds under patent enough substitutes to keep all the coconut pickers, be they Bangalas or Maoris, completely at its mercy. To the Anglo-American this is not imperialism; this is business.

Are overseas bases imperialism? Of course. America became an imperial nation when she decided to send lend-lease to support the British Empire and the three other sub-empires of that political holding company. America did not become a *possessing* or an *exploiting* imperial power, but a *protective* imperial power.

To retain bases is to retain security. It is not to acquire an exploitable empire. The aim is not trade; bases are not for the advantage of our Merchant Marine, our world air passenger system, or our business corporations. Strategy and business are separate. Moreover, "retain" does not mean "seize" or "colonize." It means to acquire by purchase, or under reverse lend-lease, sufficient acres to maintain the wharves, air fields, roads, magazines and fortifications already proven necessary to the United States by two world wars. We want bases, not colonies.

Willing to sustain the empires of Western Europe everywhere in the world, America neurotically shrinks from the naughty word *imperial* as though it were tainted. But in 19th-century Marxist dogma, a colony's resources were exploited to benefit a large industrial nation. The war has turned Marx upside down. Today, imperialism being reversed, it is the endangered colony, the appendage of empire, which exploits the protecting industrial nation.

—

The Acquisition of Bases

Acquiring bases should be segregated from the division of spoils of this war. Bases are not spoils. The United States has a claim to a share of the territorial divisions that may follow the war. This claim is proportionate to her war effort as compared to that of other powers (war effort here not to be confused with "war suffering" or "depth of defeat" or "devastation through invasion"). Spoils and bases are things apart—spoils being a matter of political prize, while bases are a matter of political stability. It is necessary to keep them distinguished from each other.

A system of permanent bases has a single purpose: to lift the political power in peacetime of the United States to equal the American wartime responsibilities on its allies' behalf—to apply in peace the security lessons of the revealed strategy of the war. Is it too demanding to suggest that political agreements be made with the subsidized powers in return for lend-lease, corresponding to the degree of help they needed? The suggestion is not made with the flinty idea of extorting advantage from a neighbor's difficulty, for statesmen have another obligation than driving hard bargains on behalf of their country. They have an obligation to lead their people in the ways of reality. But a soft and indefinite agreement does as little service to the national political ethos as to the budget.

In this sense there is no doubt that lend-lease, politically unimplemented, set back American strategic internationalism possibly as much as a generation. More serious, it set back the thought of her allies, for it ratified the mischievous Wilsonian policy of "disinterested"—hence irrational—aid, and laid grounds for them to count on a permanent military subsidy to Europe, never anchored politically or strategically.

Suspended before the American constantly is a temptation to evade the hard planning he has to do. It is so easy for the American to allow himself to think that, because the enemies of the British, French, Belgian, and Dutch Empires are the same, "it is all one war." Has it no significance that the air fields of Asia are being built with American labor, American materials, American engineering? Does the bloody sand by Paestum's old temples have no geographical significance? Have the hard coral graves of the Gilbert atolls no deeper meaning than that a force of Americans happened to die here, by gunfire, rather than at Key West of old age?

The sea has suffocated our submariners, sunk in the watery abysses of the western Pacific and the Indian Ocean, the China Sea and the Sea of Japan. Dark ocean fills the pure chamber of their minds. Their eye sockets are inlets. In the collapsed castle of their clean bones small fishes come and go with antennae for eyes. They died unnecessarily, to patch a political defeat in a diplomatic conference. How many more such riven chambers of drowned manhood must slide downward in slow zigzag—stricken, flooded, and silent—to the bottom of the great seas of the world before America controls permanent bases in the scattered waters beneath which her best young men are sleeping?

—

BASES LOADED

How does it happen that only in the third year of war the United States began to awaken to geographical commitments, and understand they must be permanently implemented? A letter from an army censor, addressed to a war correspondent [Weller—ed.] in the Southwest Pacific zone of General MacArthur, in support of his total suppression of a political dispatch with no military content, offers a clue as to why the American public is always politically uninformed, and its government spends its time diplomatically slamming the doors of empty barns. The letter reads:

We believe that a correspondent has a certain duty towards the Commander of the Forces whom he represents, and it is the Commander-in-Chief's desire that nothing of a political nature be released as coming from his staff of correspondents, and nothing that may be in any way criticizing the efforts of any Commander of any of the allied nations.

What the United States badly needs is a long cold bath of reality. There is no advantage in winning strong points overseas if the home public surrenders them. The American people have been politically bewildered about their foreign policy for fifty years. In war they are alternately drugged with the promise of bloodless and easy victory, then whipped up with official warnings that peace will be expensive and is far off. Needled with atrocity stories, flattered and exhorted with heroism, this people never leaves itself enough energy to think about its own political advantage.

One granite fact both Britain and America must keep before their eyes: This war was won not by their consummate brilliance or their close loyalty, but chiefly by the mistakes in military estimation made by a cunning but disoriented enemy leader. One cannot expect such good fortune every time. The Anglo-Saxon inventive genius in this war was never more than six months ahead of the enemy's, and at times more than a year behind. The narrowness of this technical lead should never be forgotten by the British or American peoples; it represents the margin of their victory.

The American forces, as the war goes on and they come to associate themselves with its scattered terrains, feel a sense of futility about the way they arrive, fight for, and leave (some of them by the quiet road) the raw places of the earth to which they have given so much. The development of New Guinea and the Solomons, for example, is the greatest piece of colonial expansion ever undertaken in the Pacific, nearly all of it done by American men, machinery, and money. One who has seen a skip-bombing pilot, a hero of the battle of the Bismarck Sea, take a Fortress with nine crew members off Seven Mile airdrome at Moresby amid the milky softness of the rainy tropical night, hit a hundred yards off the hard-bitten strip, and die in the space of a man's breath with all his comrades in the erupting flame of his own bombs is not likely to have leisure to reflect, even if he is aware of it, that in that splash of fire—no unusual occurrence on any war front—there was destroyed enough of value in machinery, not including men's lives, to have met the budget for the administration of Papua for ten years. Yet he senses something unbalanced, unreal, and untold in fighting for victory alone. Victory is not enough.

In a thousand years no power could get agriculturally enough from the Solomons or New Guinea what America has invested there in two years, from docks and air fields to roads and drainage systems. In New Guinea, Australia—under her mandate—will continue to exploit the gold and oil. In the South Seas the coconut plantations of the British soap cartel will resume operations, handsomely reimbursed at one to eight dollars per tree for each palm felled in their defense by U.S. forces.

Little though these considerations may mean to the American people, citizens would do well to remember that it is small satisfaction (besides being poor strategy) to spend your youth grubbing out a stake for someone else, to leave behind everything except malaria: the harbor you dug, the roads you built through the jungle, the air fields you hewed from the coral, the wrecks of your bombers in the impassable mountains, the disintegrating graves under the palms by the beach.

And does not the American home front, too, begin to need something more tangible to fight for than "it shall not happen again"? There is a sense of subtraction about the war in the United States. The young men and women are subtracted from daily life, the food is subtracted from the stores, the cars are subtracted from the streets, the money is subtracted from the paycheck, the husband is subtracted from the family, the marriage is subtracted from the maiden, the unborn are subtracted from the would-be mother, the truth is often subtracted from the news, and the politics of the war is subtracted from the fighting of it. This subtraction is due to the fact that the war is being fought, in the United States, without apparent gainful aims.

Peoples may declare war for ideals, or in self-defense. Soldiers, however, must fight and die to gain strong points. If these are renounced afterward, the war has been lost. Statesmen may convince the people it has been won, but actually it has been lost. *The cost of obtaining bases overseas is the whole cost of the war.* It is useless to pretend that any well-wishing structure of peace, or alliance of allies, can transcend the absolutes of possessive strategy. Wherever we fight is *permanently* valuable to us strategically. If not, we should not have been obliged to mobilize our industrial power and send our resources there to defend it. If the situation is dangerous for America at this spot now, it will probably be dangerous again.

In a war whose costs to the national heritage, the dowry of the American earth, are not yet measurable, political advantage can be salvaged. Only strategic bases overseas can be saved of the American expenditure. Congress was asked for a single war year to vote 100 billion dollars. It has been computed by a financial writer that the interest alone on this amount "would run the country in normal times for an entire year." A measurement of war losses in billions of dollars is childish. Cost is a measure only of the nation's willingness to indebt itself. To find out the true expenditure, and its political worth, one should inquire: How long do citizens wish this nation to exist before it goes the way of Byzantium and Knossos?

We wrest our resources from the soil, never to return, and throw them into worldwide battle. *More! More! More!* is the American battle cry. Instead it should be *Where? Where? Where?* This pair of world wars are not the last for us. We shall fight again overseas; our men will die again. The world does not change.

Does America wish to know what she has kept of victory that will protect the peace? Let her count her bases overseas.

JUST BACK

AFTER
TWO YEARS
COVERING
THE WAR
IN
SOUTHWEST
PACIFIC

"THE BIGGEST AND
FIERCEST BATTLE GROUND
IN THE WORLD"

GEORGE WELLER

Ace Foreign Correspondent Chicago Daily News . . . Awarded
Pulitzer Prize for distinguished reporting . . . Author of the
best seller "Singapore Is Silent" . . . Survivor of a chain of
hair-raising global adventures and writer of a galaxy of front
page "scoops" in leading newspapers from coast to coast
. . . An experienced and thrilling speaker.

LECTURE SUBJECT:

"AGAINST JAPS AND JUNGLE"

XV

The Home Front

While in the United States, Weller recovered his health, lectured widely on the war, wrote some of the longer pieces that appear in this book (de Gaulle, New Guinea wrecks, etc.), and fretted about missing the big story: the Allied invasion of Europe. He was unable to return to the war until the autumn of 1944.

A frequent theme was trying to describe what the conflict was like for the average soldier fighting somewhere—or waiting to fight. As he wrote once: "War is a bore when you are not running it. Its mitigations are several: the discharge of the sense of duty, the sense of participation with others in a simple common cause, and (for a surprising number) the release from civilian responsibility. But it still adds up to boredom."

—

THE HOME FRONT HAS THREE DUTIES TO FIGHTERS

Asks Support, Affection and Political Vigilance

(George Weller, who was awarded the Pulitzer Prize, be- yond question is one of the outstanding correspondents cov- ering the war. He recently returned from a three-year journey around the world which gave him a first-hand view of the fighting in the Balkans, in Central Africa, Ma- laya, New Guinea, the Solomons, and the islands of the Pacific. Now home on leave, although suffering from the *effects of malaria and burdened by a heavy schedule of writing and lecturing, he has written this article for* Illinois Mobilizes *as his contribution to the home front effort and thus to the fighting men with whom he has eaten, slept, marched and faced death.)*

Chicago, Illinois—May 1, 1944

The hardest thing for people at home in wartime is to transfer themselves imaginatively to the front where their fighting men are engaged. It is always difficult to move oneself imaginatively through time and space to an unfamiliar place. When the unknown element of battle comes into the equation, it seems nearly impossible for those at home to realize what war is like.

The first characteristic of war is not its hardship nor its danger, but the overpowering monotony. There is time for thought, for self-questioning. The question underlying much of a soldier's thinking is: "What are we fighting for?"

From Asia or Africa, from the stony villages of Italy or the wind-torn atolls of the Pacific, America comes to appear to the lonely soldier a great and amorphous creature. It is not only far away; it is unreal. News from America is complete in the sense that no important event is omitted. But it is incomplete in that the whole phenomena of American life are only sketched in.

Little mimeographed or handprinted newspapers come up to the front and they give some account of the major events at home. But the background of how people are feeling and what they are thinking is remote from the soldier.

As nearly as a war correspondent who has visited many American camps all over the world can determine, the G.I. "Sad Sack" is fighting the war for a picture. The picture may be a stained photograph of his family, or of his fiancée, wrapped and re-wrapped in a waterproof tobacco pouch at the bottom of his kit. Or it may only be a picture printed in his memory, changing and growing sharper or fading as he is buffeted about by the fortunes of war.

Field Marshal Wavell once wrote that war consists of long periods of boredom punctuated by moments of intense fear.

The pictures in a soldier's mind undergo changes due to both these causes.

Fear is not nearly so important as boredom. Fear affects only that aristocracy of our troops who go into battle, and they by no means compose the major part of the Army. It is probable that in the Pacific campaign not more than one per cent of the troops have ever seen living, non-captured Japanese. Probably not more than three per cent have ever seen General MacArthur or Admiral Nimitz.

The dispatches of war correspondents, coming usually from headquarters or the front lines, give the impression that this participation in the greatness of the war—its generalship and its fighting—are the lot of every soldier.

But they are not. The lot of the soldier is to obey orders whose meaning is unexplained to him, to dig foxholes and move on and have to dig them again the next day, to whip his bivouac into order for a visit of the general who does not turn up, to put in a request for a transfer that he cannot get and then to be transferred someplace else where he does not want to go. About the only time he is able to find himself as the individual human being and enter his own place is in his dream world of that photograph, mental and real, for which he is fighting.

The clarity of these photographs is affected by two elements: the experiences of the man in the forces, and what he hears from home. The first lies in the hands of the armed forces to shape. The second lies in the hands of people who communicate with him from home.

In relation to these two forces the soldier, though armed to the fingertips and trained to the eyebrows, is almost as helpless as a baby. He is acted upon rather than acting. What the strife of battle will make of him nobody can say. The image of the home front he gets overseas is similarly impossible to control.

There are soldiers who get nothing but oblique penciled scrawls in the shape of a letter, never any photographs, never any newspaper clippings. Never anything real to knit them up with the homes for which they are fighting. The image of the home front in their minds is most imperfect and they are more imperfect soldiers for that reason.

Men are coming home with the tidings of far places in their eyes and in their words. But while they are out overseas, there is little that they can offer in return for what they need so much from home. The writer once spent some time with an American naval outfit which had fled from the Philippines to Western Australia, part of the Asiatic Fleet. It was the beginning of the war. The men who wrote home could not say where they came from, nor where they were, nor what kind of duty they had, nor what battle action they had experienced, nor whether they had been wounded, nor where they were going next. These censorship precautions were reasonable and necessary from a military point of view. But they gave the people on the other end little to go on. And it is hard to maintain a one-sided correspondence.

One boy at Guadalcanal grew so exasperated at not being able to write home that he decided to send the family a jeep for a gift. He managed to purloin a jeep and sent it all home, part by part, wheels, chassis, hood and windshield. They caught him when he was trying to mail back the cylinder block; it was too big to go into the mailbag. Apparently he got so disgusted at himself at not being able to write anything and not having any Japanese battle flags or swords to send home that he felt he must discharge his duty in some way.

What the soldier needs most at a distance is a sense of true and undying affection for him at home. Affection does not mean pity. A moaning, slobbery letter full of misplaced anguish about danger will land in most cases in a camp where no shot has ever been heard fired in anger since the war began. It sets the soldier thinking on a vein of self-commiseration, an unhealthy note for the Army. There is something ridiculous about being in a perfectly safe place (as are nearly two-thirds of our soldiers at any one time) and receiving a letter in outrageously bathetic language.

Do not judge the quality of the soldier by the number of his decorations. Most decorations are earned and well deserved by their wearers. But many, especially in the infantry of the Marines and Army, earn decorations which they never receive. This is not because of any deliberate injustice, but simply because witnesses are required to all acts of heroism.

Often the witnesses to heroism are killed off or so badly shocked they do not remember what happened. In such cases affidavits are not forthcoming. There is no deliberate injustice about this. War, for the individual and the non-influential, is simply a great game of chance.

It becomes apparent to one who visits all the fronts that most of the talk about courage and cowardice begins about 200 yards back of the fighting line and increases in volubility until one arrives at rear headquarters, possibly several hundred miles away. Nothing like this talk is heard much at the front. Nobody wants to die for the most glittering medal that was ever hung. But everybody is willing to do his duty, not because it is brave but because it is necessary.

As the war wears on, one question lifts itself more and more often in the minds of the troops. The question is: "When shall I be going home?"

This question provides its own answer, which is: "After the victory."

Another question follows: "What do we have to do to gain the victory?"

And this question is finally succeeded by a third: "How shall we know when we have won the war?"

The new worldwide American soldier knows that he will not have won the war simply when the enemy surrenders. He knows that a sound peace must be enforced to be durable. And he is becoming more and more concerned about the terms of this peace.

The American soldier is perhaps the least educated politically of any soldier in the world today. All of his ideology is in the two photographs. But he is eager to learn more about what he is fighting for.

It is therefore necessary for civilian defense volunteers at home not only to see that metal, paper, fats and tin are salvaged, that plates are scraped clean, that gas is not wasted. It is necessary to do one thing more: be vigilant about the political terms of the peace. No soldier who has spent two years of his life defending an air field in Assam or a wharf in West Africa, or a listening post on a Pacific island, is indifferent as to what will happen to these places after the war. Having been fought for, built, or paid for by Americans, he is eager that they shall remain American.

Stories of new magical weapons that will end the war in 45 days amuse him, but he mistrusts them. What the soldier would like to know is how much political vigilance is being demonstrated on his behalf, in keeping with the fact that the American burden has been greater in terms of expenditure of resources than any other nation? What has been done, in the face of warnings that "We cannot oil another war," to guarantee that our oil resources will be replaced? How is the man fighting overseas to know that the strong points for which he has fought will remain American, and that his son will not have to fight to recover them again because of the frailty of his allies?

All these questions are political matters which interest the fighting man overseas more than which of two men is going to be president of the United States.

There are three things which the home front can offer to support the man overseas. They are: 1) material support, 2) affection, 3) political vigilance.

Of the third element the soldier, like the citizen, knows all too little. It is part of the duty of the home front to send the soldier articles, newspaper clippings, and all other information about the political direction the nation is taking in international affairs and the degree of alertness of its leaders in holding all gains made.

The next question for the home front will be re-employment of the fighting men. But at present, with the nation's alertness dulled by a domestic presidential campaign, postwar employment can wait temporarily.

Political vigilance for our international interests must come to the fore. It is overdue. The soldier overseas, while working and fighting, counts on the home front worker to let him know that America is awake and his peace is to be permanent.

This news is the best he hopes to receive.

Weller on Raid:

Forts Wade Into Flak

Daily News Man In Record Raid!

Stricken Ship Limps Home on Two Engines After Attack Near Bologna.

BY GEORGE WELLER

SPECIAL RADIO
To The Chicago Daily News Foreign Service.
Copyright, 1944, The Chicago Daily News, Inc.

Advanced Bomber Base of the U.S. 15th Air Force, Thursday, Oct. 12.—Across the blue Italian sky, dirty with thousands of puffs of vicious Nazi flak, Flying Fortresses and Liberators led this morning a cavalcade of Allied Mediterranean air power against Nazi emplacements around Bologna.

It was the greatest number of heavy bombers ever directed against a single objective in the Mediterranean theater.

As the only civilian correspondent participating in the raid, I rode in the glass nose of a Fortress, which was among the earliest to run gantlet of German flak. Scheduled to be the first over Bologna, our Fortress actually reached the well-camouflaged German bivouac area after two earlier waves had laid initial carpets of bombs.

By that time German flak had found the range, too. Before the eyes of Navigator-------- Heffron of New Orleans-------- James McCroary of Enid, Okla., a Fortress of the first wave caught fire from flak. The pilot put it in a perpendicular dive to extinguish the flames, pulled out miraculously without snapping the plane and finally disgorged seven parachutes.

"I saw them floating down into the streets of Bologna," said Heffron later.

Our Fortress, too, was already in distress as it entered its bombing run. Though the flak until then had been light—German gunners were waiting until the giants had committed themselves on their final run—one engine suddenly died.

"A small piece is torn from the left wing," scribbled Heffron in his log as we exchange glances over oxygen masks.

At that moment the inside engine on the same wing stopped. Its blackened propeller motionlessly confronted us from the side window as our chunky pilot, Lt. John Whedbee, of Stockton, Md., and the spectacled co-pilot, Lt. G. F. Cooley of Howell, Mich., fought to keep the ship in formation.

Must Held Formation.

In this case, it was necessary to hold formation, not only for protection against an unexpected fighter attack, but in order that our bombs should fall at the chosen point in the smoking carpet which had been German encampments.

Hardly had the affected engine been feathered and the ship begun to groan with an effort to hold its place, when three Messer-

(Continued on page 2, column 3.)

XVI

Flak over Italy

Hoping to get back to the Pacific and what he later called "the battles of the U.S. Navy versus MacArthur," Weller returned the long way round: first via Italy, where for about three weeks he was much hampered by British censorship. Having lived there in the 1930s—the Russian writer Gorki was his neighbor on Capri—Weller had an acute sense of how much the country had changed.

The invasion of Italy, which ultimately cost sixty thousand Allied lives and fifty thousand German, began in Sicily in July 1943. Shortly afterward, Mussolini was removed from power to a secret prison, and an armistice was signed between the Allies and the new government, which was battered between the Nazis and various partisan factions. In September, Mussolini was rescued by the Germans and installed as head of a second government in the north. Until the war's end in Europe, in May 1945, Italy would be caught in shifting, violent retributions and small civil wars.

The Allies worked their way slowly northward, and liberated Rome around D-day, in June 1944. Later that autumn, Weller arrived in time to witness part of the unsuccessful attempt to take Bologna; in the end, that important city did not fall until the following April.

Nazis Expert at Concealing Mines in Roads, Yanks Find

Rome, Italy—October 10, 1944

Singapore was lost in large part by the inability of the engineers to mine its single vertebral asphalt highway, which runs the length of the Malay Peninsula. But German engineers find similar Italian highways no obstacle to their ingenious job of frustrating the Allied advance. "Don't go there" and "Don't touch anything" are still directions which must be observed even far behind our lines.

By anticipating their own retreats far ahead of time, the Germans are able to bury mines and let nature and time aid them in concealment. When a pie-shaped hole has been cut in a highway and is sufficiently weathered by mud and rains, the hole becomes indistinguishable, even though a mine may lie beneath.

Exploiting this uncertainty, the Germans also make fake holes in the sidewalk. A tester approaches and may lose his life examining an innocent hole when the actual mine waits below his feet.

When you see a football game this fall, think of Livorno's athletic stadium, where the Germans have sown the ground thickly with mines and encouraged the turf to grow over it. From what would be sideline to sideline in the first 12 yards from the goal posts alone, engineers have dug up 64 mines of the deadliest sort.

Alert action by Lieutenant Robert Johnston of the highway transport office and an engineer friend prevented the Hotel Parco in Naples from being blown sky-high. Johnston found a loose tile in the floor of the room which was charged. The engineer then arranged a careful search and found a garbage can full of refuse, inviting immediate emptying because of the vile odor. The can, however, was riveted to the floor and 1700 pounds of TNT had been hooked up to it. Whoever lifted that garbage can would have lifted the entire hotel with it.

DAILY NEWS MAN WELLER IN RECORD RAID! FORTS WADE INTO FLAK

Stricken Ship Limps Home on Two Engines
After Attack Near Bologna

Advanced Bomber Base of the U.S. 15th Air Force— October 12, 1944

Across the blue Italian sky, dirty with thousands of puffs of vicious Nazi flak, Flying Fortresses and Liberators this morning led a cavalcade of Allied Mediterranean air power against Nazi emplacements around Bologna. It was the greatest number of heavy bombers ever directed against a single objective in the Mediterranean theater.

As the only civilian correspondent participating in the raid, I rode in the glass nose of a Fortress, which was among the earliest to run the gauntlet of German flak. Scheduled to be first over Bologna, our Fortress reached the well-camouflaged German bivouac area after two earlier waves had laid initial carpets of bombs. By that time German flak had found the range, too. Before the eyes of Navigator Lieutenant I. C. Heffrom of New Orleans, a Fortress of the first wave caught fire from flak. The pilot put it in a perpendicular dive to extinguish the flames, pulled out miraculously without snapping the plane and finally disgorged seven parachutes. "I saw them floating down into the streets of Bologna," said Heffrom later.

Our Fortress, too, was already in distress as it entered its bombing run. Though the flak until then had been light—German gunners were waiting until the giants committed themselves on their final run—one engine suddenly died.

"A small piece is torn from the left wing," scribbled Heffrom in his log as we exchanged glances over oxygen masks.

At that moment the inside engine on the same wing stopped. Its blackened propeller motionlessly confronted us from the side window. Our pilot and co-pilot fought to keep the ship in formation not only for protection against an unexpected fighter attack, but so our bombs should fall at the chosen point in the smoking carpet which had been German encampments.

Hardly had the affected engine been feathered and the ship begun to groan with an effort to hold its place, when three Messerschmitts appeared, readying to attack. My untrained eyes never caught them, but over the shoulder of Heffrom—who also was on his first raid in this theater—I saw him scribble: "One enemy fighter has been engaged by a P-38."

Though I have flown against Italian anti-aircraft fire, this was my first experience with the high-powered flak which today is Germany's chief weapon of aerial defense, as its factories labor to replenish its fighter reserves.

From the moment the first black blossom bloomed near us, it seemed as though the Nazi gunners had chosen this ship.

During the long, high-altitude ride—our oxygen masks were on for more than four hours and this was only part of the flight—I had figured that our Fortress would be on the flank nearest and most exposed to the flak surrounding Bologna.

This prediction unfortunately proved true. Though not a single black puff penetrated the heart of the formation, the sky ahead of us and beside the window was stippled with deadly black fists. Most menacing of all was a giant cauliflower-cloud of hundreds of bursts which the Nazis erected over their troops as soon as the first Forts struck.

With scant regard for the fact that their flak's constant winking might betray them to the artillery of Lieutenant General Clark's Fifth Army, already raining shells into Bologna's outskirts, the Nazis kept up a thick, compact cloud of defiant smoke puffs. The moment we crossed the Nazis' hideout the flak intensified, as though the gunners were trying to throw black dust in our eyes. We crouched lower in our metal helmets. Handfuls of thick smoke appeared ahead of the nose, seemingly as near as tobacco rings to a smoker's face. Others pockmarked the blue just above us while another set appeared and disappeared like black porpoises beside the ship.

Once I felt a sudden double bump below, approaching Bologna. Through the bottom window between my legs, I saw two strong black puffs fading to frustrated wisps of grey as the propwash blew them under the eyrie of the ball turret gunner.

Oxygen use is denoted by a black-faced dial which has a semi-human mouth with cold white lips. These lips open and shut with each breath you draw through the mask, as though the instrument were also inhaling. As the flak bloomed around us, breaths came faster and white lips parted even more rapidly. The heat of fear made our electrically-heated flying suits sweaty and the rubber mask moist inside.

Not a single bomb of the hundreds I saw cascade down through yawning bomb bays landed among Bologna's medieval skyscrapers, though its yellow walls were nearby and the Grand Piazzi visible, indenting its center. The bulk of the bombing fell between General Clark and the city—an area less than 10 miles broad.

The military motive for this gigantic effort could be read easily from the skies. The Fifth Army's artillery, looking down from the Apennines, dominates the approaches to most of the Po Valley. But these roads all intertwine at Bologna.

If the chief Nazi force entrenched between the two rivers and two roads entering Bologna is deprived of a foothold by this carpet of death, the Nazis must either withdraw or fight for the ancient city, house by house. If the latter, Bologna's beauties may succumb to war's necessities as did those of Florence.

The Fortress group which took me over Bologna was the same which saved Kasserine Pass by destroying Rommel's armor. It was among those responsible for the similar bombing at Anzio and the less successful attempt at Monte Cassino to break the mountain deadlock. For this reason, the briefing of crews—several of which have returned no more—in which I took part, before dawn in the barn of an old Adriatic farmhouse, was particularly moving. When the men shuffled in from the cold starlight, the briefing officer, Major George Sander, greeted them with the words: "Of all targets, this time we have the most ticklish one. If we hit our own troops we can cause disaster. Those kids down there are kids we went to school with, and kids we will have to live with after the war. Be careful."

Sander added candidly: "The area will be heavily defended. There are always plenty of flak-guns right behind the German front line. You will be getting the full share of their guns at this low altitude."

Sander was right.

No Heat, No Water, No Lift
in Grand Hotel de Luxe

*Tourist in Italy Would Find Courtyard a Wastebasket
and Servants Mostly Boys Who Beg Guests for Cigarettes*

Somewhere in Italy—October 18, 1944

Those "inveterate European travelers," as society columns used to call them, who are restless to see Italy in the second year of its liberation, would forgo that pleasure without regret if they could see the Grand Hotel, 1944-style. In the gilded corridors things are not what they used to be. The one-time tourist slogan—*WINTER IN ITALY*—is no longer persuasive propaganda. It is more like a challenge.

Without mentioning the smashed villages and towns where people are still combing rubble from past bombings and where running water in the town fountain is virtually the only public service restored, take a look at the Grand Hotel as it is today. Sometimes it is closed and you have to part wooden shutters in order to see the bombed interior. In some cases you can enter.

Such a hotel is usually six to eight stories high. New arrivals are placed on top floors. Social values are thus reversed, for you work your way up by working your way down.

The reason for this is twofold. Elevators, when such still are existent, are usually broken; running water exists in some rooms, but power is insufficient to lift it to the upper stories. Transients, therefore, are placed among the gilt Cupids on the top floor. After six months of hiking staircases they have worked their way down as far as the sixth floor. After a year they may be as low as the third, which ranks high.

Allied officers, temporarily the aristocrats in Italy, live three, five, sometimes eight to a room. A single naked bulb illuminates the center of the room at night. It is possible to find things (except in corners), but reading, or writing dispatches, is excluded. For drinking water a field bag has been hung in the corridor, above the absorbent sawdust scattered across the marble parquet.

At an open window this Grand Hotel de luxe offers evidence that some

Italian construction has begun, for intermittent hammering is heard. More constant is the beating sound of an accordion, played by one of Italy's young men who are living from no evident means.

. Most door locks are smashed and the keys lost. Thievery, however, is less in the hotels than on the streets, so belongings are slightly safer indoors than out.

Gone are the uniformed porters and crisped chambermaids. Instead, a pack of uncombed boys in school pants run the elevator when it works and wrestle, fight and cadge cigarettes in the corridors. They are kept in order only by cuffs from long-coated porters, who alone preserve the traditional uniform.

The hotel where your correspondent is now living has the largest wastebasket known: the courtyard window. Approximately weekly, this gigantic wastebasket is emptied by being swept out. Altogether, the Grand Hotel is not what it used to be. Anyone who misses wintering in free Italy this year will not be missing much.

—

NORTHERN ITALY A LAND OF POLITICAL CANNIBALS

Somewhere in Italy—October 27, 1944 (Delayed)

Political cannibalism, raw and terrible, is the order of the day in northern Italy as the US 5th Army presses toward Bologna, hub of the crisscrossing trunk highways of the Po and Piave Valleys.

The enormous flatland, spreading from Genoa to Trieste, is like a pond teeming with vicious life and shrinking in size every day. As the pond's edges draw in, the fish turn cannibalistic, each aiming only to be the last to die. Political creeds are fiercely devouring each other amid the ruins of Italy's lost industrial power.

Fascism was born in Turin, and northern Italy possesses, with Milan and other cities, the extremist Mediterranean worshipers of the all-powerful state. Able to find only occasional authentic members of the underground, the Fascist Republicans are turning their revolvers on passive civilian sympathizers. For a civilian to be "doubtful" is enough for him to be doomed.

Partisans claim 200,000 members in northern Italy—an estimate probably exaggerated for purposes of peace-table bargaining, but notable as an offset to the S.S. (Elite Guard) and Gestapo, which undoubtedly have the upper hand.

These underground struggles belonging to history probably will go unrecorded. It is nothing new to southern Italy to have poverty, but northern Italy has both poverty and terror.

What is going on in northern Italy today may be judged by what has occurred in southern Italy in the year since the armistice, as revealed by a diary kept by an Italian lieutenant, now in the writer's hands. The lieutenant, ill, had holed up in a village. He kept a journal of what occurred from which the following are excerpts:

October 2, 1943—In Amandola, near the Church of St. Anthony of Caldarola, the S.S. shot an Italian soldier from Bari for having a revolver (broken and empty). Before shooting him they held him more than an hour in the basin of the town fountain, forcing him to paddle his feet and pushing him down with his head underwater.

February 23, 1944—As I have requested, an Austrian deserter was brought to me, a sergeant of aviation condemned to death by the German military authority for having shown favor to 150 Italians in a concentration camp. We procured him a place to sleep. For eating he will have to make out like others, one meal daily with friendly families.

March 1, 1944—The authorities today opened the grain silos at Comunanza. Four persons were killed in the rush.

March 18, 1944—A company of Schutzstaffel men, accompanied by Fascists, arrived at Monte Fortino and searched several houses. A column of 39 vehicles, some armored, began attacking Montemonaco on our right. On the left, also on the road to Gerosa, armed parties have reached St. George Island and burned several homes. At the rock of Montemonaco they surrounded some young patriots, who fought them off with their unfit and inadequate weapons. So they called out the parents of patriots from a neighboring village and shot twelve of them.

March 21, 1944—Yesterday evening German armored cars moved into Lacentrale. Several kids trying to run away were injured. It is snowing again.

March 25, 1944—They are burning houses around Sarnano.

March 26, 1944—At four o'clock this afternoon a stranger appeared who made himself out a German Jew. Everybody caught on that he was a spy. He insisted on talking to me. Then he went around to the bar and started gambling, possibly in the hope of pulling some information out of the customers. But the alarm against him had already gone out.

This same character pretended he sympathized with the patriots of Monte Fortino. When the Germans reached our town he was taken prisoner. But he did not appear worried. He kept on smoking tranquilly and then was suddenly released.

April 9, 1944—Fascisti led by spies searched the forest where two British prisoners had been kept all winter by a family. They smashed beds and crockery in a cabin and took them all to Monte Fortino.

April 13, 1944—A group of armed Fascists arrived. They were looking for Dr. Luogo Severino as well as myself. Warned in time, I hid out in a thicket.

April 17, 1944—Fascists led by spies during the night found the cave where our friends were concealed and took three, all Englishmen.

May 1, 1944—Six prisoners of war were shot against the wall at the cemetery at Comunanza. They were said to be two British and four Americans. On this occasion German Lieutenant Horst Unrau addressed a mimeographed warning to the population. The bodies were laid away without caskets and buried, two by two, outside a small wall.

Thus ends the Italian lieutenant's diary. An American graves registration squad dug up the American and British bodies, but found no identifying marks.

—

WAR BLOWS INTO CAPRI—CLOSE CALL FOR G.I.

Somewhere in Italy—October 28, 1944 (Delayed)

The shock of war has tardily hit Capri, the high-cliffed, enchanted island of sirens, in the third week of October, a year after Italy's surrender. Nevertheless, the delayed concussion was still sufficient to blow—temporarily—Sergeant Sam Divich out of the softest job possessed by any G.I. in the Mediterranean theater.

Sam slaughtered pigs for a living back home in Steubenville, Ohio. The rugged-looking sergeant, with a boxer's profile, has been sitting on lovely Piccola Marina (Little Beach), on the seaward side of Capri, looking after the bathhouses and small gymnasium frequented by American air force officers. As was recently revealed, Capri has been a rest camp for weary fliers of the US 12th and 15th Air Forces since Naples fell a year ago.

With a dark-eyed fisher girl of Piccola Marina, Sam was thinking about what he would ask her to make him for breakfast the other morning when suddenly it seemed as though the end of the world had come.

The blast of a terrible explosion knocked Sam out.

When he recovered he found himself on the glass-littered floor. It took him a quarter of an hour to bring the Italian girl back to consciousness.

Sam's residence, which is a beach villa belonging to the English music-hall star Gracie Fields, was a mess. Its windows had been blown in, its lintels smashed. The concussion was so great that even the stone fireplace was riven in two.

Rocks on the beach, supporting Gracie's villa, were pushed apart, as though by an enormous hand. The strong smell of high explosives still came from them. When Sam got up courage he found fragments of the shell of a mine near the rocks. Capri's first taste of war had been a mine washed in from the sea by a heavy rainstorm, a year after the armistice.

—

GERMAN CORRESPONDENT TELLS REASONS WHY NAZIS CAN'T QUIT

Somewhere in Italy—October 28, 1944

How Germany, while acknowledging itself defeated, is being held together by a fantastic cat's cradle of disorganized forces and emotions, is revealed by the following conversation between a German war correspondent captured in the Mediterranean theater, and an American newspaperman. The German, who denied that he was a Nazi party member, asked that his name not be revealed because "the arrest of my entire family would follow immediately."

German: Every man in my outfit admits that Germany has lost the war. They have been convinced for more than a year now.

American: Then why keep fighting?

German: Because the Germans are told that if they yield they will be sent by the Russians to Siberia. They may not believe other Nazi propaganda, but knowing Russian tenacity, they believe this. And because most of our army has served some time in Russian winters, they would literally rather die than be sent to Siberia.

American: But why the same stubborn resistance on the Anglo-American Western Front?

German: Because the army believes that yielding there will only make it simpler for the Russians to crush in the Eastern Front.

American: Why not surrender to both simultaneously?

German: Because every Anglo-American advance is always linked by Nazi spokesmen with the danger of a "Bolshevist" victory. This is the only thing that both the army and German people fear equally. It is the only thing they fear more than Himmler's police.

American: Are the Germans aware of the Lublin* massacres?

German: Few have heard of them. All the ordinary German knows is that the secret police come and get the Jews. Where they go they do not know, and nobody dares ask. I consider the Lublin atrocities authentic, but if I had not served in Russia, I would not have known. And very few Germans know.

American: Do you think the Germans dread the Russians because they have a feeling of guilt for invading the Soviet Union and fear revenge?

German: The German people have no guilt toward Russia. They do not consider themselves responsible for the invasion. Like the army, they did what they were ordered. They feel their leaders are responsible. But they think Russia will hold the German people responsible. Also, some anti-Nazis fear surrender will mean a communist Germany, which they believe would be about the same as Hitlerism.

American: What is the attitude of the officers?

German: They have the same fear that I have described, plus another. They are afraid to surrender because whenever an important

---

*Polish region where many thousands of Jews died, in many different massacres.

officer surrenders, his family is arrested by the secret police. In such circumstances, all the alternatives are so terrible that it is easier to keep fighting than to do anything else. So every officer hopes that when the crackup comes, it will occur elsewhere than where he is, and be total. Because every incomplete defeat means worse police reprisals at home.

American: What was the effect of the attempt by the generals on Hitler's life (July 20)? Was the morale greatly shaken?

German: No, rather the reverse. From the failure of the attempt, everybody in the army perceived that even this way out was hopeless. Seeing that assassinating Der Fuehrer was impossible, the soldiers came to feel, more than ever, that nothing was left but to fight until death. And since the three Allies offer only unconditional surrender—which to the Germans means also Siberia—the Reichswehr is hearing a similar point of view from both sides.

American: Do you agree that the Junkers officers' clique is planning for an easy peace in order to make a third attempt to conquer the world?

German: I know there has been much Allied discussion along those lines. I know thousands of officers, and I consider such talk rubbish. They admit they are beaten. Their plans go no further than the predicament of the moment. Nobody is thinking about the next war. They are just wondering how to end this one. But as long as Himmler controls the situation within Germany, the Reichswehr feels it must go on fighting. If they surrender piecemeal, the officers' families will fall to the secret police. If they surrender totally—Siberia. That is the way the German army is thinking today. Whether they can fight all winter in such a frame of mind, with all confidence in Hitler as commander-in-chief evaporated, I simply can't say. When the end comes it will be suddenly.

press collect xia
   via ~~cable~~ RCA ROME 00693 *for author after*
chicagonews ~~london~~ NEWYORK *censor's consider*

        after
run ~~following~~ karpenissi story suggested foreword chicagonews

correspondent is first newspaperman reach distomo famed
                                          june tenth
martyred village greece whose massacre ~~xxxxxxxx~~ provoked
                                    july from
official statements protest ~~xxxxxxx~~ roosevelt hull ~~xxxxxxxx~~

stop following account is therefore first fully substantiaxted
        report
on spot ~~xxxxxx~~ by nonofficial observer paragraph dateline

distome november eighth delayed was story of distomo propaganda

query was tale of how town among greycliffed lower shoulders of

parnassus died before nazi guns just ~~xxxxxx~~ attempt to flag war

effort with fabricated atrocity query how did distome die querypara

to answer these questions you must sit at improvised court of inquiry

under single autumnal tree in distomos tiny square and ~~xxxx~~ meet

distomos people stop you must see their faces stop you must check

and count names of dead and ask how they died stop and you must walk

among burned out houses stop you must sit beside wounded whove not

yet died from last junes massacre stop you must count graves paragraph

order determine for himself what was true and what exaggeration xhi
                        INDEPENDENT
this correspondent been making ~~xxxxxxxx~~ investigation stop   his
           distome
unsponsored trip ~~xxx~~ undertaken without other journalist or ~~xxxxxy~~

bureaucratic influence stop conclusions are those which any responsible

person anxious only set down for history what believed exact would

affirm paragraph ~~xxxx~~ reach distomo you climb mountain highway from

levadia stop where road forks instead going right toward delphi you go

left among treeless cold hills below parnassus where icy winds play among

ravines and bearded shepherds with crooks follow tinkling bells sheep

XVII

The Liberation of Greece

Weller had witnessed the April 1941 invasion of Greece by the Nazis, and they did not retreat from the mainland until October 1944. (The Germans held Crete and other islands until May and even June 1945.) After the deaths of over three hundred thousand civilians from starvation and reprisals, liberation turned into a civil war that would continue until 1949. With the British deeply involved, Weller and other reporters were hard-pressed to make sense for readers back home of a situation of numbing complexity. I have chosen several tragic dispatches of Occupied Greece under the Nazis and those pieces that succinctly explain the civil war that followed, to which he later returned for the *CDN* and portrayed in his 1949 novel *The Crack in the Column*.

In praising it, Weller's colleague Homer Bigart (the *New York Herald Tribune*) called him "probably the best informed United States correspondent on Greece" and the civil war the "first real skirmish between Communism and the West." In the novel, Weller could be more critical of American non-policy in Greece than he could in his reporting—the "passive, critical, openhanded, complacent Americans" who could not make up their minds about who was right or wrong, and hoped they would not be forced to decide. "The great disorderly thud of the American heart could be heard, eager to be tapped for everybody and everything, everywhere, more like an udder than a heart, indiscriminate and cowlike, asking only to be asked, hinting only that it would like to be loved."

From a correspondent's perspective, there was blame laying

back home—when attention was paid at all—as to what America's responsibility was and who was doing the least dishonorable job of covering the fate of Greece and hence of postwar Europe. In mid-1945, *Time* magazine's Walter Graebner published an article criticizing the reporters in Greece months earlier, when liberation had slid into civil war. Weller, in Chungking by now, rose to their (and his own) defense, although *Time* ran little of his letter:

To support his tardy but valid point that the United States is blundering politically by withdrawing its forces from Mediterranean Europe, your skipping correspondent Graebner (*Time,* July 16) need not have paused to slur as "a pretty bad job of reporting" the work of correspondents who covered the civil war in Greece.

We American and British writers were no more "cooped up in the Grande Bretagne Hotel" than were General Scobie and his staff, who lived there and worked next door. We went everywhere unguarded, even under fire, and crossed the lines until forbidden to do so by the British military. We were never "pressed for immediate copy." We struggled rather to cut down our teeming material to the limited wordage of the military radio facilities.

Please be reminded that every line we wrote passed through censorship. No "solid bloc of pro-EAM and anti-British" ever developed among correspondents. Both American and British reporters were subdivided into many degrees of experience, observation, and understanding.

I suggest that *Time* resurrect the unpublished dispatches from its own able eyewitness correspondent, Reg Ingraham, and notes by *Life* photographer Dmitri Kessel, who photographed the Greek police opening the civil war by killing unarmed EAM marchers. Ingraham's straightforward reporting went largely unpublished or mutilated, apparently to conform to Manhattan policy. Possibly Graebner's Mediterranean account has also been editorially *gleichgeschaltet* [forced into line], in which case he deserves sympathy rather than criticism.

George Weller, *Chicago Daily News*

DELPHI, SYMBOL OF CULTURE OF ANCIENTS, BROODS OVER DESOLATION WROUGHT BY WAR

Delphi, Greece—probably November, 1944

Delphi, pinned like a reddish polkadot tie on the grey throat of Mount Parnassus, has seen in the last eight years what no mountain village should be compelled to know. From these high cliffs, where the hawks wheel against the blue, falls the pure water of the spring where the Muses once drank. But it will take time to make these waters pure again. Four years of Royalist Fascism, followed by nearly four years of Nazi occupation, have left them defiled.

When the world thinks of Greece it thinks of the Acropolis. But this is an error. Every Greek city had its Acropolis, which was simply a defensive fort. But there was only one Delphi.

Delphi was the Geneva of the ancient world. Here came not only delegates of the warring Greek cities but also Persians, Sicilians and Egyptians, testifying to the unity which transcended materialistic politics and spilled over into the realm of spirit. Up these stiff, green slopes plenipotentiaries clambered in their chitons, not chiefly to consult the oracle, nor even to dicker politically, but to assert the unity of all the known nations.

Among their self-admitted obligations was writing an honest and objective political history of their wars, which shows that Delphi has a lesson for us today. Feeling the Muses' eyes looking down on them from the cold, grey peak above, they recognized duties transcending their boundaries.

The last time I visited Delphi was in 1932. Then, as now, the sharp, dank smell of the newly crushed olives of Amphissa came up from the green valley facing on the northern edge of the ever-blue Gulf of Corinth. Greece's great question was whether the fugitive industrialist Samuel Insull* would be surrendered to American justice. Only Roosevelt's first election blanketed this

---

*British-born Samuel Insull (1859–1938) began as personal secretary to Thomas Edison and cofounded General Electric. Weller's first assignment as stringer for the *New York Times* was to interview Insull, who was hoping to avoid extradition after his holding companies collapsed. He was eventually tried in Chicago and acquitted.

then all-important matter in the American newspapers enough to permit the writer to absent himself two days from Athens.

This afternoon, as one sits by the oracle's deserted niche, the wind that sighs up the valley could tell bloody stories. What is now only the smell of olives smelled recently of smoke, and there were human hearts in the embers.

Some whim of the Nazis and Italians spared Delphi itself, and only a sole citizen here faced death. His executioners were Italian. They gave him a cigarette. While one engaged him in conversation, another put a bullet in the back of his head.

Our way to Delphi will be hard.

—

GREEKS' GREATEST PRIDE: TOWN THAT NEVER GAVE IN

Nazi Firing Squads Fail to Blot Out Kaisariani

Athens, Greece—November 2-4, 1944

Greece has between 700 and 1000 Lidices—obliterated villages where the barefoot inhabitants crouch in rags in the cold autumn rains, waiting for relief food which has not left the docks.

But Greece wants no one to forget it also has a Kaisariani, unique among hundreds of blackened communities. For Kaisariani is a village— actually, a suburb of Athens—which refused to become a Lidice. Alone among all the communities of the world which have seen their homes ripped apart by shells, this mortar-pocked, death-stricken community still survives, mutilated, but militarily as well as spiritually triumphant; living evidence that people will die to defend their homes.

Kaisariani is victorious proof that flesh and blood can be stronger here than artillery, heavy weapons and machine guns. On the eastern edge of Athens, where the barren knolls of the Hymettos, the honeyhive of Homer's time, rise brownish-grey above henhouse structures making up this community of former refugees from exchange populations of Asia Minor, spirit has triumphed over matter.

The Nazis, Greek Fascists and Fascist-led Greek police attacked this working-class suburb, this Athenian Brooklyn, time after time. Like Vienna's Karl Marxhof and Madrid's University City, it was shelled at point-blank range. At first uniformed assassins were able to fight their way into its pathetic streets which, due to poverty, have the same miniature quality as all Hoovervilles. They killed and burned, occasionally paused for rape and loot, and fought their way out. Captured defenders went to Reich-bound labor squads or, via hostage pools, to firing squads.

Kaisariani, which fought off forty-nine full-scale attacks, received a first sample of what it would soon suffer on April 23 this year. The village was suddenly surrounded by Nazis and Nazi-controlled police. Summoned to the square, 100 men were taken away to the prison at Goudi, to the hostage pool for a firing squad.

At 4 a.m. on May 1, in a city-wide attack on quarters inhabited by refugees from Asia Minor, the Germans assembled a force of about 10,000 men, mostly Nazis, and surrounded not only Kaisariani but also the suburbs of Byron and Katsipodi. A German general had been shot in Sparta, and also a major. The Nazis already had 190 Communists from Metaxas' political prison in Acro Nauplia, but required more hostages in order to make up the 200 they demanded as reprisal for their general's death. After getting them, they commenced the executions. As the trucks moved through Kaisariani to the firing range, the doomed men scribbled notes and tossed them to relatives—slips of paper now preserved in the village's shacks: *"We die for liberty." "Don't weep for us." "We give our lives for Greece."*

Truckfuls of bleeding bodies—204 in all—were taken to the cemetery in the Piraeus suburb of New Kokkinia. Somewhere women found flowers and dipped them in the blood that ran in the gutters. It required four hours for the execution squads to finish their work. The Nazis had one further formal announcement: henceforward, women would be executed.

But Kaisariani never surrendered.

A sentry system was established which made it impossible for the raiders to enter the rim of shacks without facing spears of fire from door-ways and rooftops. Finally, the raids became so costly to the enemy that their technique changed to a siege. Thus, where greater, better-armed and better-fed workmen's suburbs elsewhere in Europe succumbed, Kaisariani lived on and slowly became a fortress for the ELAS, or Communist-led guard, defending it.

In Kaisariani most houses have only one room. Sometimes there is a bed, sometimes only a mattress. Shacks are packed tight together: there are no gardens. Everyone lives by his wits. Rickets, tuberculosis, pneumonia and dysentery have been permanent residents ever since the 1923 exchange of populations with Turkey flooded Greece with non-assimilated, rootless families without rural training.

What it cost to Kaisariani to live instead of dying, to survive in its poverty instead of being destroyed, is visible in the eyes of ELAS militiamen standing by.

Their expression differs from that of their mothers and fathers. They are soldiers, men who know their arms. Back when dictator George Kondylis overthrew Greece's republic to install the monarchy with foreign support, these men knew nothing about streetfighting.

Now they know. Let any combination of interior forces or exterior nations try to bend Greece into a new totalitarianism, and they will need every gun their overseas backers can provide to take unconquered Kaisariani.

—

VILLAGE FEELS WRATH OF VENGEANCE AFTER AMBUSH BY PATRIOTS

Distomo, Greece—November 15, 1944

To reach the martyred village of Distomo, perched among the grey-cliffed lower shoulders of Parnassus, you must climb the mountain highway from Levadia.

Where the road forks, instead of going right toward Delphi, you turn left among the treeless hills below Parnassus, where icy winds play among the ravines and bearded shepherds with crooks follow the tinkling bells of the sheep and goats on the boulder-strewn slopes.

The Germans and Italians took the right fork to Arachova. In two years, they burned 173 homes in the upper and lower towns and shot 36 Greeks, including five women.

The Germans, on June 10, took the left road at the fork south toward Distomo and the village of Stiri a few miles beyond. Fifteen trucks full of Germans came from Levadia, thirty miles from Amphissa.

Before leaving the fork they tried their marksmanship and warmed their gun barrels on six persons working in fields nearby. They found it amusing to use a mortar as well as a machine gun on this small game. The Germans decided to take twelve young shepherds and farmers as hostages to Distomo in case of attack by the Greek guerrillas.

About 1:45 on that day, forty-five truckloads of Germans arrived in Distomo. They parked in the lower of its two hillside squares, near the white-plastered schoolhouse. Sensing some such "retaliation" as had laid waste scores of villages between Levadia and Salonika, and eager to propitiate the dreaded SS, Distomo's people came running with cheese, eggs, wine and bread from their meager stores. The German commander was a Greek-speaking Gestapo officer named Teos, believed to be a captain.

Apparently the Germans did not intend general murder. Their mission in the village was to search for anti-Fascist guerrillas and to plunder.

Teos ordered the Distomites indoors and SS men went through the houses, taking the proffered food, wine, and blankets, and sheep rugs as well. Teos questioned the bearded Orthodox priest, Father Sotiris Zisis, whether any *Andartes* (guerrillas) were around. Zisis replied that a small band had departed earlier.

Reassured that he could lead a party of SS men along the road to Stiri without being attacked, Teos ordered two trucks loaded with about fifty SS men in plain clothes. Around noon the party set forth. It never reached Stiri. About three miles outside Distomo it was ambushed by the anti-Fascist, anti-royalist ELAS guerrillas.

The SS men pulled out arms hidden under the seats of the trucks and replied with fire. In the fusillade five Germans were killed. At Teos' order, the party turned back. Teos himself had a bad wound in the abdomen.

It was not until Teos died just before sunset that day that the horror began. The SS went straight to Father Zisis' house with tommy guns. They already had consulted him twice, and Zisis expected a third overture. Instead he was mowed down. His twelve-month-old son was shot, his wife wounded.

The fact that any of Distomo's 2060 population survived was because of an interval that ensued when twelve bound men, caught at the crossroads, were executed. While some Distomites fled into the hills in the dead of night, others, feeling that the Nazis had slaked their wrath by killing the priest's family and the hostages, hid in their homes. They thereby wrote their own death sentences.

—

Half-Alive Survivors Tell Grim Stories

Distomo, Greece—November 16, 1944

As you stand in the tiny square of this tragic Greek village, with smoldering-eyed people gathered around you, there emerges from the small white church the murdered Father Zisis' successor. He has with him a carefully-written, alphabetized list of persons slain by the Nazis. You ask Mayor Lathas to get his own list in order to make a comparison.

The priest's list has 223 names. The mayor's has seven more, who died of wounds in the improvised hospital up the lower valley.

Nobody has tried to count the wounded, because some may not survive the winter. Like 98 per cent of Greece's obliterated villages, Distomo has received neither food, shelter, nor medicine. So you visit sixty-year-old, wizened Yanoula Limouni, lying on a bedless floor beside a tiny charcoal fire. Her head is swathed in black cloth, and she looks like a Dürer drawing of pain. A German bullet went through her right cheek and cleanly emerged from her left, leaving a large hole. She is holding a dirty bandage against it, and when she tries to talk, her unmanageable jaws make her unintelligible.

This correspondent has a leather coat that resembles a German officer's. Yanoula's two-year-old grandson, shaven-headed, ragged, barelegged Angelo Nikalaou, recoils with a wild scream and runs to his thick-bearded father, George Nikalaou. Fearfully the child rejects candy offered by the dreaded stranger, but after being told repeatedly, "American, not German," he accepts the sweet.

Angelo is motherless. His mother, Theoxoula Nikalaou, Yanoula's daughter, was tommy-gunned to death in that house with ten others, mostly women and children, while little Angelo huddled in the shadows.

The father sits Angelo on the floor and says: "What happened to mummy?" With a solemnity that wrenches the heart, Angelo bends his body over his knees and remains frozen thus. "And then?" prompts the father. Tiny Angelo, already huddled double, topples stiffly to the floor, whispering in his baby voice, *"Eisi, kai etsi"* (like this, and then like this).

You talk with grey-haired Angelis Papanghelis, who once had a bakery shop in Gary, Indiana, and later worked in the Congress Hotel in Chicago. He escaped by hiding in the cellar.

One Greek-American who died fighting was 53-year-old Athanassio Panourias, who came back to Distomo in 1928 after fifteen years in the United States. His aged father, in old-style shepherd dress, with a black cap, long white leggings, and short-skirted jacket, tells how Panourias, trapped in his house, drew his knife and got a tommy gun from one German. But two others wrested the knife from him, plunged it in his back and slit his throat.

The mayor shows you where two farmer cousins, 65-year-old Herakles Mikas and 55-year-old George Mikas, were found lying, their torsos slit lengthwise, their hands, stiff in death, attempting to hold in their vitals.

You climb the stairs to the adjacent offices of Judge Constantine Kritzopis and Miliades Kouroumbalis, government forester. From the balcony you can see the green cross over their graves in the yard.

Inside, bloodstains are still visible on the floor. The forester's 27-year-old wife was killed. His seven-year-old son, with a bullet wound in his leg, spent the night on the bodies of his father and mother.

The next room is where Judge Kritzopis' wife, 33-year-old Asteria Kritzopis, saved her girl of eight and boy of six by stuffing them under the bed. The German bullet which broke the lock is lodged in the door frame, and there are holes in the wall against which the mother died. Her throat was cut after the shooting. When the Germans left, the children came out from under the bed and fled to the home of the square-built shepherd, Sideros Kelermanes, who, thus warned, was able to save his own family.

Disbelievers should talk to the family of Marietta Philippou, 25, who offered the Germans wine and was ripped open with a knife.

The 34-year-old, shock-headed Anastasious Stathas stood in his sandals made from old tire treads. The Nazis shot his four-month-old infant while his wife, Euphrosyne, was in the next room, then riddled her chest with bullets, and finally killed both his boys, six and eight, thus exterminating his entire family.

Of Distomo's 450 houses, 62 were fired, 38 in the village itself. The Italians, who burned 29 hostages and took seven, on June 25, 1943, share honors with the SS for this.

The SS returned on June 26 of this year to burn three houses, including the home of the doctor, who was treating victims from the massacre sixteen days before.

Fixing the responsibility for Distomo on the Nazi leaders cannot be done definitely until it is determined who, besides Gestapo officer Teos, commanded the SS Panzer Grenadier outfit No. 7.

Lanky Captain Edward Kimball of Baltimore, who aided the Greek guerrillas around Levadia, has, among abundant traces of their presence that the Germans left behind, orders for neighboring operations signed by Sturmbannfuehrer Rickert, Hauptsturmfuehrer Kopfner, and Levadia's town "mayor," Obersturmfuehrer Zabel.

Were these officers responsible for Distomo? The village expects the Allies to provide the answer to these questions. Distomo's dead are waiting to see whether the British and Americans are as earnest as the Russians about seeing justice done.

—

LETTER FROM GREECE

Athens, Greece—November, 1944

For the brewing of political peace Greece is the same sort of laboratory to the world as 1936 Spain was for brewing political war. From a transatlantic distance Greece seems an alphabet soup, with ELAS, EAM, EDES, EPON and a dozen other organizations all mixed in a *macédoine*. To an observer sitting no higher above Athens than the Acropolis, however, the muddle resolves itself into simple terms.

There is left and right, just about as there was in Spain. The left is composed of a popular front of anti-fascist, anti-monarchist parties, republican by inclination. Its chief force is a communist party, receiving as yet no aid from Russia and willing to settle for a democracy and let collectivism wait.

On the right is another coalition of anti-fascist democratic elements, loosely organized. Their nucleus is royalist. The right is heavily backed by Great Britain, whose intention is to see that George II gets back his throne in spite of responsibility for four years of the dictatorial Metaxas police state. A royalist Greece fits nicely into Britain's pattern for the eastern Mediterranean.

The dominating figure in Athens is Rex Leeper, the British ambassador, whose supple policies are gradually whittling down the left and building up the right. The ambassador receives American and British correspondents separately. When they compare notes, they find his attitude toward the Communist party of Greece (the KKE) varies remarkably with his audience . . . Soviet military missions are seen in the Hotel Grande Bretagne, but they are token affairs of lonely officers whom the Greeks sometimes mistake for the despised Bulgarians.

The main question, as in France, is how to disarm the guerrillas of the left without giving them any guarantees regarding republic vs. monarchy (the plebiscite which restored George in 1935 having been strictly of the bayonet kind) and if possible how to get him back without holding a vote at all. To put this over on the suspicious guerrillas is like trying to undress a sleeping man without waking him up.

The question most frequently asked of any American in uniform is "When are the troops coming?" The Greeks do not yet know that at the Tehran conference Mr. Roosevelt introduced a campaign-year isolationism by writing off America's stake in the Balkans—or rather signing it over to Britain and Russia.

The Greeks, knowing the role that lend-lease and American aircraft played in liberating the Balkans, imagine that we remain interested in defending freedoms here. Until someone tells them that the United States is already politically on the retreat in Europe, the Greeks will probably continue in this irrational 1941 manner to expect Washington to send troops to back up its guarantees. Academy Street, a leading boulevard, became Roosevelt Road even before the Germans walked into Greece. The Nazis let the signs remain as a kind of political irony. Now they gleam with meaning again. The question is if they will turn ironical a second time. This will depend on whether Roosevelt infuses into his passive Balkan policy the vigor he subtracted during the American electoral campaign.

Athens is getting food now, but mountain villages are still starving. "People back home must be fed up with hunger stories," an American parachutist saboteur told me. He was one of the "Cloak-and-Dagger boys" who worked for months behind the Nazi lines. "If I read in my own newspaper all I've seen in these mountains the last few months," he added, "I wouldn't believe it myself."

In the region between Distomo and Karpenisi we went through one blackened village after another. People huddled between roofless walls, squatting possessively in most un-communist fashion on the last bit of private property they owned. Each rain-soaked, wind-visited and bedless stone house was soured ashen with the stain of that magnesium grenade the SS uses to demolish homes.

It is curious that while the communist bugaboo in Italy has already separated the American government from extra amounts of hush money—in the form of relief—no such corrective impulse is felt here. Some Greeks think Italy is doing better because though it was a fascist, enemy brigand state, there were millions of Italian-influenced votes in the presidential campaign—but only a few thousand Greeks.

Generous amounts of food and clothing dropped from American transport aircraft could still save lives in the snowbound, shelterless mountain villages. The idea has been proposed, but nothing done. Blown bridges block mountain roads, so the villagers simply wait and starve. Dogs, however, in villages where the SS has killed most heavily, are fat and glossy. There was a German rule that bodies of hostages must be allowed to lie where they fell for several weeks, *pour encourager les autres*. Only dogs dared ignore the regulation against approaching corpses.

The U.S. is providing, according to official figures, about three-fourths of the food and garments being unloaded at Piraeus and Salonika. The shipments are being distributed by Military Liaison, a relief organization which is nine-tenths British in personnel. Jim Landis having failed in his campaign to get lend-lease in the Middle East labelled as American, Greeks generally believe everything they get is British. The uniform of the donor counts more than the label on the can.

Europe recognizes that food distribution is a political weapon in the peace. France, Belgium and Yugoslavia have said frankly that they want the food etc., but insist on handing it out their own way. Greece is almost unique in giving uninhibited permission to UNRRA.* But UNRRA won't

---

*United Nations Relief and Rehabilitation Administration.

supersede Military Liaison until April, and meantime the predicament of need transcends all political reservations.

One incredible element has disappeared: the inflation, which topped all others known to history. A hostess at a tea party given for a member of the royal family told me that she had suffered a new kind of servant trouble. Her maids, with tearful petulance, would tear up before her face the money she paid them, in a spirit like that of the nauseated Keats flinging his uneatable supper out the window.

Historians may someday be interested in the fact that on the last day of the "old" money Hitler's drachmas were worth ten trillion to the dollar. I went to the National Bank a few days before the new drachmas, backed by American and British guarantees, were issued. An underfed clerk in seamy shoes and patched grey pre-war suit gave me a full collection of all denominations out of his own salary. He refused repayment, saying the total was too insignificant. The quisling drachmas were in fact worth less on closing day than the paper they were printed on.

The buoyancy of the Greek spirit, after four years of royalist fascism under George and Metaxas, and nearly four more years of German occupation under Hitler and the monocled ex-royalist John Rhallis [Ioannis Rallis], is hardly to be believed. It is one reason why newspapers which send correspondents from Rome to Athens find it difficult to get them back to Italy again. In Athens is none of that vacant malaise and surly recalcitrance that has been fascism's heritage to Italy. The vacuum has been filled. The Greek spirit is as full of bounce as though Hellas were being liberated every hour on the hour. Given the tools, the Greeks will certainly finish the job.

With a UNRRA scout I arrived by jeep in Lamia, a partially destroyed town in central Greece. A few minutes later a committee for children's welfare knocked at the door of the smashed house where we slept. They did not want money, food, clothing or tools, not yet: they wanted to show us the program of relief they had drawn up for themselves. One thing that impressed the UNRRA man, who had been a social worker in Denver, was that it included recreation. This professional touch, which amateur uplifters never dare include, reassured him very much. According to him, the whole thing was a good program. He accepted it on the spot, then began thinking up arguments to sell it to Military Liaison, back in Athens.

SOVEREIGNS, PARACHUTES, MULES

Delphi, Greece—December 4, 1944

More than a century ago, in the ruins of ancient Tiryns, a young American doctor crouched and held his breath while the hoofbeats of Turkish cavalry thudded by. When the enemies of the newborn republic had passed, the doctor slipped back to the wounded guerrillas in his secret mountain hospital. The doctor of Greek freedom was Boston's Samuel Gridley Howe, America's most famous 19th century physician.

Howe's tradition is on the march. Again in this war Americans have fought to expel democracy's enemies from "sacred soil." Behind Nazi and Italian lines, beside British philhellenes, dozens of Americans and Greek-Americans have joined the *Andartes,* or guerrillas. Wryly known among themselves as Cloak-and-Dagger boys, these joint Anglo-American teams have been prodding Hitler to evacuate the Balkans in general and Greece in particular.

Cloakless but well-daggered, they have dived from the wind-blown doors of C-47 troop-carrier transports into starlit Greek nights. They have landed from rubber boats amid whispers at their secret rendezvous on Aegean-Ionian headlands, while Nazi sentries fired wildly into the ominous darkness. They know how to use every weapon, from automatic rifles to diplomacy. They never shoot unless pressed; shooting gives away position. They know how to slap a handful of plastic explosive on the joint of a railroad culvert, ensuring that it will be dropped misshapenly at the bottom of a mountain gulch a few minutes later. Their best weapon is brains, yet they're all touched with a similar screwballism. Perhaps it's due to the danger, or to their peculiar tools: parachutes, mules, and gold sovereigns worth $20 and bearing the placid countenances of Queen Victoria and King George the Fifth.

At first it was the British—including Australians, New Zealanders, and other restless spirits—who started annoying Hitler in the Balkans in October, 1942. Their aim was to cut the secondary Axis supply line for Africa, which ran from Vienna to Athens to Crete and Libya.

A tiny spatter of moonlit parachutes floated unnoticed into a Hellas that was held by two Italian and five German divisions. But sabotage cannot start overnight; patriot and collaborationist bands were just getting recruited. There were Greek traitors as well as Greek patriots, and each group was subdivided from within.

The patriots were divided into liberals and conservatives. The former had a core of communists, the latter of royalists, but both gave lip service to democracy. Half the Cloak-and-Daggers' energies were spent keeping patriots engaged against Germans rather than trying to settle the future government. (An ex-N.Y.U. track captain quieted several clashes by chiding both parties in fluent Greek.)

This double-entry of arms worked because most weapons were also followed into battle by British or American officers. Borne by parachutes, the lend-lease succeeded largely due to an indivisible pair—a U.S. major and an English colonel.

The Major is a slight, tough, Texas newspaper editorialist who served with the field artillery in France in World War I. Barred by age from joining the cannons again, at fifty he became both the first and oldest American to leap from a transport plane into the Greek sky. From being a provost marshal in Cairo, the Major turned into the first American diplomat in Greece.

Howe's modern counterpart is the Doctor—a small, twenty-four-year-old Iowa dentist with earnest spectacles and a whiplash tongue. A captain, he jumped at about the same time last winter into the guerrillas' mountain stronghold. There he founded four secret hospitals for guerrillas, mostly near the birthplace of Greece's democratic parliament, at a village near Karpenisi.

The Germans searched long but failed to catch him. They burned and blew up all but a few of Karpenisi's seven hundred homes.

After being dropped in the late autumn of 1943, the Major and the Colonel traveled more than 400 miles afoot and on horseback, from one guerrilla conference to the next. When taking paratroop training in the Middle East, the Major's knees had been sprung, and the Doctor taped them to enable him to finish the required jumps. The strain of a mountain winter soon affected the Major with a double inguinal hernia. As his medical superior, the Doctor ordered him to leave Greece; instead the Major rigged himself a truss from a mule harness and kept traveling.

Arriving in the valley where the guerrillas were squabbling over the former monarchy's fascist record, the Major would interview both sides and relay his views for the British Colonel to decide what the Allied mission's attitude would be.

At Neokhori, where the Cloak-and-Daggers had a secret landing field nicknamed "Featherbed," the Major and the Colonel laid plans for the extraordinary Greece-wide explosions begun by saboteurs on August 2 [1944], which throttled the enemy route to the Mediterranean.

At a three-weeks-long talk amid the cliffs of lofty Metsovo, delegates lived in one flea-ridden cabin. When the cook sickened, the Major dished up the beans and cornmeal. ("Were it not for Major Yeary's sense of humor we might have given up right then," the Colonel said.) Placating, cajoling, revealing the misstatements of both parties, the Major and the Colonel toiled to bring leaders of the anti-fascist and anti-communist guerrillas together. A final truce was achieved this summer and led to a conference where both generals finally buried the hatchet.

The Anglo-American military missions also served with each side separately. Near the Albanian border a captain from Duluth who had dropped among the EDES immediately began building secret air fields and sowing *soverengas* near the German 22nd Corps Headquarters. The present writer reached the border only after this captain had been replaced as mission head by another, a freckled ex-University of Arizona fullback.

This Captain—snub-nosed, clean-shaven and energetic Andy Rogers— had dropped with another outfit of Greek-Americans in the middle of Peloponnesus in summer. After the dandelion puffs of parachutes scattered across the mountain, he found he had seventy mule-loads of food, arms, and explosives. Crossing the German-held route everywhere, his cavalcade traveled north until it reached Patras on the Corinth road, paralleling the blue gulf that is Greece's girdle. Exactly where the road's steepness earns the name Kaka Scala, or Dirty Grade, he deftly blew out a mile of beetling highway. Correspondents who said that the Germans blew up the road were wrong; Andy and his gang did it. Thereafter any Nazi crossing Greece by the gulf route had to take a boat or walk. (Andy thinks he might try a spell with the Chinese guerrillas next.)

Poking through cloud-obscured mountains by night, groaning transports were often unable to find a mission's landing flares. At least three crashed, costing the lives of all aboard. The Germans, unable to trap a mission in the mountains, would illumine false flares, sending transport crews into blind canyons. Unless guerrillas were on hand to aid in recovery, the parties starved.

Greek mountaineers were liable to consider the parachutes as heavenly manna. Avid shepherds, either food-hungry or money-hungry, would sometimes dash down the mountains and strip the chutes before the thinning, half-fed Allied officers could reach their supplies. Once a confused pilot "scattered stuff over half of Greece," and only 70 of 130 loads were recovered.

Though gossip between the radios of scattered missions was dangerous, word got around by a kind of underground telegraph. For example, when an Army-Navy team—a Captain and a Lieutenant j.g.—began plugging railroad bridges on the Evros River in the remotest corner of Greece, officers huddled in snow-swept huts three weeks' trek south somehow got word.

The Evros River meanders south from Bulgaria's mountains, where Turkey, Bulgaria, and Greece meet. The Army-Navy team caused so many headaches on the Pithion-Svilengrad stretch of railroad that the Germans gave up the line in disgust. For going in under Nazi fire, the Captain got the Legion of Merit and the Lieutenant a Silver Star.

The Captain, a pistol-toting cavalryman from Waco, held the liaison post at the village of Lidoriki, within sight of Amphissa's famous olive orchards. This Captain's craft was blowing bridges. Thanks to him, the serpentine road around the slopes of Parnassus to Delphi has several teeth missing.

He once had a duel of wits with the Communist leader whose party name is Ares, and who has reputedly killed more pro-German Greeks than any *Andarte* leader. The U.S. Army Colt which the Captain had lent a Greek translator had been purloined by someone, and efforts at recovery seemed less than energetic. Ares told him jovially, "Greece needs that revolver more than the U.S. Army, anyhow."

The Captain laid hands on the two guns on his hips and said, "I suppose you'd take these if you felt Greece needed them." Ares, from behind his black beard, allowed genially as how he had once been obliged to disarm a British officer and might be forced to do the same to the American. When Ares, still smiling angelically, took an exploratory step toward him, the

Texan tilted both guns and put holes in the ceiling above the guerrilla's right and left shoulders. Ares, unruffled, departed, recovered the Colt, and sent it to the Captain. They dined together and have been on terms of mutual respect ever since.

How many Nazis have been tied up by the Cloak-and-Daggers? A square-built Gaelic Major, who persecuted a stretch of Greece's dorsal railroad, obliged the Germans to deploy a thousand sentries along only forty curved, single-tracked miles between Lamia in Sperchelus Valley and Domokos in the mountains.

The soft-spoken Major led the most pretentious attack against a rail spur leading to a chrome mine at Dherli, one of Hitler's most valuable possessions. In the words of the dentist Doctor who went along to succor the wounded, "We did some damage, but got hell kicked out of us."

The Allied mission overreached by calling a general mobilization of guerrillas. The Germans sniffed an attack when shepherds who ordinarily grazed flocks in adjacent fields disappeared. The lonely station at Dherli was surrounded with barbed wire. Two reinforced pillboxes surveyed flat, coverless country in every direction; a searchlight constantly swept the tracks. The *Andartes,* gallantly led by officers of the Greek army, made the mistake of trying to climb over the barbs rather than creep under them, and fifteen paid with their lives.

Worse came when, at 7:33, two minutes after the raid's zero hour, a Nazi armored train, spitting fire from every slit, came roaring in. The raid abruptly changed into a German ambush. While the Doctor collected his wounded from a bullet-swept gully, the Major raced in alone through the wire, reached the station, and slipped through the door. The Irishman's touch on a tommy gun is famous among the Cloak-and-Daggers. He saw five Germans and two Greeks cowering against a wall. In a single sweep his gun managed to kill all the Germans, yet his sensitive trigger finger left the Greeks unharmed though swooning with fright.

Soon thereafter a 44-year-old, silver-haired American colonel, veteran of the Spanish Civil War, forsook his Middle East swivel chair to jump with the Arizona fullback Captain into northwestern Greece. Peering down into the black mountains from the transport door, he failed to see that the green light above his head was blinking: the signal pilot was telling him to jump. The Captain, with gusto, booted his superior officer through the door.

In midsummer this Colonel joined the Major's mountaineers. The night of August 19th, he led an all-American bazooka attack against a train which derailed both locomotives. Armed with only a carbine and followed by two Greek-American G.I.s, he moved in on the Nazi survivors. When he was finished, "All fire from the train had ceased."

It got so everybody put tacks under the Nazi transports. Who should drop on the "Featherbed" but a huddle of Russian officers? Their territory was actually Yugoslavia, but they stayed to watch the fun. "The Russians never attempted any political activity and had only formal contact as Allies with the Greek communists," according to mission members. Sometimes they borrowed the Anglo-American mission's radio to call Moscow from the Greek mountains. Relations between the missions were warmly cooperative.

Americans learned by working with rare Englishmen like one particular major, a stoop-shouldered guards officer who insisted in raids on wearing a formal tunic instead of practical battle dress. He set himself a quota of one train a week; his average was one and five-eighths. In the attack on the chrome mine station, just when the armored train rolled up and began sweeping the fields with Spandau fire, he remarked to the sweating Doctor, "Well, guess I ought to load my Luger now." He carried a shepherd's crook with which he gently tapped the heads of *Andartes,* like a schoolmaster, when they whispered during an attack.

A burly, genial ex-pharmacist sergeant, of Union, N.J., started having things happen to him during the summer when he was sent as medical corpsman to near Agrinion. "I enjoyed watching the Nazi trains get cut from fifteen trains daily to two," he told the writer. "It's a magnificent sight to see a locomotive blow up, and eight following cars plunge." The Nazis used a two-car buffer and often a cageful of live prisoners pushed ahead by a locomotive. The British major timed this explosion so the hostages passed but the locomotive was lifted. He is proud that his mission always had beer bought through a Greek fixer from a German canteen at Agrinion.

The Cloak-and-Dagger principle was always to attack with guerrilla support. Thus the countryside was kept united behind both forces. Once both Greek factions cooperated on the same mission, an artistic blow on a big bridge at Grigor Potamos near Lamia. EDES *Andartes* hit one bridgehead and ELAS *Andartes* the other, while British engineers crawled through the icy water and affixed their charges.

Thanks to peasant support, the missions were rarely surprised but learned to take warnings with salt. Once an officer was camped in the caves of Parnassus with explosive unloaded from his mules. A shepherd lookout came running down the mountain, crying, "Germans coming! Less than fifteen minutes from here." As the officer said: "Boy, what a flop! Took us three hours to get the explosive saddled and leave. We heard that the Jerries reached our dead campfires two weeks later."

A studious corporal who specialized in the classics at Princeton even went into the lumber business with ELAS guerrillas above Karpenisi while the SS was scouring the mountains for Americans. Money being nonexistent, the guerrillas got hold of wheat. When it reached the mountains, the corporal paid the guerrillas the price for a cubic meter of cut lumber. (In burned villages, two meters would build the interior of a house, another the roof.) Thus Greece was being rebuilt by the Cloak-and-Daggers even while being destroyed by the Germans.

In this tiny state of Rumelia, smaller than Rhode Island, 3252 patriots were executed or killed, 241 villages wholly or partly destroyed—including 78 schools and 60 churches—and 16,538 homes wiped out.

The Cloak-and-Daggers needed women to complete their work, and found plenty among the Greek patriots. They still talk of pretty Pat, who scratched and bit an SS officer in a taxi in Athens and shrieked she was being attacked when he caught her with guerrilla papers. A Greek traitor betrayed Pat, and the Nazis sentenced her to death. It cost 100 sovereigns— the expense of maintaining a mountain clinic for one month—to bribe a Nazi to let Pat escape.

There was Olga, who spread her skirts on grapes which concealed machine guns on an Athens-bound fruit truck. The Germans riding the truck kept nibbling the grapes until the machine gun cases showed, but never asked to have them opened. And there was lovely Persa Metaxas, daughter of a Greek naval attaché in London, who nursed guerrillas at secret hospitals and spent an embarrassed night between two G.I.s on a windswept air field when the mission owned only four blankets.

There were plenty of sad times. A lieutenant deftly derailed a troop train at Dhoxara, tallying 150 German casualties. The Nazis took seventeen innocent Greek hostages to the scene and hanged them. And when the Major put sixteen cars of a chrome train into the ditch at Sinia, the SS took twelve hostages from jail to the piled-up cars, shot them and placarded the names throughout the valley.

But even among the pendent bodies and burning villages, what guerrillas now remember best is the work of the Doctor, that slightly profane dentist from Iowa. There was a night when a lieutenant, of Chicago, laid a plant for a train near Pharsala and was counter-ambushed. A sergeant fell, and the lieutenant went to rescue the body. A German's grenade blew off both his shoes and left him with 57 wounds in his back. With his rectal cavity gravely perforated, he crawled up a 5000-foot mountain to the village of Phthari. Peasants carried him to a secret hospital. From September 9th to the 18th he lay on an earthen floor fighting for his life; then he was carried directly through the German lines to Featherbed Field.

The Doctor did another operation on him en route. The lieutenant lay at the field through one rainy night after another. Repeatedly, transports from Italy tried but failed to pierce the storm-held mountains. Finally a lone British Lysander cleaved the cloudbanks and came down at Neokhori, then took him off while nine fretful Spitfires waited above the clouds. The Doctor sent an invaluable corpsman out with the bleeding officer. All the way across the Adriatic he crouched under the lieutenant's stretcher stanching fresh hemorrhages. . . . The lieutenant lived.

A tall sergeant from a little tulip-growing town in Iowa jumped into Greece in midsummer, and ever since he has been close at the Doctor's side. He was with him the day when the Doctor—who had never done any surgery—did eight major operations in a row, with an open book beside him, then collapsed. When the writer last saw the sergeant by the steaming greenish springs of Thermopylae he had no time to talk about himself. But without him and others, the Doctor would never have been able to run a hospital like that at lofty Muzelou, which took 2000 patients in a single month of war, and another 1700 while Athens was toppling in early October.

"When you're not a doctor, but only a dentist, it's tough to make these decisions," said the Doctor. "I used to walk along the aisles of the dirty little churches which were my hospitals. I'd tell the sergeant, 'This guy looks too far gone for me. Give him a shot of morphine and let him die.' But if the next guerrilla looked more possible, I'd say, 'Get out that book again.

Let's try to operate on this one.' I don't know how we ever got along as
well as we did."

—

HUNGER, COLD HELP BRITISH GAIN
IN BATTLE FOR ATHENS

U.S. Stand Is Puzzle to Greeks

Athens, Greece—December 22, 1944

Republican fortunes in the Greek civil war have declined, not only because
Lieutenant General Ronald Scobie has opened his promised aerial offensive
but because of hunger and cold. From quarters of Athens beyond the barricades a stream of foodless refugees are coming, bundles in hand, fear on
every face. The air is sharp and snow is visible on nearby Mount Parnes;
Athens is totally heatless.

As this is written the air is shivering with a terrible sound of volleys of
rockets, fired by diving planes. The sound is like that made by a man in armor
sliding down a tin roof. At the end comes a solid thump as the rockets hit
home. Windows tremble. No war is so terrible as one between former allies.

A full-scale street battle is going on in the Chizi quarter, where Sherman tanks are clearing the streets and pushing down houses containing
ELAS snipers. Spitfires are strafing the suburb. But improvement in the
British position in the city center is evident; for two days the headquarters
area has been almost undisturbed by shelling. Many Greeks outside that
part of Athens are puzzled as to why, when America has declared itself neutral in this civil strife, does it not stay neutral?

America is not neutral in the eyes of the ELAS soldier who sees a huge
Sherman tank, armed with a 75-mm gun, bumping along the street looking
for him. The Sherman is an American tool, paid for by American taxpayers.
It belongs to the American government. The Greek wonders how this tank
got here. His scouts, watching unloadings at Piraeus, have the answer. It
came in one of the magnificent, ingenious landing craft made familiar by
newsphotos of Pacific landings. If the Americans are neutral, what is it
doing so far from the Pacific or Italian shores?

The Greeks are thinking that maybe they should've revolted earlier. Then they would be dealing separately with the United States—the power which pays, provides, and calls itself neutral, and (with Britain) the power which has taken upon itself to "be responsible" for this part of the Balkans.

As observers watch Greek government forces use Connecticut-made tommy guns against ELAS troops also using Connecticut-made tommy guns, they scratch their heads and wonder: Is this what lend-lease was for? Weren't the Greeks and British friends? The natural impulse of anyone, knowing his property is being used for purposes of mutual assassination— even with laudable dialectics on both sides—is to go onto the street in fron-tier-marshal fashion and take the guns away from both.

The American comes to the conclusion that maybe lend-lease has a few flaws here and there. With many billions shipped everywhere in Europe and no custodians appointed to stay with the stuff until it has been used in the Allied cause or returned to its owners, maybe something like this was bound to happen. Maybe there are better ways to maintain freedom, peace and liberty across the world than turning arms over to allies and inviting them to shoot out their difficulties. Maybe someone else neglected his re-sponsibility in the Mediterranean. Maybe it was the American.

—

TERROR, DEATH ONLY YULE FOR KIDS IN ATHENS

Bewildered, They Sit in Tatters with Void Stomachs

Athens, Greece—December 24, 1944

The Athenian child today is a bewildered, wide-eyed creature sitting in a corner watching, on an empty stomach, a world in which parents and rela-tives are jerked in and out of rooms as though by rubber bands.

What the child hears is whisperings of terror at best, at worst the terri-ble biting concussion of a low-flying aircraft machine-gunning rooftops. His world is rocked with mortars and rent with flashing artillery.

Yet not all is motion. When death touches parents, this frenzy halts. Be-tween the intervals of firing, the child may peep through closed blinds and see things once bright with familiar motion now stilled.

Why, the child may ask, does yonder green trolley car never leave its stop forty feet down the street? Suddenly a pachydermous tank swings round the corner; fire leaps from the streetcar's windows and is answered with a twist of the tank's turret cannon.

At point-blank range a shell rips through the trolley's body. Something like a doll falls from the empty motorman's vestibule, lies on the steps, then rolls into the street leaking its life into the gutter.

An hour later a man in a helmet comes and binds the wrecked trolley car in a rusty web of barbed wire which he stealthily unspins across the deserted street.

Greek children are poorest in two things, food and shoes. Though a parent with both hands raised may run full speed between the fireswept lines in the free hours between 12 and 2, hoping no sniper on the Republican or British side will make the family poorer by yet another death, what he brings home is almost nothing.

This disorderly world might be ideal from the child's view in some ways if he were less hungry. Parents are so busy either hunting food, or talking about hunting it, that the child has privacy. There are no baths, because there is no water except for drinking. But the winter cold penetrates the smashed windows. Blankets and sometimes beds have been sold. The child sleeps cold as well as fearful.

But not all the children. There are those half-dozen lucky offspring who live with their parents in the shadow of the fading Papandreou cabinet in the Hotel Grande Bretagne, girt about with red-capped British and Greek police. At the insistence of the Mae West-like British matron, the little aristocrats clear and carry dishes from the servantless kitchen themselves. Occasionally the roof is shaken by the fall of a mortar, looped over by the Republicans hardly six blocks away. But the great, bare hostelry is theirs for endless hide-and-seek games when they grow bored listening to their parents forever muttering the same names: Scobie, Macmillan, Leeper, Papandreou, Saraphis, Plastiras, Sophoulis. And they are warm and safe, fed all that is fed to the American lend-lease and British forces.

Beyond the barricades another kind of child plays a different kind of game. The ELAS Republicans have drafted boys and girls as young as seven to carry munitions. A children's committee has been formed, each member being given a sack in order to visit houses and ask everyone to contribute a few beans or a fistful of flour for the army's needs.

Love, that most essential food for all children, is not yet banished from this world. It was love for the famished children which made that father try to cross the lines, only to crumple before a machine gun. It was love that made a captured Republican woman who passed under my window, flanked by police armed with tommy guns, fill her arms with her baby and insist on keeping it.

As for the children's Christmas, that will not be possible this year. The Greeks and British are busy killing each other.

—

GUN BARRELS POINT WAY TO HISTORY ON ACROPOLIS

At the Acropolis, Athens, Greece—Christmas Day, 1944

The wind whips up the staircase of marble. The pillars of the Propylaea Gate stand white against blue skies. And as you ascend—hurriedly, because Republican snipers can still crack at your back—a British machine gun looks down on you.

Christmas on the Acropolis means a red-bereted paratrooper from Glasgow warming himself and his scrapwood fire in a niche near the Erechtheion. It means Beaufighters sweeping over the city before they plunge on the ELAS with machine guns open. It means blue smoke, swept by a bitter wind through the pillars, from burning houses on the street a pistol shot away.

The mountains are white with winter. The sky beyond the pillars is blue only in snatches. For the most part, it is gun-barrel grey.

"We consider such a prominent place unsuitable for use of mortars," says one soldier. "Mortars should be in hollows, not on prominent features. We have located observation points here for mortar and artillery, but if the ELAS claims that we have put heavy guns here, they are simply not telling the truth."

Being Christmas, the firing is slight. At our feet lies the Temple of Theseus, where Athenians once watched for Persians. They now peer through field glasses out over starving Athens. Even their glasses are covered with brown wool jerkins.

By tacit consent both parties fire as little as possible across the pure

Doric pediments, 2400 years old, testifying to the exploits of a warrior god. In almost every hollow temple foundation are empty cartridge cases.

At the walls of Themistocles you recline, the Porch of the Virgins at your back, and listen to an artillery duel on the other side of the city. Here, one once heard a huckster's cries mounting from the marketplace. All is silent except for the vengeful ripping of machine guns. Ducking quickly through the Porch of the Caryatides, you notice a Republican bullet has marred a perfect pillar. There is a little head of lead from a glancing blow and a black fan-smudge beyond.

Buried away in the museum you have Christmas dinner prepared by a private from Oldham and a sergeant from London. It is Canadian salmon, California pears, pancakes with fruit sauce, cigarettes and chocolate. You contribute chewing gum given you by Santa Claus Richard Mowrer, a fellow *Daily News* correspondent. From the museum room, where ancient figures now wear paratrooper helmets, hustles a dapper little Edinburgh padre with a book of holiday hymns under his arm.

You meet the commanding officer of the world's most precious strongpoint, young Captain David Cruden of Aberdeen, who wears silver spectacles and has made seventeen parachute jumps but never expected to land on the Acropolis.

"ELAS has hit the Acropolis with about six mortar shells since December 7," he says. "We've had one man killed, but the damage to the temples is insignificant. It's the cold wind that hits us harder than anything else."

The wintry sun of Greece's saddest Christmas is bending down the greying sky as you walk along beside the Parthenon. It is still white, still fair, still pure.

—

GREEKS ON BOMB-CAR INSURE GERMAN TRAIN
Sparta, Greece—January 4, 1945

A handsome young man at Megalopolis told this correspondent of the fiendish German method of making trains run on time. The young man's right leg was off at the knee, and he was using makeshift crutches.

A few months before the Nazis departed, Athanassios, our informant, completed one of the shortest railroading careers ever known—two weeks. He spent this in a *klemma*. This cage, which he shared with 24 other Greeks, was built on a flatcar. In the center was a two-foot silvery box of explosives.

The car was pushed ahead of a Nazi train. A car full of sand came next, a buffer against explosion. Then came a car with a Nazi sergeant sitting at an electric switch connected with the explosive. His orders were that if the train were attacked by guerrillas, he was to blow up the cage car with the twenty-five "Communists."

This system was invented because the guerrillas, aided by the Allied missions, were blowing up trains. The cage cars, in the lead, were at first used to take the explosion of the Allied mines. But when the guerrillas turned to timing their explosions, letting the car full of hostages pass, the Nazis wanted to make sure the hostages paid the price anyway, and paid it instantly. Hence the wired car.

There were six such combinations of cage cars and sand cars running out of Corinth on the three lines to the Patras, Athens and Tripolis.

Athanassios was taken prisoner as an ELAS guerrilla in a May battle. His captors, the Nazi-supported Greek security battalions, turned him over to the Germans as a Communist, which he denies ever being.

"Every morning we would leave Corinth about 7:30," he said, "hoping the *Andartes* guerrillas would not attack our train. We would get to Tripolis about 2:30 and be put into jail. Then the next morning we would come back. We got food only from the Red Cross, though sometimes in Corinth women and children would push things through the bars of the cage."

When taken out of the cage car, the twenty-five were marched past the sergeant's car and shown the red-handled switch.

The attacks on the trains stopped. There was no need for the SS sergeant to blow up the cage car. Then came the morning of July 1. The cage car was on the siding at Corinth, waiting to leave for Tripolis. Because women and children were not allowed at the station that day, Athanassios thinks it was a deliberate experiment by a captain of the SS Grenadiers, who had thought of the cage car.

However it was, the car blew up. Sixteen "Communists" were killed outright. Eight were wounded. One escaped. A Greek doctor took off Athanassios' leg; the Germans paid no attention.

The captain, however, made some changes in the cage car. He seems to
have been puzzled why nine Greeks lived. So he fitted the other cage cars
with triple explosives, a slug at each end as well as one in the middle.

As they used to say of fascism in Italy, the trains ran on time.

—

THE DURABLE QUISLINGS OF GREECE

1945

In Greek tragedy heroes suffer for inscrutable reasons. Earlier deeds of
passion pursue them—unatoned crimes not their own, not disclosed even
to them until the play approaches a close. The United States, having been
for two years the heaviest paying spectator in the marble seats of the pit,
now enters the murky Greek tragedy as a participant. The action onstage is
bloody and confused. *Why are the Greeks still at war?* we ask. From the
Greek and British actors already on the scene we get a babble of answers.
Few of them understand the chain of betrayal and treason they have
blindly set forth. Nor do we.

Greece, like other conquered countries, had a quisling movement, organized by the Germans to fight the Allied underground. In other countries,
after victory came, each chief quisling sank to death before a firing squad
or dropped twitching out of sight through a gallows' trap. The bookkeeping
of treason was wiped clean. Each nation was ready for a new start.

In Greece, alone in Europe, not one puppet was executed. Of all those
Greek constabulary officers who hung Hitler's photograph in their headquarters (where I saw it first in 1934), who organized raids on partisans'
villages, who rounded up hostages and handed them to Nazi firing squads,
who betrayed American and British officers dropped behind the lines, not
one has paid with his life.

And where today are the "security battalions" of civilian puppets who
ranged the countryside in Reichswehr trucks, sometimes under German
guard, to wipe out villages whose crime was that they fed and sheltered the
Allied underground? Such quislings served at Distomo, when the Nazis
massacred that village. Only a handful among thousands are in jail. Many

of Hitler's mercenaries are still "fighting communism," only now they wear lend-lease battle dress. Yes, they're in the army.

Where to trade or be safer than in uniform? Yet for a nation to absorb treason into its military is not easy. It is like swallowing live frogs. The outraged stomach protests. The wrigglers keep coming up again; traitors are hard to digest. That is why it is impossible for one American reporter to forget the day when an enlistment of quislings into the army first suggested itself to the Greek command.

The islet of Kranai, when Homer sang, was the sweet bower where Paris spent his first night with Helen before embarking with her for Troy. Today it is a tiny, treeless shovelful of rocks about as big as four city blocks and twice as ugly. In nearby Gytheion, connected to Kranai by a short causeway, thirty-two unarmed "communist" prisoners were slaughtered recently almost at the moment President Truman was expounding his new doctrine. The day I saw Kranai, however, it was alive with Hitler's Greeks, captive and broken. Clefts in the rocks were covered with old blankets from which greasy, frightened men popped their heads in a froglike way. I had jeeped south through the Peloponnesus for two days from Athens, in company with a British staff officer, to see these men.

The quislings were guarded and fed by a British armored car detachment. They were getting five-minute hearings from an easy-going Greek magistrate. Even the guerrilla members of the makeshift cabinet in Athens agreed it was impossible to prosecute so many thousands. So nine out of ten traitors were being pardoned. Only the highest officers, direct vehicles of Nazi orders, were held for court martial.

"Why don't you let the acquitted walk off the island?" the staff officer asked the young major.

"We've told them they're free," answered the local commander. "But they're afraid to go home to their villages. The people hate them. They're afraid of being assassinated. They won't go home unless I give each an escort of two men. Of course we haven't men enough for that."

"Of course not," said the staff officer sympathetically. Out of humaneness, or perhaps political myopia, he seemed to find nothing improper about providing an escort service for his late enemies. It was impractical, that was all, because of lack of men. A new thought struck him. "Are these troops clean?" he inquired curiously. "Do they obey orders?"

"Very clean. Very obedient. If they could, they'd like to join us."

"Would they *really?*" The staff officer was unmistakably interested. "What sort of soldiers would they make, do you think?"

"Well, sir, you can't say they've had the worst training in the world. Fritz usually knows what he's doing, doesn't he?"

A delegation of bearded men approached, asking to be heard. "We have a petition," they said. "We would like to join the new Greek army."

I thought that this sticky bid would be refused immediately, but I was wrong. We took the offer back to Athens. Other similar offers were coming in from other camps of traitors in Greece. For the time being they were tabled.

When Greece was liberated it had no army. About 11,000 Greek regulars who had rebelled in Egypt against returning to the dictatorship of King George II were penned by the British in concentration camps from Palestine to Eritrea. The remaining 5000—loyal royalists—were brought back to Greece as a *corps d'elite,* called the "Rimini Brigade" for its brief service on the Italian front, and equipped with American firepower.

Lt. General Ronald Scobie first ordered the guerrillas, who had fought three years in the mountains, to surrender Athens to the British. He then gave Athens to the Rimini Brigade. When Scobie, acting for Churchill, next ordered the guerrillas to disarm, they refused. The civil war began. The British defeated the guerrillas, with the Rimini Brigade mopping up behind lend-lease Sherman tanks and British paratroopers. Still there was only one extra battalion in the Greek army.

Then recruiting began among the ruins. The British goal was 32 battalions. Guerrillas were barred from the new army, but quislings were welcome. For the British they were still, as they had been for the Nazis, "anti-communists."

Today the frogs are safe. About 130 guerrillas have fallen before firing squads, but not one quisling. It is raining cool American dollars, and the frogs in the army are jumping with happiness. It took a long time, but finally they finish up, as they always intended, on the winning side.

P. G. C.
(Tune of Shanty Town)

It's only a shack in old Basra, Iraq,
It's a heck of a place and I'm not going back,
The sun's hot as hell, and oh! what a smell,
The Natives don't wash their feet and it's goat that they eat,
They all wear a dress and I'm forced to confess,
That I can't tell Charlie from Mamie or Bess,
There's a Queen waiting there, she has lice in her hair,
In that shack in old Basra, Iraq.

She's only a whore from old Bandar Shahpur.
A sweet Persian Maiden and need I say more.
Her price 30 riols, and not a bad deal,
When she wiggles her butt, oh! my, how you feel.
She's strictly illegit but I don't mind a bit,
And if she weren't so dusky I'd chew on her tit,
There's a Queen waiting there, she has crabs in her hair,
Just a whore from old Bandar Shahpur.

It's only a bar in old Khorramshahr,
We waded through mud from our camp so afar,
They had vodka and gin, and oh! what a din.
It's the worst goddamed place I have ever been in,
There were soldiers and sailors and Merchant Marines,
They were thinking of home and all that it means,
There's a war to be won and a job to be done,
They left that bar in old Khorramshahr.

We're stationed now in Ahwaz, Iran,
Wherever you look it's just desert sand
Where the wind starts to blow, and the dust hides the glow,
Of the moon as it shines o'er the crappy Karun,
We drink Persian beer, and there's no nooky here
And we won't get none if we stay here a year,
It's a damned dirty place; it's a lousy disgrace,
This asshole called Ahwaz, Iran.

We're in the command, but Teheran leads the band,
They are the minds, we're just hired hands,
They write letters galore, and indorsements more,
They demand more reports than there are Persian Whores.
They move supplies with a flick of their eyes,
They make inspection complete from 10,000 feet,
But we tell no lies, they're a swell bunch of guys,
The tops in the Persian Command.

XVIII

Across the Middle East

From Greece—unable to get into either Bulgaria or Rumania to cover the trials of collaborationists—Weller embarked on a six-week swing through the Middle East: Turkey, Palestine, Syria, Lebanon, Iraq, Iran, Kuwait, Saudi Arabia, Bahrain, then India (where a friend, veteran radio correspondent Lowell Thomas, stayed with him). Hal O'Flaherty had taken over from Binder as *CDN* foreign editor. Weller wrote to him on June 2, along with a list of twenty-five stories cabled or mailed:

"I went by truck the whole length of the Persian lend-lease highway. There were a lot of remarks loose in Tehran about correspondents who never got out in the roadcamps, so I made, thus, the whole trip from the Caspian to the Persian Gulf . . . I now have met almost all the principal persons American and Arab of the Middle East. For about a fortnight I have been in New Delhi battling with the problem of getting facilities and cards and permits. I think that I have this licked and shall move north soon."

Clearly he was much taken in Baghdad with the young King Feisal II, nearly ten, who would be executed by a firing squad thirteen years later. The boy's predilection for American comic books—and difficulty in acquiring them—spurred Weller to cable his superiors in Chicago to purchase complete sets of *Superman* and *Buck Rogers* for 1944–1945 and send them to the king as a gift.

I have also included one of many soldiers' verses that Weller collected through the war. This gem comes from the Americans' Persian Gulf Command.

HAIFA SIDEWALKS STRUNG WITH WIRE
AT CURFEW TIME

Haifa, Palestine—March 9, 1945

There may be towns so small the police take in the sidewalks at curfew. But at Haifa, where the pipeline from the Mosul oilfields empties into tankers, the police at curfew block certain sidewalks with barbed wire. Barricades are strung at key places to discourage both Jewish and Arab terrorist factions.

By such precautions the British preserve their two most vital securities in the eastern Mediterranean: a general security, which ensures them the upper hand in all areas strategically connected with the route to India; and internal securities, which ensure against either the Arabs or Jews gaining mastery over Palestine.

These barricades, however, represent security only on a tactical or localized level. Much more important, in a country where a mountain range divides the cities of the coastal plain from the Jordan Valley, is the system whereby railroads and highways are held. For any dissidents—whether from the Stern Gang of Jewish terrorists, or their momentarily quiet Arab counterparts—to challenge the British hold would involve cutting these roads.

Britain's answer is that specialized fortress, a "police station." The term here refers to a building almost always located in open country, with no other buildings nearby, near where the mountain highway crosses a crucial pass and above some curb where all vehicles must slow down; close enough to the highway to dominate it, but far enough away to prevent surprise attack. The station looks like something from *Beau Geste* or a flashback from India's northwest frontier. Pale yellow, it is a long building with narrow windows. The walls are thick. The tower sweeps all the valley roads. At the corners are specialized embrasures just big enough for muzzles.

There are about sixty in all Palestine, virtually invulnerable to any force not possessing artillery or bombers. Since insurrectionist armies rarely have either, the British blue-clad police—whose lower ranks include both Jews and Arabs—masters the situation. Climbing from Lake Galilee toward Nazareth, descending into Haifa's great oil dumps, following the coast to Tel

Aviv, then turning into the mountains for Jerusalem, you see everywhere these formidable guardians of Britain's Geneva-authorized mandate.

Tiberias, however, is like some Adirondack resort. Stacked on piles above Galilee's silken waters, it is one Jewish summer hotel or pension after another. Millions of dollars—mostly American—were poured into Jewish coastal cities, like Haifa and Tel Aviv, and spilled over here into this winter resort, as Manhattan's money spills in summer into the Adirondacks.

In the fervid, humid land farther down the Jordan Valley lie some of the Jewish agricultural communities, where Zionists expend their labors in Palestine's tough soil. These earnest people are rarely seen in Tiberias' comfortable hotels.

Not seen there, either, are Palestine's Arabs, who outnumber the Jews about two to one but who are economically in the minority. Their dominant characteristic is poverty.

—

ARABS' KING EXPLAINS ATTITUDE ON JEWS

Amman, Transjordania—March 13, 1945

"Creating a Jewish home in Palestine has only made for disunity," said Emir Abdullah Ibn al Hussein, king of Transjordania, in an interview today. "I doubt that the United States understands how deeply the Arab world feels on this subject. Whatever solution it is given at the peace table must be looked at with an eye which regards Arab interests as well as those of the Jews and the great powers."

Transjordania has elections, a cabinet and a popular parliament with powers to veto laws initiated by the king. Abdullah is a stocky, point-bearded man of 66, with a warm handshake and straightforward manners. Clad in a nun-grey cloak, with a gold ceremonial dagger at his waist, he wears a snowy-white headkerchief held with a white woolen ring, in desert fashion. His exceptionally small feet are clad in black cloth shoes with rubber tips. Asked whether he felt that the Arabs were better off today than after the First World War, Abdullah gave the questioner an unblinking look. "Do you want a straight-from-the-shoulder answer? That kind of answer may cause anger or resentment."

Told to fire away, Abdullah said: "The Arabs were better off then because they were in the hands of one man and were a single, united nation. They wanted to return to their ancient fatherland and see one united Arabia. Even under the Turks, they were used to high posts of responsibility, civil, judiciary and military.

"Then the peace conference imposed mandates and Zionism. King Hussein suffered a blow from the Wahabite king [Ibn Saud], and King Feisal had a mandate forced on him by the French. No one can deny that the British and French mandates brought education. What is the result? You have all kinds of colleges—French, British, even American—and all kinds of culture. There is just one culture missing: our own Arab culture. Men who felt the Arabs were one people have now grown old, and the sense of unity has been lost.

"Big nations need oil, which happens to be found in Arabia. You dispute in order to get it. Russia is seeking oil in northern Iran and Iraq, and Britain is in Iraq as well as Arabia. Neither these efforts, nor those of self-seeking politicians like those in Syria, can help the Arabs. What the Arabs need is a single unifying leader."

Abdullah spoke with a controlled sort of fire.

"In Palestine the Arabs do not want the Jews, who are already there under the Balfour Declaration, expelled," he said. "They recognize that the Jews have the same human right to live there as elsewhere on earth. But they must meet the Arabs on equal terms and not dominate them.

"I am sorry my people always seem to be complaining to those who never hear. But it is good to know, when speaking, when speaking to America, that I am speaking through a liberal press, to a liberal people, which wants only good for all."

—

HITLER FALL TO ADD TO ZIONIST ROW

Jerusalem—March 16, 1945

With Hitler tottering, Zionism, Jewry's unique effort to provide itself with a political and geographical home in Palestine, stands at the crossroads.

Arabs, even before the Hitlerite persecutions, never wanted Europe to send Jews into Palestine in such numbers as to create a dominantly Jewish state. Nor did they want America, with financial and political support, to open the door to possible Jewish control in the Holy Land. With anti-Semitism defeated in Europe (insofar as represented in Hitler and Mussolini), the Arabs see less reason than ever why "anti-Semitism should be brought here with American support." They say: "Being Semitic ourselves, we especially dislike having your Western intolerances, which do not exist in Arab countries where Jews are in the minority, solved at our expense."

Zionists here, especially the leaders of that immigration, resettlement and public utility financing company known as "The Jewish Agency," are reacting with zeal and vigor against any assertion that anti-Semitism is dead because Hitler is beaten. Zionism, they say, existed before Hitler and is destined to outlive him. In the United States—their chief source of income except for the funds brought by the immigrants themselves—they are opening a drive for about $30,000,000.

Their hand is strengthened by indignation against twelve years of Hitler's outrages and the facts that money is abundant in the war boom and contributions to Palestine are considered by the U.S. government as deductible charities.

The severe stone building of the Jewish Agency's main office in Jerusalem is intensely active. Top executives have all left for Britain or the U.S., or are packing. With Arab countries internationally represented for the first time at the San Francisco Security Conference, they are determined to battle with documents as stoutly as terrorists attempt to battle with arms.

The Zionists are less worried by the actual pressure of the Arabs than that American and Britain will "overestimate" the importance of the pressure. They say the Arab states are talking big, but that disintegrative forces and personal rivalries exist as broke loose in other postwar periods. They claim that Zionism is used by the Arab states as a lever in order to get more advantageous terms from America and Britain for oil, and strategic concessions on the Middle East.

Zionists, predicting that with Hitler's defeat anti-Semitism will only go underground, say that Europe's Jews today are more eager than ever to go to Palestine. Since American Jews are willing to supply money to make immigration possible, they say that Britain should relax the 1939 provisions permitting one Jew in Palestine to two Arabs, and further extend the almost exhausted entrance certificates. Zionist preparations to break the restrictions are the more determined as evidence increases that few Jews will return to Europe from Palestine.

Both the Arabs and Jews want Britain to end its mandate and depart, but only when their theses—which are contradictory—are carried out. Since different Britons at different times have promised Palestine to both the Arabs and the Jews, the defeat of Hitler will merely open the way for a bitter struggle.

—

YOUNG MAN OF IRAQ

King Needs His Comic Books

Baghdad, Iraq—April 19, 1945

Iraq's King Feisal II, almost ten, is a serious, sweet-mannered kid who finds it easy to win an American's heart.

In his first interview with an American correspondent, at his downtown palace in Baghdad today, Feisal said the only real care troubling royalty's brow was keeping up his stock of American cartoon books. Iraq's national budget is doing pretty well, but the king's supply of *Superman* and *Buck Rogers* comics is lamentably low. If the pistol totin' Western stories can be kept up, all will be well.

"I can swim about 50 yards—that means dog paddle and breast stroke," Feisal said modestly. "And in arithmetic, I'm through long division and working on weights and measures." Gravely, the small thin figure in a grey flannel suit, grey socks and black shoes turned the pages of a carefully penciled copybook, showing exercises with remarkably few errors. His young English athletic instructor, Theodore Sidebottom, stood nearby. Feisal spoke in a faint British accent with pauses of shy silence.

Like Yugoslavia's Peter,* Feisal has known what it is to be fatherless

---

*Peter II (1923–1970), last king of Yugoslavia; his father was assassinated in 1934. He was run out by the Nazis in April 1941, fled to Britain, and joined the RAF.

during his princeship. His young father, King Ghazi, was killed when he drove his car into a telegraph pole six years ago. His thin-faced aristocratic grandfather was Feisal I, who rode into Damascus after the last war with the British poet and adventurer T.E. Lawrence and the boy's great-grandfather, the first Arab King Hussein to whom the British promised an Arab empire as the price of his support against the Turks in that war. These almost legendary ancestors weigh heavily on the sober-faced boy king. Every day he lunches with the beautiful Queen Mother, Aliah, but her kindest ministrations cannot quite compensate for Feisal being an only child and fatherless.

Feisal has two palaces, one a yellow brick affair called Bilat Meliki, where red-coated, blue-trousered Negro and Arab guards sweep him enormous salutes, and another palace, of Walt Disney-like outlines, on the muddy Tigris near Baghdad's outskirts. The former is his schoolroom, ever fragrant with year-round blossoms in the surrounding gardens. The latter is his residence and playground.

Feisal's dearest ambition is to take an airplane ride. But such value does Iraq place on the king, that he cannot go. "The nearest I ever came was one day when they let me sit in one taxiing around the field," he said wistfully.

Feisal has found something near to a father in Regent Prince Abdul Ilah, his 31-year-old uncle. Abdul Ilah is young enough to swim and ride with Feisal like an elder brother but old enough to have authority. Of Feisal, affable Prince Abdul Ilah says: "I notice the king only asks permission to do things when he knows it will be granted. One day I took him to the air field and jokingly asked whether he wanted to fly. Feisal refused to show how much he really wanted to go up, because he knew it was impossible." Feisal's only regular playmate is Raad, a 9-year-old cousin.

All of this family are descended directly from Mohammed through the Hashemite line, and among pious Muslims they have this advantage over the Arab world's eldest king, Ibn Saud, who is not descended from the Prophet.

Among Feisal's favorite toys are American electric trains. He modestly showed me a Boy Scout map he'd drawn of an imaginary site, the X-Bar-Y Ranch in Texas. Feisal listened eagerly when told that parts of western Texas resembled Iraq, with lonely rivers and wide plains. It was evident that the Arab love of horses attracted him to American cowboys.

The plan is for Feisal to study here until fifteen, then go abroad for two years before ascending the throne at eighteen, in 1953. Feisal's future colleagues in the government are mostly products of American secondary education, since Iraq's chief pre-university schools are Baghdad College, run by American Jesuits, and the American School for Boys, run by two American missionaries.

—

ACROSS BLAZING SANDS:
They're Out for a Torrid Time

Baghdad, Iraq—April 25, 1945

Every eight days an American caravan of soldiers, paralleling ancient camel trails, travels from Tel Aviv (in Palestine) to Baghdad. The soldiers are heat-worn veterans of the battle of the Persian Gulf, the battle to supply the Soviet Union with aircraft, vehicles, supplies and food. From Baghdad the soldiers go by rail back to their posts on the steaming Persian Gulf.

To gain the relief of the green fields, mountain air and civilized atmosphere of the Holy Land, this truckborne caravan has traveled three days from Iraq. The desert journey amounts to about 700 miles each way.

The usual way for officers and correspondents to traverse the desert is by air, a three-hour journey. To find out how the Persian Gulf Command was able to maintain this trans-desert shuttle, the writer accompanied a column commanded by Lieutenant Wilbur MacDuffie of Atlanta, a tall amiable officer in a jeep. We slept two nights in the desert.

Even while the Baghdad-bound caravan was ranging itself in front of the tents of Camp Tel-Litwinsky outside the modern Jewish city of Tel Aviv, another caravan was approaching under the command of a thin brown Texan, Lieutenant John Cochran. MacDuffie and Cochran have worked out a tight schedule, in spite of heat and breakdowns, and the Mediterranean-bound and Mesopotamia-bound caravans pass each other on parallel highways of the Plain of Sharon.

"Where to?" the m.p. demanded at the gate of Tel-Litwinsky. "The Persian Gulf," answered the redheaded driver of the lead camel-truck. The caravan had sixteen ton-and-half six-wheel personnel carriers, with twelve men or more facing each other on lengthwise seats across an aisleful of luggage and provisions. The big six-wheelers had their sides lashed down with canvas against sun and sand, and three were pulling trailers containing food, spare parts, extra gas and lubricants. The next to last vehicle was the ambulance. The commanding officer, MacDuffie, dressed like everyone else in green fatigues and with a leave-is-over air, took the tail of the column in his jeep. At every breakdown in the desert, however slight, MacDuffie stopped and did not proceed until the truck was repaired.

Arabs and Jews, working in their fields, paused to watch and sometimes to wave at the caravan. They understood well the letters *USA* on the doors, but could not figure out the word "American" because it was written in Russian script, for use in northern Iran on the lend-lease line.

Just as the caravan turned from the Plain of Sharon into the often embattled Plain of Esdraelon, on a route used by Canaanites, Egyptians, Jews, Philistines, Assyrians, Persians, Greeks, Romans, French, British and other Americans en route to the former American bomber bases around Acre and Haifa, the first trucks of the new convoy just arriving from Mesopotamia were sighted. Their desert trip was over. Their canvas was rolled up, they were howling in anticipation of Tel Aviv's beaches and nightclubs, and they shouted demands for useful telephone numbers as they went into the Plain of Sharon. . . . The eastbound convoy's members waved back.

The caravan passed the place where Saul called up the Witch of Endor and the prophet Samuel. They turned into the Plain of Armageddon, with green Jewish settlements on surrounding hills. In some trucks a G.I. who had his mimeographed guide reminded his friends that Gideon, Deborah, Cleopatra, Vespasian, Pompey, Antony, Titus, Napoleon and Allenby had all passed this way. This was soldiers' country, future as well as past, for here, according to the Book of Revelation, is to be fought the final battle between good and evil.

The G.I.s are still talking about the last Palestine girls they met. "So this lil' gal says to me, 'You ain't from no New Yawk, not with thet accent you got,' an' Ah says to huh, 'Oh, yassum, Ah'm from thuh Bronx, me.' " The general view is that the Palestine girls, whether in Tel Aviv, Jerusalem or Haifa, know much about the Land of Promise beyond the Atlantic and would be glad if they could enter there.

Where Armageddon enters the Valley of Jezreel, on the way down into the Jordan, the redheaded corporal who leads—Corporal Henry Moen—

observes a column of Arab cavalrymen in a big field by the roadside. These other soldiers are members of the Druze Legion, recruited by the British from the fierce tribesmen of the Jebel Druze in southern Syria. Their fine Arab horses are brown and white, divided in patrols by colors. Every fifty miles, without orders from MacDuffie, Moen halts the column and waits for stragglers or breakdowns to catch up. When he halts here, the brigadier commanding the Druze Legion, a vigorous middle-aged Englishman, invites the Americans to come and watch the exercise.

"This is the parade we shall do on V-Day in Jerusalem," says the British officer, speaking from the back of his Arab horse.

Spilling out of their trucks, the Americans watch four patrols of Arab horses go through a complex series of interweaving chains and marches. Carrying lances with pennons, the Druzes do four- and eight-horse wheels, cakewalks, daisy chains, and in-and-out maneuvers. At the end, the Americans burst into handclapping.

With the full green length of the river below, the desert-bound Americans pass a *Sea Level* sign and continue down. They cross the Jordan where its rapids are hardly 100 feet wide, and begin ascending long zigzags into pure Arab country, the British mandate of Transjordania, kingdom of the eldest scion of the line of the Prophet. The country grows bare and thin, the grass scarce. The fort on the east side of the river is smaller and weaker than that on the west, though both are British.

Above the tumbling Jordan, just below the fort, the caravan members break out their K-ration. It is 11 o'clock, and the sun is blinding. The drivers put on their wide canvas-and-leather belts, used on the rough roads of the Irano-Russian border to prevent internal bleeding. Sergeant Linton Revill is the caravan's veteran, having helped set up its route. "We were the size of an Arab camel caravan at first," he says. "We could take only about fifty men, in four trucks. At times it looked as though the heat would lick us. Last summer it was 130° in the shade, 170° in the sun. Your body was the coolest object around, but that was always around 103°."

About two in the afternoon, on the edge of the flinty desert, the caravan pulls into camp at Marfrak in Transjordania. Everyone is thick with dust and bumped into weariness. Caution: "Park everything you have under your cot; the Arabs sometimes get through the barbed wire and reach under the tents."

In the northern distance rise the forbidding hills of the wild Jebel Druze in Syria, whose insurgent tribesmen held at bay a whole French army after the last war. Syria, nominally a free republic recognized by the United States and the Soviet Union, is restless today.

The Marfrak camp has the only American force in Transjordania, which is four-fifths composed of cooks. "Between caravans," say the desert culinary forces, "we just shoot poker and play spelling games. Once in a while we go over to the camp of the Arab Legion and see an Egyptian movie. The most fun is getting up when we damned please."

The air in Marfrak is sharp and dry. Someone proposes going out in the desert toward the Syrian border to see the Unknown City, about ten miles away. The G.I. will try anything once, and two trucks load up instantly. In half an hour, over bumping lava rocks, flint and nettles, they reach the Unknown City.

Nobody has been able to find out its name, not even the cooks at Marfrak. A city of reddish black stone, it has towers, walls, and curious external staircases. One wall is entered through an enormous stone door, cunningly swung on stone hinges. There is a huge reservoir filled with slimy greenish water. Four Roman arches stand black against the sunset, prickly with nettles. It is hard to find anything written, but a sharp-eyed corporal locates an inscription to the Emperor Valentian. When did he reign? Nobody knows.

An Arab family is living alone, amid goats and dogs, in a room of the ruins. The father, who speaks a little English, pulls out a letter from his son in Detroit. The letter has reached this nomadic Bedouin family by way of the Syrian post office at Damascus, many days' journey north.

Bedded down in tents at seven, the caravan is up at three in the morning, the heavy motors of the trucks snorting. Some G.I.s get up at two to secure forward places on the board seats of the trucks, where vibration is less. As the word "let's go" is given, a thin sliver of light is showing along the edge of the eastern horizon. At the same time humming can be heard high overhead. The transport planes that left Cairo shortly after midnight will be in Baghdad for breakfast and Tehran for luncheon. Their red and green lights show among the stars.

The torrid jump from Marfrak in Transjordania to Rutbah Wells in Iraq is by way of a lonely place of tents and sand called simply H-4. The American convoy goes through H-4 by early morning, after the third fifty-mile stop. Once the black beds of horizon-reaching lava are left behind, no birds are seen. Camels ridden by slouching, muffled Bedouins move along the skyline, but the caravan's most steady companion is the famous pipeline of the Iraq Petroleum Company, the 10-inch fuel standby of the British Mediterranean fleet, which meets the inland sea at Haifa. The pipeline can be traced by a hump of earth over it, stained black in places from leaks. The pipe is underground partly to prevent it being attacked by Arabs, but mostly to prevent it being warped by the heat.

Sometimes the American drivers hear a low buzzing behind them. Suddenly a light plane like a crop duster, flying at barely twenty feet, passes overhead, with a peering pilot inspecting the ground over the pipeline for leaks.

All morning long the highway goes toward the rising sun. Sometimes it takes a wadi, or dry riverbed, to southeast, and the sun is on the left of the road. Then it moves into a northeast wadi, and the sun is more to the right. Sometimes the sun sits directly on the road.

Before noon the caravan reaches the Iraq-Transjordanian border. It is unguarded, for no man could live there. Its marker is a single leaning metal sign, live hot in the sun. The boundary is hinted by a line of sandfilled bitumen drums, sagging and broken, which stretch a few yards into the shard-strewn desert then peter out into disappearance.

The desert now becomes, if possible, flatter and more featureless. Even the stones get smaller. Grass has long disappeared, but the only true sand is in the bottoms of the wadis. Besides the slight hump over the buried pipeline, and the abandoned bitumen drums, the only companion of the caravan is the telegraph line. Exactly 26 poles to the mile, and marked to fractions, the poles tell precisely how many hot miles remain to Baghdad and the life-giving green banks of the Euphrates and Tigris. When the caravan stops for the breakdowns to catch up, the G.I.s throw stones at the metal poles, which ring when hit.

Here, in the hottest part of the desert, the company has piled stones over the pipeline. The stones absorb the heat, keep the desert below in shadow and hence cooler, and thus reduce shrinkage and expansion in the pipeline.

At 384 miles from the Mediterranean, the caravan pulls into Rutbah.

The caravan's members are too hot and bump-happy to do anything but fall on their cots. Spectacles are covered with dust, and the camp is putting up a losing fight against flies and sand. Oil tins are used for almost everything, from basins to latrines.

A cook from Rutbah once went out into the desert hunting gazelle. He became lost. An airplane found him five days later, raving and naked, with acute sunburns and what the doctors called "almost complete dehydration." His eyeballs were white, with only a small black pinpoint for each pupil.

The caravan is up with the stars on its third morning. In the light before dawn the road can be seen covered with yellowish objects the size of cartridges. Motionless, they are crushed flat as the trucks pass over them. "Those are locusts," says one G.I. "If we could pick them up and string them on wires, we could sell them to the Baluchi guards at our camp for 20 rials (60¢) a kilo. They eat them."

By dawn the locusts, numb from the cold desert night, begin to wake up and flutter feebly away at the roar of the oncoming caravan. By seven they are weaving across the road. By nine the air is alive with them, big and bright yellow, with staring eyes. They fly into the windshields of the trucks, turning them into a mash of yellow. They slip through the crevices in the tarpaulins and flutter around wildly inside the trucks.

Since Rutbah both pipelines and telegraph poles have veered away, taking a more direct route to Baghdad. At the fifty-mile stops the G.I.s face the clouds of oncoming locusts and throw handfuls of stones at them.

The trucks, now looking as though bombed with eggs, set out again. The desert turns from grey to a reddish clay color. To the north, about noon, is seen the cobalt waters of Lake Habbaniyeh, fed by underwater leakage from the Euphrates. Then the great river is reached, with its low mud houses. The trucks descend into the "fertile crescent" of Mesopotamia, and in midafternoon cross the Tigris, past the castle of the boy king Feisal II, and reach Baghdad.

It seems as though the travelers would never want to stir again. But when the tall blond campmaster arranges for two trucks to take volunteers to Babylon, fifty miles away, many are ready to go. Amid its mud-brick and bitumen ruins they see Nebuchadnezzar's hall, and the enigmatic lion of Iraq. And then they are ready to go back to the oven-like posts of the Persian Gulf.

IT MAKES YOU CRAZY

Khorramshahr, Iran—May 11, 1945

With a thermometer outside the heat stroke center showing 111 degrees in the shade at 3 p.m., the military police here, and in Ahwaz eighty miles north, all agree it is unseasonably cool for May. It ought to be warmer than this, right now.

Someone walks in and says, "It's 146° in the sun in the motor pool right now." "We hit that in the shade in August," comes the response.

In the desert cities, probably the largest and ugliest military slums in the world, the day begins at seven and ends at one in the afternoon. In the afternoon you just breathe, eat salt tablets, drink water and if lucky enough to wangle a ride, go to the Anglo-Iranian Oil Company's pool on the island of Abadan.

But the m.p.s keep right on working. They were just eighteen, most of them, when formed in Chicago. This is their third summer in the Persian Gulf Command. They have the official air corps weather records for their first year, back when they thought statistics would be believed. For May, June, July and August 1943 the *lowest* recorded temperatures were 72°, 104°, 108° and 92°. The average shade temperatures for the same months were 110°, 116°, 122°, and 126°.

The average heats in the afternoon sun, where they work, were 162°, 166°, 170° and 172°. The *hottest* it got for this Chicago-in-Persia was 171° in May, 181° in June, 177° in July and 177° in August.

In Ahwaz, the town in the desert where the railroads from the twin ports of Khorramshahr and Bandar Shapur join, one G.I. says, "In 22 months I've lost 37 pounds. It did me good but I still didn't like it." Says another, "The sun dries up the liquid in the corner of your eyes and pulls the skin out of shape, so you can't focus." Advice? "Swing your washed-out underwear twice around your head and it's dry."

In this heat you sweat, but dry off so quickly you don't realize what is happening. Then your clothes turn white; that's salt from your body, the only trace left of your perspiration. After a scorcher, one 6-foot-5-inch sergeant from Chicago, 32 months married and 28 months overseas, looks like a lighthouse.

"We desert rats," attests a corporal, "understand how the South felt after the Civil War. That's the way we feel about those correspondents who write articles about how swell life is in the desert without ever coming here." The company politician puts it like this: "Persia for the Persians; that's our motto."

In the shimmering heat that makes the telegraph poles ripple to the horizon like a snake, you cross the last stretch of desert to where the Shatt-al-Arab slides lifelessly into the Gulf. The door to Khorramshahr is two 20-foot pedestals with a traffic island. On the right side of the road, where northbound truck convoys can see it, is an arrow and RUSSIA. Khorramshahr has many such gates, like a stockyard for humans, where the m.p.s work with the British, in their red-rimmed caps.

Elmer Stoneberg says, "We broke down in the desert and were out there for fourteen hours. I'd read about prospectors out west holding stones in their mouths to keep saliva flowing, so we did that." John Urban, who was on the truck that found Stoneberg, says, "His tongue was hanging out about a foot."

But these men have competition. The two towns of Andimeshk and Dizful, glowering at each other across a tepid desert river, are the hottest places on earth. Andimeshk is an American railroad center, where the trains that have been broiling their way across the desert change to double engines to meet the mountain grades. Dizful, with a claimed record of 189°, is the dwelling place of a unique underground people who prefer the blindness of cool caves to the blindness of the sun.

Between the towns, on the stone bridge above the muddy rapids of the Karun River, stand the American military police, frying in their white helmets. They have a special burn on right now, because another Chicago newspaper asserted that the temperatures reported from Iran were impossible.

"There's no sense telling people how hot it gets here," they say. "They wouldn't believe us, anyway. A thermometer hung out in the sun broke. You spill a glass of water and hardly any reaches the ground. Heat! Yeow! I don't even want to hear the word—that one syllable puts a guy through a million agonies in this unfair country. Iran is a hot shower, just without the water. In Dizful it gets so hot you can hardly breathe. And I don't know which is worse, Andimeshk or hell, never having been in hell yet."

"Weather like this is hard on chaplains," admits a man of the cloth. "It deprives us of half our talking points."

—

Soldiers' Verse from a War Correspondent's Notebook

Persian Gulf Command
(Tune of "Shanty Town")

It's only a shack in old Basra, Iraq,
It's a heck of a place and I'm not going back,
The sun's hot as hell, and oh! what a smell,
The natives don't wash their feet and it's goat that they eat,
They all wear a dress and I'm forced to confess,
That I can't tell Charlie from Mamie or Bess,
There's a queen waiting there, she has lice in her hair,
In that shack in old Basra, Iraq.

She's only a whore from old Bandar Shahpur,
A sweet Persian maiden and need I say more.
Her price 50 rials, and not a bad deal,
When she wiggles her butt, oh! my! how you feel.
She's strictly illegit but I don't mind a bit,
And if she weren't so dusky I'd chew on her tit,
There's a queen waiting there, she has crabs in her hair,
Just a whore from old Bandar Shahpur.

It's only a bar in old Khorramshahr,
We waded through mud from our camp so afar,
They had vodka and gin, and oh! what a din.
It's the worst goddamned place I have ever been in,
There were soldiers and sailors and Merchant Marines,
They were thinking of home and all that it means,
There's a war to be won and a job to be done,
They left that bar in old Khorramshahr.

We're stationed now in Ahwaz, Iran,
Wherever you look it's just desert sand
Where the wind starts to blow, and the dust hides the glow
Of the moon as it shines o'er the crappy Karun,
We drink Persian beer, and there's no nooky here
And we won't get none if we stay here a year,
It's a damned dirty place, it's a lousy disgrace,
This asshole called Ahwaz, Iran.

We are in the command, but Tehran leads the band,
They are the minds, we are just hired hands,
They write letters galore, and endorsements more,
They demand more reports than there are Persian whores.
They move supplies with a flick of their eyes,
They make inspection complete from 10,000 feet,
But we tell no lies, they're a swell bunch of guys,
The tops in the Persian Command.

to be forwarded by airmail to Mr. Hal O'Flaherty, Foreign Editor, the
Chicago Daily News, after censorship at New Delhi...
    from George Weller, Chicago Daily News, at an advanced base
                        ******

WITH ADVANCED AMERICAN JINGPAW RANGERS IN EASTERN BURMA, June 22---

This small secret airfield wants to remain secret, but sees no

reason why it should remain small. Tiny planes, old and temperamental,

race along its flooded green runway, lift into the low monsoon clouds,

and make their way between rain-squalls to the bands of American-led

Jingpaw hillmen fighting behind Jap lines. The field's location must

remain secret. But the Jingpaw leaders at "Paddy's Ricefield" have big

beans, big ideas. Here is their brochure (all prices subject to

revision in the event of a banzai attack by the Japs).

        Flying (all combat time qualifying you for any of the
        medals in L-1 or L-5 planes)

Straight flying over friendly area $10.00 per hour
    (stunting $1.00 extra per stunt)

Flying where there might be Japs $15.00

Flying where there definitely are Japs $17.00

Flying where there is ground fire $20.00

Flying where there is anti-aircraft fire $40.00

Parachute jumps $10.00 per jump
    (behind enemy lines $5.00 extra)

One plane landing behind Jap lines $25.00
    (qualifying you for Silver Star)

Rescues at risk of life and limb $100.00

Purple Hearts obtained at no extra charge..."bull sessions" with

our pilots a nightly feature...our planes feature constant contact

with the ground by "walkie-talkie"....

            You too can be photographed at the front !
        (all types of uniforms and weapons furnished)

XIX

From Burma to China

From New Delhi in June, Weller wrote to his editor: "I may disappear for a week or ten days on a special job. Do not be worried if you do not hear from me, or tell anyone who inquires that you knew it was in the offing."

This was Weller's two weeks behind Japanese lines with the Jingpaw Rangers, young Burmese guerrillas led by intrepid American officers. Originally, he was to parachute in—his training in New Guinea made it feasible to get to the story— but at the last minute he was landed on a secret airstrip "seemingly no longer than a bowling alley" by a tiny plane coming to take away a wounded Ranger. This world of improvisatory war and constant movement, where roads "are only places for planting ambushes" and those "taken by Japs die slowly and with torture," was ideal for Weller. "They cannot reveal even to their wives what they're doing. Some have ceased writing home. One Ranger, surrounded by Japs, had a letter dropped with his ammunition supplies. It contained divorce papers served by his wife's lawyer. Her love could not outlast his enforced silence."

I have included the full magazine-length treatment of the story rather than dispatches that the newspaper ran—both included descriptions of Japanese waterboarding. Weller then set out to drive the harrowing, curlicue "Burma Road" to China (a crucial supply route before the British had lost Burma), reopened at the insistence of U.S. general Joe Stilwell. Weller ended up in Chungking, and until August he covered border

clashes between Communist and Nationalist forces. In a couple
of weeks, following the atomic bombs, the war with Japan would
be over.

—

Asia's Little States Pin Hopes on U.S.

New Delhi, India—May 28, 1945

The Balkans of southeast Asia stand on the threshold of freedom. These
include Burma, Thailand, Indo-China, the Federated Malay States, and
the Dutch East Indies. All have national movements which desire self-
government without excluding guarantees of their sovereignty by the
great powers.

The Japanese, when evacuating the Asiatic Balkans, leave behind in
each country grants of "independence," which are political time-bombs.
The dying Japanese idea of a Greater East Asia Co-Prosperity Sphere* may
be revived at the outbreak of the next European or Middle Eastern war if
the United Nations cannot win back the confidence of Asiatics.

As in the European Balkans, these peoples look to the United States as
the key to what they hope will be more liberty. But though American
seapower, directed against the Philippines, has been largely responsible for
weakening the doomed limb of the Jap empire, America political policy is
nonexistent. Complete obscurity surrounds the question of what attitude
the United States intends to take toward the aspirations of freed people
and the traditional rights of their European protectors.

The most to be said of the American position in southeast Asia is that it
is still publicly uncommitted. At Tehran President Roosevelt acceded to dividing the European Balkans into spheres of Russian and British influence.
Though the 15th Air Force (with the Soviet army) was the strongest factor
in the crisscross strategy which liberated the Balkans, Roosevelt signed

---

*Japan's justification for World War II—to dominate China, Malaya, the Netherlands
East Indies, the Philippines, Burma, Thailand, and the rest of the Pacific, thus creating
an Asia for Asians. Publicly announced in 1940, the policy had been in force for years.

away all but a rubber-stamp role for the United States. Despite American airmen having sacrificed their lives over Ploesti and Sofia, Rumania and Bulgaria are now barred to the American press. Today not one country in the Balkans except Albania is without a foreign army on its soil. These precedents make Asiatic nationalists watch Burma as a test case of their probable destiny. Will the United States accept its responsibilities, or turn them over to other powers as it did in Europe?

As Asiatics see the issue, Truman's hand is perfectly free. It is hazarded that the United States may delay formulating its attitude until a landing has been achieved on the Chinese coast. The American habit of acting militarily first and letting a political policy tag along afterward is as much a mystery here as in the Middle East. The Asiatic view toward America now is: "It's later than you think."

—

CONFLICTING VIEWS ON EMPEROR

New Delhi, India—May 30, 1945

Two conflicting cries directed to Superforts [B-29s] bombing Japan come from the lowly Allied bleachers at China's back door. "Kill that Emperor! Kill him!" yells one savage chorus. "Let him alone. We need him," comes an opposing singsong.

Neither party is thinking about nice questions like whether the royal line should endure or Japan become a republic. They think of the Emperor in practical soldiers' terms. Their views about the Emperor depend strictly on whether he can get them out of the monsoon—their hot, humid present environment—by Christmas.

One school thinks that every palace of the Emperor should be plastered by Superforts in the hope of sending Heaven's Son heavenward. Then, as they opine, Japanese resistance would collapse. But the other school of bleacherites says: "What if the Emperor does meet with a super accident from a Superfort? Where does that leave us? It may leave us digging these disagreeably determined little men out of their holes for the next ten years. No, what we want is for Japan to remain unified until its surrender under the Emperor. Because only the Emperor can uproot wholly this tiresome Co-Prosperity Sphere which takes so much trouble now."

Ask either party in the bleachers what ought to happen to the Emperor after he has whistled the last Japanese infantryman down from a sniper's tree-nest, or out from a foxhole, and all you get is a baffled stare. Where do umpires go after games, anyway? Who cares? Certainly not Asia's bleachers.

—

BEATEN JAPS FIGHT ON IN BURMA

New Delhi, India—June 4, 1945

Dead on its feet in rain-sodden Burma, Japan's army nevertheless bitterly refuses to lie down. British imperial forces hold every major city except Moulmein, which planes crack every time the clouds open, attempting to diminish the Jap pullout south toward Bangkok, capital of Thailand.

But Japan's retreat is no rout. It is a stubborn, well-calculated withdrawal, with every jungle road held milestone by milestone. The northern part of their army is seeking refuge in the Shan Hills. If it succeeds, they will still be able to claim a foothold in Burma as they do in bypassed New Guinea and the Solomons.

It is essential for the Japanese to practice frugality, because if the Americans land in China, both land and sea routes from the enemy homeland will be cut and their Southeast Asian command can expect praise but little wherewithal. The Jap aim in clinging to parts of Burma is less to harass than to form a kind of bucket brigade along which the last man, the last bag of rice and the last grenade may be passed eastward.

—

SAFE AND COZY BEHIND THE JAPANESE LINES

Bhamo, Stilwell Road, Burma—July 7, 1945

The idea that this war, despite military and political censorship, is being better reported than all its predecessors has reached such general acceptance that a man who doubts it finds himself on a par with one who throws acid at an oil painting. As news the war is yielding to the peace; as history the war is still unaccepted. Ian Hamilton, one of the good war correspondents of the earlier, European conflict, once said that history had to be written on the day of the event. By break of the following dawn, he observed pessimistically, the facts have put on their uniforms.

It would be helpful, certainly, if history could be written immediately on the scene, before rain has filled the shellholes, before the bodies are covered, and before the general begins to yearn for a samurai sword. Such promptness has not, of course, been achieved in this war. It cannot be attained by correspondents in any way. If an event is great, like a mighty landing on a defended beach, it is also critical. Since it is critical, the correspondents cannot describe it fully in public, where the enemy would benefit. So it must be described afterward, and afterward is too late. If an event is small but brimming with meaning, it is often accidental, and never becomes known but at second or third hand. At a distance of hours, even minutes, it is already exaggerated, adulterated or deformed. A day is distortion, a week is deadly. Thus correspondents find themselves forever writing not about what they saw, but what they just missed seeing. What happened was malice and blood, but at the time the correspondent was face down in a foxhole, his weaponless hand clasping his exposed neck, or a plane-leap away on an aircraft carrier, previewing history on a radar screen. It is for these unavoidable reasons, plus a few others, that the remarkable exploits of the American Jingpaw Rangers behind Japanese lines in Burma, which have been going on for more than two years, must already be regarded, in a historical sense, as forever lost. Narratively speaking, nobody was there. And an invisible condition, though ideal from the point of view of a guerrilla, simply baffles a historian.

Of course, there are records. The United States is long on keeping records. There are flimsies of the unemotional messages that were flashed to these guerrillas, sometimes when they were surrounded by search columns of *kempeitai,* the Japanese military police. "All other battalions now engaged. No other units are near enough to help you," says one message, needing no gloss.

The messages that flew over the heads of the Japanese back to the American headquarters contain few gifted or sententious passages. Their style goes like this: "Food drop fell outside our perimeter. Saw Nips get it. Please try another tonight, or if pilots unable, tomorrow morning." . . . "Holed up in caves because our Shans took a powder. Our coordinates are unchanged. If possible drop us Chinese mortarman and about six Kachins preferably with Bren guns and our mail." . . . "Our Gurkha outpost on his six o'clock sked says that village Mong-sa has been visited by Indian believed Jap agent. He asked headman location our camp. Headman played dumb. Gurks think that he may have letter from Japanese commander to me, this being excuse for visiting our camp." . . . A sheaf of such messages, assembled by correspondent or historian, adds up to nothing. Yet it is as close to the event, as near to a contemporary battle record of what the Jingpaw Rangers have been doing in Burma, as exists.

As this is written, the Jingpaw Rangers are still fighting in the rear of the Japanese lines. It is mid-monsoon, not a good season for war. Yet a Ranger outfit still sits alone on the highway near Loi-lem, east of the Japanese fortifications on the mountain escarpment at Taunggyi. Their presence, won by six weeks' fighting, blocks the otherwise free retreat of two Japanese divisions into Thailand. They have beaten off dozens of attacks. Yet their work is almost unknown. In communiqués of the Southeast Asia Command they are rarely mentioned. (The guerrillas do not resent their omission, but attribute it to security.)

Only three correspondents have served in the field with the Rangers in the past year; the two besides this writer were both sergeants with army publications. No civilian correspondent save the writer has ever been with a Ranger detachment behind the Japanese lines, an undertaking which has been open to all and is not nearly so risky as it sounds. An editor of the *Reader's Digest* spent some time in residence at Ranger headquarters when it was in Myitkyina (the place India-Burma veterans mean when they speak of "Mishinaw"). A sergeant commanding a company of Shans, an eastern Burman people whose devotion to war is desultory at its best, was able to keep his men beyond their enlistment by reading the resulting article to them, and assuring them that if they chose to fight all the longer they would be famous. The Shans, after thinking it over, decided that they still wanted to go home a while, make a few children, and return after the monsoon . . . History is something the guerrillas do not exactly shun, but they have found that history shuns them.

The American task of raising and equipping a native army in Burma was not one of drafting or shanghaiing unwilling cannon fodder. The British call these tobacco-skinned little men "levies," but the term is inexact. The several native tribes who serve under this wholly American command have not been coerced into service. They are volunteers. They have simply been asked whether they wished to do their Jap-fighting under the American flag for a rupee (30¢) a day and have responded affirmatively.

To like wholeheartedly an ally is a rare thing, but it has occurred in Burma between the hill tribes and the Americans. The highlanders of the Shan States, a great area of northeastern Burma as different from the rest of the country as Mexico is from the United States, have respect, admiration and what seems like affection for Americans. They have proved willing to follow Americans into very questionable situations, such as into open space through the door of a tinnily rattling C-47, or uphill into the ominous, chugging fire of a Japanese heavy machine gun. They have been the more willing, perhaps, because in proportion to the trail of Japanese corpses they have littered across the scene, the losses among these skimpily trained riflemen, most of whom are less than twenty years old, have been unbelievably small.

The job of a guerrilla is disrupting enemy communications and sowing sabotage. Killing, as in gangsterdom, is incidental and opportunities to kill are often passed by. Yet the Jingpaw Rangers, in their two years fighting behind the Japanese, have managed to kill, so to speak with their left hands, 5466 fully vouchered enemies, and to capture and bring back 63 more. Only 160 natives have met death, many of them accidentally. The American deaths total three. Vertical warfare directed at the Japanese rear has proved by far the most economical offensive in the East. But the Shan people consider these one-sided results only natural because they are covered, and as they believe protected, by a close-woven chain mail of blue tattooing. These indigo whorls, extending from the neckline to the wrists and below the kneecaps, are invulnerable to Japanese fire. "As a matter of fact," one American officer told me with wonder, "bullets go through every part of their clothing without touching the tattoo marks. I don't know why it is, but cartridges seem to take a curve the minute they see a Jingpaw."

Quite without knowing it, the natives of the Shan States who responded to Stilwell's call for 10,000 guerrillas have been proving two things new in

American history: that an American G.I., be he only a private bucking for pfc, can lead ably natives of all levels of civilization, from the most primitive Kachins to the Christianized, educated Karens; and secondly, that native guerrilla bands, operating in tropical country behind enemy lines, supplied, organized and commanded by Americans, can soften the advance of a mechanized army (here the British Imperial forces plus some Chinese troops) in a degree as great if not greater than similar underground movements of more intelligent and more patriotic partisans in the Balkans and Western Europe.

None of the motives of Greece's ELAS, of the Chinese Communists, of the Philippine patriots have induced these strong-minded regionalists of eastern Burma to fight under the American flag. They are partisans only in the sense that they do not like foreigners. Especially they dislike the southern or lowland Burmans. What attachment the hill people feel toward the British is founded on appreciation for London's treating them separately from the rice-puddlers of the Irrawaddy delta. The Japanese, in setting up a puppet play of Burman independence, mistakenly played ball only with the Burmese of the Irrawaddy. Consequently the highlanders who eventually made up the American guerrillas distrusted Japan from the beginning. Besides, the Japanese gave two of the Shan States to Thailand. When American air power was infused into the campaign, making it possible to nourish British ground forces exclusively by parachute, doubt vanished. The people of the Shan States have an Asiatic inclination to be with a winner.

When the first Americans leaped into empty air to muster these Burmans—whose tiny, flatchested women wear white shirtwaists all the time and smoke cigars in the middle of their mouths—the Japanese Imperial Army was the only force east of India. In France, the Low Countries and the Balkans, large and self-contained partisan armies already existed to meet in-dropping guerrilla leaders; in northern Burma there was only political paralysis. Thus the Jingpaw Rangers were an experiment not only in harassing the enemy from the rear, but in initiating and raising a hostile army right under his nose.

The people of eastern Burma are not united even among themselves. The Karens and Kachins, the best fighting people, come from the extreme south and extreme north and can converse with each other only through the hated *lingua franca* Burmese. Many Karens are devout Baptists of the

American sect. They do not fight on Sunday except under duress, because it interferes with the four or five services they like to hold on that day. The Kachins, on the other hand, are animists. They believe that human affairs are in the hands of nats. A nat is a small, vicious spirit who lives in rivers and trees, and not invisibly, either. A Kachin cannot merely imagine a nat; he can actually see him. When he sees him, he shoots him. The thousands of Japanese who have fallen to the Rangers have mostly been rubbed out by threes and fours. The number of nats, seated in bushes or flying through the air thumbing their noses, who have been picked off by the Kachins is simply countless.

A singular fact about the Rangers, who have done more to protect the Burma Road into China than any other force of like numbers, is that there are very few Burmese among them. Besides the hill-born Karens and Kachins, there are Gurkhas and Chinese, who speak Burmese but are not even truly Burman. A Burman is anyone native to Burma. A Burmese is a lowlander of the Irrawaddy delta.

Nearly everything is a little bit special or tricky about the Rangers. Its Gurkhas, for instance, are not the same breed as the true-born Gurkhas of Nepal who have served a century, father and son, as part of the Indian army. These Gurkhas are immigrants of the second or third generation in Burma, and do not belong anywhere in particular. Even the Chinese in the Jingpaw Rangers are peculiar. They are renegades, drifting sons of the great, fertile mother beyond the Yunnan mountains. The nat-beset Kachins, who are themselves immigrants from Tibet, hate the Chinese. Chinese troops in Kachin country are not given the freedom of the village, but sometimes take it. And the final tribe mustered by the parachuting American officers, on the old guerrilla principle of having every indigenous tribe represented in your force no matter how unmartial they may be, was the Shan. The Shans are a torpid, unbelligerent clan of bullock-slappers and elephant herders who live smack between the Baptist Karens and the animistic Kachins, believe in a transcendental Buddha and will have none of either of their neighbors.

Stilwell's notion of having all these tribal irreconcilables fighting under a single American command in eastern Burma, that is, between Lord Mountbatten's* Anglo-American force in western Burma and the escape

---

*Supreme Allied commander of the Southeast Asia Theatre.

corridors into Thailand, was one that could be entertained only in a country where the force itself could be subdivided as never to get in intestinal squabbles. A united effect was actually achieved no less through the conciliatory leadership of the Americans who led individual companies, than through the topography of the country, which was ideal for warfare against a common enemy by tribal elements in themselves dissident. The companies of course had to be gathered by tribe, for they neither sang *Jesus, Lover of my Soul* in the same dialect nor saw the same nat sitting in the ear of an elephant. The country itself kept them apart, as guerrilla bands should be, and prevented any ELAS-EDES controversies arising between them.

The Shan States, lying between Burma and the borders of China and Thailand, where most of the Rangers' fighting has been taking place, resembles upstate New York, or the Columbia Valley just above Portland. It is a country of bamboo brakes and rice paddies, like most Burma, but it is also a country of mountains, brooks and big timber. Even in monsoon time, when the rest of Burma is killingly damp and hot, the nightly mists of the Shan States are cool instead of suffocating. Its valleys are not thickly jungled, but lie open, clear and beautiful.

Seen from the air, as pilots of the unarmed, low-flying grasshopper planes of the Jingpaw Rangers see the Shan States, Burma resembles an extended golf course, of brilliant green meandering along endlessly north-south between heavily jungled hills. There are level pastures, like golf greens, beside the villages. It has been the business of the Rangers to convert secretly these pastures into drop grounds for arms and food, and later into air fields for the use of their tiny L-1 and L-5 planes.

It was the aim of the Japanese, after American and British fighters had swept the Japanese air force out of the sky, to try through patrols and espionage by native agents to locate these drop grounds and the nearby American forces and to wipe them out with superior numbers, supplies and firepower, the advantages of an army that is being needled in the rear by guerrillas.

Guerrillas take to this sort of open golfing country better than to continuous dense jungle. The course suits their game. A happy sequence of Japanese medal players tees off solemnly from a village, having murdered and looted their fill, and starts down the fairway. At some elbow hole, where the fairway bends around the rough, they are suddenly enfiladed by machine-gun fire. Grenades burst among them. They dive into the nearest bunker, the roadside ditch, pulling in their wounded after them. Bunkered thus, they return fire in a burst of explosion shots, using knee mortars for niblicks. By the time the following foursomes have overtaken and reinforced them, and the sportsmen have collected their spirits for a *banzai* charge, their ambushers have departed, leaving only a few .303 clips, the waxed wrapper of a bar of American tropical chocolate, a few clumps of crushed grass and a faint smell of unwashed bodies. The Rangers have escaped into the rough.

In about two years of fighting, by alternating southeast and southwest zigzags the Rangers have gone halfway the length of Burma, as far as 150 miles behind the Japanese front. They began fighting early last year around Myitkyina, helping the Marauders. Once 150 Kachins aided another battalion to relieve a thirteen-day siege when a force of Marauders were surrounded. Myitkyina settled, they zigged southwest to persecute the Japanese fighting the British in the Imphal valley. Here an American detachment blew up what was apparently the main Japanese munitions dump, some 400,000 pounds of shells, grenades and cartridges. The blast broke up a breakfast of fifteen Japs a few yards away. This spring the guerrillas zagged southeast to gnaw the underpinnings from the Japanese defenses before Lashio, the key to the old Burma road. To do this they stealthily built and maintained a big transport strip 16 miles outside a village called Hsenwi, only an hour by road from Lashio. For nearly three months, in a country dominated by the Japanese army and infested with Japanese sympathizers, the guerrillas kept this air field open and busy, a miniature LaGuardia 60 miles ahead of the most advanced Allied troops. Finally in April, zigging southwest again, the Rangers managed in about three months' fighting to win two open battles with Japanese field forces. Finally they single-handedly took the town of Loi-lem as the summer monsoon broke, blocking the only Japanese route of escape into northern Thailand.

The Americans in the Rangers, when you come to know them, seem no more adapted for this kind of Iroquois warfare than the fellow you roomed with at college. The educational level is high; even their latrines have alumni magazines as standard reading matter. But they are a mixed lot. Their commanding officer is a tall, 31-year-old regular army colonel, plainspoken and alert. Some of the Rangers come from the navy, the marines and even the coast guard, but most are army amateurs. The best "kicker"—that extremely essential person who stands in the windy open door of a cargo plane, reads the panels on the ground, and determines whether food and arms can safely be dropped without falling to the Japanese—is a sergeant who resembles Henry Fonda and once served in the Polish army. Like all Rangers, he has many talents. He not only can pack a parachute, but knows how to persuade a trembling Kachin to walk through a transport's empty door into space. He does this by pointing steadfastly out into vacancy and saying repeatedly *teekhai,* an Hindustani word meaning "goods." Of tens of Americans and scores of natives who have jumped deliberately, without previous training, the parachute of none has "come a streamer," that is, failed to open. Ranger luck in vertical warfare does not always hold, however. On one occasion a Ranger light plane, forced by monsoon clouds to swoop low over a complex of green dumplings held by guerrillas and Japanese, overshot the determined hill and dropped a set of orders into the Japanese camp.

Though the Rangers have been mentioned casually in the Asiatic news, the curtain of censorship has risen enough to give an ankle-high view of them.

Another secret item about the Rangers is the location of between two and three hundred air fields they have built behind Japanese lines, almost all of which are now back in the confines of the British Empire. About twenty of these fields are long and solid enough to accommodate big planes. Although they are located in one of the most important regions in Asia, strategically speaking, no overtures for their future use by American air forces have yet been made.

The anonymity of the Jingpaw Rangers has political disadvantages for the United States. There are few Britons, for example, who realize that the southward march of imperial forces to Rangoon was made possible in good part by the exploratory slashes delivered by the Rangers in the Japanese rear. A guerrilla force has done a great deal if it merely annoys an enemy with sporadic attacks, even if ineffective. The aim is that he should be forever looking over his shoulder, expecting trouble behind him, like a fighter pilot.

The Rangers have ways of making sure the enemy takes a long look. Say a Japanese division is holding off an Anglo-Gurkha-Indian division at some roadblock, a typical situation. An important Japanese ammunition dump is perhaps two miles in the rear. The Japanese infantryman in his foxhole feels a puff of air tap at the back of his helmet, and turns to see what it is. He hears a first explosion, then sees a column of black smoke lift in his rear. Soon he hears the uneven pumping of shells ineffectually exploded, shells his artillery will never use. Any soldier knows, under such circumstances, that retreat is likely.

Recently I spent several days with the most forward Jingpaw companies. By this time most of them were no longer encircled by the Japanese, but were fighting frontally. This circumstance had arisen because the Japanese were so harassed by guerrilla pinpricks in their rear that they had decided to unload a few assets. They did this by shortening their front at the points where the Rangers were most troublesome behind it. The Jingpaw intruders, who had been muddling things in the rear, found themselves cold-shouldered outward to the Japanese flank. I learned with some surprise that they considered this flanking position that had been thrust on them far less comfortable than when they were what they sometimes call "safe and cozy behind the Japanese lines." They felt this way because while no army can protect itself against airborne invasion from the rear if it has no air force, all armies get very worked up when they find a force on their flank. An army seems to mind being tickled in the rear more than being stabbed in the back.

One of the Ranger officers with whom I stayed behind the Japanese lines was gently critical of a recent film called *Objective, Burma!,* which he had not seen—the guerrillas do not yet have cinema in the Japanese rear—but which he had read in synopsis in a movie periodical. (All kinds of reading matter is dropped to the Rangers; they get so many Sunday newspapers that the average guerrilla hideout is a gaudy litter of red and yellow comic pages.) "As I understand it," said my friend, "Errol Flynn is trying to lead back a whole company of paratroopers into our lines after their having destroyed a radar station inside the Japanese lines. He keeps losing men and manages to get back with only a few. Now I don't want to play expert, but all I can say is that Flynn must be a hell of an officer. You can drop me anywhere in the Japanese rear in Burma with a company of Rangers—American or Jingpaw, I don't care—and I'll bring back every man alive, except perhaps one or two

I'd lose in the original assault. More likely I wouldn't lose even one man, and we'd have plenty of fun and games coming in. People don't realize how much safer it is behind the Japs than in front of them."

Once a party of Rangers found a camp full of Japs waiting for dinner, killed all five cooks, and sped away. This was an ideal guerrilla action. In killing by driblets more than 5000 Japanese, some of them two weeks' foot march behind the front, the Rangers have tried to strike a nice mean between that amount of losses which worries the enemy and that amount which makes him furious. Worried, the Japanese loses initiative and gets discouraged and scatterbrained. Furious, he is likely to set out like a Nazi on a general sweep of extermination. In such sweeps he includes all villages in his path. There was an early time when the Japanese in Burma stood for law and order. Soldiers who looted soon felt an officer's revolver at their heads, and went into the hereafter dishonorably. The old Burma Independent Army, when it tried to become a partisan government, was put down as thoroughly as the British liquidated ELAS in Greece. But in retreat the Japanese have turned completely vicious.

A certain West Pointer, who has a close relative still in Japanese hands, has pondered more deeply about being a guerrilla than his brother officers. In a conversation I had with him ten miles beyond the most advanced British lines, within an easy walk of the Japanese mountain stronghold of Taunggyi, he told me: "I borrowed my creed for this job from an Englishman who did this work in France. Once he went ashore from a submarine and killed the Luftwaffe's six best bombing instructors in a few minutes. He told me, 'In this work you have to be without fear, without pity, and without remorse. Without fear because otherwise you won't take on the job. Without pity because otherwise you won't carry it out. Without remorse because otherwise you won't sleep afterward!' " My host looked quietly at a yellow-clad Buddhist priest sitting in the sun and added, "My men are almost all Christian Karens who have escaped after being tortured by the Japanese. We are proud of one thing. We have never tortured anybody."

Twice I have been with Ranger outfits which were under attack by Japanese patrols, or "being bumped," as the Rangers put it. I heard few orders. For a stranger it would have been difficult to discern who was in command. It is hard to tell an American officer of the guerrillas from an enlisted man. Insignia are almost never seen. "I have been with this outfit two years," a corporal told me, "and never yet received a direct order." It is something new to hear a sergeant address a lieutenant colonel as "Butch," or refer pleasantly to his superior in his presence as "the Beast of Buchenwald." To realize at the same time that the mystic discipline of the chain of command still holds firm under the surface, and has not been broken, is exhilarating.

The Japanese, listening these days to our walkie-talkies conversing from top to top off the 400-foot green dumplings south of Loi-lem, must frequently be perplexed at the words they overhear. In order to test, when addressing troops, the honesty of an interpreter, a habit of inserting a little double-talk has grown up among the officers, and now often creeps into their radio conversations. "Frottix on the litteraw" is a specimen commonly heard. Since the glib guerrilla interpreters never have any difficulty translating this phrase into the native dialects, the Americans have been forced to conclude that "frottix on the litteraw" has some sort of pan-meaning east of the Irrawaddy which was not perceived when they invented it. . . . The great sticklers for speech among the guerrillas are the Kachins. They refuse to be called Kachins, because in Burmese the word means "sour-bitter." They prefer to be known as Jingpaws, which in Tibetan means "cannibals."

A Ranger column, even though it strikes hard, moves with un-blitzlike slowness. Its only vehicles are two-wheeled bullock carts, drawn by the grey, lowbrowed beasts that plod the flooded paddyfields. Sometimes the guerrillas have used elephants, but they have found them uncertain beasts. Elephants have been known to give away a promising ambush by a snorting trumpet of anticipation. They move silently enough through the jungle, but they leave behind a trail of disengaged leeches, clinging lightly to bushes and reaching thirstily for the bodies of men on foot. "When you see a bush ahead of you at a turning that seems to be alive and waving at you," one Ranger told me, "you do not need to look at the trail for elephant prints. Take off your combat boots and you find them full of blood. The leeches get in through the eyelets." Bullocks, loving water like hippopotami, can traverse almost any river, while elephants are sometimes swept away. One guerrilla elephant, caught by his chain on a rock, spent five hours "whirling in the current like a watch." Bullock carts, which look like American prairie schooners sawed in half and covered with bamboo mesh instead of canvas, cost the Rangers two rupees (60¢) a day.

The creeping guerrilla columns, bounded on the one hand by the dozing water beasts, leap directly on the supply side to the fastest vehicle known to man. The C-47s of the Combat Cargo Command, which at one time were supplying 300,000 men in Burma exclusively by air, are the long leg of the compasses which make up for the uneager, splay-legged bullocks. Unless the monsoon's mists hang too low on the mountains, or there is not enough sun to blink a signal to a searching plane, the guerrillas can always be sure that Combat Cargo will not let them starve. Occasionally a spell of mis-drops or bad weather can put them temporarily on a diet of bamboo shoots and tadpole stew. But I have had two meals that I remember about fifteen miles behind the Japanese lines which were better and more various than what is served to the wallahs at the Imperial Hotel in New Delhi. A typical message from such an outpost, not intended to be sardonic, reads: "We have been feeding DC pilots. Have enough food but are completely out of cream and sugar. Please send us same."

Ranger teams usually consist of two to ten Americans, with riflemen from as few as ten up to and over three hundred. Almost all guerrillas wear the brown broadbrimmed Gurkha hat, and they like it double-lashed with a leather thong in front, cowboy style. Below that they generally wear green fatigues, green canvas jungle sneakers that come calf-high and dry out quickly, and a belt with a revolver and a grenade or two. The natives dress exactly the same, except that they have carbines instead of .45s. The minimum combat team is two Americans, an officer and radioman. The commanding officer is expected to do the most dangerous work himself, laying explosives under bridges, preparing ambushes and blowing up enemy supplies.

It is this last job which is the real test of a clever guerrilla. "No matter how often our supply dumps are moved," complained a Japanese officer, "they always seem to get blown up." His troubles were due to the guerrillas a single Ranger force was able to throw out around his chain of camps.

It is improbable that any outfit under the American flag is more knowledgeable about Japanese tactics almost on a folksy level. The Japanese naturally have a special distaste for the guerrillas. When one is captured, torture almost invariably ensues. A favorite device of the *kempeitai* in Burma is the water mask, an apparatus that straps a man's mouth open while water is poured into him. When he is inflated like a bladder, the Japanese m.p.s sit or jump on him until he talks or his organs burst. When the Japanese find the body of a Ranger they often cut off some part, usually his hands. The Rangers have no explanation for this mutilation. Perhaps it is obscurely connected with the fact that the Japanese, in lieu of sending home the ashes of a fallen soldier, nowadays cut off the end of his thumb, cremate that and send it to his family. After one recent ambush, where the guerrillas festooned a 120-yard stretch of road with simultaneously fused grenades, 104 cremated thumbs were sent to Japan.

To know what it means to be a guerrilla leader you have to spend a night lying flat in the rain with a telephone cramped against your ear, waiting for a message and listening with the other ear to the trigger-happy Kachins or Shans firing from the edge of your perimeter. Are they shooting Japs or nats? A silent green arc of Japanese flare rises from outside your farthest foxhole. Perhaps it is a signal for a concerted *banzai* charge. The frightened bullocks clamber to their feet, lowing wildly and struggling at their pickets. More flares greenishly scratch the night around you. The methodical Jap is tapping around the edge of your perimeter, like a blind man learning the outlines of a city block. The attack may come tonight or it may not come until tomorrow night. The danger hours are around nine, about two, and just before dawn. And then when your men—some of them only fourteen or sixteen years old, nearer Boy Scouts than soldiers—have tired of wasting ammunition, the dawn finally arrives. The Japanese, a night animal by preference in his attacks, has pulled back to sort out what he has learned. You may have to change your perimeter to cross him up, or you may have to break camp. Anyway, you can light your first cigarette.

You are drowsing over your morning coffee when a far-off vibration starts the air humming and thrumming. The murmur grows, too constant and undiminished to be the sunrise gong in the village. And then suddenly, with a roar, a C-47 comes thundering over the green hill of your outer perimeter. Your Jingpaws, rubbing the silver bells in their left ears, arise from their trenches and wave upward at the plane's blind, froglike nose. As it stammers overhead you cry out, "Somebody get out those panels!" and your *jemidar* rushes to see it done. You polish your signal mirror on your knee, and get it winking. Then the plane begins its circling. First, from about 300 feet the rice sacks are pushed out, five or six at a time. Freedropped, they hit hard and heavy. Then, while your bullock carts are being hitched to go out and get the rice, the grey-green plane's door expels other packages, their fall stayed just under and behind its tail by the abrupt opening of cotton parachutes. What is floating before you is probably salt, sugar, flour, K-ration and ten-in-one. Then, after new circlings, there descend under other canopies your ammunition, grenades, cartridges and the long black tubes that hold mortar shells. Finally, with a courteous special pass of the plane all to itself, there follows a last red rayon chute with a small and curious package, probably medicine but possibly mail. It will be half an hour before the bullock carts get everything collected and bring it in.

The transport gives the green, new-cut *bashas* where you are living a buzz so low the bamboo poles tremble, scaring the crows and the crickets into silence. The kicker, near enough to be discernibly grinning, waves his hand from his open door like a railway mail clerk, and suddenly the plane is gone over the hill again, and the motors fade away and the silence descends. You can see the first bags of rice being heaved up by your coolies into the first bullock carts. It is quiet; the jungle is still awed. For a moment, during the drop, you are back at Binjan, at Myitkyina, at Bhamo, places where there are movies, nurses, adjutants and beer. Then, as the crickets take up again, and the crows venture their first remarks, you realize that you are alone once more with your Jingpaws, and that there are Japanese all around you. You are alone, that is, until darkness again circles the world and reaches Burma.

—

Rainy Monsoon Giving Road Acid Test
Bhamo, Burma, on the Stilwell Road—July 9, 1945

Almost six months old now, Asia's most valuable and strategic highway, extending from Ledo, Burma, to Kunming, China, is at the halfway point in meeting its stiffest test, the monsoon. Will new stretches built by American engineers survive rising floods? In some places bridges have already been swept away and replaced. Will these temporary bridges endure?

I have just completed a low-level trip in a grasshopper plane over the first 367 miles of the road from Ledo to Bhamo. Though some bridge sites were torn by violent floods and strewn wreckage, long columns of American trucks still plodded faithfully toward China. Tomorrow I will join one such convoy, driving a jeep, which I hope will achieve the whole 707-mile drive from Bhamo over the Yunnan mountains and the Salween and Mekong rivers to Kunming.

The last *Chicago Daily News* correspondent who drove the Burma Road was Leland Stowe, just before the road was sealed in December, 1941. In those days it ran from Rangoon north through Burma, veering east at Lashio. Now, instead, the road begins high in the Himalayan foothills of Assam and runs one-third of its length south before turning east into China. In a remarkable series of articles Stowe revealed that pilfering, squeeze, graft, and misuse of lend-lease materials prevailed. This drew strong protests from Chinese authorities in Washington. One of my aims is to determine whether this security situation has improved since the road reopened.

The Burma Road is now in every sense an American highway, studded with American convoy stations, automotive repair companies, and hospitals. American investment is gigantic. Our engineers keep the twin-lane route open by a constant battle with landslides and mutilations of the surface caused by the unceasing trucks. Nothing ever comes down the most valuable highway of America's Asiatic battle. Everything goes into China without anything coming out, and that "everything" is American.

The revival of the Burma Road was urged by General Stilwell, but opposed by Lord Mountbatten as impractical. As Mountbatten claimed, most of the tonnage—now nearly 50,000 a month—is carried by American Transport Command "Hump fliers" from numerous air fields around the Chabua-Ledo area. But the Burma Road has made it possible for thousands of trucks (which could never have flown) to go to China under their own power. It has made possible the American-built pipeline and newly-completed telephone line which parallel the road and are serviced along it. The Burma Road thus does three jobs which aviation never could.

On a cost basis, like everything else in the war, it is impossible to determine whether we are getting our money's worth. If the United States adopts a vigorous foreign policy in this area, something may be recovered in future highway tolls. But the cost of all we now supply to China is so colossally high in transport terms that valid comparisons are impossible.

American critics of the quantity furnished China under lend-lease often overlook this. They compute lend-lease on the factory side, omitting the huge distribution overhead. If the costs of transportation and delivery are included, the true generous dimensions of America's aid to China are revealed.

The eventual opening up of China's coastal ports will modify but not dismiss the permanent importance of the road in American foreign policy. China is now divided into Communist Kuomintang and Japanese-occupied. Whatever divisions persist after the war, free entry into China remains important for America's interest.

The Burma Road is the twin of the American-built highway from the Persian foothills in the Caucasus to the Persian Gulf. The former is the eastern back door into Asia and the latter is the western. The Persian road is vital in determining the balance of power in oil on which the United States depends to replenish overdrawn resources. The Burma Road is the key to Anglo-Russo-Chinese relations, wherein all the great powers are involved.

—

LUCK AND NINE GEAR SHIFTS MAKE
ANYONE A MOTORIST

Burma Road Deserves Its Title: "Infernal Gate"

Kunming, China—July 18 & 25, 1945

You too can learn to drive the Burma Road. You can, that is, if mud is your preferred habitat, if you can skirt a precipice by inches and not go over, if you can sleep in a rain-soaked bedroll, shave by a side mirror, and live off K rations eaten sitting on the hood of an overheated motor. And learn to drive with a trailer.

Americans call it the Burma Road. The Chinese call it the Infernal Gate. You have to travel it to find out how much better is the Chinese name for that 700-mile rollercoaster of mud from Bhamo to Kunming—the best argument, in monsoon time, for air travel.

I have just finished driving the Burma Road in a lame convoy of battle-worn American vehicles. My steed was a war-weary, road-saddened jeep with no speedometer, defective tires, imperceptible brakes, no tools and no relief driver. Behind this pathetic orphan rattled a helpless trailer, striving with guileful persistence to drag the entire combination over precipices whose sides are already littered with the carcasses of far better vehicles. Bravely lettered with the words *Chicago Daily News,* this pathetic tandem struggled in mud so high that the frogs were staring in over the dashboard and multi-ton bulldog tractors occasionally were required to pull us through. Repeatedly this sponge-bath on wheels was passed by long columns of brand new lend-lease jeeps driven by Chinese soldiers.

China needs vehicles. What China needs, America tries to provide. That is why over a thousand miles from India through Burma to China is one squirming, swimming, bumping line of American vehicles. That's why Americans taking convoys through—nameless sergeants, lieutenants, captains and plain G.I.s who wallow like swine and whom nobody cares about—gradually go grey. You can look over the road's outside edge and wonder how they do it.

The problem children are the big trailers which have to fight their way around bends and start minor avalanches when their corners tear away the earthen embankments. The grades tilt up to 16%. In thirteen places you climb over passes more than 7200 feet high. That means you must have complete mastery of either the nine possible forward gear shifts of a jeep, or the fifteen of a big truck. When you come to one of the half-mile-long mudholes called a camp, you have to be able to back your vehicle-trailer combination as well as manage it in forward speeds. A trailer will jackknife seemingly without provocation and be found biting at your elbow when you think it is stretched out tailwise behind. Front-wheel movements are reversed, as everyone knows, in going backwards. But in going backwards with a trailer, they are reverse-reversed for the starting impetus, then must be changed to plain-reversed. A trailer asked to back at too sharp a curve rises in the air on one wheel, making piteous sounds. If these fail, it tries to turn over.

While all this is happening there are always seven Chinese urchins at hand, grinning and calling "Ding hao!" (super-okay) with thumbs upraised.

Every convoy is broken down into sections called "serials." You stay in position unless you break down. When the convoy commander was at the top of a serpentine road up a mountain he could talk with the sub-commander of his last section just crossing a bridge below. "Hello, C-serial, this is Charley-Charley. We are about ten miles ahead of you and 4000 feet above. I can see you crossing the bridge but I do not see the wrecker. Over."

"Hello, Charley-Charley. You do not see the wrecker because the mess-trailer in B serial fell out with a broken spring. The wrecker stayed with him. Over."

Every convoy on the Burma Road goes armed, even though bandit attacks have almost ceased. The road camps do not provide any guards, and the tired drivers have to stand their own sentry duty. The military police control the camps and the hours of departure, which are usually from four to seven in the morning. You get up an hour and a half before you leave and you do your own grease job which has to last two hundred miles. A hundred miles of Burma Road is considered equal to a thousand miles of American highway in wear and tear.

The style of thought of Americans on the Burma Road is optimistic, but sardonic. Here is what the m.p.s have to say to their guests at Mong-Yu, the last stop in Burma before Wanting, the Chinese border station. Their placard reads:

Take a look at the side walls of the tents you occupy tonight. The convoys before you have taken down these walls and used them as rugs, mattresses and drapes . . . Saki is Bu-How (no good). We use it for a gas substitute here, so if you want to drink it, go ahead. But wait till you get back home . . . Villages are off-limits. The women may look good to you, but don't let that fool you. The bugs are here if you are really looking for them . . . Keep the villagers out of your convoy area. They will steal you blind when your back is turned. But any native you see walking post is an American soldier who has done more to lick the slanties than many of you will get to do or have done. Treat them with respect. Most were given discharges from the army at an age when you were in high school.

At the Salween River gorge, which is something like the Grand Canyon done in green, I saw a truck which had fallen about 100 feet straight down, then caught on a jutting rock. In its suspended ominousness it suggested the Infernal Gate more than do those ferociously cannibalized, wheelless, motorless skeletons flanking the roadside which salvagers have hauled up from limbo. When Americans get through salvaging the cargo and whatever else they can of martyred trucks, the Chinese start in. The result looks like a rusty shell cast aside by a mammoth beetle. Some are bullet-ridden, for it is not long since Japanese Zeros veered like butterflies through the valleys, scourging the convoys. But today when you see, as our convoy did, the body of an American negro G.I. at the roadside, stiff in death, and hear a report that three drivers were killed at Mong-Yu last week, you know it's the Infernal Gate, not the Japs, which led these unmentioned heroes through a gate even more infernal.

"I keep ready to jump any second," is the remark you hear most often, for almost every curve is blind and unmarked. One merit is that little traffic is coming at you. Anything coming toward you, in Burma Road slang, is "reverse lend-lease."

Almost three hundred convoys of all sorts, lengths, and make-ups have mastered the Burma Road since it was opened in late January. At that time the seven hundred miles from Wanting, the Chinese border post, to Kunming were smooth by Asiatic standards. Now they're rowelled, rutted and puddled. My average speed actually driving was about seven miles an hour. My average progress for ten days of infernalization was three miles an hour. The clouds overhead buzzed and murmured day and night with hump aircraft, traveling at 200 miles an hour.

Anyone who crawls through the Infernal Gate with grease in his mouth and mud in his hair is a soldier, a war correspondent, or crazy. Any two guesses are right.

20/8/45

Announcement by Commander

Both Japan and the Allies stopped the fighting under an agreement and Truce will be signed shortly. Then the war which has lasted almost four long years will be all over. We know you are tired of the life in the war prison[...] We can imagine how happy you are now. Your long cherished hopes to be with your loved ones will be fulfilled. We are not enemies now. We are friends with one another. We want to see you go back where your loved ones are and begin to enjoy your normal lifes.

At present we don't know exactly when you start for your homeward journey. We will let you know as soon as the date is announced by the army. Until then let us have [...] life. We will help you that you may be able to start for home safely. On the other hand you are requested to keep orderly lifes, and observe the rules and regulations till then.

The Commander

XX

Japan Defeated

Weller was in Chungking, China, when both atomic bombs were dropped (August 6 on Hiroshima, August 9 on Nagasaki) and Japan surrendered (August 14). He hurried to the Philippines, along with hundreds of other reporters, to join MacArthur's invasion force for the treaty signing. He almost immediately ran into trouble with the general's censors—a blockade over his story (now lost) about Corregidor, a Gibraltar in the mouth of Manila Bay. Many American servicemen had been killed or captured bravely trying to defend this U.S. base for five months in 1942 (see Chapter XI). When it was finally taken back by MacArthur's adroit paratroops in February 1945, thousands of enemy died in tunnels dug at the top of the island. Weller, in Manila, fell afoul of a captain in charge of censorship:

"Having seen and described Japanese skulls from Buna to Myitkyina, I saw no harm in mentioning that there was one skull still underfoot in the exploded tunnels of the Rock. 'You can't mention that skull; it would allow the enemy to know we have not been able to bury their dead respectably,' said this unusually deft player. 'But there is no enemy,' I said, a little wildly, perhaps. 'Japan caved in early this month. Didn't the news come through channels yet?' The censor, without replying, took a nice easy stance and thudded my Japanese skull into the corner wastebasket. The perfect ending to four years of censorship."

The August 22 dispatch ("The Iron Curtain of Censorship") was also totally killed. It provides a preview, only a week after

Japan had caved in, of MacArthur's muzzling of the press as a fundamental technique.

More complicated questions are raised by Weller's first dispatches from Tokyo, "an ashtray filled with the cigarette butts of buildings." These dispatches, from September 1, were passed by the censors but never published by his newspaper. One was about the radiation effects of the atomic bomb; another would have been the earliest on-the-ground graphic descriptions of the fire-bombings of Tokyo, here described by Weller as a frying pan. (Despite what some historians have suggested was a conspiracy of silence, accounts of these firebombings did appear in the mainstream American press a week later.)

Following the treaty signing in Tokyo Bay on September 2, Weller was the only correspondent who flew south to an island *kamikaze* base near the southern tip of Kyushu on September 3 to ostensibly cover the landing of American forces. He sent one dispatch the next day, turned in another late the following night to be transmitted, and before dawn on September 5 got a boatman to take him across to the mainland. Then he caught a succession of trains to Nagasaki, where—posing as a U.S. colonel—he spent four days exploring the ruined city (September 6–9).

On September 10 he made his way north forty miles to Omuta and the largest Allied prison camp in Japan, Camp #17, with seventeen hundred American, British, Dutch, and Australian POWs who had survived years of malnutrition, disease, torture, and forced labor in coal mines. Though some prisoners had seen both atomic bombs explode, Weller's presence was their first proof that the war was over. These events are all recounted in his censored dispatches, in *First into Nagasaki*. I have included one POW dispatch found after that book's publication.

I have chosen to conclude this volume with a short story that Weller wrote after leaving Nagasaki by ship for Guam via

Okinawa, Saipan, and Iwo Jima. It takes place in a POW camp evidently modeled on Omuta #17. "Departure, with Swords and Ashes" was sent to his agent, Harold Ober, from Guam, and published by the *Saturday Evening Post* in the issue of March 23, 1946. This popular weekly magazine often carried Weller's fiction and journalism, yet the delay suggests that editors thought it better to wait before running such material. The five-thousand-word story includes details of the camps after the recovery teams arrived that did not make it into any of the dispatches, written now not with a reporter's but with a novelist's eye.

Omuta #17, which the bulk of Weller's censored POW dispatches describe, was one of the harshest such camps in Japan. Its facilities were somewhat better than others'; there was bathing water a few months a year. Its thirty-three buildings, originally laborers' quarters built by the Mitsui Coal Mining Company, had some ventilation—a liability during winter. The coal mines were about a mile walk from camp. Theoretically, men were given a day off every ten days, though sometimes they worked for four weeks straight.

The owner of the mines, Baron Takaharu Mitsui (1900–1983), a graduate of Dartmouth and world famous as a philatelist, was head of one of the two most powerful industrial families in Japan (along with Mitsubishi), and among the wealthiest men in the country. His mines produced half of its coal, though those at Omuta had been closed down in the 1920s as unsafe. He was well aware of the work and living conditions of the POWs, having visited the camp several times in his open touring car. Like other companies that used Allied prisoners—Kawasaki, Mitsubishi, Nippon Steel—Mitsui paid a leasing fee per prisoner of two yen per day, and the government kept the money. Though the prisoners were supposedly paid a wage that was a minuscule fraction of this, very few received anything.

Because of this prisoner slave labor, such vast companies maintained full production throughout the war. Due to the delay between surrender and the occupation, they were able (unlike equivalent German companies) to obliterate a damning paper trail before the Americans arrived. They persuaded MacArthur's representatives that it was in no one's interests to slow down Japan's recovery by holding millionaire industrialists legally and financially responsible for what they had done in wartime. Indeed, many returning American POWs were ordered by intelligence officers never to speak of their experiences under the Japanese unless given military clearance; some were compelled to sign documents to this end.

The story is rooted in actual events. For example, it describes the Baron Mitsui figure (here called Baron Satsumai) asking the prisoner recovery team over for tea; Major Toth, senior officer among the prisoners, refuses to go, and the head of the recovery team cannot understand why. There is also a discussion of the food trading among U.S. prisoners that so shocked other POW nationalities and which Weller mentions only once in his *Chicago Daily News* dispatches.

—

Japs, Yanks Begin Talks

Manila, Philippines—August 20, 1945

Talks between MacArthur's staff officers and Japanese military envoys, which recessed at noon today, are reducing to military terms the political problem of a peaceful occupation of Japan.

The talks are being conducted in Manila's former City Hall, one of the less shell-smashed ruins of public buildings. These talks are on what might be termed a police level between Japanese forces and the Allies, with Americans in the leading role as negotiators. Although focused into perhaps unnatural brilliance by being the first contact between victor and vanquished, the talks do not pretend to touch on the central political issues which will eventually determine America's future in Asia. It is as though police chiefs of two rival towns with a long record of hotheaded rivalry were meeting so that the next encounter of explosive forces can be managed with the fewest possible broken heads.

It is neither a peace conference, a political conference, nor even a surrender conference, but merely a preliminary to a surrender conference. The business of the talks is merely to determine how the U.S. forces shall enter that strategically no longer very important part of East Asia which comprises the Japanese home islands. America's main geopolitical question remains how to control Japan's relations with the Asiatic nations, but it is uncertain whether any progress has been made on this point. While the protection of U.S. interests in the triangle of Korea, Manchuria and North China is still militarily obscure, the home islands at least may be said to be already under MacArthur's control.

While businesslike and straightforward in tone, without recriminations or emotions, the two days of talks have been shadowed by future uncertainties. No foreign nation has ever occupied Japan before. In the delegates today there was nothing submissive or broken. These Japanese, although they talked frankly—"sincerely" was the adverb used by one MacArthur spokesman—conducted themselves with the same air of being spiritually intact as characterized by the Emperor's statements and the Domei News Agency's self-righteous broadcasts.

[With a punctiliousness more appropriate for the victor than the vanquished, Japan informed General MacArthur by radio tonight that Allied parties bent on rescuing prisoners and internees in Mukden, Kijo and Hong Kong have been "made to return to their base." The Japs coolly suggested that "visits by Allied officers and men before arrangements are made, even if notified in advance, are likely to hamper the realization of our desire to effect smoothly and satisfactorily a cessation of hostilities and a surrender of arms."]

These two days of technical military talks have been merely a red, white and blue version of Wainwright's surrender of U.S. forces at Corregidor and Percival's of British at Singapore. What the Americans are after politically in Asia is as foggy as ever, and—judging by the behavior of these delegates— Japan is whipped but does not consider herself tamed.

THE IRON CURTAIN OF CENSORSHIP

(This story was never published. Weller scrawled on it:
"Killed by censorship.")

Manila, Philippines—August 22, 1945

The iron curtain of censorship was clamped down today at MacArthur's headquarters on all details regarding the coming occupation of Japanese-held territory. In the meantime, Tokyo Radio and the Domei News Agency continued to pour forth a flow of purported details of how, when, and where all Japanese-held territory was destined to be occupied.

This curious situation of the vanquished announcing the details of a coming surrender which the victor grimly refuses either to confirm or to deny can be considered typical of the Pacific situation today. Whereas in Germany, British, American and Russian armies did their occupying first and their talking afterward, Japan seems to be—at least in the eye of MacArthur's headquarters—just as much a problem in logistics and military secrecy after the "unconditional" surrender as before.

In some senses, this attitude of supersecrecy is undoubtedly justified. Never conquered before in her history, Japan is still a land of the unpredictable. But the paradox has arisen that while MacArthur's planners have been forced to put most details of the forthcoming occupation in Japanese hands in order to insure their success, they cannot—for reasons which may well be good and sufficient—reveal them publicly.

Meantime, without hindrance or even rebuke, Japanese Radio continues broadcasting to the world that the first American party will land by plane at Atsugi Airdrome on the west side of Yokohama next Sunday, and that the main naval landing will occur on Tuesday at Yokosuka. Because—by reason of many imponderables—responsibility for security has shifted to the Japanese, the initiative for announcements is also theirs, causing some observers to inquire: "Say, who's surrendering here, anyway?"

[*The rest of the dispatch is missing.*]

FREEDOM AT HAND FOR POWS

Manila, Philippines—August 25, 1945

Freedom itself will be enough for 32,000 Allied prisoners about to be released in Japan, but hundreds of officers and men are now working to make that freedom sweeter for their comrades awaiting liberation.

On a cool green hill twenty miles from the dusty chaotic rubble of ruined Manila, a camp of green tents is growing. It is quiet and beautiful. Visiting there today, the writer found the hills like the rolling country of Wisconsin or Michigan. A Dutch prisoner of war—an officer who escaped from Java by submarine at the same time as the writer—thought the countryside was more like Java. Either way, it is perfect because at the 29th Replacement Depot some 7000 Americans will taste liberty in company with some 5000 Dutchmen. Down the road about a mile is the 5th Replacement Depot where some 15,000 British, 5000 Australians and 1000 Canadians will go. These "repple depots" now converted into "recovery centers" face outward on beautiful Laguna de Bay, a freshwater lake about fifteen miles across. Smoky blue mountains shoulder themselves up against the horizon and a delightful breeze never stops blowing.

Pitifully little is actually known about who or where our prisoners are in Japan. Some information is on hand regarding the location of prison camps. Nearly half those in Japan are within two hundred miles of Tokyo. But due to Japanese noncooperation, almost nothing is known about which soldiers are where.

The Japanese have offered to assemble all prisoners in seven camps at key points. Whether this offer will be accepted is unknown. One high officer in recovery duties told me today that otherwise the recovery from the Japanese islands might take forty-five to sixty days from the American landing on Sunday.

Our records on prisoners are naturally fragmentary because of the circumstances under which we lost the Philippines. For example, the writer has searched for two days to find the names of Maywood's famous 192nd Tank Battalion. The best available information here is five names of officers, but none of enlisted men. Their location is simply unknown and will not be disclosed until Japan and Asia itself are searched.

The men who head the recovery teams and the transit camp to American soil are unsparingly energetic and imaginative. Many tents of this "Freedom House" are pitched on Japanese cement. The enemy selected this site above the lake for a medical supply base. Each of the four battalions in the depots has about 180 men and officers, and can care for 5000 ex-prisoners—but it won't be for long. The aim is that none will stay more than five days before being hustled off to the United States. Everybody is expected to eat from five to eight meals daily—or upward. Originally the mess tables were corrugated in order to keep the boys from dreaming over their coffee. But now, by order of Captain Edward Healy, they are being flattened out. "Let 'em dawdle all they want," says Healy.

—

BOMB'S FATAL EFFECTS CONTINUE

(This dispatch is stamped *Passed By Censors,* but was never published.)

Tokyo, Japan—August 31, 1945

The atomic bomb holds first place over any other element as the cause of Japan's decision to surrender, according to Japanese civilians with whom I've talked.

At first the authorities held down newspapers from announcing the bomb's effect on Hiroshima, but leakage began after four or five days. Now the newspaper *Asahi,* with two million circulation, is planning a book detailing the bomb's effects on Hiroshima and Nagasaki.

Japanese censorship was doubly effective because internal circulation was almost halted, and therefore refugees from Hiroshima—and therefore the truth—could not reach Tokyo masses even by gossip.

When authorities decided to inform people of what might be in store for them, [Japanese] Army members of the Censorship Board had cushioning stories released saying that people in white shirts with sleeves escaped burning, and also that those underground went unscathed. The last story was partly true since the only survivors came from dugouts.

The government was compelled to release the truth by the fact that many who escaped—as they thought—the effect of the atomic bomb with light wounds went to live with relatives in other cities and died as much as a week after.

Sadao Maruyama and Keiko Sonoi, an eminent stage actor and movie stage actress, were living in Hiroshima. Both escaped. Maruyama came to Tokyo. After three or four days he began claiming that he felt excessive warmth in his stomach. After five days, the warmth had turned to burning. At the end of a week he suddenly cried to the friend with whom I talked, "I feel as though my insides were burning out." He rushed to the bathroom, guzzled water and stepped into a cold shower where he abruptly died. An autopsy showed his entrails eaten away.

Actress Sonoi, after Hiroshima, went to Kobe and telegraphed Tokyo, "I am happy to have been saved." She had only a small swelling of her wrist. But the swelling spread and soon covered her whole body. Her hair fell out. In approximately a week, she too died.

These seemingly healthy persons who died many miles from Hiroshima many days afterward were the actual breakers of censorship, who compelled the military to allow the truth to be told about Hiroshima. Small wonder that some Japanese have been asking correspondents: "When will we get scientific equality?"—meaning the secret of the atomic bomb.

—

TOKYO IN RUINS

(This dispatch is stamped *Passed By Censors,* but was never published.)

Tokyo, Japan—August 31, 1945

With American troops still confined to their perimeters around Yokohama and the Yokosuka naval base, the occupation is still not being felt by Tokyo and the rest of Japan. MacArthur and his host generals—like George Kenney, Carl Spaatz, and Lt. General Robert Eichelberger—spent their second day in Japan establishing headquarters on "Consular Row" in Yokohama. With Japanese coastal emplacements now nullified, the prohibition on residences overlooking this magnificent harbor has become a dead letter, and several generals and admirals acquired seaside villas. Businesslike machine guns guard the approaches to these streets, but the air of tension has almost dissipated. Every one of MacArthur's six-foot paratroopers has a post, but the powder keg feeling has gone away.

The Japanese fear of the American occupation was due to governmental propaganda emphasizing that Americans plundered and raped wherever they conquered. Ninety-nine per cent of Japan's masses are still enmired in this propaganda and will not know better until proof is offered. Yokohama is an example in that the chief of the civil police force "suggested" that all women and girls should leave Japan's first seaport by August 26, two days before the American landing, in order to protect their virtue. One result was that the streetcar system instantly broke down because all motoresses and conductorettes fled. Now they are returning. But in Tokyo many daughters have been sent to the country by families for the same reason. American officers treat this situation with a kindly tolerance slightly mixed with derision. "Our boys won't look at the girls unless the girls look at them," one general told the writer.

Long trains of open cars filled with soldiers headed for demobilization pass through Tokyo's railyards. Their attitude is dumbly obedient, but they are also full of health and vigor. Squads marching along the streets give the impression of discipline and purpose, contrasting with the disintegration for which they are destined.

With light rains and the low-lying clouds, fighters and *bekos*—the Japanese name for B-29s, meaning "B-babies"—swept continually over Tokyo. Their flights were random and appeared more for sightseeing than security. Few Americans like Major Winslow Lewis of New York, with thirty-nine unbelievable months in B-25 bombers, managed to get through to Frank Lloyd Wright's Imperial Hotel, whose lava-born walls are all intact and only one wing's floors burned out. Among those greeting Americans was Father Bruno Bitter, a German Jesuit who for two years taught summer courses in economics at Loyola and is now the rector of Jochi Catholic University. Only one wing of this university has been burned, and only one building at St. Paul's American Episcopalian University. The former American School, for pupils from kindergarten to high school, was wholly unscathed.

The B-29 raids of March 10 and May 25 will go down in Japan's history as the worst, the former because an area about four miles square became a frying pan for approximately 100,000 people—more than a third of Tokyo's deaths for the whole war—and the second raid because it was carried out in a wind of typhoon proportions.

The March raid hit the triangle between Sumida Creek and the Arakawa River. Factories with industrial tenements were the target. The Japanese excuse their failure to provide air-raid shelters here by saying that they lacked the concrete for service shelters against a blast, and wherever they went underneath the river or the harbor, water flooded shelters. B-29s first outlined the district variously called Koto Honjo or Fukagawa with Pathfinder firebombs. The inhabitants were penned in by a circle of fire, and huddled Japanese-fashion in the center. Then main waves of bombers filled in the pattern with a deadly result. Even workers who slipped through the ring of fire found themselves unable to cross the two rivers, for bridges and also barges were burned. Yet most perished from the smoke of suffocation rather than through actual burning.

The May raid was decisive, because it showed that flames would leap across even firebreaks under windy conditions. It also demonstrated that the little red engines of the Tokyo Fire Department could not hold back the flames except where buildings of heavy stone gave them occasional protective shelter.

Americans are being asked by the liberal press to be patient about coming to terms with Japan. The English-language daily *Nippon Times,* successor to the *Japan Advertiser,* says that although Potsdam conditions were accepted with "unwarranted slowness" and Manila envoys were tardy in going toward MacArthur, Americans should make haste slowly. "The complexities of the political machine even normally cause the Japanese government to move with a slowness which may appear strange to efficient Americans." The paper pointed out that three elements made certain that Japanese cooperation with Americans would be genuine and not merely a masked docility. The first reason is that the Japanese are "feverishly anxious" to fulfill terms because this is the first hurdle to rehabilitation. "The quickest, surest way to redemption lies in a quick, complete atonement." The other two guarantees, according to the paper, are that the Japanese are naturally good sportsmen, a sense of injury is harbored by only a few, and many Japanese were already favorable to Allied aims. "It is to be hoped that when American correspondents secure the opportunity to study the new Japan at first hand, they'll see fit to discard their attitude of suspicion." The *Nippon Times* has been edited for three-and-a-half years by Kazuo Kawai, a former instructor in history at the University of California.

The first G.I.s who enter Tokyo after MacArthur receives the surrender will find little worth buying as souvenirs. Across the burned empty lots fronting the Ginza, Tokyo's Michigan Boulevard, the writer picked his way into a shattered department store. Only the bottom-most of about ten stories was open and offered foolish cheap ornaments and outdated maps of the one-time Greater East Asia Co-Prosperity Sphere. No clothing whatever was on sale.

The yen, once three to a dollar, is now fifteen to a dollar. Meat is obtainable on the black market for about seven dollars a pound.

—

Spying Eyes Haunt Jap-American Girl

Tokyo, Japan—September 1, 1945

"That girl looks American," said one American newspaperman to another as we stood on an elevated train platform in the Ginza district of downtown Tokyo.

We were awaiting the train to Yokohama; the girl was going the other way. We crossed the platform and in the next hour found what it was like to be a *Nisei* ("the other way")—a young, pretty girl, pronouncedly American in appearance, yet partly of Japanese blood—in wartime Tokyo.

"Every time the B-29s came over, Mother used to say, 'Why don't they hurry up and rescue us?' It seemed so terribly long," said the girl.

Her mother is a Cincinnati woman who was married to a Japanese student in the United States, came to Japan with him, and found that it was not a land of cherry blossoms and dolls but police and Spartan living. She separated from her husband and earned a living for herself, two daughters, and her own mother by working in an American oil company.

Nothing about the girl on the elevated platform was Japanese except a trace in the corners of her eyes and flashing white teeth. Her accent, her frankness, her quick laughter were all American. But almost every other sentence she spoke had the word "police" in it.

Before the correspondents spoke with her, both she and they were simply members of the crowd without being particular objects of attention. The moment they approached her, a gawking and not particularly friendly crowd in rainy-day clogs and military caps gathered.

"I'm sure someone will see me talking with you and report me," she said. "There are always several police spies around."

The girl explained that she had made the trip from her suburban home in order to get a copy of the *Nippon Times,* Tokyo's English-language newspaper.

"For two weeks we've been too frightened to go into town and find out what's happening. All we do is work in our garden and hope the Americans come. We've been very short of money since I lost my job at a French bank in April."

The two newspapermen first tried to persuade her to come with them to the American-held area, around Yokohama. She said: "I could never go there. The police are worse there even than in Tokyo. I could not get home, and my mother would worry."

She had difficulty grasping the idea that it was now the Americans who were in control of Yokohama's police and she would be safe.

Government officials tried to get her to go to work on Tokyo Radio as a kind of assistant to Tokyo Rose.* (Tokyo Rose is now supposed to be "too ill" to receive newspapermen.) "I went to the studio one day. I saw many American prisoners doing broadcasting. It seemed as though I could too, if they did. We needed money badly. But I decided I could not do it and feel right. So I just let the police think whatever they wanted, and stayed home."

The correspondents took her to Yokohama and introduced her to the 8th Army's leader, Lt. General Eichelberger, who started her on the route to working for the Americans. She was not promised a job, but was given hopes of one.

She wanted to know what was the new dance music in America; her last record was *Deep Purple.* She had never heard of *Oklahoma!* Why hadn't

---

*Generic name invented by U.S. soldiers for (as it turned out) a number of different Tokyo Radio women broadcasting propaganda, in English, throughout the war.

she tuned in on Tokyo Rose, who had all the latest records? "Because we were not allowed sets that could hear her. Those broadcasts were just for Americans, not for Japanese."

The correspondents then commandeered a Japanese army truck and took her back to the Yokohama elevated station. Her face was beaming, but she had a final question: "You both keep talking about G.I.s. What's a G.I.?"

"Lady, you're going to find out—and soon."

She entered the elevated turnstile alone and was gone, with her head full of worries about the police.

—

HIROHITO IS ACES WITH JAPS AFTER RESTORING PEACE:

Increased Popularity Makes Staying on Throne a Sure Bet

Tokyo, Japan—September 4, 1945

Emperor Hirohito is here to stay. Any talk of his abdicating or being forced to abdicate can be forgotten. Acceptance of President Truman's terms for the first defeat in Jap history merely has brought the *Tenno,* as the Emperor is known to his subjects, more respect and affection than ever before. If the Allied intention is to "use" the Emperor and discard him later, they are already beaten. But if their intention—as seems likely—is to retain him permanently, they have succeeded.

The reason why the imperial tradition and the Emperor himself have emerged on top is because his acceptance of peace terms has caused the whole nation to heave a gasp of relief. For months peace had been their unspoken thought. As the insular empire fell before MacArthur and Nimitz, and the British (with American aid) gained in Burma, and Chinese troops recovered the Ledo Road, the Japanese saw their empire shrink. Then the terrible raids of *bekos,* B-29s, taught them that the choice was between death and defeat, with defeat inevitable anyway.

But nobody dared say what was obvious to all: that the Empire's new armor still left Japan naked. The thought police were everywhere. The thought police have two independent bureaus of spies, listeners and informants: the political department of civil police, and the political department of gendarmerie which was under the war department. To eavesdropping agents of these two bureaus—the latter of which has been "abolished" by the present liberal government—it would have been treason for anyone to say that Japan should accept the Potsdam terms. In the eyes of any civilian it would have been worse than treason; it would have been poor form. But meantime unventilated resentment was piling up against the hopeless course of the war. Relatively few had lost sons in battle, yet the home islands were seared with death.

There was admiration for the army and navy, as well as for courageous individuals, especially kamikaze pilots. But this was combined with impatience at the operation, by military officials, of domestic food and manufacturing controls. The military clique would have been able to maintain civilian loyalty much longer if its interference in internal economics had not made the home front chaotic.

The Achilles' heel of the military, which gradually deprived them of public support, was the misorganization of civil powers of production that they had so optimistically seized. This dissatisfaction turned to applause for the Emperor. But the Emperor's successful legerdemain, which both saved Japan and gathered the common people's loyalty around himself instead of around the military, naturally cost him much support among officers. The attitude of some was boldly expressed after the surrender when kamikaze pilots dropped pamphlets over Tokyo—this was never mentioned by Tokyo radio and was suppressed by censorship—reading:

There must be no surrender for the Tenno. We cannot believe that our Tenno can have surrendered to the enemy. No doubt surrender terms have been cooked up by those crafty high officials who surround the Tenno. We of the Navy Air Corps intend to act independently. People, don't believe what is written in the newspapers, and broadcast. Cooperate with us like true Nipponese. These leaflets fluttering from the skies were boldly signed *Commander, Navy Air Corps,* without any name.

Threats like these made Japanese envoys to MacArthur at Manila express the fear that their returning plane might be shot down by kamikazes, and throw a veil of secrecy over its schedule. Those staff officers who cooperated with MacArthur were regarded as belonging to the peace clique around the Emperor, hence as traitors to the officer class which desired to go on fighting.

When the kamikazes asserted they would act independently of the Emperor, they made as serious a blunder in gauging public opinion as the ground officers did in being caught with the squalling baby of misfired production. Kamikazes had been portrayed in movies before taking off for flights whence none ever returned; they were lionized. Like other military officers, they got to thinking they were statesmen. But when they asserted their freedom from the Emperor's will, they overreached. Their impudence went sour, and people sneered at their placing themselves above the throne. Their last ace—selfless devotion to the Emperor—had been trumped by an insolence so great it disgusted Tokyo's straphangers.

Behind this duel, which the Emperor has won with American help, lies an explanation of why Royal Premier General Prince Higashikuni is encouraging free speech and an uncensored press. Japan's royal circles have not gone suddenly insane over democracy. But everything the long-muzzled newspapers say about the military is a nail in its coffin, and a spangle on the Emperor's white horse.

—

Lower-Grade Japs Polite, Higher-ups Cool in Kanoya

With American Forces Occupying Kanoya, Kyushu, Japan—September 5, 1945

Encountering no resistance other than giant mosquitoes, the three-day-old American occupation of southern Kyushu is dickering with Japanese officials and firmly digging itself in. This *Chicago Daily News* correspondent was the only newspaperman to arrive with them.

Kyushu is mountainous, fir-covered country of rich green valleys and few farms, sharply in contrast to Tokyo's thick industrial suburbs. At sunset last night, the first landing ships grated on the coarse beaches of Kagoshima Bay, about one mile north of the fishing hamlet of Takasu. Takasu is a picturesque village whose shores are littered with the corpses of shot-down Japanese aircraft, and lies three miles inland over rolling country from Kanoya airstrip and town. Unloading began during the night, and by today the first six-wheel trucks of heavy wireless equipment began to rumble through the streets of deserted coastal villages. Big troop-carrying aircraft from Okinawa circled noisily at the edges of the valley, waiting their turn to descend on the single runway of Kanoya's two which remains usable.

Kanoya is one of the *kamikaze* (suicide pilot) fields for the raids which cost our shipping dearly around Okinawa. On these concrete airstrips talks of the Divine Wind were held with pilots—none of whom ever returned, and whose commander pledged to follow them to eternity. Now these strips are in the hands of unsuicidally-minded Americans.

It is a tribute to the selectivity of the intense bombing southern Japan has suffered that hardly a village has even a window broken. American fliers seem to have avoided civilian targets completely. This forbearance is in contrast with the long steel-cobwebbed ruins of hangars of which Kanoya has literally miles. Hardly ten square feet of roofing can be found intact. As a sympathy-getter, Japanese in Tokyo are making the most of the fact that American bombs hit not only factories but the tenements around them. But Kyushu's people speak with little dread of the bombings though they confess that the fighter raids, particularly by P-51s harassing truck traffic along the roads, bothered them greatly.

Barbed wires have been removed from the beaches where the Americans are landing, but closely interwoven fortifications, particularly along cliff edges, demonstrate how costly storming them would have been. The strongest points are also rich in fakes: wooden anti-aircraft guns complete with revolving gunners' seats, and phony tanks intended to draw American fire.

In dealing with Americans the lower-class Japanese sailors and soldiers are willing workmen, but their superiors vary in their degree of cooperation. When embarrassing or disadvantageous questions are put by Americans, the reply is sometimes "That man is not here," or "We do not know," though the contrary is proven true. The official tone, however, is cool but helpful.

Each evening Colonel Norman Sillen, the air force officer commanding this operation, confers with the Japanese civil military committee. The baldish Japanese major general sits across a table in the small hotel with the colonel beside him doing all the talking. The Japs also have two foreign office men sent from Tokyo to see that the Americans remain within the conditions of the Manila conference. Behind these Japanese are two tables of interpreters who are also all Japanese. Sillen handles these negotiations alone and seems somewhat outnumbered.

The Japanese are pedantically insistent that agreements be written down and hunt carefully for hidden traps or catches. For example, when one agreement said that negotiations would on go with "Japanese officials," the Japanese said that "governmental officials" must be so described or otherwise the Americans would be empowered to deal separately with any Japanese of their own choosing.

Characteristic of Japanese insistence on the letter of the law was their sending back to a camp somewhere in the north an American prisoner of war who managed to reach Kyushu. They insisted that no Americans had the right to give themselves up until freed. The landed Americans were ignorant that their comrade had reached Kanoya before the Japs bundled him north again.

—

MORE CHINESE PRISON CAMPS DISCOVERED

(This dispatch was censored and never published.)

Omuta, Kyushu, Japan—September 13, 1945

Acting on a hint from Chungking radio that many Chinese POW camps remain undeclared by the Japanese and undiscovered by Allied authorities, American officers who only recently ceased being prisoners themselves nearby have today discovered two such secret camps.

One camp near Kumamoto, traced and found by Navy Lieutenant Edward Little, proved a regular Shangri-La whose chiefly civilian prisoners had not even been told by Japanese authorities that the war was over. This camp is still under Japanese guard, and the Japanese only permit escorted prisoners to leave the walls. They are receiving 300 grams of rice daily and are without doctors or medicine, shoes or clothing. These civilian prisoners, mostly accused of unsympathetic acts against the Japanese, had been engaged by their captors in building air fields.

Another camp, with rooftops not marked as the Manila agreement specified, was found by Warrant Officer Houston Sanders. This camp, the third discovered by Americans near Omuta, has 546 Chinese soldiers captured in the Shenai drive. (Eighty were executed by the Japs since their arrival seventeen months ago.) About sixty per cent suffer deficiencies of vitamins A, C, or B_6.

Both Little and Sanders were formerly captives at Corregidor.

—

DEPARTURE, WITH SWORDS AND ASHES

A Short Story

"We made a pretty good showing at *tinko* tonight, considering," said Borum, the conscientious master sergeant of Camp 34, to Major Toth, the American veterinarian from Bataan, whom the Japanese had appointed commandant of prisoners.

"Considering what?" said Major Toth.

"Well," said Sergeant Borum defensively, "considering that it's been such a strain, waiting here for the recovery team. Every prisoner would like to go over the hill and turn up in Nagasaki or Kobe. Everybody knows he wouldn't be blamed for jumping the gun a little, not after three years' waiting."

"How were our percentages at *tinko* tonight?" asked the major.

"Dutch ninety-nine per cent, British ninety-five per cent, Aussies seventy-eight per cent and Americans sixty-nine per cent present," said Borum. "There might be a few of our guys shacked up around here, but most of them have probably thumbed a ride to Okinawa or Manila by now."

"I haven't seen Captain Ralston all afternoon," said the major. Captain Ralston was in charge of the four-man recovery team which had liberated the camp the day before.

"Baron Satsumai asked the whole recovery team over for tea," said Borum, his mouth commencing a smile. His smile, during his imprisonment, had acquired a peculiar and ironical Japanese twist, and often signaled a double meaning.

"The baron and baroness are sure polishing that old apple," said Major Toth mildly.

"Oh, they're just mending their fences," said Borum, diluting his irony with tolerance. "It's natural. After all, we'll be gone in a few hours. But another outfit is moving in to occupy and stay."

There were twenty-three square wooden boxes, each with a name and serial number painted on the plain yellow wood, stacked beside the major's desk. They contained the ashes of the American dead, two of whom had been beaten to death in the guardhouse. Major Toth rested his hand on the topmost box as he turned to look out the window, broken in the last bombing and half patched with paper.

The major could see outside in the prison yard the giant statue of a greenish-black miner, tall and inspirational—an idealized Satsumai miner towering above the doll-like buildings. At the feet of this behemoth of industrial propaganda two Americans were making a business deal. Halborn, a bearded seaman second captured at Cavite, was disposing of a sword to Mendoza, a 200th Coast Artillery gunner from Bataan. Mendoza, a clean-cut kid from Albuquerque, had lost four fingers the first winter, when the rotten, mushy ceiling of the mine, abandoned till the Americans arrived, vomited coal by tons on him as he picked at what the prisoners called the long wall—that is, the most advanced part of the coal face.

The deal was closed. The sailor walked away scratching his beard. Mendoza, acting on a buyer's impulse, turned and entered the prison office, swishing his new sword before him and setting the fat flies buzzing wildly.

"Hello, Captain Toth," he said. "Hello, Borum. Look, this sword I just bought, captain, I wanted to ask you—"

"Major Toth, since yesterday," reminded Borum gently under his breath. "And how about throwing a *kirei* to your commanding officer?"

Mendoza threw the salute. "Sorry, sir," he said. "Congratulations."

All three of them grinned; these promotions were part of the wild fantasy of their new freedom, all unreal, totally incredible.

The New Mexican kid held the salute, his skinny half-naked body at stiff attention. His garrison cap was hand-stitched from the tail of the O.D. shirt of a prisoner who was now ashes. His black slit-toed sandals looked like flappy comedian's shoes on his thin feet. His neck bones and backbone showed through his pale skin. Among the ulcers on his legs Toth recognized the old one which Lieutenant Bernstein, the medical officer, had nourished and kept alive with cap lantern acid, so that Mendoza, after his amputation, would not have to go down the shaft again. It was the most famous of Camp 34's many acid-fed ulcers; it had flourished nineteen weeks, and even in its present fossilized or emeritus condition it still had an eye like a devilfish.

"I hope you don't want to go home on points," said Toth.

Ralston's talk of the first day, in which he explained how hard the point system was going to be on the occupying army, was derision to the prisoners.

Mendoza relaxed, ignoring the question. "Sir, this sword. Take a look at it. Halborn owed me four rice rations and two cigarettes and a pickle. It's a legal debt, because it goes back to before you made trading food illegal. Now he offers me this sword to wipe out the debt. He's got a better one for himself, but this is the one he offers me." He held out the sword, once a cheap prop to the authority of some sergeant now flown on the wings of fear.

Major Toth took the sword, withdrew the blade until he saw rust, then shoved it back. "Good souvenir," he said.

Mendoza looked relieved as well as grateful; it's always shaky business discussing souvenirs with officers; now he had authority on his side. *I showed it to Major Toth,* he could say, if someone asked him. But he wanted a little more assurance.

"Now here's what I wanted to know, sir," he said, taking a big breath. He spoke very distinctly and emphatically. "Will they take these swords away from us in Okinawa or maybe in Manila when we board the plane for the States?"

Major Toth looked at Borum. Sergeants know everything. Borum looked back at Major Toth. This time he did not know. This question was from the outside world, beyond Camp 34, beyond even Nagasaki.

"Who told you they took swords away?" asked Toth.

"That corporal on the recovery team, when he was getting our serial numbers this morning."

"He was just trying to beat down the price," said Borum quickly. "You hang on to your sword. Don't let it go, no matter what they say. . . . Isn't that right, major?"

"I don't know," said Toth with a hesitancy unusual for him. "I might tell you that you could keep it, and still some brass hat might order you to turn it in."

A shadow was falling on him of the old bewilderment, the uncertainty that rottenly underlay everything in camp life, that supported the hunger, the dysentery, the stolen food parcels and the mail destroyed before one's eyes, and the corrupt ceilings of coal. Doubt was the mole of camp life, the mole under the miners.

He looked at Borum and Mendoza and it struck him how Japanese they appeared. Their hair, thin from malnutrition, was cut in that surly down-pulled cowlick affected by the Japanese infantryman. So was his own, for that matter. Under their patched trousers, he knew, they wore not shorts, but breechclouts. By sale, theft and compromise, Japan had crept in and occupied the fortress of each man's body. The Christmas before last, when he had had diarrhea, Borum had sold his own Bataan knife and fork for three rations of rice for him, and had eaten with nothing but chopsticks for nineteen months. Often he caught himself thinking whole sentences in Japanese.

Mendoza was still looking at the sword, and Toth felt impatient with himself for not being able to put his fears to rest. It reminded him of the afternoon when, after repeated rumors leaking through from Korean tunnels that Germany had surrendered, Lieutenant Kashihami had called him in. Because an Aussie had struck a foreman, Kashihami publicly had struck him, the Allied commandant, at morning *tinko*. But in the afternoon Kashihami offered him a cigarette. "Hitler has died," said Kashihami.

Was it a trick? Had Hitler really died? Or was Kashihami trying to bait him on something else? Nothing the Japanese ever said or did was unmotivated, except when they hit you, and that was like a reflex.

As the three prisoners stood looking at the sword, a jeep grated to a stop in front of the giant miner. Captain Ralston swung free his long legs and jumped out. He had a thin, pointed face, full of energy, and healthy black hair with something electric about it. To Major Toth, the hair of all the Americans on Ralston's recovery team appeared thick with an almost artificial brushiness. Their skins seemed unnaturally clear and ruddy, like girls on a magazine cover. Their strapped fieldboots were heavy, they carried their revolvers lightly in their shoulder holsters, and there was a hint of unexpended violence in their purposeful walk.

Captain Ralston came in, and Sergeant Borum and Mendoza saluted him. "Well, major, it looks as though our last train would be ready about two in the morning," he announced. "The slanties may go for an atrocity now and then, but say what you like, when you want a special train whipped up, they're right on the ball." Holding up his fingers, he ticked off his triumphs, "We got the Dutch out at eleven, the British at five, the Aussies and Wake Island civilians will be gone by seven, and I think we can turn the camp over to the Chinese and be aboard the train by one in the morning."

Not so fast, not so fast, the major wanted to say. *We've been here twenty-three months. Don't yank us out by the roots. Give us a little time.*

"Mendoza here has a sword," he said. "He wants to know whether they'll take it away from him in Okinawa."

"Let's see the sword," said the captain, with the air of a professional.

He had been hardly five days on Japanese soil, but on swords he had already a collector's eye. He drew the blade and looked at it frowningly. "Looks like a sergeant's, maybe from the military police," he muttered.

"That's right, a *kempeitai* sergeant," said Mendoza eagerly. "Can I get it through, do you think?"

Major Toth, watching Ralston finger the blade with connoisseur's precision, found himself inquiring silently where the brush-haired younger officer had been on an afternoon in April three years ago.

On the afternoon, two of General Homma's sergeants had arrived at Toth's camp on Bataan and by gestures indicated that they wanted to borrow a roll of toilet paper. When it was provided they went methodically around the circumference of the camp, tying little bowknots of toilet paper in the bushes. They then posted guards and explained that any American or animal who went outside the toilet-paper lines would be shot.

On that afternoon, Toth reflected, this healthy captain was probably sitting in some auditorium, sweating out an officer-candidate examination. And now Ralston was a captain of swords, while he was a captain of ashes.

Ralston had made up his mind about the sword. He looked Mendoza square in the eyes, deadly serious. "Try to get it through," he said. "If the MPs try to take it away, make them show you the ruling. But whatever you do, don't sell it to the Navy in Nagasaki. You can always get a better price in Okinawa or Manila."

Mendoza gave him a beaming Mexican smile, took back the sword, sheathed it, saluted and walked out.

"Captain Ralston," said Sergeant Borum. The captain turned readily to him. "Sir, there are a couple of things a lot of the men have been wanting to ask you. We haven't heard any news, you know, for a long time." The captain nodded encouragement. "First, can you tell us whether Bing Crosby is dead?"

"Bing is very much alive," said Ralston, picking him up quickly, as though he had been waiting and prepared for this very question. "So is Benny Goodman and so is Jack Benny. Those were just rumors that circulated around the camps in southern Japan."

"Who is dead, then?" asked Borum searchingly. "Who did those rumors actually refer to?"

"Nobody's dead," said Ralston cheerfully. "Nobody big that I know of." He began to pick up recovery forms from Toth's desk, and Toth observed that they were the forms for the deceased men whose ashes were in the boxes.

Ralston slid them unseeingly into his briefcase.

Suddenly he raised his head and looked at Borum sharply. "Of course, Roosevelt's dead," he said. "They certainly told you that, didn't they?"

"At the time, our officers thought it was just a new Jap trick," said Borum with his Japanese style of self-apologetic timidity. "You know, psychological warfare. They were always experimenting with little lies, testing our reactions."

"No," said Ralston, not greatly interested. "Roosevelt definitely died, right after Yalta. Yalta was a conference. Truman succeeded him— Truman—*T-r-u-m-a-n*. Bing and all that old gang, they're fine. Even Errol Flynn. . . . Major, would you care to ride over to the club with me in the jeep? I'd like to coordinate with you on a few things."

When Ralston and Toth drove through the open gate, the sun had gone down and the skeletons of the collieries stood out against the dark red in the west. Ralston turned on the headlights.

The Korean miners coming off shift, their lives unchanged by the liberation of the Americans, walked with sunken shoulders along the black, coal-saturated road on their way to their bunkhouses.

Toth lit a cigarette. Ralston at the wheel looked at it and saw it was Japanese. "Throw that nail away," he said. Toth looked inquiringly. "Throw it away, sir," said Ralston with a wink. The major still hesitated. The young captain reached a thick, freckled arm across the wheel, took the cigarette gently from the major's lips and threw it on the road, where two Koreans immediately sidled toward it. "Here," said Ralston, passing over a silver cigarette case. "Take an American smoke." He watched Toth light up, smiled, and then continued smiling ahead as he guided the jeep over the bumpy tracks of the Satsumai coaling yards.

"Now major," Captain Ralston said, "I've got a couple of things to check with you. First, did your engineering detail paint 'gone' in white on the roofs of all the buildings?"

"Finished them this morning," said Major Toth.

"Then that takes care of the drops," said Ralston. "It's like stopping the milk when you close an apartment. I'll have Nagasaki send confirmation to Saipan that we don't need any B-29 stuff, and tomorrow drops can go to the Chinese camps. Good. Now, what else was there? Oh, yes, ashes. You didn't have a camp chaplain, did you?"

"I used to read the services myself," said Toth quietly.

"Well, can you take care of the ashes, then?"

"All right."

"Have you got some sort of flag?"

"We've got a crude sort of camp flag we made out of parachute canopies from the drops," said Toth. "Do we need a flag before we get to Nagasaki?"

"As a matter of fact, we do. You see, major," said Ralston, "when we pull in on that train to the wharf siding at Nagasaki, things are going to get a lot more elaborate than here. But fast. Clean clothes, fumigation baths, Red Cross girls, a big Navy swing band, ice cream, telegraph blanks. Then those big white Navy hospital ships, and the admiral on his cruiser out in the middle of the harbor. So we have to watch appearances as we come in, especially about things like ashes."

"I always planned to take care of the ashes myself," said Major Toth. "Borum is packing all the boxes together in one big box the shape of a coffin. He and I will sit with it in the baggage car."

"How about the flag?" said Captain Ralston.

"Well, just before the train gets in to Nagasaki we can drape the flag over the big box."

"I should think the colonel ought to be satisfied with that," said Captain

Ralston, reasoning aloud. His young face cleared and relaxed. "That's about everything, I guess." He took a cigarette and lit it from Toth's. "Thanks. Everything on the serious side, that is. Now that we're cooking, how about a little recreation tonight? Feel like a little party?"

"What kind of party?"

"A geisha party, of course," said Ralston gaily.

They turned in to the driveway of the club where the executives of the Satsumai banks and mines used to meet when they came down from Tokyo. The Allied officer prisoners had moved in there at the baron's invitation after the B-29 drops began, two weeks before the arrival of Ralston and the recovery team.

"Who's giving the party?"

"The baron," said Ralston. "It's for the recovery team and the American officers of the camp. He told me to invite you."

"Did the baron tell you anything about working conditions in his mine?" said Toth. "Did he tell you that the mine had been abandoned as nonproductive before we arrived? Did he tell you that our boys lost their legs and arms stripping out the coal, knocking out the supporting pillars for less than a cent a day?"

"Well, I didn't push him too hard on that," said Ralston. He had the guarded air of an arbiter between extreme dissenters. "We're not war-crimes commission, you know; this team is strictly limited to prisoner re-covery. I just let the baron do the talking. He took his M.A. at Berkeley and enjoys showing off the slang he knows. He admitted conditions were de-plorable, but he said he was helpless. I get the impression that the military ran the mine over his head and never gave him much leeway to intervene."

"Did he tell you whether he knew about Pappy Ryan being beaten to death, and Bos'n Bill, and why the fellow we called 'Mother' Williams went mad?" Something indignant was stirring in Toth, deep below his prisoner's passivity. "Did he show you any of the clubs the size of baseball bats that were used on our men? Did he tell you why Doc Bernstein walks with a limp?"

"He didn't touch on any of that," said Ralston soothingly. "Maybe he knew about it, maybe he didn't. The baroness was there, and perhaps he didn't want to speak about that stuff before a lady. They both said they sympathized, and the baron kept repeating how much he admired you, now that he knew you."

Disgust turned in Toth's stomach.

"Two weeks' admiration, after two years' starvation," he said with unashamed bitterness. "You know what we call that around Thirty-four? We call it 'atomic love.' "

They entered the red-carpeted lobby of the Satsumai clubhouse, which was high-ceilinged and western, and resembled a Brussels brothel.

"I want you to understand this geisha thing," said Ralston uneasily. "It's just a way of having a hot dinner on the mine's expense account. This team isn't going to pull any shady stuff with the geishas. But I understand the girls cook the dinner, right at the table."

"I don't really like having the baron as host," said Toth, "either inside the camp or outside it."

"But the baron isn't even going to be there himself," protested Ralston. "He's in national mourning. It's just a little party for us."

No host, thought Toth. A sort of butlers-and-maids ball for Americans. "I guess I'll spend the evening packing," he said, as gently as he could.

"Bitter against them, aren't you?"

Toth thought a little. "I guess I don't have the same chivalric spirit as the baron," he said.

Toth was halfway up the stairs, at the landing with the big vase, when Ralston called up, "Hey, major, you know something?"

"What?"

"You've got damned good self-control."

"What do you mean by that?"

"Turning down this geisha party, I mean. Quite aside from what you feel about the baron, it must be a long time since you were—well, near a girl—"

"I don't want to be close to a geisha," said Toth.

"Are you married?"

"Yes and, furthermore, I've been lucky with letters, seven in the three years."

"Look," said Ralston, as though remembering something that had been on his mind a long time, "is it true that ninety per cent of the conversation in a camp like this centers around sex?"

"If you want to know what we actually talked about, it was food. Half the men in camp kept recipe books, full of imaginary dishes they'd made up. They were always exchanging new recipes. I know I dreamed more about food than about my wife. We were always hunting for new twists for dishes without rice in them."

It was the literal truth, but he could see, as he climbed the softly carpeted stairs, that Ralston was disappointed and perhaps did not believe him. What the hell, who could come from outside and see the baroness pouring tea and the Nip girl motormen stopping the streetcars to let you pass and even the *kempeitai* ducking their little shaven heads, and believe it ever happened? All the most feared guards had disappeared—Fishface, the Growler, Donald Duck and the Fresno Kid—with their *kabokos* and their whips of motor belting and their challenges of *"Sabis?"* ("You want a gift?") followed by a bone-breaking blow. Gone, all gone. It was ending up in a love feast, with swords and a few ashes.

The major had the club valet bring him up some eggs and camp buns with a package of K rations. He made a dry supper in his room. Then, after hearing Captain Ralston drive away in his jeep with Lieutenant—now Captain— Bernstein, he got out the seven letters from his wife. It was Thursday, his night for reading the letters, and he saw no reason for disturbing a routine that had been so satisfying to him.

He opened up the photograph of his wife and placed it on his bureau. He laid out one cigarette, two matches and a canteen of water. Then he undid the first letter, dated August 3, 1942. "Darling—" He read carefully and avariciously. If you read very slowly and pulled up hard at the periods, stopped and waited there awhile, you could sometimes wring out a new, an absolutely new thought from an old letter. You could not do this if you read the letters oftener than once a week. But if you waited a week, you could almost always find a new meaning in an old sentence. And one new thought often led to another. You could make a rereading of a single letter stretch out as long as a quarter of an hour.

This night, however, he fell asleep. When he awakened, the bedside lamp had been turned off. There was moonlight in the room, and before a cloud covered the moon he saw that Borum was in the big chair. He turned on the bed lamp. Borum did not stir. There was a faint smell of liquor in the air. Borum lay in the chair with his baldish head at an angle and his prison-crimped ears inattentive; he snored.

Borum was surrounded by a small collection of prizes. On the carpet were a mine lantern, a pick and the white-faced dial of the clock from the timekeeper's office. Hooked in his fingers were two Japanese lieutenant's epaulets, a little muddy, as though from struggle. And between his patched knees stood a sword, a big two-handed sword with a case in violet velvet and a crusted handle. When the bed creaked as the major put his feet on the floor, he straightened up.

"The geisha party is over, major," he said, yawning, rubbing a dry hand over his face and wetting his lips. "The Chinese have taken over the camp. The train is in. Captain Ralston sent me back with the jeep for you."

"Where are the ashes?" said the major.

"Downstairs in the jeep, with our flag over them. It looked like rain, and I had nothing to cover them but the flag. I don't think those parachute colors will run."

The major went to the porcelain bowl, where a generation of Satsumai executives from Tokyo had washed. He splashed water on his face, dried himself and came back. He stood over the sword and looked down on it.

"Is that Kashihami's sword?" he said.

"Yes, sir," said Borum.

"Why did you take it?" asked the major gravely.

Borum hesitated. "Sir, camp discipline ceased at ten-forty when the Chinese took over. Is that right?"

"Keep building. That'll do for a foundation. Keep building."

"Well, we heard that the baron had arranged a big wind-up scene for the geisha party. Lieutenant Kashihami was going to present Captain Ralston with his sword." Borum's face assumed a stubborn look. "Now, we figure Kashihami's sword belongs more to you than to Captain Ralston. If he doesn't get it, why, he'll never miss it. So, when Kashihami came out to the *benjo* to relieve himself, we jumped him."

"Did you kill him?"

"No. We just sort of degraded him. He never went back to the geisha party. Without his sword, he couldn't."

The major looked at the sword. He considered ordering Borum to return it, but it was not long before he changed his mind. "How am I supposed to get it to Nagasaki?" he asked.

Sergeant Borum now seemed very sober. "I tried it for the length in the coffin with the ashes, and it fits fine," he said.

"Thank you, then."

"You're welcome, major." Borum got up and began to put his other prizes into his musette bag. Toth was careful not to see the lieutenant's epaulets. "Time we were leaving for the station," said the sergeant. "I'll manage both the musette bags, if you want to take your sword."

The sword's lightness delighted Toth's hand. He followed Borum through the door. On the threshold he paused, drew the unblemished blade, and cut a small, almost dainty notch in the edge of the door. Sheathing the sword he descended the stairs, holding the scabbard carefully in front of him.

Outside it was raining, exactly as Borum had predicted. Major Toth put his sword in the coffin with the boxes of ashes, and as Borum started the engine he drew the coarse flag tight over the whole lash-up.

[Written on U.S. Navy hospital ship *Haven,* en route from Nagasaki to Okinawa, Saipan, Iwo Jima, and Guam, September–October, 1945.]

Acknowledgments

Quite a few people took part in pulling this book together.

If anyone deserves the most thanks, it is a fine young journalist, David Farady. Undaunted by the size of the task, he flawlessly transcribed entire campaigns and called my attention to details in the original dispatches that I would otherwise have missed. I am also very grateful for David's astute editing advice as numerous complex problems came up, time and time again.

Many decades after their deaths, for doing their best to keep scrapbooks of my father's clippings throughout the war, I owe an enormous debt both to my grandmother, Matilda Weller, and to "Uncle" Russell Churchill, a Boston theater director who was my father's best friend for thirty years. (He also introduced my parents.) Without those scrapbooks as a starting point, my task would have been considerably harder.

Bob Herguth Jr. and Monifa Thomas of the *Chicago Sun-Times* helped me ascertain what little of my father's Japanese reporting bypassed censorship of many kinds to appear in the *Chicago Daily News*. At the New York Public Library, David Smith attacked the same mystery from another direction.

For a more massive research problem, Smith also led me to Lucy Lyons at the Northwestern University Library, who in turn led me to her colleague, Dan Schuld. Despite what many think, even great newspapers vanish easily; it is no simple task to lay one's hands on, say, the *CDN* for 1943–1944. Without Dan's exactitude and patience, there would've been significant gaps in this chronicle, along with much guesswork. His care and energy went far beyond the bounds of professionalism.

Kirk Williamson, a photographer with considerable experience at dealing with historical images, faced yet again—as he had with Nagasaki and the POW camps—the challenge of the many pictures my father took, as well as the task of giving life to the paper trail of relevant cables, documents, and permits.

Thanks also to agent J. P. Pappis and his superb Polaris Images, who handle worldwide rights on my father's photos. Everyone at Polaris has been tireless.

The following either answered difficult questions or steered me in the right direction: John Burke, David Erlanger, Barry Feldman, Hazel Hammond, Damiana Koutsomiha, Alen MacWeeney, Vicki Syroglou, Lisa Tuite, Randy Warner, and especially the all-knowing Craig Tenney of my father's longtime literary agency, Harold Ober Associates—a family relationship that has endured for seventy years.

William H. Bartsch, a friend of my father and a military historian who specializes in the early Pacific War, generously offered his unparalleled knowledge in assisting me with *"Luck to the Fighters!"* and answering many other questions. His forthcoming book, *Every Day a Nightmare,* promises to be the work my father dreamed of: the complete story of the American Army pursuit pilots who opposed the Japanese aerial onslaught against the Netherland East Indies. (I also found much helpful background material in Bartsch's earlier books, *Doomed at the Start* and *December 8, 1941: MacArthur's Pearl Harbor.*)

The following comrades-in-arms helped enormously with my essay: Rex Baird, Kevin Buckley, Dan Connell, Barnaby Conrad III, Jeff Donovan, David Farady, Eddie Lazarus, Kylée Smith, and Donna Wolfe. As always, I am indebted to them for close readings and asking the right questions. Geo Beach and Greg Gibson, in particular, were with me every step of the way with their customary patience, sustaining humor, and wisdom.

At Crown, I am deeply grateful for the support of my fearless editor, Sean Desmond (I had thought editors this conscientious were extinct), his assistants, Julie Miesionczek and Stephanie Chan, and my publicist, Rachel Rokicki. I also wish to thank the book's original editor, Luke Dempsey, and publisher, Steve Ross.

I have been very fortunate to have Henry Dunow as my literary agent and close friend of twenty years; the crucial balance between those roles has been central to a bond I value enormously. At the Dunow, Carlson, and Lerner Agency's New York headquarters, Jeff Moores unknotted myriad problems.

My father would, I know, wish me to thank the community of San Felice Circeo, Italy, for many kindnesses across five decades.

Lastly, it is my wife, Kylée, who saw me through the intense odyssey of seeking out the diverse contents of this book. Only she can fully appreciate the irony of a single organized volume culled from the terrifying original chaos of moldy steamer trunks, crates of dusty newspapers, sheaves of utterly disorganized carbons, and scattered letters and ragged cables and meticulous expense reports adding up to another story, missing from the dispatches, at which I have tried to hint. It was she who faced my father's thousands of wartime photographs and found their hidden messages that, indeed, changed my notion of what his war had been. She was much loved by him and much saddened by how, as the years went on, the past seemed to slip from his grasp. This book, in its determination to retrieve the past, is as much her accomplishment as mine.

Index

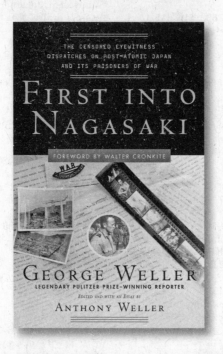